BOOKS BY ROBERT LECKIE

HISTORY

None Died in Vain: The Saga of the American Civil War
Delivered from Evil: The Saga of World War II
The Wars of America: A New and Updated Edition
American and Catholic: The Catholic Church in the U.S.
Challenge for the Pacific: The Struggle for Guadalcanal
With Fire and Sword (edited with Quentin Reynolds)
Strong Men Armed: U.S. Marines Against Japan
Conflict: The History of the Korean War
The March to Glory: 1st Marine Division's Breakout from Chosin

AUTOBIOGRAPHY

Helmet for My Pillow   *Lord, What a Family!*

BELLES LETTRES

These Are My Heroes: A Study of the Saints
Warfare: A Study of War
A Soldier-Priest Talks to Youth

FICTION

Ordained   *Forged in Blood*
Marines!   *Blood of the Seventeen Fires*
The Bloodborn   *The General*

FOR YOUNGER READERS

The Battle for Iwo Jima   *The World Turned*
The Story of Football   *Upside-Down*
The Story of World War Two   *1812: The War Nobody Won*
The Story of World War One   *The Big Game*
The War in Korea   *Keeper Play!*
Great American Battles   *Stormy Voyage*

THE WARS

A NEW AND UPDATED EDITION

OF AMERICA

Volume I

Robert Leckie

HarperPerennial
A Division of HarperCollins*Publishers*

☆

To Charles Watters
Compassionate Priest and Brave Chaplain
Who Was Killed by Friendly Fire in Vietnam
While Hastening to the Side of a Wounded Soldier.
Simple and Direct, He Was, as Jesus Said of Nathaniel:
"An Israelite, Indeed, in Whom There Is No Guile."

A hardcover edition of this book was published in 1992 by HarperCollins Publishers.

THE WARS OF AMERICA, VOLUME I *(Updated Edition)*. Copyright © 1968, 1981, 1992 by Robert Leckie. All rights reserved. Printed in the United States of America. No part of this book may be used or reproduced in any manner whatsoever without written permission except in the case of brief quotations embodied in critical articles and reviews. For information address HarperCollins Publishers, Inc., 10 East 53rd Street, New York, NY 10022.

HarperCollins books may be purchased for educational, business, or sales promotional use. For information please write: Special Markets Department, HarperCollins Publishers, Inc., 10 East 53rd Street, New York, NY 10022.

First HarperPerennial edition published 1993.

LIBRARY OF CONGRESS CATALOG CARD NUMBER 92-54863

ISBN 0-06-092409-8

98 97 96 95   RRD(H) 10 9 8 7 6 5 4 3

Contents

Maps

Preface

☆

Twenty years ago while discussing war with a Pakistani friend I was astonished to hear him, a Moslem, declare that Islam had never been aggressive. The sons of Mohammed, he insisted, had fought only in self-defense. A few minutes later I found myself maintaining that America had never been imperialist. "Not really," I said. "After all, we gave the Philippines their independence." Now it was my friend's turn to be scornful. "*You* gave *them* their *independence*?" he mocked. Blushing, I realized that my own chauvinism had been no lovelier than his: if I could look upon the Crescent as a bloody scimitar, he could regard the Cross as a sword carried upside down.

The point here is not so much to echo Robert Burns's plea for the gift "to see ourselves as others see us," but rather to accept Voltaire's remark that the study of one's nation's history makes one a better and more loyal citizen. Knowing his national history, a man is less likely to deny the undeniable and more inclined to take the good with the bad and put all into true perspective. This, then, is the purpose of this book: to put the wars of America into perspective.

It is an attempt to show not only how our wars were fought but also why they occurred, as well as to illustrate what this country has gained or lost by appeals to arms. Equally, it is an attempt to portray the men who made and fought in these wars. When military history becomes a dreary compendium of maps and maneuvers, of calibers and compass bearings, as it so often does, the reason usually is that the writer has left out the human heart. War changes, its materials and its methods change, but the hearts of men do not. That is why Marshal Saxe could say, "The human heart is the starting point in all matters pertaining to war," and that is why this book attempts to come down heavily on the human side. I agree with the Englishman who said he liked geography less than biography "because that's about maps, but the other is about chaps." And if, in following this sublime lead, this book sends a few scales flying from the hides of those antediluvian myths—America, the peace-loving nation; man, the peace-loving animal—then I will consider myself to have performed a small service in the interest of international sanity. Obviously, during an age in which an exchange of pushed buttons might very well end mankind's career upon this planet, it would be helpful to understand men as fighting creatures and our own nation as perhaps the fightingest society since the advent of modern warfare. Yet, though America can become martial, she has never been militarist. The distinction is a great one, and it is hoped that a knowledge of American military history may help us to maintain it. To this end, once again, this book was written.

Space limitations in a book of this scope have precluded the listing of a bibliography. A comprehensive one was simply out of the question, while a selected bibliography could well have run to another forty or fifty printed pages. In its place, I have included a list of recommended books and would refer the reader to Colonel Vincent J. Esposito's excellent and longer list in *The West Point Atlas of American Wars,* two volumes, New York: Praeger, 1959. Much of the research for this book was based upon that list.

It should go without saying that, apart from World War II, Korea and Vietnam, in which I had a personal interest, this work depends upon published sources. Nor do I pretend to have read everything published about every American war. When it is considered that one may collect more than 25,000 volumes and articles on the Civil War alone, it may be seen that the problem was not one of finding material but of choosing from it. Therefore, to have gone over ground already spaded by abler men before me would have been not only impossibly time-consuming but also pretentious.

Space limitations have also compelled me to confine reference notes to direct quotations. To footnote every statistic or observation would have been to number every third or fourth sentence. In the interest of smoother reading, all spelling and punctuation has been modernized, except where a certain echo from the past seemed appropriate. All dates are for the Time Zone in which the event occurred, and, to avoid an impression of that precision so rare in warfare, figures for casualties, the size of armies or the number of their arms, as well as the distances they have marched or sailed to battle, are usually rounded off to the nearest zero.

Finally, let me acknowledge my great debt to my editors: to the late Cass Canfield and to Norbert Slepyan for their kindly assistance on the original edition of this work published in 1968; to Corona Machemer for the same reasons on the revised and updated edition of 1981; and to M. S. ("Buz") Wyeth and Daniel Bial for their suggestions, patience and tact on this new, updated revision of 1992—to Mrs. Clarice Browne, librarian at Roxbury (New Jersey) High School, who kindly lent me copies of news magazines I was unable to obtain—and, of course, to my dear wife, who actually runs this lash-up as top kick and mess sergeant, for typing the manuscript while wearing her third hat of company clerk.

ROBERT LECKIE

Polliwog Pond
Byram Township, N.J.
September 23, 1991

PART ☆ I

The Colonial Wars

1

☆

In the spring of 1609 Samuel de Champlain prepared to make war upon the Iroquois. Only the previous autumn, soon after Champlain had planted the settlement of Quebec atop a high cliff commanding the broad St. Lawrence, a young Ottawa chief had come to him to propose such an expedition.

The Indian told the Father of New France that the Iroquois were the most ferocious savages in the American wilderness. Known as the Five Nations—Mohawk, Oneida, Onondaga, Cayuga and Seneca —they were the dread of surrounding tribes: killing, torturing, eating or enslaving them, while imposing upon some the humiliating epithet of "women" or exacting from others a ruinous tribute. Should Champlain join with this Ottawa and his kinsmen, as well as with the Hurons and Algonquins, who were also the Frenchman's friends, he might make himself the ally and the leader of all the tribes of Canada. His cannon and arquebuses—his "thunderhorns" as the Indians called them—would surely humble the haughty Iroquois.

Champlain consented, for here was the opportunity to seize power among the savages, and thus carry out French policy in the New World. Unlike those English who had settled at Jamestown in 1607 or the other English who were to come to Plymouth 13 years later, the French did not hold aloof from the Indians but rather mingled with them. They were not in the New World for gold like the Spaniards or land like the English, but rather for furs, for glory and for God. In one way or another, either by gaining the confidence of the Indians or by cowing them, they sought to bind the red men together under French leadership so that Canada's valuable trade in furs might be secured and expanded, and so that the Crown and the Cross might be pushed deeper, ever deeper, into the westward wilderness.

For these reasons, Samuel Champlain joined the war party. He lifted the war hatchet and watched the war dance. Then he dined at the war feast and the following morning—June 28, 1609—he led the war party south to the Iroquois country.

A few days later Champlain came upon a frothing white torrent that marked the rapids of the lower Richelieu. His light sloop could not pass, and he sent the sloop and eight of his 11 Frenchmen back to Quebec while the Indians bore their boats around the rapids. Then Champlain and two other Frenchmen entered war canoes. They paddled upriver and glided into that lovely long lake that was to bear Champlain's name. To either side rose towering forest walls growing darker in the July heat.

Champlain and his Indians paddled on. They intended to move south along Lake Champlain into narrower, lovelier Lake George, and then strike overland to the Hudson River, which they would descend to fall upon some Mohawk village. St. Lawrence River–Richelieu River–Lake Champlain–Lake George–Hudson River, in that order or the reverse, this was the watery warpath of the Iroquois and their enemies, just as it became for 150 years the invasion route of the warring French and English.

But Champlain and his savages did not traverse its length. On July 29 they lay encamped at the foot of Lake Champlain on a promontory which was probably the site of Fort Ticonderoga. A few hours after dark they made out a flotilla of Iroquois war canoes approaching from the south. Both Indian bands exchanged war cries, and then the Iroquois landed on the same shore to erect a barricade of logs in preparation for the morning's fight.

On that morning, Champlain and his fellow Frenchmen vested themselves in steel armor and seized their short, stubby matchlocks in their hands. Each of the three Frenchmen then entered a different canoe and lay hidden on its bottom. The canoes were paddled toward the Iroquois camp. They were beached in sight of the enemy barricade. After Champlain's savages went ashore, their steel-clad allies stealthily slipped from the canoes and followed behind.

Soon the Iroquois began filing out of their makeshift fort. There were about 200 of them. They also were "armored." Some carried shields of wood or hardened hide, or wore vests made of twigs bound by fiber. The Iroquois advanced steadily toward their foemen from the north. Shaken, the allies parted ranks and Champlain strode forward.

"I looked at them," Champlain wrote,

and they looked at me. When I saw them getting ready to shoot their
arrows at us, I levelled my arquebuse, which I had loaded with four balls,
and aimed straight at one of the three chiefs. The shot brought down two,
and wounded another. On this, our Indians set up such a yelling that one
could not have heard a thunder-clap, and all the while the arrows flew
thick on both sides. The Iroquois were greatly astonished and frightened
to see two of their men killed so quickly, in spite of their arrow-proof
armor. As I was reloading, one of my companions fired a shot from the
woods, which so increased their astonishment that, seeing their chiefs
dead, they abandoned the field and fled into the depth of the forest.[1]*

Exultant, the allies closed on the Iroquois camp. They took the
scalps of the fallen—both living and dead—and took prisoners on
whom they commenced those foul tortures which turned the stomach
of their mighty ally.

But Champlain's horror at the spectacle of Indians drinking the
blood or eating the hearts of their victims would have been magnified
up to the limit of even his considerable endurance had he suspected
that his victory in this first pitched battle between French and Indian
on American soil would produce in the hearts of the vanquished
Iroquois a horrible ache for revenge.

The Father of New France had bequeathed to his heirs a legacy of
terror.

In 1641 the Iroquois were ready. An entire new generation had
brooded over the insult dealt to the brethren of the Long House.
Only fear of the French thunderhorns had restrained them. But now
Dutch traders at Fort Orange—renamed Albany after England
acquired New York and New Jersey—had supplied them with firearms.

With these in their hands they boasted that they would wipe the
Hurons, the Algonquins and the French off the face of the earth.
They vowed that they would carry the "white girls"—the nuns of
the colony—back to their villages. Regarding themselves as peerless
warriors destined to conquer all mankind, they went on the warpath:
in the west the Senecas and the others attacked the Hurons, while
in the east the Mohawks struck at the French and their allies.

There were between 700 and 800 Mohawk braves, 300 of whom

* Notes begin on page xv.

carried arquebuses, and they came very close to exterminating the 300 French colonists at Quebec, Three Rivers and Montreal.

In parties of ten to a hundred men, they paddled down the river that gave them their name, entered the Hudson at Albany, and stole north along the traditional invasion route. Reaching the St. Lawrence, they lay in ambush for canoes coming downriver with cargoes of fur or outgoing boats bringing supplies to the missions and trading stations in the Great Lakes region.

No one was safe from them. To hunt or fish alone was to risk the war whoop, the sudden shot—and the scalping knife in the brain. Small parties of French soldiers or bushrangers who rushed to the scenes of ambuscades rarely found more than a mangled corpse or heads stuck up on poles, and sometimes, scrawled on trees stripped of their bark, the crude picture writing of the Iroquois vaunting their latest massacre and promising destruction to all who opposed them.

Against the Indian allies of the French they aimed a particular ferocity. They drove the Algonquins from their hunting grounds deep into the wilderness, pursuing them there to destroy their camps and boil and eat the enemy slain in the sight of the survivors. "In a word," wrote the missionary Father Vimont, "they ate men with as much appetite and more pleasure than hunters eat a boar or stag."[2]

But those who were merely killed and eaten were comparatively fortunate, for the Iroquois had brought the practice of torture to an indescribable degree of perfection. In justice to them, it must be stated that none of the Indians regarded cruelty as being wicked. Indeed, its very opposite—pity—was a weakness in their eyes. Compassion in a warrior seemed nothing less than cowardice. To eat the heart of a fallen foe or to drink his blood was to partake of the dead man's courage. To torture a prisoner was not only pleasant; it gave an enemy the opportunity to show by his stoicism that he was a brave man. At times a victim's fortitude so excited the admiration of the Iroquois that they conferred upon him the highest honor, adoption into one of the five tribes.

Nevertheless, they were savages, and if some well-manicured moderns may be able to rationalize their cruelty as being nothing but the ungentle customs of primitive peoples, those who suffered under it had a different explanation.

"They are not men, they are wolves!" a Frenchwoman sobbed, after describing how her baby was burned before her eyes.[3]

Human wolves that they were, they would have devoured New France had they possessed the slightest understanding of the art of warfare or of that discipline which is the chief mark of a military organization. The Iroquois, however, could only make forays or raids. A battle was won or lost in an instant's rush. Stealth and surprise comprised their tactics. A siege was to them an incomprehensible bore, to maneuver in the open a madness. Even so, skulking in the forests by day, charging with a yell out of the dark by night, the Iroquois struck terror into the hearts of the French and came close to achieving the extermination of their enemies.

Gradually, however, the warpath wore them out. Their victories exhausted them, their villages fell silent, and by the year 1660 the Iroquois could count only 2,200 warriors, of whom more than half were adopted prisoners from the Hurons, Eries, neutrals and various Algonquin tribes.

Nevertheless, the Iroquois remained a threat to Canadian security down to the last chapter in the history of New France. Goaded back onto the warpath by the British, they repeatedly hurled themselves against the French and their Indian allies; and it was not until 1763, when the Peace of Paris made Canada a British colony, that they could forget those humiliating shots fired on the shores of Lake Champlain.

That the tolerant French rather than the haughty English should have been the first to incur the wrath of the red men is one of the ironies of American history. True enough, French policy toward the Indians was not one of unmixed altruism: if souls were to be won for the Cross, there were also furs to be gained for the Crown. Yet on balance the French treatment of the Indian tribes seems to have been more humane.

French agents lived in Indian villages and learned their languages. The Indians were befriended and flattered. Whenever they visited a French fort they were saluted with cannon and rolling drums. They were given medals and French uniforms and flags. Their customs—even the most savage ones, especially when they could be turned against the English—were rarely mocked or ridiculed.

It was otherwise with the English. First and foremost, the English colonists sought land. They had come to stay. This, of course, joined to the corollary necessity of learning to govern themselves, was to prove their strength; just as the paternalistic character of the French colony was to be its undoing. But in the beginning this passion for land was the disturbing quality which the Indians marked in the English. Not only the Indians, for Roger Williams, the famous fighter for religious tolerance, once observed: "I fear that . . . God Land will be as great a God with us English as God Gold was with the Spaniard."[4]

English officials were often overbearing in their dealings with proud Indian chiefs. More often than not, the English emissaries among the Indians were the fur traders who were universally hated and despised as "rum-carriers." Some Indians who had beheld the swift, curt justice of French military law were filled with contempt for slower English civil courts, confusing the Englishman's elaborate machinery for safeguarding civil rights with a weak uncertainty. Finally, although there were Protestant ministers such as John Eliot who were as zealous for souls as their Papist rivals to the north, Puritanical colonial legislatures passed blue laws applying to all Indians, converted or no. Thus, in Massachusetts, Indians as well as whites were liable to the death penalty for blasphemy, interpreted to be the denial of God or deprecation of the Christian religion; while in Plymouth no Indian was allowed to fish, hunt or carry burdens during the white man's Sabbath. Such intolerance only served to aggravate the Indian's growing anger at the greatest provocation of all: the shrinking boundaries of his ancestral home.

True enough, the colonists were scrupulously careful to obtain titles to Indian lands; nevertheless it was difficult for the red man to realize that in bartering away hunting preserves for guns or horses or casks of rum he was actually giving up all rights to hunt or fish there or to grow corn on unused parts of it. It might be that the genial Massasoit, friend of the Pilgrims and chief ceder of Wampanoag land, did not complain; but his far fiercer son, King Philip, came to see that the inexorably expanding whites would not be satisfied until they had all the land.

King Philip received his bizarre name after his father had asked the General Court in Plymouth to give English names to his two oldest sons, Wamsutta and Metacom. The English, recalling the kings of ancient Macedon, named the former Alexander and the latter Philip. On the death of Massasoit, in 1661, it was Alexander who succeeded to the chieftainship.

The new sachem quickly showed that he did not share his father's easy trust of the English. Although he did not attack them, he tried to rule his people independently of them. Summoned to appear in Plymouth to give evidence of his loyalty, Alexander refused to go. But colonial soldiers made him go, and he was subjected to a haughty and humiliating interrogation, during which time he contracted a fever that killed him.

King Philip succeeded him, fired by a burning resolve to avenge his brother's death and a determination to wean his people away from the corrupting influences of the white men. Although Philip was only 24, the fame of his ability as an orator and ruler was already great. More warlike and decisive than his brother, he saw with a painful clarity that there was no possibility of compromise for his people: they would either be overwhelmed by the colonists or they would turn and drive the whites into the sea. He realized early that his own outnumbered forces were fragmented, cut up by the sharp knife of tribal jealousies. By the time of the outbreak of King Philip's War in 1675 there were about 40,000 whites in New England, all of whom would certainly close ranks in the face of Indian menace, against 20,000 red men who would rather worry some old bone of tribal contention than rally to a common danger.

Nevertheless, King Philip prepared his war. For 13 years he patiently sought to bind the Indians into a unified whole. By the end of that period, however, it did not appear that he could rely upon more than half of them. Nor did it seem that he could produce any valid reason for taking up arms.

Then, in January, 1675, John Sassamon, a Christianized Indian who had been educated at Harvard College and had served as Philip's trusted aide, came to Plymouth to reveal to Governor Josiah Winslow all the details of Philip's "conspiracy" against the colonists. A few days later Sassamon was found murdered in a pond. The enraged authorities immediately blamed King Philip. They arrested three Wampanoags, and put them on trial. Philip protested that the whites had no right to try red men for crimes committed against other Indians. But the trial went forward, the three men were found guilty, and on June 8 they were hanged.

Twelve days later a group of young Wampanoags came into the settlement at Swansea and shot some cattle. A young colonist retaliated by wounding an Indian—and then, painted and feathered for war, Philip's braves came swarming out of Mount Hope. They surrounded Swansea and shot down settler after settler, until, by the night of June 21, 11 English had received their death wounds.

New England was shocked. From Boston and Connecticut, parties of hastily formed militia came hurrying to Plymouth's rescue. Philip quickly evacuated Mount Hope. His position on the peninsula in Narragansett Bay was untenable. He moved west to the mainland of Rhode Island, while the colonists occupied Mount Hope. From there, Benjamin Church, a colonist knowledgeable in Indian affairs, led a party eastward in pursuit. But they blundered into country infested with rattlesnakes, to the disgust of Church, who thought his men were more afraid of the rattlers "than the black Serpents they were in quest of." Suddenly the "Serpents" appeared and drove the colonists back to Mount Hope.

King Philip now had his war. It had been forced upon him unawares and there was nothing to do but to unleash the ferocity which might rally all the wavering tribes to him while paralyzing the English will to fight. Moving rapidly he struck against settlements in Rehoboth, Taunton and Dartmouth, forcing the residents of Middleborough to flee their village and spreading the dread of his name right into nearby Plymouth. Soon, as he expected, news of his triumphant sorties brought hordes of other tribesmen to his side. Gradually, the fire and ruin, the blood and agony of the tomahawk and the flaming arrow were spread up and down the Connecticut River Valley. It was warfare as barbarous and as pitiless as the horror which the Iroquois spread along the St. Lawrence. Massacre followed massacre, and midnight raids succeeded daylight ambush. With such terror Philip hoped to paralyze the English. But Philip had underestimated his foes. He was the first of the enemies of this country to mistake the peaceful man for the pacifist, and to confuse unreadiness for war with unwillingness to fight. So also were these colonists the first Americans to expose the guardians of their frontiers to a hopeless and bloody fight against overwhelming odds. Even so, the dripping hatchet plunging into the brains of defenseless women and children was also to cut away the last restraints of the English. All their own disciplined ferocity was now let loose upon the Indians. Scalps were taken, bounties were offered for Indian heads, and captive red men were sold into slavery in the Mediterranean and the West Indies.

Six months after Philip had begun his war, the crucial battle was fought on the west side of Narragansett Bay, where the United Colonies of Massachusetts, Connecticut and Plymouth had raised a force of a thousand men. A few miles to the southwest of them 3,000 Indians commanded by the Narragansett sachem Canonchet were entrenched in a fortified village built on an island in a marsh known as the Great Swamp.

On December 19, a cold, snowy day, the colonists marched toward the fort. They crossed the frozen marsh and came upon a walled village protected by masses of felled trees and piles of brush heaped in front of a stockade. There was one gap in the walls, directly opposite the colonists, and they charged it.

Fighting for their lives, the Indians drove the English back with a volley of musket fire. But the colonists rallied and charged again. They fought their way inside the village, and a fierce hand-to-hand fight raged among the wigwams. Then the English set fire to the lodges and the battle swirled on amid flames and smoke, until, as the dusk of a bitterly cold night began to descend, the Indians broke and fled. Now the flames were beyond control, engulfing the Indian dead and wounded, so that, in the words of Cotton Mather, 600 men, women and children were "terribly barbikew'd."

Such a defeat might have discouraged a less ardent spirit than Philip. But he fought on, assisted by the able Canonchet, with whom he had made rendezvous in central Massachusetts. Throughout the winter Philip counseled his allies: burn every house, destroy every village, kill every white man. Before the thaws of spring set in, the war parties set out along the frozen streams and terror was renewed. Town after town was put to the torch. Canonchet struck steadily south until he had reappeared near the scene of his Great Swamp defeat, and King Philip devastated Rhode Island and swept east into Plymouth itself, burning 16 houses.

Of 90 white settlements in New England, 52 had been attacked and 12 had been destroyed. The flower of its manhood was perishing in the battle. However, at the very peak of success, with his goal of utter annihilation almost within his grasp, Philip's own weaknesses became rapidly and ruinously apparent. He had no solid base of operations, no inpregnable position to which he might return to regroup and replan. He had no stores. His war parties lived off the land. Now it was spring and the Indians, denied old hunting and fishing lands, needed to search out new ones if they were to prevent their women and children from starving. And so, one by one, the war parties slipped away, to be defeated piecemeal by the rallying colonists or to be brought over to the English cause.

In April Canonchet was trapped and captured. He was sentenced to be shot. "I shall die before my heart is soft, or I have said anything unworthy of myself," the proud chieftain said before his death.[5] His loss depressed King Philip. It discouraged Philip's followers still more. One by one, the war bands deserted their chief. One of them went straight to the enemy. A chief dispatched by Awashonks, squaw sachem of the Sakonnets, came to Benjamin Church and said: "Sir, if you will please to accept of me and my men, and will head us, we will fight for you, and will help you to Philip's head before the corn be ripe."[6]

Church accepted. Plymouth authorized him to lead a party of colonists and the treacherous Sakonnets against Philip. On July 20, 1676, Church surprised Philip in a swamp, killing or capturing 173 Wampanoags. Philip escaped, but his uncle and adviser was among the slain; his wife and son were among those captives sold into slavery. Now the manhunt began in earnest. Philip flitted from haunt to hideout, never tarrying for fear some new piece of treachery would betray him. His followers were now few. After one of them advised Philip to make peace with the English, he ordered the man killed—setting in motion the final betrayal. The executed man's brother, an Indian named Alderman, deserted to Church and promised to lead him to King Philip.

The Indian leader, like a wild beast coming home to die, had returned to his ancestral stronghold at Mount Hope. In the dead of the night of August 11, 1676, Church led 18 English and 22 Indians across the bay to the peninsula. They surrounded Philip's camp. To the rear of the camp, Church stationed an ambush. Then, at dawn, he attacked.

Driven from their quarters by volleys of musket balls, the startled Wampanoags reacted as Church had envisioned; they turned and fled. Most of them ran straight into the ambush. One of them came sprinting toward a man named Caleb Cook and the traitor, Alderman. Cook's gun misfired, but Alderman's double-barreled weapon roared twice. The fleeing Indian toppled to the ground. Alderman ran forward and rolled the body over. It was King Philip, and there was a hole in his heart and another one two inches above it.

Thus ended King Philip's War. It had been the opening round of a racial conflict which was to rage intermittently for two centuries until it came to its climax on the Western plains. And if the colonists of New France had learned about war by fighting Indians, so had the settlers of New England.

Soon they would be fighting each other.

2

☆

In American folklore the myth of "the most peace-loving nation in the world" still persists. But the fact is that American history is not only concurrent with the annals of American arms, but is as firmly woven into it as a strand of hemp in a rope. Probably it could not have been otherwise, for the birth of both the English and French colonies in the New World was simultaneous with the birth of modern warfare.

Even before the New World was colonized, the Spanish had revolutionized war by introducing an improved matchlock musket and fielding units of professional foot soldiers called infantry. (The name derived from the custom of adopting Spanish princes, or *infantes,* as the honorary colonels of various formations.) With their new though clumsy six-foot muskets, the Spanish foot soldiers were invincible, and their advent opened the age of modern infantry tactics. Deployment and maneuver on the open plain supplanted siege warfare.

However, the true beginning of modern warfare was probably the Thirty Years' War (1618-48), and its true parent was the great Swedish captain, Gustavus Adolphus. It was this warrior king who placed the modern emphasis on infantry firepower. He saw that the real arbiter of battle was the foot soldier holding the hand gun; he shortened and lightened his muskets and increased the number of musketeers while decreasing the number of pikemen. Gustavus Adolphus also introduced modern military discipline into his army and organized the service of supply. He was the first to make widespread use of artillery in the field, using bombardments to cover the shock charges of his cavalry. After Gustavus Adolphus, the heavy, ponderous formations of the Spanish infantry were obsolete, and European kings everywhere adopted the Swedish soldier's light and mobile battalions.

None of these changes had any effect on far-off America. Throughout the Thirty Years' War only one small ripple of Anglo-French conflict backwashed over American shores.

In 1629, while Protestant England came to the side of the French Huguenots resisting Catholic France, an expedition was mounted against Quebec. Samuel Champlain still commanded the struggling settlement then, although he had only 16 starving men inside his rickety fort when Lewis Kirke sailed up the St. Lawrence and summoned him to surrender. Forced to capitulate, Champlain was taken to England as a prisoner. Three years later an Anglo-French treaty brought him his freedom.

Once again the colonists of both crowns were left alone, and they left each other alone. All their fighting was against the Indians, and although their discipline and weapons were always superior, their tactics were scarcely more refined than the bush warfare of the red men. Arms as an art, still less as a profession, was not known in America, and it was not until 1672 that a professional soldier on the new European model arrived in the New World. He was Louis de Buade, the Count Frontenac, a fiery and tumultuous war dog. When Frontenac sailed up the St. Lawrence and entered the widening basin of Quebec, he saw the young city crowning the cliff above him. "I never saw anything more superb than the position of this town," he wrote. "It could not be better situated as the future capital of a great empire."[7]

Ten years later Frontenac was sailing back to France. By his own lights, and by the standards of those days, he had served his King faithfully and well. He had planted Fort Frontenac on the shores of Lake Ontario, thus guarding the routes of the fur trade; but he had also quarreled with the Bishop over the sale of brandy to the

Indians (from which illicit traffic he probably profited), and with the Intendant over the exercise of power. In fine, Frontenac had made too many enemies, and it is safe to say that, as he left, only those friendly Indians who called him the greatest of the *"Onontios,"* or governors of Canada, were sorry to see him go.

In 1689, a crusty and audacious 70 years of age, he was back—and with his arrival came the first blows of New France against New England during the War of the Grand Alliance.

The colonists called this conflict King William's War, and the name is significant. Although Americans generally are fond of pretending that the religious intolerance which erupted in the Thirty Years' War failed to infect the forefathers of America, the fact is that those doctrinal disputes which sundered Christendom were from the very beginning a powerful influence upon American history. Those Pilgrims who fled England to escape the persecution of the Anglican Church set up a harsher and more intolerant persecution of their own once they had planted the New Jerusalem on the uncontaminated shores of Cape Cod. They abhorred the Catholics of New France as idolators and were in turn despised as heretics.

The War of the Grand Alliance was "King William's" to the colonists because William of Orange was a Protestant prince sworn to guarantee Protestantism in England. James II, whom he had supplanted during the "Glorious Revolution" of 1688, was a Catholic who had already attempted to restore that faith in England. Now, in 1689, as Frontenac returned to New France, the Catholic James supported by the Catholic Louis of France was trying to regain the English throne.

Frontenac's first mission was the capture of New York, with explicit instructions to expel all settlers except any Catholics found willing to take an oath of allegiance to the French King. He was foiled by foul weather, which delayed his arrival until September —far too close to winter for military operations. Nevertheless, the religious motive was already present on both sides; and in all the Colonial Wars, as also partially in the Revolutionary War, the religious thrust was never very far away from its emotional twin of racial pride.

Actually, the New York operation was far too grandiose for the forces at Frontenac's command. He arrived at Quebec to find only 700 or 800 soldiers there and the colony itself in terror. Iroquois

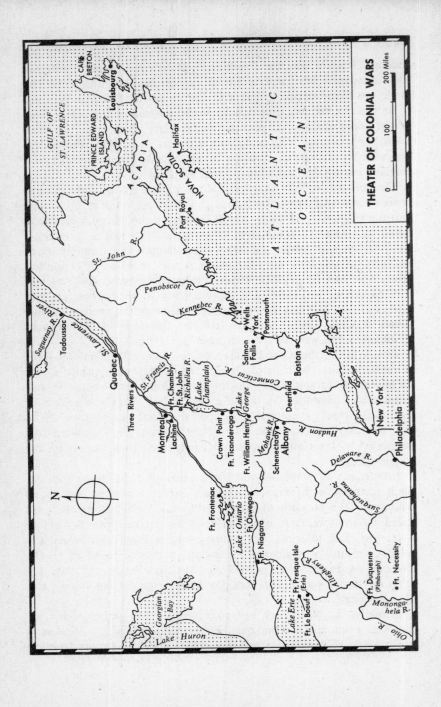

THEATER OF COLONIAL WARS

0   100   200 Miles

had come howling and murdering along the borders again. Frontenac himself inspected the bloody ashes of the massacred settlement at Lachine. He had also, to his disgust, arrived too late to prevent his frightened troops from destroying Fort Frontenac; and Canada's Indian allies, terrified by the English-oriented Iroquois, were on the point of deserting to the enemy.

Frontenac decided that he could only retain his allies, and give a check to Iroquois arrogance, by attacking the English to the south. He formed three war parties: one at Montreal, one at Three Rivers and one at Quebec. In that order they were to strike at Albany, the border villages of New Hampshire and those of what is now Maine. The Albany foray, the largest, was to depart first.

It consisted of 210 men, of whom 96 were Indians. The remainder were Frenchmen, and most of these were *coureurs de bois,* that is, "runners of the woods," or bushrangers, a hardy breed of Canadian to whom the forest was home. Like their English counterparts, the American rangers, they were romantic figures of a vanished era. Equally at ease in bucksin or in homespun, dreaming beside the campfire or drunk inside the gambling hall, they could stalk wild beasts as skillfully as any savage—and they could also take a neat scalp.

The Montreal party left in mid-January, 1690, in the dead of winter. They moved on snowshoes, clad in hoods or blanket-coats, with hatchets, knives, tobacco and bullet pouches dangling at their belts, pipes slung about their necks in leather cases, arquebuses in their mittened hands and packs on their backs. Supplies were dragged over the snow on Indian sledges.

Turning left at the Richelieu, they shuffled up that ribbon of ice and debouched on Lake Champlain.

It was a bitter march, and the French gradually came to realize that to attempt Albany would be folly. They would attack its outpost, Schenectady, instead. Reaching the Hudson, the march became even more miserable. A partial thaw had set in and Frontenac's wretched warriors were forced to stumble through slimes of mud and slush, up to their knees in icy swamp water. The weather changed again, to a whistling snowstorm.

But if the weather was against the French and Indians, the complacency of the Dutch burghers in Schenectady was in their favor. The Dutch laughed aside all warnings from Albany, and carried their derision to the length of leaving the settlement gates open with two snowmen as mock sentinels.

The raiders slipped past the snowman at the northern gate. Schenectady slept on. The raiders peeled off, left and right, until, between the palisades and the rows of silent houses stood ranks of French and Indians. And then the night silence was split with the screeching of the war whoops, the doors of the houses were burst open, the tomahawks came plunging down—and the butchery began.

"No pen can write, and no tongue express, the cruelties that were committed," wrote Peter Schuyler. "The women bigg with Childe rip'd up, and the Children alive throwne into the flames, and their heads dashed against the Doors and windows."[8]

In all, 60 persons were killed—of whom 22 were women and children—and between 80 and 90 were taken prisoners. By noon the village of Schenectady was a pile of smoking ashes. Even the Mohawks were shocked when they came upon it a few days later. And Albany was terrified, as were New Hampshire and Maine, when springtime brought the news that raiding parties of French and Indians had destroyed the settlements of Salmon Falls and Casco Bay in like barbarous blood baths.

To Count Frontenac in Quebec the reports were cause for jubilation. "You cannot believe, Monseigneur," he wrote to the Minister in Paris, just after Schenectady, "the joy that this slight success has caused, and how much it contributes to raise the people from their dejection and terror."[9]

The raids may have lifted Canadian hearts, but they had not cast down English ones. Frontenac had not only failed in his second objective; he had created exactly the reverse reaction. Far from being cowed, New York and New England were in a fighting mood. Like King Philip before him, the Count Frontenac had mistaken the temper of his enemy.

The English colonists planned to retaliate with a land-and-sea assault upon Canada. Colonial militia—400 from New York, 350 from Connecticut, Plymouth and Massachusetts—were to rendezvous at Albany with nearly all of the Iroquois, and then advance on Montreal by way of Lake Champlain. Massachusetts alone was mounting the water-borne attack. It was at first intended to fall on Quebec. But the Bay Colony could not afford such an expensive expedition.

Her treasury was empty. French privateers operating out of Port Royal in Acadia (modern Nova Scotia) had been scourging her commerce. Why not, then, take Port Royal? It would put an end to that shark's sanctuary and would give New England command of the entrance to the St. Lawrence. It was agreed, and seven ships carrying about 500 militia were placed under Sir William Phips.

Phips is one of the most remarkable figures in colonial history. Born one of 26 children by the same woman, he was reared in poverty at a rude settlement on the banks of the Kennebec, tending sheep until the age of 18. Then he took up carpentry. Next he came to Boston to marry a widow, better born, better-off and better along in years than himself. In Boston he learned to read and write and to aspire to the command of a king's ship and possession of "a fair brick house in the Green Lane of North Boston."

Phips achieved far more than both dreams combined. Like countless Americans to follow him, he went hunting for sunken treasure. After one fruitless expedition during which Phips, a tall and powerful man, quelled two mutinies, he persuaded the British Admiralty to subsidize a second quest. This time Phips found the wreck of a Spanish galleon in the West Indies and took from it treasure valued at £300,000, and he came home a rich man and a knight.

On May 11, 1690, Phips put his militia ashore at Port Royal and summoned the French Governor, Meneval, to surrender. Meneval had only about 70 soldiers holding a ramshackle fort, and he pulled down his flag with alacrity.

Meanwhile, the overland attack on Montreal was floundering badly. Fitz-John Winthrop, the commander, had met nothing but trial and setback. Only a few reluctant Iroquois had joined his forces. Disputes between the men of the colonies, and quarrels within the New York militia, disrupted discipline. Smallpox reduced Winthrop's strength and scared off the three western tribes of the Iroquois. Finally, there were not enough canoes to ascend Champlain. Winthrop decided to return to Albany after sending Captain John Schuyler forward to make a successful but minor raid at Laprairie.

Frontenac had been at Laprairie. He had rushed there from Montreal—where he had delighted his Indians by seizing a tomahawk and joining them in a whooping war dance—but then, convinced that the English would not attack in force, he had returned to Montreal and then to Quebec.

He arrived in time to gird his beloved "capital city of a great empire" for the all-out assault launched upon it by Sir William Phips.

The triumphant Phips returned from Port Royal to find Boston throbbing with preparation for a much bigger venture: the capture of Quebec.

England had been asked to supply arms, while Massachusetts got ready the ships and men. Even though the Bay Colony's funds were short, it was believed that the plunder of Canada's capital city would more than offset outlays for the expedition. Accordingly, 36 ships of all sizes were assembled and a call for volunteers was issued. After enlistments failed to produce the desired number of men, the colony calmly impressed the rest.

In all, the expeditionary force numbered 2,200 sailors and soldiers, if raw farmers and fishermen may be so designated. At their head was Sir William, a bluff, coarse adventurer-turned-merchant whose military experience consisted of a victory by summons. Beneath him was John Walley—"Major" Walley, now—one of the colony's most respectable citizens, and therefore, by the standards of a merchant republic, eminently qualified to command men in battle.

But vain considerations for the arts of war would have seemed a contradiction to the race chosen by the God of Battles. These citizen-soldiers of New Jerusalem—all these Jonathans and Sauls and Calebs, these Abrahams and Israels and Jedidiahs—could they possibly fail in the holy war against the idolators of the north? Was the New Jerusalem not to be the instrument of God's vengeful wrath upon the New Canaan? Certainly it was, and to suggest that the Almighty's own purpose might be thwarted was to utter a blasphemy. Just to be sure, however, the populace was exhorted to do penance, a day of fasting was ordained, and the Lord was imprecated to look with favor upon the instruments of His will.

Meanwhile, the reply from England had come and the answer was no. King William was too busy with James II in Ireland at that moment. Nevertheless, the expedition sailed. Phips had already waited too long to begin operations, and he left Nantasket on August 9, 1690.

Contrary winds delayed Phips for three more weeks, and it was well into October before he arrived. During that time, Frontenac had fortified Quebec. Entering the basin with the city on the cliff before him, Phips also contemplated a bristling fort. Still, he had taken one French fortress simply by raising his voice—and he summoned Frontenac to surrender. The count's reply to the young subaltern who brought the summons was: "No, I will answer your general only by the mouths of my cannon, that he may learn that a man like me is not to be summoned after this fashion. Let him do his best, and I will do mine."[10]

Sir William called a council of war. It was decided to land at Beauport, a town just below Quebec. The St. Charles River emptied into the St. Lawrence between Quebec and Beauport. Major Walley would take his men up the St. Charles to a ford, cross and strike at the rear of Quebec. The smaller ships would sail up as far as the ford to give fire support. Once the English soldiers had begun attacking Quebec's rear, Phips and the heavier ships would bombard the city from the basin. Neither Phips nor Walley seems to have known that Frontenac had constructed a line of fortifications behind the city. Nor did they pay much attention to French prisoners who told them of a place a mile or two above Quebec where a little-known path led upward to the heights. Seven decades later a red-haired British general named Wolfe would scrutinize similar information a bit closer.

Daylight was fading as the council of war reached its conclusions. At nightfall the colonists heard the peal of fifes and the roll of drums from atop the cliff. The English asked a prisoner named Granville what it meant.

"Ma foi, Messieurs," he answered, smiling, "you have lost the game. It is the governor of Montreal with the people from the country above. There is nothing for you now but to pack and go home."[11]

It was true. Quebec had been reinforced just in time. About 800 men—regular soldiers and unruly *coureurs de bois*—had come downriver to enter the city shouting and singing, to swell the garrison to 3,000 armed men, and to make Sir William's slim chances of success even narrower.

Nevertheless the assault went forward. Walley took some 1,300 militia ashore at Beauport. They were met by a delaying force of 300 sharpshooters. Slowly, taking casualties, Walley's men drove the Canadians back. They gained the St. Charles and made camp

for the night. In the morning they would rendezvous with the fireships and move upriver.

Unfortunately, the impatient Sir William had gone into action.
With neither Walley nor the smaller ships as yet on the St. Charles,
he had opened fire on Quebec. Actually, it was Frontenac who had
opened fire on him. From the Château St. Louis perched on the
brink of the cliff, the count had watched the biggest English ships
leave their moorings and sail into position under the town, and he
fired the first shot in a furious cannonading that reverberated in one
long re-echoing crash around the basin of Quebec. The English ships
spat flames and shot, and the cliff belched back with fire and ball.
Next day, the duel was resumed. But now the British Crown's failure
to provide adequate ammunition, yoked to the colony's faith in God
rather than in gunnery practice, began to tell.

The French were superior in shot and in skill. Their 18- and 24-
pounders battered the biggest English ships. One cut off Phip's flagstaff and the Cross of St. George fluttered into the river, to be rescued
as a prize by Canadian boatmen. Infuriated, the colonists turned
their guns on a banner of the Holy Family floating from the spire
of the cathedral. They missed it, and the jubilant French—whose
priests and nuns had not neglected to imprecate the Virgin for direct
hits—promptly proclaimed a miracle. However, as Parkman dryly
observed, "The miracle would have been greater if they had hit it."

Riddled and listing, Sir William's ships retired from the combat.
He had attacked prematurely, he had exhausted the slender supplies
of ammunition needed for the moment when Walley pressed his
attack from the rear—and he had, in effect, lost the entire battle.
Walley, to his credit, tried to persevere in an impossible situation.
Though his small fireships never appeared, probably because their
masters also owned them and were loath to risk them under Frontenac's cannon, he still attempted to press on to the ford. But he
never crossed the St. Charles. Frontenac, with battalions of regulars,
militia and Indians, crossed it instead to oppose Walley's frozen
troops. A series of inconclusive actions was fought, and four days
after they had landed at Beauport the English withdrew to their
boats.

The capture of Port Royal and the unsuccessful attempt against
Quebec were the only military expeditions of note in King William's
War. Once they were over, the fighting degenerated into an exchange

of bloody border raids, until, in 1698, England and France ended
the War of the Grand Alliance with the Peace of Ryswick.

In that same year Count Frontenac's heart ceased to beat. That
very summer he had marched once more against the dreaded Iroquois,
but in November he took to his bed in his chamber in the Château
St. Louis. He died there, in his 78th year, and New France went
into deep mourning.

Perhaps it was understood that something more than a governor
of Canada had breathed his last. An era was also perishing. Cartier,
La Salle, Champlain, Jogues, Joliet, Marquette, all those bright and
shining names which ennoble the history of France in the New
World, all these had come before the fiery count from the Pyrenees,
and now Frontenac was also dead.

Soldiers and explorers and martyrs were to be replaced by grafting
officials, vain and petty governors and worldly priests. It was almost
as though the death of Frontenac had been concurrent with the death
of the dreams of Louis XIV. All the glory and dominion that the
Sun King sought had been his throughout most of the seventeenth
century. Now the eighteenth was at hand, and with it disaster for
Louis and for France.

3

☆

From a purely military standpoint, it would seem that the
advantage during the next three Colonial Wars lay with the French.

Feudal in structure and directed by the strong hand of a centralized
government, New France was almost as military as Sparta. Its settlers
or *habitants,* as the ordinary French people of Canada are called to
this day, were not loosely scattered through the forests as were their
southern neighbors of New England. Rather, they were strung out
in settlements on either side of the St. Lawrence. A cannon shot from
Montreal or Quebec sent them running for the forts. An order from
the governor mustered them as militia.

Moreover, the French spent the five-year truce conferred upon

America by the Peace of Ryswick in preparing for the second round of battle. New France's seaward flank had been secured by the restoration of Port Royal to the French Crown. Now, with the power of the Iroquois broken by Frontenac, the way was clear to pen the English colonies between the Alleghenies and the sea. A fort had been built at Michilimackinac at the point where the waters of Lake Michigan enter Lake Huron, and another was erected at Detroit to command the confluence of Lake Huron and Lake Erie. Eventually there was a chain of forts stretching westward from Montreal to the Mississippi; then, with the planting of a new French colony at the mouth of the Father of Waters, French lines of communication reached from the Gulf of the St. Lawrence to the Gulf of Mexico.

Such formidable activity did not seem to trouble the English colonists. More commercial than military, fragmented as a whole and perhaps even looser in its democratic parts, the English society on the Atlantic was quite naturally re-engaged in growth and gain. It was, at the beginning of the eighteenth century, a community of some quarter-million souls. That was perhaps five times larger than the colony on the St. Lawrence, thanks not so much to greater immigration as to a birth rate that was already the astonishment of Europe.

. In the South, tobacco made the Chesapeake aristocrats prosper; in the middle colonies it was land and trade; and in the North trade alone. In the Southern and middle colonies—all, except for New York, distant from Canada—there was little fear of French incursions, and little disposition to succor either New York or New England should trouble recommence. True enough, the South and the middle had Indian troubles, but nothing to compare with the howling hell that could burst on the Northern borders upon a fresh outbreak of hostilities between England and France.

And that was to occur after Louis of France had cast his covetous eyes on the crown of Spain.

In simplified terms, the War of the Spanish Succession began because King Louis claimed the Spanish throne for his grandson, Philip of Anjou. In justice to the French King, however, he was all but forced to make that claim. Had Spain gone to the rival house of Austria, the old French fear of encirclement would have been realized. But when Louis followed up his justifiable claim by a series of unwarranted aggressions, and then excluded English merchants from the Spanish colonial trade, the war began. It was a commercial war to the death. Because King William had died of injuries suffered in a fall from his horse, and his sister-in-law, Anne, now reigned in England, the Americans called it Queen Anne's War.

Queen Anne's War brought a return of the scalping horror to the borders between New England and Canada. Then, in 1704, a band of French and Indians sacked the sleeping village of Deerfield in western Massachusetts. With this, New England became enraged. Major Benjamin Church, the old Indian fighter of King Philip's War, was so infuriated that he mounted his horse in Tiverton, Rhode Island, and rode all the way to Boston. He arrived with both himself and his horse in a froth and the poor beast staggering. Church had by then grown so stout that he could not pursue Indians into the woods unless accompanied by a sergeant detailed to hoist him over fallen trees. Nevertheless, he was the only veteran soldier in the colony, and Governor Dudley at once agreed to let him lead an expedition of retaliation.

As usual, Massachusetts was not quite ready for war, and Church was unable to do more than to invade Acadia to destroy Saint-Castin's fort and burn a few houses at Grand Pré. An attempt at Port Royal in 1707 ended in failure after a brief exchange of shots that can best be described as a token fight. Still, the border outrages continued, until at last the exasperated English colonists decided that the only way to end them was to conquer Canada itself.

Captain Samuel Vetch of Boston, the prime mover in this scheme, was sent to England to solicit the help of the mother country. By the time he arrived, Vetch had expanded the plan to include the capture of Newfoundland and the expulsion of the Spanish from Florida. Then he wrote: "Her Majesty shall be sole empress of the vast North American continent."[12]

Queen Anne, however, could be quite content with Canada alone, and Vetch returned to Boston in 1709 empowered to execute a campaign which was to end with himself installed as governor of the conquered province. Montreal was to be attacked by land and Quebec by water. New York with 800 men, New Jersey with 200, Pennsylvania with 150 and Connecticut with 350 were to furnish a total of 1,500 men to be mustered at Albany by the middle of May. This force, under Colonel Francis Nicholson, was to strike at Montreal by way of the Champlain route, while a British squadron bearing five regiments of regular troops—around 3,000 men—and 1,200 militia from Massachusetts, New Hampshire and Rhode Island sailed up the St. Lawrence to invest Quebec.

New York and Connecticut promptly furnished their troops. But New Jersey, far removed from the fires of border warfare, gave no men at all; and Pennsylvania, ruled by pacifist Quakers, supplied only £3,000 with the quaint proviso that the money should not be used to kill people.

Nevertheless Colonel Nicholson was able to move up the Hudson with a force of 1,500 men. He built a stockade fort where Fort Edward now stands and cut a rough road to Wood Creek, which led to Lake Champlain. Then, while canoes were made and flatboats were brought upriver and dragged to Wood Creek, and after an inconclusive brush with a French force which seemed to return to Montreal as suddenly as it had appeared in New York, Nicholson sat down to await word of the arrival of the British fleet in Boston.

The New England soldiery encamped near Boston Harbor also awaited the British squadron. Each morning they arose and searched the horizon for the welcome sight of sails. Days became weeks and weeks months, and as the New Englanders fidgeted and Captain Vetch wrote imploring letters to England, a malignant dysentery broke out in Nicholson's camp far to the west. Men dropped by the scores. The able-bodied were busy tending the sick one day and burying the corpses the next.

At last, as autumn turned that dark green wilderness into a glowing riot of rubies and topazes, the disgusted Nicholson was forced to accept the fact that land operations against Canada were now no longer feasible, and he withdrew to Albany—his men cursing Vetch and swearing that he should be hanged. On October 11 the unfortunate Vetch received a letter from England advising him that the troops promised him had been diverted to Portugal instead.

Though deeply disappointed, the dogged New Englanders did not give up all hope of reprisal; once again they lowered their sights from Quebec to Port Royal. England was again persuaded to provide ships, and in 1710 Massachusetts again rounded up its semidrilled throng of farmers, mechanics, plowboys, clerks and apprentices. The soldiers of 1709 were asked to enlist again, this time lured by the promise

that they might keep the muskets supplied them. Once again, when volunteers fell below quotas, the colony calmly drafted the reluctant. Seamen were impressed by the forefathers of that nation which would fight a war to protect its seamen from British press gangs, and the parents of those sturdy provincials who would make mock of the dainties and delicacies in the elaborate war train of Gentleman Johnny Burgoyne did not hesitate to vote 20 sheep, 5 pigs, 100 fowl and 1 pipe of wine for the table of General Nicholson. A dinner was held at the Green Dragon Tavern in honor of Nicholson, Vetch and Sir Charles Hobby, the British squadron commander, and on the following morning, September 18, the expedition numbering about 40 ships, large and small, sailed for Acadia.

Six days later the fleet threaded the narrow entrance to Port Royal. One ship was driven on rocks and sank with the loss of 26 men, but the others anchored safely in sight of the fort. Without interference from the French garrison under Subercase, the new Governor of Acadia, Nicholson began putting his troops ashore. By the following day, September 25, the English had landed four battalions comprised of 400 British marines and about 1,500 militia—no slight achievement in an era when transports were always at the mercy of the wind and the tides.

Moving against the fort, two battalions under Vetch attacked from the north, two under Nicholson from the south. The French harried them with cannon and small arms, but the English continued to move forward until they had occupied ground within artillery range of the fort. Then their own artillery was brought up and emplaced. On October 1, after a desultory—and probably perfunctory—exchange of shots, Subercase asked for terms. Once more the golden Bourbon lilies came fluttering down Port Royal's flagstaff; the French soldiers—about 250 men—came marching out with drums rolling, colors flying and arms reversed; the English troops went marching in, the Union Jack went up the pole, the Queen's health was drunk—and in the morning the distressed French ladies of the fort were treated to a breakfast by the English officers.

For the third time irate New Englanders had responded to Canada's border attacks by seizing the capital of Acadia. This time, however, the city which Nicholson renamed Annapolis Royal in honor of Queen Anne remained British. Eventually, the entire province of Acadia fell to the British Crown.

However, one more expedition—the mightiest of all in Queen Anne's War—was mounted against Quebec.

The third attempt upon the capital of Canada was organized by the mother country, and it sprang from political motives. The new Tory ministry in England was eager to discredit the Duke of Marlborough, whose stunning victories over the French and Spanish had made him the darling of the Whigs. The Tories reasoned that if France could be evicted from America, it could be shown that this triumph would be of greater value to England than all Marlborough's victories, which were already being belittled as of more benefit to Holland and Austria than to Britain. So the new Tory ministry looked across the sea to America. A force of 12,000 men was to be raised to assault Quebec. The sea command was given to an armchair admiral named Sir Hovenden Walker and the ground forces were to be led by Mrs. Masham's brother Jack. Mrs. Masham was the new royal favorite, and her brother, Jack Hill, a man of immense social grace and no military ability, had been promoted to general.

Perhaps the most competent high commander in the entire expedition was the colonial General Nicholson, who was again to move against Montreal by way of Lake Champlain.

Walker and Hill sailed into Boston in June, 1711. They had 9 ships of war, 2 bomb ketches and about 60 transports and supply ships, carrying 7 British infantry regiments, 600 marines and artillery. After picking up 1,500 colonial militia, they steered for the St. Lawrence.

Although it was only August by the time they had reached it, Admiral Walker was already full of misgivings about the Canadian winter. He could think of nothing but ships stove in by freezing ice and men perishing of cold and hunger. "I must confess the melancholy contemplation of this," he wrote later, "for how dismal must it have been to have beheld the seas and the earth locked up by adamantine frosts, and swoln with high mountains of snow, in a barren and uncultivated region; great numbers of brave men famishing with hunger, and drawing lots who should die first to feed the rest."[13]

However, calamities of a different order afflicted Walker's fleet. Because of his own poor seamanship eight transports and two other ships were driven ashore and wrecked during a fog. Perhaps 900 persons perished, and a witness has written: "It was lamentable to hear the shrieks of the sinking, drowning, departing souls."[14] Shaken,

Walker called a council of war. Both he and Jack Hill were eager for an excuse to withdraw. They learned from the ship captains' report that they could not sail up the St. Lawrence without experienced pilots. Walker was aware that Sir William Phips had done that very thing 30 years ago; nevertheless, in the face of opposite—and indignant—counsel by such colonials as Samuel Vetch, he sailed back the way he had come.

At the foot of Wood Creek, prepared to enter Lake Champlain, General Nicholson heard the disgraceful news. "Roguery!" he cried, tearing off his wig and hurling it to the ground. "Treachery!" he screamed, stamping on the wig.[15] Recovering his composure, he ordered his forts burned and marched his force of 2,300 men back to Albany again.

Walker's ordeal was not quite ended. As the British fleet sailed up the Thames, a sailor attempting to steal gunpowder accidentally blew up the flagship, *Edgar*. Five hundred more men were lost in this tragic conclusion to the most ambitious of all projects to conquer Canada. The commanders sent out to eclipse the glory of the great Marlborough had accepted defeat without unsheathing their swords.

4

☆

The debacle on the St. Lawrence made the Tories eager to end hostilities, and in 1713 the Treaty of Utrecht brought the War of the Spanish Succession to a close.

England, Holland and Austria had fought to prevent the union of France and Spain under a Bourbon king, but the war ended with a grandson of Louis of France firmly seated on the Spanish throne. Nevertheless, both France and Spain were exhausted. France was forced to cede Acadia, Hudson's Bay and Newfoundland to England, while Spain handed over Gibraltar at the mouth of the Mediterranean and the sentinel island of Minorca inside it. Both France and

Spain granted England important trade concessions, while Spain, by leasing to England the slave trade to Latin America, indicated to what woeful depths her once proud fleets had sunk.

The British lion had not only obtained its customary share, it had grown stronger at sea at the expense of its ally—but foremost maritime rival—the Dutch Republic. Holland had supplied only three-eighths of the naval forces, against Britain's five-eighths, but she contributed 102,000 soldiers against Britain's 40,000. By accident or design, the Dutch exhausted themselves in an unfamiliar land war while Britain became supreme upon the sea. She was the queen of the waves, not only in her invincible navy but also in her merchant fleet. As Mahan writes: ". . . she was *the* sea power, without any second. This power also she held alone, unshared by friend and unchecked by foe."[16]

Posted now in the Mediterranean, America and the West Indies, Britain began to build that far-flung empire which dazzled the world for two and a half centuries; and she achieved this because she was conscious of the unique value of sea power, as her rivals in the House of Bourbon were not. Her conscious policy was the destruction of the French and Spanish navies and the strengthening of her own. Ports and harbors and strategic islands, not kingdoms, were the objects of her desire; and she sought them as outlets for trade and as bases for her fleets. She could cross no enemy's land frontier, but she could strike at them all from the sea. Without borders of her own, the sea gave her the world for her neighbor.

It was the new Kingdom of Prussia which convulsed Europe again. Once a mere duchy on the Polish border, Prussia was proclaimed a sovereign state in 1701 by the Margrave of Brandenburg, who thereafter became known as King Frederick I of Prussia. After his death, his son, Frederick William, succeeded to the throne.

Frederick William infected Prussia with its demonic spirit of militarism. He was obsessed with his army, with his tall grenadiers whom he had kidnaped from every corner of the world, and with whom he mated tall women similarly enslaved. But Frederick William did not live to lead his splendid army into battle. Instead, it was his son, Frederick II, who lifted the sword the father had forged.

Frederick swung at Austria, because that empire had been left helpless with the death of Emperor Charles VI in 1740. Charles's dominions were bequeathed to his daughter, Maria Theresa, and his will had been guaranteed in advance by the chief powers of Europe. But not a sovereign kept his word. Led by young Frederick of Prussia, who almost at once marched into Maria's province of Silesia and seized it, a pack of bejeweled jackals flocked forward to despoil the beautiful young queen's realm. After Frederick came Spain, Bavaria and then France. England, ever anxious to preserve the balance of power, as well as the Hanoverian holdings of King George II, rushed to Austria's side. Holland followed. Maria Theresa fought back, and the War of the Austrian Succession—the conflict which the colonists called King George's War—had begun.

The first blow struck for King George in America came from the new colony which had been named Georgia in his honor.

In the summer of 1740, James Oglethorpe, Georgia's founder, decided to evict the Spanish from the first European settlement in North America: St. Augustine. Then Florida would fall to the Union Jack and the Atlantic seaboard would be English from the Bay of Fundy to the Gulf of Mexico. But the Spaniards foiled him. They reinforced St. Augustine from Havana, and Oglethorpe's motley of 2,000 English and Indians sailed back to Georgia sunburned and hungry.

Three years later, the commander at St. Augustine, Don Manuel de Monteano, attempted a reverse expedition. He hoped to expel the English from the weak colony which stood as a buffer between New Spain and the rich and populous Carolinas. Even Virginia—and thus the entire South—would be annexed to Spain.

Monteano's force was much larger than Oglethorpe's had been. About 50 ships carrying about 6,000 men and artillery sailed up to St. Simon's Island off the Georgia coast. Here Oglethorpe had entrenched himself with a few thousand American Rangers and wild Highlanders from Scotland, and here he proved himself a more capable commander on defense than on offense. Though outnumbered, he took ship and struck boldly at the Spanish vessels; after which he returned to land, forced Monteano into attacking him piecemeal, destroyed the pieces, and finally frightened the Spaniards off with a bogus letter which, planted on Monteano by an "escaped" Spanish soldier bribed for the occasion, warned of the approach of a huge English fleet.

The first and only land clash of any consequence between England and Spain in North America had ended in stalemate. There was no more colonial fighting under the Southern sun. Thereafter, the Colonial Wars were fought within the familiar gloom of primeval forests or the mistbound coasts of the North.

Louis XIV had hated to give up Acadia. He had even offered to bar French fishermen from those Newfoundland coasts which they had patrolled for centuries if the English would allow him to keep those lands now called Nova Scotia. But all that he could obtain by way of compromise was the restoration of Cape Breton Island just a few miles east of Acadia. Even in this, the English ministers at Utrecht were not wise; in relinquishing Cape Breton Island they at once destroyed the military value of Acadia.

King Louis saw that the island wilderness was the true guardian of the St. Lawrence, and before he died he caused a port to be fortified to that end, and against the day when war would be resumed and France might attack New England and attempt to recover Acadia.

The new port grew into a fishing village of 4,000 persons. It became a harbor so well defended and a privateering refuge so secure that it was called the "Dunkirk of America." And it was named Louisbourg in the king's honor.

The power of Louisbourg was demonstrated when the French captured Canso and attempted but failed to take Annapolis Royal. Obviously, Acadia was at the mercy of the new French base on Cape Breton Island. Because of this, and because the French had renewed their border warfare, the colonists of Massachusetts decided to capture Louisbourg.

Governor William Shirley invited other colonies as far south as Pennsylvania to join the expedition. As usual, all but the New Englanders declined, and even Rhode Island did not provide troops in time for battle. Of the force finally assembled, 3,300 came from Massachusetts, 516 from Connecticut and 454 from New Hampshire, of which 150 were paid by Massachusetts. Some of these men—particularly the hardy borderers from Maine—had fought in the recent war against the Norridgewock Indians; but few, if any, had the sort of experience required for siege warfare against the ramparts and casemented batteries of a fortified town.

"Fortified towns are hard nuts to crack," Benjamin Franklin had written to his brother in Boston, "and your teeth are not accustomed to it. But some seem to think that forts are as easy taken as snuff."[17]

In Boston such good advice was regarded as typical of pacifist Philadelphia. Tough nut or no, Louisbourg and its Papists had already been consigned to the jaws of the Lord. What Cotton Mather once called "the wheel of prayer" was whirring night and day. The very man whom Governor Shirley had appointed to lead the expedition was known to be a pious man of God. William Pepperrell, a highly successful merchant as well as a man of extreme good sense—though no military experience, as he would himself declare—counted many clergymen among his friends. With him at the very moment Shirley appointed him a lieutenant general was none other than George Whitefield, that squint-eyed breather of fire whose archangelic voice had summoned New England to its Great Awakening. At the moment, that revivalist frenzy seemed to be subsiding, and another of Pepperrell's clerical friends was already complaining: "The heavenly shower [is] over; from fighting the devil they must turn to fighting the French."

Pepperrell himself would have preferred to continue with the devil, for he was aware that his forces included not an officer of experience, not even an engineer. Nevertheless he was persuaded to accept. Whitefield, meanwhile, was persuaded to supply a motto. He offered, *"Nil desperandum Christo duce,"* or "Despair not when Christ leads." Old Parson Moody, he of the iron lungs and marathon sermons, also joined the crusade against the antichrist. He brought along an ax to hew down his abominable altars.

Such was the crusading character of the expedition, and it was this ardor of intolerance which brought Parson Moody and General Pepperrell and 90 ships and 4,200 raw recruits to Louisbourg on the morning of April 28, 1745.

To enter Louisbourg basin would have been suicide. Even the warships of the British squadron which had joined the colonists would not attempt it. Instead, they blockaded the port.

To the east or the right of the town itself was a small entrance barely a half-mile wide. Commanding this was the "Island Battery" mounted on a rocky island to the west or left of the entrance. Directly ahead of the entrance on the basin's north shore was the "Grand

Battery." Ships attempting to force the harbor would be raked port and forward. So General Pepperrell sagely decided to put his troops ashore at Flat Point, three miles west of the town.

The Chevalier Duchambon, Governor of Louisbourg, sent 120 men to repulse them. Although Duchambon had 560 regulars and 1,400 militia, he probably did not send a larger force because he could not rely on rough and untried conscripts or soldiers ready to mutiny over pay and rations. So a Captain Morpain led his handful of defenders to Flat Point. They dug in, awaiting the English rowing toward them. Suddenly the English veered away, as though they dared not risk the surf boiling over Flat Point's rocky coast. Captain Morpain relaxed. He began to flatter himself on a bloodless repulse. But then, to his dismay, he saw that more English boats had been lowered away and that the reinforced body was rowing madly for Fresh-Water Cove another two miles to the west.

Morpain and his French soldiers went flying up the coast. But they were too late. The invaders were already ashore. Turning, they fell upon the French, killed six and captured six, and routed the rest against only two of their own men wounded. More and more boats came bobbing through the surf and soon General Pepperrell had a firm beachhead.

Louisbourg had been flanked.

On May 2 Captain William Vaughan, a bold though sometimes rash man, led 400 troops through the hills to the northwest of the town. His men saluted Louisbourg with three rousing cheers, and the inhabitants, surprised by the ragged and disorderly appearance of this crowd of colonists, were also startled by their vigor. Then Vaughan marched to the hills to the rear of the Grand Battery and put a supply of naval stores to the torch. Thick oily coils of smoke swirled skyward, to the dismay of the occupants of Louisbourg— and to the unseemly fright of the troops holding the Grand Battery.

Imagining that Vaughan had come to attack them, they hastily spiked their guns, threw gunpowder into the well and withdrew to the town in boats—leaving 30 of the King's good cannon to fall into the hands of Vaughan, who quickly occupied the battery in their absence. Soon a squad of soldier-mechanics had drilled out the cannons' spiked touchholes, and, in the words of an *habitant* of Louisbourg: "The enemy saluted us with our own cannon, and made a terrific fire, smashing everything within range."[18]

The ragged rabble which the civilian Pepperrell commanded was amazingly constant and cheerful. They built an encampment near Fresh-Water Cove, making tepees by stretching old sails over poles, or building sod huts with spruce boughs for roofs. They unloaded boats by wading up to the waist through ice-cold surf, and at night they threw themselves down, dripping wet, on soggy ground discharging the mists and chills of the thaw.

Next, in tatters and sometimes barefoot, they began dragging Pepperrell's cannon eastward toward Louisbourg. The first attempt to move a gun through the intervening marsh resulted in the loss of the piece, which vanished in the slime. Sledges of timber 16 by 5 feet were then made; cannon were placed on top of them, and teams of 200 men harnessed in breast straps and rope traces, sloshing through knee-deep mud and mush, began hauling them over the marsh. But this could only be done under cover of night or thick fog. Toiling "under almost incredible hardships," as Pepperrell was to write in admiration, they got the guns in place.

Battery after battery was planted under the strangely languorous nose of the Chevalier Duchambon. Louisbourg was hammered from the west, northwest, north and northeast. In all, the bellowing of five new batteries had been added to the cannonade issuing from the captured Grand Battery. Still, Duchambon sent forth no sallies to destroy the guns that were destroying him. Perhaps he still feared mutiny, although mutiny would seem less dangerous than the torrent of balls that was shredding Louisbourg's walls and forcing a terrified citizenry to take refuge within stifling casements.

It may also have been that Duchambon was aware that the New England army was in dire straits. Their food supply was low, ammunition was running out, Louisbourg's cannon and the accurate small-arms fire of the French soldiers had whittled their ranks, and diarrhea and fever had ravaged the remainder. In all, Pepperrell had only 2,100 men fit for duty. The disadvantages which always work against the besiegers in siege warfare were beginning to work in Duchambon's favor. And if the French ship Vigilant arrived with promised reinforcements, he might still be saved.

Vigilant, carrying 64 guns and 560 men and munitions and stores for the relief of Louisbourg, was commanded by the Marquis de la Maisonfort. On May 19 *Vigilant* came upon a small English cruiser. The little Englishman attacked. *Vigilant* replied with broadsides. The cruiser fled, still firing; *Vigilant* pursued, and found that she had been led straight into the massed guns of a British squadron. Maisonfort and his men fought gallantly, but after 80 men had been lost, the French commander was forced to strike his colors.

British sea power had saved Pepperrell's army and doomed the French. "We were victims devoted to appease the wrath of Heaven," wrote the *habitant,* "which turned our own arms into weapons for our enemies."[19]

Nevertheless, Duchambon did not know that he was doomed until after the English had also incurred the Heavenly wrath.

The impetuous Captain Vaughan was certain that the Island Battery was the key to Louisbourg. Capture it, and British troops could enter the harbor while Pepperrell's men stormed the town from the land. Vaughan proposed this before news of *Vigilant's* fall reached Pepperrell.

After midnight of May 23, about 300 men clambered into boats beached off the Grand Battery. It was a dark night and they hoped to gain the Island Battery undetected. They used paddles to make no noise. A rising wind also covered their approach. The leading boats reached the island's breakers, drove boldly through them, and scrambled ashore—still unseen.

And then they gave three cheers!

Island Battery "blazed with cannon, swivels, and small-arms." A withering fire plunged into these foolish commandos, and into the following boats piled up on the shore. The English fought back bravely. They even succeeded in placing a dozen scaling ladders against the walls of the fort, but with daybreak it was hopeless to fight on. Those who did not escape surrendered, to the number of 119. In all, English losses were 189, or more than half of the attacking force.

The only pitched battle had ended in an English defeat, although Louisbourg was already undone. The town's fate was sealed when Pepperrell wisely decided to mount another battery on Lighthouse Point across the harbor entrance from Island Battery. The Lighthouse guns gradually reduced the island to impotence. All was in readiness for a final land-sea assault jointly commanded by General Pepperrell and Commodore Peter Warren, commander of the British squadron. It was to commence June 15. On that day, Captain Joseph Sherburn at the advanced battery, wrote in his diary: "By 12 o'clock we had got all our platforms laid, embrazures mended, guns in order, shot in place, cartridges ready, dined, gunners quartered, matches lighted to return their favours, when we heard their drums beat a parley; and soon appeared a flag of truce, which I received midway between our battery and their walls."[20]

Duchambon was asking for terms. Two days later Louisbourg was occupied by the English. "Never was a town more mauled with cannon and shells," Pepperrell wrote to Governor Shirley, "neither have I read in History of any troops behaving with greater courage."[21]

He was right. The disorderly rabble had taken a fortified city with the bold precision of troops trained in siege warfare. Pepperrell's New Englanders had won the only outstanding engagement of King George's War. True, there would be skirmishes to follow, and a French fleet more powerful than the English one which Admiral Walker and Jack Hill had led to disaster and disgrace in the last war was to encounter ordeals even more dreadful and to achieve as little in its attempt to retake Louisbourg and succor Canada.

Even if it had done so, its success would have been superfluous. Much to the indignant disgust of *"les Bastonnais,"* the Peace of Aix-la-Chapelle which ended the War of the Austrian Succession in 1748 returned Louisbourg to the French Crown.

5

☆

Aix-la-Chapelle solved next to nothing,
It gave Europe a breathing spell during which the contending powers realigned themselves, and it bestowed upon the American colonies of England and France a fitful peace soon to degenerate into undeclared war.

Both colonies knew that they could not remain at peace. Between their rival claims and conflicting ambitions there could be no compromise.

France claimed the continent from the Alleghenies to the Rockies, from Florida and Mexico to the North Pole. She possessed the two great waterways—the St. Lawrence and the Mississippi—and two bases of operations in Canada in the north and Louisiana in the south. Moreover, by the middle of the century she had occupied all the points controlling the waterways between Montreal and New Orleans and had even entered New York to plant a stone fort at Crown Point on Lake Champlain. The English colonies had thus been penned between the barrier of the Allegheny Mountains and the Atlantic Ocean. France desired to keep them there while she explored and exploited the vast American interior.

The English, however, not only rejected the French claim, but also aspired to enter the interior—not to exploit but to settle. Should they break out of the Allegheny enclave, they would cut New France in two. To prevent this, the French began to seal off the passes to the west.

They built a fort at Presque Isle on Lake Erie, at the point where the city of Erie, Pennsylvania, now stands; and then cut a road about ten miles long to French Creek, placing at the road's end another outpost called Fort Le Boeuf. They could now cross Lake Erie from Canada to Presque Isle, march overland to Fort Le Boeuf and follow French Creek to the Allegheny River, descending that swift stream to the Ohio River. This was done in 1753. Just before winter, the French evicted an English trader from his house at Venango, the place where French Creek enters the Allegheny.

Venango was France's farthest outpost. It was a clearing in the wilderness, caught between the steady roar of merging waters and the eternal silence of the forests. One day in December the three French officers who occupied the house there thought that they heard the thud of horses' hoofs approaching. A tall young Englishman came riding out of the woods.

He was only 21, but he was already a commanding figure. Tall at six feet three inches, strongly built, his angular cheeks pitted by the scars of the smallpox which had threatened his life a few years before, his humorless eyes full of his unbending determination,

Major George Washington of the Virginia Militia had come to Venango on a mission for Governor Robert Dinwiddie.

Washington had been in Williamsburg at the end of October, 1753, just after Governor Dinwiddie had received the King's approval for his plan to evict the French from the Ohio country. His Majesty promised military equipment, and in the meantime Dinwiddie was to warn the French that they were encroaching upon English lands and to call upon them to retire. Although the icy hand of winter would soon hold the Ohio in its grip, Dinwiddie, an aggressive man, wished to notify the French before they could build any more strong points. Who better than Washington to carry the message?

On Dinwiddie's orders, Washington assembled his party: horses, baggage, four orderlies and hostlers and a veteran of the Dutch army named Jacob van Braam who said he could speak French. On November 15, 1753, they set out for the Ohio country. It was a difficult journey, over strange terrain and beneath the cold rains of the dying autumn. But on December 4 Washington and his companions rode out of the dripping woods at Venango.

The French officers there greeted Washington with flawless courtesy. They also tried to lure his Indians to their side. Failing in this, they suavely refused the young Virginian's message and sent him up French Creek to Fort Le Boeuf to their superior officer, Legardeur de St. Pierre. At Le Boeuf, Washington presented Dinwiddie's demand that the French leave the Ohio country. It was politely refused by St. Pierre. "He told me," Washington wrote later, "that the country belonged to [the French]; that no Englishman had a right to trade upon those waters; and that he had orders to make every person prisoner who attempted it on the Ohio, or the waters of it."[22]

On December 16, bearing St. Pierre's reply, Washington and his party started downriver for Venango. They hurried, plying their paddles furiously, for the creek had begun to freeze. Leaving Venango, Washington discovered that his horses which had been quartered there were too feeble to carry riders. They dismounted and began to walk. Snow was falling regularly. The temperatures fell. Some of the men were so frostbitten they had to be left in a temporary shack. Washington pressed on grimly, eager to get the French answer to Dinwiddie as soon as possible. If he delayed, he might be snowed in until spring, when the French would be already on the move. Eventually, the young major struck out on foot with his guide.

"I took my necessary papers, pulled off my clothes, and tied myself up in a match coat. Then with gun in hand and pack at my back, I set out with Mr. Gist, fitted in the same manner."[23]

They were shot at—and missed—by a false Indian guide. Attempting to cross the Allegheny by a log raft, Washington was thrown into the icy water—only saving himself by throwing one long arm across the raft. But both men could not pole through the current to either shore, and they waded ashore on a little island, spending the night sheeted in ice. In the morning, to their inexpressible joy, they beheld the treacherous river locked in a silent white vise of ice. They crossed, and on January 16, 1754—exactly one month after his departure from Fort Le Boeuf—George Washington placed the French refusal in Governor Dinwiddie's hand.

At the age of 21 the Father of America had already entered his nation's history.

With hindsight, it seems incredible that New France should have even thought of victory in the contest for North America. By 1754 the continent held barely 80,000 Frenchmen, of whom only 55,000 were in Canada. In contrast, the English colonies numbered 1,250,-000 souls. They were richer, they lived in a less exhausting climate, and some of them possessed infant industries capable of producing some of the necessities of war. However, where New France was military and feudal, they were peaceful and democratic. A Canadian governor, usually a veteran military commander, had only to issue his order to send canoes and bateaux swarming down the rivers to the Ohio country. A colonial governor had no such power over people extremely sensitive of their liberties and their right to self-rule. Abhorring war and waste, loving peace and gain, they could rarely be made to see that in the America of that day war was only slightly less avoidable than the continent's twin scourges of smallpox and malaria.

Moreover, there were 13 governors whereas Canada—the actual instrument of French policy—had only one. Canada was unified in race and religion, as the 13 colonies were not. Anticipating the pluralist character of the American nation, the colonies were a welter of races and creeds and a mosaic of differing interests and forms of government. New England was, of course, almost wholly English and Puritan and representative. But other colonies, though

predominantly Anglo-Saxon, included many more races. Pennsylvania was a conglomerate of English, Germans, Irish, Dutch, Scotch-Irish (or Ulster Scots) and Swedes. They were Anglicans, Quakers, Lutherans, Catholics, Presbyterians and Moravians, to say nothing of lesser-known sects already beginning to splinter and resplinter under the double impetus of border life and the American ideal of private judgment. Delaware, New York, New Jersey and Maryland had racial and religious variety to a lesser degree, and there were large settlements of Ulster Scots on the western borders of North Carolina and Virginia.

Virginia herself differed almost as much from New England society as did Canada. She was Anglican, and her tobacco-growing aristocracy openly adopted the airs of those cavaliers of King Charles I whom the Roundhead ancestors of the Puritans had detested. Virginia society was nearly as finely structured as Canadian feudalism, a pyramid based on the Negro slaves in the field and rising upward through indentured servants and other poor whites—all unlettered—proceeding next to the despised though literate merchants and mechanics, and then to the farmers and smaller planters, most of whom struggled and schemed to rise to the apex of the structure where the great landowners resided and ruled with almost regal elegance.

Finally, only New York and New England, under the guns and hatchets of the French and Indians, could be made to see that England's war with France was also their own. Even Virginia, mother of so many American captains, kept "out of it" until the French began to invade those western lands which Virginia considered her own. Even so, Governor Dinwiddie's attempts to raise forces to evict those French illustrates how even an aroused aristocracy was reluctant to take the rough road to war.

The Burgesses gave Dinwiddie a most frugal grant of money, and then, jealous of their prerogatives, placed that in the hands of a committee of their own. Of the other colonies to whom Dinwiddie appealed for help, only North Carolina—also claiming western lands—replied with men and money of her own.

The final proof of French capacity to move and English reluctance to take preventive action came when Dinwiddie attempted to fortify that point which today is called Pittsburgh and which then was a fork of land where the confluence of the Allegheny and Monongahela gives birth to the great Ohio River.

"The land in the forks," young George Washington had written, "I think extremely well situated for a fort, as it has the absolute command of both rivers. The land at the point is twenty or twenty-five feet above the common surface of the water; and a considerable bottom of flat, well-timbered land all around it, very convenient for building."[24]

Dinwiddie resolved to fortify the Ohio forks and in February of 1754 he sent a band of backwoodsmen to seize them and build a fort there. In the meanwhile, he argued with the Burgesses over funds, began rounding up independent companies of British regulars, and got half of the Virginia militia regiment of 300 men moving toward the Ohio under young Washington, now a lieutenant colonel. Before the Governor could get the other half moving, the French came bobbing down the Allegheny, took the English fort by summons, demolished it and replaced it with a larger one of their own.

Fort Duquesne now held the West for France.

Lieutenant Colonel Washington was just across the Alleghenies—perhaps 110 miles southeast of Duquesne—when he heard of the disaster. Immediately, he began pushing northwest to establish a forward base for the arrival of reinforcements and artillery. On May 28, 1754, halfway to Duquesne, he surprised an advance party of French.

Jumonville de Villiers, the French leader, was slain in the first volley. After Washington's Indians had brained and scalped the wounded, there were 10 French dead, 1 wounded and 21 captured, against Washington's losses of one wounded. It had been the youthful commander's first fight, and he was elated at the near-perfect result. In fact, his biggest difficulty came in keeping his fierce ally, Half King, from killing and scalping his prisoners. Half King swore that he would be avenged on the French for killing, boiling and eating his father.

But Washington dissuaded him, after which the young Virginian withdrew ten miles to a place called Great Meadows. Here he threw up a ramshackle stockade aptly named Fort Necessity. Meanwhile, all Canada and later France seethed with rage over the "murder" of Villiers by "the cruel Vvasington [*sic*]." The dead man's brother, the Sieur Coulon de Villiers, came marching hotly from Montreal to avenge "*l'assassin*." On July 3 his 900 men clashed with Washington's 400 at Fort Necessity.

The French quickly drove the English into rain-filled trenches, and then they carefully shot down every horse, cow or dog within the fort. In a half-hour the English realized that their transport and meat were gone. By nightfall it was obvious that the English were beaten, and the disconsolate young Washington, certain that a glorious career had ended before it had barely begun, sent his old comrade Jacob van Braam out into the night to ask for terms.

The French were generous. They could not have known that van Braam had mistaken the French word for assassination for the word death and they were pleased that Washington was willing to acknowledge his crime of murdering Jumonville. Unaware of a concession he would certainly never have made, Washington capitulated. Next day the English were accorded the honors of war.

Drums beating, colors flying, arms sloped, they marched out of the slime of Fort Necessity while the Indians went rushing in to plunder all that had been left behind. Though the English attempted to show a proud face, they were weary and hungry, many of them carried wounded men on their backs, and they had barely enough powder and ball to drive off the hostile Indians who harried them along the 60 miles back to Wills Creek. A heart-breaking march had begun, and the youth who led it never forgot the day that it started.

It was the fourth of July.

6

The skirmish with Jumonville de Villiers and the fight at Fort Necessity were the tiny sparks which set battlefields blazing in the Old World, in India and in North America.

As yet, neither England nor France had found it convenient to make a formal declaration of war; and the Seven Years' War was still 19 months away. Nevertheless, both France and England seemed content to allow their colonists in the New World to continue to strike at each other in what was nothing less than a head start on the fourth and final round in the Anglo-French war for empire.

Again, the early advantage seemed to lie with the French. Coulon de Villiers' victory over Washington had brought almost all of the wavering western Indians to their side. Flanked by the Spanish of Florida and the French of Louisiana in the South, by the French in the West and the North, with the sea at their backs, divided and disorganized, the 13 colonies at last resolved to act.

A congress was convened at Albany and the famous Indian agent, William Johnson, was sent to the Iroquois to persuade the Five Nations to remain loyal to the English. At the Albany congress, however, neither the colonies nor the Crown could sink their mutual distrust, and the famous plan for union proposed by Benjamin Franklin was rejected by the Crown because it gave too much power to the colonies and by the colonies because it gave too much power to the Crown. Neither side was willing to relinquish governmental functions to the central council proposed by Franklin.

So the colonies continued to flounder along their separate ways, and as they did the French mother country prepared their destruction. Eighteen ships carrying six battalions of regulars—3,000 men in all —sailed from France for America. With them went their commander, the German veteran Baron Dieskau, who had served under the great Marshal Saxe, as well as Canada's new governor, Pierre François Rigaud, Marquis de Vaudreuil, son of an early governor of the colony.

England, however, learned of the French preparations. At once, plans were made to send two regiments of regulars to America, and Admiral Edward Boscawen was ordered to intercept the French force sailing for Canada.

Boscawen stationed his squadron off the mouth of the St. Lawrence. But a fog which had scattered the French fleet also enabled all but two of the ships to elude Boscawen and arrive safely at Quebec and Louisbourg. The other two—*Alcide* and *Lis*—were attacked and overpowered by the British, and two French battalions were taken prisoner. With this action of June 8, 1755, the two mother countries at last crossed swords.

Major General Edward Braddock commanded the British and colonial forces in America. Short, stout and choleric, Braddock was as brave as he was bullheaded, and he had not been in America very long before he had condemned most colonials as a crowd of ignorant sloths, reserving a special contempt for colonial troops.

Braddock was schooled in the tactics of European warfare which had been developed since the turn of the century. After the flintlock had replaced the firelock, and with the development of the socket bayonet, infantry tactics had been simplified. Four kinds of infantry —pikemen, musketeers, fusiliers and grenadiers—were now reduced to one general type of foot soldier armed with bayoneted flintlock. He was drilled incessantly and subjected to a barbarously brutal discipline, which made him, in effect, a battlefield automaton.* He fought in the open against other automatons also taught to wheel and to dress ranks amid the very smoke and stress of battle, to load and advance, fire and reload—and to drive home the assault with the bayonet under the smoke of the final volley.

A musket's killing range was only a few hundred paces, and firing was not very accurate; in fact, the British fire drill of the period did not include the order "Aim." The object was not so much to riddle the enemy as to frighten him and pin him down for the shock action of the cavalry. Such tactics, adjusted to terrain and weapons as tactics always are, were almost the opposite of American bush fighting in which the forests imposed a premium upon dispersion, cover and accuracy. To say that Braddock could not or would not see this difference is only to say, after all, that he was an ordinarily competent commander not gifted with the insights of genius. New wars are always being fought with the fixations of the old, and Edward Braddock was no exception to that dreary axiom as he reached Wills Creek on the tenth of May to take command of his army.

Braddock had a fourfold plan for eviction of the French. He would personally lead the operation against Duquesne, while another force destroyed Fort Niagara on Lake Ontario, a third reduced the French bastion at Crown Point on Lake Champlain and a fourth sailed to Acadia to rid that province of the French forever. All these points were to be attacked at once, neither Braddock nor the colonial governor seeming to question the feasibility of coordinating multiple operations in a wilderness passable only along its waterways or by painfully cleared roads, and in an age when all forms of transport were still at the mercy of the weather.

For his own expedition against Duquesne, Braddock had some-

---

* In 1712 a British guardsman was sentenced to 12,600 lashes and nearly died after he received the first 1,800.

thing over 2,000 men divided among 1,400 British regulars in bright red coats, perhaps 450 Virginia militia—those contemptible "blues" of whom Braddock said "their slothful and languid disposition renders them very unfit for military service"—about 300 axmen assembled to cut the road, and an unknown number of Indians. Of these, Braddock would lead an advance force of 1,500 men while Colonel Thomas Dunbar followed with the remainder. At the end of May, working parties began cutting the road.

The French had decided not to await the English. Scouting reports had made it clear that the approaching enemy possessed enough artillery to batter down even the stout log walls of Fort Duquesne. Accordingly, the Sieur de Contrecoeur ordered Captain Daniel Beaujeu to ambush Braddock's force.

Beaujeu was aware that the terrain would probably force the British to cross and recross the Monongahela. About seven miles from Fort Duquesne lay the second or lower ford which would allow the enemy to return inside the triangle again. It was a place made for ambush, and on July 8 Beaujeu led about 900 men—650 Indians, 100 French, 150 Canadians—southeast toward it.

Unfortunately for Beaujeu, half of his Indians strayed away from him during the day's march, and he was unable to prepare his ambuscade. On July 9, under the covering guns of an advance party led by Lieutenant Colonel Thomas Gage, Braddock's army successfully recrossed the Monongahela. Only seven miles of easy going now separated the English from Fort Duquesne. The men were in high spirits. Some officers predicted that before they reached the French fort the enemy would blow it up.

George Washington was also jubilant. Though racked with pain and weakened by an illness which had kept him an invalid with Colonel Dunbar's rear echelon, he had risen from his pallet on a jolting pack wagon, fastened a pillow to his horse's saddle to ease the agony of riding, mounted and overtaken Braddock so that he, George Washington of Mount Vernon, the first Englishman to lay eyes on the site of Fort Duquesne, might also have the honor of witnessing its fall.

Gradually, the marching column straightened out. From point to point it measured 2,000 yards. There were guides in front and flankers to either side. All seemed secure as Harry Gordon, the army's engineer, rode forward looking for the guides. Suddenly they came running back to tell him that they had seen the enemy. Then Gordon saw a white man in Indian dress come sprinting through the woods. It was Beaujeu. Behind him were about 300 French and Indians, also approaching on the run. Beaujeu caught sight of the scarlet coats behind Gordon. He stopped. He waved his arms to right and left, and Gordon stiffened in the saddle to hear the blood-curdling Indian war whoop. Then Beaujeu's men parted and vanished in the woods on either side of the English, and began raking both flanks.

Gage's troops wheeled into line almost immediately. Shouting "God save the King!" they discharged volley after volley. They killed Beaujeu and sent his Canadians flying away in fright. Captain Dumas, now in command, rallied the Indians, who had stood their ground. They hid behind trees or fallen trunks, they crouched in gullies or ravines, and thus invisible they poured a heavy fire into the close-packed red coats of the British soldiery.

Soon the British fell silent. In their ears was a frightful cacophony. The endless yelling of the Indians, the screams of their own stricken, the rolling musket fire of the battle, all were picked up and sent reverberating through the encircling gloom of the forest. Rare was the British regular who saw his enemies, and rarer still was the survivor who ever forgot that whooping and screeching.

Only the despised Virginians seemed capable of fighting back. A party of them led by Captain Thomas Waggener dashed for a huge fallen tree. They threw themselves down behind it and began picking off red men flitting from cover to cover or darting to the road to scalp a dead or wounded soldier. But the British regulars mistook their only friends for foemen and they opened fire on the Virginia rear, killing many colonials and forcing the rest to withdraw.

Now from a hill to the English right came a plunging fire. Demoralized and then terrified, the redcoats fired volley after volley into thin air. They riddled the trees and chipped the rocks. Some of them tried to take cover like the colonials, but their officers would not allow them. They yanked them erect or away from trees and strode among them with bared swords, crying angrily: "Stand and fight!" Back came the pitiful plea: "We would fight if we could see anybody to fight with."[25] And so, rather than disperse, they stood fast; they huddled together, shrinking from the bullets that swept among them, presenting to their tormentors larger and ever larger targets of red.

Suddenly the rumor spread that the French and Indians were attacking the baggage train in the rear. Gage's men turned and ran. They thundered over St. Clair's working party, abandoned their cannon to the enemy, and came tumbling eastward into the ranks of the British main body even as General Braddock led these soldiers forward.

Now both British regiments were mixed and confusion reigned unchecked. The towering fury of Braddock riding among them failed to rally this disorganized mass. How could it have? Braddock beat his men with the flat of his sword rather than allow them to adopt the "cowardly" cover which is the only way to fight in a forest. He refused George Washington's request to allow him to take the provincials against the hill on the right in Indian style. Instead, he ordered Lieutenant Colonel Ralph Burton to storm the height with dressed ranks. Burton obeyed. He rallied a hundred regulars, who followed him until he fell wounded, after which they melted away.

Gage was also wounded, as were Horatio Gates and Braddock's two aides, Robert Orme and William Morris. The carnage among the officers was frightful. Mounted, resplendent in laced regimentals, the English leaders were choice targets. Sir Peter Halkett was shot dead. So was young William Shirley, son of the Massachusetts Governor. Of 86 officers, 63 were killed or wounded.

Washington himself had four shots through his clothes, and two mounts were shot from under him. Braddock lost four horses, mounted a fifth—and took a musket ball that passed through his right arm and pierced his lung. He fell gasping into the bushes beside the road.

It was then that the retreat which Braddock had ordered became a frenzied rout. The English simply turned and fled for the river in their rear. Some of them were scalped by pursuing Indians even as they plunged into the ford. Washington saw that it was useless to attempt to rally them on the right bank of the Monongahela. Instead, he came to Braddock's side, placed the wounded general in a cart, and conveyed him across the river.

Behind him, howling hideously, the Indians took possession of the field.

It had not been possible to rally the fleeing army on the left bank of the Monongahela, either. Throughout the horrible blackness of the night of July 9, the routed remnants of Braddock's army stumbled steadily southeastward. All along the road back were the sounds of lost horses blundering blindly through the bush, of soldiers cursing as they stumbled over the dying bodies of men who could crawl no longer, or of other wounded crying piteously to be carried away from the dreaded scalping knives of the red men.

Nor was it possible to make a stand when Dunbar's camp was reached, 50 miles back. Here the wagons were burned, cannon and cohorns burst and their shells buried, barrels of gunpowder stove in, and food scattered through the forests. Here, too, the wounded bulldog Braddock came to the end of the trail.

He had remained silent throughout the day and night of the tenth, looking up only to say, "Who would have thought it?"[26] Another day passed in giving orders, and then, after another prolonged silence, Braddock added, "We shall better know how to deal with them another time."[27] Next day, cursing his redcoats while praising his officers and "the blues" of Virginia, Edward Braddock died.

Washington buried him with the honors of war. The corpse was lowered into a short, deep trench. It was covered without a marker. To efface the grave from the sight of marauding Indians, the defeated army passed over it on the retreat to Wills Creek.

7

☆

While Braddock was marching to his defeat, the colonies were launching the remaining three operations in his fourfold plan to evict the French. Of these, the expedition to Nova Scotia was the most successful.

Although the Acadians, who were the sole inhabitants of Nova Scotia, had taken an oath of allegiance to the British King, the French from Canada had begun to encroach upon these now English lands. They had built a fort at Beauséjour on the isthmus linking Nova Scotia with present-day New Brunswick.

This fort was captured on the lucky chance of an English shell having pierced a French bombproof at the moment when its occupants—the officers of Beauséjour—were sitting down to breakfast. Six of them were killed, and the English, having only just begun their bombardment, were astonished to see a white flag waving above Beauséjour's ramparts.

With Beauséjour fallen, the English proceeded with the roundup and expulsion of the Acadians from their more than a century-old home. Militia visited settlement after settlement to tear these sturdy though illiterate peasants away from the harvest and march them to deportation points. About 6,500 Acadians were deported or driven into the wilderness. Their settlements were destroyed, their possessions were seized, and they themselves were herded aboard ships and distributed among the English colonies where, alien in race, language and religion, they passed a miserable existence. Others entered Canada, only to be cruelly exploited by their fellow Frenchmen. Another group reached Louisiana, where their descendants dwell to this day; and still more, having endured an odyssey of indescribable travail, finally made their way back to their homeland.

Thus the cruel mass deportation which, although defensible on military grounds, remains the one crime staining the otherwise admirable record of British colonialism in America. It is true that the Acadians were always a Trojan horse inside Nova Scotia. In faith and race truer to the French Crown than to the British, and maintained in that attitude by their priestly leaders, they were ever ready to rise for France. To prevent this, they were deported. This is the reason, though never the justification, for the uprooting of an entire people; nor does it explain why the Acadians were stripped of most of their possessions before being scattered like barren seeds on unfriendly soil.

In the meantime, while this virtual writ of attainder was executed against an entire province, the French began a counterattack from Canada.

The Marquis de Vaudreuil, the new governor of Canada, had intended to send Baron Dieskau and the newly arrived French regulars against the English outpost of Oswego on Lake Ontario. However, papers of General Braddock found on the Monongahela battlefield gave away the English design against Crown Point and

Dieskau went to Lake Champlain instead. Finding that General William Johnson was farther south in Fort William Henry at the foot of Lake George, Dieskau attacked him there.

He led 700 French and 600 Indians against 2,200 men holding a fixed position, and the result was all but foreordained. The English, skillfully led by General Phineas Lyman, who took command after Johnson was wounded, repulsed charge after charge. Baron Dieskau was himself wounded. He sat helpless behind a tree while his forces fled before the English sallying fiercely from the fort. He turned to see an enemy soldier aiming his musket at him. He signed to the man not to shoot. But the soldier did, sending a bullet across Dieskau's hips, leaping on him and commanding him in French to surrender.

"You rascal!" Dieskau roared. "Why did you fire? You see a man lying in his blood on the ground, and you shoot him!"

"How did I know that you had not got a pistol?" the indignant soldier replied. "I had rather kill the devil than have the devil kill me."[28]

More soldiers fell on the defeated general, stripping him of his clothes. Then they took him to General Johnson, who treated him kindly. Johnson's Mohawk allies, who had lost their great sachem Hendricks to Dieskau's soldiers, would have done otherwise. They burst into Johnson's tent in a fury and demanded his prisoner. Johnson refused, and they filed out, glancing fiercely at Dieskau.

"What did they want?" Dieskau asked.

"What did they want!" Johnson repeated forcefully. "To burn you, by God, to eat you, and smoke you in their pipes. . . . But never fear. You shall be safe with me, or else they shall kill us both."[29]

Johnson was truer to his word than he was to his purpose of expelling the French from New York. He still could have sent General Lyman to Lake Champlain to follow up the advantage gained at Lake George. But he did not, probably because he was already jealous of Lyman. Contenting himself with strengthening his fort, while the French quickly reinforced Ticonderoga, he allowed the opportunity to slip away. A cold and raw November arrived, and with it came mutiny and desertions among the men. At a council of war presided over by Lyman, to whom Johnson was now willing to transfer responsibility, it was voted to withdraw.

William Johnson's outraged army jeered him all the way home, but the reluctant general was still able to make himself a hero abroad. He had already flattered King George by renaming Lac St. Sacrement after him, and now he proceeded to name his stockade there Fort William Henry in honor of one of the king's grandsons, and to change Fort Lyman to Fort Edward to compliment another. Then he wrote a long account of the fight at Lake George in which he exaggerated both its value and his own part in it, while neglecting to mention Lyman's name. Mightier with pen than with sword, William Johnson was made a baronet and Parliament gave him a gift of 5,000 pounds.

And Crown Point remained French.

Fort Niagara also remained French.

Governor Shirley of Massachusetts led about 1,500 men to Oswego on Lake Ontario, and there, staring across the lake toward Fort Frontenac, he came to the unhappy conclusion that the French outpost made it impossible for him to move to his west or left to attack Fort Niagara. If he did, the French in Frontenac would merely cross the lake to take Oswego and occupy his rear. So he left part of his force in Oswego to strengthen the garrison and returned to Albany.

Of General Braddock's fourfold plan to destroy the French in America, only the minor operation against the Acadians had succeeded.

8

☆

Although France and England had already declared war, the general European conflict known as the Seven Years' War did not begin until 1756.

It was started by Frederick of Prussia, and England, forsaking her old ally in Austria, and still anxious to protect her sovereign's lands in Hanover, again sided with Prussia. France once more made com-

mon cause with Maria Theresa of Austria, while Czarina Catherine
of Russia also came to Maria's side. Catherine had been insulted by
Frederick, who called her "the Apostolic Hag," and she brought
Sweden with her against her detractor.

Frederick's taunts also annoyed Maria Theresa, and they had
enraged Madame de Pompadour. Pompadour ruled France. From
being the mistress of the libertine Louis XV, she had become his
procuress—and therefore his master. Frederick had called Pompadour "Mademoiselle Fish," in a biting reference to the favorite's
mother, reputed to have been a fishwife. Thus three angry women
were allied against the captain of his age, and he was to chastise
them more severely with his sword than with his tongue.

Unfortunately for Canada, Pompadour's pique led her to neglect
America. She sent 100,000 troops to help Maria, but could spare
only 1,200 for the New World. However, Canada did get a splendid
new military chief: Louis Joseph, Marquis de Montcalm-Gozen de
Saint-Véran. Scholarly and courteous, Montcalm was also a veteran
soldier who had been in many battles and been frequently wounded.
He sailed for Canada in April, 1756.

Opposing him was a new British commander: the Earl of Loudoun.
Akin to Braddock in his contempt for the colonials, Loudoun was
also of the same irascible temper. He was not, however, as energetic.
He arrived in America in July, 1756, sat still while Montcalm destroyed Oswego, and did not move until the spring of 1757.

Then he sailed against Louisbourg, found it defended by a mighty
French fleet, and sailed back to New York in disgust. Meanwhile,
his unsuccessful expedition had left Fort William Henry exposed to
the French in Ticonderoga. On August 1 Montcalm left that fort with
about 7,500 men. He sailed down Lake George. For the last time the
French and their Indian allies took the watery road to the English.
In swarms of canoes and hundreds of bateaux, with oar, sail and
paddle, while Canadians in buckskin and French regulars in white
coats mingled with naked savages radiant as rainbows, the twin
perfections of civility and barbarism glided down King George's
beautiful lake to fall upon his fort at the foot.

Fort William Henry fought back valiantly, but it never received
the reinforcements it needed. Using European siege tactics, Montcalm worked his artillery ever closer to the English position, at last
compelling its surrender after his guns were within point-blank range.

And then his Indians went screeching out of control, rushing inside the helpless fort to slaughter the sick and wounded in their beds. A French missionary named Roubaud witnessed the butchery and wrote: "I saw one of these barbarians come out of the casemates with a human head in his hand, from which the blood ran in streams, and which he paraded as if he had got the finest prize in the world."[30]

Nor could Montcalm curb the frenzied Indians as the English began to depart for home. They fell whooping on the rear of the New Hampshire regiment and dragged off 80 men. Montcalm rushed among them, crying, "Kill me, but spare the English!"[31] The massacre continued. In all, 50 prisoners were killed, and perhaps 200 more carried captive to Canada. There, many of them were ransomed by the French, who also bought back the clothes which the Indians had torn from the backs of their terrified captives.

Nevertheless, the massacre was a bloody breach of honor. Montcalm's only excuse for not using his own troops to restrain the Indians was that to do so would have lost the red men as allies. This he would not do, and the Indians and their grisly trophies were still with him when he burned Fort William Henry and withdrew to Montreal.

English defeat in the New World had been joined by English reversal in the Old. In 1757 the inept Duke of Cumberland, son of the King, was defeated in Hanover by the French, and Britain's great ally, King Frederick of Prussia, was unable to prevent a Russian army from invading his kingdom. Yet Frederick rallied in the year's last two months to crush the French at Rossbach and rout the Austrians at Leuthen. The tide was turning, and in London an event occurred which prompted Frederick to say: "England has long been in labor, and at last she has brought forth a man."[32]

The man was William Pitt, Pitt the Elder, the Great Commoner, the father—if ever there has been one—of the British Empire. First and foremost, William Pitt sought the destruction of France. It was his policy to fight her and to crush her wherever she was found: in Europe, in India, in Africa, on the seas and especially in America. Pitt saw at once that the three keys to the New World were Fort Duquesne, Ticonderoga and Louisbourg-Quebec, and he opened his campaign to conquer a continent with another assault upon the French base at Louisbourg.

On the morning of June 1, 1758, Louisbourg's southeastern horizon was fringed with the sails of the English. A fleet of 22 ships of the line, 15 frigates and 120 transports under Admiral Boscawen had arrived with Major General Jeffrey Amherst and 12,000 soldiers, of whom only 500 were colonials.

Inside Louisbourg were about 3,200 French regulars, besides a body of armed inhabitants and some Indians. Five ships of the line and seven frigates lay inside the harbor. However, the fortifications were not completed and ramparts made with bad mortar had already begun to fall down. Breaches in the wall were stuffed with fascines. But the Chevalier de Drucour, Governor of Louisbourg, was an able soldier who was determined to fight.

Colonel James Wolfe was perhaps even more eager for battle. His reckless battlefield gallantry had already amazed his colleagues and impressed William Pitt, and now he was to lead the assault on Fresh-Water Cove. This was the crescent-shaped beach which William Pepperrell's colonials had seized to begin their successful siege of 13 years ago, and Amherst was going to try to duplicate that maneuver —with the added diversion of a double feint at Flat Point and White Point closer to the town.

About a thousand white-coated Frenchmen held the beaches from White Point to Fresh-Water Cove. Wolfe had perhaps more than that. After a few days of high surf and fog, the English went over the side into their landing boats and pulled for the little quarter-mile beach lying between two piles of rocks.

The French opened up. Volleys of grape and musketry raked the English. Wolfe raised his hand to withdraw, but three boats of light infantry either missed his signal or ignored it. They rowed on, driving through the surf and landing among the leftward rocks. They leaped ashore. Wolfe saw them and ordered his other boats to follow. Another party of ten men hurdled the rocks and ran up the beach. French fire cut down half of them. Now other boats battled through the breakers. Some were hurled upon the rocks and stove in, others were broached or overturned, emptying their occupants into the surf. Infantrymen and grenadiers, weighted with cartridges, went down. Some arose without their muskets, others never got up. But the assault was going forward against a nearby French battery, and Colonel James Wolfe, his long lank red locks tied neatly behind his head, only a cane in hand, was leaping among the rocks, urging his men forward and calling upon others to come into line.

Now another division of British came ashore to Wolfe's right, and the French, fearing to be cut off from Louisbourg, broke and ran for the woods.

Once again Louisbourg had been flanked, and now the reduction of the fort was begun in steps almost identical to those of Pepperrell's campaign.

Amherst made his camp between Fresh-Water Cove and Flat Point, brought his guns and supplies ashore, and prepared to work his trenches and batteries forward within range of the fort. The French again abandoned the Grand Battery on the north shore of the harbor (although this time they left it useless), and Colonel Wolfe took 1,200 men around to Lighthouse Point just opposite the Island Battery. Once more British cannon pounded the island's guns into silence, while Amherst's siege works snaked closer and closer to Louisbourg. The English guns roared night and day. Louisbourg's rotten walls crumbled and fell apart.

On July 26 the last of the French guns before the town were silenced and the walls so breached as to admit an assault. At that point, Drucour asked for terms. Amherst and Boscawen were stern. Their master in London desired an end to the French in the New World. There would be no honors of war so that men allowed to depart with their arms sloped might one day return with muskets leveled. No, the garrison must surrender as prisoners of war.

Drucour refused. He would fight on, and he sent his reply by messenger. The courier had hardly departed before Intendant Prevost came to Drucour, beseeching him to spare the town and its inhabitants further ruin and misery. He warned of the dangers of exposing the people and their possessions to an assault by storm. Drucour submitted. He sent another messenger to recall the first one, and notified the English that he accepted their terms.

For the last time in history the golden Bourbon lilies fluttered down the flagstaff at Louisbourg. In England there was great rejoicing at the news of the victory. Cannon were fired and the captured flags of Louisbourg were hung in St. Paul's. Throughout New England bells were rung and bonfires lighted from Boston to Newport.

Most ominous for New France, the tall, thin, nervous redhead who had been foremost in the battle sailed home to England on fire for the final thrust up to Quebec.

Pitt had recalled Loudoun and allowed the American command to devolve upon the next in line, Major General James Abercrombie.

Pitt thought of Abercrombie only less disdainfully than he had thought of Loudoun, but even the Great Commoner could not ignore certain influences at court. Moreover, Pitt was hopeful that the real commander of the expedition against Ticonderoga would be Abercrombie's junior, Brigadier Lord Augustus Howe.

Howe was the younger brother of two other Howes—Richard and William—who appeared ten years later in American history, one as an admiral and the other as a general of British arms. Like his brother William, who had been with Amherst at Louisbourg, Augustus was an excellent soldier. Moreover, he was one British commander who respected the colonials. He had served with the Rangers led by Captain Robert Rogers, and he insisted that the 6,350 regulars, as well as 9,000 colonials, whom Abercrombie was to lead against Ticonderoga, learn to live and fight as the Rangers did.

On July 5 the Ticonderoga force embarked from the ruins of Fort William Henry upon the shining surface of Lake George. Rogers and his Rangers led the way in whaleboats, Colonel Gage—the veteran of the Monongahela who remained in American history for yet another war—was behind with the light infantry, and then Lord Howe with the main body.

The following day the army began landing on the western shore of the lake. It was intended to march around the rapids of Lake George's outlet as they ran northeast and then turned west to Ticonderoga. In this way, the English could attack the French fort from the rear.

Lord Howe and Major Israel Putnam went forward to reconnoiter. They encountered a party of about 350 French which Montcalm had sent down to harass the English. A sharp fight began, and Lord Augustus Howe fell dead, shot through the chest. With one shot the French had saved themselves.

"In Lord Howe the soul of General Abercrombie's army seemed to expire," Major Thomas Mante wrote. "From the unhappy moment the General was deprived of his advice, neither order nor discipline was observed, and a strange kind of infatuation usurped the place of resolution."[33]

Worse, from wavering and hesitating, Abercrombie moved to the conviction that he must do something—anything—and he attacked Montcalm exactly where that astute Frenchman expected him.

Montcalm had deduced that Ticonderoga was not to be attacked from the front, and he had ordered a huge breastwork constructed on a ridge behind the fort. Even officers had stripped to the waist to join the throng of axmen bringing thousands of trees crashing down. When completed, the breastwork stood eight to nine feet high. Firing platforms were provided behind it, and the entire line was zigzagged so that the front could be swept with flanking fire. On the sloping ground in front of the breastwork the French also built an abatis. An entire forest was felled with the trunks pointing inward to the breastwork and the sharpened boughs of the treetops outward toward the approaching English.

Such a formidable position should not have been assaulted. Instead, Abercrombie might have waited for his cannon to be brought up from Lake George to batter the breastwork down; or he might have occupied Mount Defiance overlooking the redoubt and directed a plunging fire into it. Best of all, he could have left a holding force in front of Montcalm while marching through the woods to occupy the road to Crown Point in his rear. Turning the French line in this way, he could have starved Montcalm into submission, for the French had only a week's provisions. But Abercrombie, outnumbering Montcalm 15,000 to 4,000, superior in equipment and supply, holding the initiative and operating at the end of a shorter and unmenaced supply line, chose to storm a fixed position!

The result was disaster. The English fought bravely, and so did the French. "God save the King!" roared the red-coated English, and the French in white cried out *"Vive le Roi!"* and *"Vive notre Général!"* Seven times Abercrombie pressed the assault and each time his men were repulsed in blood and agony. At last, he ordered a retreat. Two thousand dead, wounded and missing had been sacrificed to his foolish conviction that men in the open with muskets could overwhelm men behind breastworks with muskets and cannon.

The second phase of Pitt's threefold campaign for 1758 had failed because "Mrs. Nanny Cromby," as the embittered English soldiery called their general, had not cut his enemy's supply line. Against Fort Duquesne in the third phase, the English succeeded because they did cut it.

This maneuver was undertaken on the initiative of Lieutenant Colonel John Bradstreet. Sailing up the Mohawk River at the head of 3,000 men, he reached Oswego, crossed Lake Ontario and captured and destroyed Fort Frontenac. By this action he severed the

French supply line to the west and left Fort Duquesne at the mercy of the advancing English. Thus it was that the prediction made under Braddock was at last fulfilled: as the English, with George Washington again among them, approached Duquesne in November of 1758, they heard a great roar followed by explosion after explosion. Rushing forward they found that the French had blown up their fort and fled up the Allegheny.

Now it was the turn of the English to fortify the forks. As the year ended they began to build the bastion called Fort Pitt on the site of the modern city of Pittsburgh. With this, they won the West and cut New France in two. Canada was now flanked on the west by Fort Pitt and on the east by Louisbourg, and her capital city of Quebec lay open to attack.

9

☆

When the Duke of Newcastle complained to King George II that James Wolfe, the 32-year-old soldier whom William Pitt had chosen to capture Quebec, was not only too young to command such an important expedition but was also slightly demented, the old King looked up and growled: "Mad is he? Then I hope he will bite some of my other generals."[34]

In fairness to the protesting duke, James Wolfe certainly did not look or act like a "normal" British officer. Tall, thin and very awkward, pallid in complexion and constantly picking at his cuffs and buttons with long, tapering fingers, he seemed more of a sissy than a soldier. He did not even wear the customary military wig, but allowed his bright red hair to grow loose and long, pinning it together at the back of his head like any jackanapes. Yet James Wolfe's pale and bulging blue eyes were hard, and they usually blazed with a zealous fire.

He was a soldier born and bred. He was one of two sons of an

Anglo-Irish colonel of marines, and he had got himself attached to his father's regiment at the age of 13. Only the ill-health which afflicted him throughout his life prevented him from entering battle at that age. Yet at 15 he was an ensign; at 16 he was his battalion's adjutant fighting at Dettingen; and at 18 he was aide-de-camp to the brutal General "Hangman" Hawley during the Jacobite rising of 1745. Wolfe rather liked Hawley, cruel as he might be to the defeated Highlanders. Like St. Paul he was "approving everything that was being done against them." There was much of Saul of Tarsus in James Wolfe. He too was intense, ugly and zealous, thirsting to fight for the King just as Paul hungered to serve the Lord. It was this very single-mindedness that had impressed William Pitt. That was why he had given him command of the chief operation in another three-pronged campaign with which Pitt intended to complete the destruction of the French in America during the year 1759.

Amherst was to take Ticonderoga and move on Montreal by way of Lake Champlain, General Prideaux was to take Fort Niagara on Lake Ontario and open the way to Lake Erie and the West, and Wolfe was to crack the hard nut at Quebec.

Certainly this would be the most difficult of all three operations. Wolfe, however, was supremely confident, so much so that he prevailed upon the caste-conscious British Army to allow him to select two of the three brigadiers who were to accompany him.

One was Robert Monckton, who had commanded the Acadian operations in 1755, and the other a capable officer named James Murray. Monckton was only six months older than Wolfe and Murray only two years older. Thus there were three general officers 34 or under, to whom was added a fourth only a few years older: the Hon. George Townshend. Townshend had not served in the army as continuously as the others, but he did have a reputation for coolness under fire. Once, as he watched an attack, an exploding shell blew off the head of a German officer standing near him, splattering Townshend with gore. "I never knew before," Townshend murmured, calmly mopping his chest with a handkerchief, "that Scheiger had so many brains."35 Clever and quarrelsome, Townshend was also an artist of talent whose savagely funny caricatures had lost him friends and led him to the field of honor. He did not, of course, get along with Wolfe, who disliked him from the first; but the youthful commander put on a face of politeness while arranging for his departure in February of 1759.

The night before Wolfe sailed, he dined with Pitt and Lord Temple, Pitt's brother-in-law. Toward the end of the meal he suddenly jumped erect, drew his sword and rapped on the table for attention. He then began striding around the room flourishing his sword while boasting of his military prowess and threatening his enemy with doom; after which he turned and walked from the room without a word.

"Good God!" Pitt exclaimed. "That I should have entrusted the fate of the country and of the administration to such hands!"[36]

The Great Commoner might have felt better for his country had he known that his guest, a teetotaler, had been drinking a little wine.

Admiral Charles Saunders commanded the fleet which was to transport Wolfe's army to Quebec. In all, he was to have some 170 sail manned by some 18,000 seamen. Part of his force, under Rear Admiral Philip Durell, had been sent ahead to blockade the St. Lawrence so that the French could not reinforce Quebec.

But Admiral Durell did not enter the river, choosing to stay clear of its treacherous ice, and the French did get men and supplies into the fortress city on the cliff. With them was the Sieur de Bougainville, whom Montcalm had sent to Paris. Bougainville stepped onto the strand of the Lower Town bearing a copy of an intercepted letter from General Jeffrey Amherst.

It revealed the English plan.

Montcalm had planned to resist Amherst at Lake Champlain and Fort Niagara. Now, seeing the major thrust directed at Quebec, he prepared to meet Wolfe there.

First, under Vaudreuil's orders, all French ships were sent upriver to be out of harm's way, and to release about 1,000 sailors for duty in Quebec. Vaudreuil, and Montcalm as well, was confident that Quebec's guns could prevent the English from getting above the city to cut the supply line westward to Montreal. Confident also that the fortress on the cliff was impregnable, Vaudreuil entrusted its defense to the Chevalier de Ramesay with about 2,000 men, and allowed Montcalm to move the main body east along the St. Lawrence.

Montcalm built a line about seven miles long. His left rested on the gorge and falls of the Montmorenci and his right on the St. Charles. The mouth of the St. Charles was guarded by a boom of logs chained together and two sunken ships mounting cannon. A mile up the St. Charles was a bridge of boats which linked Montcalm's right with Quebec. In the center of this bristling line of men and redoubts was the little town of Beauport, and there Montcalm made his headquarters.

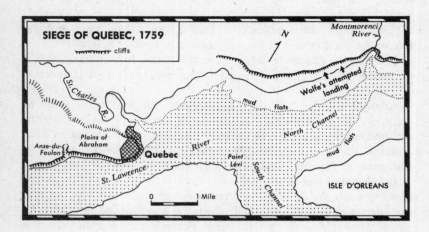

Thus Quebec's only weak point, its landward flank on the left, had been protected against encirclement. The city with its 106 guns was inaccessible from its sheer front and from its impassable heights on its right. Even if the British landed on the unoccupied south bank of the St. Lawrence, they could not possibly force the stream.

All that Montcalm needed to do was to hold his position until October, when the advent of the harsh Canadian winter would force the English to retire. He had 14,000 men, besides his Indians, and Amherst's letter indicated that Wolfe would have only 12,000.

Wolfe had only 8,500 men, of whom many were those Americans whom he despised as "the dirtiest, most contemptible, cowardly dogs that you can conceive."[37] He accepted them, nevertheless, and after he arrived at Louisbourg he divided his army into three brigades under Murray, Monckton and Townshend. While at Louisbourg, Wolfe received a letter from his mother informing him that his father had died. At once, he put on the sleeve of his red coat the black armband of mourning, which he wore constantly, and which was to become as familiar to his men as the little ornamental cane he wore slung at his hip like a toy sword.

On June 5, 1759, a foggy, windless day, the English fleet began working slowly and with flapping sails out of the harbor at Louisbourg.

When the British fleet came up the St. Lawrence about 60 miles below Quebec, it was flying the French flag.

Canadians to the fleet's right cheered and hugged themselves for joy. They had been dreading the appearance of the enemy armada, and now, it appeared, relief from France had come instead and they were saved. Jubilant river pilots quickly launched their canoes and put out to the ships. They clambered aboard, but instead of a smile and the promise of a fee, they met a pistol and a pledge of sudden death if they did not work the vessels through the treacherous Traverse ahead.

Aboard the leading transport *Goodwill,* one enraged pilot vowed that Canada would be the graveyard of the British Army and the walls of Quebec would be hung with English scalps. Captain Killick, the ancient master of the *Goodwill,* angrily pushed the Canadian aside and went forward to the forecastle to guide the ship through himself. The pilot shouted that the ship would be wrecked, for no French ship had ever attempted the Traverse without a pilot.

"Ay, ay, my dear," old Killick shouted back, fiercely shaking his speaking trumpet, "but, damn me, I'll convince you that an Englishman shall go where a Frenchman dare not show his nose."[38]

Behind *Goodwill,* the captain of the following ship was alarmed to learn that *Goodwill* had no pilot.

"Who's your master?" he yelled, and Killick replied, "It's old Killick! And that's enough."[39]

Leaning over the bow, the old man chatted gaily with the sailors in the sounding boats, giving his orders easily while pointing out the different shades of blue and gray indicating the depth of the water, warning of submerged ridges marked by telltale ripples or the sudden disturbance of smoothly flowing waters. Eventually *Goodwill* emerged from the zigzag Traverse into easier water. Killick put down his trumpet and handed the ship over to his mate. "Well, damn me," he snorted. "Damn me if there are not a thousand places in the Thames more hazardous than this. I am ashamed that Englishmen should make such a rout about it."[40]

Gradually, all the following transports were safely through. The fleet was moving now through the South Channel. To the right lay the lower tip of the Island of Orléans, an island about 20 miles long and five miles wide in the center of the broad St. Lawrence. Off the island's upper tip was the basin of Quebec and four miles across the water was the city itself.

Here, on the 26th of June, the fleet anchored. That night, 40 American Rangers under Lieutenant Meech landed on the Island of Orléans and drove off a party of armed inhabitants. In the morning Wolfe's army began coming ashore to build a base camp. A few days later, General Wolfe went forward to a high point on the island's tip to examine his objective, and it was then that he saw the true magnitude of the mission on which Pitt had sent him.

High, high above him, beautiful and white in the sunlight, was the city. He could see the stone houses, the churches, the palaces, the convents, the hospitals, the forest of spires and steeples and crosses glinting beneath the white flag whipping in the breeze. Everywhere he saw thick square walls and gun batteries, even along the strand of the Lower Town straggling out of sight to his left beyond Cape Diamond. To his right as he swung his glass slowly like a swiveling gun, Wolfe perceived the entrenchments of Montcalm. He saw the sealed mouth of the St. Charles and the thundering falls of the Montmorenci guarding the French left flank. He saw the little town of Beauport and the mud flats before it beneath the grape and muskets of Montcalm's redoubts. From left to right he saw steep brown cliffs scarred with the raw red earth of fresh entrenchments, the stone houses with windows reduced to firing slits by piles of logs, and behind them the tops of the Indian wigwams and the white tents of the regulars. If Wolfe could have seen beyond Cape Diamond to his left, he would have been appalled by natural obstacles more formidable than Montcalm's fortifications. Here for seven or eight miles west to Cape Rouge rose steep after inaccessible steep, ranges of cliffs atop which a few men might hold off an army, all ending at another river and waterfall like the Montmorenci.

James Wolfe held his telescope delicately. A soldier near him noticed the marks of scurvy on the back of his long thin hands. No one spoke except his engineer. Wolfe listened mutely, silencing him with a gesture and gazing eagerly at what appeared a likely landing place or a flaw in his enemy's line; but then, shaking his head petulantly, he moved on. At last, he snapped his telescope shut and strode back to camp.

Wolfe had seen that he could not land upriver or between the St. Charles and the Montmorenci as the colonists under Sir William Phips had done six decades before. In fact, there did not seem to be any place to land. As he was to notify William Pitt, he had gazed upon "the strongest country in the world."

That night a black thunderstorm drenched his troops. After it had passed, sentries on Orléans Point thought that they heard movement on the river. They saw flashes of light and the glow of torches and heard the sound of excited voices—and then the world seemed to explode.

Sheets of fire shot up from the river, roar after roar shook the camp, while the air was filled with flying pieces of burning wood and whizzing bits of metal. The sentries turned and ran. As they did, the flames and the roar pursued them like dragons from hell, belching out columns of suffocating smoke and drenching the air with the sulphurous reek of their breath.

The French had launched their fireships downriver against the English fleet anchored off the island. Flames ran up masts and sails like fiery snakes and then vessels soaked in pitch and tar and stuffed with bombs, grenades, old iron, fireworks, rusty cannon swivels and muskets loaded to the muzzle burst apart like floating volcanoes. But the French sailors had applied their torches too soon. Before the fireships could drift down on the English vessels and ignite them, British sailors had jumped into their boats, rowed bravely within range of the blazing hulks, secured them with grappling irons, and towed them ashore where they were allowed to burn themselves out.

The fireship fizzle depressed the Marquis de Vaudreuil, who was watching glumly from the steeple of the little church at Beauport. He had spent two million francs on this military bauble, and had hoped, with characteristic naïveté, that it would drive off the British with one stroke.

Unfortunately for the defense of Canada, the Marquis de Vaudreuil fancied himself a conqueror. Jealous of Montcalm's military prowess, he sometimes pretended that Montcalm's victories were won by Vaudreuil. Such vanity disgusted Montcalm, who already despised the Governor for failing to check the corruption of the greedy officials around him. With the Governor and the general thus divided, delay and indecision were bound to ensue, and this was at once apparent when Wolfe moved to bring Quebec under bombardment.

On June 29 Wolfe seized a tip of land called Point Lévi across the South Channel from the Island of Orléans. Between this point and Quebec the St. Lawrence narrowed to a width of less than a mile. On June 30 Monckton's brigade came ashore in force and began to emplace Wolfe's guns. By the time the French moved to evict the English from Point Lévi, it was too late. They were there in force, and soon their guns were pounding the cliff city's walls.

Next, Wolfe moved to draw Montcalm out of his secure fortifications. Leaving a light guard around the camp on the Island of Orléans, he landed Townshend's and Murray's brigades on the east bank of the Montmorenci, just across from Montcalm's left flank. Wolfe now had thrice divided and dispersed his army into a light guard at Orléans, Monckton at Point Lévi and himself with Townshend and Murray east of the Montmorenci. It would seem that he had offered Montcalm a marvelous opportunity to overwhelm any one of these divided forces and to gobble up the English Army piecemeal. However, Wolfe was confident that the English fleet could rapidly concentrate his separated army at any given point. Thus, having lured Montcalm out into the open, he could bring him to decisive battle.

Montcalm, however, refused the bait. He did not fear Wolfe's army as much as the one General Amherst was leading against Ticonderoga. If Amherst could come up Lake Champlain, he might capture Montreal and threaten Montcalm's rear. Montcalm was delighted to have two-thirds of Wolfe's army bogged down among the mosquitoes and skulking Indians of the woods across the river.

"While they are there they cannot do much harm," he said. "So let them amuse themselves."[41]

On the night of July 12 a rocket exploded above the river between Quebec and Point Lévi and Monckton's cannon roared into life.

Both the first and the second salvos fell into the river, and cries of derision rose from the French. But the English gunners eventually found the range. Shells began bursting among the wharves and streets of the Lower Town and some even shook the walls of the Upper Town itself. Soon the French batteries were belching back. A furious artillery duel raged throughout the night, and it continued to roar intermittently for the next two months.

On the night of July 15 an English shell set fire to a building in the Upper Town. High winds carried the fire to the cathedral, which burned to the ground within an hour. A week later another fierce fire all but demolished the Lower Town. Soon the Lower Town was a shambles and the crowded streets of the Upper Town were not safe for passage. One by one, sometimes in family groups, the residents of the crumbling city began to flee to the sanctuary of the countryside.

Meanwhile, the siege continued. Wolfe's batteries on the Montmorenci made life unpleasant for the troops on Montcalm's left flank, and Montcalm's sharpshooters cut down the rashly curious English who visited the gorge of the river to marvel at its cataract. Both sides languished in an alternating ordeal of heat and rain, both sides skirmished and both sides took scalps. The American Rangers and soon the British regulars became as proficient in this grisly art as the opposing Indians and *coureurs de bois* until Wolfe had to issue an order prohibiting "the inhuman practice of scalping, except when the enemy are Indians or Canadians dressed like Indians."

Wolfe's brigadiers had repeatedly advised him to try forcing the northern shore above Quebec, but the general had just as frequently declined; and on July 23 he proposed to storm the very heart of the enemy line.

In front of the gorge of the Montmorenci there was a ford during the hours of low tide. Townshend was to cross here with 2,000 men. Meanwhile, another 2,000 would be embarked up the St. Lawrence and brought downstream opposite Beauport to make a feint there. Wolfe's true object was the camp of Lévis on the Montmorenci.

In midmorning of July 31, the 64-gun frigate *Centurion* sailed downriver and anchored off Lévis's camp, while a pair of 14-gun catamarans worked in close to the shore. It was now high tide and the river flowed full against the sandy beach beneath the cliffs. *Centurion* and her tiny twins opened up, battering the French redoubts on the beaches. From Wolfe's camp east of the Montmorenci and Monckton's batteries to the west at Point Lévi came an artillery crossfire aimed at the clifftops. For two hours the thunder of the cannonade continued, and the basin of Quebec echoed and re-echoed once more to the thump of discharging guns and the crash of exploding shells. Yet Lévis with about 11,000 men carefully concentrated underground was barely scratched, demonstrating the imperishable truth that when artillery fires at positions built to deflect it, its bark is worse than its bite.

Montcalm, however, was momentarily perplexed by the boated British force rowing back and forth opposite Beauport. But as the promenade became prolonged, he became convinced that the assault would come against Lévis, and he rode down to the Montmorenci through ranks of cheering, white-coated men crying, *"Vive notre général!"*

In the afternoon the tide turned to the ebb. Gradually the dark sedge of the mud flats became visible. Wolfe, standing in an open boat, cane in hand, flushed with the exultation of battle, gave the order to attack.

As Townshend began crossing the ford, the first wave of grenadiers and Royal Americans rowed cheering for the mud flats.

But the boats were swept downstream and many of them were stranded on mud ridges. The French on the heights poured a plunging fire into them. Wolfe in his boat shouted orders to delay the assault. The tide was not low enough. The French fire continued. Three times splinters struck Wolfe and his little cane was knocked from his grasp by a round shot. At length he ordered the first wave in again. The boats beached on the broad expanse of mud. Shouting and challenging each other, the grenadiers and Royal Americans floundered forward in wild disorder. The French in the redoubt on the sand fled at their approach. The English seized the redoubt, but then the French on the heights delivered a heavy fire among the redcoats milling about below.

To the rear, all was confusion. Monckton's men were ashore and Townshend's troops were already over the ford. Boats were piling up, and no one seemed to know what to do. At that moment, without orders from Wolfe or even from their own officers, the grenadiers took the battle into their own hands.

They went storming up the heights to get at their tormentors above them. Thick scattered raindrops had begun to fall and the heat was oppressive as the English swarmed up the slopes. French fire scourged them. Their breath came faster. Sweat stained their uniforms, and the ground beneath their boots became a slippery morass. Straining for handholds, using their muskets as crutches, rolling downhill to be stopped by a bush or a fallen comrade, they continued their ascent into the very throats of the twinkling, flashing muskets of the French. And then the skies darkened, the clouds opened up and a torrent of rain fell on all that wild scene.

It squelched the battle. Wolfe sounded the retreat, and as the last of the living grenadiers and Americans came sliding downhill again, while the entire assault force withdrew in good order to their boats, the rain stopped and the Indians on the heights drew their scalping knives and came clambering down among the fallen.

Wolfe had lost 443 men killed and wounded without harming a single Frenchman in an aborted battle that should never have been begun. His plan of attack upon the heart of a fixed position was not only scatterbrained in its conception but also blundering in nearly every detail of execution down to the boating of troops at flood tide in the morning for an assault to be launched at dusk and on the ebb. By the defeat of the Montmorenci, Wolfe lost the respect of almost all his staff officers, including the heretofore intensely loyal Monckton.

Townshend was particularly savage in his criticism and even the fire-breathing Murray regarded the entire affair as stupid and foolhardy. Admiral Saunders was also alienated after Wolfe sent him a copy of the draft of his ambiguous despatch to Pitt. Saunders accused Wolfe of giving the navy an unfair share of the blame, and Wolfe meekly promised to remove the objectionable parts of the letter. Meanwhile, Wolfe, his health failing every day, vented his rage upon other victims. First, the grenadiers were excoriated in a scathing General Order, and next the Canadians on the south banks of the St. Lawrence were informed that because of "the most unchristian barbarities against his troops on all occasions he could no longer refrain from chastising them as they deserved."[42]

East and west, parties were sent forth to scourge the Canadian *"canaille."* Night after night the residents of Quebec could see the glow of burning villages. Montcalm also watched this savaging of his countrymen, but with no intention of ending it. He would not be drawn into open battle under any circumstances, and thus the tormented Canadians were caught between two fires. Where Wolfe was wasting the countryside in an effort to starve Quebec and force the militia to desert to defend their homes, Montcalm kept the militia in check by threatening to turn his Indians loose on their families.

Meanwhile, Quebec was collapsing under the hammer of Monckton's artillery. Fires in the Lower Town were a daily occurrence, and in the Upper Town 167 houses were destroyed in a single dreadful night. On August 10 a shell crashing into a cellar set a vat of brandy afire and burned down many buildings, including the beautiful Notre Dame des Victoires. Most of the city fronting on the river was in ruins.

Worse, rations in the town and for the army encamped beside it were growing short. Vaudreuil's assurance that the English could not get upriver had been shattered by the audacity of the British fleet. Beginning on July 18 and with every fair wind thereafter, English ships had run the gantlet of Quebec's guns until a sizable flotilla had been assembled upstream under Vice Admiral Charles Holmes. Thus supply ships coming downriver from Montreal were frequently intercepted by Holmes's ships, while a shortage of pack animals made supply by land along the river's northern shore very difficult.

The ships, however, worried Montcalm most. Wolfe was now able to make thrusts against the northern shore to the west of Quebec. To oppose him, Montcalm sent Bougainville above the city with 1,500 men. He was to guard about 15 to 20 miles of clifftop against the English. He did, twice driving Murray off with losses. A third time, Murray landed at Deschambault and burnt a building and all the spare baggage of the regular officers. For once, Montcalm was alarmed; but then his good humor returned. He had received news indicating that General Amherst could not possibly come to Wolfe's assistance that year.

Amherst had occupied Ticonderoga and then Crown Point, after the French had blown up the first and abandoned the second. Then General Prideaux had carried out the assault on Fort Niagara. Although Prideaux was killed, the French fort had been surrendered to Sir William Johnson. Thus, with his countrymen driven from Lake Champlain and Lake Erie, it appeared to Montcalm that his right or western flank at Montreal was in extreme danger. Amherst particularly might ascend Champlain to fall on Montreal. But Amherst had dawdled at Crown Point and could not possibly assault Montreal before winter.

"Two months more," Montcalm said of the English, "and they will be gone."[43]

Toward the end of August it appeared that Montcalm was right. Wolfe's army was melting away. He had lost more than 850 men killed and wounded since June, and disease and desertions were daily reducing his strength. Worse, the general himself was gripped by an indecision nearly as destructive to discipline as his own feuding with his brigadiers. Then, on August 20, Wolfe fell ill of a fever. He lay in an upper room of a French farmhouse on the Montmorenci, his thin body racked and his white face haggard with pain. On the 25th he began to recover, and on the 29th he sent his three brigadiers a message:

"That the public service may not suffer by the General's indisposition, he begs the brigadiers will meet and consult together for the public utility and advantage, and consider of the best method to attack the enemy."[44]

Monckton, Murray and Townshend conferred. They advised Wolfe, as they had often done before, to seize a position on the north shore between Quebec and Montreal. Thus he would force upon Montcalm the choice of fighting or starving. Wolfe agreed. He not only embraced this heretofore unacceptable proposal eagerly; he went even farther. He would ascend the inaccessible heights beneath the Plains of Abraham under the very nose of Quebec. Montcalm, cut in two, would *have* to come out to fight.

Wolfe did not immediately disclose the details of his plan to his brigadiers. He divulged it only at their insistence and at the eleventh hour. Nor will history ever know how he came to adopt it, after having previously rejected all counsel to force the stream above Quebec.

It has been said that Wolfe was on the edge of despair. He had told his intimates that he would not go back defeated "to be exposed to the censure and reproach of an ignorant population." The very news that he could expect no help from Amherst might have strengthened him in that resolution so often born of desperation. Wolfe was that sort of soldier: audacious in adversity, delighted to look into the face of calamity and spit in its eye, genuinely determined to triumph or to die trying.

It has also been said that Wolfe was anxious to make one more attempt on the city before the advent of winter forced the fleet to depart. On September 10 Admiral Saunders assembled his officers and informed them that he thought the time had come to leave. Saunders had about 13,000 men under his command. With their ships they represented about a quarter of the strength of the British Navy. He could not risk being frozen into the St. Lawrence. Moreover, ice floes were already beginning to form in the Gulf of St. Lawrence. All of Saunders's officers agreed, including Holmes, but Wolfe, upon being advised of this decision, rushed to Saunders's flagship and told him of his plan. He advised the admiral that he was going to send 150 picked men up a secret path to the Plains of Abraham. If they could overpower the light guard posted there, then his main body would follow. But if they could not, then Wolfe would agree to return to England with Saunders.

Wolfe is said to have seen this secret path while studying the heights west of Quebec. Examining a little cove called the Anse-du-Foulon, he is said to have spotted outlines of a path winding up the side of the supposedly inaccessible cliff. Then, observing that there were only a few tents pitched on the clifftop, he is supposed to have concluded that the guard there was light.

This is the generally accepted explanation of why Wolfe changed his mind about the northern shore and came to choose the Anse-du-Foulon. But because it assumes too much while accepting the implausible fable of Wolfe suddenly seeing the path "through a glass darkly," and because Wolfe did deliberately destroy the September entries in his diary, it is not too much to posit the possibility of treachery.

Although history offers no incontrovertible proof of betrayal at Quebec, it does encourage a suspicion that there might have been. Montcalm himself gave the reason why. Having long ago secretly informed Paris of the corruption in Canada, as well as Vaudreuil's failure to suppress it, he had said: "Everybody appears to be in a hurry to make his fortune before the colony is lost; which event many perhaps desire as an impenetrable veil over their conduct."[45] Obviously, with Canada destroyed there would be little likelihood that the corrupt officials would be brought to book, and it would certainly be to the advantage of any or all of them to inform James Wolfe of the existence of the Anse-du-Foulon. Again, because Wolfe destroyed his September diary entries, it cannot be said definitely whether or not this happened.

However, it is known that Vaudreuil, who was constantly accompanied and advised by the false Intendant Bigot, did countermand an order of Montcalm's and left the Plains of Abraham themselves unguarded. The crack Guienne Regiment under a capable colonel was moved from the Plains back to the line of the St. Charles. Moreover, the guard of 100 men which Montcalm had placed at the top of the Anse-du-Foulon was fatally crippled.

It had been commanded by Captain St. Martin, a regular officer hand-picked for the duty by Montcalm; but Vaudreuil replaced St. Martin with the Chevalier Duchambon de Vergor, a crony of Bigot whose career as commander at Beauséjour was distinguished by corruption on one side and cowardice on the other. Where St. Martin had refused to allow the Canadians in his command to go home to help in the harvest, Vergor granted leave to 40 men on the condition that they also put in a few hours of work on Vergor's farm.

Finally, the clifftops between the Anse-du-Foulon and Cape Rouge were not even well patrolled on the night of Wolfe's attack. On that night the patrol commander, Captain de Remigny, lost his three horses. One was stolen and two were lamed.

Thus the possibility of treachery at Quebec. The facts, of course, are no more than suggestive of this possibility. Yet, even if they are not conclusive proof of it, they should not be summarily rejected in the interest of preserving the romantic idea of Wolfe on a river bank suddenly espying the chink in Montcalm's armor. Montcalm himself knew of the path, and he said to Vaudreuil: "I swear to you that a hundred men posted there would stop their whole army."[46] He was right, but there were not 100 men but only 60 under the untrustworthy Vergor, and the Guienne Regiment which was to come to their assistance had been sent away. Whether or not Wolfe knew of this belongs to the limbo of unanswerable questions. What does belong to his lasting glory, however, is the masterly preparation which he made for this attack.

First he began the difficult withdrawal from the Montmorenci. Next he made a feint at Cape Rouge held by Bougainville, and during the next few days he drove Bougainville and his men into weary distraction by having the ships of Holmes's flotilla drift upriver with the flood tide and drift downriver on the ebb, forcing the French to march and countermarch to remain abreast of the English fleet. To delude Montcalm into believing that the movement above the town was a diversion for another attack against his fortifications east of Quebec, he asked

Admiral Saunders to deploy his main fleet in a demonstration off Beauport. Finally, two deserters told Wolfe that Bougainville was sending a convoy of provisions down to Montcalm on the ebb tide on the night of September 12. Wolfe immediately saw the possibility of sending his own boats down ahead of the convoy so as to deceive the French sentinels, and he gave that order. Wolfe could not know that Bougainville had postponed the provision convoy, but neither did Bougainville inform the sentries below that the familiar store ships were not coming.

On the night of September 12 all was in readiness. The stars were visible, but there was no moon as perhaps 4,800 English began drifting upriver. Bougainville, wearied by the promenade of the past few days, was confident that they would only drift downriver again. In fact, the Sieur was going to spend the night farther west at Jacques Cartier. The desirable, and accommodating, Madame de Vienne, wife of one of Bigot's subordinates, was at Jacques Cartier. Below Quebec, Saunders was lowering boats filled with sailors and marines, his guns were thundering, and the Marquis de Montcalm was massing troops at the wrong point ten miles below the Anse-du-Foulon.

At two o'clock in the morning of September 13, 1759, the tide began to ebb. A lantern, its light shrouded from the northern shore, was hoisted to the main topgallant masthead of the *Sutherland*. It was the signal to cast off, and the boats of the English began slipping silently downstream.

General James Wolfe stood mutely in one of the foremost boats. Suddenly the general began to speak in a low voice. He was reciting Gray's "Elegy in a Country Churchyard," which he had only just memorized. His aides listened quietly. Wolfe finished, and said softly, "Gentlemen, I would rather have written those lines than take Quebec."[47] An embarrassed silence followed. No one believed him. Wolfe said no more. Perhaps he was reflecting on the prophetic line:

The paths of glory lead but to the grave.

Unchallenged and ignored, the boats had been gliding downstream for a full two hours. Now the tide was bearing the lead craft with Wolfe's spearhead—24 volunteers who were to surprise Vergor— toward the towering shore. Suddenly there was a shout.

"Who goes there?"

No one spoke, and then Simon Fraser, a young Highland officer who spoke French, shouted back: _"France! And long live the King!"_

"What regiment?" the sentry persisted.

"La Reine," Fraser shot back, aware that part of this unit was with Bougainville.[48]

The sentry was satisfied and the boats drifted on, one of the men giggling aloud in relief. Again the challenge. A sentry had come scrambling down the cliff face to stand at the water's edge and demand the password. Again a French-speaking Highlander, Captain Donald McDonald, gave the answer.

"Provision boats!" he hissed, deliberately disguising his accent with a hoarse whisper. "Don't make such a bloody noise! The English will hear!"[49]

The sentry waved them on. The English could see the gray of his cuff against the black of the cliff behind him.

On the boats drifted, and now the current was running strong and they had rounded the headland of the Anse-du-Foulon. The sailors broke out their oars and rowed desperately against the tide. But the spearhead boats were swept too far downstream. Undaunted, McDonald, Fraser and their men leaped out. McDonald and Captain William Delaune led the party softly up the cliff face. The figure of a sentry materialized out of the gloom above them. He shouted down at them. Still hissing his hoarse whisper, McDonald told him that he had come to relieve the post.

"I'll take care to give a good account of the English if they land!"[50]

On the shore of the cove below, General James Wolfe and two aides crouched helplessly in the dark, their ears straining for the sound of firing. It came, and Wolfe despaired.

Above, the sentry had hesitated for too long. There were 24 shadowy figures around him before he could reply, and then the English charged with blazing muskets. Captain Vergor came dashing out of his tent barefooted and nightshirted. He fired two pistols wildly into the air before he turned and sprinted for Quebec at the head of his departing troops. A musket shot pierced his heel and he fell screaming.

It was then that Wolfe's despondency changed to a fierce, wild joy for he had heard the huzzahs of his triumphant volunteers. Quickly he gave the order for the second wave to land. In came the boats, and and soon the cliff face was crawling with British soldiers. Among them was James Wolfe. Diseased, weakened by bloodletting, never strong, he was climbing on his magnificent will alone; and as he got to the top, the empty boats of the first wave were returning to the packed transports for the rest of his troops.

Now the guns at Point Levi and the Island of Orléans had joined those of Saunders firing on Beauport. Soon Beauport's batteries were thundering back, followed by those at Quebec and at Samos to the west of the Anse-du-Foulon. Wolfe immediately sent Colonel William Howe's light infantry against that battery menacing his rear, and the British silenced it.

By dawn the last of Wolfe's sweating soldiers had struggled up to the undefended Plains of Abraham. Some 4,800 soldiers began to form and to march into a north-south line parallel to and about three-quarters of a mile distant from the western walls of Quebec.

That was how the Marquis de Montcalm saw them as he rode up in a drizzling rain.

Montcalm had been completely deceived by Saunders's feint. Nevertheless, he rode over to Quebec that morning with the Chevalier Johnstone, a Scots Jacobite who had been given a commission in the French Army. En route, a messenger informed him of the British landing. Montcalm set his horse on the path to Vaudreuil's house. From there he could see clearly to those plains which had once been owned by a French pilot named Abraham Martin. He could see the red lines of British soldiers stretching from the St. Foye Road on their left—and his right—to the cliffs of the St. Lawrence. Faintly, skirling on the wind, came the wail of the Highlanders' pipes. The enemy array stood motionless, as though awaiting inspection, their regimental colors drooping in a gentle rain.

"This is serious,"[51] Montcalm said gravely, and ordered Johnstone to ask Governor Ramesay of Quebec for the garrison's 25 fieldpieces. Johnstone clattered off and Vaudreuil came out of his house. Shaken, he spoke a few words to Montcalm, and went back inside. Montcalm rode off to find his command disorganized by a welter of orders and counterorders given in an atmosphere of distrust and dislike. Ramesay would surrender only three of the 25 cannon and Vaudreuil had refused to allow the Beauport troops to move up to Quebec.

Eventually, Montcalm conferred with his officers. Should he attack now or wait until Bougainville could move on the British rear? If the French waited another hour or possibly two for Bougainville, the British could improve their position. If he attacked now, he would have to do it without Bougainville and the troops withheld by Vaudreuil, but he might also strike the British before they could dig in. His officers, afraid that Vaudreuil might appear at any moment to issue additional hamstringing orders, were for immediate attack. Montcalm agreed. He sent his troops out to the Plains of Abraham.

Out they marched to the last battle of New France. All that was French, all that Samuel de Champlain had planted 150 years before on the cliff above the river, was to be defended here this day. Golden lily and gilded cross, dream of an empire stretching to the Rockies, fervor and faith and feudalism, all that had nourished or corrupted the martial and colorful little colony along the great river was at stake on the plains beyond. Through the narrow streets they thronged, white-coated regulars in black hats and gaiters and glittering bayonets, troops of Canadians and bands of Indians in scalp locks and war paint; out of the gates they poured, the battalions of Old France and the irregulars of the New, the victors of Fort Necessity, the Monongahela, Oswego, Ticonderoga and Fort William Henry, tramping to the tap of the drum and the call of the bugle for the last time in the long war for a continent.

With them rode their general. He had never seemed more noble to his officers and men. Mounted on a dark bay horse, he was a splendid figure in his green-and-gold uniform, the Cross of St. Louis gleaming above his cuirass. "Are you tired?" he cried. "Are you ready, my children?"[52] They answered him with shouts and as he swung his sword to encourage them, the cuffs of his wide sleeves fell back to reveal the white linen of his wrist bands.

In splendid composure, the English watched the French arrive. Since dawn, when the high ground less than a mile away had become suddenly thronged with the white coats of the tardily arriving Guienne, the redcoats had been raked by Canadian and Indian sharpshooters. After Ramesay's three cannon had begun to punish them, Wolfe had ordered them to lie in the grass.

James Wolfe had put on a new uniform: scarlet coat over impeccable white breeches, silk-edged tricorne on his head. He walked gaily among his reclining men, making certain that they had loaded their muskets with an extra ball for the first volley, pausing to chat with his officers. Wolfe ignored the enemy sharpshooters and exploding shells. A captain near him fell, shot in the lung. Wolfe knelt and gently took the man's head in his arms. He thanked him for his services and told him that he would be promoted when he was well again, immediately sending off an aide .to Monckton to make sure that his promise was carried out should he be killed that day.

The desired battle had arrived, and James Wolfe was exalted. All his black moods and indecision had vanished clean away. His step was light, his voice was steady and his pale face shone with confidence. Although he did outnumber Montcalm 4,800 to 4,000, it was the quality rather than the number of his troops which gave the English general his assurance. He had trained them personally and he had taught them to stand in awesome silence until their enemy was close enough to be broken by a single volley.

Toward ten o'clock the French began coming down the hill, regulars in the center, regulars and Canadians to right and left, and Wolfe ordered his men to arise and form ranks. On came the French, shouting loudly, firing the moment they came within range, two columns inclining toward the English left, one to the right.

The English stood still.

Gradually the French lines became disordered by Canadians throwing themselves prone to reload, but they still came on, crying out and pouring a musket fire into the silent English.

"Fire!"

A single volley as loud as a cannon shot struck the French not 40 yards away. Again a volley, and then a clattering roll of muskets, and then, in the lifting smoke, the English saw the field before them littered with crumpled white coats, and the French, massed in fright, turning to flee.

"Charge!"

The British cheer and the fierce, wild yell of the Highlanders rose into the air, and the pursuit was begun. Redcoats with outthrust bayonets bounded after the fleeing enemy, Highlanders in kilts swinging broadswords overhead leaped forward to decapitate terrified fugitives with a single stroke.

James Wolfe joined the charge. He had already taken a ball in the wrist and had wrapped a handkerchief around it. Now, leading the Louisbourg grenadiers, he was wounded again. He pressed on, but a third shot pierced his breast. He sank to the ground. He was carried to the rear. He was asked if he wanted a surgeon.

"There's no need," he gasped. "It's all over with me."

He began to lose consciousness, until one of the sorrowing men around him shouted, "They run! See how they run!"

"Who run?" Wolfe cried, rousing himself.

"The enemy, sir. Egad, they give way everywhere!"

"Go one of you to Colonel Burton," Wolfe gasped, "and tell him to march Webb's regiment down to Charles River, to cut off their retreat from the bridge." Turning on his side, he murmured, "Now, God be praised, I will die in peace!" and he perished a few moments later.[53]

The Marquis de Montcalm was also stricken. His horse had been borne toward the town by the tide of fleeing French, and as he neared the walls a shot passed through his body. He slumped, but kept his seat rather than let his soldiers see him fall. Two regulars bore him up on either side. He entered the city streaming blood in full view of two horrified women.

"*O mon Dieu! O mon Dieu!*" one of them shrieked. "The Marquis is dead."

"It is nothing, it is nothing," Montcalm replied. "Don't be troubled for me, my good friends."[54]

But that night he was dying. His surgeon had told him that his wound was mortal. "I am glad of it," he said, and asked how much longer he had to live. "Twelve hours, more or less," was the reply. "So much the better," Montcalm murmured. "I am happy that I shall not live to see the surrender of Quebec."[55] He died peacefully at four o'clock the next morning.

Wolfe had fallen knowing that he had won an important skirmish, Montcalm perished aware that his army was routed and demoralized, but neither knew that all was won and all was lost.

Another year passed before the seal was placed on the Battle of the Plains of Abraham as the crowning victory in the 150-year war for a continent. Only a few hours after Wolfe's triumph, Bougainville appeared in the west with about 2,000 men and was repulsed by Townshend. That night, Vaudreuil panicked and abandoned Quebec, fleeing to Montreal in the van of a terrified army which had hastily quit the Beauport line leaving tents and cannon behind. Although the infuriated Levis rallied these remnants and prepared to march against the English, the town was surrendered before he could arrive. The British Army, now under Murray, passed a terrible winter in Quebec; and in the spring Lévis appeared outside its walls with a superior force. Murray rashly left the city to attack him, was driven back after losing a third of his army, and Quebec was now besieged by the French.

By then, however, a sea battle perhaps more important than the land war in Canada had been fought between the English and the French. Admiral Sir Edward Hawke met Admiral Conflans at Quiberon Bay, decisively defeating him to break the back of French naval power and to win control of the Atlantic for England. Thus it was an English and not a French fleet which sailed up the St. Lawrence on May 16, 1760. Murray was relieved and Lévis forced to withdraw to Montreal. There, Amherst, now in command in America, applied the final blows.

Murray advanced up the St. Lawrence, Haviland ascended Lake Champlain, and Amherst descended the St. Lawrence from Lake Ontario. Trapped east, south and west, Lévis was forced to capitulate.

Canada had been conquered, and the French and Indian War was over. A few years later the Peace of Paris ended the Seven Years' War in Europe. France ceded her colony on the St. Lawrence to England, retaining in America only that vast though vaguely defined region called Louisiana. France had emerged from the conflict a wreck: only five towns in India remained to her, her navy was gone and her finances were in the ruin which was to produce the French Revolution. England and Prussia were all-powerful: the one to rule the waves, the other to rack Europe.

England had beaten France, and she had won an empire. And yet she was already in danger of losing the fairest jewel in that imperial crown. As the Count Vergennes had warned:

"Delivered from a neighbor they have always feared, your other colonies will soon discover that they stand no longer in need of your protection. You will call on them to contribute toward supporting the burden which they have helped to bring on you, they will answer you by shaking off all dependence."[56]

This they would do indeed.

PART ☆ II

The War of the Revolution

1

☆

In Boston one day in 1761 the courthouse was packed to hear the fiery James Otis attack those detested Writs of Assistance—virtual blank-check search warrants—with which Parliament hoped to crush smuggling in America. Otis was a flame of eloquence, and at one point he electrified his audience with the declaration: "Taxation without representation is tyranny!"

It was the birth cry of American freedom, and it became the rallying call of all those colonial forces whose aims were converging upon a demand for independence; but at the time it passed almost unheeded. A young lawyer, John Adams, who was in the courtroom that day, did not forget Otis's immortal challenge. Nor did his radical cousin, Samuel Adams, who swore that to have no say in how they would be taxed reduced the colonists "from the character of free subjects to the miserable condition of tributary slaves."[1] Most other colonial leaders, however, failed to second Otis's fundamental challenge to Parliament's right to make laws for the entire Empire.

Across the Atlantic, far from the towering forests and great rivers of America, King George III and his ministers heard nothing. They were too busy with the Seven Years' War. Two years later the Peace of Paris made Britain the world's foremost colonial and maritime power. King George and his ministers then turned to the task of repleting an exhausted treasury and of paying off a huge public debt of some £ 136,000,000. Certainly the colonists who had also profited from the four Anglo-French wars would be willing to help. Had they not been relieved of their old fear of Canada? Surely they would agree that it was expensive to maintain some 6,000 soldiers in America, troops who were even then engaged in putting down Pontiac's rising in the West.

No proposition could have been more reasonable, providing that the colonies bore the slightest resemblance to the "grateful daughters" who existed only in the mother country's imagination. Neither George nor his ministers nor most of the bribed or blindly obedient members of the King's rubber-stamp Parliament had even been to America, and they could not have known that the colonies regarded the conquest of Canada merely as having ended their need for British protection. If Britain could have appreciated the spirit of independence which frontier life and decades of self-rule had implanted in the colonial character, or realized how the colonies loathed standing armies as a threat to liberty, she would certainly have reflected before imposing taxation from London or demanding that British redcoats be quartered in private homes.

There was the tragedy. The men who ruled Britain thought that they were dealing with men like themselves, English gentlemen in the Georgian mold. But the colonists were not. They were Americans, and it would not be long before a Virginia gentleman would say: "There ought to be no New England men, no New Yorker and so on, but all of us Americans."[2] As Americans they were not yet democrats or republicans, but they were the most fiercely independent breed of men ever to tread the earth. And yet, convinced that these Americans were as submissive to Parliament as any home-grown Britisher, Britain called upon them to help pay the cost of empire.

In 1764 the Sugar Act was passed. It was intended to replace the old Molasses Act of 1733, which the colonists had either ignored or sidestepped through smuggling. It raised the import duty on sugar, imposed other levies, and cut the tax on molasses in half. It was, on the whole, a wise and sincere attempt to strike a balance between colonial planters in the West Indies and merchants in America. But the Sugar Act exploded in the colonies like a bomb.

First, the halving of the tax on molasses was an empty gesture made to conceal the very real fact that Britain intended to *collect* this duty. Smugglers and evaders accustomed to the old, unenforced Molasses Act were in for hard times. So was a colonial distilling industry so huge that in 1750 Massachusetts alone had 63 distillers. American rum—the popular drink of the ordinary man—was distilled from molasses. Obviously, both maker and drinker were opposed to price increases which would follow *any* collectable duty. They swore they would not pay the new one, and one colonial hooted that Britain's attempt to stop smuggling would be as foolish and costly as "burning a Barn to roast an Egg."[3]

In its preamble the Sugar Act stated that it was enacted to help pay the costs "of defending, protecting and securing" America. It was a *taxing* measure. This the colonists and particularly the Yankees of New England found abhorrent. A committee of the Massachusetts House of Representatives under the redoubtable Otis challenged Parliament's very *right* to tax the colonies, declaring that such measures "have a tendency to deprive the Colonies of some of their most essential Rights as British Subjects, and . . . particularly the Right of assessing their own Taxes."[4]

Where or when the colonists got this novel idea was immaterial. What mattered was that they now had a cause: taxation without representation is tyranny. Parliament, not King George, was the tyrant. The colonists were as loyal subjects of the British Crown as any Englishmen, but they, not the British Parliament, would impose their own taxes. This was the idea which such artful propagandists as Samuel Adams were spreading abroad while the colonists evaded the Sugar Act, and an attempt to enforce the long disobeyed Navigation Acts, by bringing the techniques of smuggling to a state of near-perfection.

In 1765 Britain countered with the Stamp Act. Once again Parliament thought that it was only asking the colonies to share a burden already borne at home. Englishmen had long been accustomed to buying revenue stamps to be affixed to all legal documents, commercial paper, ship charters, bills of lading, titles, and even newspapers, pamphlets and playing cards. But the Americans had not. They were infuriated to be informed that if they did not purchase stamps all their transactions would be declared illegal and their press would be closed. This, a taxing act undisguised, simply could not be accepted; and the bellow of protest which followed the Stamp Act made the uproar against the Sugar Act seem comparatively a bleat of dissent.

In Virginia, the House of Burgesses met in the lovely rose-brick-and-white town of Williamsburg to hear the fiery back-country lawyer, Patrick Henry, suggest that just as Caesar had had his Brutus and Charles I his Cromwell, some good American should stand up for his country. There was a cry of "Treason!" and Patrick Henry quickly apologized to the Speaker, vowing that he was ready to shed his last drop of blood for George III.

Still, an open defiance of the Crown had been spoken, and Patrick Henry was in the forefront of the radicals pressing for passage of the famous Virginia Resolves. Even though the most inflammatory of the Resolves were eventually killed, they were reprinted throughout the colonies as though passed in their entirety, and so increased the uproar against the Stamp Act that Massachusetts called for a congress of colonial representatives.

In October, 1765, the Stamp Act Congress convened in New York. It expressed its loyalty to the Crown and "all due subordination" to Parliament, but firmly stated that since the colonies had no representatives in Parliament they could not be taxed by that body. Only their own legislatures could tax them, the colonies continued, adding the practical argument that the stamp taxes were so heavy that they precluded the buying of English goods and would thus be harmful to English trade.

Meanwhile, up and down the coast, associations called the Sons of Liberty were formed. They were particularly powerful in Boston, where Samuel Adams had already organized the old Guy Fawkes Day brawlers into mobs responsive to his will. He turned them loose in August after one Andrew Oliver had been named Stamp Officer. Blacksmiths and cartwrights, tavernkeepers and fishermen, and some "mechanics" whose soft white hands suggested a readier acquaintance with quill and ink than with turnspit or tar, they gathered in the glare of torches and lanterns, and went roaring off to Oliver's house. They smashed his windows, shook his doors, and hanged him in effigy. Glad to get away with his life, Oliver quickly resigned his commission. That same month mobs burned the records of the Vice-Admiralty Court—destroying all evidence of smuggling tolerated in the past—and sacked the office of the Comptroller of Customs, finally moving against the fine mansion of Governor Thomas Hutchinson. In a frenzy of rage misdirected against a man who had spoken and written against the Sugar and Stamp Acts, the mob wrecked his splendid dwelling, destroyed his furniture, defaced his paintings and ruined the finest collection of books and manuscripts in America by burning most of them or scattering the pages through the streets.

Down in New York City violence erupted with the arrival of a shipment of stamped paper. Old Cadwallader Colden, the acting governor and scholarly correspondent of Linnaeus, Benjamin Franklin and Dr. Samuel Johnson, was nearly frightened out of his wits, shutting himself up in Fort George while the howling mob reduced the gilded splendor of his coach to a pile of smoking ashes. Then the mob rushed uptown to the home of the fort's commander, breaking into the wine cellar to nourish their "patriotism" before falling upon the house in a paroxysm of vandalism.

So it went from Maine to South Carolina, and as barbaric as the mobs might have been they quickly achieved their purpose of intimidation: stamp officers resigned in droves. Came November 1, 1765, the day the act was to go into effect, and the American seaboard went into mourning.

Flags flew at half-staff, minute guns were fired, and muffled bells tolled a dirge. No one bought stamps and all business was at a standstill. Political or economic death, however, was not the goal of the colonists, and soon unstamped newspapers appeared and business was resumed as usual—without stamps. The law was simply disregarded.

But it was still on Britain's books and therefore an irritant. To remove it, the colonies organized a boycott of British goods. It worked, for America was Britain's chief customer. With British factories and shops closed and thousands out of work, Britain's manufacturers and merchants petitioned Parliament to repeal the offending law. Parliament complied, although its members tried to save face by insisting that if the Stamp Act had been ill-advised, Parliament still possessed the *right* to pass it.

Nevertheless, news of the repeal brought joy to America. It was succeeded by an outburst of gratitude and loyalty lasting about a year. Then, in early 1767, Charles Townshend took over effective leadership of Britain as Chancellor of the Exchequer. No friend of America, he believed that he "understood" the colonists. They objected only to "internal taxes" such as the Stamp Act but would not oppose "external taxes" such as duties on imports. So the famous—or infamous—Townshend Acts were passed. They imposed duties on imports from England of glass, certain painters' materials and tea. Proceeds were to pay the salaries of the colonial governors and judges, who had been paid heretofore by colonial legislatures and had been therefore beholden to them. Writs of Assistance were also revived, and provisions made for a reorganized and vigorous customs service directly responsible to the British Crown.

The Townshend Acts proved how thoroughly their author misunderstood the Americans. The colonists made no fine distinctions between external and internal taxes: they hated all taxes with a fine fervor fortified by their recent "victory" over the Stamp Act. Those Writs of Assistance which had called forth Otis's immortal cry were still anathema to them, and they were not going to cooperate in the death of smuggling. From Massachusetts came a circular letter urging concerted action again. Britain responded by ordering the colonial governors to force all legislatures to drop all opposition to the Townshend Acts under pain of dissolution. Such steps were taken in half of the colonies, and only succeeded in stiffening opposition.

As practical as they were political, the Americans simply renewed the boycott of British goods. Nonimportation Agreements were made and the Sons of Liberty began roving the night streets again. In June, 1768, royal officials attempting to seize John Hancock's sloop, *Liberty,* were attacked by a Boston mob and the Commissioner of Customs was driven to the sanctuary of Castle William on an island in Boston Harbor.

Stung, Britain sent two regiments of infantry into rebellious Boston. They landed in October, 1768, and Boston coolly refused to quarter or supply them. Two more regiments arriving in later months got the same cold-treatment. Their commander found that he had to rent quarters and purchase provisions. Moreover, to their astonishment, the British redcoats found themselves vilified as "foreigners" and as "lobster-backs," a derisive reference to the British Army's custom of enforcing discipline by flogging.

Hostility degenerated into mutual hatred, with the inevitable result coming on March 5, 1770. On that day a crowd of Bostonians hurled snowballs, stones and insults at a group of British soldiers. Some of the mobsters struck at the soldiers' muskets with clubs and dared them to fire. The redcoats lost all patience and discharged a volley straight into the crowd. Eleven citizens fell, three of them instantly killed and two more mortally stricken. This became known as the "Boston Massacre."

Bells were rung and drums beat to summon militia. The whole town poured into the streets and two companies of musketmen surrounded the Town House. Rebellion, at least in Boston, might have exploded right then and there had not Governor Hutchinson quieted the crowds and had the troops withdrawn to Castle William.

Eventually, the Townshend duties were repealed, not through the belligerence of Boston but through the boycott. British exports to America had been cut in half, and in April, 1770, all of the acts but the tax on tea were abolished. With this gesture of conciliation, a period of quiescence ensued in America. Even the boycott fell into desuetude and Samuel Adams began to grieve for the slow death of the spirit of independence.

But the spirit was only sleeping, and it came awake again June 9, 1772, with the affair of the *Gaspee*. A British armed schooner of that name had run aground near Providence while pursuing a smuggler. Once more the drums beat to arms, and that night eight boatloads of volunteers boarded the *Gaspee,* wounded her commander, overpowered the crew and put the King's ship to the torch.

Britain was outraged. King George had been publicly affronted. A royal proclamation was issued offering a reward for information leading to the arrest and conviction of the *Gaspee* culprits, and a royal commission was formed to investigate the insult. But there was no one to claim the reward nor to cooperate with the royal commissioners, and Britain discreetly dropped the matter. There was no point in expanding a single incident into the *cause célèbre* which might disturb the otherwise placid colonies.

The colonies, however, had done slumbering. When Britain attempted to influence the colonial courts by paying judges out of the royal treasury, Massachusetts countered successfully with offers of higher pay. Next Samuel Adams proposed the organization of Committees of Correspondence to act as links between the various towns of Massachusetts; other colonies followed suit and an effective communications network was eventually established between them. It was now 1773, the amiable but inept Lord North was in charge of His Majesty's government, and the East India Company was frantically begging him to do something about the American refusal to buy its tea.

King George had kept the tax on tea because he believed "there must always be one tax" to maintain the right to tax. The Americans, however, thought otherwise and calmly evaded the duty by buying mostly smuggled tea. This, among other things, had brought the East India Company—in which the government had an interest—face to face with bankruptcy. A huge backlog of seventeen million pounds of tea had piled up in its warehouses in Britain. Concerned, Lord North's government agreed to reimburse the company for the import duties it had paid in England. The company was also to be allowed to export its tea directly to its own warehouses in America—thereby cutting out American importers—and to pay a duty which would still make East India tea cheaper than the smuggled brands bought by the Americans. The colonists would thus be getting tea cheaper than it could be bought in England. Surely they would be delighted.

They were infuriated.

The Tea Act threw conservative colonial merchants straight into the arms of the radical Sons of Liberty. Dealers in smuggled tea determined to prevent the introduction of a cheaper product into the colonies, and legitimate importers, enraged at the "monopoly" granted the East India Company, now flocked to the mass meetings under the Liberty Trees. Once again political and economic forces were joined, and soon American ship captains were refusing to ship East India tea aboard their vessels. The astutely agitating merchants of Philadelphia had branded anyone who approved of the Tea Act as "an Enemy to his Country,"[5] and "the whole country was in a blaze from Maine to Georgia."[6] Like the stamp agents before them, the new tea agents hastily resigned rather than risk tar and feathers and a ride out of town on a rail.

Now it remained to prevent receipt of the tea. In Charleston no consignee being bold enough to step forward to claim the cargo, it was seized by customs officers and left to rest for three years until the new state of South Carolina could make use of it. At Philadelphia and New York the captains of the tea ships saw fit to carry their cargoes back to England. And in Boston a group of Samuel Adams's "Mohawks"—Sons of Liberty disguised as Indians—climbed aboard three tea ships on the night of December 16, 1773, broke open the tea chests and threw the contents in the harbor.

The Boston Tea Party enraged King George. Boston, that "sad nest," that hotbed of treason, and Massachusetts, that schoolhouse for rebellion, were to be brought to heel. Boston itself was to be closed as a port, leaving Marblehead and Salem the only Massachusetts ports. Massachusetts was to suffer in its charter: its Assembly was to continue to function but its upper chamber, the Council, was to be appointed by the King. Lesser judges, sheriffs and other officials were to be appointed by the Governor, the King's man. Town meetings, the heart of self-rule in the colony, were to be held only once a year to elect officers, and otherwise only by permission of the Governor. Anyone indicted for a capital offense connected with a riot or revenue laws was to be tried either in England or in another colony, and, finally, troops were to be quartered in Boston.

These were the four Coercive Acts, which the now-seething colonies decried as the "Intolerable Acts." Not every Englishman approved them, nor were they passed by a unanimous Parliament. One by one the Coercive Acts were opposed and denounced in the Commons by such eloquent pleaders for a policy of conciliation as Burke, Barre, Conway and Charles James Fox, and in the House of Lords by William Pitt, now Lord Chatham, who was rapidly losing his faculties as well as his influence. In each case, it was the royal will that prevailed. The rod was out and the colonies were to be chastised, much as the Whigs of the opposition might argue that such a course would only provoke American confederation and rebellion, perhaps even American independence.

2

☆

A cold rain fell from a codfish sky on that momentous May 17, 1774, when Lieutenant General Thomas Gage arrived in Boston to take command of His Majesty's troops in America and to assume office as Governor of the Province of Massachusetts Bay.

The enforcer of the Coercive Acts—for Gage's two hats, or sticks, had been given him to beat both port and province to their knees—met with a mixed reception. Those patriots who greeted him with chill propriety remembered that it was Gage's troops who had perpetrated the Boston Massacre, and they deduced grimly that he was come again to destroy their liberties. Those Loyalists who welcomed

him warmly recalled Gage's service with Braddock at the Monongahela, with Abercrombie at Ticonderoga, and as the American commander in chief whose troops put down Pontiac, and they rejoiced
to receive just the man who would make Yankee Doodle dance.

It was not long, however, before this handsome, dignified and
dedicated soldier discovered that Yankee Doodle preferred to call
the tunes himself. For weeks after Gage's arrival church bells tolled
dolefully, prayer and fasting were proclaimed and mourning badges
displayed. Gage's answer was to put the Boston Port Act into effect
on June 1 with a sweeping totality that left the town paralyzed.

"Did a lighter attempt to land hay from the islands, or a boat to
bring in sand from the neighboring hills, or a scow to freight to it
lumber or iron, or a float to land sheep, or a farmer to carry market-
ing over in the ferry-boats, the argus-eyed fleet was ready to see it,
and prompt to capture or destroy it."[7]

Such Draconian thoroughness succeeded only in making a martyr
of Boston. Though many abruptly unemployed people fled to the
countryside, most of Boston's 20,000 inhabitants remained within
the city. And they did not starve, for the rest of the colonies rallied
to Boston's side. Flour, cattle, fish and other foods came pouring
into the blockaded city from all over New England. From the
distant Carolinas came supplies of rice, from Delaware money—and
even Quebec sent a thousand bushels of wheat. Boston was abjured
to stand firm, to refuse to ransom her economic life by paying for
the destroyed tea.

Boston did not waver, and on June 17 the General Assembly of
Massachusetts met in Salem to protest removal of the capital to that
place. Gage sent an order dissolving the Assembly, but the doors
were locked against his emissary. Inside, the aroused Assembly made
its historic proposal for a Continental Congress of the colonies and
elected delegates to represent Massachusetts.

Shortly thereafter Gage's task of subduing these stiff-necked Yankees was made even more difficult. The Quebec Act had been passed
by Parliament and signed into law by King George. It was probably
the most statesmanlike measure of George's stormy reign, and yet
it came at absolutely the wrong moment for the American colonies.
Extending the Province of Quebec to include those French-speaking
settlements in the valley of the Ohio and the Illinois country, the law
also recognized French civil law and the Roman Catholic Church in

Canada. Thus the abhorred religion was to be guaranteed in the North and a fresh obstacle to colonial expansion was erected in the West. It was as though Canada had never been conquered, and the colonies saw red. Meanwhile, the Continental Congress met in Philadelphia.

No new nation a-borning was ever blessed with as many able political midwives as those who gathered in Philadelphia on September 5, 1774, to attend at the birth of American freedom. Nor was this a "vagrant Congress," a motley assembly of a "rabble in arms." Few delegates were as radical as Sam Adams or Patrick Henry or Richard Henry Lee of Virginia. Many of them were conservatives such as wealthy Joseph Galloway of Pennsylvania, Charles Carroll of Maryland, or the Rutledges of South Carolina who feared "the low Cunning, and those levelling principles" of New England. Most of the delegates were moderates like John Jay or James Duane of New York, John Adams of Massachusetts—probably the most respected man at the Congress—and, of course, George Washington of Virginia, tall, wide-hipped, narrow-chested, still the most imposing figure in the Congress, but now, after his marriage to the wealthy widow Martha Custis, more renowned for his social position and vast plantations than for his military talent.

Did these men intend to break with Britain? Did they seek independence? "There is no man among us," said John Adams, "that would not be happy to see accommodation with Britain."[8] The fiery, radical ideas revolving in the great, palsied, shaking head of Sam Adams were not shared by this assembly. But then Paul Revere galloped into town, his saddlebags bulging with news from the north. Massachusetts had defied General Gage and set up its own Provincial Congress. The explosive Suffolk Resolves had been passed. They were read out before a hushed and thrilled Continental Congress: the Coercive Acts were "the arbitrary will of a licentious minister"; they were "murderous law," and because of them the streets of Boston were "thronged with military executioners";[9] the Quebec Act was "dangerous to an extreme degree to the protestant religion and to the civil rights and liberties of all America."[10] Therefore the Suffolk Resolves advised that Massachusetts form its own government to collect taxes and withhold them from the royal government until the Coercive Acts were nullified. The people of the colony were to arm and form their own militia. The most severe economic sanctions must be brought to bear on Britain.

The hearts of the radicals lifted. The standard of implacable opposition was at last being raised. Moderates also were carried away. Swarms of shouting delegates engulfed the men from Massachusetts. Without changing a comma, the Congress adopted the Suffolk Resolves. Then, calling for the third and most stringent boycott of British goods, it served notice on Parliament that the colonies were no longer bound by its laws outside purely commercial regulations. The King was politely informed that his prerogatives must conform to the Americans' ideas of their liberties and his authority.

No one had yet spoken of rebellion or independence or an appeal to arms. But the American Revolution had begun.

In Boston the war which was fought to preserve that revolt was beginning to sputter.

General Gage had been steadily accumulating troops. He called for workmen to build barracks. None came forward. Though unemployed, no one cared or dared to work for the "lobster-backs." Gage sent to New York and Halifax for workmen, and the Bostonians began a campaign of sabotage. Brick barges were sunk, straw for soldiers' beds was burned, and wagons were overturned. Enraged, Gage countered by sending soldiers over to Charlestown and Cambridge to seize colonial powder and cannon. The troops carried out his orders, but their little foray gave Massachusetts an opportunity to carry out a dress rehearsal for the later reality of mobilization.

News of the seizure spread swiftly throughout the province. Details of the coup were so magnified that the Continental Congress heard the absurd news that Gage had bombarded Boston. Nevertheless, by the day following the seizure some 4,000 armed and angry men had come crowding into Cambridge, while all over New England other men were on the march. Gage blinked and took note. Now he began to fortify the narrow neck of land linking Boston to the mainland. The Provincial Congress replied by appropriating the huge sum of £15,627 to purchase military supplies. It called for the organization of "minutemen," named three generals to command its militia, set up a Committee of Safety under Dr. Joseph Warren to take over its own duties once it had ceased to exist, and then, on December 10, having set up all the apparatus for rebellion, dissolved itself.

Gage too late proclaimed all the acts of the vanished Provincial Congress as treasonable. His attempts to undo its mischief were like the sound of a cannon trying to overtake the flash. Everywhere in New England men were drilling on the green. Guns and powder were being stolen from British forts. Colonial supplies were increasing. To counter American thefts of munitions Gage sent a British expedition to Salem on February 26, 1775. It met colonial militia under Colonel Timothy Pickering at an open bridge.

Pickering refused to obey the British demand to lower the drawbridge. Finally, a Salem clergyman intervened. He persuaded the militia to lower the bridge on the British promise to march only thirty rods into the town and return. This was done, but the redcoats discovered nothing but the Yankee willingness to fight.

Marching home they passed through the town of Northfields, where a nurse named Sarah Tarrant called to them from an open window: "Go home and tell your master he has sent you on a fool's errand and broken the peace of our Sabbath. What, do you think we were born in the woods, to be frightened by owls?"

Stung, one of the soldiers pointed his gun at her, and Nurse Tarrant scoffed: "Fire, if you have the courage—but I doubt it."[11]

A month later the fierce spirit of resistance sweeping through America had caught fire in Virginia. There, Patrick Henry arose in the House of Burgesses to declare:

"There is no retreat but in submission and slavery! Our chains are forged. Their clanking may be heard on the plains of Boston! The war is inevitable—and let it come! I repeat it, sir, let it come!

"It is in vain, sir, to extenuate the matter. Gentlemen may cry, 'Peace! Peace!'—but there is no peace. The war is actually begun! The next gale that sweeps down from the north will bring to our ears the clash of resounding arms! Our brethren are already in the field! Why stand we here idle? What is it that gentlemen wish? What would they have? Is life so dear, or peace so sweet, as to be purchased at the price of chains and slavery? Forbid it, Almighty God! I know not what course others may take; but as for me, give me liberty or give me death!"[12]

The choice was not a month away, and the gale from the North ringing with the clash of arms was already making up on the road from Lexington to Concord.

3

☆

King George and Parliament, ignoring the petitions of the Continental Congress, had moved to subdue that "most daring spirit of resistance and disobedience"[13] existing in the colonies. More oppressive measures were passed, capped by the Fishery Act forbidding New Englanders to trade with Great Britain, Ireland and the West Indies and banning them from the Newfoundland fisheries.

Angered beyond restraint by this dreadful blow at its economy, Massachusetts replied by reviving the Provincial Congress. The members of that body, seated in chambers so cold that many of them kept their hats on, placed the province on a virtual war footing. Then, once more turning the military apparatus over to Dr. Warren and the Committee of Safety, the Congress adjourned.

That was on April 15, the day after General Gage received his "get-tough" orders. Force was to be quickly applied before the rebellion could spread, Gage was told, and the leaders of the Provincial Congress were to be arrested. Gage, a practical soldier, realized that the latter instruction was not possible. Although Dr. Warren was known to be in Boston, Sam Adams and John Hancock were out in the vicinity of Concord and John Adams was still farther away. At Concord, however, lay the Committee of Safety's arsenal. Gage had been kept minutely informed of its growth by none other than Dr. Benjamin Church. This urbane grandson of the old Indian fighter of the same name had fallen hopelessly in love with a lady, and because he needed money to keep her, he betrayed the Committee's secrets to Gage.

Resolved to seize the stores of arms at Concord, Gage collected his best troops—the grenadier and light infantry companies—and placed them "off all duties 'till further orders" to learn "new evolutions." The patriot spies, however, knew what Gage hoped to "evolve." Boston patrolmen under Paul Revere had seen the transports hauling up their whaleboats for repairs. They guessed correctly that an expedition was being prepared to go by boat from Boston to Cambridge and thence take the road to Concord about 20 miles away.

Next morning Warren sent Revere riding to Lexington to warn John Hancock and Sam Adams to be ready to flee. Revere returned that night and arranged "that if the British went out by water we would show two lanterns in the North Church steeple; and if by land, one."[14] This is the famous "one if by land, two if by sea" of Longfellow's poem, but Revere did not intend that "I on the opposite shore will be." The lanterns were to rouse the Charlestown countryside.

During daylight of April 18 Gage sent mounted officers out to patrol the Concord road and to keep it free of rebel couriers. That night his elite troops—from 600 to 800 men—were awakened by sergeants shaking them and whispering to them. Startled, unaware of their destination, knowing only that their packs were full for a march, they slipped out of the barracks unknown to their sleeping comrades. Having stolen away from their own quarters, they marched openly to Boston Common where they formed ranks under the lackluster eyes of their commander, fat, slow-thinking Lieutenant Colonel Francis Smith. Fortunately for Smith, Major John Pitcairn of the Royal Marines was also coming along. Although Pitcairn has gone into some American histories as a profane and bloodthirsty boor, he was actually a gallant gentleman and a fine officer. At half-past ten the British were ready to move, and by then Dr. Warren had sent William Dawes and Paul Revere flying from Boston to warn the countryside.

Dawes took the longer land route over Boston Neck to Cambridge and thence to Menotomy (now Arlington) and the road west to Lexington and Concord. Revere, booted and swathed in a greatcoat, had himself rowed over to Charlestown. At eleven o'clock he sprang onto a waiting horse and clattered off.

Behind him two lanterns began to glow in the steeple of old North Church.

"The regulars are out!" Paul Revere cried, his excited voice rising above the hoofbeats of his horse. "The regulars are out!"

He was, with Dawes, warning every "Middlesex village and farm," cupping his hands to his lips to shout at lighted windows, tossing

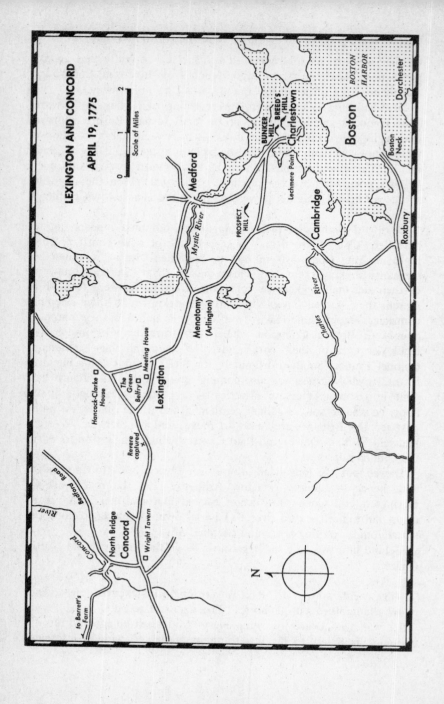

LEXINGTON AND CONCORD
APRIL 19, 1775

Scale of Miles
0   1   2

BOSTON HARBOR
Dorchester
Boston
Boston Neck
Roxbury
Charlestown
BUNKER HILL
BREED'S HILL
Lechmere Point
Cambridge
Charles River
PROSPECT HILL
Medford
Mystic River
Menotomy (Arlington)
Lexington
Hancock-Clarke House
The Green
Belfry
Meeting House
Revere captured
Concord
North Bridge
Wright Tavern
Bedford Road
Concord River
to Barrett's Farm

N

gravel at darkened ones, then riding on, his mount's hooves ringing boldly in the still darkness, the sweat on its hide forming puffs of foam.

At Lexington, Revere rode up to the home of Parson Jonas Clark. Sam Adams and Clark's cousin, John Hancock, were staying there. Revere shouted to the guard to let him in, and the guard yelled at him to stop making so much noise or he'd wake the family.

"Noise!" Revere roared. "You'll have noise enough before long. The regulars are coming out!"[15]

Adams and Hancock were awakened. They dressed and fled. It was then after midnight, and as they crossed a meadow Adams said to Hancock: "What a glorious morning this is!" Seeing his friend puzzled, Adams added: "I mean for America."[16]

It was not such a glorious morning for Paul Revere. After Dawes arrived in Lexington an hour later, the two set out for Concord. They were joined by young Dr. Samuel Prescott, who was returning home from a long evening of courting. The three rode on, spreading the alarm. Halfway between towns they were intercepted by Gage's outriders. They scattered. Revere rode into a pasture, where he was cornered and captured. Dawes wheeled and galloped back to Lexington. Dr. Prescott jumped a low stone wall and went clattering off for Concord, where he roused the militia.

The countryside had been warned, and back on the road from Charlestown the clear cold dawn of April 19 fell on the long columns of British redcoats marching into Lexington.

Colonel Francis Smith's soldiers were fuming. It was bad enough being perpetually damp from the waist down because of that moist white paste called pipe clay with which they were supposed to keep their breeches impeccably white, but now those same pants were stained with mud and the men were sopping from the chest down.

The whaleboats had put them ashore at Lechmere Point in knee-deep water. Then, after their fathead colonel had kept them waiting two hours for rations, he had led them into a backwater of the Charles in which they had been forced to wade up to their chests. No sooner had they begun squishing and squelching away for the Yankee lair at Concord than shots and ringing bells and scampering feet to either side of the road made it clear that there was to be no surprise. The only surprise that day would be if any of the officers knew any of the men they commanded. Their own officers were sick or on detached service. In their place were volunteers, thrill-seekers and smooth-chinned subalterns out for a lark. Some of them did not even come from the crack "flank" companies but wore the silly cocked hat of the line.

At Menotomy there was a surprise. Alarmed by outriders' reports that the rebels had been warned, perhaps prompted by Major Pitcairn, Colonel Smith made a wise decision: he sent an express rider back to Boston with a request for reinforcements. It was then about three o'clock in the morning. The men had been on their feet for five hours, and they continued to slosh forward, burdened by perhaps sixty pounds of equipment—packs, belts, bayonet scabbards and cartridge boxes—hampered by stiff and awkward clothing, and still clutching their ten-pound muskets, the famous Brown Bess of England.

But the guns' barrels and metal fittings were no longer brown but brightly burnished like the socket bayonets fitted to their muzzles, and these rows of gleaming barrels and glittering blades were visible from afar to the handful of patriots drawn up on Lexington Green.

Captain Jonas Parker and about 70 men had formed on the green. They stood inside a triangle formed by three roads. The road to Concord was at its base. Parker's men stood about a hundred yards above it, and they could clearly see the steady, awesome approach of the British advance guard under Major Pitcairn.

"There are so few of us," one man said, "it is folly to stand here."

"The first man who offers to run shall be shot down," Parker warned.[17]

Major Pitcairn ordered his men into line of battle. The rear ranks ran forward at the double to line up with the others and form two sections three men deep. They shouted and cheered as they ran.

"Stand your ground!" Parker ordered. "Don't fire unless fired upon. But if they want to have a war, let it begin here!"[18] Some men shook their heads and drifted away.

Pitcairn rode forward crying, "Lay down your arms, you damned rebels, and disperse!"[19]

Parker finally saw that this situation was impossible. He ordered his men to disband, taking their weapons with them. Pitcairn called repeatedly to them to lay down their arms. Shots crashed out (from the British on the road or from patriots behind a wall, history will never know), a British soldier was wounded and two balls grazed Pitcairn's horse.

"Fire, by God, fire!" a British officer cried, and a volley of British ball tore through the Americans. "Soldiers!" Pitcairn called. "Soldiers, don't fire! Keep your ranks. Form and surround them."[20] But the regulars, taunted for months in the Boston prison cage, driven mad by their frustrating march, were not to be checked. Pitcairn swung his sword downward as the signal to cease fire, but they replied with another crash of musketry, and then, after the rebels fired a ragged return, they cheered and charged with the bayonet.

The militia fled. Brave Jonas Parker stood alone. He had fired once and been wounded. He stood like a stricken bull in the arena, reloading to fire again—and British bayonets cut him down.

Eight Americans lay dead on the Green and ten more had been wounded. Only that single British soldier had been hurt—and that was all that there was to the Battle of Lexington. The British officers re-formed their exultant men, Colonel Smith came up with the main body, and then, with drums beating and fifes squealing, the redcoats swung west on the last six miles to Concord.

The alarm bell rung in Concord after the arrival of young Dr. Prescott had brought three companies of minutemen and one alarm company of old men and boys tumbling into town. Many of them joined Colonel James Barrett hurrying over the North Bridge that crossed the Concord River on the road west to Barrett's house, where most of the province's munitions were stored.

Much of these had been sent farther west the day before, but the minutemen still had to lug barrels of musket balls, flints and cartridges into the attic and cover them with feathers. Powder was hauled into the woods and a plowman dug furrows in which muskets and light cannon were laid while the earth from other furrows covered them over.

Meanwhile, other militia companies from other towns and villages were arriving in Concord. Eventually they numbered about 400 men under the nominal command of Colonel Barrett. Most of these men were stationed on a ridge overlooking North Bridge from Barrett's side of the river. They stayed there, watching, while the British marched into town unhindered.

Colonel Smith and his staff went to a tavern to refresh themselves, carefullly paying for all that they ordered, while four companies of light infantry crossed North Bridge and went up the road to Barrett's house. Behind them, three other companies of light infantry guarded the bridge, fanning out on both sides of the river. Inside Concord, the grenadiers, with a courtesy that should make the twentieth century blush, began searching houses. One huge grenadier retreated, red-faced, before a determined old lady brandishing a mop, and a grenadier officer in another house politely accepted the falsehood that a locked room was occupied by an invalid when it actually contained military stores. Still, they found 100 barrels of flour and sent them splashing into a millpond, followed by 500 pounds of bullets. But the flour barrels were not stove in and the bullet sacks were not slashed, and almost all of these supplies were salvaged. However, gun carriages found in the Town House were set afire, and then put out after the grenadiers realized that they might also set the Town House blazing. Dragged outside, they were relighted—and that column of smoke spiraling lazily into the sky above Concord's elms and oaks was seen by Colonel Barrett's men on the hill.

"Will you let them burn the town down?"[21] an officer asked Barrett, and Barrett replied by ordering the militia to march to the defense of the town and not to fire unless fired upon. In column of twos they came down, these "embattled farmers" of history, marching silently to the beat of drummer boy Abner Hosmer with Captain Isaac Davis, the Acton gunsmith, at their head.

At North Bridge Captain Laurie of the light infantry watched their approach in surprise. He sent back to town for reinforcements. Colonel Smith ordered a few companies of grenadiers forward, "but put himself at their head by which means he stopt 'em from being [in] time enough, for being a very fat heavy Man he wou'd not have reached the Bridge in a half hour tho it was not half a mile to it."[22]

Suddenly Laurie was nervous. The long column of Americans was coming straight down the steep hill to the bridge. His own men were uneasy. There were no better troops in the world, but today they were strangely unruly. Unfamiliar officers were having trouble forming them after Laurie pulled his outposts back to the Concord side of the bridge. Laurie wanted the front-rank men to fire, peel off and run to the rear to reload, thus exposing the second-rank men who would do the same and so on. Smartly executed, it was a fine maneuver designed to rake the approaching Yankees with a steady fire. But it was done clumsily that day. The first British shots fell short in the river. One of them whistled by the ear of Captain Timothy Brown.

"God damn it, they are firing ball!" Brown exclaimed.[23]

They were indeed, and now they had the range. Captain Isaac Davis was knocked down dead. Little Abner Hosmer toppled beside him with a ball through the brain. Two other Americans were wounded.

"Fire, fellow soldiers!" an American officer pleaded. "For God's sake, fire!"[24]

The first full American volley of the Revolutionary War crashed forth. Three redcoats—the first Britishers to die in that war—fell lifeless, and nine more were wounded. Then the Americans cheered, for the British were withdrawing! Leaving their dead and one wounded man lying on the road, they rushed back to town in disorder. They met and mingled with Smith's tardy grenadiers and were finally re-formed and faced toward the Americans.

But the undisciplined Yankees pursued for only a few yards before breaking ranks. Some went back across the bridge to carry off the bodies of Davis and the little drummer boy, but most of them returned to the ridge. Perhaps they were amazed by their own "victory" over the regulars. Perhaps also they did not want to be caught between Smith's force and the four companies of light infantry who might return from Barrett's house any minute.

Silence came over North Bridge. The Yankees stared at the crumpled red-and-white forms of the fallen foe. They saw a gangly farmer come over the bridge. He had an ax in his hand. One of the sprawled soldiers stirred. The farmer panicked, struck at him with his ax and ran off. The soldier sank back onto the road.

Now came the tread of marching feet. The light infantry was returning from Barrett's house. They had found nothing. They were disgruntled, then frightened to see their dead comrades and the "scalped" soldier. Their step quickened. They began running. They went tearing around the bend on the double, and the Americans on the hill to the left let them pass without firing a shot.

It was now ten o'clock, and in Concord Colonel Smith was preparing to leave. He hired carriages to carry his wounded and at noon the silent columns trudged back the way they came.

> Yankee Doodle went to town
> Ariding on a pony,
> Stuck a feather in his cap
> And called it macaroni.

Earl Percy was marching to Colonel Smith's rescue with a force of 1,000 men and two cannon, and his fifes and drums were derisively playing "Yankee Doodle" as they struck confidently over Boston Neck. Passing through Roxbury a schoolboy is supposed to have laughed so hard at the tune that Percy asked him why. The boy replied with a mocking reference to a ballad that went:

> To drive the deer with hound and horne
> Erle Percy took his way.
> The child may rue that is unborne
> The hunting of that day!

On every side of the British column the Americans were gathering. Towns and hamlets too far away to fight at Lexington or Concord had sent militia hurrying to the scene. Some dispatched only a few dozen and others as many as 300 men. In all, perhaps 4,000 Americans were gathering along that 16-mile gantlet running back to Charlestown.

They fired from behind stone walls or from trees. They took long-range pot shots from houses or rushed boldly to within a few yards of the line of march and blazed away. Redcoat after redcoat slumped into the dust. Smith's hired carriages were piled high with wounded. But the patriots did not escape unscathed. Smith sent his light infantry out on the flanks. They surprised groups of militia in the hollows and put them to rout. They doubled back on themselves and took the unsuspecting Americans in the rear. They cornered them in houses and shot them down or drove their slender bayonets into them. And because they had taken as much as men can be expected to endure, they set fire to the houses or wrecked them.

But the militia were hydra-headed. Each time an American was killed or put to flight or merely quit the battle, two more arrived to take his place. And the galling fire from both sides of the road continued.

It not only tore British flesh; it fragmented British discipline. Smith's column became a disorderly crowd of men. Soldiers broke ranks to ransack roadside houses or taverns for food and whatever they could carry off. Nearing Lexington, Smith halted and ordered Pitcairn to hold off the Americans while he re-formed his ranks. The Americans swarmed around Pitcairn's rear guard and opened fire. Riflemen lying behind a pile of rails blazed at Pitcairn, conspicuous on an elegant horse. The horse plunged, threw Pitcairn, and ran into the American

lines, carrying off Pitcairn's set of fine horse pistols. The rear guard
was driven in and Smith was forced to renew the retreat.

Now the dreadful pace was killing. Men who had been on their
feet for more than 20 hours were wilting. The light infantry were exhausted from the ordeal of covering the flanks. Some soldiers were
breaking ranks in a stumbling run. Men continued to fall—from American musket balls or fatigue—and the redcoats' ammunition was running out. Entering Lexington the British were on the verge of breaking
into a rout. Officers had to stagger around their hurrying men to confront them with bayonets and warn them to slow down or die. And
then, at three o'clock in the afternoon, they beheld the black hats
and scarlet coats and white breeches of Percy's brigade formed in a
hollow square. Too tired to cheer, they passed through their saviors'
ranks and sank to the ground, "their tongues hanging from their
mouths, like those of dogs after a chase."[25] Percy's pair of 6-pound
cannon kept the Americans at a respectful distance while Smith's
exhausted men rested.

Meanwhile, American reinforcements were arriving. General William Heath came out to Lexington and so did Dr. Joseph Warren.
Neither man saw the opportunity lying at hand. If a force could have
been sent downroad while the redcoats rested, Percy's retreat could
have been sealed off. A party of axmen could have been formed to
fell trees across the British path. Neither tactic was adopted, although
it must be said that the Yankee "army" was actually only a great
crowd of armed and angry farmers, each fighting individually and
entering or leaving the fight at his whim. Nor were they the crack
shots of legend, either. When Percy resumed the retreat some time
after three o'clock, the Americans again buzzed about his flanks like
swarms of bees. The finest of targets lay under the muzzles of their
muskets, and even though that weapon's projectile falls harmlessly
to the ground after 125 yards, they still should have been able to
slaughter the defenseless enemy.

Still, they continued to torment them all the way to Charlestown.
And the British fought back. They were burning and ransacking every
roadside house now, and at one point the flankers drove a party of
patriots into a house and bayoneted 12 of them to death. At Menotomy
40 Americans and 40 British fell. At Cambridge a mile and a half of
continuous battle was begun. Redcoats and men in homespun fought
each other at close quarters, with bayonets and clubbed muskets.

Again and again Percy halted his column and unlimbered his little cannon. They spat, drove the Americans off, the gunners limbered up again, and the guns and carriages became covered with the scarlet coats of the wounded and fatigued. At last Percy's battered force crossed Charlestown Neck into Charlestown under the protecting muzzles of the British ships. The Americans fell back, darkness came, and the bloody retreat from Concord was over.

British casualties were 73 killed, 26 missing and probably dead, and 174 wounded, a total of 273 out of about 1,800 men engaged. The Americans lost 49 killed, 5 missing, and 41 wounded, a total of 93. If a battle's importance were to be measured by its casualties, Concord and Lexington would have been trifling indeed. But the shots "heard round the world" had been fired, and the Revolutionary War—one of the most momentous in history—had been started.

Next day, Percy's troops were hardly safely across the Charles before the vanguard of thousands of armed New Englanders rushed into Cambridge. Works were thrown up outside the city, an army arose on the plain and the siege of Boston was begun.

4

☆

The day after Lexington and Concord a British ship arrived in Boston Harbor with Lord North's "peace proposal." The King's minister, realizing that he had been too harsh to the Americans, offered not to tax those colonies which voluntarily paid their share of the cost of empire.

His Lordship, however, was too late with much too little. Americans were generally too enraged even to consider this evasion of the issue of the *right* to tax, and one of them exclaimed: "An armed robber who demands my money might as well pretend he makes a concession by suffering me to take it out of my own pocket, rather than search there for it himself."[26]

Meanwhile, couriers from the Committee of Safety had gone galloping north and south ever since the first American perished at Lexington. At ten o'clock that fateful morning, Israel Bissell went pounding out of Watertown bound for points south. Two hours later the horse beneath him fell dead, but Bissell mounted a fresh horse and clattered on: New York . . . New Brunswick . . . Princeton . . . Philadelphia. Other express riders carried the news farther south, and before the month of April was out it had spread across Virginia and was en route to South Carolina.

In Virginia a British major named Horatio Gates knew that Lexington meant war. Like Thomas Gage now commanding in Boston, Gates had been wounded at the Monongahela. Gates, however, had left the service to become an American planter. He was definitely on the colonial side. So was another former British soldier, General Charles Lee. Thin, ugly and irascible, fonder of dogs than of men, this soldier of fortune was considered by many Americans to be the ablest military man in America. Charles Lee was certainly—as he would personally insist—more experienced than that Colonel George Washington whom he had just visited at Mount Vernon.

Washington also heard the news from the North, and it so affected him that he packed the old red-and-blue uniform he had worn under Braddock and took it to Philadelphia with him for the second session of the Continental Congress.

The Congress was due to convene on May 10.

Dawn of May 10 crept across Lake Champlain and the stone walls of Fort Ticonderoga. Ethan Allen realized that the fort would have to be rushed immediately if surprise were not to be lost. Turning to address his Green Mountain Boys, he stood just a bit forward of Benedict Arnold at his side to make it clear that he, Ethan Allen, by orders of the Connecticut Assembly, not Arnold, representing Massachusetts, was in command of the expedition.

"I now propose," Ethan Allen said, "to advance before you and in person to conduct you through the wicket-gate. For we must this morning quit our pretensions to valor, or possess ourselves of this fortress in a few minutes. Inasmuch as it is a desperate attempt—which none but the bravest of men dare undertake—I do not urge it on any contrary to his will." He paused. His great figure was growing more distinct in the half-light, and he seemed to dwarf the short, stocky Arnold. "You that will undertake," Ethan Allen called, "poise your firelocks!"[27]

All obeyed, and they marched off three ranks deep toward the fort on a venture that was not actually that "desperate." Ticonderoga was held by only 40-odd British soldiers—most of them unfit for service—under Captain William Delaplace and Lieutenant Jocelyn Feltham. Still, neither Allen nor Arnold nor their 83 men knew this as they went charging toward the wicket.

A sentry saw them, pointed his musket and pulled the trigger, but it flashed in the pan, and the sentry ran back into the fort to sound the alarm. The Americans pursued, crying, "No quarter! No quarter!" Another sentry slightly wounded one of Allen's officers with a bayonet, and huge Ethan Allen lifted his sword to cut him down. Taking pity, he softened his blow to a saber cut on the face and went on up a staircase with Arnold.

At the top of the stairs stood Lieutenant Feltham clutching his breeches.

"Come out of there, you damned old rat!"[28] Allen roared, and the astonished officer asked by what authority these men had intruded on the King's domain.

"In the name of the Great Jehovah and the Continental Congress!"[29] Allen bellowed, waving his sword over Feltham's head. Then, demanding "the Fort and all the effects of George the Third" upon pain of a general massacre, Allen brought Captain Delaplace hurrying down the stairs. Delaplace promptly handed over his sword and Fort Ticonderoga.

The gateway to Canada, with all its priceless artillery, was in American hands.

The capture of Ticonderoga startled Congress. Many of the delegates there had comforted themselves with the argument that the "ministerial troops," as the King's soldiers were called, were to blame for Lexington and Concord. But now colonials had attacked and captured a royal fort. The fact that they were openly opposing King George III sank deeper into the minds of the delegates as debate began over such matters as general defense, although the possibility of reconciliation with Britain was also discussed.

Colonel Washington, in charge of a committee "to consider ways and means to supply these Colonies with ammunition and military stores," was delighted to hear that Ticonderoga had yielded about 60 cannon and mortars. Washington, appearing daily in his uniform now, was also pleased with accounts of the fighting in Massachusetts. He assured John Adams and other powerful delegates that Americans could stand up to British regulars. Still, the prospect of fratricidal war oppressed him, and he wrote to a friend:

"Unhappy it is, though, to reflect that a brother's sword has been sheathed in a brother's breast and that the once-happy and peaceful plains of America are either to be drenched with blood or inhabited by slaves. Sad alternative! But can a virtuous man hesitate in his choice?"[30]

On May 25 King George's unhesitating choice of "sad alternative" arrived in Boston Harbor aboard the frigate *Cerberus*. A "triumvirate of reputation," Major General William Howe, Major General Henry Clinton and Major General John Burgoyne had come to America to give aid and advice to the faltering General Gage, already earmarked for recall.

William Howe was probably the most outstanding of this trio of hand-picked generals. It was Howe who had led his light infantry up the slopes of the Anse-du-Foulon to the Plains of Abraham. Now, 46 years old and grown heavier through indulgence in food and drink, he was still handsome in the florid fashion of the period. Like his older brother, Admiral Lord Richard ("Black Dick") Howe, who soon joined him in America, he was of very dark complexion. He was also, like his brother, a strange choice to subdue the colonists: both Howes were grateful to the Americans for having placed in Westminster a statue of their oldest brother, Lord George Augustus Howe, the beloved leader killed at Ticonderoga in 1758. They had agreed to serve against the colonies only on direct orders from the King.

Henry Clinton needed no such urging. A colorless career soldier, he was the only son of an admiral and former governor of New York. His military career began at 13, when he purchased a lieutenant's commission. At 20 he was a lieutenant colonel and a major general at 34. Three years later he boarded the *Cerberus,* chosen for his reputation as a planner.

"Gentleman Johnny" Burgoyne's reputation was of a different order. Wit, playwright, member of Parliament and *bon vivant,* he shared

William Howe's passion for the pleasures of the gaming table and the boudoir. Yet Gentleman Johnny seems also to have been a good soldier. He had not only astounded his officers by insisting that they read or learn something of mathematics, but also shocked them by treating soldiers as human beings who were not to be trained "like spaniels by the stick." Unfortunately for Burgoyne, his sharp tongue got him into trouble before he arrived.

Hearing that 5,000 British regulars were being cooped up by a force of raw colonial militia only twice their number, he exclaimed: "What! Well, let *us* get in and we'll soon find elbow-room."[31] Stepping ashore May 25, Burgoyne heard himself hailed as "General Elbow-Room."

The truth of the situation was exactly as Gage had been describing it for London. Yankee Doodle would not dance until more troops were sent to America. Even then, subduing the colonials would be difficult. First, the countryside was hostile: there were many loyal Tories but they so feared the Sons of Liberty that they would only be good for acclaiming a victorious army. As a result the problem of a supply line 3,000 miles long was magnified. Next, the road networks were poor and the ruggedness of the countryside, with its multiplicity of rivers, made battle in the accepted European style unlikely. Third, even though British sea power gave Gage the advantage of being able to move anywhere against these coastal colonies, there was no single centralized capital the capture of which might bring capitulation. There were, in effect, 13 different subcapitals.

All London's witty contempt for the Yankee "cowards," now being so drolly relayed by Gentleman Johnny Burgoyne, would not raise the siege of Boston. A criminal amnesty from King George would not make the "army of thieves and vagrants" melt away. Generals such as James Grant might taunt Benjamin Franklin with the remark that, given a thousand grenadiers, "he would undertake to go from one end of America to the other and geld all the males,"[32] but even Grant would have to admit the impossibility of transporting just a thousand men from one end of this wild continent to the other. Bombs, not bombast, were needed—to say nothing of a little fresh beef.

By June the British in Boston were on lean rations. "However we block up their port, the rebels certainly block up our town, and have cut off our good beef and mutton," one of Gage's officers wrote home. "At present we are . . . subsisting almost on salt provision."[33]

Outside Boston, the colonial army under General Artemas Ward had problems of its own. Ward at 48 was himself sick of "the stone," and he was having difficulty disciplining his militia. Ward dared not try to take the town. He had no siege guns to batter it, nor enough troops to storm it. The seacoast towns of the four New England provinces had withheld their militia against the possibility of invasion by the ever-present British fleet.

So as the Army of Massachusetts, or, more properly, of New England, sat down before Boston and waited for something to happen, the Continental Congress down in Philadelphia soberly began debating whether or not impetuous New England was dragging the whole continent into war.

Benjamin Franklin had written from London that war must be the unanimous will of all 13 colonies. Not all of them, however, particularly those of the South, were anxious to take up arms. Many conservative delegates such as Duane and Farmer John Dickinson of Pennsylvania had revived the spirit of conciliating the Crown.

Then, from the Massachusetts Committee of Safety came a petition for Congress to adopt the Boston army as its own. Many delegates recoiled. Even George Washington was not now sure that war was inevitable. But John Adams, now the spokesman for New England, was determined not to allow the other nine colonies to split away from the Northern four. He arose in Congress to make clear the common danger. Let New England fall and the other colonies, one by one, beginning with New York, would feel the rod. John Adams spoke of an American army recruited from all the colonies. He had already decided who should command it. Not a professional such as British-born Charles Lee, general by grace of the King of Poland, but rather a native-born American. Should he be from the North which had fielded the army before Boston, or from the middle or Southern colonies which seemed to be wavering?

On June 14, with John Hancock in the president's chair, John Adams began describing the man he wished to nominate as the American commander in chief. John Hancock listened hopefully.

"A gentleman whose skill as an officer, whose independent fortune, great talents, and universal character would command the respect of America and unite the *full* exertions of the colonies—"

John Hancock's face fell. A Northern man had been ruled out.

"—a gentleman from Virginia who is among us here, and who is—"

There was a stir. The tall man in uniform had risen quickly to his feet and bolted for the library.

"—George Washington of Virginia."[34]

There was a swelling hum of voices, raised first in surprise, as well as, from New Englanders, some resentment. John Hancock's face fell farther when his old friend, Sam Adams, arose to second his cousin's motion. Washington, in the library, might have been a bit chagrined to hear Edmund Pendleton of Virginia say that although the colonel was a decent man, he had lost every big battle he'd been in.

Debate continued until the next day, June 15, when Washington appeared and heard Hancock say: "The President [of Congress] has the order of Congress to inform George Washington, Esquire, of the unanimous vote in choosing him to be General and Commander-in-Chief of the forces raised and to be raised in defense of American liberty. The Congress hopes the gentleman will accept."[35]

The gentleman would, but with the modesty which was one of his finest traits:

"Mr. President . . . I . . . declare with the utmost sincerity, I do not think myself equal to the command I am honored with. As to pay, Sir, I beg leave to assure the Congress that as no pecuniary consideration could have tempted me to have accepted this arduous employment at the expense of my domestic ease and happiness, I do not wish to make any profit from it."[36]

He would keep an account of his expenses, and this was all he asked Congress to pay.

After selection of the leader came the choice of his lieutenants. Artemas Ward, of course, was the first of them as a major general; then Charles Lee; Philip Schuyler, the wealthy Hudson River patroon who was so influential in New York; Israel Putnam to satisfy Connecticut; and finally, as a skilled professional adjutant to handle Washington's staff work, his neighbor from Virginia, Horatio Gates.

Appointments of brigadiers followed as Congress quibbled over questions of priority or tried to assuage wounded provincial pride. In the meantime, General George Washington prepared to take command of the army which had preceded him to battle. Before he could, a fresh gale, clamorous with the clash of arms, blew down from the north.

5

☆

To beat General Gage to the high ground above Boston the Committee of Safety directed its army to seize and fortify Bunker Hill.

General Artemas Ward called a council of war at which both he and Dr. Warren expressed their reluctance to move. Ammunition was low and there were only 11 barrels of powder in the entire American camp. Moreover, Bunker Hill out on Charlestown Peninsula between the Charles and Mystic rivers was exposed to the guns of the British fleet and could be easily cut off at the rear on Charlestown Neck, an isthmus so narrow that it was flooded at high tide.

Such considerations did not deter Major General Israel Putnam, who assured the council: "The Americans are not at all afraid of their heads, though very much afraid of their legs. If you cover these, they will fight forever."[37] The council agreed, so completely, it appears, that no one bothered to ask Putnam how troops were to "fight forever" after their ammunition ran out. But then, it was not customary to challenge "Old Put."

At 57 years of age, Putnam was still an imposing figure with his bear's body, his bull's voice and his great round owlish head. He was also a legend. He had been with Lord Howe on that fatal patrol at Ticonderoga, he had narrowly missed being burned at the stake by Indians, he had been a prisoner of the French at Montreal and had been shipwrecked while leading an expedition against Havana. Such was his great courage and capacity for inspiring men that no one dared to suggest that Old Put seemed to excel at narrow escapes from avoidable traps. On the night of June 16 he led about 1,200 men into a fresh cul-de-sac.

Dressed mostly in homespun dyed the colors of the colony's oak and sumach bark, wearing broad-brimmed hats and clutching old Brown Bess muskets from the colonial wars, with here and there an ancient Spanish fusee, they marched across Charlestown Neck in the darkness. Ahead of them was Old Put riding a fine horse, his saddle holsters stuffed with the splendid pistols once owned by Major Pitcairn of the Royal Marines. Beside Putnam was Colonel William Prescott, another colonial veteran but a man as practical as Old Put was impetuous.

Prescott sent a patrol into Charlestown to watch the enemy while his main body marched to Bunker Hill and then along a ridge leading east to Breed's Hill, which was closer to Boston. For a time Prescott, Putnam and others argued about whether it was best to fortify Breed's or Bunker. Colonel Richard Gridley, an excellent engineer, cut them short with the warning that they were wasting precious time. So they agreed to place the main works on Breed's while fortifying Bunker Hill to cover any retreat. Then Gridley marked out the lines of a redoubt, and the tall lean Prescott gave his iron-armed citizen-soldiers a single order: "Dig!"

They did, and with such astonishing fury that a marine sentry aboard the *Lively* staring through the dissolving mists of the hot moist dawn of June 17 started in disbelief at the sight of the red raw earth of the Yankee positions. *Lively* almost immediately opened fire, but an angry order from Admiral Samuel Graves silenced her guns. Soon, however, the entire fleet was booming away, while the surprised British commanders gathered in a council of war.

Henry Clinton proposed that the British attack across Charlestown Neck in the rebel rear. But Gage and William Howe, who was to command the expedition, decided rather to land on the peninsula and march around the Mystic River side of the redoubt to get in the American rear. It was a good plan, although Clinton's, being based on the obvious fact of British sea power, was probably better. However, the tide was against the British. Before Howe could begin landing at the appointed place, six precious hours had been granted the Americans.

Putnam and Prescott took every advantage of the respite. Prescott drove his men relentlessly. They were thirsty and hungry and wilting in the heat, but he insisted that they build a breastwork from the redoubt down the Mystic side of the hill. Cannon balls smashed among them. One of them tore off the head of happy young Asa Pollard, leaving his torso a spouting stump. Prescott saw his horrified men faltering and he jumped up on the parapet of the redoubt, striding back and forth to prove that the shot had been a lucky one.

On Bunker Hill to the rear, Old Put was in a rage of command. He was everywhere along the line, putting units into place, stiffening the spines of the unvaliant, trying but failing to get cannon out to Prescott's redoubt. Twice Putnam rode his horse across shot-swept Charlestown Neck to ask for reinforcements, and twice Ward refused him. Eventually, at the urging of the Committee of Safety, Ward sent out the New Hampshire regiments of John Stark and James Reed.

Colonel John Stark was the true commander of this force of about 1,200 frontiersmen. Though they were splendid sharpshooters, they had no ammunition. On the spot in Cambridge they were issued two flints apiece, a gill of powder and a pound of lead cut from the organs of a Cambridge church. Stark sent them back to quarters where they made up fifteen cartridges apiece. Men with bullet molds made musket balls, men without them hammered out slugs of lead.

Leading his men on the four-mile march to the front, Stark took them through enemy naval shelling at such a deliberate pace that young Captain Henry Dearborn of the leading company suggested that he rush the cadence.

"Dearborn," Stark said calmly, "one fresh man in action is worth ten fatigued men."[38]

At Bunker Hill Stark paused to survey the battle front.

At one o'clock in the afternoon, with raving fifes and rattling drums, some 2,300 British redcoats came ashore at Moulton's Point. General Howe immediately began studying the American position. He saw at once that he could not turn Prescott's left so easily. The Yankee commander had built a breastwork out in that direction. Moreover, Howe saw numerous bodies of men farther back on Bunker Hill and mistook them for an American reserve. Then he saw a column of men —Stark's sharpshooters—come marching along the ridge to Breed's Hill, and decided to call for reinforcements of his own.

In that second delay, Prescott again improved his position. The sight of the British forming on Moulton's Hill made it clear to him that there was still a gap yawning between his breastwork on the left and the Mystic River. So he sent some Connecticut troops and two cannon back to a stone-and-rail fence about 200 yards to the left rear of the breastwork. The fence ran down to the Mystic bank, and it seemed good enough to block Howe's flanking attempt.

Colonel Stark did not agree. Coming up to the rail fence Stark saw that it ended on the bank of the river, but that beneath it was a narrow strip of open beach along which four men might pass abreast. Taking his best shots, Stark put them on the beach behind a barricade built of stones. Then he posted the rest of his force along the rail fence. Now Prescott had about 1,400 men holding positions: the redoubt, the breastwork, the rail fence and the beach wall. Suddenly, to his surprise, Prescott saw Dr. Warren enter the redoubt.

Warren was a dashing sight in his white satin breeches, his pale blue waistcoat laced with silver and his carefully combed blond hair. Because he had just been appointed a major general, Colonel Prescott saluted him and offered him command.

"I shall take no command here," Warren said. "I came as a volunteer with my musket to serve under you."[39]

The fiery young revolutionary mounted the firing platform alongside the men who had flocked to his standard of rebellion.

Howe was ready.

He had about 2,500 men evenly divided between himself on the right at Moulton's Hill and Brigadier General Sir Robert Pigot on the left in the town of Charlestown. Pigot was to take the redoubt, Howe would attack the breastwork and rail fence. Howe drew up his men in three ranks and told them he expected them to "behave like Englishmen and as becometh good soliders," adding: "I shall not desire any one of you to go a step further than where I go myself at your head."[40]

Howe ordered his artillery to commence firing. It did, and suddenly fell silent. The guns' side boxes contained 12-pound balls instead of 6-pounders. Howe's fieldpieces were useless.

On the British left, American snipers in the houses of Charleston began whittling the redcoats. General Pigot complained to Admiral Graves, who sent orders to burn the town.

Ships in the harbor and batteries planted on Copp's Hill in Boston began showering Charlestown with red-hot ball and "carcasses," hollow iron balls pierced with holes and filled with pitch. Within a few moments Charlestown caught fire, to the great delight of Gentleman Johnny Burgoyne, who stood on Copp's Hill watching the scene with Henry Clinton.

Charlestown was one great blaze. Whole streets of houses collapsed against each other in walls of flame, ships on the stocks began burning, the high steeples of the churches were like great flaming spears, and everywhere was the hiss of flames and the crash of timbers.

On the British right, Howe was changing his formations. He drew off his light infantry and put them in columns of four along the Mystic beach. There were about 350 of them, and they were to storm the Yankee beach wall at bayonet point.

Opposite Howe's main body behind the breastwork and the rail fence, burly Israel Putnam rode up and down the lines roaring the immortal words: "Don't fire until you see the whites of their eyes! Then, fire low."[41]

Behind the Mystic wall Colonel Stark went Putnam one better, dashing out about 40 yards to nail a stake into the ground. "Not a man is to fire until the first regular crosses the stake," he yelled.[42]

The attack commenced.

Pigot's men climbed steadily toward the redoubt. Some nervous Americans opened fire before they were in range. Prescott swore he would kill the next man who fired. A young Yankee officer ran along the parapet kicking up the leveled muskets. Pigot's redcoats came steadily up the slope.

On the right Howe's men marched down Moulton's Hill, across a lowland, and up the slopes of Breed's against the silent breastwork and rail fence. It was hot. Neither the tall bearskins of the grenadiers nor the cocked hats of the line had brims to keep the sun out of a man's eyes. The regulars stumbled in thick grass reaching to their knees. A brick kiln and adjacent ponds broke their ranks and they had to re-form. Sweat began to darken the armpits of their scarlet coats. Men began to gasp beneath burdens of 60 pounds and more. Still they came on.

Along Mystic beach the light infantry—Howe's favorite troops— were trotting to the attack with outthrust bayonets. In the front were the dreaded Welsh Fusiliers.

Now all was thunder and flash and flame, Charlestown blazing, batteries crashing, naval guns roaring, echo and reverberation rolling over water and earth, while overhead, now exposing, now concealing, drifted the billowing white clouds of gun smoke.

The light infantry were running now.

The Welsh Fusiliers went slanting past Stark's stake, and the little wall ahead of them exploded in a crash of musketry.

The Fusiliers swayed and went down. Great rents were torn in the attacking column, but the King's Own Regiment swept forward to fill them. They ran on, while behind the fence the Yankee sharpshooters with empty muskets gave way to men with loaded ones.

Another dreadful volley crashed out, and the King's· Own went down in heaps.

Now the picked flank troops of the 10th Regiment were called upon. Officers ran among the reluctant, beating them with swords. Surely it would not be possible for the rebels to fire a *third* volley in so short a time. Once again the lines of scarlet and sun-tipped steel slanted forward, and there *was* a third volley—and that was all on Mystic beach.

Ninety-six dead redcoats had been left sprawled upon its bloodclotted sands, and even though his plan was wrecked at the pivotal point, Howe pressed his charge forward. Two ranks of men, grenadiers in front, came at the breastwork and the rail fence. Flame and smoke belched forth and tightly dressed ranks of red and white were instantly transformed into little packs of stunned and stricken men. Again and again the American weapons spoke, and men spun and toppled or went staggering away streaming blood. Every man in Howe's personal staff was either killed or wounded. It was a wonder that the general himself, in the forefront as he had promised, was not scratched. But he was mortified to see his vaunted regulars sprawling in heaps under the guns of ignorant peasants, and then, when he heard that Pigot was also thrown back in what was little more than a feint against the redoubt, there came upon the heretofore invincible William Howe, as he was to write later: *"A moment that I never felt before."*[43]

He recalled his troops, sent for more reinforcements and began reforming.

The Americans were exultant. They had met and beaten the finest troops in the world with but little cost to themselves. Colonel Prescott went among them, praising them and reminding them that the battle was not over. He encouraged them to stand fast, keeping to himself the fact that a steady trickle of desertions had drained his forces like a leaking pipe. The redoubt was down to 150 men.

There were many more men to be had back on Bunker Hill, but they refused to come forward. Putnam stormed among them, sometimes beating reluctant soldiers with the flat of his sword, but he only got a few to follow him back to Breed's.

Worse, he got no ammunition.

A quarter-hour after his first bloody repulse, Howe was attacking again.

His plan now was to avoid the beach wall. The light infantry had rejoined Howe's main body. They were to attack the rail fence while Pigot and Howe threw all that they had against the redoubt and the breastwork.

On the left, Pigot depended chiefly on John Pitcairn and his marines. They got to within a hundred feet of the silent Yankee fort, and then the wall of flame gushed forth again. Pitcairn sank to the ground mortally wounded. His son, also wounded, held his dying father in his arms. "I have lost my father!" he cried in anguish, whereupon the marines are said to have echoed: "We have lost our father!"[44]

On the right before the breastwork, the regulars there were also being sickled to the reddening earth, and the shaken Howe called for a bayonet charge. An incessant stream of fire poured from the American lines. The British light infantry was riddled. Some 38-men companies had only eight or nine men left. A few had only four or five. On the left Pigot was staggered and actually retreated. For the second time, Howe withdrew.

Reinforcing regiments had been sent to Prescott, but Putnam found the men of one of them scattered on the safe side of Bunker Hill. Fat Colonel Samuel Gerrish lay flat on the ground. He told the livid Putnam that he was "completely exhausted." Old Put snarled that he was, rather, completely cowardly—and ran among Gerrish's shrinking violets knocking some of them to the ground with his sword.

Two companies, however, did arrive in time to give some comfort to Prescott. But for every man he got, he lost three. Whenever a wounded man had been taken to safety, there were, in a cowardly dodge as old as arms, as many as twenty "volunteers" to carry him.

Most men had enough ball to repulse a third assault, but there was precious little powder. Cannon cartridges had to be broken open and their contents distributed.

Re-forming below Prescott, the British had reinforcements and all the necessary ammunition. Four hundred marines and regulars had responded to Howe's call for fresh men. Henry Clinton had crossed the river to collect all the guards and walking wounded he could find and join Pigot's force. Cannon were brought into play. A demonstration was made against the rail fence while Howe hurled himself against the breastwork in the center and Pigot-Clinton struck at the redoubt on the left.

"As soon as the rebels perceived this," Lord Francis Rawdon wrote to his uncle, the Earl of Huntingdon, "they rose up and poured in so heavy a fire upon us that the oldest officers say they never saw a sharper action. They kept up this fire till we were within ten yards of them. They even knocked down my captain, close beside me, after we had got into the ditch of their entrenchment."[45]

But the redcoats had reached the ditch, and after the American fire "went out like a spent candle," they leaped down from the parapet into the open redoubt. From three sides they came. Little General Pigot, too small to leap into the fray, climbed a tree outside and swung himself into it.

Still the Americans fought, most of them without bayonets of their own.

"Twitch their guns away!" Prescott roared. "Use your guns for clubs."[46]

Barehanded or with clubbed muskets the Americans actually tore guns out of the hands of the regulars. But more and more redcoats were pouring over the walls, and Prescott shouted: "Give way, men! Save yourselves!"[47]

Prescott fought on himself, his sword clanging against bayonets and gun barrels. His loose linen coat probably saved him. The bayonets cut it into tatters, but missed his flesh. Prescott was finally borne out of the rear gateway on the tide of retreating Americans. As he left, he passed a figure in a blue waistcoat steadily directing a covering action for the withdrawal. Outside, Prescott joined Putnam in directing a running fight from one fence or wall to another, until their force had crossed Bunker Hill and gone across Charlestown Neck onto the mainland.

Nevertheless, it was in this retreat that Americans suffered most of their casualties. One of them was found at the redoubt exit. The body had been stripped of its waistcoat, but from the quality of the blood-stained ruffled shirt it was obvious that the dead man had been a person of importance. A British officer rolled the body over and gasped in surprise.

Dr. Joseph Warren was dead.

6

☆

British casualties in the Battle of Bunker Hill had been staggering. Of 2,400 engaged, 1,054 had been shot, of whom 226 were killed. It is doubtful if British regulars had ever before suffered in such proportions, and this at the hands of a rabble in arms.

Although William Howe was not a physical casualty, he was certainly a spiritual one. Howe never forgot that moment he had never felt before. The curtain never came down upon that bloody tableau at the back of his brain, and William Howe, having formed his military character upon the ardor and daring of his mentor, James Wolfe, now turned slow and cautious.

American casualties totaled about 450—most of them suffered during the retreat—of which about 140 were killed. Unfortunately, once the Americans came to realize that they had won a victory, the indestructible myth of the invincible minuteman was born. Raw and ragged militia had given more than they got to the world's finest troops; therefore all Yankee Doodle need ever do was to get his dander up and grab his musket. This fallacy had happily overlooked the fact that the Americans were behind fortifications while the redcoats were in the open, and was based on the assumption that the great carnage among the British was due to Yankee marksmanship. There had been some sharpshooters at Bunker Hill, especially among Stark's frontiersmen, but the most nearsighted neophyte could hardly have missed packed scarlet ranks at 50 feet. No, the New England militiaman was never a crack shot. He was a plowboy or a mechanic and he was too far away from the wilderness to develop prowess with firearms.

He was also, from the standpoint of discipline, a very poor soldier, and once the ennobling fervor of battle had deserted him, he slipped back into his old slothful ways. What George Washington always excoriated as the New England "leveling principle"—that every man is as good as the next one and maybe even a little better—made it almost impossible to enforce discipline. Privates who had "listed" in the cause of freedom would not be regulated by officers whom they had helped to elect. Officers so chosen did not dare to push their constituents about, and it was not uncommon in the American camp to find a captain shaving a private or a lieutenant fixing a corporal's musket, both officers being anxious to please old customers. The camp itself was a huge, smoking, filthy hobo jungle in which each man cooked his own mess and latrines ("necessary houses") were built cheek by jowl with sleeping quarters. On one occasion a colonel who was the army's chief engineer was seen carrying his ration of beef to his tent, where he intended to cook it himself "to set the officers a good example." The Reverend William Emerson, grandfather of Ralph Waldo Emerson, has described that scene:

Some [tents] are made of boards, some of sailcloth, and some partly of one and partly of ye other. Others are made of stone and turf, and others again of birch and other brush. Some are thrown up in a hurry and look as if they could not help it—mere necessity—others are curiously wrought with doors and windows done with wreaths and withes in ye manner of a basket.[48]

The reverend thought the camp's variety a beauty, but General Washington, who took command in Cambridge on July 3, considered it a most unmilitary mess.

Washington was already depressed to learn that he had only 14,500 men to command, few trained engineers, a dearth of artillery, no war chest and only enough powder to issue his men nine cartridges apiece in case of British attack.

Discipline, however, was the chief problem. It became Washington's chief duty to make these liberty-loving individualists understand that in armies which fight for freedom, liberty must give way to regulation. He began by insisting upon respect for authority and the display of rank ranging from his own blue chest riband to the stripe of green cloth on a corporal's left shoulder. Where Washington could not persuade, he punished.

Although the American commander seems to have discouraged some of the more barbarous punishments then in vogue, he was not loath to use the whip. Once he asked Congress to increase the number of allowable lashes from the Biblical 39 to 500. Congress wisely refused, while sympathizing with its military chieftain's enormous problems in trying to form an army on the very field of battle.

Washington was especially anxious to cashier cowardly or conniving officers, and in August he reported:

> I have made a pretty good slam among such kind of officers as the Massachusetts government abound in . . . having broke one Colonel and two Captains for cowardly behavior in the action on Bunker Hill—two Captains for drawing more provisions and pay than they had men in their company—and one for being absent from his post when the enemy appeared there and burnt a house just by it. Besides these, I have at this time one Colonel, one Major, one Captain and two Subalterns under arrest for trial.[49]

Gradually, the inflexible and sometimes irascible gentleman from Virginia produced a measure of cleanliness and order in the camp. Old latrines were filled up and new ones dug. Offal and carrion were burned. Company messes were set up and inspected regularly, loose women were run out of camp, and drunken soldiers were flogged. Although there were never enough blankets or muskets, and the men were still generally clad in homespun, a kind of military organization was developed.

A 720-man regiment of the "line" was formed consisting of 8 companies, each company having 1 captain, 2 lieutenants, 1 ensign, 4 sergeants, 4 corporals, 2 "Drums and Fifes," and 76 privates. These were new regiments, of course, for the marvel of forming an army on the battlefield was to be surpassed by the miracle of recruiting a new one to replace it.

Constant recruitment was necessary because the American soldiers believed in going home after the battle. Their enlistments expired January 1, 1776—some said December 1, 1775—and they had withstood every attempt to make them re-enlist. Thus General Washington had to face the melancholy fact that the army he was molding would melt away at year's end. He had also to contend with the fact that each of the colonies, in effect, was fielding armies of its own, often offering higher bounties than Continental Army recruiters, as well as the reluctance of the more Southern colonies such as Georgia and South Carolina to contribute troops to the Continental Army at all.

On the other hand, Maryland, Virginia and Pennsylvania came through splendidly. From the western wildernesses of these colonies came about 1,500 backwoodsmen, "remarkably stout and hardy men: many of them exceeding six feet in height." They had to march from 400 to 700 miles to reach the camp. Old Daniel Morgan, still bearing the scars of the flogging he had received under Braddock, put his men on horses and rode them 600 miles in 21 days. Not a man was lost by sickness on the way.

These men in leather hunting shirts and moccasins carried a new weapon: the Kentucky rifle. This was the long, slender and graceful gun which German and Swiss gunsmiths in Pennsylvania had designed for the American frontier. Whereas a musketman rarely could hit a man beyond 60 yards, a rifleman could put ball after ball into a seven-inch target at the range of 250 yards.

If the rifle had not been so slow-loading and if it could have been fitted with a bayonet and placed in the hands of a marksman who would accept discipline, the American arsenal would have been augmented in truly splendid style. However, the endless pop-popping of unruly frontiersmen at British redcoats far out of range drove George Washington to distraction, to say nothing of the rifleman's custom of freeing any of their comrades confined in the guardhouse for misdemeanors. They were of use later on in the Revolutionary War, but not at Boston, and Washington wished that they had never come.

Negro soldiers presented another problem. There were quite a few Negroes, both slave and free, in the New England army. One of them, Salem Poor, fought with great bravery at Bunker Hill. Crispus Attucks, one of the first American martyrs in the Boston Massacre, was a Negro slave. Actually, the problem was not Washington's but Congress's. At first, Congress decreed that no Negroes be re-enlisted in the Continental Army. But then Washington reported that "discarded" Negroes were discontented and might join "the Ministerial Army" opposing him and that he was therefore re-enlisting Negroes. Congress aquiesced, but insisted that only freedmen were acceptable.

The problem—like Washington's annual headache of forming a new army—lasted throughout the war. Southern colonies were not eager to imperil their "peculiar institution" of slavery by placing muskets in the hands of slaves. Yet the British were promising freedom to those slaves who would fight for the King against their former masters. Many slaveowners, especially in the Northern and middle states, were only too pleased to send a slave to war as substitutes for themselves. Finally, if it was embarrassing that the fight for freedom might also preserve the institution of slavery, it was equally shameful to raise an army of slaves under the flag of liberty. There was never any real solution to this complex problem. As might have been expected, the colonies most dependent upon slavery put no Negroes in the field, while the others, to the degree of their freedom from this evil, enlisted slaves and gave them, in the phrase of Alexander Hamilton, "their freedom with their muskets."

Hamilton, incidentally, was himself typical of the higher type of patriot flocking to the American standard. This bold and brilliant young captain of New York artillery eventually became one of Washington's most trusted aides. Another able officer whom the commander in chief first met in Boston, was his chief of artillery, Henry Knox. Fat, amiable and forceful, Knox had kept a bookstore in Boston and had read enough about guns to amaze the British professionals who came to his shop. Knox's friend, Nathanael Greene of Rhode Island, a handsome man who limped and was asthmatic, also emerged as a top commander as well as one of Washington's most intimate advisers.

General Charles Lee was also in Boston, followed, as ever, by a pack of yapping hounds, and surrounded by a circle of admiring yokels listening to him speak with easy expertise of such esoteric things as redans or flèches or chevaux-de-frise.

In the meantime, William Howe took command of the British Army, poor "blundering Tommy" Gage having been recalled. Howe, however, showed himself no more aggressive than his predecessor. Rather than sally forth to assault George Washington, a general as helpless as a man standing on one foot, he preferred to dally with lovely Mrs. Joshua Loring while Mrs. Loring's husband merrily seized the property and possessions of Boston's patriots and fed them to his accomplices at rigged auctions.

With the arrival of winter, both armies postponed hostilities.

Congress had taken charge in America. Although there was as yet no true American government, and the Continental Congress had no legal foundation for its actions, it had assumed responsibility for conducting the war. It had adopted the New England army, appointed its officers, drawn up a military code, set up a Postal Service under

Benjamin Franklin, named commissioners to deal with the Western Indians, issued paper currency, and, finally, found itself incapable of resisting the Canadian magnet.

At first, Congress attempted to coax Canada into joining the rebellion, but after the Canadians refused they decided to conquer her instead. Those two incompatible comrades of Ticonderoga—Ethan Allen and Benedict Arnold—had already been to Philadelphia to offer their services for a Canadian expedition, but the delegates, while generally adopting their advice and plans, chose General Philip Schuyler as the leader.

It was a bad choice. An able aristocrat and an ardent patriot, Schuyler was better fitted to counsel than to command. Fortunately, he had a fine deputy in Brigadier Richard Montgomery. Like Horatio Gates, Montgomery had fought in the French and Indian War as a British officer, later leaving the service to settle in the colonies and marry an American of wealth and family. Montgomery urged the dilatory Schuyler again and again to move quickly down the lake-and-river chain against Montreal. At last, on August 28, 1775, he took the bit in his own teeth and embarked a force of about 1,000 men on Lake Champlain.

With him was Ethan Allen. The tiger of Ticonderoga had promised to lead his Green Mountain Boys on the expedition, but the Boys had "diselected" him and Allen appeared at Ticonderoga as a regiment of one. Major John Brown, a polished and urbane lawyer with a surprising aptitude for war and the woods, was also present.

Sailing down the Richelieu on September 5, Montgomery's lookouts could see smoke rising from the British fort of St. John's. Here Montgomery began his siege, stationing his gunboats in the river to protect his own rear and sending Ethan Allen and John Brown around the British flanks—Allen to take charge of a body of rebellious Canadian volunteers waiting downriver, Brown to strike at the enemy supply line.

While the siege of St. John's was slowed down by cold and rain and sickness, these two daring spirits met in the enemy rear and decided to take Montreal by themselves. Brown had about 200 men, Allen about 100. Brown would attack above the town, Allen from below. But Brown failed to make an appearance. Allen, nevertheless, decided to go it alone. News that "Ethan Allen, the Notorious New

Hampshire Incendiary" was outside the gates threw the town "into the utmost Confusion."

Sir Guy Carleton, commanding there, remained calm. He sent a mixed force of about 250 regulars, volunteers and Indians out the Quebec Gate to attack the American. Seeing their approach, the men on Allen's flanks fled into the woods. Allen began a fighting retreat, but was surrounded and forced to surrender.

Allen's capture failed to discourage Montgomery. Eager to conquer St. John's before winter closed in, the American commander floated gun batteries past the fort to force the surrender of Chambly in its rear. Then he stepped up his attacks on St. John's until, on November 3, the fort surrendered.

Ten days later the swift-moving Montgomery received the surrender of Montreal; too late, however, to prevent Carleton's escape. A few days after that he received word from Benedict Arnold to join him at Quebec.

Arnold had come to Washington at Boston an angry and frustrated man. His great scheme had been given to Schuyler, and his personal honesty in his military accounts had been questioned. Washington, who appreciated Arnold's dash and daring, soothed him with command of a second invasion of Canada.

He was to go up the Kennebec River and then down the Chaudière to assault the old fortress of Quebec while Montgomery engaged Carleton at Montreal. Hundreds of musketmen and riflemen bored with the siege of Boston volunteered for the expedition. Altogether Arnold had about a thousand men, among them 19-year-old Aaron Burr and Captain Daniel Morgan, when he began, in late September, a march that ranks as an epic ordeal in American history.

First, the bateaux which were to carry them up the Kennebee from Fort Western (present-day Augusta) were made of green wood and badly built. They came apart. Often they had to be carried or hauled upriver against boiling rapids. Going down the swift-running Chaudière some smashed into rocks and the men aboard were lost. Floundering, stumbling against one another, the men waded for days over one stretch of nearly 180 miles.

After provisions gave out, the Americans ate soap and hair grease. They boiled and roasted their bullet pouches, moccasins and old leather breeches and devoured them. They killed and ate the dogs that accompanied them. There were dropouts and slow death and mass defections along the way. At one point Lieutenant Colonel Roger Enos refused to go on and withdrew his division of 300 men. Undaunted, Arnold pressed forward. On November 9 his ragged band burst from snow-cloaked forests onto the south bank of the St. Lawrence. They marched upriver to Point Lévi on the Isle of Orléans. They were ragged and bearded. Their feet were shod in raw skins. Their clothes hung in tatters over bodies that were but bags of sticks. There were only 600 of them. They had taken 45 days, not the estimated 20, to cover 350, not 180, miles. But they had arrived, and they were going to attack Quebec.

For all his doggedness, events were thwarting Arnold. He had collected canoes and dugouts to make a night crossing of the St. Lawrence and ascend the cliffs to the Plains of Abraham as James Wolfe had done. Quebec was held by a mere handful of marines and regulars and a weak body of about 500 militia. Arnold was certain he could not fail. But for two straight nights the winds blew so strongly that he could not cross. In the meantime, Lieutenant Colonel Allen Maclean had arrived in Quebec with about 100 veteran soldiers. Their coming heartened Quebec's defenders and raised their number to about 1,200.

Arnold still thought that in a stand-up fight his hardy band could scatter the militia and overwhelm the remaining regulars. At nine o'clock on the black night of November 13, the first detachments began crossing to the Anse-du-Foulon, now Wolfe's Cove. They landed and kindled a fire to revive a lieutenant who had fallen overboard and been towed through the ice-cold river. The rest of the Americans crossed on the following night.

Now Arnold led his men up to the Plains of Abraham, routing a force of militia there. He sent a flag of truce to Quebec to demand its surrender. His emissaries were routed by cannon ball. Then Arnold was driven off as the frigate *Lizard* sailed upriver to cut off his rear and Maclean prepared to attack with 800 men.

Miserable again, with many of their number barefoot, the invaders retreated to Pointe aux Trembles. Here, on December 2, they saw with elation the topsails of a schooner coming downriver. It was Montgomery with reinforcements of 300 men.

Montgomery had brought with him captured British clothing: great white blanket-coats with caped hoods, heavy blue overalls, sealskin moccasins and fur-tailed caps. Arnold's freezing men joyfully damned them for their tardiness and donned the winter clothes. Then, about a thousand men strong, the hardy little American army marched back to Quebec.

Once there, it became plain to Montgomery and Arnold that they could not conduct a siege. They had no heavy guns to batter Quebec's walls, they could not possibly endure an entire Canadian winter encamped outside the city's gates, smallpox had broken out, food was short, and, worst of all, the enlistment of Arnold's New Englanders expired at year's end. They decided to attack, even though Sir Guy Carleton had entered the town and raised the number of its defenders to 1,800 men. On the first snowy night they would storm the Lower Town, Arnold attacking from the north, Montgomery from the south.

The afternoon of Saturday December 30 snow began falling. It thickened. The wind rose. By early morning of the 31st a blizzard was howling about Quebec. Snow mixed with hail whistled into the faces of the Americans moving to their positions. They ducked their heads and shielded their firelocks with their coats. At some time after four o'clock, signal rockets burst red in the blackness above them and the Americans began marching.

Within Quebec drums began beating and bells tolled. Officers ran through the streets shouting, "Turn out! Turn out!" Guy Carleton's formidable barricades in the Lower Town were quickly manned.

On the left of the American pincers, Montgomery's division was slipping and sliding down the slopes toward the road from Wolfe's Cove to Cape Diamond. Men carrying unwieldy scaling ladders could barely struggle through drifts six feet deep.

On the right Arnold's force of 600 men left the suburb of St. Roche and stole silently past the Palace Gate. They veered right and a sudden blaze of musketry from the ramparts above raked them. Men fell. They moved on, Arnold leading an advance party of about 25 men, including Daniel Morgan. Behind them came 40 artillerists dragging a 6-pounder on a sled, and behind them came the main body.

Arnold and Morgan came to a narrow street blocked by a barricade. They called for the 6-pounder. It had been abandoned. A gun in the barricade fired but did no damage. Arnold called for a charge.

Out of the snow they came, yelling, rushing to the barrier, and firing through its gun ports. The British fired back. Arnold fell with a ball in his leg. Bleeding freely, he was helped away while huge Daniel Morgan took command. The Old Wagoner mounted a ladder set against the barrier, calling upon his men to follow. A blaze of fire tumbled him back into the snow. He had a bullet through his cap and another through his beard. Shaking himself, Morgan leaped erect, climbed the ladder again and jumped over the parapet. Others followed. The defenders fled. The Americans were inside the Lower Town. Another barrier lay ahead, but the Americans did not attack it. Instead, they decided to halt to await the arrival of Montgomery.

Richard Montgomery's force had also come to a barricade. Soldiers began sawing at it. Montgomery and his officers tore at half-sawed posts with their hands. They pulled it down and passed on, no more than 60 or 70 of them, the remainder of the division having been disorganized and scattered by the storm.

Now a blockhouse confronted them. Inside were about 50 men and four little 3-pounders charged with grape. The British blew on their slow matches and awaited the American approach. Montgomery came on. His men faltered. He called to them through the storm, "Come on, my good soldiers, your General calls you to come on."[50]

Montgomery, Aaron Burr, a few other officers and about a dozen men rushed forward. They were within a few paces of the blockhouse when a sheet of flame and a hail of grape and musket balls raked them. Another burst, and it was all over.

Montgomery lay dead. So did most of his officers. Only Burr and a few men got away.

To the north, inside the Lower Town, the Americans under Morgan were fighting desperately. Carleton had sent a force of 200 men and cannon out the Palace Gate to take them in the rear. Morgan's men were trapped. They began to surrender. Morgan fought on. He set his back against a wall. Tears of rage and despair flowed down his face as he stood there, his sword uplifted for his last blows. His men implored him to give up. He shook his head. Then Morgan saw a clergyman in the crowd and called: "Are you a priest?" The man nodded, and Morgan handed him his blade with the words: "Then I give my sword to you. But not a scoundrel of these cowards shall take it out of my hands."[51]

Two bursts of gunfire, an able maneuver by Carleton, and the attempt to storm Quebec had been repulsed. More and more troops were to be fed into the project, but Carleton was not to be dislodged. In the spring, as in the days of James Wolfe, a British fleet came up the St. Lawrence to raise the siege.

The American army had to retreat, Montreal had to be abandoned, and in July of 1776 the demoralized wreck of Montgomery's once proud little army washed back upon the shores of Lake Champlain. The attempt to conquer Canada, the most ambitious American expedition of the Revolutionary War, had ended in humiliating defeat.

7

☆

By New Year's Day of 1776, General Washington's army had melted away to about 10,500 men.

A month previous the Connecticut regulars had set the example of homegoing, insisting that their enlistments were up on December 1. All attempts to dissuade them had failed, most notably the perverse performance of General Charles Lee.

"Men," Lee roared, after "entreating" them with curses and insults, "I don't know what to call you. You are the worst of all creatures."[52]

The troops merely laughed, and at the appointed time they marched home, ignoring the hisses and groans of the comrades they left behind, the showers of stones and the mocking blandishments of the women of the camp. Even Washington lost his temper and wrote of the "dirty, mercenary spirit" of the men "upon whom I reckoned" and who now had "basely deserted the Cause of their Country."

In fairness to these men, however, it must be made clear that they *had* enlisted for eight months only, that the practice of enlisting for specified short terms—for the "campaign," as it was called—was customary, and that very few ranking officers, the wealthy Washington in particular, were called upon to make sacrifices comparable to those demanded of most of the junior officers and all the enlisted men.

While they served, their farms went uncared for or their trades were gobbled up by stay-at-homes. They had served long enough, they argued, and now it was someone else's turn.

Fortunately for Washington, thousands of men in the Massachusetts and New Hampshire militias decided that it was their turn. They poured into Washington's camp while the time-expired regulars jeered at them as "Long-faced People," and marched home. The new arrivals did not intend to stay long, either, but they at least gave Washington a respite in which to recruit men and rebuild his army, and they were numerous enough to keep Howe contained in winter quarters.

Actually, Washington might well have attacked at this time, and he regretted not having done so. The British Army was in frightful condition. Smallpox was at work and food was short. Howe tried desperately to maintain order and discipline, but not so desperately as to forgo the charms of blonde Betsey Loring. His officers also amused themselves. The Old South Church was turned into a riding academy, and dramatic plays—heretofore banned in Boston—were performed in Faneuil Hall. *The Blockade of Boston* was a burlesque of Washington and his ragtag army and Washington was invited to attend for the pleasure of being hanged. The American replied by raiding Bunker Hill on opening night. British officers dressing up as women heard the alarm and rushed off to battle in petticoats.

British and Tory hopes that the patriots might be quitting were momentarily raised at the sight of a red flag flying in present-day Somerville. The familiar combined crosses of St. George and St. Andrew were visible. But they were only in one corner, and the rest of the flag was covered with 13 alternate stripes of red and white. It was the first American flag, and as it was flung to the breeze the booming of a 13-gun salute celebrated the birthday of the Continental Army.

The Americans were not quitting, they were getting bolder—and soon in that eventful month of January, 1776, Tom Paine would teach them to regard even the King as their enemy.

"How impious," Tom Paine wrote in the pamphlet *Common Sense, "is the title of Sacred Majesty applied to a worm, who in the midst of his splendor is crumbling into dust! . . .*

"Of more worth is one honest man to society, and in the sight of

God, than all of the crowned ruffians that ever lived."

Having had at King George III—the "royal brute"—Tom swung hard at the arguments for reconciliation.

"To be always running three or four thousand miles with a tale or a petition, waiting four or five months for an answer, which, when obtained, requires five or six more to explain it in, will in a few years be looked upon as folly and childishness."

And then came the ringing call for freedom which was to electrify the colonies and to bring thousands of waverers to the side of the rebellion:

"O ye that love mankind! Ye that dare oppose not only the tyranny but the tyrant, stand forth! Every spot of the old world is overrun with oppression. Freedom hath been hunted around the globe. Asia and Africa have long expelled her. Europe regards her as a stranger, and England hath given her warning to depart. O receive the fugitive, and prepare in time an asylum for mankind!"

Such were the logic and the rhetoric which inspired the men of Washington's new Continental Army as they toiled frantically to install the guns which Colonel Henry Knox had brought from Ticonderoga.

Even the ordeal of Arnold's march to Quebec hardly surpassed the feat of bringing those heavy guns down from the mountains of the northern lakes in the dead of an American winter. They were loaded on barges, but the barges sank and Knox calmly had the guns grubbed up. They went on sleds to cross frozen lakes and rivers, and sometimes the ice broke and the cannon sank and had to be recovered again. Snow fell and the roads froze and Knox's "noble train of artillery" was packed on sledges. Up and down the Taconics the column toiled, over the Berkshires, men shouting warnings as the sledges began to gather momentum down the snowy slopes, horses and oxen panting and wheezing as they hauled the guns across the valley floor and up the next hill. Sometimes the poor beasts perished in the traces, but there were always replacements, and on January 18 the convoy at last lurched into Framingham.

Eventually all 59 pieces of ordnance—from 24-pound cannon to stubby little cohorns or mortars—would go into Washington's 14-mile line around Boston. On the nights of March 2 and 3 the regulars began mounting the biggest guns on Dorchester Heights below the city. They built forts. So great was the surprise of the British who beheld them in the morning that one officer said they were made by "the Genii belonging to Aladdin's Wonder Lamp."[53]

The guns and works on Dorchester were even more serious than those which had menaced Boston from Bunker Hill, and Howe immediately called a council of war. It was decided to evacuate the city.

On March 17 the last of Howe's soldiers and 1,000 Tories sailed from Boston Harbor for Nantasket Harbor. Ten days later this woe-begone fleet of perhaps 170 vessels set sail for Halifax.

Triumphant, the patriots rushed into the city that had been the center and the symbol of the rebellion. Now it was Tory property that went under the auctioneer's hammer. Now it was Tory homes that sometimes went up in flames while the owners were stripped, tarred, feathered and ridden out of town on a rail. No one hates more than hostile brothers, and even the British themselves were not hated so venomously as were those Loyalists whom Howe was forced to leave behind.

From Maine to South Carolina they were lashed through the streets, pelted with rotten eggs or forced to go down on their knees to damn the King and his ministers. One Tory is on record with the quaint lament that he had "had the misfortune to affront one of the Committee men, by not giving his Daughter a kiss when I was introduced to her. This has offended the old man so much, that . . . he has several spys to watch my actions. Sorry I did not give the ugly Jade a kiss." Washington himself wanted the more notorious Tories hung as an example to the rest, and Governor Livingston of New Jersey said: "A Tory is an incorrigible Animal: And nothing but the Extinction of Life will extinguish his malevolence against liberty."[54] Before the war was over the patriots were forcing all secret Tories to declare themselves by imposing oaths of loyalty to the United States. Those who refused were fined, imprisoned, deprived of civil rights or, as the new states seized upon this handy means of raising revenue, dispossessed.

Witch hunt though this was (although it never led to stake or gallows), it is difficult to see how the patriots could have acted otherwise. The Tories were a dangerous fifth column. They were nearly as numerous and fully as able as the patriots, and they were so inimical to the revolution that the man who conducted the war from England always believed that it would be won by a Tory uprising.

Lord George Sackville had been convicted of cowardice at the Battle of Minden in 1759 and adjudged "unfit to serve His Majesty in any Military Capacity whatever." Yet King George III began 1776 by making Lord George Secretary of State for the American Colonies. With his name changed by an inheritance to Lord George Germain, *"that man,"* as he was described by indignant accusers, undertook "to engage the people of America in support of a cause which is equally their own and ours."

Germain's "people of America"—Tories—were numerous in the colonies south of Virginia. It was believed that the appearance of a British force there would bring thousands of Loyalists rallying to the old red flag. Germain thus approved a Southern expedition already planned. Henry Clinton was to command the troops, with young Lord Charles Cornwallis as a second. The fleet would be under Admiral Sir Peter Parker.

The British counted on the fierce Scottish immigrant Highlanders of the North Carolina interior, who hated the seaboard aristocracy, to seize Carolina ports. But then trouble in Ireland and contrary winds delayed the fleet's departure—while in Carolina the kilts came out on schedule.

In February of 1776 the clans began gathering. With the skirl of the pipes on the wind, with knives tucked into tartan hose, swords at the belt and muskets on their shoulders, all of the McDonalds and McDowells, the Campbells and Camerons of the North Carolina west were marching behind General Donald McDonald toward the port city of Wilmington on the coast.

There were about 1,500 of them, and out to meet them came 1,000 patriots under Colonels Richard Caswell and John Lillington. The patriots came to Moore's Creek Bridge and crossed it. They began to dig in, until their leaders realized that it was not wise to fight with their backs to water. They returned to the other side of the stream and dug in afresh.

In the soft daylight of February 27, General McDonald's Highlanders came to Moore's Creek Bridge. They saw the empty trenches and concluded that the patriots had fled. They rushed the bridge, and a single crashing volley of musketry smashed them to the ground. Up from their trenches rose the patriots to counterattack, to shatter the kilted ranks and slaughter them in a merciless pursuit.

Moore's Creek Bridge was a Tory disaster. North Carolina stayed firmly in the rebel camp, Georgia and South Carolina stiffened against the King, and Henry Clinton and Sir Peter Parker found no Loyalist enclave awaiting them when they joined forces off the Carolina sand bars.

So they hoisted anchor and sailed for Charleston farther south.

During that balmy May while the British fleet plunged south toward Charleston, two gentlemen met in Paris. The Comte de Vergennes had recently become Foreign Minister of France, and he saw in the American Revolution the opportunity to avenge his nation upon the detestable English. Pierre Augustin Caron de Beaumarchais, famous for his play, *The Barber of Seville,** was a passionate lover of liberty and avowed friend of the Americans.

Vergennes did not yet dare to make war upon Britain. He could, however, simply assist her enemies, the colonies. Vergennes invited Spain to do likewise, and was accepted. A secret fund of one million livres was set up. A dummy trading company to purchase munitions "privately" was created.

In May the firm of Hortalez et Cie., under the amiable management of Caron de Beaumarchais, began "acting" for the Americans. During the year 1776-77 as much as 80 percent of the Continental Army's powder would come through Hortalez and Beaumarchais. It was very good powder, made by a scientist named Lavoisier.

Charleston was the most important American port south of Philadelphia. It was also the most heavily defended.

Throughout the month of May reinforcements from Virginia and North Carolina had been hurrying to Charleston. None other than Charles Lee came down to take command. By dawn of June 4, when the horizon bristled with the masts and sun-gilded sails of the British fleet, there were some 6,000 men holding a series of fine fortifications.

To the south of the harbor lay James Island with Fort Johnson. Across the harbor mouth was a sand bar, and inside of it on the main-

---

* And later *The Marriage of Figaro.*

land and guarding the city were batteries at Haddrell's Point. To the north of the harbor was Sullivan's Island with the redoubt of palmetto logs which was to bear the name of its builder, Colonel William Moultrie. Farther north across a narrow strip of water called The Breach lay Long Island, unoccupied and undefended.

The fort on Sullivan's Island was obviously the key to Charleston. Colonel Moultrie had confidence in its walls of palmetto logs enclosing a fill of earth 16 feet thick. Moultrie believed that they would soak up British cannon balls like a sponge. Moreover, the fort had 30 guns, though very little powder, and the garrison of about 450 men was confident and actually eager for action. Moultrie improved his position while the British wasted time sounding for a channel across the bar. By June 7 they began entering the harbor. On June 9 Clinton put 500 of his 2,500 men ashore there. His plan was to cross The Breach to Sullivan's Island and attack the fort from the north while Parker's ships battered it from the south. Lee sent a force of about 800 men to Long Island to counterattack, but then recalled it and placed the troops at the northern tip of Sullivan's Island. In the meanwhile, Clinton put the remainder of his force ashore on Long Island. The two armies confronted one another across The Breach while Admiral Parker's ships consumed another two weeks working their way over the bar.

On June 28, as the British ships roared a thunderous cannonade, Clinton's grenadiers and light infantry jumped into The Breach. Many of them vanished in holes seven feet deep and Clinton called for boats. But many of these ran aground in shallows a foot and a half deep. Once it was seen that The Breach was an impassable moat of deeps and shallows, Clinton's regulars could do no more than growl at the Americans across the water while the battle for Charleston became a fight between a fleet and a fort.

The bomb ketch, *Thunder,* began the British fleet's attack by hurling shells at the fort. Then the rest of Parker's fleet sailed to battle stations. Close inshore of the fort were *Active,* 28 guns; Parker's flagship *Bristol,* 50; *Experiment,* 50; and *Solebay,* 28. Stretched farther offshore away eastward were *Actaeon,* 28; *Sphynx,* 20; *Syren,* 28; *Thunder* and the armed ship *Friendship* with 28 guns.

The British were highly confident. The wind was right, it was a clear day, and the fort seemed to be answering weakly. Then *Thunder* realized that her bombs were falling short. Rather than come in closer and perhaps foul the other ships, she increased the powder charges in her mortars. The first supercharged shots broke the mortar beds and *Thunder* was of no further use.

Now the American guns were replying with a slow and awful accuracy. *Bristol*'s cable was shot away. She lay end-on to the fort and was raked horribly. Twice her quarterdeck was cleared of every person except Parker, and Sir Peter, to his lasting mortificiation, had the seat of his trousers shot off and his behind singed. *Experiment* suffered just as badly.

Within the fort, sweat-drenched Americans were scorched by a hot southern sun and sometimes by the muzzle flashes from 30 cannon in continual blaze. Colonel Moultrie cheered his gunners on, while men with fire buckets full of grog darted along the fire platforms to refresh the thirsty. Gradually the artillery duel rose to such a frightful roar that even the veteran General Lee, who had come over to the island, was astonished. Once a combination of three or four British broadsides struck the fort with such force that Moultrie feared another such salvo would shake it down.

Then the fort's flag disappeared. British sailors cheered while American onlookers in Charleston groaned. They believed the fort was surrendering. Inside the redoubt, Sergeant Jasper cried to Moultrie: "Colonel, don't let us fight without our flag!"

"What can you do?" Moultrie replied. "The staff is broke."[55]

Jasper's reply was to run outside the fort, seize the flag, and then, fixing it on a sponge staff, set it upright again while British shot and shell crashed all around him. A cheer arose from Charleston as the blue flag with its white crescent and the word "Liberty" whipped in the breeze again.

Now three of the British second line of ships upped anchor and tried to move around the western end of the island. They wanted to batter the fort on its flank and bring their guns to bear on a plank bridge behind the island. All three ships ran aground. *Actaeon* and *Sphynx* fouled each other, *Sphynx* losing her bowsprit. Eventually, two worked free, but *Actaeon* was immovable.

As night fell the jubilant Americans could hear their shots crashing into her, and eventually she was set afire.

Night also marked the end of the battle. At eleven o'clock, horrified at the carnage aboard their ships, mortified at having been so mauled by the tiny American fort, the British slipped their cables and stole off into the night.

Charleston had held, the glory of Fort Moultrie had entered American history, and it was two years before the British would think again of "the people of America" who dwelt in the South.

8

☆

Parliament had voted to raise an army of 55,000 men to crush the rebellion, but the King's subjects did not rally to his cause.

Among the officer class there was much sympathy for the colonists, while the English yeoman had never been keen on the poor pay and brutal discipline of British Army ranks. Press gangs, judges and tavernkeepers had always been the King's chief recruiters, and so, faced with a spectacular lack of enthusiasm in his own people, King George went looking for hirelings.

He found them in the principalities of Germany: Brunswick, Waldeck, Anhalt-Zerbst, Anspach-Beyreuth, Hesse-Hanau, Hesse-Cassel. Eventually some 30,000 German mercenaries were hired for the American war, and because more than half of these were supplied by the Landgrave of Hesse-Cassel, all were called Hessians.

Britain promised to pay all expenses of the soldiers, as well as $35 for each soldier killed, $12 for each one wounded, and over $500,000 annually to the Hessian Landgrave alone. Thus the subjects, rather the human chattels of the German princelings, were often worth more slaughtered than on the hoof.

The decision to send them against Britain's descendants in America was the last of George's fatal blunders, He had rejected the colonies' Olive Branch Petition asking for a peaceful reconciliation, he had used harsh language in proclaiming the colonies in a state of rebellion, his Navy had wantonly burnt Falmouth, and now the King was sending mercenaries against the colonies, just as he did against foreign foes.

Americans were now convinced that there was nothing left to do but break the last ties that bound them to him.

In the fateful summer of 1776 Thomas Jefferson told John Adams that he ought to make a draft of a declaration of independence. Adams declined, and Jefferson, pressing him, asked: "What can be your reasons?"

"Reason first," Adams replied, "you are a Virginian, and a Virginian ought to appear at the head of this business. Reason second, I am obnoxious, suspected and unpopular. You are very much otherwise. Reason third, you can write ten times better than I can."

"Well," Jefferson said, "if you are decided, I will do as well as I can."[56]

Jefferson did draw up a declaration, after which Congress, much to the anguish of its redheaded author, toned down its language and cut out about a quarter of it. Jefferson's impassioned attack on slavery, which he blamed on the King, although he was himself a large slaveholder, did not get past his Southern colleagues. The vituperation poured out on King George personally—language which Jefferson may or may not have had from his friend, Tom Paine—was also deleted. On July 4, after much debate, the Declaration of Independence was adopted.

John Hancock signed first, with a great bold flourish, and said: "There, I guess King George will be able to read that!"[57]

One by one, the others signed, radicals, moderates and conservatives, all united now in their determination to be "Absolved from all Allegiance to the British Crown." There were the Adamses of Massachusetts, openly jubilant that "the river is passed, and the bridge cut away"; there was the wealthy Marylander, Charles Carroll of Carrollton, a Catholic island in a Protestant sea, signing because "I had in view not only our independence of England, but the toleration of all sects professing the Christian religion."[58] The Lees of Virginia signed, one before and one behind a beaming Thomas Jefferson. So too did Benjamin Franklin, his wise eyes still twinkling over his quip. "We must all hang together, or assuredly we shall all hang separately." After the Pennsylvanians came Caesar Rodney of Delaware. No odder-looking man ever lived than this bold bantam with a face hardly larger than an oversize apple. But Caesar Rodney had ridden 80 miles through a storm-tossed night to put Delaware on the side of the declaration and swing the Congress toward independence. Now all argument was done. All signed, 56 delegates from 13 colonies, pledging to each other "our Lives, our Fortunes, and our sacred Honor." Four days later—July 8—the Declaration of Independence was published. Philadelphia heard for the first time those noble ideals and ringing phrases which still have the power to move hearts.

When in the Course of human events . . .
We hold these truths to be self-evident, that all men are created equal,
that they are endowed by their Creator with certain unalienable Rights,
that among these are Life, Liberty and the pursuit of Happiness. . . .

Philadelphia took the news calmly. After all, the debate had been common knowledge. But it was different elsewhere in this new-born "country." Bells tolled and bonfires burned up and down the coast. Savannah burned King George in effigy. New York pulled down his statue and Connecticut melted it down for bullets, while Boston tore George's arms from the State House and burnt them along with every other vestige of His Majesty that could be found.

Thus it was an exultant and defiant United States of America, not 13 cowed and submissive colonies, which greeted Admiral "Black Dick" Howe when he arrived in New York Harbor empowered to talk of peace.

Lord Howe's "peace" overtures began with a letter to "Mr." Washington, which the American commander coldly refused to accept. Next General Howe sent a letter to "George Washington, Esquire," as well as an emissary who claimed that both Howes had been specially nominated as peace commissioners by the King. Washington received the emissary but discovered that all that the Howes had power to do was to grant pardons. Since no fault had been committed, Washington said, no pardon was needed—and he coolly dismissed his guest.

After this exchange, the Howes decided to attack New York. The general had come down from Halifax to Staten Island with a large body of regulars, the admiral had come from Britain with the Hessians, and Henry Clinton and Sir Peter Parker soon came limping up from Charleston with their men and ships. General Howe now had an army of 32,000 superbly armed and equipped troops to hurl against 19,000 ragged, untrained Americans in New York. His

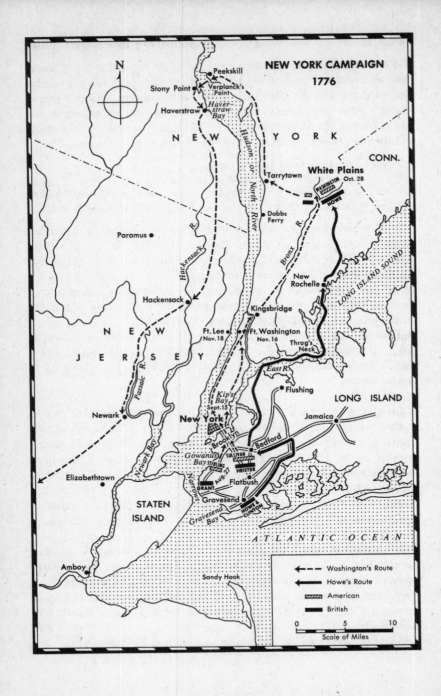

brother led a fleet of ten ships of the line, 20 frigates mounting 1,200 guns and hundreds of transports. Britain had never before sent out such an armada. She had spent the staggering sum of £850,000 to organize and supply it.

On August 22 the troops began landing on Long Island.

Washington clearly understood the importance of New York. "It is the Place that we must use every Endeavour to keep from them,"[59] he wrote to its commander, Brigadier General Lord Stirling.* Control of New York City meant command of the Hudson and access to the lake-and-river chain to Canada. If the British held it, they could cut off New York City and New England from the rest of the colonies.

But Washington did not yet appreciate British sea power. He believed New York could be held against it, when, actually, Manhattan Island and the other islands clustering around it were highly vulnerable to amphibious attack.

To defend it Washington divided his force into five divisions under Putnam, Greene, William Heath, Joseph Spencer and the garrulous John Sullivan of New Hampshire. One division held the northern end of Manhattan Island where Kingsbridge linked it with the mainland, three held the southern end where the mile-square town of New York was located, and the fifth under Greene was across the East River on Long Island.

Greene built works on Brooklyn Heights, which rose 100 feet above water and commanded New York. But then he came down with malaria, and was evacuated to New York. Command passed to John Sullivan, who was in charge when Howe began landing 20,000 troops at Gravesend Bay.

Great white sails flooded the bay. Longboats, galleys and flatboats crowded with scarlet coats and green-clad Hessian Jaegers rowed away from them toward shore. The sun made a million points of light on bayonets and burnished buckles, on flashing white oars and on the instruments of the bands playing lively marches to spur on "Black Dick" Howe's bluejackets. By noon Howe had 15,000 men ashore—a feat which modern amphibious commanders with motor-

---

* William Alexander, "Lord Stirling," is probably the only peer in American history, although his claim to the Earldom of Stirling was rejected by the House of Lords.

powered ships might well admire. Three days later he received another 5,000. By then Israel Putnam had replaced Sullivan as the
Long Island commander.

Putnam knew nothing of Long Island's terrain or its troops. He
continued Sullivan's dispositions. On the American right were about
1,700 men under Stirling. On the left was the main body under Sullivan. To the rear guarding Brooklyn were works held by Putnam's
reserve. In all, say 5,000 men held Long Island. Unfortunately, although Putnam had posted troops to watch the roads, he had neglected
to cover the vital Jamaica Pass opening on the Jamaica Road to
Sullivan's rear.

William Howe knew of both pass and road and was planning to
pivot a turning movement on them.

Howe's left under the American-hating Major General James
Grant was to attack Stirling and hold him in place. The center composed of Hessians under General Philip de Heister was to strike
at Sullivan and the American main body. Meanwhile, Howe's main
body would slip through the Jamaica Pass and follow the Jamaica
Road into Sullivan's rear.

At nine o'clock the night of August 26, Howe's main body under
Clinton, Percy and Cornwallis began moving out. Tories led them to
the pass. At dawn the British stole through and turned left down the
road to Sullivan's rear.

To the left, Grant had begun attacking Stirling, who had reminded
his men that the general opposing them had boasted he could geld
every male in America. Stirling's men fought valiantly. They not
only repulsed Grant's regulars but also tried to seize a British-held
height. Grant, however, was content with keeping the Americans
engaged.

So was Heister with the Hessians in the center. He waited until
two cannon shots signaled the successful turning of Sullivan's position. They came, and the Hessians lunged forward, bands playing,
some of them singing hymns. The Americans met them with the oaths
and profanity characteristic of all English-speaking troops since the
"Goddams" who fought Joan of Arc. Resistance was fierce, at first.
But then came reports that Howe's main body was in the American
rear, and Sullivan's troops panicked and ran.

The Hessians moved among them mercilessly. They had been told by their English officers that the Americans gave no quarter, and they spitted many of the ragged rebels on trees or slaughtered entire groups of men who had laid down their arms.

Caught between two fires, the American main body was completely routed, and Sullivan himself was captured trying to rally his troops in a cornfield.

On the right, Stirling's men fought on. They were now surrounded on three sides. Lord Cornwallis had come down the road to attack their rear, Grant charged them on the right, and the Hessians hit them in the front. Too late, Stirling ordered a retreat. Many of his men trying to escape through the Gowanus marshes were drowned in the attempt. The rest broke and scattered through the woods. Stirling himself then deliberately surrendered to the Hessians rather than to the detestable Grant.

Long Island was a decisive British victory, and it could have been a greater one if William Howe had consented to his subordinates' pleas to storm the American redoubts at Brooklyn. Some British officers were livid with rage when Howe ordered their eager troops to retire. But those crumpled redcoats of Bunker Hill still lay in heaps at the back of Howe's brain, and he would not again assault Americans behind fixed positions. Instead, he decided to take Brooklyn by regular approaches, thus missing an opportunity to end the war with one blow, for Washington was at Brooklyn and had brought over reinforcements.

Troubled and heart-sore, Washington saw, next day, the first of the British trenches begun. On the following day he held a council of war and decided to evacuate Long Island.

To do it he relied upon luck, darkness and John Glover's regiment from Marblehead.

They were called infantry, these men of Marblehead, but they had the look of men of the sea. They marched with a sailor's rolling gait. They wore cocked hats of the line, but also the short blue jackets and loose white trousers of the sailor. Their faces were grizzled from salt and their hands curled from oar and line. They spoke a language of their own: a stern man was "hord-horted," a barrel of tar was a "tor-borrl" and a useless man was a "froach." Their colonel, stocky John Glover, was a soldier happier to obey than command when he was on land, but on this dark night of August 29 he and his men were on water.

With similar men of the Salem regiment they took charge of the small boats which Washington had wisely collected in advance. They brought them bobbing up to the Brooklyn ferry landing. Men bent beneath loads of baggage and equipment came marching silently down to the waiting boats. No lights were shown. No words but softly whispered commands were spoken. Then the wind blew northeast against the Americans. The ebb tide ran so strong that even the Marbleheaders could not make the crossing. Suddenly, the wind veered to the southwest, lessened and subsided. All seemed well.

But all was not well. At two in the morning Major Alexander Scammel, Washington's aide, told General Thomas Mifflin that his boats were waiting and he must march at once. Mifflin objected. His was the covering party. He had stationed sentries and advanced posts close to the British to observe their movements. He *couldn't* leave. Scammel, however, insisted—and Mifflin pulled his men out.

On the way to the ferry landing Washington came riding up on his gray horse. He reined in in astonishment and halted the column.

"Good God!" Washington exclaimed. "General Mifflin, I am afraid you have ruined us by unseasonably withdrawing the troops from the lines."

Mifflin retorted angrily that he had only obeyed orders. Washington said he had not, and Mifflin burst out: "By God, I did! Did Scammel act as an aide-de-camp for the day, or did he not?" Washington admitted that he had, and Mifflin snapped: "Then I had orders through him."[60]

Composed now, Washington told Mifflin that it had all been a dreadful mistake, and requested him to return to his covering position. Mifflin obeyed, and the evacuation continued.

Toward morning and the daylight that would reveal the boats to the guns of the British fleet, a fog set in. It enabled Mifflin's covering force to be withdrawn without mishap. Not until then did the British take note of the strangely silent Yankee trenches. When they opened fire and charged, they found them empty.

Out on the water a young Connecticut lieutenant named Benjamin Tallmadge peered through the swirling mists of the fog and saw the last man step down the slippery steps of the landing into a boat. He was very tall and wore a blue sash across his breast.

9

☆

Washington had saved his army by perhaps the most brilliant feat of his career. But it was still a retreat, and his star would seldom sink lower than during those doleful days following the evacuation from Long Island.

John Haslet, the capable colonel of the Delaware Regiment, wrote to Caesar Rodney: "Would to heaven General Lee were here is the language of officers and men."[61] Worse, Washington did not seem to know what to do about New York itself.

Nathanael Greene, recovered from malaria, had wisely recommended burning the city and withdrawing. The British would take it; anyway it was two-thirds Tory—so why not spoil the prize? Congress, however, instructed Washington not to harm the city, and he decided to defend it as well.

Meanwhile, the Howes, jubilant over the Long Island victory, aware of the deteriorating morale in the American camp, decided to have another try at talking peace. Congress was approached, and John Adams, Edward Rutledge and Benjamin Franklin were chosen to confer with Admiral Lord Richard Howe. They met aboard his flagship on September 11.

Once again, the admiral was forced to confess that he could only grant pardons. Only after the colonies had surrendered would the mother country consent to discuss peace terms. He told them that he could not even receive them as members of Congress, since King George recognized no such body. John Adams replied that the Americans were perfectly willing to be received "in any capacity his Lordship pleased, except in that of *British subjects*."

Shaken, Lord Howe said that if America fell he would lament "as for the loss of a brother," whereupon Franklin put in gently: "My Lord, we will do our utmost endeavors to save your lordship that mortification."[62]

The meeting ended with Lord Howe's affection for America severely strained, and four days later his brother began attacking New York.

British warships in the East River opened fire on American fortifications at Kip's Bay in the area of present-day 34th Street. British and Hessian troops began crossing the river in flatboats, and the Americans rose and fled before the enemy put foot on New York soil.

Washington rode to Kip's Bay in a fury. "Take the walls!" he cried to his fleeing troops. "Take the cornfield!" But only a few obeyed. In a paroxysm of rage, Washington dashed his hat on the ground and bellowed: "Are these the men with whom I am to defend America?"[63] He snapped his pistol at them, he beat them with his cane—privates, officers, even a colonel and brigadier general. But they kept on running, flinging away muskets, knapsacks, even their coats and hats—anything that could slow down their flight from troops they had not even seen.

Washington sat his horse blinded with rage or despair. He paid no attention to a party of Hessians within 80 yards of him. He would have been killed or captured had not an aide seized his bridle and hurried him away.

Howe now had another opportunity. He might cut off Israel Putnam and 4,000 men to the south if he plunged straight across the island. But he moved slowly again, not, as a charming legend suggests, because Mrs. Robert Murray beguiled him and his officers with cakes and wine while Putnam made his escape, but because he had obtained his first day's objective and was satisfied.

Next day his forces turned north or right toward the Americans' entrenchments in Harlem. They moved swiftly. A British bugler began to taunt the patriots with the notes of the fox chase. Stung, Washington sent out troops to nip off the British detachment. Then, seeing an opportunity to inflict real damage on the enemy, Washington fed in more units. So did the British. A two-hour bullet-for-bullet battle began raging. Finally, about 1,800 Americans under Greene, Putnam and George Clinton sent the Anglo-German army backpedaling through an orchard. In high spirits, the Americans had to be restrained from charging full tilt into a large body of British reinforcements pushing north under Cornwallis.

The engagement brought drooping American heads high. More important, it was a national victory. Troops from all the colonies behaved bravely, and for once the Southerners and Pennsylvanians left off sneering at the "dastardly, cowardly" New England troops.

After that action, Howe, still neglecting the opportunity to get onto the mainland and cut off Washington's escape, contented himself with accepting the acclaim of New York's grateful Tories.

The moment the redcoats marched into the town at the foot of Manhattan Island, they were overwhelmed by throngs of weeping, shouting Loyalists. Women as well as men carried British officers around on their shoulders. The rebel standard was torn down and trampled under foot and the King's hoisted in its place.

Then the witch hunt began. Rebels or suspected rebels were rounded up, especially those who had been overheard to vow that they would set fire to the town rather than allow the British to occupy it.

In the early morning of September 21, by accident or design— history does not know—New York *was* burning. By the time the alarm was given the fire was out of control. Whipped by high winds, flames believed to have begun in a shed near Whitehall Slip howled through street after street. Hovels went up, fine mansions, Dutch houses dating back to Peter Stuyvesant, wharves, churches—all were collapsed and consumed. Frenzied women and children were driven from house after house, until finally they could only lie down on the common, mingling their screams and shrieks with the cries and curses of the citizens and soldiers who had spilled outdoors to fight the blaze. But buckets were few and the supply of water was scanty, and the holocaust continued to spread, engulfing Trinity Church. Soon the church's steeple was "a lofty Pyramid of fire." Flames ate away the outer shingles, exposing timbers which quickly began burning themselves. Finally, with a great hissing roar and a shower of sparks, the entire structure came crashing down.

Meanwhile, mob frenzy had overcome the Tories. They seized suspects and strung them up without trial. Some were even thrown screaming into the flames.

At last, the wind changed and the fire was brought under control. What Nathanael Greene had wished and Congress had forbidden had come to pass. New York was gutted and of very little use to William Howe. Next day the angry general confronted an American officer accused of being a spy. He had been captured on Long Island the night of the fire. His name was Nathan Hale. He was about 24, well educated and completely composed as he admitted to Howe that he had been observing British troop movements for General Washington.

Howe curtly ordered him hanged without the grace of a trial. Hale asked for a clergyman. He was refused. He requested a Bible. He was turned down. A gallows was erected at what is now 52nd Street a bit east of First Avenue. The noose was slipped around Nathan Hale's neck. He stood there calmly, his light blue eyes betraying no inner fear, and he said: "I only regret that I have but one life to lose for my country."

Then the noose tightened and life passed from the body of the first martyr of American arms.

Far to the north, Benedict Arnold was headed for battle again. General Horatio Gates had placed Arnold in charge of a rickety, makeshift fleet with which the Americans hoped to hold Lake Champlain against the ships and soldiers of Sir Guy Carleton, issuing south from Canada.

Arnold had once cruised his own ships in the West Indies, and knew something of the water. He was also spoiling for a fight, having been humiliated at Quebec and still being harassed by government bodies demanding an accounting of public funds in his care. In such mood, he helped direct construction of galleys and gundalows made of wood as green as the amateur sailors whom Gates had recruited from his regiments. Jerry-built as they were, the boats would float and the guns would fire. Arnold sailed down the lake and took position off Valcour Island about 50 miles north of Ticonderoga.

Up the lake came Carleton with gunboats of seasoned wood prefabricated in Britain, a huge raft called the *Thunderer* mounting heavy guns poked through thick wooden walls, and about 9,000 infantry. On October 11 Carleton's superior force passed Arnold's hidden fleet at Valcour, spotted it, and doubled back into the battle.

It was fought at almost musket range. Americans and British poured shot and shell into each other while Carleton's Indians on shore raked the rebels with small-arms fire. Arnold himself aimed the guns of his flagship, *Congress,* until that rickety craft was riddled and aflame and had to be abandoned. Eventually, British superiority told. One by one Arnold's ships were hunted down and sunk. Only six survived, limping back to Crown Point where they were burnt. Arnold and his men took to the woods to return to Ticonderoga.

Yet, though the British had won a tactical victory, they suffered a strategic loss. Carleton did not press on to Ticonderoga as he might have done. He did not even tarry at Crown Point and thus hold an advanced base for a fresh expedition in the spring of 1777. Instead, wary of the approaching winter, he withdrew to Montreal.

Benedict Arnold's desperate delaying action had prevented a fatal link-up between Carleton and General Howe, now moving north from New York.

Just as the Battle of Valcour Island was ending, the deliberate William Howe at last began to move. He had dawdled for nearly a month in New York. Then, on October 9, British warships sailed up the Hudson between the batteries at Fort Lee in New Jersey on their left and those of Fort Washington in Manhattan on their right. Sunken hulks in the river, a famous network of chains and booms, had failed to stop them from getting into Washington's right rear.

Howe now moved to get into Washington's left rear. He took his main body up the East River and through Hell Gate to land at Throg's Neck, and then still higher on the mainland at New Rochelle.

To forestall this double envelopment, Washington left 2,000 men in Fort Washington and 4,000 under Greene in Fort Lee and quit Manhattan to build a strong camp at White Plains in Westchester County. On October 28 Howe attacked Washington's right flank at Chatterton's Hill.

British and Hessians struck at the hill frontally while Colonel Johann Rall moved to hit the American right flank. But Rall did not get into position in time, and the Americans on Chatterton's Hill were able to pour a heavy fire into the frontal attack. The British withdrew and re-formed, Rall got into place on the flank, and the attack went forward again, forcing the Americans to abandon the hill.

General William Howe had another chance to destroy Washington. He was in position on his flank and could roll him up. But he did not move. Questioned later by the House of Commons on this decision, he refused to answer "for political reasons." Cornwallis, a Whig like himself, supported his silence. Whatever the reason—a hope that mild means would end the rebellion, perhaps even desire to vindicate Whig predictions of American independence—the lost opportunity did not reappear. Heavy rains prevented a renewal of the attack, and on the dark night of November 1 Washington marched from his lines into a new and stronger position at North Castle behind the Croton River.

Washington now expected Howe to move higher up the Hudson or cross into New Jersey. Instead, the British chief struck at Fort Washington on Manhattan.

On November 16 Howe called upon the fort to surrender or have its garrison put to the sword. Colonel Robert Magaw, the commander, swore to fight to the end. The next day, floating batteries in the Harlem River and the guns of a man-of-war in the Hudson burst into a roaring barrage, and the attack surged forward.

Howe had about 13,000 men divided into four columns converging on the fort from every side. Colonel Magaw had nearly 3,000 men, actually far too many for such a constricted position. At first, the Americans fought valiantly. They took an especially dreadful toll among the Hessians attacking from the north. But the Germans came on through the redoubts and masses of felled trees. General William von Knyphausen, their commander, tore at the branches with his hands. Drums began to beat, oboes blew, and lines of music-loving Hessians in tall brass miters swept on toward the fort.

They drove the Americans ahead of them. Fort Washington filled with swarms of beaten men. It became a slaughter pen exposed to British cannon, and Colonel Magaw surrendered it. Still the Hessians came on with their bayonets, angered because they had borne the brunt of British losses. They had to be restrained from bayoneting prisoners. Even some of Howe's officers thought that their general should have slaughtered the garrison as he had threatened. They said that he would not have been held accountable by the rules of war then prevailing, and that he "would have struck such a panic as would have prevented the Congress from ever being able to raise another Army."[64]

That army was fast vanishing. Howe, moving quickly for once, sent Cornwallis across the Hudson against Fort Lee, forcing Nathanael Greene to decamp hastily without his guns and supplies. Greene joined Washington at Hackensack. Cornwallis pursued.

Slowly, slogging over roads that fall rains had turned into a slop of mud, Washington began his miserable retreat across New Jersey. Again and again he got off dispatches to Lee in North Castle urging him to join him with the main body. Desertions were melting his force like powder in the rain. He was down to barely 3,000 men. If Lee could come down and gather up intervening units, Washington might have 10,000 men—at least on paper. But Lee, for reasons of his own, did not move.

Onward, in alternating fury and despair, Washington led his wretched scarecrows. With the oncoming raw cold of a Northern winter they suffered more. Through the Watchung Mountains they trudged, into Newark, out of it . . . into New Brunswick, and away again with Cornwallis nipping at their heels. Behind them, the numerous Tories of New Jersey were breaking out their British flags and welcoming their "saviors" in red coats. Into Trenton the rebels dragged their long tail of retreat. Washington began collecting all the boats on the Delaware, even as Congress prepared to flee from Philadelphia to Baltimore.

It was Howe who was on Washington's heels now, and he was dallying as usual. He might have gotten to the Delaware ahead of Washington, but his men did not enter Trenton until the last of the Americans were crossing the river.

Safe on the other side, George Washington fired off letter after imploring letter to Charles Lee. All depended on his bringing his troops south from New York. In another few weeks enlistments in the Continental Army would expire. The outlook was at its darkest. Pennsylvania had sent him only a few thousand men and New Jersey almost none. If the army was not quickly replenished, the general wrote to his cousin Lund Washington, "I think the game will be pretty well up. . . ."[65]

10

☆

On the morning of December 13 General Charles Lee finished his breakfast and began to write a letter to General Horatio Gates. Lee was in a tavern in Basking Ridge, New Jersey. He had finally departed North Castle on December 2 with the bulk of Washington's army. Two days' march from Pennsylvania the army had halted to make camp, while General Lee rode to the tavern four miles away.

Lee's aide, James Wilkinson, stood at the window listening to the scratching of the general's pen as he wrote:

"The ingenius maneouvre of Fort Washington has unhinged the goodly fabrick we had been building. There never was so damned a stroke. *Entre nous,* a certain great man is most damnably deficient. . . ."[66]

Lee ended his letter with another blast at Washington and a forecast of doom. He was just about to sign it when Wilkinson cried: "Here, sir, are the British cavalry!"

"Where?" Lee cried in incredulity.

"Around the house," Wilkinson yelled, watching with horror as about 30 dragoons under Colonel William Harcourt neatly opened files and went galloping around the tavern to surround it. Lee jumped up in alarm.

"Where is the guard?" he shouted. "Damn the guard, why don't they fire?"[67]

Wilkinson caught up his pistols, thrust Lee's letter into his pocket and ran outside to look for the guard. Behind him, Lee was coldly rejecting a maid's suggestion that he hide himself in a bed. Outside, Wilkinson saw the British dragoons chasing Lee's guard away from the tavern. Shots were fired at him, and he ducked back inside.

Then he heard Harcourt's voice saying, *"If the general does not surrender in five minutes, I will set fire to the house."* There was a pause, and the threat was repeated. Two minutes later Wilkinson heard a voice say, *"Here is the general. He has surrendered."*[68] There was a loud shout of triumph, the trumpet sounded the assembly, and Lee was mounted on Wilkinson's horse standing saddled at the door. He was bareheaded, in slippers and blanket coat with his collar open. He was not happy to find himself captive in the hands of his old regiment.

With a clatter of hoofs the jubilant Harcourt bore off the prize which was to bring him his own general's star.

Many Americans were as dismayed by Lee's capture as by the loss of New York. Even Washington, aware of Lee's criticism of him, continued to overvalue the general's abilities. He, too, was crushed

—although the arrival of Lee's troops softened the blow.

But only temporarily. In two weeks' time most of Washington's 6,000 men would be leaving. Very few of them were re-enlisting. Fewer were willing to join the Continental Army. General Howe—now Sir William as a reward for his summer victories—thought so little of this rag, tag and bobtail, about-to-vanish army that he had withdrawn into winter quarters in New York, leaving a chain of posts to hold New Jersey. The cause of the revolution was at its nadir, and Washington had to move swiftly lest it collapse and fall apart.

He had already conceived his counterstroke, but first he must rally his men. On December 23 he had them formed in ranks to have Tom Paine's first issue of *The Crisis* read to them:

"These are the times that try men's souls. The summer soldier and the sunshine patriot will, in this crisis, shrink from the service of their country; but he that stands it now, deserves the love and thanks of man and woman."

Words do not often inspire beaten soldiers, especially men who are threadbare and hungry and cold. But these words did. A thrill of patriotism and purpose ran through Washington's ragged ranks. They were ready for their general's great scheme, and that was simply to attack.

He *had* to attack. He had to forestall the enemy before the Delaware froze and became passable, and he had to rally the dying rebel cause. Across the river from him lay about 3,000 Hessians under Colonel Carl von Donop. They held a six-mile line from Bordentown up to Trenton. About half of them were at Trenton, and Washington proposed to strike them with three forces.

Brigadier General John Cadwalader would cross downriver with about 2,000 men to engage von Donop's Bordentown force and prevent reinforcements being sent north to Trenton.

Brigadier General James Ewing would cross opposite Trenton with about 900 men to capture a bridge and seal off the Hessian escape route south to Bordentown.

Washington himself would make the main attack with about 2,400 men. He would cross the Delaware above Trenton on Christmas Night and march downriver to make a surprise assault an hour before dawn.

As the daylight of Christmas, 1776, began fading into a storm-tossed night, the American troops under Washington began to move toward McKonkey's Ferry. Here were gathered the boats Washington had collected, and at their oars were John Glover's blue-coated Marbleheaders. Snow mixed with sleet blew into the faces of the men.

Near the ferry, General Washington was preparing to mount his horse. Major Wilkinson presented himself with a letter from General Horatio Gates. "By General Gates?" Washington asked, astonished to hear that his Northern commander was in the vicinity. "Where is he?"

"I left him this morning in Philadelphia."

"What was he doing *there?*"

"I understood him that he was on his way to Congress."

"On his way to Congress!" Washington repeated.[69] Without asking leave, the confidant of Charles Lee had gone hurrahing off to Baltimore to bask in the admiration of certain Congressmen who might also agree that "a certain great man is damnably deficient." Lee a captive, and Gates . . . what? Without a word, Washington rode off to join his troops.

Colonel Johann Rall, the hero of Fort Washington, commanded at Trenton. Rall had contempt for the Americans. He agreed with General Grant at New Brunswick that he could "keep the peace in New Jersey with a corporal's guard." Fine fighter that he was, Rall believed that when a soldier went into winter quarters he should address himself to women and wine. He had built no redoubts around Trenton as Colonel von Donop had ordered. He had only a few pickets stationed along the roads.

On Christmas Day Johann Rall awoke with the customary hangover. He dressed leisurely, listening to the serenade played by shivering Hessian bandsmen standing outside his window. He prepared to celebrate the Nativity in the hearty German manner.

At night, after the festivity, there was a minor scare when a roving American patrol shot up the picket guard. The troops were called to arms, but very soon returned to quarters. Colonel Rall dropped in on a supper party at the home of a wealthy Trenton merchant. There were wine and cards. Near the middle of the night there was a knock on the door. A Tory had come with information for the colonel. Rall would not see him. The man wrote a note informing Rall that the American army was on the march. A servant delivered it. Rall stuck it into his pocket, unread. Eventually, his heart gladdened with wine, Colonel Rall went home to bed.

Outside his window the storm mounted in fury.

The Americans had been enjoined to silence. No soldier was to break ranks under pain of death. They stood huddled by the ferry landing, ducking their heads into their collars against the rising howl of the storm. Their firelocks were hopelessly wet, but Colonel Knox's artillerymen had kept the cannon touchholes dry.

The men entered the boats. Thin, jagged cakes of ice came floating downriver to strike the boats so hard that Glover's Marbleheaders had difficulty keeping afloat. Washington had hoped to have his troops on the Jersey shore by midnight, but it was not until after three o'clock that Knox's booming voice announced that the crossing was completed.

Washington formed his forces into two divisions. John Sullivan would take his division—which included John Stark's sharpshooters—down the river road. Nathanael Greene's division, accompanied by Washington, would march on Trenton along a road two miles farther inland. Sullivan would hit the bottom of the town, Greene the top. The Americans began marching. The roads were slippery. Cruel ice cut through flimsy footwear and drew blood. In the morning, Major Wilkinson could follow the route by the bloodstains in the snow.

But down the roads they marched, steadily slipping up on the still-sleeping enemy. With daylight, just before eight o'clock in the morning, both columns reached their destination—and both flushed Hessian pickets and drove them in.

"*Der feind! Heraus! Heraus!*" the pickets shouted. "The enemy! Turn out! Turn out!"[70]

Lieutenant Jacob Piel heard the shouts and rushed to alert Colonel Rall. He hammered on his door. Rall, in his nightclothes, poked his head out the window. Piel told him he had heard firing. Rall withdrew his head and a few minutes later came rushing downstairs in full uniform. He formed his own blue-coated regiment on King Street. The scarlet-coated Lossbergs marched to the right to take over Queen Street parallel with King, while the black-coated Knyphausen Regiment made up the reserve. But at the top of both King and Queen streets stood the American artillery.

Two guns to a street, but would they fire? Captain Alexander Hamilton's gunners stuck their matches in the touchholes. The cannon roared and shook. American cheers mingled with the shrieks of Hessian soldiers stricken by grapeshot. Rall's regiment was fragmented and driven back. The other brace of cannon cleared Queen Street, but the Lossbergs mounted their own cannon and fired back. The Americans charged. Captain William Washington and Lieutenant James Monroe led their men right into the cannon's mouth. They captured them, although both were wounded—a liability which eventually would be a political asset to President James Monroe.

Sullivan's men at the bottom of the town were attacking from the west. Green's division extended its right flank to join Sullivan, while more of Greene's units worked around to the rear or the east of the town. If General Ewing had crossed to hold the bridge over Assunpink Creek, the Hessians were caught in a box.

Ewing had not crossed. The bridge lay open, and perhaps 400 Hessians were escaping over it. The remainder, however, could not get away. Even with wet firelocks the Americans fought with conquering fury. "Use the bayonet," Washington ordered. "I am determined to take Trenton."[71] Some Americans ran inside the houses to dry their pieces or pick the touchholes clear. They acted as snipers when Rall re-formed his shattered troops and tried to counterattack, and they sent two bullets into Rall's body. The Hessian commander fell from his horse, fatally stricken, and that was about the end of the battle.

Sullivan's troops now held the bridge, and the escape gap was plugged. One by one the Hessian regiments surrendered. In all, about 920 Hessians had been captured, about 25 were killed and 90 wounded. Two Americans had been frozen to death on the march, but not one was killed in the battle: two officers and two privates were wounded.

General George Washington stood radiant on the field. When Major Wilkinson rode up to him to announce that the last enemy regiment had grounded arms, his face actually shone and he extended his hand in thanks.

"Major Wilkinson," Washington said, "this is a glorious day for our country."[72]

11

☆

It had been a glorious day. From the depths of despair the American people rose to the heights of exultation. Sir William Howe was staggered. He could not believe that "three old established regiments of a people who made war a profession should lay down their arms to a ragged and undisciplined militia."[73]

Howe stopped Cornwallis from sailing home to Britain and sent him out to take command in New Jersey, while he gathered reinforcements and prepared to join him.

Washington, meanwhile, was hailed as a military genius. His reputation, tarnished by defeat and retreat, glittered as never before. A grateful Congress voted him powers that made him a virtual military dictator, and the general was quick to use them in forming a new Continental Army. While battalions of militia inspired by the Trenton victory were marching to his side, Washington persuaded his regulars to re-enlist for six weeks for a bounty of $10. He ordered his forces in New York to march to winter quarters in Morristown, New Jersey, and told Cadwalader and Ewing, who had belatedly crossed the Delaware, to join him in Trenton. Then he himself went back across the river to renew the offensive.

To Washington's surprise, Cornwallis, unlike Howe, moved rapidly to meet him. On January 2, 1777, Cornwallis marched from Princeton toward Trenton with a force of about 5,500 men, the flower of the British Army. A brigade of about 1,200 was left behind as a rear guard under Lieutenant Colonel Charles Mawhood. They would rejoin Cornwallis the next day.

Cornwallis and his main body came up with Washington on a ridge in the late afternoon. The American pickets were driven in. Washington, with his back to the Delaware, was in a bad position. Cornwallis's officers urged him to attack then and there. Sir William Erskine is supposed to have said: "If Washington is the general I take him to be, he will not be found there in the morning."⁷⁴ Cornwallis replied that the men were tired from marching all day. He would "bag the old fox" in the morning.

That night Washington's officers held a council of war. They knew that their situation was desperate. Highhearted as the Continentals might now be, they could not hope to repulse a superior force. British batteries, British bayonets, British discipline had to prevail. Then someone, perhaps Washington himself, made an audacious proposal: why stay on the defensive when the offensive beckoned? Why not steal away from Trenton and attack Princeton in Cornwallis's rear? Farther back lay New Brunswick with the British war chest of £70,000. It was agreed, even though a thaw had made a muck of the only known road. Then the weather changed. The road froze. A party of 400 men was detailed to work loudly with pick and shovel within earshot of the British. Baggage and guns were sent on ahead. Wheels were wrapped in rags to muffle their noise. At one o'clock in the morning of January 3, leaving his campfires burning brightly, "the old fox" led his men softly into the enemy rear.

It was, again, a nightmare march. But dawn of January 3 came at last, bright and frosty, as the Americans neared Stony Brook two miles outside the town. Washington sent General Hugh Mercer's brigade to hold the bridge while Sullivan with three brigades took a road to the right into Princeton.

Marching out of Princeton, meanwhile, came Colonel Mawhood and his regulars.

Mounted on a little brown pony, Mawhood clattered over Stony Brook bridge ahead of his men. Suddenly, to his left he caught the flash of arms. Yankee rebels were emerging from a wood. They were Hugh Mercer's advance guard, but Mawhood thought that they were the backwash of the American army "defeated" at Trenton. He sent mounted officers to intercept them while pulling his brigade back over the bridge. Then he led them on the double for an orchard on that side of Stony Brook. The Americans raced him for it and beat him. They quickly fortified a hedge and a gun duel ensued. Mawhood called for the bayonet, and the sight of British steel broke the American ranks.

General Mercer and Colonel Haslet tried to rally the men. But the bayonets overtook Mercer. A rifle butt drove him to the earth. He arose brandishing his sword, but seven bayonets drove into his body, and he fell dying. Haslet was shot through the head, and Mercer's brigade fled.

They poured back over the road and washed around the tall man on the big white horse, leading the main body toward the sounds of battle. He waved his hat and cried, "Parade with us, my brave fellows!"[75] and galloped down the road to within 30 yards of Mawhood's advancing regulars. The redcoats were astonished. They raised their muskets. One of Washington's aides covered his eyes in dread. A volley crashed out and smoke concealed Washington from all eyes, but when it parted he was still there, erect and valiant, calling his men forward.

They did not come. But then troops from Sullivan's division came hurrying to the rescue. Mercer's men were re-formed. Yelling battle cries, they charged the British and forced them to retreat down the road to Trenton. Washington led the pursuit, crying, "It's a fine fox chase, my boys!"[76] But the British dragoons successfully covered Mawhood's withdrawal.

In Princeton, meanwhile, Sullivan's troops had successfully stormed the town. About 200 British were cornered in Nassau Hall. Captain Alexander Hamilton's gunners put one ball into the building, and they surrendered.

Far away in Trenton, Lord Charles Cornwallis heard the distant sound of guns and guessed that the vanished old fox had bared his fangs again.

Washington's men were simply too tired to march the mere 18 miles to New Brunswick. Holding a council of war on horseback, Washington decided to leave Princeton immediately and make for Morristown. There he could rest within a defensive position from which he could attack Howe's flank should he move against Philadelphia or up the Hudson.

It was a heart-breaking decision. As the general later wrote to Congress: "Six or seven hundred fresh troops, upon a forced march, would have destroyed all their stores and magazines" at New Brunswick, "taken . . . their military chest . . . and put an end to the war."[77] But there were no such men, and the exhausted Americans straggled wearily out of town.

With the British Army's treasury threatened, Cornwallis made directly for New Brunswick and allowed Washington to escape to Morristown. It was the only course to follow, but as his Lordship was to write ruefully to Lord George Germain: "The unlucky affair of Rall's brigade has given me a winter campaign."[78]

That "campaign," it would seem, was waged against the helpless New Jersey countryside. Stung by the upstart Yankees, claiming the miserable eighteenth-century soldier's privilege of pillage and plunder, the British and Hessian regulars burned and looted and raped the winter away. In Princeton they maliciously burned all the firewood available to inhabitants whose own homes and orchards had also been burned, slaughtered and carried off cattle and destroyed mills.

The Hessians were the more proficient at plunder, which they regarded as the means of making their fortunes. Wherever they passed, anything movable was carefully piled up on wagons and carried away. Friend or foe, it made no difference. No Jaeger sergeant could read Sir William Howe's writs of immunity, and he would not have heeded them if he could: booty was booty.

To Britain's dishonor, the treatment of prisoners was something far more cruel and without any plea of custom or "uncontrollable soldiery" to excuse it. British prison ships were floating horrors in which men fought for food or for air, "some swearing and blaspheming, some crying, praying and wringing their hands and stalking about like ghosts and apparitions; others delirious . . . raving and storming; some groaning and dying—all panting for breath; some dead and corrupting."[79] One prisoner wrote: "The air was so foul at times that a lamp could not be kept burning, by reason of which three boys were not missed until they had been dead ten days."[80]

Lord Francis Rawdon believed it was necessary to ravage the countryside to teach "these infatuated wretches" a lesson. His Lordship also found the ravishing of American women highly entertaining, writing:

The fair nymphs of this isle [Staten Island] were in wonderful tribulation, as the fresh meat our men have got here has made them riotous as satyrs. A girl cannot step into the bushes to pluck a rose without running the most imminent risk of being ravished, and they are so little accustomed to these vigorous methods that they don't bear them with the proper resignation, and of consequence we have most entertaining courtmartials every day.[81]

"Of consequence" also: the Tories began turning patriot, and the atrocities of Lord Cornwallis's "winter campaign" helped to guarantee the safety of Washington's army in its hill fastness at Morristown.

12

☆

Washington had intended to stay in Morristown only a few days, but he was forced to remain there nearly five months.

It was a cruel sojourn. On March 14, 1777, Washington reported that he had less than 3,000 starved and freezing scarecrows to command. In desperation, he used his dictatorial powers to commandeer provisions. But he could not outlaw smallpox, which ravaged the camp.

At last the patriot cause brightened. About 22,000 muskets and other supplies arrived through the good offices of M. de Beaumarchais. Eventually men to shoulder them also began to arrive, not in a trickle or a flood, but in a steady small stream that was to be characteristic of Continental Army recruiting. Washington now had a force of about 9,000 soldiers, not including the Northern army with which General Horatio Gates was guarding the lake-and-river chain.

That summer two notable recruits appeared: one a huge self-styled baron, a German-turned-Frenchman named Jean de Kalb, the other a slender youth who was truly both French and noble and whose name was the Marquis de Lafayette.

Lafayette joined Washington's staff or "family," and was with him when he marched to intercept Sir William Howe's attack on Philadelphia.

The British plan of campaign for 1777 was for General John Burgoyne to lead a large force from Canada down to Albany, where he would make junction with General Sir William Howe moving up the Hudson.

Howe, however, decided to move into Pennsylvania first. He informed Lord George Germain that numerous Loyalists there would rally to his standard. Howe also believed that by drawing Washington into Pennsylvania he would make Burgoyne's invasion of New York State easier. Finally, the British commander was confident that he could finish off Pennsylvania and Washington in time to return to New York to help Burgoyne.

On July 23, after an unsuccessful attempt to trap Washington in New Jersey, Howe sailed for the mouth of the Delaware River with 260 ships and about 15,000 soldiers. He did not, as he had intended, sail up the river to take Philadelphia. Reports that the Delaware was too difficult to navigate and too well fortified to storm decided him in favor of sailing up the Chesapeake Bay instead.

On August 14 he began landing at Head of Elk in Maryland. Fifty miles away to the northeast lay Philadelphia, the "capital" of the rebellion. Howe began marching toward it. Hearing of his movement, Washington moved to head him off—and on September 11, 1777, the armies collided at Brandywine Creek.

The Brandywine is marked by numerous shallow crossings or fords. Washington, holding the east bank of the stream, chose to guard most of them. His left rested on Pyle's Ford, his center at Chad's Ford, while his right held Painter's and Brinton's. Smaller forces watched other crossings higher up, but Trimble's Ford seven miles north of Chad's was neglected.

And Howe was making for Trimble's.

Howe was duplicating his turning movement of Long Island. Von Knyphausen had been sent against Chad's Ford to hold the Americans in place while Howe with Cornwallis and the main body secretly crossed the Brandywine above them, swung south and came down on the American right rear.

Washington sat calmly still for the knockout blow. As on Long Island, he braced himself for a frontal assault. And then, in the forenoon, came two messages warning him of Howe's march to Trimble's Ford. Washington was amazed. The enemy had divided his forces! Eager to take advantage of Howe's "blunder," Washington divided his own and ordered the parts to cross the creek and attack.

Just as the movement began, a message came from Sullivan on the right advising Washington that there was no enemy on the road to Trimble's Ford. The American commander relaxed, until a hatless, coatless, bare-legged farmer named Thomas Cheyney was brought to his headquarters. The British were across the Brandywine, Cheyney shouted. He had seen them and they had fired on him and chased him. Washington's staff smiled superior smiles. Obviously the man was a Tory out to deceive them. Cheyney turned on them wrathfully. "I'd have you know I have this day's work as much at heart as e'er a blood of ye!" he yelled.[82]

Cheyney dropped to his knee and drew a map in the dust, marking the exact place where he had seen the British. Washington shook his head in disbelief.

"You're mistaken, General!" the farmer cried. "My life for it you're mistaken. By hell, it's so! Put me under guard till you find out it's so!"[83]

Washington hesitated, torn by doubts. But then a courier arrived from John Sullivan reporting that the British were in the rear of his right and were coming down. Stunned, Washington ordered Sullivan to march to Birmingham Meeting House a mile to his right rear and halt the British there. Sullivan obeyed. He occupied a hill in the enemy's path, but by then it was too late.

British bayonets again broke the Yankee ranks. The entire left of Sullivan's new line was swept away. Down at Chad's Ford, Knyphausen began attacking the Americans under Mad Anthony Wayne.

Washington was no longer deceived. He realized that the sound of cannon booming up at Birmingham Meeting House signaled the main attack. Hesitating no longer, he at once ordered Greene to march to the rescue.

Meanwhile, the Americans under Sullivan were rallying and fighting desperately. Young Lafayette, ardent for battle, had galloped up from Chad's and was with them. Five times the Americans were driven off their hill, and five times they returned to drive the enemy off. But the issue was not in doubt. A force twice their number backed up by four 12-pounders could not be denied.

Still, Greene was hurrying north. Washington was with him, goading on a reluctant old man who had been forced aboard a horse to act as guide. "Push along, old man!" Washington roared. "Push along!"[84] Above him, the Americans were giving way. British and Hessian soldiers brandishing bloody bayonets were turning an orderly withdrawal into a stampede. All seemed lost for the American army and the American nation.

And that was when the vanguard of Greene's column arrived, opening its ranks to allow the terrified fugitives to pass through and re-form, and then closing firm again to halt the onrushing British. Below, at Chad's Ford, Knyphausen's attack had broken through. But the Americans were retiring in good order. Eventually darkness came and the Battle of the Brandywine was over.

Howe had again outmaneuvered and defeated Washington. Nevertheless, the American had again managed to save his army. Nor were his men downcast. Some of them, as they retreated to Chester and thence to Germantown, were actually proud of how they had held off the regulars in a stand-up fight. Many of them were actually saying, "Come, boys, we shall do better another time."[85]

Actually, they did worse. In the early morning of September 21, British forces under Major General Charles Grey surprised Anthony Wayne's division at Paoli's Tavern. Grey had ordered his men to march with unloaded muskets, removing their flints to guard against accidental discharges. "No-Flint" Grey's men caught the Americans silhouetted by the light of their own campfires and routed them with a fierce bayonet charge. Some 300 Americans were killed or wounded, 100 more were captured, and reports of so-called "atrocities" at the "Paoli Massacre" caused fleeing Congressmen to dig their spurs into the hides of horses carrying them from threatened Philadelphia to the safety of York, Pennsylvania.

On September 26 Howe entered Philadelphia. He received a liberator's reception and he became convinced that he had come at last to the Land of the Tories. Notifying Mrs. Loring to join him —escorted by her husband, of course—Howe relaxed his vigilance. He divided his army, keeping one force in Philadelphia and a larger one in the unguarded suburb of Germantown.

Washington, seeing his chance, attacked.

From Washington's position roughly north of Germantown four roads ran down into the British camp. Washington proposed to follow all of them. He had been reinforced, and now possessed about 9,000 Continentals and about 3,000 militia. Howe in Germantown had about 9,000 regulars.

On the night of October 3 four American columns struck south for Germantown. On the right were militia, then Sullivan, then Greene, then more militia. Sullivan and Greene in the center, of course, packed the main punch. After they attacked the British, the militia to either side would hit Howe's flanks and crumple them. It was an elaborate plan, nothing less than that classical "double envelopment" so fatally attractive to commanders since Hannibal had first made it work at Cannae 2,000 years previously.

Hannibal, however, had never had Washington's problems. The American proposed to send untrained officers and men on a 16-mile night march over four widely separated roads, and then launch them in a single coordinated stroke that would surround the world's finest troops under the command of an able tactician. Yet he almost pulled it off.

Sullivan's column caught the British by surprise. They drove the vaunted light infantry back. Astonished, Howe leaped on his horse and rode to the front to rally his old outfit.

"For shame, light infantry!" he cried. "I never saw you retreat before. Form! Form! It's only a scouting party."[86]

To give him the lie, and to warm the hearts of the men he had scolded, the "scouting party" exploded a charge of grape over Howe's startled head—and the Americans came charging forward.

"Have at the bloodhounds!" they cried. "Revenge the Paoli Massacre!"[87]

Wayne's soldiers killed British troops even after they had laid down their arms. Their officers could not restrain them, and the butchery continued even though "many of the poor wretches . . . were crying for mercy."[88] Then, for the first time in the war, British bugles sounded the retreat. Fighting doggedly, the red lines fell back—and the ragged Americans pursued.

Gradually pursued and pursuer lost sight of each other in a fog which mingled with the smoke of battle. Under cover of it, a party of about 120 British slipped into a large stone house owned by Justice Benjamin Chew. The Chew House lay directly in the American path. It could have been by-passed while a small rear guard contained its garrison, but Henry Knox, fighting by the book, insisted on reducing it with artillery. Washington agreed, and precious time was lost in futile battering at a "fort" that refused to fall. At last, Washington ordered his troops on. But where was Greene?

Nathanael Greene with two-thirds of the American army had not yet appeared. Misled by a guide, he came up an hour late. Still, his men were able to drive back the British on Wayne's left as planned.

But then one of Greene's divisions blundered in the smoke and fog into Wayne's rear. At that moment Wayne became convinced that the blasting at the Chew House behind him meant that Sullivan was in trouble back there. He wheeled his division around—and ran into the lost division. Both American forces fired on each other and fled, and the departure of Wayne left Sullivan's left flank completely exposed.

Already striking at Sullivan's right and front, the British sent a counterattack roaring into the gap on his left—and with that the tide turned. Sullivan gave way. His men panicked. Soon the entire American army panicked. Washington again tried to rally them by exposing himself to the hottest fire, but it was of no avail. Many of the men were out of ammunition. Running past Washington they held up empty cartridge boxes. "We ran from Victory,"[89] Anthony Wayne wrote bitterly afterward, but these men had marched all night and fought all morning, and been undone chiefly by the blunders of their commanders.

And so Washington, with the tents of the enemy and victory within his sight, was born off into darkness and defeat on the crest of a flood of cursing, jostling, frightened soldiers. He had fought Sir William Howe for the fifth time and had lost again. But once again he had not lost his army. Undaunted, rocklike, he reformed his shattered remnants and led them off to the gloomy hills of Valley Forge.

13

☆

Early in 1777 a new betting book was opened at the exclusive Brooks's Club in London, and the first entry was made by a handsome dandified man who wrote: "John Burgoyne wagers Charles (James) Fox one pony* that he will be home victorious from America by Christmas Day, 1777."[90]

---

* Fifty guineas or 52½ pounds.

It was thus that Gentleman Johnny Burgoyne set out to execute his scheme for humbling the colonies. Burgoyne was to lead a large Anglo-Hessian force down the lake-and-river chain from Canada to Albany. A second smaller force under Lieutenant Colonel Barry St. Leger was to advance east on Albany from Oswego. Once both forces were joined, communications would be established along the Hudson linking Albany with New York.

Burgoyne arrived in Canada in May and found the troops in good condition after a mild winter. He had about 7,200 regulars, half British and half German, about 400 Indians and perhaps 250 Canadians and Tories. He also had three excellent lieutenants, Major General William Phillips, a veteran and skilled artillerist; Major General Baron von Riedesel commanding the Hessians; and Brigadier General Simon Fraser, the Highlander who had beguiled the French sentries for Wolfe at the Anse-du-Foulon.

In June, with a huge artillery section of 138 guns, with an enormous baggage train equipped to serve Burgoyne's elegant table, as well as to provide amenities for such women of the expedition as the blonde Baroness von Riedesel, her three little daughters and Burgoyne's mistress, the expedition set out for Ticonderoga.

The fort itself had been strengthened by the Polish engineer Kosciusko, but the American northern army had been weakened by quarrels between Generals Schuyler and Gates. As a result, there were only about 2,500 Americans under Major General Arthur St. Clair. Worse, Gates had positively forbidden the fortifying of Sugar Loaf Hill to the southwest of the fort. It completely commanded the American position, but Gates insisted the steep hill was inaccessible. Game-legged Benedict Arnold climbed it himself to disprove Gates, but the general would not budge.

There it stood, inviting, when scarlet coats again became visible through Ticonderoga's leaves, and it was not missed by General Phillips. He consulted his Swiss aide, Lieutenant Twiss, who told him that by using ropes wound around trees and calling forth much sweat the guns could be hauled up Sugar Loaf.

They were, even as a furious exchange of musketry and artillery began between besieger and besieged, but once the guns were emplaced, the battle was over. St. Clair saw the British looking down his throat, and he discreetly abandoned Fort Ticonderoga.

Burgoyne at once ordered a pursuit. The British were momentarily delayed at Hubbardton, where the Americans fought a stubborn delaying action, but von Riedesel saved the day by placing himself at the head of a company of Jaegers and marching through the forest to the rescue with his band playing his country's battle hymns. Elated, Burgoyne pushed on to Skenesboro; but St. Clair eventually eluded him and reached Fort Edward in safety with most of his troops.

Now Burgoyne had to choose one of two ways of continuing his southward march. He could return to Ticonderoga and move across Lake George and so on to the Hudson, or he could strike out overland from Skenesboro toward Fort Edward. The second way was the most difficult through terrain he had himself called "impassable." Yet he chose it. It is said he was persuaded to choose it by the Loyalist Major Philip Skene, founder of Skenesboro, who stood to profit by a new road cut from his colony to the Hudson. But Burgoyne himself feared to encourage the patriots by a "retrograde motion."

Whatever the reason, Schuyler skillfully took advantage of Burgoyne's blunder. He sent a thousand axmen to make Burgoyne's straight way crooked. They felled huge trees "as plenty as lampposts upon a highway about London."[91]

They destroyed every bridge and multiplied the area's numerous water obstacles by digging ditches. Schuyler sent out couriers to warn the inhabitants to drive off their cattle, and even induced them to burn their unharvested grain. He made a labyrinthine hell and a scorched earth of Burgoyne's southward path, and then, as the toiling British inched their way toward him, he withdrew from Fort Edward to Stillwater on the Hudson.

On July 29, three weeks from the day he had landed at Skenesboro, Burgoyne reached Fort Edward. It had taken him three weeks to advance 23 miles, seven of which had been over uncontested water. Exhausted, Burgoyne rested—while his Indians began exploring the surrounding countryside. One small but fateful band captured a young American woman named Jane McCrea.

Beautiful Jane McCrea was in love with her former neighbor, David Jones. But Jones was a Loyalist serving with Burgoyne. To be near him, Jane came to live with her patriot brother near Fort Edward. Hungering for news of the man she hoped to marry, Jane often visited the cabin of fat Mrs. McNeil, a cousin of the British General, Simon Fraser.

Because of these connections with Burgoyne, neither woman feared death or violence when Burgoyne's painted Indians broke into Mrs. McNeil's cabin. They were afraid, of course, but not for their lives. So Jane was placed on a horse and taken away to Burgoyne's camp, while other Indians struggled with the difficulty of getting her obese friend mounted. At last Mrs. McNeil went swaying off, clad in her chemise.

To her surprise, she arrived at Burgoyne's camp first. She was taken to Fraser. Red-faced, the general rushed to cover his huge cousin with his greatcoat. Then Jane's captors appeared.

They were trailing a scalp of long silken hair.

They had quarreled over Jane and had settled their dispute by killing her.

John Burgoyne was shocked. He had already been ridiculed for the high-flown speech in which he had enjoined tenderness upon his savages. He resolved to execute Jane's killer. But his officers, like generations of French and English officers before him, pointed out that to do so would alienate his Indians. Burgoyne reluctantly agreed, and the story of the brutal murder of Jane McCrea—embellished and magnified by patriot propagandists—soon enflamed the countryside with patriotic anger.

It was white-hot in the hearts of militia gathering across the border in New Hampshire and Vermont.

"I have three thousand dollars in hard money," Speaker John Langdon is supposed to have told the General Court of New Hampshire. "I will pledge my plate for three thousand more. I have seventy hogsheads of Tobago rum, which shall be sold for the most it will bring. These are at the service of the State. If we succeed in defending our homes, I may be remunerated. If we do not, the property will be of no value to me. Our old friend Stark, who so nobly susstained the honor of our State at Bunker's Hill, may be safely entrusted with the conduct of the enterprise, and we will check the progress of Burgoyne."[92]

General Stark said he would lead the brigade. But it would be a New Hampshire Brigade only. He wanted no truck with that Congress which had snubbed John Stark (as it had snubbed Benedict Arnold) by promoting green and untried junior colonels over his head. So Stark gathered nearly 1,500 men and marched them toward Manchester in Vermont 20 miles north of Bennington.

Here, General Schuyler ordered Stark to join him in the south at Stillwater. Stark refused. He took his orders from the New Hampshire General Court and no one else. Major General Benjamin Lincoln rebuked Stark, and so too did Congress later on, but John Stark had already decided that Bennington was the place to be. He marched his men south, leaving word for Colonel Seth Warner and the Green Mountain Boys to join him at Bennington.

Baron von Riedesel did not believe that his Brunswick Dragoons could take the American wilderness much longer. They needed horses. They were ridiculous on foot. Wearing enormous 12-pound jack boots, they were constantly tripping over the long broadswords trailing from their hips, and their short heavy carbines were not made for forest warfare. Men in great cocked hats with long white plumes might be the envy of the Indians, but they were also unenviable targets as they stumbled along in tight, thick coats, stiff leather breeches and huge gauntlets nearly elbow length. No, the Brunswickers needed mounts. Riedesel told Burgoyne so, and the British commander, now also in need of cattle for his hungry men, as well as horses to replace those hundreds which had perished in this sweltering green hell of a province, decided to send out a foraging expedition to the Connecticut River valley.

A force of about 500 men under Lieutenant Colonel Friedrich Baum was to secure these badly needed supplies. Their expedition was to be a secret one, and therefore, in the curious custom of the day, a German band was going along, plus 150 of those blundering Brunswickers.

The target for the raid was Bennington.

Colonel Baum's "stealthy" advance was so harassed by militia hanging on his front like a swarm of bees that he became uneasy and sent back to Burgoyne for reinforcements.

Lieutenant Colonel von Breymann was quickly dispatched with about 650 men and two guns. Using parade-ground formations in the woods, Breymann hurried to the rescue at the rate of about one mile an hour.

On August 15, a rainy day, Baum's force nearly collided with Stark's brigade marching down from Bennington along Walloomsack Creek. Baum immediately took a position on high ground and dug in. Next day Stark attacked.

He did not launch a headlong frontal assault. Instead, he sent knots of men in shirt sleeves idling forward. They wore the Loyalist white paper badge in their hats. Major Skene, who had accompanied Baum, told him they were Tories. Baum allowed the men to get onto his flank and rear. It was then that Stark is supposed to have uttered his famous battle cry:

"There, my boys, are your enemies. You must beat them, or Molly Stark is a widow tonight!"[93]

Baum's Indians and Tories quickly fled, but his regulars fought on until their ammunition was exhausted. The Brunswickers drew their swords and tried to cut their way out. But the enraged Yankees herded them back into the slaughter pen. Baum fell dying and only nine of his 374 Germans escaped death or capture. At noon it was all over, which was just when Breymann arrived with reinforcements.

So, too, did Seth Warner with reinforcements for Stark. Between them they fell on Breymann so ferociously that they sent him thrashing backward with casualties of about 230 dead, wounded and captured. Stark lost only 30 killed and 40 wounded during both actions.

General Burgoyne, who seemed to have forgotten Bunker Hill, was stunned. Once again, like William Howe, he had underestimated the American capacity for rising to crisis. But the Battle of Bennington was only the first—though perhaps the heaviest—of the blows that fell on Burgoyne's head. Far to the west, a second was also being delivered.

Barry St. Leger had moved with his mixed force of Tories, Indians and regulars from Oswego on Lake Ontario toward Albany, where he planned to make juncture with Burgoyne. Between him and the Mohawk River, however, stood Fort Stanwix with about 750 men under Colonel Peter Gansevoort and Lieutenant Colonel Marinus Willet. On August 3 St. Leger confidently invested the fort.

Once again the Americans rose to the occasion. Eight hundred New York militia flocked to the standard of General Nicholas Herkimer, and marched to relieve Stanwix. Molly Brant, the Mohawk widow of Sir William Johnson, notified St. Leger of their approach, and Joseph Brant, her brother, laid an ambush in a wooded ravine near Oriskany. Herkimer blundered into it. A dreadful fire swept his ranks, and yet the Americans refused to panic. They had seen the faces of their despised Tory neighbors in the woods around them, and they fought back in a vicious, bullet-for-bullet, knife-for-knife melee.

Herkimer, mortally wounded, lay with his back against a tree, pipe in mouth, giving his orders. As the battle continued, Willet in Fort Stanwix led a sally against the weakened British camp. He captured and sacked it. Hearing of the enemy in their rear, the Indians and Loyalists fled and Herkimer's force withdrew.

St. Leger, however, rallied his men and reinvested the fort. During a howling night storm, Willet crept through enemy lines to reach Schuyler's camp at Stillwater and plead for relief. Schuyler consented, and was at once assailed by his critics for "weakening" the northern army. Enraged, the "damned Dutchman" bit his pipe stem in two and called for a volunteer brigadier to command the expedition. None stepped forward.

Benedict Arnold, at last a major general, eagerly took command. With a thousand volunteers he moved toward Stanwix. Arnold's plan was to frighten the enemy by a ruse revolving around a half-crazy prisoner named Hon-Yost Schuyler. Arnold told the man's mother he was going to hang Hon-Yost unless he returned to St. Leger with a report that the Americans were coming in overwhelming strength. The woman persuaded her half-wit son to agree. Holding her other son as a hostage, Arnold had Hon-Yost's coat shot full of holes and set him hurrying to St. Leger. Next, he dispatched a friendly Oneida Indian to confirm the half-wit's tale.

Hon-Yost arrived in St. Leger's camp. The Indians asked him how many men Arnold had. Hon-Yost pointed to the leaves of the trees, at which point the Oneida Indian arrived to support him. That was enough for St. Leger's red allies. Seizing supplies of rum and clothing, they fled. The Loyalists followed, and St. Leger quickly withdrew to Oswego, leaving his tents behind him.

He would not make rendezvous with Burgoyne that fall.

Burgoyne now knew that his situation was desperate. He could expect no help from Howe. The very day that St. Leger had invested Stanwix, he had received a letter from Sir William saying: "My intention is for Pennsylvania, where I expect to meet Washington, but if he goes to the northward and you can keep him at bay, be assured I shall soon be after him to relieve you. After your arrival at Albany, the movements of the enemy will guide yours."⁹⁴

If Burgoyne had ever expected to effect a juncture with the main British Army, it must have been clear to him then that it was now out of the question. He had to push on to Albany. And yet the Americans between him and that city were growing stronger daily.

Horatio Gates now commanded the Americans. Congress, searching for a scapegoat for Ticonderoga, had removed Schuyler on August 4. But by August 19, the date of Gates's arrival at the Ameriman works at Stillwater, the "damned Dutchman" had all but reversed the situation. Nevertheless, the northern army belonged to Gates, and it was growing into a force between 6,000 and 9,000 men. Burgoyne could not sit still while his enemy swelled into an over-powering force. On September 13, 1777, he crossed the Hudson and began pushing south.

Six miles north of Stillwater was the rolling ground known as Bemis Heights. The Americans had fortified this ground. But they had neglected a height on the far left. Burgoyne saw it. Possession of it would command the American positions just as Sugar Loaf had been the key to Ticonderoga. Burgoyne ordered Reidesel to move against the American right along the Hudson River, he himself would strike the patriot center at a place called Freeman's Farm, and Fraser would swing wide to the right to take the hill.

On September 19, a cool, clear day with the grass bright with frost, the assault began. Almost immediately Americans in the treetops spotted the movement of scarlet coats and flashing steel. Headquarters was notified. Arnold, who commanded the American left, wanted to attack at once at Freeman's Farm. Gates demurred. He wanted the British to come to him. Meanwhile, the British drove in the patriot pickets at Freeman's. Arnold again expostulated, and Gates reluctantly gave him Morgan's riflemen and Henry Dearborn's New Hampshire Regiment. They were too successful. Morgan's sharpshooters all but annihilated Fraser's advance guard, but then, pressing the pursuit too eagerly, they too were routed. Morgan stood almost alone, tears of chagrin coursing down his seamed face, while he sounded his famous turkey call to rally his men to him. They returned, and Arnold, having checked Fraser on his left, began probing for the British weak spot.

He found it between Fraser and Burgoyne at Freeman's Farm. Here he eagerly fed in fresh regiments. A pitched battle ensued. Now the Americans drove the British back and seized their guns. But they could not fire them because the gunners had carried off all the linstocks holding the slow matches. When the Americans attempted to haul the guns away, the British came charging back with the bayonet.

American riflemen in the trees then trained their sights on British officers and gunners. They scourged them. General Phillips riding up to see to the guns found every artillery officer save one shot down and 36 out of 48 artillerymen stricken. Phillips called for four more guns and got them, but they soon ran out of ammunition. Again and again the British tried to carry the day with their favorite weapon, the bayonet. But the Americans repulsed them.

Now Arnold saw his chance. The British center under Burgoyne was faltering. He needed only a few more men to strike the knockout blow. He appealed to Gates and was refused. Late in the afternoon Gates changed his mind, but he sent the reinforcement to the left rather than the center. The golden opportunity had passed, and Baron von Riedesel was already marching up from the British right to stiffen Burgoyne. The Americans retreated, and as night fell the Battle of Freeman's Farm came to an end.

The British occupied the field and were the technical victors. However, they had lost between 500 and 600 men and the Americans only slightly more than 300. Burgoyne was weakened for the next round, and even as it was preparing, the Americans were busy in his rear, recapturing almost all of the lost positions around Ticonderoga and threatening to sever his line of communications.

Burgoyne *had* to try again, or else retreat ignominiously into Canada. Henry Clinton in New York with Howe's rear guard had promised help, but Clinton was moving slowly. He did not move against the patriot forts on the Hudson until October 3. He stormed them successfully, after some bitter fighting, and wrote cheerfully to Burgoyne: "*Nous y voici,* and now nothing between us but Gates. I sincerely hope this little success of ours may facilitate your operations."[95] Unfortunately, the courier whom Clinton sent north was captured by the Americans and forced to vomit up the silver bullet containing the message.

A few days later one of Burgoyne's couriers finally reached Clinton, and the alarmed general immediately sent a fleet upriver to burn Kingston while he hastened back to New York to collect reinforcements. By then, however, Burgoyne was attacking at Bemis Heights.

Three months in the American wilderness had so frazzled Burgoyne's troops that they were little better than animated bags of bones. Yet, in spite of this, perhaps because of this, Burgoyne resolved on a last desperate fling. Over the objections of some of his generals, he called for another swing at the American left. About 1,500 men would attempt to turn it. If they were successful, more would be fed in. Unknown to Burgoyne, the chances of success were higher than usual, for Horatio Gates had relieved Benedict Arnold of command.

Gates's reports of Freeman's Farm had ignored Arnold's leading role. Arnold angrily challenged Gates on the issue and then demanded a pass to Washington. Gates was only too eager to comply, but then Arnold's officers persuaded him not to leave. Nevertheless, Gates took over the left wing while Benjamin Lincoln held the right. Thus, when the British scarlet was again sighted through the trees on the left, it was Gates who ordered Daniel Morgan "to begin the game."

It was not long after Gates's holding action began, however, before a short stocky man on a big brown horse came sweeping onto the field. Cheer after cheer and man after man followed Arnold as he led a headlong charge against the British center. With his unerring eye, Arnold had found the soft spot, and an entire German unit collapsed. Now Arnold saw that Simon Fraser was skillfully rallying the enemy. He turned to Morgan and asked him to bring Fraser down. Morgan called for Tim Murphy, a legendary Indian fighter and rifleman. Murphy climbed a tree and aimed his double-barreled rifle.

His first shot creased the crupper of Fraser's horse. The second parted the horse's mane. Alarmed, Fraser's officers tried to draw him away. Fraser refused, and Murphy's next shot killed him.

With his fall, the last hope of British success perished. They withdrew to the shelter of earthworks, and it was then that Arnold called for the crusher. Spurring his horse, he rode against the left of the position. He and his men were repulsed. Riding madly across the line of battle, Arnold commandeered another general's brigade and sent it smashing into the earthworks and swept the enemy clean away.

Now a redoubt on the British right held by Breymann was exposed. Collecting two more regiments, Arnold came riding down on it. Breymann was mortally wounded, but Arnold was also shot—in the same leg that had been hit at Quebec. It was then, with the redoubt carried, with Burgoyne's main position open on his right and rear, that an officer sent by Gates came up to Arnold with orders to return to quarters before he did something rash.

Arnold returned on a litter and the battle quietly fizzled out. Burgoyne had lost 600 men, the Americans 150, and the Battle of Bemis Heights had been the last nail in the coffin of Burgoyne's army.

Leaving 500 sick and wounded, Burgoyne withdrew to Saratoga. Gates quickly built entrenchments across the Hudson. By October 11 he had Burgoyne completely surrounded. Gentleman Johnny called four despairing councils of war. At length he accepted black reality: surrender.

Even so, he asked for terms; and Gates, fearing that Clinton might come up in his rear, allowed Burgoyne to name his own. But then Burgoyne, also aware of Clinton's approach, began to stall for time. Gates threatened to renew hostilities and Burgoyne signed the famous "Convention" of Saratoga whereby his exhausted little army of less than 5,000 men laid down its arms on October 17.

Ticonderoga, Bennington, Stanwix, Oriskany, Freeman's Farm, Bemis Heights, Saratoga—all those separate actions which, woven together, form the single tapestry called the Battle of Saratoga—had culminated in one of the most decisive victories in the history of mankind.

Saratoga's effects were immediate and enormous. It spurred Congress to adopt the Articles of Confederation and send them to the separate states for ratification. More immediately important, the American victory at Saratoga brought the Bourbons into the war against England. France, watching warily, threw off all pretense of "neutrality" once Burgoyne's defeat and the surrender of a British army became known. On December 12 the Count Vergennes met with the American commissioners in Paris. Two months later he signed an alliance with the United States and after that declared war on Britain. Spain followed suit in 1779, then came Holland, ordering her Dutch West Indies to increase their aid to the Americans. Catherine of Russia followed, organizing a League of Armed Neutrality which deterred British trade. There was no longer any need of Beaumarchais and his little deception at Hortalez et Cie. Now ships and soldiers and supplies in great quantities came flowing out to America from France.

Back across the Atlantic sailed Gentleman Johnny Burgoyne. Perhaps he remembered what Charles James Fox had said to him after he had recorded that wager for victory in the betting book at Brooks's:

"Be not oversanguine in your expectations. I believe when next you return to England you will be a prisoner on parole."[96]

And he was.

14

☆

The good news from Saratoga came to Washington adulterated with the sour taste of the so-called Conway Cabal.

General Thomas Conway was an Irish-born officer of the French Army. It is his name that describes a "plot" that was actually not a plot but a haphazard coalescing of Washington's numerous critics. Among these were Samuel Adams, John Adams occasionally, Richard Henry Lee and other powerful Congressmen. They wished to replace Washington with the popular Gates.

The glory of Saratoga had served to exaggerate the shame of Germantown and the Brandywine, and since Gates had been careful to claim credit for that victory it was he who was named president of the revived Board of War. Technically, he became Washington's superior. Next, Congress named Conway as Inspector General, much to the indignation of Washington, who held Conway in contempt.

Actually Conway was a competent professional, but his tongue was unfortunately as sharp as his sword. He had already written Congress criticizing the drinking habits of Lord Stirling, after which he wrote a letter of high praise to Gates and asked if he might serve under him. In that letter, Conway was critical of Washington.

Major James Wilkinson, Gates's aide, saw Conway's letter. He mentioned it to a friend who was Lord Stirling's adjutant. Stirling was informed, and with happy malice passed the information along to Washington. Now Washington, probably using the pen of Alexander Hamilton, wrote a stinging rebuke to Conway, who denied all criticism. Gates heard of this and dashed off an angry letter to Washington protesting his innocence of disloyalty and demanding to know who was spying on his correspondence.

Washington named Wilkinson. Gates turned on his aide so furiously that Wilkinson challenged him to a duel. Gates declined the honor. But Conway did not decline when General John Cadwalader later challenged *him* to a duel, and he was so badly wounded in it that, believing himself near death, he wrote a letter of apology to Washington. Conway eventually recovered and returned to France

Before he did, however, Gates made a grievous error. He and his Board of War proposed an "irruption" into Canada. When it became clear to Congress that such an expedition was foredoomed to bloody humiliation, Gates's popularity declined and the Board of War's prestige sank to a low from which it never recovered.

Thus the Conway Cabal, and if history has shown that Gates probably did not desire Washington's hat, the fact remains that Washington and his officers thought that he did, and that criticisms raised by Congressmen safe in their snuggery at York were heard by men passing through the ordeal of that dreadful winter at Valley Forge.

It was not the cold (actually it was a mild winter) that made the Continentals suffer so, but rather a bungling quartermaster department and the selfish avarice of American farmers and merchants. Soldiers at Valley Forge went hungry because nearby farmers preferred to sell to the British in Philadelphia for hard cash, because New York's grain surplus was diverted to New England civilians and the British in New York City, and because Connecticut farmers refused to sell beef cattle at ceiling prices imposed by the state. Soldiers went half-naked because merchants in Boston would not move government clothing off their shelves at anything less than profits ranging from 1,000 to 1,800 percent. Everywhere in America there was a spirit of profiteering and a habit of graft that made Washington grind his teeth in helpless fury. In response to his appeals, Congress passed the buck by authorizing him to commandeer supplies. This he was reluctant to do among a people supposed to be trying to throw off the yoke of a tyrant. When he was forced to do it, the results confirmed his fears.

And so every night for too many weeks sticklike soldiers stuck their heads out of their smoky huts to cry, "No meat! No meat!" Firecake and water was their food, bloody footprints in the snow their sign. Their clothes were so ragged and blankets were so scarce that they often sat up all night rather than fall asleep and freeze to death. Although they had little sustenance themselves, body lice managed to feed on them. Lafayette was horrified to see soldiers whose legs had frozen black and who had to be carted off to hospitals that were little better than death terminals to have their limbs amputated. One bitter Continental wrote: "Poor food—hard lodging—Cold Weather—fatigue—Nasty Cloaths—nasty Cookery—Vomit half my time—smoak'd out of my senses—the Devil's in it—I can't Endure it—Why are we sent here to starve and freeze . . . ?"[97]

Officers fared hardly better, and the sight of them wrapped in filthy blankets astonished Lieutenant General the Baron von Steuben, former aide to the King of Prussia, upon his arrival at Valley Forge.

He had not been a lieutenant general for very long, he was not a real baron, his service with King Frederick had been very brief, and his last rank in the Prussian Army had been that of captain. However, a wise French minister of war, recognizing both Steuben's abilities and the fact that he needed some fancy titles to impress the Americans, had invested him with a counterfeit nobility. Eventually the Americans became aware of the deception, but by then they could not have cared less.

Steuben was the father of the American Army. Seeing what he saw at Valley Forge, he told Washington that no European army could ever have endured such hardship, and then set himself to give the hardy Continentals the discipline and uniformity that they so grievously lacked. He established his own system of drill, adapting the Prussian method to American conditions, and substituted it for the differing drills of the various states. Then, having endeared himself to the officers by holding a party at which no man with a whole pair of breeches might attend, he horrified them by insisting that they drill their men in person.

In this republican army the officers let the sergeants handle drill, some of the higher ranks lived in comfortable houses far away from the rows of filthy huts, and others made servants of their soldiers. Steuben, the Prussian, changed all this—and he did it by example.

Here was a lieutenant general standing in the mud or snow waving his arms and howling in German, French and bastard English at privates who thought a bayonet was for roasting meat over a fire. And the troops loved him. He made them obey, but he also made them laugh. Shrewd showman that he was, Steuben let them. Once, having blown up at a particularly slow company, he turned to a young officer named Benjamin Walker and gasped:

"*Viens, Valkaire, mon ami, mon bon ami! Sacré!* Goddam de *gaucheries* of dese *badauds. Je ne puis plus.* I can curse dem no more."[98]

By spring Washington had an army that could march and maneuver, and he was eager to use it against the British departing Philadelphia.

When Benjamin Franklin was informed that Howe had captured Philadelphia, he shook his head and said, "No, Philadelphia has captured Howe!"[99] Franklin was right. Howe and his officers gave themselves over to balls, theatrics, horse racing and wine, much to the despair of the Tories, who wanted the British to go out and destroy the Yankee vermin in their nest at Valley Forge. Howe's dalliance with blonde Betsey Loring so exasperated the Tories that one of them wrote:

> Awake, arouse, Sir Billy,
> There's forage on the plain,
> Ah, leave your little filly,
> And open the campaign.[100]

Howe, however, would open no more campaigns. He had asked Lord George Germain to relieve him from "this very painful service," and in May of 1778 he handed over the American command to Sir Henry Clinton, now also a Knight of the Bath. Before Howe departed, he was honored at an extravagant pageant called the "Mischianza."

It was organized by the dashing Captain John André, who had passed the winter courting the lovely Peggy Shippen, daughter of a wealthy Philadelphian. Peggy did not attend the Mischianza, because her father would not permit her to wear Turkish bloomers like the other beautiful young Loyalists for whose smiles British officers, mounted as knights of old, shivered lances and crossed swords until the small hours of the morning of May 19.

As the Mischianza was breaking up, Howe was informed that Lafayette was in the vicinity with a large force. Actually, the young marquis was only on an armed reconnaissance. But Howe scented a last opportunity and tried to trap "the boy." It was then that von Steuben's value to the American cause became evident. Feinting and maneuvering precisely with disciplined troops, Lafayette made his escape.

On May 24 Howe sailed for home, having advised the Loyalists to make their peace with the patriots. Tory consternation turned to despair after Sir Henry Clinton announced that he was moving to New York. Clinton was acting on Germain's orders.

Germain knew that a large French fleet under Comte Charles d'Estaing was sailing for America. The French could bottle up Lord Howe's ships in the Delaware and catch Clinton's troops between themselves and Washington. So Clinton was making for New York, and he chose to go overland rather than give Washington the chance to make a cross-Jersey dash into the city before he could arrive by sea.

Clinton placed 3,000 grieving Tories aboard Admiral Lord Howe's ships, as well as two Hessian regiments of whose loyalty he was not sure, and then, as the ships dropped down the Delaware, he and Lord Cornwallis led the British Army across the river into New Jersey.

On June 27, with his forces strung out for a dozen miles along the road to Sandy Hook, he stopped to bivouac for the night at Monmouth Court House.

Washington's plan was to attack Clinton's rear guard at Monmouth, and the man who was eventually to lead the operation was General Charles Lee.

Lee had been exchanged. He had also been changed. He had spent his captivity advising his captors how to crush the Americans, and he had returned to his old comrades convinced that they could not win. Lee scoffed at Steuben's drill and swore that the Americans could never hope to meet European troops on even terms. During the council of war called by Washington after he had caught up to Clinton it was Lee who argued most vehemently against attack. When Washington decided otherwise and offered Lee the command of the advanced corps which was to strike Clinton, Lee refused it. But then, seeing the corps grow to a force of about 5,000 men, he changed his mind and rode forward to supersede Lafayette.

Clinton had started out on the road to Sandy Hook at about eight in the morning of June 28, 1778. He left behind a covering force of about 1,500 or 2,000 men. Lee proposed to cut off and destroy this force. But he had no definite plan of battle, his commanders had no idea of what to do, and the Americans moving along the road toward the British at Monmouth became an uncoordinated mass. Individual unit fights began. Clinton, hearing them, turned about to come to the rescue of his rear guard. He placed his troops on the east side of the road facing the Americans on the west side.

Lee ordered Lafayette to attack the British left. Lafayette did not believe he was in position to attack. He moved to a different position, unmasking the other divisions, which quickly began falling back. Soon all the units were pulling back, Lafayette among them, and then Lee gave the order for retreat.

Whether or not Lee had actually averted a crushing blow by Clinton, as his defenders later maintained, whether or not he had led the withdrawal with a smug spirit of I-told-you-so, the fact is that Washington did not want a retreat. He was coming east along the road with his main body. When he rode up on the great white horse presented to him that day by Governor Livingston of New Jersey and found himself surrounded by streams of backpedaling soldiers, he lost his temper in the most spectacular outburst of his career.

His face livid, sitting his horse like the splendid equestrian figure he was, Washington came galloping down on Charles Lee with all the wrath of the God of Battles. What he actually called him is not certainly known. There are many versions, but the best description came from General Charles Scott, who was there and later recalled: "Yes, sir, he swore that day till the leaves shook on the trees. Charming! Delightful! Never have I enjoyed such swearing before or since. Sir, on that memorable day, he swore like an angel from heaven!"[101] ·

Ordering Lee to the rear, Washington stopped the retreat. He stopped it by his magnificent presence, riding easily among the men, re-forming them, inspiring them by his calm courage. Galloping down the road to Monmouth, he halted two retreating regiments, and ordered them to hold the advancing British until he could re-form the American line behind them. Choosing high ground just west of a ravine, Washington put Greene on the right, himself in the center, and Stirling on the left. Behind him Lafayette commanded the second line, while Wayne held an outpost in Washington's front.

Cheering and charging with typical fury, the British struck first at Stirling's men on the left. A desperate hour-long battle punctuated by an artillery duel ensued. Men fought each other in sweltering 100-degree heat. Everywhere soldiers were fainting from fatigue. And here, as Steuben watched with satisfaction, Washington was at last able to maneuver like an eighteenth-century general. Stirling's position was saved when American regiments wheeled into line under fire and worked around the British right flank, forcing them to retire.

Clinton next hurled his finest troops against Greene on the right. Cornwallis personally led the assault. But volley after volley of American musketry, thickened by the shot of an artillery crossfire, repulsed the British.

Meanwhile, Wayne in the front-center was also under attack by a force led by Lieutenant Colonel Henry Monckton. "Forward to the charge, my brave grenadiers!" Monckton cried, and the scarlet waves surged forward. "Steady, steady!" Wayne cautioned his men. "Wait for the word, then pick out the king-birds!"[102] Wayne gave the word at 40 yards, and the volley that crashed out was so devastating that it broke the attack. Monckton fell so close to the Americans that they leaped out to seize his body and his battalion colors.

Wayne then withdrew, outflanked on either side by a fourth British line—but by then the battle was over. Both sides occupied the field that night. Washington lay under an oak tree with Lafayette beside him. At midnight, however, Clinton arose and led his men quietly away. He had saved his rear guard and thus, if there was any victor, it was he. Washington had not accomplished much in a military way, but his men had fought the British regulars to a standstill in open battle. A new spirit now informed a new American army.

Meanwhile, an old war dog was snapping his last. Outraged, Charles Lee demanded a court-martial. He was found guilty of disobedience, of making "an unnecessary and, in some few instances, a disorderly retreat," and of disrespect of his commander in chief. Lee was sentenced to a year's suspension from the service and Congress approved the sentence. Hearing his fate, Lee is reported to have cried: "O that I were a dog, that I might not call man my brother."[103] Later he wrote an insulting letter to Congress which boomeranged with his dismissal from the service.

And so Washington's chief military critic had passed from the scene. After Monmouth Washington's position as commander in chief was secure. After Monmouth also the two main armies did not meet again. The War of the Revolution was fought by detachments and subordinate units, while the old golden lilies of France, once detested in America, reappeared beside that new standard of "thirteen stripes alternate red and white, [with] thirteen stars white in a blue field."

15

☆

The Comte d'Estaing had taken too long crossing the Atlantic. He had held practice maneuvers en route and he arrived off the Delaware capes on July 8, 1778, ten days too late to intercept Admiral Howe's vulnerable transports.

Howe had also ferried Clinton's troops across the Lower Harbor into Manhattan, after which he put about to block d'Estaing's entry into the port. Here, the new Franco-American alliance met its first test. Would d'Estaing, with a fleet nearly double the strength of Howe's, risk crossing the bar at Sandy Hook to close with the British? The answer was no.

The French admiral spent ten days cautiously taking soundings. His best chance came on July 22 when wind and a high tide raised 30 feet of water over the bar, but d'Estaing bowed to the warnings of his pilots and stood away to the south.

New York, the very hub of British power in America, had been spared. Perhaps it had been spared because the French admiral was not too eager to end the war with a single blow and thus free Britain to turn all her power against his own country. History does not say, but the fact remains that the Franco-American alliance was, at its outset, put to a severe strain.

Washington was disappointed at the missed opportunity, and within the next few days reports of British-led Indian massacres of western settlers increased his dismay. On July 4—to mock American independence—Colonel Sir John Butler struck at the Wyoming Valley in Pennsylvania. Hundreds perished. Men were burnt at the stake or thrown on beds of coals and held down with pitchforks while their horrified families were forced to witness their torment. Others were placed in a circle while a half-breed squaw called Queen Esther danced chanting around them to chop off their heads. Soon the entire frontier was in flames, with Washington unable to come to its rescue.

All the commander in chief's resources were at that moment directed toward recovering Newport from the British. Sullivan with about 10,000 men divided between Greene and Lafayette had marched north of the vital port city to make rendezvous with d'Estaing's 4,000 French soldiers. But Clinton and "Black Dick" Howe acted quickly to discomfit them. Clinton collected a force of 5,000 to come to the aid of General Pigot, who held Newport with about 3,000 troops, while Howe, now reinforced, crowded on all sail for Rhode Island.

Hearing of Howe's approach, d'Estaing re-embarked his troops and sailed out to meet Howe. Sullivan was furious, but the Frenchman would not change his mind. On the night of August 11 the ships of both fleets were scattered by a violent storm, and both had to sail away for repairs—Howe to New York and d'Estaing to Boston.

In the meantime, the French withdrawal had so disgusted Sullivan's militia that more than 5,000 of them went home. Sullivan had to backpedal furiously away from the eagerly pursuing Pigot, and the Newport expedition ended in a fiasco. Sullivan was openly critical of his allies, and there were some tense moments in Boston after a French officer was killed during riots between sailors and soldiers of both nations—but tempers eventually cooled, especially after d'Estaing sailed away for Martinique on November 4.

A week later Walter ("Hellhound") Butler, the bloodier son of Sir John Butler, ravaged the patriot settlement of Cherry Valley in western New York. Assisted by Joseph Brant, Butler put the town to the torch. Then, with the American frontier being pushed back and ravaged, the British moved south.

In November of 1778 Clinton sent about 3,500 regulars and Tories under Lieutenant Colonel Archibald Campbell against Savannah, a port which not only offered entrance into the most southern colonies but also linked them with the West Indies. Campbell was to be assisted by General Augustine Prevost, marching up from St. Augustine in Florida.

Opposing them was Major General Robert Howe with about 1,000 Georgia and South Carolina militia. Howe took position to the east of Savannah with his right resting on a swamp and his left on rice paddies. Campbell feinted through the paddies while another column, led by a Negro slave, slipped through the swamp and turned the Americans' right. At that juncture Campbell converted his feint into a strike and both columns closed on the patriots, putting them to rout and inflicting about 500 casualties against a handful of their own lost.

The date of Savannah's fall was December 29, and after that the British, now under Prevost, set about clearing Georgia.

Up north, both Washington and Clinton had gone into winter quarters, the British in and around New York, Washington in a great arc beginning in Middletown, New Jersey, not far from Monmouth and stretching on through West Point and Fishkill in New York and thence east to Danbury, Connecticut.

It was a mild winter and the troops were relatively comfortable, a small blessing for which the harried Washington found it difficult to be thankful after having seen the campaign of 1778 begin so brightly only to fizzle out in the end.

16

☆

    While the chief commanders and their armies wintered in the North, fighting flared in the South and on the western border.

    In Georgia, capture of Savannah had been tantamount to conquest of the state. After the arrival of General Prevost the state was once more subjected to the Crown, and as 1779 began, Georgia's inhabitants "flocked by hundreds to the King's officers, and made their peace at the expense of their patriotism."[104]

    Soon Prevost moved against South Carolina, where he was opposed by Benjamin Lincoln commanding about 3,000 ragged Continentals and untrained militia. There ensued a series of marches and countermarches, skirmishes and small pitched battles, clashes between Tories and patriots marked by brutality and depredations on both sides, and although the British regulars certainly could claim most of the victories, the net result of the campaign was that Prevost withdrew to Georgia, and South Carolina remained in the rebel camp.

    In the West a dashing frontiersman named George Rogers Clark struck a sharp blow at the British. Acting for Virginia, which was anxious to nail down its old claims to the Northwest, Clark had begun clearing the Illinois country during the previous summer by capturing posts at Kaskaskia and Vincennes. But then the British under the unsavory Colonel Henry Hamilton—the "Hair-buyer," as he was known to the settlers—recaptured Vincennes. Hearing of this, Clark rushed to Kaskaskia about 150 miles to the southwest. In early February he led a tiny force of 130 men, half of them French, against Vincennes. Few marches in American history equal the ordeal which awaited Clark's men. Torrential rains and floods barred their path. Much of the time they floundered through icy water up to their chests. Men who sank beneath the surface were fished up and placed in canoes. But Clark urged them on, ever onward, until at last they debouched before Vincennes. Here Clark deceived Hamilton's superior force by marching his little band back and forth to create the impression of a thousand men approaching. That was enough for Hamilton's Indians. Then, after Clark's sharpshooters began picking off the fort's defenders, Hamilton asked for talks. To make up Hamilton's mind, Clark had five Indians, who had been captured with scalps in their possession, tomahawked in full view of the garrison. Hamilton surrendered Vincennes.

Although Clark had given British power north of the Ohio a severe check, he had not destroyed it—if only because he could not capture Fort Detroit. As a result, warfare of the savage border kind was to be renewed in the Illinois country.

Meanwhile, with the advent of summer, General Washington moved to retaliate against the British and Indians who had ravaged the Wyoming and Cherry valleys the year before. He sent General Sullivan and about 5,000 men to destroy Iroquois towns and to capture Fort Niagara, the base for their raids. Niagara, however, was not taken, although the Indians were severely scourged by Sullivan leading one column up the Susquehanna from the Wyoming Valley and General James Clinton pushing up the Mohawk Valley with another. No less than 40 Iroquois towns were destroyed and the people of the Long House were struck a blow from which they never completely recovered. Standing crops were ruined, granaries burned and orchards cut down. In the cruel winter of 1779-80 which followed, hundreds of Indian families starved to death. Still, the British and Indians were not completely suppressed, and it remained for the kingdom of Spain to deal Britain her most severe blow in that summer of 1779.

On June 16, 1779, Spain declared war on Britain, and at once seriously complicated the problem of subduing the American colonies.

The British fleet, already spread thin over the vast new empire, now found it necessary to reinforce Gibraltar and Minorca. The West Indies came under the threat of a Spanish fleet at Havana and a French fleet and army at Santo Domingo. D'Estaing began to take island after island away from Britain, with the result that Sir Henry Clinton had to send 8,000 regulars from New York to the West Indies.

Clinton was so gravely weakened that he began considering the evacuation of New York. This was not done, but Newport, which had resisted both the French and the Americans the year before, was abandoned without a shot.

Then, in August, the mother country herself came under the guns of a Franco-Spanish fleet. For the first time since the Spanish Armada was routed in 1588, the "island set in a silver sea" was threatened with invasion. In his alarm, King George III tried to rally the people by reminding them how valiantly the subjects of Queen Elizabeth had met the same threat two centuries previously. His oratory was not needed, however, for the vast enemy fleet turned out to be only a "huge mob of ships." On August 16 as the combined fleets came in sight of Plymouth a storm drove them out of the Channel never to return. The Bourbons "talked big, threatened a great deal, did nothing, and retired."[105]

The only sailor who really twisted the British lion's tail in that year of 1779 was a renegade Scots captain named John Paul Jones.

British atrocities in America had so enraged the leaders of the Revolution that at one point Benjamin Franklin proposed the burning of English and Scottish cities in retaliation, and Congress authorized expeditions to set fire to London and burn the Royal Palace to the ground.

In the first years of the war, however, no daring firebrands volunteered to carry the torch across the sea. Most American sea captains were too busy taking profits as privateers. Armed with letters of marque authorizing them to take enemy ships as prizes—that is, to wage war for private profit—they took to the sea in such numbers and with such success that in 1777 Benjamin Franklin could declare that American shipping had grown richer by privateering than it had by commerce. Gradually, however, British privateers evened the score. The British Navy bottled up the Continental Navy in home ports, and it did not appear likely that Franklin's schemes of retaliation would ever be realized—until John Paul Jones stepped forward.

Born plain John Paul, Jones had knocked about the world as a cabin boy, ship's mate and finally a captain. Charged with murder in the West Indies, he proved his innocence but then faced a second charge of cruelty to his crew. With that, he changed his name and came to live in America. There, like many other British liberals, he became convinced that the Americans were upholding the rights of mankind against the forces of repression.

In 1778, in command of the *Ranger,* Jones attacked the English town of Whitehaven and burned ships in port. He also invaded Scottish soil, and soon he had so terrified the British coast that Lord North planned to send a special squadron against him as soon as Britain was free of the fear of Franco-Spanish invasion. Then, in September, 1779, Jones put out from France with his flagship *Bonhomme Richard,* 42 guns; the 32-gun frigates *Alliance* and *Pallas,* and the brigantine *Vengeance,* 12. At dusk of the 23rd, off the coast of northeast England, they sighted a British convoy escorted by *Serapis,* 50 guns, and *Countess of Scarborough,* 20.

Jones at once signaled his ships to form line while he made for *Serapis* in *Bonhomme Richard.* For some reason, *Alliance* stood off at a safe distance, while *Pallas* went after *Countess of Scarborough,* eventually capturing her. Undismayed at this lack of support, Jones engaged the heavier *Serapis.*

Richard's first broadside resulted in disaster: two of the three heavy guns on her engaged side burst, killing the crews and blowing up the deck above them. For fear of a repetition, the third gun was abandoned. Still undaunted, Jones put himself alongside *Serapis* and lashed both ships together. There they lay in the moonlight for two and a half hours, pounding each other at point-blank range.

At first it seemed that *Serapis* would prevail. Her guns splintered *Richard*'s rotten timbers and sent them flying. She scored numerous water-line hits and set *Richard* to leaking badly. And one by one she knocked out Jones's main battery of 28 12-pounders. Jones had only three 9-pounders left. All around him fires were breaking out and the pumps were falling behind the leaks. Still, he fought on. When one of his gunners called out to *Serapis* for quarter, he broke the man's skull with his pistol. When the captain of *Serapis* shouted for verification of the gunner's appeal, Jones bellowed back: "I have not yet begun to fight."[106] And when the British attempted to board him, he led the fight that repulsed them.

Yet, as badly as *Richard* had been hurt below, she had begun to conquer aloft. Under the direction of American officers, French marines in *Richard*'s fighting tops had cleared the enemy rigging of British seamen and had begun to pour a heavy fire into *Serapis.* Sniping, hurling grenades and combustibles, they cleared the Britisher's upper decks. Then a grenade thrown into a pile of cartridges on a lower deck set off a chain of explosions that racked *Serapis* from bow to stern. A half-hour later *Alliance* appeared and took up a raking position off the Britisher's bow. Some of *Alliance*'s shells struck *Richard* by mistake, but enough of them landed on *Serapis* to force the British captain to strike his colors.

By then *Bonhomme Richard* was a floating wreck, and Jones was compelled to transfer to *Serapis*. Nevertheless, he had won. By his refusal to submit, the indomitable John Paul Jones had humbled British naval pride, given the Continental Navy its greatest victory and bequeathed to the United States Navy one of its most cherished traditions. After his triumph, however, except for privateering and a few sea skirmishes, the American battle for freedom was fought exclusively on land.

The most that Sir Henry Clinton had been able to do in the North was to launch a series of destructive raids into Connecticut and to seize the Hudson River forts at Verplanck's Point and Stony Point. His objective in Connecticut was to lure Washington out of his new headquarters at West Point. But Washington, though angered by the frightfulness of the British raids, refused to budge. Instead, he sent Mad Anthony Wayne out to retake Stony Point.

Wayne led about 1,200 men of the American Light Infantry, the Continental Army's new elite. Remembering what "No-Flint" Grey had done to his own troops at Paoli's Tavern, he ordered most of his men to attack with bayonets only. On the night of July 15 all the inhabitants in the Stony Point area were taken into custody. Dogs on the line of march were destroyed to prevent their barking.

Moving along the river bank, wading through two feet of water, Wayne's men moved out silently. Just after midnight, under the guns of the fort, they parted into three columns and moved to the attack.

British sentries spotted Wayne's column on the right and opened fire. Wayne fell, stunned by a ball that grazed his skull. He got up on one knee and shouted to his men to go forward. Angered by his fall, the American light infantrymen went yelling against the fort. They overwhelmed it, and had to be restrained from using the bayonet to avenge Paoli.

It was a perfect little victory. Against American losses of 15 killed and 83 wounded, the British suffered 63 killed, about 70 wounded and 543 men captured. Only one man got away, and Wayne's triumph —even though Washington eventually evacuated Stony Point—forced Clinton to abandon his intention of a campaign in New Jersey.

Instead, he too evacuated Stony Point, and Verplanck's as well, sending the garrisons south to help defend Savannah against the French.

Washington hoped that Count d'Estaing would help him capture New York, and he daily awaited word that the French fleet had been sighted off the Delaware capes. But d'Estaing thought differently. Turning from his West Indies plunder, spurning the most valued prize, Jamaica, he sailed with his troops to recover Savannah from the British.

On September 12 about 3,500 French soldiers sailed up the Savannah River, came ashore and took up position south of the town. Three days later they were joined by Count Casimir Pulaski's mounted legion of 200 horsemen. On the 16th Benjamin Lincoln appeared with 600 Continentals and 750 militia. D'Estaing now had about 5,000 men against about 2,400 British, of whom the vast majority were Tories. If he attacked immediately he would undoubtedly overwhelm Prevost. Instead, he tried to take Savannah by summons. The wily Prevost asked for a truce, which he used to strengthen his position and await the arrival of Lieutenant Colonel Maitland from Port Royal to the north.

Maitland's march seemed hopeless. The French held the sea and Lincoln's army blocked him by land. Still, though ill of malaria himself, he led 800 regulars through a swamp, crossing the Savannah River under cover of a fog to make a most welcome addition to Prevost's fighting force. And then d'Estaing delayed further, deciding to try to take the town by regular approaches.

The first trenches were opened September 23, and on October 3 nearly 50 land guns, plus those of three ships in the river, began battering the city. Its fall seemed inevitable, and yet d'Estaing could not wait for it. Reports that Admiral "Foul-Weather Jack" Byron* was en route to Savannah with a British squadron made him fear for his ships. Storms of the season might scatter them. So he decided to attack Savannah.

* Grandfather of the poet.

Three columns were formed. One under General Count Dillon was to march to the British right rear and try to enter the town through the Sailor's Gate. A second under General Isaac Huger was to make a feint at the British left, while a third, the main blow, struck at the British right on the Spring Hill Redoubt.

Unfortunately for the Franco-Americans, Sergeant Major James Curry of the Charleston Grenadiers overheard the plan and revealed it to the British after he deserted. Prevost at once sent Maitland and a force of regulars to strengthen the Spring Hill Redoubt.

Early in the morning of October 9 Dillon's men began moving toward the Sailor's Gate. They blundered into a swamp, came out into the open and were repulsed by British fire. Dillon ordered a retreat. On the British left Huger made his appointed feint and Prevost calmly ignored it. Thus when d'Estaing and Lincoln sent the main body hurtling toward the Spring Hill Redoubt, the British were braced to receive them.

This they did with a dreadful hail of musketry and interlocking artillery fire which tumbled the American spearheads in heaps. On came the South Carolina Continentals led by the "Swamp Fox," Lieutenant Colonel Francis Marion. They reached the redoubt's parapet. Two officers raised their flag and were shot down. Another officer met a similar fate, and Sergeant Jaspar, who had bravely rescued the flag at Fort Moultrie, attempted it again at Savannah and was killed.

With Americans and French now milling wildly about outside the redoubt, Maitland launched a counterattack. The redcoats rushed from their fort and fell upon the enemy with fury. But they could not break them. A savage hand-to-hand fight raged for an hour, until the allies were finally driven back.

On their left, Count Pulaski and his legion tried to save the day with a cavalry charge. But a crossfire broke them up and the gallant Polish nobleman was himself killed. That was the end of the attempt to storm Savannah. D'Estaing refused Lincoln's plea to continue the siege operations. Stunned by losses of about 250 dead and 600 wounded, against British casualties of about 150, he re-embarked his troops and sailed away.

The French had failed a second time, to the great delight of the British and growing numbers of Southern Tories, and to the deep dismay of Washington entering winter quarters at Morristown for a second time.

Nothing in the history of the trials of the Continental Army, not even the ordeal of Valley Forge, compares to the cold white crucible of that second winter at Morristown. It was so cold that New York Harbor froze over. Howling blizzards lashed Morristown. Often officers as well as men were buried beneath deep drifts after the wind had blown their pitiful ragged tents away. Other soldiers without tents or blankets, barefoot and half-naked, struggled to build rude huts out of the oak and maple trees around them.

"We have never experienced a like extremity at any period of the war," Washington wrote, and soon he was complaining that his men lived off "every kind of horse food but hay." Another day he wrote: "We have not at this day one ounce of meat, fresh or salt, in the magazine."[107]

Food supplies grew scantier rather than more abundant. And once again, while the Continentals suffered and died, the countryside waxed fat and flourished. Washington's only choice was to commandeer supplies, and just as he feared, he was hated for it. The situation was summed up by Alexander Hamilton, who wrote: "We begin to hate the country for its neglect of us. The country begin to hate us for our oppressions of them."[108]

As the Continentals suffered, Congress struggled with the evil which was the chief cause of their misery: runaway inflation.

On the one hand there was a shortage of goods because of the British naval blockade and a boycott of British manufactures. On the other there was a demand aggravated by the requirements of the armed forces. Into this situation came unscrupulous merchants and speculators: the one raising prices again and again, the other "cornering" articles in short supply and controlling the market for them. Washington hated these wreckers of the American economy with a white-hot ferocity and he once wrote: "I would to God that one of the most attrocious of each State was hung in Gibbets upon a gallows five times as high as the one prepared by Haman. No punishment in my opinion is too great for the man who can build his greatness upon his Country's ruin."[109] But there was no way that Congress could check profiteers from amassing huge private fortunes. In rage, the Continentals blinked at the opulence of bloated rich men; starving, they heard of dinners in Philadelphia at which as many as 169 different dishes were served. Paid in Continental dollars, the army might have found it cheaper to wear or eat that near-worthless paper.

Paper currency was perhaps the chief cause of inflation. Not only Congress but every one of the 13 states had its own issue. The states refused Congress's plea to cease printing, and some even passed laws protecting their paper money. As a result, the paper printed by Congress became less and less acceptable. Congress had to print more and more currency in larger and larger denominations. Because there was little gold to back up this paper blizzard, the value of the Continental dollar fell. In 1776 four Continental dollars were worth one in gold, but by the end of 1779 the ratio was as high as 100 to one, and the phrase "not worth a Continental" was born.

In desperation, Congress repudiated the dollar, declaring on March 15, 1780, that 40 Continental dollars equaled one in gold. By this step Congress wiped out $200 million in debt, but it worsened the plight of the small wage-earner and the Continental soldier, who was paid in Continental paper.

If he had unwisely hoarded his meager pay, he was ruined. If he tried to buy anything with such money, he was rebuffed by farmers and merchants who demanded hard coin, or else twice as much as he thought his money was worth. Thus, as Washington wrote, "The long and great sufferings of this army is unexampled in history,"[110] and a Loyalist poet could confidently predict:

> Mock-money and mock-states shall melt away,
> And the mock troops disband for want of pay.[111]

As the campaign of 1780 opened, he looked like a true prophet.

17

☆

As the year 1780 began, Sir Henry Clinton moved to subjugate the South.

He still believed, with Lord Germain, that the South was Toryland. With Georgia now restored to the Crown, using Savannah as a base, he planned to conquer the Carolinas, then Virginia, after which, with his army augmented by a huge influx of Tories, he would reduce the Northern provinces. If he could not conquer the North, he could at least save the South for the Crown.

To begin, Clinton chose Charleston where he had begun before and failed. He arrived there on February 11 with 6,000 regulars and his second-in-command, Lord Cornwallis. Clinton moved slowly. Not until March 7 did he begin to erect batteries on the west bank of the Ashley River opposite the town.

Clinton's delay seemed a godsend to his opponent, Benjamin Lincoln. He began drawing all available troops into Charleston. Even the reinforcements sent south by Washington were quartered there. In the end this was a disastrous decision. About 5,000 men representing the American Army in South Carolina had been placed inside a noose.

Clinton, whose strength had risen to 10,000 men, began drawing the noose tight. Holding the Ashley River south of the town, he extended his line to the Cooper north of it. Then he moved to cut off communications by sea and by land. By sea, the British fleet took advantage of a thunderstorm to run past the once fearful batteries on Fort Moultrie; by land, the bold and brutal cavalry leader, Colonel Banastre Tarleton, routed a small force of American horse and militia which held Lincoln's communications open 30 miles up the Cooper. With his siege works inching ever closer to Charleston, Clinton at last began raining cannon balls and red-hot shot on the city. Haddrell's Point on the waterfront was carried on April 18 and the invincible Fort Moultrie fell on May 6. On May 8 Clinton called upon Lincoln to surrender. He refused, and Clinton's batteries began taking Charleston apart preparatory to an all-out assault. On May 12 Lincoln surrendered.

It was a dreadful defeat, a mass surrender of some 5,500 men, not to be equaled in the history of United States arms until the capitulation on Bataan in 1942.

Clinton made wise use of his victory. He turned a deaf ear to the clamoring of Tories eager for rebel blood and turned to the wholesale granting of pardons and paroles. His policy was so successful that more than 2,000 men volunteered to fight for the King, provided they served against Frenchmen or Spaniards, and a British officer observed: "The most violent Rebels are candid enough to allow the game is up."[112] And then Colonel Tarleton delivered what appeared to be the knockout blow.

His American legion of mounted Tories defeated a force of American cavalry under Colonel Abraham Buford. After the Americans were driven together in a mass, with white flag flying and arms grounded, the Tories fell upon them with sword and bayonet. That was "Tarleton's Quarter," a byword for the slaughter of surrendered men; yet it seemed to have stamped out the last sparks of opposition.

Sir Henry Clinton sailed back to New York leaving Cornwallis in charge. His Lordship took objective after objective at his leisure. He drove the patriots underground and Marion and Thomas Sumter into the swamps. South Carolina seemed a sure quarry, until the Tories got out of hand.

They started taking revenge for years of ill treatment, and because the state's Loyalists and patriots were evenly divided, nothing less than a civil war began in South Carolina. Men shot at each other in the woods and on the streets of towns. It was death by ambush, not face-to-face confrontations. Long after the war a magistrate boasted that he had shot down 99 Tories in cold blood and regretted that peace had prevented him from rounding out the score. And as Cornwallis's campaign began running into difficulty, word was received that the unabashed rebels were hurrying a force south to contest him.

At first it was the huge, ascetic Baron de Kalb who galloped south to collect and rally the scattered Americans. But because he was a foreigner who had no influential friends in Congress, someone else was sought as over-all commander in the South. Washington preferred Nathanael Greene, but Congress chose Horatio Gates.

Gates took over from de Kalb supremely confident. Fortune did seem to be smiling upon him. First, 3,000 Southern militia had swelled his command to 5,000 men, more than twice the number Cornwallis led. Second, as he advanced south rebels-turned-Tory turned rebel again. Third, he had heard that Cornwallis had returned to Charleston leaving Lord Rawdon in command at Camden. Gates decided to force a battle at Camden. His force was to begin marching to the attack at ten o'clock on the night of August 15. Before they did, they dined on half-cooked meat and half-baked bread with a dessert made of corn meal mush mixed with a medicinal molasses that turned out to be a physic. "Instead of enlivening our spirits," said Sergeant Major Seymour, it "served to purge us as well as if we had taken jallap."[113] So they moved out on a sullen sultry moonless night, the men constantly breaking ranks to relieve themselves. Before they met the enemy, they were sick and weary.

Cornwallis, who had returned to Camden, was also moving— toward Gates. The two forces met in an open pine forest between two swamps. Tarleton's Tories charged the American cavalry and drove them back, only to be repulsed themselves. Both sides awaited daylight. With it, the British light infantry assaulted the American left. It was the scarlet regular with his bayonet against the ragged militiaman with his musket, and the militia broke and ran.

They unmasked the left flank of de Kalb's Continentals on the American right, and the huzzaing British poured through the hole and struck de Kalb's rear. No braver fight was ever fought by the Continentals. Men from Maryland and Delaware rallied around their gigantic leader. De Kalb's horse was shot from under him, and he fought on foot. A saber laid his head open; he fought on.

As he did, Gates tried to rally the militia running away without their weapons. He failed, and fled himself. De Kalb battled on, still confident of victory. Cornwallis hurled his entire force of about 2,000 against this valiant band of 600. De Kalb called for a bayonet charge. Cheering, the Americans nearly burst the wall of scarlet surrounding them. Ball after ball staggered de Kalb. With his last stroke he cut down a British soldier, and then fell dying from 11 wounds.

That was the end at Camden, and it was also the end of the American Army career of General Horatio Gates. Before Gates stopped flying he had reached Hillsboro, North Carolina, 240 miles from the battlefield. No general ever fled his army more precipitately. "It does admirable credit to the activity of a man at his time of life,"[114] Alexander Hamilton jeered.   To the British victories at Charleston and Camden was added Tarleton's resounding defeat of General Sumter two days later. The South appeared lost to the rebel cause, and as the year 1780 turned toward fall, Benedict Arnold in the North was preparing to sell the Hudson River to the enemy.

Benedict Arnold loved money. He also loved beautiful Peggy Shippen, the fair friend of Captain John André and other British officers. Unlike some of her friends, Peggy had escaped ostracism when the patriots returned to Philadelphia in 1778. Because Peggy's father would not let her wear Turkish bloomers she had missed the Mischianza, and since nonattendance at that gala farewell to Sir William Howe had been made the test of loyalty, Peggy was acceptable to the Americans.

Above all to Major General Arnold, now in command in Philadelphia. On April 8, 1779, Arnold married Peggy and brought her to live with him in the Penn house surrounded by elegance and a staff of liveried servants. Such opulence was beyond a general's salary, and Arnold was already accused of using his position to make money. He was also awaiting court-martial on those old charges of misuse of public funds. Moreover, Arnold, probably the most capable field commander on the American side, had been repeatedly passed over for promotion and had been personally snubbed by Washington for having the effrontery to hold a lavish party at Valley Forge.

To a man of Arnold's hot and haughty temperament insults and snubs always rankled. Moreover, he liked money and he needed it to keep his Peggy happy, and in May of 1779 he asked a china dealer named Joseph Stansbury to visit his house. Stansbury, though a political trimmer, was secretly sympathetic to the Crown. Stansbury, anticipating a profitable sale to Mrs. Arnold, was astonished when "General Arnold . . . communicated to me, under solemn obligation of secrecy, his intention of offering his services to the commander in chief of the British forces."[115]

Stansbury went to New York and got in touch with none other than John André, now a major and chief of British intelligence. André opened correspondence with Arnold and found, to his dismay, that the American general was no high-minded idealist ready to betray rather than see his country fall under French influence, but rather a hardheaded haggler who wanted his 30 pieces of silver to be very large indeed. André dropped the correspondence.

In 1780 a court-martial found Arnold guilty on two counts and sentenced him to be reprimanded by Washington. Congress confirmed the sentence and Washington carried it out. In May of that year Arnold reopened his correspondence with André. This time he baited the hook with secret documents. André and Clinton, who had returned from Charleston, were impressed. They were delighted when Arnold succeeded in waggling command of West Point from Washington, and they settled down to arrange that vital fort's betrayal to them.

Arnold bargained like a fishwife. He wanted so much per head for every soldier he surrendered to the British. In all, £10,000 and a general's commission would do. Clinton agreed. He sent André to confer with Arnold on the details. André sailed up the Hudson on the sloop-of-war *Vulture* and met Arnold on the west shore below Haverstraw on the night of September 21. Before André could return to the *Vulture,* fire from American batteries drove the sloop downstream.

André, disregarding Clinton's instructions, decided to return to New York by land. He put on civilian clothes and put the documents that would damn Arnold inside his stockings. On September 23 he was captured in Tarrytown. Warned by a bungling though innocent American officer, Arnold left his wife and child and rode breakneck to his barge on the Hudson. He was rowed to the *Vulture,* to whose skipper he surrendered his enraged rowers.

Washington arrived at Arnold's headquarters a bare hour after the traitor's flight. In rage and in sorrow, he was able to take the precautions guaranteeing West Point. He tried to capture Arnold, but failed. So he ordered Major André hanged.

Clinton tried to dissuade him. André was the only officer for whom this cold commander had any affection, and he made every effort to save him. But Washington was adamant. He could not forget what had happened to Nathan Hale, and André went to his death with great composure.

The British kept their part of the bargain. They made Arnold a brigadier general, awarded him £6,315 even though he had failed to deliver the fort, plus a yearly pension of £500 for his wife, £100 for each of his children, and in 1798, after service against the French, 13,000 acres of land in Upper Canada (the Ontario Peninsula).

Arnold served his new masters well, even though he was never popular with them. They had bought an able traitor, but they felt uneasy about breaking bread with him.

18

☆

There was one ray of light during that dark summer of 1780, although some patriots found it too painfully bright.

The Count Vergennes, evidently convinced that the Americans could not beat Britain by themselves, sent the patriots one form of assistance that they did not desire: troops. Some 5,000 soldiers under the veteran Comte de Rochambeau began landing at Newport on July 12, and many patriots who had hoped to win their freedom themselves felt rebuked by the presence of white-coated Bourbon soldiers on American soil.

"I am fond of an alliance," said General Nathanael Greene, "but I wish for the honor of America that liberty may effect her own deliverance. I should like supplies from our friends, but wish to fight all the battles ourselves."[116]

In truth, this was just what the Americans could not do. Washington's own army had not only melted away again; it was living on short rations hardly better than the winter fare at Morristown. An acute shortage of horses and wagons made it impossible for him to do anything but stand on the defensive, while Congress itself was near bankrupt and the country was sunk deep in lethargy. Thus the arrival of the French encouraged the commander in chief, even if he too was reluctant to have a foreigner take Columbia's other hand. Washington hoped that the states would now give him the men and means to strike a knockout blow. But they did not. By the middle of July only about 1,000 men had rallied to the colors. It was not possible to reopen the campaign, and even the ever-hopeful Washington lamented: "I have almost ceased to hope."[117]

The British Navy put a period to that remark. Though it had not been able to intercept the French fleet, it arrived off Newport in numbers sufficient to bottle up the French ships and to render Rochambeau's army inactive for the rest of the year. British warships also blockaded another French fleet and 5,000 more troops in the harbor at Brest.

So the dark summer passed, to be succeeded by a fall made blacker by the treachery of Benedict Arnold, and then the rebel sun rose high again over a Southern eminence called King's Mountain.

After Cornwallis had routed Gates he moved north from Camden to enter North Carolina. Before he left he detached Major Patrick Ferguson to cover his left or inland flank. Ferguson was a remarkable soldier. He had invented a breech-loading rifle which could be fired five or six times a minute, and he was a campaigner fully as arduous and as thorough as the more famous Banastre Tarleton.

However, Ferguson's merciless pillaging of the Carolinas enraged a breed of hardy Scots-Irish frontiersmen dwelling west of the mountains in what is now Tennessee. Hunters and Indian fighters, crackshots with their long-barreled rifles, these horsemen could go on campaign with a blanket, a knife and a bag of parched corn mixed with maple syrup. They were not rebels, but they hated Ferguson, and they were enraged when he told them to cease their opposition lest he cross the mountains to destroy them.

Rather than await their own ruin, they went to meet him. Their numbers swelled to 1,000 by men of similar breed from Virginia and the Carolinas, led by Colonels Isaac Shelley, John Sevier, William Campbell, Charles McDowell and Benjamin Cleveland, they caught up with Ferguson at King's Mountain.

Ferguson had about 1,200 men, all Tories. In fact, Ferguson was the only Britisher present. He believed that he held a strong position atop King's Mountain. It was a level summit about 500 yards long and 70 to 80 yards wide, broadening to 120 yards at its northeast end. Here Ferguson established his camp, defying "God Almighty and all the rebels out of Hell to overcome him."[118]

Up they came, climbing the mountain's steeps in nine parties forming a long narrow horseshoe enclosing Ferguson. "Here they are, boys!" Colonel Campbell shouted at his men at one end of the horseshoe. "Shout like hell, and fight like devils!"[119] The Tories shoved plug bayonets into their musket muzzles and routed Campbell's men with a charge. But the Americans took to the trees and began firing up the slope with deadly accuracy.

So it went: as each American corps burst in upon Ferguson's men to be driven away with bayonets, another struck him elsewhere, and all the while a deadly fire came crackling from the treetops ringing him round. Soon the Tory position was hopeless. Even so, Ferguson would not surrender. Twice he cut down white flags raised into the air, and at last, trying to cut his way out, he was shot from his horse and died with one foot caught in the stirrup.

Now the rebels turned to butchery. They could recognize their enemies—some of them neighbors or relatives—among the Tories, and they called out by name those men known to have killed or plundered patriots. Shouting, "Buford! Buford! Tarleton's Quarter!"[120] they herded the terrified Tories into a knot and scourged them with bullets and bayonets. Campbell rode among them crying, "For God's sake, quit! It's murder to shoot any more!"[121] They were finally restrained, before the victory of King's Mountain was turned into a shameful slaughter.

It was a fine victory. Only 200 Tories sent out earlier on a foraging expedition were able to escape. Hearing of Ferguson's defeat, Cornwallis began backpedaling into South Carolina.

The tide of the war was turning in the South.

19

☆

On New Year's Day 1781 the men of the Pennsylvania Line mutinied at Morristown, killed one of their officers, and began marching on Congress in Philadelphia.

They had not been paid for a year, they were half-naked and starving, and many of them claimed that they had enlisted for three years, not the duration. They were also high on holiday rum.

Anthony Wayne cut short his own New Year's celebration to ride into the Morristown encampment to quell the mutiny. The men told him their quarrel was with Congress. When he persisted, they fired shots over his head. Wayne retorted by tearing his coat open in anguish and daring them to kill him. They replied that they had no desire to hurt any of the Line's officers, and they marched off toward Princeton with guns and baggage.

They were orderly, and they even seized two spies sent into their midst by Clinton and handed them over for trial and execution. From Princeton the mutineers marched to Trenton, where they were met by Joseph Reed, president of the Pennsylvania Council.

Washington, meanwhile, was faced with an agonizing decision. He did not want the mutiny to spread, but he feared that if he used force to halt it—as he wished to do—he might provoke an unfavorable reaction among the rest of the Continental Army units. In the end, by promising part of the back pay and discharging many of the men who claimed three-year enlistments, the problem was settled.

And then the smaller New Jersey Line quartered at Pompton mutinied over similar grievances. This time Washington used force, rather than risk losing his whole army. General Robert Howe and a strong force of New England Continentals surrounded the Jersey mutineers in their huts, paraded them without arms, and singled out the ringleaders. Then twelve of the most guilty mutineers were forced to shoot two of the ringleaders, and the mutiny was quelled.

That was how the New Year began for General Washington, and then, as had happened the previous black fall, there was good news from the South.

Nathanael Greene took command of the ragged Southern army in Charlotte, and promptly broke the biggest rule of the art of war: he divided his forces in the face of a superior foe. By all the accepted maxims this meant that he had given Cornwallis the chance to destroy him in detail, to devour the parts one by one. Greene, however, had the insight to see that classic precepts presume normal situations, and the situation in North Carolina was far from normal.

Greene knew that his tatterdemalions could not meet Cornwallis's regulars, who outnumbered them 4,000 to 3,000. Yet he could not risk a demoralizing retreat. Better, then, to divide his army in two and send each part to operate against the British flanks while irregulars such as Marion and Sumter struck his rear. Thus divided they could live off the country and be mobile enough to elude the equipment-heavy British.

One detachment under Daniel Morgan was to move west from Charlotte while the other under Isaac Huger, accompanied by Greene, would move east. If Cornwallis in the center lunged to his right, he would unmask Camden and the town of Ninety Six to Morgan on his left. If he struck at Morgan on his left, Greene could dash downcoast to Charleston. Cornwallis saw this, and he realized that he too must divide his forces. Banastre Tarleton with about 1,100 men went galloping west to dispose of Morgan, and on January 17, 1781, the two small armies collided at Cowpens.

Daniel Morgan chose to fight in what looked like a trap. He held a plain dotted with widely spaced trees in which Tarleton's superior horsemen could easily maneuver, and he had his back to the Broad River. But the Old Wagoner knew his men. If he secured his wings on swamps, as he said later, his militia would have vanished through the bogs, and if he crossed the river, half of them would abandon him. He wanted no hope of retreat, so that his men would fight the dreaded Tarleton with the desperation of the doomed, and he was certain that his dashing enemy would charge straight ahead rather than nibble at his exposed wings.

So Morgan put about 150 picked riflemen forward in a skirmish line. About 150 yards behind them were about 300 militia under Andrew Pickens, and back another 150 yards on the crest of a hill was his main line of about 400 Continentals under John Howard. Again to the rear, behind another hill, were about 100 horse under the fat but capable William Washington, the cavalryman who had been wounded at Trenton.

The sharpshooters in front were not to open fire until the enemy was within 50 yards, and then they were to aim at "the men with the epaulets." They were to deliver two volleys, and then fall back on Pickens's militia. The militia were then to fire only two volleys, before retiring around the American left to the rear of the main line on the hill, there to re-form as a reserve. Morgan promised them they would be perfectly safe. He also informed every man of his plan so that no one would be alarmed at the withdrawals.

Tarleton came on. His legion cavalry rode at the sharpshooters. A scathing fire sent 15 riderless horses off the field, and the Tory cavalry fled, never to be induced to re-enter the battle. Now the main British line moved forward, dragoons on either wing. Here was the crux of battle. If the militia showed their customary reaction to bared British steel, they would flee. But Pickens's men stayed, firing and loading and firing again to send two volleys into the scarlet line. Then they began running to the left as planned, to get behind the Continentals on the hill. The militia on the right had the farthest to go, and the British dragoons came thundering down on them.

Suddenly out of the American right rear Washington's horsemen came riding. They fell upon the astonished dragoons with whistling sabers, routing and pursuing them while all Pickens's men gained the rear and re-formed.

But the impetuous British had taken Pickens's retirement to mean the start of the customary retreat, and they came shouting against the main line of Howard's Continentals. Kneeling on the hill, the Americans poured a plunging fire into the enemy. Still, the British advanced. Tarleton put his Highlanders on his left. They stretched beyond the American right. Howard saw that he was being outflanked. He called for his right-hand company to face about. Then they were to wheel and form a right angle to the main line and face about again to blunt the British flanking movement.

But they faced about and marched to the rear, and the whole line followed suit.

Morgan came rushing up to Howard, shouting, "What is this retreat?"

"A change of position to save my right flank," Howard replied.

"Are you beaten?" the Old Wagoner yelled, and Howard shot back scornfully: "Do men who march like that look as though they were beaten?"[122] Morgan nodded, and dashed off to find Howard's men a second position between the two hills.

Tarleton, sensing victory, pursued. His men broke ranks and rushed forward. William Washington, whose pursuit of the dragoons had carried him ahead of the American lines, saw the British confusion. He sent word to Morgan: "They're coming on like a mob. Give them one fire, and I'll charge them."[123] Morgan gave the order to the Continentals; they faced about and blazed away from the hip. The scarlet line crumpled and Howard cried: "Give them the bayonet!"[124] So it was that an American cheer and American blades went forward, just as Washington's cavalry burst upon the enemy flank and rear like a tornado. After that Pickens's re-formed militia struck the Highlanders down, and the Battle of Cowpens was over but for an individual and inconclusive mounted skirmish between Tarleton and Washington.

Banastre Tarleton himself rode off, his brilliant plumed helmet drooping in a defeat that was nearly total: nine-tenths of his force had been killed or captured, against only 12 Americans killed and 60 wounded.

Cowpens was the American Cannae, it was the glittering small gem of the Revolution, and it was brought off by an American back-woodsman who, like the great Hannibal himself, was merely adapting himself to men and terrain. Moreover, Cowpens made the way of the wary Nathanael Greene easier as he waged his war of attrition against Cornwallis. No one described the war he fought better than

So it went, as the American Army moved like an infuriating wraith before the pursuing Cornwallis. First, the enraged earl tried to catch Morgan, but the Old Wagoner rejoined Greene. Together, they withdrew into Virginia. Nearly exhausted, his little army dwindled to 1,900 men, Cornwallis gave chase. Greene recrossed the border, gathering forces until he had 4,400 men under his command. On March 15 Greene met Cornwallis at Guilford Courthouse, employing a line of battle similar to Morgan's at the Cowpens. British bravery and skill routed Greene's militia and broke his first two lines, and Greene wisely withdrew, having so badly mauled Cornwallis that he was compelled to fall back on Wilmington 200 miles south.

Lord Rawdon now took up the pursuit of Greene. He caught him, beat him but could not crush him at Hobkirk's Hill on April 25. Rawdon also was forced to withdraw after Marion cut his line of communications, and Greene took his army to the High Hills of Santee to pass the dreadful Carolina summer in comparatively cool surroundings. Then, on September 8, he met the British again at Eutaw Springs in South Carolina. The Americans had the battle won, and would have won it had they not fallen upon supplies of rum in the camp of the routed British. Re-forming, the British snatched the victory out of Greene's fingers.

But they had not beaten him. Greene had suffered tactical loss after tactical loss but had carried out his strategy. He had actually forced Cornwallis to abandon South Carolina and to march into Virginia instead, where he joined forces with Benedict Arnold and Phillips.

Thus was laid the foundation for the conclusive victory of the Revolution. Lord Cornwallis, steadily gathering his Virginia forces until they numbered 7,200 men, eventually led them into a little tobacco-trading port named Yorktown.

20

☆

On May 21, 1781, General Washington and Count Rochambeau met in Wethersfield, Connecticut, to plan a summer campaign.

They knew that the French West Indian fleet under Admiral de Grasse was going to be available, and Washington wished to use these ships for an assault upon New York. It was agreed that the Continental and French armies would join above the city to await the fleet's arrival, and a frigate was sent to Haiti to inform de Grasse of this plan.

Unknown to Washington, Rochambeau had privately advised de Grasse that he preferred Chesapeake Bay as an area of operations. To a sailor the Chesapeake was more attractive because it was closer and deeper, and de Grasse agreed with Rochambeau.

Thereafter de Grasse acted with a vigor and vision not always characteristic of a French admiral. He sent the frigate dashing back with word of his own intentions, he procured 3,000 regulars from the island governor, he raised from the governor of Havana the money needed by the Americans, and he took aboard American coast pilots that he had long ago requested from Rochambeau.

De Grasse also did what no British admiral answerable to a mercantile nation would have dared to do: he allowed French merchant ships to sail home unprotected and ordered about 200 others to mark time in Haiti until his return. Then, with his entire fleet of 28 ships of the line, sailing an indirect and less frequented route, he made for the Chesapeake.

In New York, Sir Henry Clinton had intercepted a number of letters from Washington and Rochambeau. From them he learned of the action concerted against New York. Alarmed, he sent to Lord Cornwallis in Virginia for 3,000 troops—and so set in motion the final event of the British campaign in the South.

Between Clinton and Cornwallis there had been almost nothing but dispute since Cornwallis, cheered on by Lord George Germain, had begun acting independently of his superior in New York. The basic difference was that Clinton wanted to campaign in Pennsylvania and Cornwallis preferred Virginia.

After Nathanael Greene and a fratricidal countryside disabused Cornwallis of his hopes of victory in the Carolinas, the earl had hurried to Virginia. There he joined Phillips and Arnold, who had been busy ravaging the Virginia country around the Chesapeake.

Then, after he received Clinton's call for reinforcements, Cornwallis began marching for Portsmouth as the point to embark them. Lafayette, then in Virginia trying to capture Arnold, struck at Cornwallis on July 6 at Green Spring. Cornwallis, always eager to catch "the boy," very nearly did. But darkness saved Lafayette, and the disgruntled earl moved on.

Thereafter he received from Clinton a welter of conflicting orders: first, to send the troops not to New York but to Philadelphia; second, to send them to New York after all; third, to retire to Yorktown on the peninsula between the James and York rivers; fourth, to go to Old Point Comfort instead, but also to fortify Yorktown if necessary; fifth and finally, to keep all the troops himself if he thought that he needed them, but to hurry to New York whatever he could spare.

Cornwallis inspected Old Point Comfort and decided against it in favor of Yorktown, and he went there in August.

Cornwallis considered himself secure so long as Britain controlled the sea. British ships entering Chesapeake Bay had easy access to Yorktown. They could supply him, reinforce him or evacuate him. French ships, of course, could seal off the mouth of the Chesapeake and thus make Yorktown very vulnerable to siege by land. But neither Cornwallis nor Sir Henry Clinton believed this to be likely.

After the French and Continental armies—each about 5,000 strong —had met in July, Washington and Rochambeau made an armed reconnaissance of New York. Washington was dismayed. Clinton's works, defended by 14,000 troops, were far too strong. The American began to think of campaigning in the South. And then, on August 14, came the wonderful news that de Grasse was en route to the Chesapeake with 28 big ships and 3,000 men!

Washington at once fell in with the Chesapeake plan. He dashed off orders to Lafayette to keep Cornwallis cornered in Yorktown. The French squadron in Newport under Admiral de Barras was ordered to the Chesapeake with Rochambeau's siege artillery. It left on August 27, making a wide circuit to avoid the British.

Next, efforts were made to convince Clinton that New York was still the allied objective. Staten Island was made to appear the staging area for an assault. Roads toward it were improved. A party of French in nearby Chatham, New Jersey, began making bake ovens as though for a siege. Leaving 3,000 men above New York, Washington sent 2,000 across the Hudson into New Jersey. The French followed. A leisurely march toward Chatham began. On August 29 the troops were making for Morristown–New Brunswick, and Clinton still believed them bound for Chatham.

But on the next day the Americans and French began marching briskly south toward Chesapeake Bay and Yorktown.

The British knew of de Grasse's departure for the Chesapeake, and the formidable Admiral Sir Samuel Hood had sailed from the West Indies with 14 "liners" to intercept him. Hood took the direct route, and arrived at the bay three days ahead of de Grasse. Poking inside, seeing nothing, Hood withdrew and made for New York, where he joined Admiral Samuel Graves with five liners. Graves, still the indecisive leader he had been at Boston six years ago, was senior to Hood and he took command. He sailed on August 31 for the Chesapeake, hoping to prevent de Barras with Rochambeau's guns from joining de Grasse.

Two days later, Sir Henry Clinton realized with horror that Washington and Rochambeau were after Cornwallis. He could not overtake them by land, and he dared not try the sea without the protection of Admiral Graves.

That commander, meanwhile, was dumfounded to find de Grasse's fleet inside the Chesapeake. Seeing his enemy, de Grasse immediately slipped his cables and stood seaward for battle—parading his ships with slow majesty to impress his strength upon the enemy. With only 19 sail and 1,400 guns against 24 ships and 1,700 guns, Graves knew himself to be overmatched. Still, with the aggressiveness typical of the British Navy, he seized the advantage of being windward of the French, and gave battle.

Graves's directions, however, were as confused as the seamanship of some of his captains, and de Grasse quickly brought his superior firepower to bear. The French mauled five British ships so badly that Graves hauled off. De Grasse kept to sea for five more days, deliberately luring Graves away from the Chesapeake so that de Barras might slip inside. De Barras did, de Grasse joined him, and the British, more badly outnumbered than before, sailed sadly north for New York.

All the way down to the Head of Elk, where Lord Howe had landed four years previously, George Washington had chewed on the question: Where is de Grasse? He had not heard of him since receipt of that letter in mid-August. On September 2 Washington had written Lafayette: ". . . my dear Marquis, I am distressed beyond expression, to know what is become of the Count de Grasse, and for fear the English Fleet, by occupying the Chesapeake . . . should frustrate all our flattering prospects in that quarter."[126]

He still had no word as his Continentals reached Head of Elk and began embarking in boats for Williamsburg on the James. The French, still elated from their wild reception in Philadelphia, followed. As Rochambeau and his elegant aides neared the landing on the Virginia shore they saw a straight tall figure in blue and buff waving his hat wildly, almost capering for joy.

Rochambeau stepped ashore and a beaming Washington rushed up to embrace him. Then French hats went soaring into the air, for Washington had informed them that de Grasse held the Chesapeake, Cornwallis was cut off, 3,000 French reinforcements were already ashore and, in the words of another Virginia general, "we have got him handsomely in a pudding bag."[127]

Without help from the sea, Cornwallis was caught—and he knew it. He had about 700 men across the York River in Gloucester, but they were cooped up and would remain cooped up by a Franco-American force three times their number.

The remaining 6,500 men held a series of fortifications curving around Yorktown on its landward side. On the morning of September 30, to the great surprise of the allies, Cornwallis abandoned his outer redoubts. His reason was that Clinton had written him promising ships to break the blockade and 5,000 troops as reinforcements. Cornwallis thought he could hold out better by concentrating his forces.

The allies, however, quickly occupied the redoubts, and then on October 6 work was begun on the first parallel about 600 yards from the lower end of the town. The trench was to run down to the water's edge. Diggers toiled throughout the night, sweating profusely in that moist heat which had already spread sickness through both camps. Heavy guns were dragged into place, and on October 9 a French battery on the left opened up. Then the American battery on the right began blasting, with Washington firing the first shot, and a British frigate on the York was driven to the Gloucester shore.

On the next night two bigger batteries began roaring. The French set another frigate hopelessly afire, and two transports were destroyed. In all, 52 guns were battering the town, and Cornwallis wrote ominously to Clinton: "We have lost about seventy of our men and many of our works are considerably damaged; with such works on disadvantageous ground, against so powerful an attack we cannot hope to make a very long resistance. P.S. 5 P.M. Since my letter was written (at 12 M.) we have lost thirty men. . . . We continue to lose men very fast."[128]

Clinton and the admirals, meanwhile, had only belatedly begun a rescue operation. But the limitations of New York's dockyards made the work of refitting proceed with agonizing slowness. It was hoped to be ready by October 5, then the 8th . . . the 12th . . . But the 12th passed and the fleet still had not sailed. Clinton was beside himself. At last, on October 17, 7,000 troops were embarked and the ships began dropping down Sandy Hook—only to be forced to wait two more days for favorable winds and tides. In the meantime, some 16,000 French and Americans drew ever closer to Cornwallis's beleaguered 7,000, and a second parallel only 300 yards away from Yorktown was begun by Steuben and his engineers.

As the trench approached the river edge, its builders were raked by fire from two British redoubts close to the water. Washington decided to storm them. The French took the left in a stirring charge, climbing the parapet with cries of *"Vive le Roi!"* and forcing its garrison of Hessians and British to throw down their arms.

Alexander Hamilton led the Americans against the one on the right. Now grown fond of the bayonet, the patriots went at it with unloaded muskets, clawing their way through the abatis, crossing the ditch and leaping over the parapets. From all the British lines came a storm of shells and musket balls. Washington, watching the assault, was cautioned by his aide: "Sir, you are too much exposed here. Had you not better step a little back?"

"Colonel Cobb," Washington replied gravely, "if you are afraid, you have liberty to step back."[129]

And so both redoubts were won, the second parallel was extended down to the river and the second nail driven into the British coffin. On the morning of October 16, Cornwallis sent out a force of 350 men to capture and destroy the batteries in the second parallel. In a brave charge, the British succeeded in entering both positions and in spiking some guns, but they were eventually driven back and the guns restored to service.

So desperate now that he was losing his judgment, Cornwallis attempted a wild escape across the river through Gloucester. He expected to burst through the Franco-American force there and proceed to New York by forced marches. That same midnight he began embarking his troops, but a violent storm broke upon him and forced him back into Yorktown.

That was the end.

In the morning of the 17th, two days before Clinton's relief force made the open sea, the allies opened on the town with a dreadful cannonade. One by one the British works collapsed. There was no answering fire, for the British had exhausted their ammunition. Soon a redcoated drummer boy strode onto a parapet and began to beat a parley. He could not be heard in all that thunder, but he was seen. The guns fell silent and a British officer advanced to be blindfolded and led to Washington.

He asked for a 24-hour armistice. Washington granted him two hours. He returned with Cornwallis's surrender terms, including a condition that his army be paroled to Britain. Washington insisted that the enemy surrender as prisoners of war, and Cornwallis submitted.

At noon of October 19, 1781, the gay military music of the French sang out, and for the last time the vivacious white-coated soldiers of France went into line on American soil. Into line opposite them, moving proudly across trampled fields to the Celtic lilt of fifes and drums, went the tall Americans in brown or hunting shirts and here and there in blue and buff. George Washington rode up on a great bay horse and stood at their right. Across from him Rochambeau and Admiral de Barras sat their horses. To the right of them Yorktown's main sally port was flung open. Faint on the wind came the mournful beat of drums and the melancholy squeal of fifes. Out rode Brigadier General Charles O'Hara. With stupefying bad grace, Cornwallis, pleading illness, had sent a deputy to surrender for him.

Bewildered, O'Hara rode first toward Rochambeau. But the count, by a gracious inclination of the eyes, directed him to Washington. Slightly flustered, O'Hara approached the tall Virginian. Washington indicated General Benjamin Lincoln. Deputy must surrender to deputy, and O'Hara handed over Cornwallis's sword. Lincoln returned it, and called for the surrender to begin.

Out they came, the scarlet-coated British and their Hessian allies brilliant in blue and green. Out came the German mercenaries, striding briskly, stacking their arms neatly, then the British, moving along slowly, their faces sullen, some of them already weeping. Down went their arms in a disorderly crash. Drummer boys stove in their drums, infantrymen smashed their musket butts and stomped on their cartridge cases. Officers pouting like schoolboys avoided the eyes of their captors.

Above the clatter of grounded arms and the hoarse cursing of broken-hearted soldiers rose the music of the British bands bringing the War of the American Revolution to its effective close with the prophetic notes of "The World Turned Upside Down."

PART ☆ III

The War of 1812

1

☆

When the news of Yorktown reached Lord North in London, he shuddered as though shot, threw his arms wide and cried: "O God, it is all over!"[1]

It was indeed, although fighting sputtered on for another year, chiefly on the western borders. On March 20, 1782, North's ministry fell, to be replaced by a Whig government eager to end the war. Even though the British naval victory in the Battle of the Saints in the following April served to retrieve British prestige, while weakening Franco-American bargaining power, the Whigs still sought peace at almost any price.

On January 20, 1783, hostilities ceased between Great Britain and the United States. In Paris, meanwhile, peace commissioners worked out an agreement to restore Minorca and the Floridas to Spain, cede Tobago in the West Indies and Senegal in Africa to France, and leave the United States free west to the Mississippi, north to Canada and south to the Floridas. On September 3, 1783, the Peace of Paris formally brought the War of the Revolution to an end, and on November 23 the British Army sailed home from New York.

To the astonishment of the world, Britain's upstart daughter had humbled her powerful mother. But now, confident in its knowledge of the natural history of revolutions, the world settled down in supercilious expectation of Yankee collapse. If the Confederation did not go the dissolving way of all unions pasted together by the mere exigencies of war, then some man on horseback—General Washington, perhaps?—would certainly establish a military dictatorship.

But General Washington had already squelched the one occasion in American history on which the military acted as though it sought political power. That had been in the winter of 1782-83, when the officers of the Continental Army encamped at Newburgh, New York, asked Congress for what was actually the barest relief of financial distress caused by war service and inflation. Congress refused, and the officers flew into a rage. There appeared two inflammatory papers known as the Newburgh Addresses and believed to have been written by Major John Armstrong, an aide of General Gates and a close friend of the ubiquitous Major James Wilkinson.

The Newburgh Addresses told the officers "that the slightest mark of indignity from Congress now must operate like the grave and part you forever; that, in any political event, the army has its alternative."[2] Should peaceful measures fail, the author continued, the army could march to the west and defy Congress.

To Washington this was at best mutiny, at worst insurrection. He met the challenge by making a surprise personal appearance in the hall where the angry officers had gathered. He appealed to their patriotism and explained the difficulties in which Congress found itself. Then, with a deft, sure touch characteristic of the leader who had guided this ragtail army through eight despairing years, he began to read a letter, paused—and drew a pair of spectacles from his pocket. The officers were surprised. They had not known that Washington's sight was failing. "Gentlemen," he explained, "you will permit me to put on my spectacles, for I have not only grown gray, but almost blind, in the service of my country."[3] Overcome, with many of them openly weeping, the officers voted to leave their problems in Washington's hands. Eventually he persuaded Congress to grant pensions acceptable to officers and men alike.

At the outset, then, the danger of military despotism was avoided and the new American nation was saved by the one man who could have killed it. The second danger—that the jealous bickering of 13 sovereign states would tear the fabric of Confederation apart—was less immediate though probably more grave.

Through the Articles of Confederation and the fact that Congress had simply seized the reins of government, the United States had been able to wage successful war. But the problems of government remained, chief among them the question of how to induce the states to surrender enough of their sovereignty so that all might be served by a single national government. The Articles did not supply the answer. They denied Congress the vital taxing power and they could not be amended without unanimous consent. In a union already divided by the sectionalism of North versus South and beset by the mutual distrust of large and small states, unanimity was not possible. Congress, being a new government, overawed no one. In fact, it was held in wide contempt. Driven from Philadelphia in June, 1783, by mutineers of the Pennsylvania Line, it wandered like a waif from Princeton to Annapolis to Trenton and finally, in 1785, to New York. Two years later Congress's basic weakness was laid bare by the rising of Massachusetts farmers known as Shays' Rebellion.

A sound money policy supported by heavy taxes had left the Bay State's farmers destitute. Farms and cattle were sold to satisfy court judgments for taxes or debts. The farmers tried to stop the courts from sitting, and they set up committees of correspondence, just as the leaders of the Revolution had acted against Parliament. But now these leaders were conducting the state government and they threatened the farmers with the gallows. The farmers paid no heed. They grew stronger and more aggressive and they called upon Daniel Shays, a distinguished soldier of the Revolution, to lead them. Shays tried to prevent the Supreme Court from sitting at Springfield, and it was here that his attack on both the courthouse and the Confederation arsenal was shattered by artillery fired by loyal state militia. After a few more, lesser defeats, Shays fled to Vermont. Massachusetts wisely treated his followers with clemency, and a newly elected legislature moved to alleviate their hardships.

Nevertheless, Shays' Rebellion alarmed the nation, delighting those Tories who saw in it the first crack in the American façade. Massachusetts had appealed to Congress for help, and Congress had been able to do nothing. Even those Americans who had feared the formation of a strong national government now favored revision of the Articles of Confederation. On May 25, 1787, the Constitutional or Federal Convention convened in Philadelphia for this "sole and express purpose."

The Founding Fathers of the United States (only four of fifty-five Convention delegates were sixty or over) did not so much revise the old Articles as devise an entirely new government as set forth in the Constitution. Congress received taxing and other important powers and was expanded from a single chamber into a House of Representatives elected by the people and a Senate selected by the more conservative state legislatures. A strong executive power vested in a President was also provided, as well as a Supreme Court.

Thus was born the American system of the division of powers—legislative, executive and judicial—acting as checks and balances on each other. In Congress the people as manifested by the popularly elected House was balanced against property as expressed by the Senate. Civilian control of the military was guaranteed by making the President commander in chief, and the President in turn was checked by giving the House the power to determine the size of the armed forces. Finally, excesses by either legislative or executive powers could be checked by a Supreme Court empowered to interpret the Constitution.

In four months, then, these political carpenters raised a stout roof over the new nation. They wrote a Constitution which, intended to serve 4 million people and 13 states for a generation, still guides 249 million Americans and 50 states while remaining, after the tests of nearly two centuries, one of the triumphs of practical politics. Above all, these men were practical. They were not doctrinaires, like the French and Russian revolutionaries who eventually replaced old tyrannies with new ones. They were experienced in the arts of self-rule. "Experience must be our only guide," John Dickinson told the Convention, "reason may mislead us."[4] And so these supreme realists proclaimed the rule of law, making no attempt to reconcile such irreconcilables as freedom and authority, populace and property, but rather balancing the one against the other so that neither might gain a clear ascendancy to establish either extreme of anarchy or oligarchy.

The Constitution was adopted, and on September 13, 1788, the Continental Congress passed the resolution ending its own life and putting the new govenment into operation. The First Congress was chosen, and then the presidential electors who made George Washington their unanimous choice. On April 30, 1789, Washington was inaugurated in New York.

The form of government which, in all its fundamental characteristics still governs the United States of America, had entered history.

The new government began life without money or an administrative system, with no navy or marine corps, an army down to 672 officers and men—and with war clouds still hovering over the horizon.

Britain had not withdrawn from her seven northwest posts as she had promised. Rather, after dividing Canada into the provinces of Lower and Upper Canada* (modern Quebec and Ontario), she planted Upper Canada's seat of government at Fort Niagara on the American side of the border. Britain also continued to sell arms to those Indians who were one of the young Republic's chief enemies.

To counteract British influence in the Northwest, the United States proposed to build a fort on the Maumee River. In 1791 about 2,000 men—the entire American Army—marched toward the Maumee under General Arthur St. Clair. The Indians, believing the fort aimed at them, prepared an ambush. St. Clair blundered into it and was put to rout with casualties of more than 900 men.

Elated, the Indians boasted that they would drive the "long knives" back across the Ohio. Britain encouraged them, for Britain hoped to block American expansion with an Indian buffer state. In the meantime, while the House of Representatives began an investigation which ended in placing the blame for the defeat on no one, the United States began to suffer at sea.

Without a navy to protect them, American merchant ships in the Mediterranean had fallen prey to the pirates of the Barbary Coast. Captured American seamen were held for ransom. Until it was paid they languished in prisons or toiled in chains at the oars of Algerian war galleys. Congress, forced to choose between war or tribute, talked belligerently of reviving the Navy but actually did nothing. Then it appropriated $54,000 to ransom the sailors at $2,000 a head and appointed John Paul Jones to negotiate a treaty of tribute with the Dey of Algiers. Fortunately for Jones's honor, he died before he could complete his ignominious mission; unfortunately for the seamen, they were to suffer many more years in captivity before the Republic at last faced up to the war-or-tribute decision.

Meanwhile, the first ripples of the tidal wave unleashed by the French Revolution of 1789 were lapping at American shores. American sympathy for their republican brothers in France rose to near-hysterical devotion after the French decreed "a war of all peoples against all kings." That was in 1793, the same year in which Britain and the French Republic went to war. Love for France thereupon

---

* "Upper" or "Lower" Canada then did not relate to north or south but "up" or "down" the St. Lawrence and the Great Lakes chain. Thus "upper" was actually western and "lower" was eastern.

became synonymous with hatred for England, especially after British naval vessels began seizing American ships with cargoes bound for France. Britain claimed that any enemy property was good prize, whether or not it was carried in a neutral ship. The Americans countered with the principle, "Free ships make free goods." Actually, the debate was academic; Britain had no intention of allowing America to supply her French enemy, and she had the ships to prevent it.

A war clamor arose in America. Washington, determined to avoid foreign entanglement, sent John Jay to Britain to prevent war, and also to persuade the British to evacuate the Northwest forts. In the meantime, however, Upper Canada had built a new fort on the Maumee in what is now northwest Ohio. Indians, grown confident since their defeat of St. Clair, were encouraged to attack American settlements. They did, and Washington called on Anthony Wayne to restrain them.

Wayne spent the winter of 1793-94 at Greenville, Ohio, which he had named for his old friend, Nathanael Greene. In the spring of 1794 he moved out with a force of perhaps 2,500 men, regulars whom he had personally trained, as well as a few hundred mounted Kentucky riflemen. The Indians, between 1,500 and 2,000 from a half-dozen different tribes, retreated back toward the Canadian fort. They turned to fight at Fallen Timbers, a wide swath which a tornado had cut in the woods northwest of present-day Defiance. Hidden among twisted trunks and branches, the savages were all but invisible. But the Americans in four columns marked by the white, red, yellow or green plumes of their officers' hats were unmistakable targets.

On August 20 the battle began with a charge of American dragoons against the Indian left. White horsehair plumes flying, sabers glittering, the mounted Americans galloped through an intense fire, leaped the timber barricades and fell upon the enemy with flashing steel. On the right, infantry and riflemen fired one volley and charged with the bayonet. It was over in less than an hour. The Indians, as they admitted later, "could not stand up against the sharp ends of the guns."[5]

Thus the critical year of 1794 was crowned with American military success. The prestige of the national government rose higher in 1795 as the Indians ceded the southeastern corner of the Northwest Territory, together with Vincennes, Detroit and the site of Chicago; it soared again in 1796 when the British withdrew from the Northwest forts.

Federalism, however, had reached its high-water mark. The rival theories of Alexander Hamilton and Thomas Jefferson had come out into the open and clashed, and in that collision political parties and the American two-party system were born. Hamilton's Federalists believed in an industrial America run by men of wealth and talent, while Jefferson's Republicans rallied under the standard of agrarianism and democracy. It was rule-by-the-best versus rule-by-the-most. The Federalists, political parents of today's Republicans, were realist and empiricist and they mistrusted the people; the Republicans, from whom the modern Democrats have descended, were idealist and rationalist and they trusted the people too much. Actually, the differences between the parties were never so distinct, shaded as they were by local rivalries and religious, racial and social disparities. But they were crystallized in 1794 when the war between Britain and France found the Federalists opting for Britain's conservative society and the Republicans backing republican France.

That war had repercussions in America, after John Adams became President by a narrow margin and took office in 1797. By then the French Revolution had been drowned in the blood bath of the Reign of Terror and the French Directory had become the arrogant afflictor of the Western world. Its armies, led by that very Napoleon Bonaparte who eventually destroyed the Directory and made France his own, had been victorious everywhere. Of all the Western nations, only Britain, Russia and the United States had not come to terms with France. Cheered on by the Republicans, the French fell upon the American merchant fleet with a ferocity that made previous British spoliations seem comparatively gentle. Distressed, Adams sent a mission to Paris.

It was received coldly. Foreign Minister Talleyrand sent a trio of minor officials (identified only as Monsieurs X, Y and Z) to inform the Americans that negotations would only be opened after a $250,-000 bribe had been paid to Talleyrand, and a $10 million loan be granted to France. News of the XYZ Affair enraged America and rocked the Republicans; the rallying cry of "Millions for defense but not one cent for tribute" provided support for President Adams's policy of armed neutrality.

The policy actually was nothing less than declaration of a naval war with France. Congress revived the Navy and Marine Corps, expanded the Army, and sent such famous ships as the *United States, Constellation* and *Constitution* swaying down the ways. These and other warships were authorized to capture French armed vessels wherever they might be found, and in actual battle they gave far more than they got. Meanwhile, the Army prepared to repulse an anticipated French invasion of America. George Washington put on his sword again to command this force of 3,000 men, which he found to be a distasteful motley of "the riff-raff of the country and the scape-gallows of the large cities." Fortunately, the British Navy bottled up Napoleon in Egypt and there was no French invasion. In 1799 the French government turned conciliatory and the Naval War with France quietly entered history.

The following year the Federalists lost power, never to regain it. Federalist intolerance as exemplified by the Alien and Sedition Acts —attempts to persecute the foreign-born and curb criticism—helped to establish Thomas Jefferson and his Republicans in office.

In Jefferson, the United States got a President eager to save money by cutting back the armed forces, although it was he who founded the Military Academy at West Point and although within a few months of his inauguration the U.S. Navy had found its true battle birth in the wars with the Barbary pirates.

By 1801 the United States had paid Morocco, Algiers, Tunis and Tripoli—the Moslem states of the Barbary Coast—$2 million in ransom for captured seamen and in tribute to allow American ships to sail the Mediterranean unharmed. In May of that year the Pasha of Tripoli declared war on America in an attempt to squeeze more tribute money out of her.

To everyone's surprise the pacifist Jefferson responded by rebuilding the Navy which had done so well in the Naval War with France and which he had almost personally scrapped. It did not immediately spring into being, but by 1804 Commodore Edward Preble was able to appear off Tripoli with a task force built around the *Constitution*. Preble shelled the Pasha's fortress. Unfortunately, the frigate *Philadelphia* was grounded on a reef off Tripoli. The Pasha imprisoned its crew, and floated the frigate free preparatory to making use of it himself.

It was then that young Stephen Decatur slipped into the harbor at night, boarding and capturing the *Philadelphia* and setting her hopelessly afire. And as the Pasha's naval ambitions went up in flames, he was assailed on his landward flank by one of the most implacable haters in American history.

William Eaton, the American consul at Tunis, writhed under the shame of the tribute. The author of perhaps the angriest and most anguished reports in State Department annals, he could write: ". . . recall me, and send a *slave* accustomed to abasement to represent the nation."[6] Convinced that the French consul in Tunis was in cahoots with the Bey "to milk the United States of every pailful of tribute the docile republic might yield,"[7] he denounced him in the presence of the consuls of Sweden and Great Britain and then publicly horsewhipped him in a Tunis street.

Eaton also hated the Pasha of Tripoli, who had usurped his brother on the throne, and he proposed to put the brother, Hamet, back in power on condition of his friendship for the United States.

Hamet agreed, and Eaton with the approval of the American naval commander in the Mediterranean station began rounding up his "army." It was commanded by Lieutenant Presley O'Bannon of the Marines and included 6 or 7 other marines, a naval midshipman, 40 Greeks, 100 of the flotsam of Europe and Asia coughed up on the shores of the Levant, a squadron of mounted Arabs under Hamet Pasha and a fleet of camels. Eaton's plan was to march from Alexandria to Derna 500 miles away, and then to advance on Tripoli another 500 miles westward. On March 6, 1805, the march began. It was a dreadful ordeal: burning sands and brazen sun by day, cold and sometimes mutiny by night. Eaton and O'Bannon drove their motley forward. On April 27 they attacked Derna. Three American brigs bombarded the city from the sea, while O'Bannon led a charge on the fort. It fell, and for the first time Old Glory flew over an Old World fortress.

But the formidable Eaton was not to complete his design. A highly chastened Pasha had requested peace and been granted generous terms. His captives were ransomed, his tribute was continued and his city of Derna evacuated. Chagrined and embittered, Eaton resigned from the service of his country. Yet the War with Tripoli had taught the Barbary powers to respect the U.S. Navy and the American flag. Perhaps more important in a military way, the exploits of Eaton and O'Bannon lived on in the annals of the Marine Corps. O'Bannon's charge on the shores of Tripoli was commemorated in the first stanza of the Marines' hymn, as well as in the hilt and blade of a Marine officer's sword, and it embarked his Corps on its long career of victory and valor.

The war, then, was a success, even if the Barbary bribery was to continue until 1816; and to this military achievement the unmilitary Mr. Jefferson, who also detested the shifting diplomacies of Europe, was to add in 1803 the diplomatic coup of the Louisiana Purchase. Derided as it was at the time, the purchase of the Louisiana Territory for $15 million from Napoleon (who had secretly recovered it from Spain) was a stupendous event which advanced the American frontier to the Rocky Mountains. Out of this huge province came four new states and parts of nine others, and with the Union already expanded to 17 states through admission of Vermont, Kentucky, Tennessee and Ohio, the continental expansion of the United States was already in full career not 15 years after Washington had taken his first oath of office. In 1805 its advance parties penetrated to the Western Ocean, when Captain Meriwether Lewis and Lieutenant William Clark made their overland expedition to and from the Pacific.

So much territory, as loosely defended as it was loosely defined, naturally attracted the attention of adventurers—chief among them former Vice President Aaron Burr. After the Republicans had dropped him in the election of 1804, Burr had entered into a conspiracy with some New England Federalists who hoped to secede from the Union and form a Northern Confederacy. New York State was to be the keystone of this Federalist arch, and Burr tried to capture its governorship. He was defeated, mainly by the efforts of Alexander Hamilton. Enraged, Burr seized upon a pretext—a reported slur on his character—to challenge Hamilton to a duel. Hamilton, who had no need to prove his courage, unwisely accepted. The two met at Weehawken across the Hudson from New York. Hamilton missed deliberately, but Burr took careful aim and sent a ball into Hamilton's abdomen. So perished, after 30 hours of intense pain, one of the great men of American history. Even more than Washington he was the true soldier-statesman, able to write as well as fight, to execute as well as propose.

Indicted for murder, Burr fled into hiding off the Georgia coast. When Congress reconvened in 1804, he calmly resumed his duties as Vice President until his term expired in March, 1805, after which he went west to organize what seems to have been nothing less than a conspiracy to make himself emperor of Mexico and to set up an independent republic in Louisiana. Yet if plots and conspiracies came naturally to this bold bantam and ruthless charmer, they were also common to the age. Districts run by sturdy and honest men who went "up west" out of disgust with the fumbling Confederation had already flirted with Spain, while Nolichucky Jack Sevier's fiercely republican State of Franklin often acted as though it had seceded from the Union. Nor were the Creoles of Louisiana happy when the Stars and Stripes were unfurled at New Orleans and the notes of "Yankee Doodle" came squealing into their cultivated ears. Therefore it was not surprising that Burr should win the friendship of such men as Andrew Jackson of Tennessee, that filibusterers should flock to his cause or that the Catholic Bishop of New Orleans should give him his blessing. In such times also it was almost automatic that Burr should find an accomplice in James Wilkinson, then commanding general of the American Army, federal governor of the Louisiana Territory—and Spy No. 13 in the pay of Spain. The conspiracy might very well have succeeded had not Wilkinson—finding even his duplicity unequal to the challenge of remaining a loyal conspirator, citizen and spy at one and the same time—decided to betray Burr.

Burr was taken in disguise within a few miles of Spanish Florida and brought to trial for treason. Much to the consternation of Jefferson, and to the credit of American jurisprudence, he was acquitted on strict adherence to the constitutional definition of treason. Indicted again for high misdemeanor, he fled to Europe.

By then, 1807, the threat to American security—or at least to national honor—was external again. Britain and France were locked in the duel-to-the-death known as the Napoleonic Wars, and once again America was to find her own destiny yoked to the fortunes of Anglo-French conflict.

2

☆

The magnetic chain of events drawing the United States into her second war with Great Britain began in 1805. In that year Napoleon stood poised to invade England. However, Lord Nelson won the great sea battle of Trafalgar, reasserting British supremacy at sea and ending Napoleon's hopes of invasion. Instead, like Louis XIV before him, the Corsican conqueror turned inward on Europe. After a series of lightning conquests he was supreme there.

Once again France, all-conquering on land, confronted Britain, invincible at sea.

Both sides tried to strangle each other economically. Britain issued Orders in Council proclaiming a blockade of Europe and the right to capture ships which did not submit to her regulations, while Napoleon countered with decrees closing European ports to Britain and stating his right to seize any ship dealing with the British.

The United States, largest neutral carrier in the world, was caught in an economic crossfire. But she suffered more at the hands of the British, who sailed right up to the shores of America to enforce their blockade, seizing ships and impressing American seamen. Britain claimed that the impressed sailors were deserters from the Royal Navy. Actually, most of them were. They had fled the poor pay, rotten food and brutal discipline of the British Navy, and many of them had signed on American vessels where life was far more pleasant. A few of them had become naturalized American citizens, although most merely obtained "protection" papers which could be purchased for as little as one dollar. Britain, intent only on maintaining the force of 150,00 seamen required to keep the Navy operative (she impressed her own subjects as well), proclaimed the principle: "Once an Englishman, always an Englishman." She recognized no naturalization process (neither did the U.S.), and especially not those spurious protection papers. However, British captains who stopped and searched American vessels were often arrogant. They also equated ability to speak English with proof of English birth, particularly if it was spoken by powerful or agile men, and so, many an American sailor was dragged off to serve under the detested Union Jack.

Impressment, more than anything else, outraged that growing sense of "national honor" which America, like all young nations, possessed in supersensitive degree; the inevitable blow-off came in the "*Chesapeake* incident" of June 22, 1807.

With guns unprepared for action, the U.S. Navy frigate *Chesapeake* had been only ten minutes out of Norfolk when the British frigate *Leopard* hailed her and claimed the right to examine her crew. *Chesapeake* refused. *Leopard* promptly poured three broadsides into her, sent officers aboard and carried off four seamen. One of these sailors might have been British, but the other three were an American Negro, an American Indian and a native of Maryland—and all four were not mere merchant seamen but sailors of the U.S. Navy.

National indignation nearly catapulted the United States into war with Britain. Jefferson, however, thought that he had a substitute for war. He would teach both contending powers, and especially Britain, the lesson of "peaceable coercion." Britain's chief customer was the United States, which was in turn the largest neutral carrier of goods to England. If he could cut off Britain's market and reduce the flow of her imports, Britain would be brought to terms. Thus in December of 1807 Congress by a close vote passed the Embargo Act. It forbade any U.S. ship to sail from a U.S. port for any foreign port.

This was Jefferson's noble experiment, and it was a notable failure. It did not humble Britain, but rather enriched British shipping at the expense of American, played into Napoleon's hands, nearly wrecked the American economy and came close to provoking the secession of mercantile New England. It was repealed on March 1, 1809, three days before Jefferson handed over his office to his protégé, James Madison.

Madison, a superb scholar and statesman but a shy and inept politician, sincerely sought an understanding with Britain. Unfortunately, his efforts were torpedoed by George Canning, the British Foreign Secretary. Madison's next move made him a foil for Napoleon. Congress had offered to resume trade with whichever belligerent removed its restrictions. Napoleon pretended to revoke his decrees. Madison, led to believe in his sincerity, tried to persuade the British to make some concessions too—which was exactly what Napoleon wanted. The British, however, were not deceived. They demanded evidence of Napoleon's sincerity. America could produce none simply because Napoleon's agents were still confiscating American ships.

The situation worsened. National honor became more and more outraged with each new offense. There were not only exponents of war with Britain, but also advocates of war with France—to say nothing of those Republicans who, eager to escape the imputation of Francophilism, proposed a "triangular war" with both.

Such a course was lunacy undiluted, and if it was never really seriously proposed, it does indicate that there was ample cause for war with either power. But Britain was the primary target of rage simply because she was the chief maritime offender and because the practice of impressment was so irritating. And Britain was also very vulnerable in her province of Canada.

The elections of 1810-11 brought the "war hawks" to Congress. Young men impatient with the slow processes of diplomacy, many of them Westerners who blamed Britain for the Indian border menace, they were hot for war and they seized control of the House by electing the eloquent and militant Henry Clay as Speaker. After Clay packed the important committees with war hawks like himself, war with Britain was advanced another giant step. There also began a debate which might have been comic were its consequences not so tragic. Westerners and Southerners who had never smelled salt water thundered for war for "Free Trade and Sailors' Rights," while those shippers and sailors who presumably should have been the first to fight for freedom of the seas swore that they would never lift a finger against Britain.

In truth, both sides had ulterior motives. The shippers had been growing rich under a British licensing system which allowed them to evade the blockade, and the sailors were delighted to see impressment put an end to competition from British deserters who would work for less money. Among the war hawks the maritime grievance was only a cover for their real purpose: the acquisition of more land. Not only the fertile woods of Upper Canada beckoned, but also the lands of the Indians as well as those of Spanish America. Napoleon's invasion of the Spanish homeland had set the disintegration of the Spanish Empire in motion; President Madison had already confirmed the seizure of most of West Florida by American adventurers, and now East Florida lay ripe for the plucking. On one score only were the war hawks trumpeting the truth: their hatred of Canada as the source of British support for the Northwestern Indians.

Already, by the spring of 1810, the great Shawnee chieftain, Tecumseh, had begun his desperate defiance of white imperialism. With his brother, a reformed drunkard called the Prophet who claimed supernatural powers, Tecumseh had traveled from tribe to tribe, binding his Indian federation together. Tecumseh taught renunciation of the white man and all his works, not only his dreadful firewater which drove the Indians insane,* but even his productive tools and skills. Tecumseh wished the Indians to remain hunters. To do so they had to fight for their Great Lakes hunting grounds. In 1810 they began the battle by attacking outlying white settlements. In the following year William Henry Harrison moved against them.

Harrison, a thin, wiry man whose frugal habits made him as tough as a squirrel, was not exactly a typical frontier leader. Devoted to the Roman classics, he had also aspired to study medicine, but finally turned to the army, much to the delight of his father-in-law, who said: "He can neither bleed, plead nor preach, and if he could plow I would be satisfied. His best prospect is in the army; he has talents, and if he can dodge well a few years, it is probable that he may become conspicuous."[8]

Harrison had become conspicuous enough to be appointed Governor of Indiana Territory, and in 1811 he led just over 900 regulars and militia into northern Indiana. It was not Tecumseh, but his brother the Prophet, who opposed him. On November 6 Harrison encamped outside the Prophet's town near Tippecanoe Creek. He expected a conference with the Indians in the morning. The Prophet, however, had brewed a "hell broth" which told him to attack the white men. More magician than military man, he turned the unplanned assault over to other chiefs and retired to a hill to chant those incantations which were to seal Harrison's doom.

In the dark and rain-swept cold of the morning of November 7, 1811, the Indians attacked with a yell and a rattle of musketry. Harrison, asleep, jumped to his feet, mounted an aide's bay staked outside his tent by mistake, and rode off in darkness toward the battle. His aide, singled out on Harrison's gray mare, was killed. Three times the Indians attacked, and each time they were driven back with losses. In the end they fled, and Harrison burned the Prophet's town to the ground.

Although the fame of the Battle of Tippecanoe eventually made Harrison an American President, and also deluded the war hawks into thinking that American militia were enough to lay Canada at the feet of Congress, defeat did not restrain Tecumseh. It merely threw him more firmly into the British camp; and after bitterly re-

* Unlike the white man, who usually drank to relax or be merry, Indians drank to get drunk. If there was not enough firewater for all, then a few were chosen to fulfill the purpose of drink: intoxication.

buking his brother for the folly of his attack, he turned once again
to savaging the American frontier.

Thus the war hawks, surer than ever that Britain was supplying
Tecumseh and hounding him on, rattled the saber louder. National
honor had now been outraged on the landward flank, and Americans
were reminded how the unholy alliance of redskin and redcoat had
bloodied the American frontier during the Revolution.

To these three causes of war—maritime insult, Indian outrage,
lust for land—was added a fourth when the British blockade began
to produce a depression in the South and West, the centers of anti-
British feeling. Ironically, American boycott of Britain had also
produced economic distress in England. Receipts of American food
crops had fallen to a trickle, exports to America had dried up, and
the harsh winter of 1811-12 was made more unbearable by the
failure of English crops. Starved and jobless English workmen began
to riot while merchants and manufacturers beseeched the government
to rescind the Orders in Council and reopen American trade.

It took that event unique in British history—the assassination of a
prime minister, Spencer Perceval—to place in power a ministry willing
to make the change. On June 16, 1812, London announced that the
Orders in Council had been suspended.

However, while Parliament had hesitated, Congress had acted.
The House voted 79 to 49 in favor of war with Britain, and the
Senate by 19 to 13. On June 18, two days after Britain had removed
the chief cause for war, President Madison signed the declaration
which began the War of 1812.

3

☆

If it is true that the War of 1812 was begun for the covetous
purpose of conquering Canada, then much as its proponents might
be criticized for their greed, they cannot be blamed for their timing.
Canada was defenseless. Britain, engaged against Napoleon in Spain,

could spare only about 4,000 regulars—reinforced by about 3,000 trustworthy Canadians—to defend an open border running about 1,700 miles. Moreover, British North America numbered less than 500,000 souls, many of whom were French-Canadians indifferent to the cause of British arms, as opposed to about 7,500,000 Americans. If ever the time for attack was ripe, this was it.

America, however, was incredibly unprepared. Her Navy was in comparatively good shape, but her ground forces were a marching mockery of the war whoops raised by Henry Clay and his war hawks the day war began. There were less than 7,000 men in the regular Army. True, Congress had voted an increase of 50,000 men, but in the first six months of hostilities only 5,000 men volunteered to serve in "Mr. Madison's War." To this could be added about 50,000 militia, available for use only as the loyalty and politics of the state governors might dictate.

Commanding this force were ranking officers who seemed to be prodigies of senility or incompetence.

Henry Dearborn, the senior major general, had fought with John Stark at Bunker Hill and marched to Quebec with Benedict Arnold. He had also served as Secretary of War, in which office he distinguished himself for his reluctance to apprehend Aaron Burr. Latterly whatever ardor he possessed had been smothered in the soft life of the Boston customhouse. Taking the field again at the age of 61, he was nicknamed "Granny" by his troops.

Thomas Pinckney, another Revolutionary War veteran, was 62, and, in the words of a ranking Congressman, "as fit for his place as the Indian Prophet would be for Emperor of Europe."[9]

The senior brigadier was James Wilkinson: Wilkinson of the Conway Cabal, the friend of the author of the Newburgh Addresses, secret agent of Spain, treacherous accomplice of Aaron Burr, and, at the age of 55, an officer renowned for never having won a battle or lost a court-martial. After Wilkinson came four more brigadiers about 60 years of age, all sharing the distinction of never having commanded a regiment in battle, and chosen on the basis of family, wealth, politics or service in the Revolution. These were the top commanders who, together with officers of field rank whom young Captain Winfield Scott scorned as drunkards or drones, were to lead the lightning war envisioned by President Madison and his penny-pinching Secretary of War, William Eustis.

Eustis had been a military surgeon during the Revolution. After Benedict Arnold's flight from West Point, he administered restoratives to the shocked Peggy Shippen Arnold. He switched to politics after Shays' Rebellion and was later rewarded with the War Department,

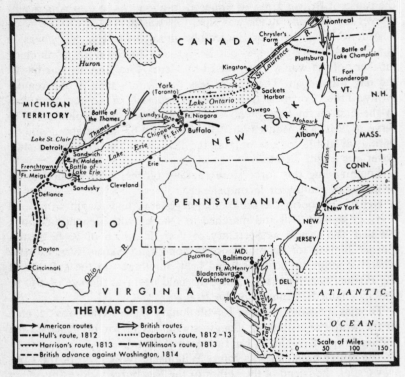

THE WAR OF 1812

→ American routes   ⇨ British routes
—·— Hull's route, 1812   ······ Dearborn's route, 1812–13
—▾— Harrison's route, 1813   —·—·— Wilkinson's route, 1813
— — — British advance against Washington, 1814

Scale of Miles
0   50   100   150

where he found his chief delight in writing advertisements for bids on Army supplies detailed down to the last biscuit. Eustis probably knew less about war than the shy, scholarly Madison, and between them they dribbled along a series of "proposals" for the conquest of Canada which, in retrospect, appear to be the negation of prudence erected into a plan.

Detroit, in the heart of hostile Indian country, and menaced by the British across the Detroit River in Fort Malden, was vital to the defense of the Northwest Territory. In February of 1812, four months before the declaration of war, William Hull, the Governor of Michigan Territory, came to Washington to discuss Detroit's defenses. So did General Dearborn. Both Hull and Dearborn insisted that the key to the Northwest was naval control of the Great Lakes. At the time, this was possessed by the British. Britain also, according to the pessimistic Hull, possessed in her regulars and Indian allies the power to subdue the Northwest. The problem, then, was whether or not there was time to build a Great Lakes fleet before the British moved. And then the gloomy Hull made an enigmatic about-face.

He assured Eustis that the British could be forced to abandon Upper Canada merely by menacing them with an army placed in Detroit. British ships on Lake Erie would then fall into American hands and the nation would be spared the expense of building a Great Lakes fleet. From what depth of fatuous optimism Hull dredged up this fantastic proposal is not known, but the prospect of getting a vast province and a lakes fleet free-for-nothing was certainly appealing, especially to the parsimonious Eustis. Madison, accordingly, made no provisions for building an American fleet. Worse, out of these purely defensive considerations came the "plan" for Canadian conquest.

Madison approved Dearborn's proposal to launch a major operation down Lake Champlain against Montreal while supporting thrusts were made into Upper Canada from Sackets Harbor, Niagara and Detroit. Thus an army was not merely to garrison Detroit; it was to move across the river into Canadian territory. And Hull would command it, though reluctantly. Silver-haired and venerable at 60, "a short, corpulent, good-natured old gentleman who bore the marks of good eating and drinking,"[10] Hull had insisted that a younger man should lead. But Madison persuaded him to accept the rank of brigadier general, and in April he went out to Ohio to take command. Dearborn went to Albany to prepare for the Montreal operation.

There was no detailed plan for either Hull or Dearborn. There could not be any time set for coordinated attacks, as such a plan required, because Congress had not yet declared war. Democracies, unlike dictatorships, cannot set invasion dates beforehand and then calmly go about faking "incidents" to justify them. Democracies are given to that debate which precludes timetables and guarantees late starts. They are not always united, either, as President Madison found out when, on April 15, he asked for the Massachusetts militia for use against Montreal.

Massachusetts refused. Governor Caleb Strong coldly informed

Madison that militia were for federal use only, to suppress insurrection or repel invasion, and since neither exigency was imminent, Yankee Doodle was staying home. So were the Connecticut militia, and the message to Madison was clear: Westerners wanted this war, let them fight it. Westerners, however, were too far from the Lake Champlain region to be of immediate use, as were the regular troops scattered in garrisons across the country. Therefore the major stroke against Montreal was blunted at the outset.

Meanwhile, William Hull was marching toward Detroit serenely confident that General Dearborn was organizing the Montreal and Niagara expeditions which were to coincide with his. Hull had taken command of about 1,200 Ohio volunteers on May 25. He introduced himself with an eloquent speech which fired every breast. On June 1 the march began. On June 10 Hull was reinforced by a regiment of regulars, and eventually his army numbered about 2,000 men.

War had not yet been declared, nor had Hull been authorized to invade Canada, but he certainly must have expected orders to do so. As he marched, he drew farther and farther out of reach. Thus he had no way of knowing how hopeless the situation on his eastern or right flank had become. The Montreal operation was not only definitely bogged down, but the assault from Niagara was already a travesty. Only a handful of New York militia had gathered along the Niagara frontier, where they milled around leaderless, waiting for Granny Dearborn to appoint their commander.

Hull plodded on. His men cut such a clean slice through the forest that parts of it were still visible as late as the Civil War. At the end of June, Hull reached the Maumee or Miami River. To his delight he found the schooner *Cuyahoga* there. He decided to load it with his heavy equipment and send it up to Detroit, freeing himself for faster movement. Unfortunately, he also put aboard a trunk containing his instructions and his army muster rolls. As *Cuyahoga* set sail for Lake Erie, Hull hurried through the forests, eagerly awaiting those dispatches from Eustis which would inform him that the nation was at war. He did not receive word until July 2, four days after the British had been alerted, and then only by ordinary mail which a conscientious postmaster had forwarded from Cleveland. On the same day the British captured *Cuyahoga* as it attempted to slip past Fort Malden and enter Detroit.

Hull's mission and strength were now known to the enemy.

Major General Isaac Brock was the Governor General of Upper Canada. He was a superb soldier, decisive, energetic—and an aggressive foil to his cautious superior, Lieutenant General Sir George Prevost. Prevost, Governor in Chief of all Provinces, was impressed with the weakness of his position, and on July 10 he warned the impetuous Brock not to attempt any stroke that might unite the bickering American states. Brock was to remain on the defensive.

Brock, however, had different ideas. He had long ago realized the importance of naval power and built the ships which gave him command of Lake Erie. He knew that neither his Indians nor his militia were reliable unless he immediately took them on the offensive, and he was prepared to order them out against Detroit and Fort Michilimackinac once war began. However, Brock was also certain that the main American blow would fall on the 40-mile Niagara frontier between Lake Erie and Lake Ontario, and here he waited on the defensive while Hull moved against Detroit far to the west.

Hull reached Detroit on July 5. It was then a community of about 800 souls, including Hull's own daughter and grandchildren. The fort was a square enclosure of about two acres which was within gunshot of the British shore, but did not itself command the Detroit River. Hull might well have considered himself in a trap, for he was 200 miles above his base, and his line of communications, running 60 miles along the edge of Lake Erie, was menaced from the water by British ships and on land by hostile Indians. Moreover, he was responsible for the welfare of perhaps 5,000 American civilians in the area.

Hull did not act confidently. His troops, eager to win the war in time to be home for summer harvesting, chafed at the delay in attacking British and Canadians clearly visible across the river at Sandwich (part of present-day Windsor). Hull, however, told his importunate officers on July 9 that he had no authority to enter Canada. But that same night orders to that effect were received, and two days later his army began marching downstream as though to cross the river at Fort Malden 12 miles below Sandwich. The British immediately gathered their men inside Fort Malden, and at daybreak of the following day, July 12, Hull's army crossed at Sandwich without opposition.

News of Hull's bloodless coup filled the nation with rejoicing. But on July 16 Hull began to take counsel from his fears. On that day

Colonel Lewis Cass found a lightly guarded bridge only about four miles above Malden. He attacked and seized it. Aware that he had exceeded orders, he asked for permission to hold this vital crossing. Hull vacillated. Instead of seeing that Cass had penetrated the enemy's defenses, he preferred to believe that Cass had needlessly exposed his rear. Finally, he left the decision up to Cass, and that worthy officer —who came very close to becoming an American Vice President— retired in disgust.

The golden chance had been muffed. Along all the British frontier from Sandwich down to Malden there were not 500 men, of whom only 100 were regulars. Now was the time to storm Malden, but Hull timidly marked time. He sent off letters to Governor Meigs of Ohio pleading for supplies, and the British intercepted them and blocked the supply train. He pleaded again and again for a diversion out of Niagara, but Granny Dearborn was dragging his feet. On August 6 Hull mustered his courage and ordered an attack on Malden. Next day he canceled it, turned around, recrossed the river and took up a defensive stance in Detroit. The crossing at Sandwich had been the high point of the campaign.

Meanwhile, the resourceful Isaac Brock was already flying to the relief of Malden.

General Brock heard of Hull's entry into Canada on July 20. He immediately sent Colonel Henry Proctor and 60 regulars to reinforce Malden, called a special session of the provincial legislature to vote supplies, and then dismissed its members after they refused to suspend the Habeas Corpus Act. Certain now that Niagara was not the critical point, he embarked a force of 240 militia and 40 regulars on Lake Erie and crowded on all sail for Malden.

The value of control of the lakes was now apparent, yet not a single American hand was lifted to detain Brock as he sped toward Malden. He arrived there on August 13, and soon met Tecumseh, who had also arrived with 600 warriors. Having read the captured *Cuyahoga* papers, as well as other intercepted American documents, Brock judged that his enemy, though more numerous than he, was very low on morale. He proposed an immediate attack. Delighted, Tecumseh drew his knife and cut a map of the area on a roll of birch bark.

On August 14, while Brock made his preparations, Hull sent a relief expedition south in a last desperate attempt to bring supplies into Detroit. Making a wide circle to avoid ambush, the column became lost in the woods. Next day Brock took his regulars and militia across the river three miles below the fort. Playing on Hull's fears, he sent him a surrender demand, warning of what might happen if his Indians became angered by a prolonged siege. Hull had the wit to reject it, and Brock promptly ordered his shore batteries and two gunboats into action. Cannon shot shook the American fort, and Hull's guns began to reply—but faintly. Next Brock planted a document alluding to "5,000 Indians" in Hull's hands and dressed his untrained militia in the scarlet coats of British regulars. That night Hull learned that Tecumseh and his warriors had crossed the river below Brock and had moved inland to cut off the return of his relief column. Fatigued and exhausted, his spirit began to sink under the weight of multiplying fears.

As daylight of August 16 came, William Hull began to fall apart in the presence of his men. He sat on an old tent with his back against the rampart. His voice trembled. He avoided the contemptuous eyes of those officers who wanted to fight. In his agitation he stuffed quid after quid of chewing tobacco into his mouth until the brown spittle began to spill out and run down his beard and vest. Hull could think of nothing but the safety of the cut-off relief column or of an Indian massacre that would include his own daughter and grandchildren. Cannon shot still shook his fort, four men fell, the militia began to desert, and so William Hull sent his son to signal the surrender.

For the first and only time an American city unfurled a white flag to a foreign foe, and it was seen with incredulous delight by Isaac Brock and his soldiers as they came marching up the hill.

The surrender of Detroit was not only the most disgraceful episode in the annals of American arms; it was the first of a series of Western defeats sufficient to shake even Henry Clay's faith in the invincibility of Western frontiersmen. Hull, stunned by the news of the fall of Fort Michilimackinac, had sent orders for the evacuation of Fort Dearborn, the site of modern Chicago. Captain William Wells arrived with these instructions on August 12. However, a friendly Indian chief warned the Americans not to leave the safety of the fort, explaining that "leaden birds had been singing in his ears." He was ignored. The soldiers with their women and children left the fort on August 15. Less than an hour later they were overwhelmed by 500 red men who killed half of them and imprisoned the others.

Captain Wells was beheaded, after which the Indians cut out his heart and ate it.

Now, with the entire frontier laid open to Indian incursion, 2,000 Kentucky militia were called out to punish Indians in the Illinois country. With typical bombast their general, Congressman Samuel Hopkins, described his army as the best he had seen "in the western country or anywhere else." The closer Hopkins's army came to the Indians, however, the more unruly it became. After the red men set the prairies on fire, the "flower of Kentucky" wilted and went home.

The Northwest frontier now lay wide open to invasion, the British were over the border at Detroit, and hundreds of frightened Western settlers began leaving their homes.

America's military weaknesses and internal divisions were never so naked as during the storm of reproach and recrimination which followed the Northwest disasters. Federalists could not conceal their delight at the dismay of the war hawks, while these thwarted conquerers screamed in concert for the head of William Hull.* Even Thomas Jefferson went so far as to say: "The treachery of Hull, like that of Arnold, cannot be a matter of blame for our government."[11] However, as Henry Adams has observed, if any man was responsible for Hull's failure it was Thomas Jefferson, whose unyielding pacifism excluded military efficiency and unity from the American system. Even then, while Jefferson's protégé Madison yearned for the military victory which might retrieve his political fortunes in the election of 1812, the American military posture was a chaos of conflicts and confusions.

Madison wanted to raise a second Northwestern Army to retake Detroit. He thought of naming James Monroe, his Secretary of State, to command this and all other northern armies. But the people of the West took the matter out of his hands. They thought of William Henry Harrison, the 39-year-old hero of Tippecanoe, and a Kentucky caucus elected Harrison major general of militia.

Harrison hastened toward Fort Wayne, then besieged by Indians. Meanwhile, the federal government decided to make him a brigadier

---

* Two years later a court-martial convicted Hull of cowardice and sentenced him to dismissal and death, but President Madison spared Hull's life.

general junior to James Winchester, who, at 61, seemed to satisfy the Federal preference for silver hair. But Winchester was a Tennessee aristocrat who was not loved in the West, as Harrison informed Madison. And so, under pressure of a state's action, Madison on September 17 gave Harrison the Northwestern command.

Harrison was to have an army of 10,000 men and to recapture Detroit in a rapid autumn campaign. But he could not traverse the road cut by Hull's army because his own force was five times as big and the autumn rains had made an impassable quagmire of it. So Harrison decided to wait until winter had frozen the lakes and rivers and made them passable. Winter, however, was slow in arriving that year, and Harrison was frustrated in his hopes of striking at Detroit before 1813.

In the meantime, the focus of the fighting shifted to the Northeastern front.

After the fall of Detroit, General Brock hastened back to the Niagara frontier. En route, he discovered that Prevost and Dearborn had agreed to an armistice! Prevost, hearing of the suspension of the Orders in Council, had at once sent an emissary to Dearborn in Albany. Dearborn, distracted and disorganized, looked upon a truce as a godsend. Although the armistice did not include Detroit, Dearborn assured Eustis that "it will not probably have any effect on General Hull or his movements." In other words, the left arm did not need the right arm. Madison angrily repudiated the agreement, but not before Brock had had the time to organize his meager force of 1,600 soldiers and 300 Indians in mutually supporting positions along the 40-mile Niagara River.

By October some 6,000 Americans had gathered across the Niagara from Brock's 2,000. Most of them were militia, undisciplined, poorly fed and supplied. But they had at last received a commander, General Stephen Van Rensselaer, a distinguished Federalist whom the Republicans appointed to give the campaign a nonpartisan coloring. Unfortunately, he had no military experience whatsoever. To compensate for this deficiency, Colonel Solomon Van Rensselaer, a relative and a Revolutionary War veteran, was named as his aide.

The new general's militiamen were eager to fight, threatening to go home unless the shooting started soon. So General Van Rensselaer drew up a plan for a double crossing of the Niagara. General Alexander Smyth with 1,650 regulars was supposed to move out onto Lake Ontario and come in on the rear of Fort George, located at the point where the river empties into Ontario. Van Rensselaer's own force would cross opposite Queenston, about ten miles upriver.

Smyth, however, did not wish to cross the river below Niagara Falls. He wanted to cross above the cataract at a point in the neighborhood of Buffalo, at the southern end of the Niagara, where he was based. Smyth, therefore, sat still.

Van Rensselaer went ahead. On the morning of October 11 all was in readiness—except that an American officer, either from ignorance or treachery, rowed across the river in a boat containing all the oars and left it there. Undaunted, Van Rensselaer made another attempt on the rain-swept night of October 12-13.

Colonel Van Rensselaer led about 200 men across the river. They landed successfully, but were discovered about four o'clock in the morning. The British-Canadians opened fire, and the Americans charged and scattered them. Down at Fort George, General Brock was awakened in surprise. He had expected the main blow to come from Fort Niagara almost directly opposite George. Instructing his gunners to open a restraining fire on Niagara, he hurried upriver to Queenston.

There the Americans had ascended the heights under Captain John Wool, who took charge after Van Rensselaer was severely wounded. And as Brock hurried to the battle scene, Lieutenant Colonel Winfield Scott, 26 years old and 6 feet 4 inches of muscle and righteous insubordination, came galloping down from Buffalo without so much as a by-your-leave from the uncooperative General Smyth.

Brock, meanwhile, had reached Queenston just as the Americans on the heights began firing down on a British gun. Charging down the hill, the Americans took the piece. Brock led a countercharge and was shot in the breast and killed.

Now, at about two o'clock in the afternoon, the towering Scott had come over to Queenston and taken command from Wool. He had between 700 and 800 Americans to hold off a British force which had swelled to about 1,000. Brock's system of supporting positions had gone rapidly into effect. Obviously, the Americans needed reinforcements.

But not a man of the militia so bold to fight would come to the side of their embattled comrades. They said there were no boats, but only half had been swamped or carried off by the Niagara's swift currents. They were asked to cross in detachments, but they still refused. The distraught General Van Rensselaer rode among them and pleaded with them to cross. One well-equipped militia company consented, but just as the men began stepping into the boats the sound of firing was heard from Queenston Heights and they changed their minds.

Not a soldier crossed the river, and Scott's outnumbered force braced for the enemy's assault. It was begun by the Indians, who charged splendidly. Then the British-Canadians crashed out a single volley and followed with the bayonet. The Americans gave way and broke. Many of them tried to hide along the steep banks of the river, but they were caught and killed. Others attempted to swim the turbulent Niagara and were drowned. Most of them surrendered, including Colonel Scott.

Once again a small but able British force had humbled an American military mob; but this time, with the death of General Brock, the Crown had won a Pyrrhic victory. No soldier of Brock's stature appeared on the British side for the remainder of the war. Meanwhile, the American cause passed from the tragicomedy of Queenston Heights to the travesty of Black Rock.

Alexander Smyth had replaced Van Rensselaer, who had resigned in chagrin. Smyth, more writer than fighter, spent much of his time composing ringing declarations. "Friends of your country!" he told his soldiers. "Ye who have 'the will to do, the heart to dare!' the moment ye have wished for has arrived! Think on your country's honors torn! Her rights trampled on! Her sons enslaved! Her infants perishing by the hatchet! Be strong! Be brave! And let the ruffian power of the British king cease on this continent!"[12]

Thus, hurling his exclamation points like spears, Smyth rallied a force once again grown to 6,000 men for another assault on Canada. In the early morning of November 28 a small advance guard crossed the river from the vicinity of Black Rock. The Americans seized two enemy batteries near Red House. As daylight approached, 2,000 men climbed into waiting boats. Barely out on the river, Smyth suddenly and unaccountably called off the entire expedition.

Smyth's soldiers were so enraged, however, that their general was forced to reschedule the assault for December 1. Before that date Smyth told his troops: "The general will·be on board. Neither rain, snow or frost will prevent the embarkation. . . . While embarking the music will play martial airs. *Yankee Doodle* will be the signal to get under way." The general's officers, however, objected to sending Yankee Doodle across a river in broad daylight into the mouths of enemy guns. General Smyth promptly called a council of war at which his officers vetoed his proposal. Seeing a chance to get off the hook, General Smyth agreed and climbed down.

Now his men were so infuriated that they began shooting off their muskets, some of them in the general direction of General Smyth's tent. And that was the end of the Niagara fiasco.

Meanwhile, at Sackets Harbor on the eastern end of Lake Ontario there was simply no invasion whatever.

At Lake Champlain, General Dearborn had at last moved north, taking some 6,000 or 8,000 men up to Plattsburg on the lake. The Canadians countered by sending 1,900 men south from Montreal. On the night of November 19 the Americans and Canadians collided in a skirmish on the Lacolle River. The Americans captured a blockhouse, the Canadians fled, and then the Americans got lost and began firing on each other. After his militia suddenly remembered their constitutional rights and refused to cross the border, General Dearborn went into winter quarters.

Disgrace at Detroit, ignominy at Niagara, a blank at Sackets Harbor and a fizzle on Lake Champlain: thus had the 1812 campaign to conquer Canada concluded in the most inglorious chapter in American military history.

4

☆

Because of its reliance on unruly militia and white-haired generals the United States had failed shamefully in that Canadian conquest which was the true object of this war for "Free Trade and Sailors' Rights." But at sea, where battle was almost an afterthought, the brash young American Navy sailed forth to astonish the old queen of the waves.

Britain then was a sea monster of 600 ships, of which 120 were ships of the line and 116 were frigates. Roughly corresponding to a modern battleship, a ship of the line usually mounted 74 or more guns, although some carried as few as 50. Frigates—equal to a modern cruiser—were armed with 32 to 44 guns.

At the outbreak of hostilities, Britain had only one 64-gun ship of the line and seven frigates near the American coast. To oppose them, the United States had 16 seagoing vessels and about 200 gunboats. The gunboats, imposed on the protesting Navy by Jefferson in his belief that they were a cheap solution to coastal defense, were widely scattered and in varying stages of disrepair. Even in the best condition, gunboats were of use only inside harbors and not out on the stormy ocean where sea power holds sway. Only 12 of the seagoing ships were of value, but of these the seven frigates were superb.

They had been built by the Federalists when the Naval War with France threatened, and they might have had sister ships of the line had not the Jeffersonian Republicans worked their "chaste reformation" of the armed forces. Now they were the delight of the Madisonian Republicans: sturdy, swift ships heavily timbered and planked to repel enemy shot, able to throw heavier broadsides than the British frigates; and yet, with their clean lines and great spread of sail, capable of outrunning anything afloat.

This small navy was also well trained and efficient. Most of its captains were veterans of the French and Tripolitan fighting. They were eager to clash with the British, those doughty though arrogant sea dogs who looked upon all other sailors with disdain and contempt.

The *Constitution* had been called "Old Ironsides" because her live-oak planks had been forcefully bent into place without benefit of that steaming process which was believed to weaken wood. She was commanded by Captain Isaac Hull, the nephew and adopted son of William Hull. On the morning of July 18, 1812, just as his unfortunate uncle began to falter at Fort Malden, Hull fell in with four British frigates: *Shannon,* 38 guns; *Belvidera,* 36; *Aeolus,* 32; and *Guerrière,* 38. Following them but out of sight was the battleship *Africa,* 64.

Constitution, rated at 44 guns but actually carrying 54, could outfight any single frigate but not four of them. As the British quartet began closing in, Hull prepared for a fighting withdrawal.

He cut away part of his stern rail and mounted a long 18- and 24-pounder aft. He widened his cabin portholes and poked 24s through them, and because it was a windless day he put out his boats to try to drag himself out of range. So did the British, putting all their boats at *Shannon*'s disposal. Finding himself in fairly shallow water, Hull stopped towing and began to kedge. That is, a cutter carried a small anchor forward and dropped it so that all hands might tug on the attached cable and thus haul the ship ahead. Kedging laboriously, *Constitution* began to crawl away from her pursuers. Then *Shannon* began to work two kedges, drawing closer until *Constitution*'s stern guns spoke and forced *Shannon*'s cutters to keep a wary distance. So it went throughout the day, while the sweating, cursing sailors of both nations alternately rowed or dragged their ships through a glassy sea. Night gave them respite, but in the morning Hull saw that *Africa* had joined his pursuers.

Towing and kedging were renewed until noon, when a breeze sprang up. Quickly Hull ordered his tired sailors to swarm up the rigging and saturate the sails. He began to empty his ship of ten tons of drinking water to lessen her draft by one inch. Still the lighter British craft came closer.

Hull had a set of skysails made and set. All other sails were set and trimmed to the greatest advantage, close by the wind—and with the freshening of the wind at noon the beautiful American ship began to draw away from her pursuers. Two hours later she was plunging toward Boston at nearly 13 knots and the British were dwindling specks to her stern.

Rotund little Isaac Hull was not content with having taught the British a lesson in seamanship. He wanted battle with them, especially with Captain James Dacres of the *Guerrière,* who had repeatedly challenged the Americans to come out and fight him. Reconditioning his ship, Hull sailed from Boston on August 2. On August 19, three days after his uncle's surrender at Detroit, about 750 miles east of Boston, Hull's lookouts sighted the sails of *Guerrière.*

Both ships immediately began maneuvering for "the weather gauge," that is, to get to the windward of the enemy. Each wanted to be able to rake the other without being raked. But Hull and Dacres maneuvered with such skill that neither could gain the advantage. *Guerrière* opened fire at long range, blasting away in a starboard broadside that fell short. Dacres next wore ship, that is, turned in a half-circle so as to bring his portside guns to bear. This time his cannon balls went shrieking high over *Constitution*'s topsails.

Suddenly Hull set extra sail and closed quickly on the surprised Dacres. Hull waited until he was within half-pistol shot—50 feet—and then cried to his crew: "Now, boys, pour it into them!"[13]

Old Ironsides's forward guns, double shotted with grape, roared and flamed. They riddled *Guerrière*'s rigging, ripped her sails and reddened her decks with blood. Hull leaned over the rail, eager for a closer look, and split his tight buff breeches down the rear seam. His men shouted with laughter, and bent to the guns.

Running before the wind, nearly abreast of each other, both ships exchanged fire. Gradually the superior American guns and gunnery began to tell. After a quarter-hour *Guerrière* was a cripple. Her rear mast fell overboard just as her main yard gave way in the middle. Slowing with reduced sail power, she allowed Old Ironsides to steer across her bow into the coveted raking position. *Guerrière* now could fire only a few forward guns, while *Constitution* could bring all guns to bear to blast the Britisher lengthwise. Hull seized the opportunity. He raked Dacres with his starboard guns, wore ship, and raked him with the port battery. Marine sharpshooters in Old Ironsides's tops poured musket fire into *Guerrière*'s decks. Now the ships swung close and the Britisher's bowsprit caught in *Constitution*'s rigging. Both captains cried: "Boarders away!"

Marine Lieutenant William Bush leaped to the rail to lead his men aboard the enemy. He was shot through the head, falling back on *Constitution*'s deck just as the wind filled her sails and broke her free of *Guerrière*. Now Ironsides's sharpshooters took a toll of British seamen clearly visible on the enemy's decks. American gunfire cut away the Britisher's foremast and then the mainmast. Dacres, streaming blood, gallantly ran up a new Union Jack on his stump of foremast—but the battle was over. Her decks slippery with blood, her hull riddled, her masts and canvas gone and her rigging shredded, *Guerrière* was a helpless hulk dipping and rolling in the sea. Dacres fired a surrender shot to leeward and pulled down his flag.

Although Hull was forced to burn his prize, his victory was indestructible. It shone like a lone beacon of hope throughout the military eclipse of the Northern campaign. In one half-hour, says Henry Adams, Hull and his men had raised the United States to the rank of a first-class power. Never before had a British frigate struck to an American, and in Britain the *Times of London* reported: "The loss of the *Guerrière* spread a degree of gloom through the town which it was painful to observe."[14] The *Times* observed that *Guerrière* had fallen to "a new enemy, an enemy unaccustomed to such triumphs, and likely to be rendered insolent and confident by them."[15]

True enough, for even the Federalists of New England joined the general rejoicing, and even "the cautious Madison was dragged by the public excitement upon the element he most heartily disliked."[16]

Tasting blood and eager for more, the Navy's fiery young captains were granted a freedom of action rare in the usages of warfare, and they quickly put to sea in three squadrons of three ships apiece. As they did, the *Times of London* thundered: "But above all, there is one object to which our most strenuous efforts should be directed —the entire annihilation of the American Navy."[17]

The Thunderer of Fleet Street was disappointed. On October 18 the American sloop *Wasp,* 18 guns, Master Commandant Jacob Jones, came upon the British sloop *Frolic,* 19, Captain Thomas Whinyates, as she escorted a convoy of six merchantmen from Honduras to England. The seas ran high, and the merchants ships made safely off while the two sloops closed for broadside battle.

In such seas one ship would be now above the other on the crest of a wave, now below in a trough, and serving the guns was a difficult feat. Yet the Americans firing their port guns were able to catch *Frolic*'s starboard rising on the roll of the waves and put holes in her hull. *Frolic*'s starboard battery, fired on the roll as *Wasp* dipped into the trough, went screaming over the American's head or through her rigging. Thus *Wasp* quickly gained the advantage. As the ships drew closer, an American seaman named Jack Lang leaped to the rail waving a cutlass and jumped down on *Frolic*'s deck. Lang had been an impressed seaman, he was thirsting for revenge, and his impetuous action touched off an American boarding rush which brought *Frolic*'s colors fluttering down.

Once again the Americans had shown their superiority with guns, although their exultation was to be short-lived. While they struggled to bring *Frolic* home as a prize, the big 74-gun ship of the line *Poictiers* came up to free *Frolic* and take *Wasp* as prize. Nevertheless, *Wasp* had won another American victory, and 12 days later Captain Stephen Decatur made a third British warship dip her colors to Old Glory.

The hero of Tripoli commanded the *United States,* sister to Old Ironsides. Off Madeira on October 25 he fell in with the 38-gun *Macedonian.* The British ship, though fleet, was heavily outgunned, especially in long-range pieces. Decatur stood off at a distance and pot-shotted *Macedonian* to death. His highly trained crew loaded and fired with such speed that they outshot the British two to one, and Captain John Carden struck his colors. Although the British ship was a floating wreck, Decatur managed to bring her back to Newport, the only British frigate ever brought into a United States port as a prize.

And so the glorious six months passed, capped on December 29 by *Constitution*'s toe-to-toe slugging victory over the evenly matched British frigate *Java.* True, the Americans had only won a handful of single-ship victories and had not even challenged a ship of the line. Yet the Yankee seamen with their beautiful swift ships had shown the world that they could sail at least as well as and certainly shoot better than the old sea dogs of Britain. More, they had forced the *Times* to ask the incredible question: "What is wrong with British sea power?"[18]

5

☆

Re-elected for a second term and heartened by a glittering string of naval victories, President Madison began 1813 looking hopefully toward the Northwest, where William Henry Harrison stood poised to redeem American military fortunes.

Harrison's army had entered on the cruel ordeal of the Northern winter. It had dwindled to 6,500 men. Some of them were mutinous, especially the fiercely independent Kentucky long knives who held down the army's left wing at Fort Defiance under General Winchester. Nevertheless, Harrison decided to get closer to Detroit. He ordered Winchester to move from Defiance up to the Maumee Rapids. In early January, at the head of about 1,200 men, Winchester moved out.

His soldiers marched through snow two feet deep, harnessing themselves to sledges to pull their gear. At the front of the column men floundering through the drifts gradually packed them smooth, so that men at the rear slipped and fell or flailed their arms to keep their balance. Then the temperature rose and it began to rain. The soldiers slogged through slush and mud or splashed through water floating atop the rotten ice of thawing streams and ponds. Living on half-rations, soaked, their teeth chattering, lacking axes to fell firewood or utensils to cook with, they plodded on—reaching the rapids on January 10.

Winchester had begun building a fortified camp and gathering supplies, when he received an appeal from American settlers at Frenchtown (now Monroe, Michigan) on the River Raisin. The Americans said their lives were endangered by 100 Indians who were inside the town with about 50 Canadian militia. Frenchtown was 35 miles north of the rapids, 100 miles away from Harrison's main body and only 18 miles south of Fort Malden. Thus it was within easy reach of the British. Nevertheless, Winchester decided to succor Frenchtown, persuaded, perhaps, by the fact that his men had reached that point of exasperation where they were eager to fight anyone.

On January 17 Colonel William Lewis and 550 men began marching north over frozen terrain and in bitter cold. On the next day they reached the little settlement of 30 families and attacked the Indians and Canadians. After a two-hour fight the Americans cleared the village. Two days later, General Winchester came up from the rapids with 300 additional men. He set up a camp that was an invitation to disaster, leaving most of his force stationed on the north bank of the River Raisin while he himself set up headquarters a half-mile south of the river. The sight and smell of his ragged and half-mutinous long knives were too much for Winchester's elegant senses. And so, to the folly of placing men with their backs to a stream, and then trying to command them from the other side, Winchester added the dereliction of ordering no night pickets or night patrols.

Up in Fort Malden, meanwhile, it was clear to General Henry Proctor, the successor to the fallen Brock, that the Americans were incredibly far off base—although he could never have imagined that they were also off their guard. Taking about 1,200 men—half of them Indians under Roundhead and Walk-in-the-Water—he began stealing south. On the night of January 21, under cover of a raging snow-storm, he came within reach of the Americans. He put his artillery and his regulars in his center and his Indians and militia on his right and left flanks. Opposite him the American left was protected by a picket fence, while the right was only partially guarded by a crude rail fence.

Two hours before daylight of January 22, 1813, with the snow still falling, Frenchtown was suddenly shaken by artillery fire and the rattle of musketry. War whoops were heard. Almost at once the American right was overwhelmed. Within a few minutes 100 soldiers were scalped by Indians who had gotten into the rear. General Winchester, blundering to the front to rally his men, was taken prisoner.

On the left, however, about 400 men under Major George Madison fought with bravery and skill. They repulsed charge after charge. Came a lull in the battle and they saw a white flag approaching. Their hearts soared, for they thought that it was a flag of truce. But it was rather a British officer bringing a message from Winchester to the effect that he had surrendered his entire army, themselves included.

Chagrined, Madison sent back the reply: "It has been customary for the Indians to massacre the wounded and prisoners after a sur-render. I shall not agree to any capitulation which General Winchester may direct, unless the safety and protection of all the prisoners shall be stipulated."[19] Proctor raged that he would not accept dicta-tion, but in the end he agreed and Madison surrendered.

Proctor kept his word by stripping his prisoners of some of their clothing, robbing them of their money and forcing them to drag his sleds to rest his horses. His wounded prisoners were left behind without guards. An American who had asked for help for the wounded was told: "The Indians are excellent doctors."[20] So Proctor deserted them on the grounds that he wished to flee the area before Harrison could come up and attack him. As soon as he departed, the Indians became drunk and began scalping the wounded. They set fire to one houseful of them, and as those able to rise rushed to the windows to escape, they beat them back into the flames with tomahawks.

Thus the allies of the noble Proctor, and as Proctor hurried north to regain the safety of Fort Malden, Harrison, from whom he fled, was also burning Winchester's post at the Maumee Rapids and hastening south. Thirty-six hours after the Battle of Frenchtown the two enemies were 60 miles apart. A week later Harrison returned to the rapids with 2,000 men. He built a fortified camp on its south bank and named it Fort Meigs after the Governor of Ohio. Ordering up all troops in his rear, he collected a force of 4,000 men which he planned to hurl against Malden. February 11 was fixed as the day of advance, but on that day the roads were sheeted with ice and impassable, and the expedition to Malden was canceled.

So ended, in defeat, massacre and disgrace, the Western movement against Upper Canada. Although his contemporaries were kinder to Harrison than to Hull, and would one day make him President, the fact is that William Henry Harrison had done less with more. He had not even gotten across the Maumee River. The men whom he led, and in whom he had great faith, were obviously superior to those who had followed Hull into Canada. A British officer has left a description of them:

Their appearance was miserable to the last degree. They had the air of men to whom cleanliness was a virtue unknown. . . . It was the depth of winter; but scarcely an individual was in possession of a great coat or cloak. . . . They still retained their summer dress, consisting of cotton stuff of various colors shaped into frocks, and descending to the knee. Their trousers were of the same material. They were covered with slouched hats, worn bare by constant use, beneath which their long hair fell matted and uncombed over their cheeks; and these, together with the dirty blankets wrapped round their loins to protect them against the inclemency of the season, and fastened by broad leathern belts into which were thrust axes and knives of an enormous length, gave them an air of wilderness and savageness.[21]

They were neither pretty nor perfumed, but hard with the lean toughness of adversity, and such men, given the leader to inspire and organize them, have always been invincible. However, America had yet to find its leaders. The penny-pinching William Eustis had done his country the great kindness of resigning, but Madison had replaced him in the War Department with John Armstrong, a leading Republican politician from New York who was also the author of the mutinous Newburgh Addresses as well as the crony of the treacherous James Wilkinson.

Despite his record, Armstrong was not disloyal—just personally ambitious. Nor did he fail to see, as Hull and Harrison had also seen before closing their eyes to the fact, that naval control of the Great Lakes was the key to the Western campaign. But as Armstrong assumed office on February 5, 1813, the lakes were still frozen—and out on the open Atlantic the British Navy was demonstrating the risks that are taken when a young nation with a small navy and a long coastline defies the greatest sea power in the world.

Although the American single-ship victories continued into 1813 —notably when the 18-gun *Hornet* under the gallant James Lawrence defeated the 16-gun *Peacock* in February—they could at best only scratch the iron façade of British sea power. Unshaken, the Admiralty paid the Americans the ultimate compliment of ordering heavy frigates the equal of *Constitution* and her sister furies to be built, instructed its captains to be more respectful of Yankee fighting abilities and called for improvements in gunnery training. It also began to enforce a blockade of the exits of the Delaware and Chesapeake.

The blockade was ordered after Britain realized that suspension of the Orders in Council had not brought peace. President Madison still insisted that the British stop impressing seamen, and this, of course, Britannia would never do. So the blockade was begun, and later extended north to Long Island and south to the Mississippi, carefully excluding New England for the purpose of encouraging antiwar sentiment there.

Vice Admiral John Borlase Warren was charged with enforcing the blockade and by February, 1813, he had at his disposal 17 ships of the line, two 50-gunners, 27 frigates and about 50 smaller vessels. With the years, as his fleet grew steadily larger, he turned the screws of the blockade tighter and tighter. The American economy was strangled. Exports, which had been as high as $130 million in 1807, fell to $25 million in 1813 and to $7 million the following year. Import duties, which had yielded $413 million in 1811, fell to less than half that amount in 1814.

The blockade also bottled up coastal shipping, with the result that a dreadful burden was placed on land transportation. It took 46 days for a wagon to move from South Carolina to Philadelphia, and the poor roads were so thronged with wagons that on one occasion, no less than 800 of them were counted waiting in line before a Pennsylvania ferry. Prices soared. Sugar quoted at $9 a hundredweight in New Orleans sold for $21 in New York in August, 1813, and by December had risen to $40. A hundredweight of rice that sold for $3 in Savannah brought $12 in Philadelphia.

Not content with strangling the American economy, the Admiralty ordered Admiral Warren to bring the war home to the Americans in the Delaware-Chesapeake area. Warren thereupon sent Captain John Beresford in the 74-gun *Poictiers* to the Delaware. Beresford appeared before Lewes, Delaware, and shelled the town after its inhabitants stubbornly refused to hand over 25 live bullocks as he demanded. Lewes fought back with old Revolutionary War cannon, and in so doing launched the famous du Pont powder dynasty.

Pierre du Pont de Nemours, a French intellectual who might have lost his head to the French Revolution's guillotine had not it first cut off Robespierre's, came to America with his two sons. Although he returned to France, the sons remained and built a powder factory. When Lewes came under attack, the du Ponts rushed powder there, and the militia, who had provided themselves with cannon balls by "capturing" British ones that missed their mark, actually disabled a British boat and drove Beresford off. But the British returned, and this time Admiral Warren teamed up with his second-in-command, Admiral Sir George Cockburn.

No better team for chastising civilians could have been chosen. Warren, a religious man who had once wavered between the quarterdeck and the cloth, and was now vice president of the Halifax Bible Society, was as quick with a torch as with a text. Cockburn was simply a crusty old salt who delighted in the discomfiture of landlubbers, especially those who were enemies of the Crown.

Cockburn entered the Chesapeake in the early spring of 1813, engaging first in cleaning out the hen roosts and pigsties in the area around Lynnhaven Bay. Next he ravaged Frenchtown, Maryland, put Havre de Grace to the torch and sailed up the Susquehanna 60 miles to destroy a cannon foundry. Carrying plunder and pillage to other areas in the upper Chesapeake, he turned south in June to join Warren and 3,000 regulars in an attack on Norfolk.

There were two objectives: the frigate *Constellation,* anchored near the town, and the Portsmouth Navy Yard. But an amphibious assault on Craney Island which guarded Norfolk was hurled back on June 20 by Americans fighting coolly and shooting accurately under the command of Brigadier General Robert Taylor. Frustrated,

Warren and Cockburn vented their spite on the little village of Hampton. Here the British lost all restraint. As one officer who was later to command the British Army in India noted in his diary: "Every horror was perpetrated with impunity—rape, murder, pillage—*and not a man was punished*."²² Warren tried to place all the blame for Hampton on a unit of French prisoners who had elected to serve with the British rather than languish in prisons, but the vice president of the Halifax Bible Society deceived no one.

Nor was Warren able to destroy the Chesapeake's privateering sanctuaries. Before the war ended there were 526 Yankee privateers swarming out of American coastal cities to strike British commercial shipping and take a total of 1,334 prizes. Even more effective were the U.S. Navy's fighting ships: 22 of them captured 165 British vessels.

Warren's fleet was eager to bottle up those fighting ships which had been caught in port. Among these was *Chesapeake,* the frigate already famous—or notorious—for its humiliation by *Leopard* in the impressment incident of 1807. *Chesapeake*'s new commander, Captain James Lawrence, did not value such celebrity. He was eager to prove that his victory over *Peacock* at the helm of *Hornet* had been no happy fluke. He was, in fact, too eager, for his crew was not yet properly trained, and the ship then watching Boston was the formidable *Shannon,* the frigate which had nearly caught *Constitution* the preceding August.

Like *Chesapeake, Shannon* was rated at 38 guns but actually carried more: 52 to the American's 50. She was commanded by Captain Philip Broke, a British sailor who did not neglect his guns. Broke had personally seen to the mounting of his ordnance and had daily drilled his men in their use. He sent Lawrence a challenge to meet him "ship to ship, to try the fortunes of our respective flags."

Lawrence sailed from Boston on June 1. Broke awaited him at sea between Cape Ann and Cape Cod. Without preliminary maneuver both ships closed to half-pistol shot and began battering each other with broadsides. Cannon roared mouth to mouth. Grapeshot swept the decks, iron balls burst wooden walls, shells exploded, canister flamed with spreading death, and marines of both sides swayed in the rigging while pouring musket shot into the enemy below. Soon both ships were floating charnel houses. But within 15 minutes

Shannon's better-trained gunners had exerted their superiority over *Chesapeake*'s mixed crew. Still, the Americans fought on, especially after Lawrence received his death wound. As he was being carried below, he uttered the famous command that became the motto of the United States Navy.

"Don't give up the ship," he gasped. "Fight her till she sinks."[23]

They did not give up until the cutlasses and grenades of a British boarding party made all further resistance madness. But her flag was never struck by an American hand.

Nevertheless, *Shannon*'s triumph had restored British naval pride, and was also the beginning of the end for America's deep-water fleet. Only two more victories remained for the graceful ships which were the precursors of the beautiful Yankee clippers, and then, one by one, the others were taken or bottled up in port until, in 1814, even the far-ranging *Essex* was caught and destroyed on a Pacific reef.

It was not, however, the end of the U.S. Navy. Far away westward on the warming water of Lake Erie the words of the dying Lawrence echoed in the heart of a young sailor named Oliver Hazard Perry.

Master Commandant Perry had gone to sea at the age of 11, and had fought in the wars with the Barbary pirates. In 1812 he wrote to Commodore Isaac Chauncey, commander of the budding Great Lakes fleet, applying for command of the Lake Erie flotilla being built at Erie, Pennsylvania. Chauncey replied, "You are just the man I have been looking for,"[24] and in March of 1813, at the age of 28, Perry arrived on the shores of Lake Erie.

He hurled himself into the task of building his flotilla and training the men to sail and fight it. He beat the bushes for carpenters, combed the wilderness for blacksmiths, scavenged for scrap iron to make the mounts for his guns, went to the foundries to observe the casting of his shot, and sailed downriver to Pittsburgh to set up a supply line. By the end of May two 20-gun brigs were launched. Soon a trio of gunboats followed. Five ships, however, were not enough to wrest control of Lake Erie from British hands. If only the young commander could free five other ships then stationed at Black Rock on the Niagara River. Unfortunately, the enemy in Fort Erie stood between them and Perry.

Then there began a chain of events in which Perry not only participated but of which he became the chief beneficiary.

Soon after John Armstrong assumed office as Secretary of War he proposed a Northeastern campaign aimed at Montreal. Yet when the orders were received by General Dearborn, Montreal, which was certainly his true objective, was not mentioned. Dearborn was told to take Kingston at the western end of the St. Lawrence River with alternate objectives at York (present-day Toronto) or Forts George and Erie.

Dearborn consulted with Chauncey and after both men grossly overestimated enemy strength at Kingston, that project was dropped and the Northeastern campaign faced farther away westward to York and Fort George.

York was assaulted on April 27 when Chauncey's Ontario ships put ashore 1,600 men under the capable Brigadier General Zebulon Pike.* Pike's soldiers drove off a small force of British regulars and Canadians, and seized the harbor batteries and magazines. They burned a half-built, 30-gun frigate which would have been a valuable addition to the British Ontario fleet, and destroyed naval supplies destined for Lake Erie. And then one of the magazines blew up with a tremendous explosion, raising a deadly shower of stones, one of which crushed the life out of General Pike. In all, 53 Americans were killed and 150 wounded, while 40 Canadians perished and 23 were wounded. The cause of the explosion was not known, but some of the Americans began to think that it was an enemy trick. They thought angrily of "retaliation," ignoring the fact of the Canadian deaths and their own status of invaders, and they began to plunder and loot. They carried off the mace and royal standard of Parliament, and then set fire to the Parliament buildings; and in so doing, even though they might have been aided by capricious Canadians, they created in Canadian hearts a thirst for retaliation in kind which would be satisfied all too soon. That was all there was to York: the wanton burning of the capitol of Upper Canada, the more profitable burning of a ship and naval stores.

At Fort George there was even less military profit. Here, General Dearborn had about 4,000 men against 1,300 under the command of Brigadier General John Vincent. His spearhead troops were led by Winfield Scott, who had been exchanged and promoted to colonel. On May 27 ships commanded by Oliver Hazard Perry bombarded the fort's crumbling wall while his seamen rowed Scott's spearheaders

* He was also the explorer for whom Pike's Peak was named.

through a wild surf. Reaching the beaches, the Americans were momentarily checked by a handful of defenders. But then, gathering force, they burst through. Bringing artillery ashore, Scott put the fort under fire, and Vincent abandoned it.

Vincent's garrison, not moldering old Fort George, was the true objective. But the British got away, chiefly because Scott was wounded and could not pursue, and the vacillating Dearborn was not ashore to give the order. Vincent ordered his garrisons at Fort Erie, Queenston and Chippewa to join him, and withdrew westward along the lake to Burlington Heights.

Two days later the British struck at the American rear. General Sir George Prevost with 800 men appeared at Sackets Harbor and forced a landing, only to be repulsed by the resolute defense maintained by Brigadier General Jacob Brown. With his line of communications thus guaranteed, Dearborn tardily turned to the pursuit of the retreating Vincent.

About 3,000 men under Brigadier Generals William Winder and John Chandler tried to catch Vincent with 1,600. On the night of June 5 the Americans set up camp at Stony Creek, ten miles from Vincent's bivouac. Early the following morning, 750 British regulars struck them in a surprise attack, scattered them and took Winder and Chandler prisoner. Next a force of 600 Americans under Lieutenant Colonel Charles Boerstler surrendered to 400 Indians and 50 regulars.

With this freshest of fiascoes along the Niagara frontier, the fumbling career of Granny Dearborn came to an end. President Madison requested, and received, his resignation. And yet out of Dearborn's mismanagement had come an indirect but enormous advantage. Merely by acting, he had forced Vincent to withdraw his garrison from Fort Erie, thus freeing Perry's ships at Black Rock to sail up the Niagara into Lake Erie.

Perry harnessed the vessels to oxen to tow them through the Niagara's swift current. Reaching the open waters of the lake, they spread sail and made for the sheltering long arm of land that formed the harbor at Erie. Now there were ten ships in Perry's flotilla, and the youthful commander was elated.

On July 12, however, he was saddened to hear of the death of James Lawrence, an officer whom he much admired. In tribute to the *Chesapeake*'s fallen captain, he named his own flagship *Lawrence*. Her sister ship was called *Niagara*.

Now Perry's problems were of a different order. He needed men. Again and again he wrote to Chauncey back at Sackets Harbor, imploring him to send men. Even as Chauncey procrastinated, or sent him the raked-over leavings of his own command, the Navy Department ordered Perry to do battle on the lake. Stung, Perry wrote Chauncey: "For God's sake, and yours and mine, send me men."[25] Chauncey sent him 60 sickly sailors, and Perry turned to recruiting his own crews by offering farmers and woodsmen the princely pay of $10 monthly for four months' service or the duration of a battle, whichever was shorter.

Even so, by mid-July he had only 300 men, and Perry was as nearly frantic as a man of his stability might become; for continued delay gave the enemy time to finish the powerful brig *Detroit,* still on the stocks near Fort Malden. And as the American waited for more reinforcements, warfare flared afresh in the Northwest.

With the coming of the spring of 1813 General Harrison's force in Fort Meigs had dwindled down to about 1,000 men. Harrison appealed to Governor Shelby of Kentucky, who sent forward about 1,200 men under General Green Clay. As the relief force approached Meigs, General Proctor moved out of Malden with 500 regulars, 500 militia and 1,200 Indians under Tecumseh and Roundhead.

The British force reached Fort Meigs on May 1, set up batteries on both sides of the Maumee River and attempted to pound the fort into submission. Just before midnight of May 4, Harrison received word that Clay's relief force was coming down the Maumee on flatboats only two hours away. Harrison decided on a daring plan to raise the siege of Meigs.

Clay's troops were to destroy the British artillery on the north side of the river while Harrison's sallied out of Meigs to take the guns on the south side. About 800 of Clay's men were to land on the north bank, spike the cannon, and then fall back into their boats before the British could get into action. Then these men would join Clay, who with the remaining 400 soldiers was to land on the south bank to cut his way into the fort.

On the south bank the plan worked to perfection. Harrison's men rushed out of Meigs to take the south battery and General Clay got safely into the fort with his 400. On the north bank 800 men under Lieutenant Colonel William Dudley quickly carried the enemy battery and spiked the guns. But then too little leadership and too much zeal betrayed the American cause. One of Dudley's details had wandered off and became engaged with Indians. Instead of falling back to the boats as planned, Dudley went to the aid of the detail. His men charged the Indians, broke them and pursued them through the woods up to the British camp. With this the British counterattacked the American front while more Indians struck the flanks. About 600 men were killed or captured. Dudley was taken and tomahawked as the Indians began to renew the horrors of the River Raisin while Proctor looked on indifferently.

But this time Tecumseh was present. He rushed in among his murdering warriors, who had already taken twenty scalps. He knocked one down with the flat of his sword, seized another by the throat and swung at a third. "Are there no men here?" he roared, and the slaughter stopped. Enraged, Tecumseh ran to Proctor to demand to know why his Indians had been allowed to kill prisoners. Proctor said, "Your Indians cannot be controlled. They cannot be commanded." Tecumseh's face twisted in contempt. "You are unfit to command," he told Proctor. "Go and put on petticoats!"[26]

Despite the Dudley disaster, Fort Meigs had been saved. On May 9, with his Indians deserting and his militia clamoring to go home to plant crops, Proctor raised the siege and returned to Malden.

Two months later he came back, and failed again. Disgruntled, he dropped down the Maumee, reached Lake Erie and coasted east to the Sandusky River. He went up the Sandusky determined to take Fort Stephenson, an American outpost so vulnerable that Harrison ordered it abandoned. Its commander, Major George Croghan, thought otherwise. "We have determined to maintain this place, and by Heaven we will," he told Harrison.[27] He did. As the British and Indians charged they were mowed down by his Kentucky sharp-shooters and a single cannon called "Old Betsey" spewing out grape and nails. Proctor thought that Groghan's fire was the severest he had ever seen, and he gave up his offensive to return to Malden.

The date was August 1, one day before Commodore Perry began taking his flotilla over the bar at Erie.

Perry used "camels" to float his ships over the bar. Floats were placed on either side of a ship, filled with water and sunk to a depth just below the ship's portholes. Then timbers were run through the portholes, coming to rest on the decks of the camels to either side, after which the water was pumped out of the camels and as they rose they lifted the ship with them and floated over the bar.

By August 5 Perry had his fleet out in open water, and he began searching the lake for the British. But the enemy fleet was still in Malden under Captain Robert Barclay, a veteran sailor who had lost an arm at Trafalgar. Perry returned to Erie, where he resumed his demands for more men. On August 10 he got 90 of them, headed by young Lieutenant Jesse Elliott, whom he placed in command of *Niagara.* Perry still needed marines, however, and this shortage was eliminated when General Harrison sent him 100 Kentucky marksmen. With their easy discipline, these sailors in buckskin might have turned out to be a new trial, but they turned to like old salts after Perry explained the demands of shipboard life. Now all that the eager American commander needed was a battle, and he got it on the morning of September 10, 1813, when the one-armed Barclay brought the British fleet to Perry's new base at Put-in-Bay.

Because of so many variables in guns, number and tonnage, it is almost impossible to estimate which was the stronger fleet. Suffice it to say that Perry, with nine ships to Barclay's six, held a slight edge. Otherwise they were evenly matched, Barclay possessing superior long-range artillery, Perry being stronger at close range. Barclay planned to fight at a distance and defeat his enemy ships in detail; Perry was eager to close to bring his carronades into action.

Perry's plan was to sail his own ship, *Lawrence,* supported by *Caledonia, Scorpion* and *Ariel,* against Barclay in *Detroit*—most powerful ship on the lake—and *Hunter* and tiny *Chippewa.* Elliott with *Niagara* would fight Barclay's second ship, *Queen Charlotte,* to which she was superior, while *Somers, Porcupine, Tigress* and *Trippe* took on *Lady Prevost* and *Little Belt.*

Slowly the American ships beat their way out of the harbor. Their decks were strewn with sand to prevent them from becoming slippery with blood. Outside stood the British ships, freshly calked and painted, with their red hulls gleaming and their polished brass glittering in the autumn sun. At first the weather favored the British, but then the wind changed and Perry held the weather gauge. Suddenly an American cheer rolled toward the British ships. Perry had unfurled his standard, a nine-foot square of blue on which white letters a foot high proclaimed the words of the dying Lawrence: "DON'T GIVE UP THE SHIP." Then the British cheered. Their bands had begun to play

"Rule, Britannia"—and out of the mouths of *Detroit*'s cannon came the first shots of the battle.

Lawrence was *Detroit*'s target. She took a punishing fire as she sailed down the British line in an effort to reach her adversary. Then *Queen Charlotte* joined *Detroit*, and *Lawrence*'s ordeal was nearly redoubled. *Charlotte* was free to pound Perry's flagship because Elliott in *Niagara* was not closing as ordered. Elliott stood off at a distance firing only a few long-range guns.

For two hours the British pair blasted away at *Lawrence*. They took her apart, cannon by carronade, spar by sail, brace by bowline, and they shot her hull into a sieve. Undaunted, Perry fought on alone. Of 103 men who began the fight, 83 were either killed or wounded. Perry stood upon the blood-clotted sand and cried: "Can any of the wounded pull a rope?"[28] A few crawled to his side to help put a dismounted gun in place. It was *Lawrence*'s last gun, and Perry fired it to let the fleet know that he was still in action. But Elliott in *Niagara* still stood at a distance. All seemed to be lost, except for Perry.

The American knew that he had given as well as taken punishment. He knew that with a fresh ship he could turn the tide of battle. Hauling down his blue banner, he leaped into a boat with his 13-year-old brother, Alexander, and four seamen. They began rowing toward *Niagara*. Perry stood in the stern until the seamen pushed him down. A British broadside went over their heads. The water around them was dimpled with musket shot, but the little boat passed miraculously through. Coming aboard *Niagara*, Perry took command. He ordered Elliott to bring up the three schooners which had also lagged behind. *Lawrence* was now drifting out of control, her flag pulled down, but before the British could move to possess her, Perry returned to the fight.

Swift and straight, *Niagara* burst the British line. On the port side her batteries battered *Chippewa, Little Belt* and *Lady Prevost*; on the starboard they thundered and flamed at *Detroit* and *Queen Charlotte*. *Detroit* tried to turn, and fouled *Queen Charlotte*. Perry's gunners took aim at the tangled ships and shot them both to pieces. With the first- and second-in-command on each of his vessels either killed or wounded, with his remaining arm shattered, Barclay surrendered *Detroit*. Eventually his other ships were overcome, and the battle was over before dusk.

Now the battered *Lawrence* had run up her flag again, and a feeble cheer rose from the living and wounded men aboard her who still had breath to spare. Aboard *Niagara,* Oliver Hazard Perry took an old envelope from his pocket. He held it against a navy cap and penciled a message to General Harrison, waiting anxiously ashore. Perry wrote: "We have met the enemy and they are ours."[29]

Barclay's defeat unmasked Proctor at Fort Malden, and that jittery general, fearing American revenge for the River Raisin massacre, quickly prepared to flee. Tecumseh soon realized that Proctor was about to withdraw and leave the Indians to shift for themselves. He confronted him and said: "We must compare our Father's conduct to a fat dog that carries its tail upon its back, but when affrightened drops it between its legs and runs off."[30]

Nevertheless, Proctor would not stay, as he had promised the Indians, and Tecumseh realized that he would have to go with him. "We are now going to follow the British," he told his people glumly, "and I feel certain that we shall never return."[31]

As Proctor began withdrawing, William Henry Harrison moved to the attack. Governor Shelby had come to Lake Erie with 3,000 Kentucky volunteers. Harrison also had the services of Congressman Richard Mentor Johnson with 1,000 mounted volunteers. But Proctor got away. Harrison found Fort Malden and the nearby town of Amherstburg still burning. On September 26 Detroit was reoccupied, after which the pursuit of Proctor began.

Johnson's horsemen crossed the Detroit River and gave chase by land while Perry's ships tried to sail through the river into Lake St. Clair in an effort to cut off Proctor's rear. Neither was quick enough, for Proctor had reached the Thames River and was moving up its banks. On the night of October 4 he halted at the modern town of Thamesville and prepared for battle. Tecumseh gathered his warriors. He took off the sword denoting his rank as a brigadier general in the British Army and said, "When my son becomes a noted warrior, give him this."[32] He forecast his own death, just as his elder brother Cheeseekau had done in the Carolinas when Tecumseh was a young boy. "Brother warriors," he said, "we are about to enter an engagement from which I shall not return. My body will remain on the field of battle."[33]

In the morning Tecumseh was more cheerful. He hunted up

Proctor and spoke to him in a forgiving mood. "Father, have a big heart! Tell your young men to be firm and all will be well."[34] Proctor's conduct, however, was not likely to make many men stand firm. His army was aware that he was giving battle reluctantly, that he preferred flight to fighting. Yet his battle position was fairly strong.

It lay between the river on the left and a large swamp on the right. In its middle was a smaller swamp. Most of the British troops were between the river and the small swamp. Indians under Tecumseh were between the small and large swamp.

Harrison planned to make an infantry frontal assault against the British, but then, learning that the enemy regulars were drawn up in open rather than close order, he called on Richard Mentor Johnson's mounted Kentuckians. Just before the attack, Johnson decided on his own that the space was too narrow for 1,000 horsemen. He divided his regiment in two, one battalion under his brother James to ride at the British, the other under himself to charge Tecumseh's Indians between the swamps. The bugle sounded and the homespun dragoons on their ragged mounts swept forward crying, "Remember the Raisin! Remember the River Raisin!"

On the American right James Johnson's cavalrymen burst the British line. Leaning from their saddles, the Americans swung their tomahawks and scattered the regulars in terror. General Henry Proctor became so frightened that he jumped into his carriage and clattered away from the battlefield. The Americans pursued in delight. They did not catch Proctor, but they took hundreds of prisoners and captured about $1 million in supplies, including guns taken from Burgoyne in 1777, then lost at Detroit by Hull in 1812.

On the American left, Tecumseh's warriors waited until the American horsemen were within a few paces before pouring a heavy fire into them. Perhaps 20 saddles were emptied. Richard Johnson was among the wounded, but he stayed with his men as they seized their rifles and leaped from their horses to engage the Indians on foot. American infantry hurried forward in support, and the Indians charged.

One of them came at 64-year-old Colonel William Whitley. Both men fired and both fell dead. Another Indian rushed with upraised tomahawk at the bleeding Johnson. Johnson shot him through the head and fell down unconscious. In one of these two encounters— probably the first—the gallant Tecumseh was killed. His fall did not decide the Battle of the Thames, for British defeat was already guaranteed with the American charge and Proctor's flight. But the death of this noble Indian leader was also the death of his vision of a confederacy of Indians hunting, as their fathers had hunted, across vast and untroubled stretches of American plains and forest.

Tecumseh's body was never found. It was believed to have been borne off in the night by his sorrowing warriors, and his final resting place remains as much a mystery as the name of the man who killed him. Richard Johnson never claimed the credit, although his followers claimed it for him during the election of 1836 which made Johnson Vice President. What is known, however, is that vengeful frontiersmen as barbarous as the butchers of the River Raisin stripped the skin from a body mistakenly believed to have been Tecumseh's and cut it into razor strops. "Tecumseh razor strops" eventually appeared in fashionable Washington.

Harrison's victory had ended British power in Upper Canada, crushed the Indians and redeemed the Northwest Territory. All this had been made possible by the earlier and more important victory which Perry had won on Lake Erie. Together the two battles raised the American flag for good over northern Ohio, Indiana and Illinois, and over the territory out of which Michigan, Minnesota and Wisconsin were formed—in other words, most of the modern Midwest, that rich, thriving, clanging, fertile territory which is at once the breadbasket and the toolshop of America and the iron heart of the continent.

And the Midwest was won for America chiefly because an ardent young captain would not give up his ship.

6

☆

Upon the resignation of Henry Dearborn, command in the Northeast passed to Major General James Wilkinson, and thus, in Ganoe's phrase, "age and infirmity gave place to age and fatuity."[35]

"The selection of this unprincipled imbecile was not the blunder of Secretary Armstrong,"[36] Winfield Scott claimed long afterward; but the fact is that Armstrong, though aware of Wilkinson's shortcomings, had no wish to offend his old comrade in arms from the Battle of Saratoga. So he was merely going to make him Dearborn's chief of staff!

"Come to the North, and come quickly!" Armstrong wrote to Wilkinson in New Orleans. "If our cards be well played, we may renew the scene of Saratoga."[37]

Few men could answer an urgent summons more slowly than Wilkinson. He received the letter on May 19 and arrived in Washington on July 31. By that time Dearborn had resigned and Wilkinson by virtue of his seniority became the ranking general. No choice, however automatic, could have been more odious. Even though Wilkinson's occupation of Mobile while he commanded the Southern Department turned out to be the only American acquisition of territory during the war, his rise disgusted every decent officer in the service. Armstrong compounded this repugnance by placing Wilkinson over Major General Wade Hampton, his archenemy. For years these two men had led rival factions in the Army. To exalt one over the other would be certain to divide the service, but to prefer the scheming and unscrupulous Wilkinson to the honorable though harsh Hampton was to give a kiss to vice and a kick to virtue.

At the outset Hampton refused to command at Lake Champlain unless his orders came directly from the War Department. Only when his and Wilkinson's commands were combined would he take orders from the crony of Aaron Burr. Armstrong agreed. Wilkinson, however, did not. He wrote Armstrong: ". . . if I am authorized to command he is bound to obey; and if he will not respect the obligation, he should be turned out of the service."[38] Armstrong did not agree with this, but neither did he tell Wilkinson that he did not.

Thus another American attempt on Montreal was begun with its two chief commanders cooperating like a mongoose and a cobra, after which the Secretary of War made his contribution to unity by getting into a wrangle over strategy with his own general in chief.

Armstrong had moved the War Department to Wilkinson's base at Sackets Harbor! It is said that he did so to slip the tight reins held on him by Madison. It is also said that he wanted to ride herd on Wilkinson. Whatever the cause for this unusual move on the part of a civilian war chief, Armstrong quickly found that Wilkinson was already unfit to command. By October he had fallen ill of fever. "He was so much indisposed in mind and body," according to General John Boyd, "that in any other service he would have perhaps been superseded in his command."[39] But Wilkinson was never so sick as to stop giving orders or to forbear from quarreling with Armstrong.

Wilkinson, apparently thinking little of Harrison, had originally wanted to clean out the Niagara frontier and attack Malden. Armstrong vetoed this with the remark that a movement west "but wounds the tail of the beast." Montreal was the beast's true heart. But the louder Armstrong spoke for Montreal, the more Wilkinson veered toward Kingston. In the end Wilkinson demanded written directions to abandon Kingston, and it was agreed to take Montreal first and *then* come back and seize Kingston: in other words, the beast's heart first and then its hindquarters.

Actually, neither man expected to capture either Kingston or Montreal. Wilkinson went so far as to ask for authorization to surrender should disaster threaten, and Armstrong secretly ordered Hampton to provide winter quarters for the army at a point 80 miles short of Montreal. In other words, he intended no serious movement on Montreal.

Unfortunately for some 10,000 Americans who had put their trust in this perfidious pair, the farce was to be played out. Wilkinson with about 6,000 men was to descend the St. Lawrence, where he was to meet Hampton with about 4,000 men, and together they would move on to Montreal. As was the custom set by their colonial forebears of a century before, the Americans did not get started until autumn plumed the woods in red and gold and the nights were chill with the breath of approaching winter. On October 17 about 300 boats carrying Wilkinson's men sailed north for the mouth of the St. Lawrence. Heavy gales scattered them, and it was not until November 5 that they had regrouped and begun sailing downriver. Behind them Commodore Chauncey's gunboats bottled up Kingston to prevent the British from following on Wilkinson's rear. To the left of the American flotilla, British guns on the northern bank made their passage difficult. But they faltered on, and as they did, Secretary Armstrong returned to Washington.

Meanwhile, Hampton had begun moving westward from his base at Lake Champlain. He reached Four Corners (New York) on the Chateaugay River and took up a position from which he could either join Wilkinson, cut the British communications to Upper Canada or move against Montreal. Appreciating this, Sir George Prevost sent about 1,500 French-Canadians against Hampton. Prevost had not always been sure of the loyalty of these Gallic troops, but in the Battle of Chateaugay on October 25-26 they fought Hampton's men with enough enthusiasm to dispel Prevost's doubts and to force Hampton to fall back. It was then that Hampton received Armstrong's orders to build winter quarters for the army. "This paper sank my hopes,"[40] said the disillusioned Hampton.

As Hampton's part in the camaign came to an end, about 1,000 boated British troops slipped out of Kingston to follow Wilkinson's flotilla. They snapped at his heels, even as the artillery on the river banks struck his left flank. At last General Jacob Brown was landed with an advance guard to clear the north bank of the St. Lawrence and a flanking movement was ordered. But the rear was left open until, on November 11, 1813, General Boyd took 2,000 men ashore and deployed them at a place known as Chrysler's Farm.

Here, in alternating snow and drizzle, while his troops attacked bravely across a field of mud and slush, Boyd attempted to crush the British force from Kingston. But he was defeated, and that was the end of the campaign. Wilkinson, learning that Hampton was not moving to meet him, flew into a rage and ordered Hampton's arrest. Then he changed his mind and decided to throw the responsibility on Armstrong. In the meantime he turned south, ascended the Salmon River and went into winter quarters in New York.

Never again did American arms menace Montreal, if, indeed, this monstrously mismanaged expedition actually ever had endangered the city. Why, it may be asked, was it ordered? Did Armstrong, as Wilkinson and Hampton both insisted, deliberately order an impossible campaign so as to bring the blame of failure on their heads? History does not know, although it has been maintained that Armstrong's motive was to rid himself of his decrepit generals so as to take the field himself as the American general in chief. If he did—and it is difficult to place any other interpretation upon his actions—then he was eminently successful, for the Montreal fiasco disposed of the last of the graybeards: Wilkinson, Hampton and Morgan Lewis. But field command never did devolve upon John Armstrong. He was already in odium in the White House, and by stripping the entire Northern border of troops so that not a regiment stood guard between Detroit and Sackets Harbor, he invited disaster along the Niagara frontier.

The British did not have to fight to recover Fort George, held by about 500 men under the militia general, George McClure. Most of McClure's men were near the expiration of their enlistments, and as the holiday season neared they began going home. McClure could neither restrain them nor persuade them to re-enlist, and so he moved his remaining force of 100 men across the river to Fort Niagara. But before he did he wantonly burnt the town of Newark, leaving its residents homeless in the frightful Northern winter. McClure said he wanted to deny the British winter quarters, but the truth was that the only building left standing was the army barracks.

Retaliation for this American atrocity, together with the burning of the capitol at York, was quick and dreadful. As the Americans in Niagara prepared to observe Christmas, a British force including 600 Indians slipped across the river. Someone had left Fort Niagara's front gate open. Yelling for revenge, the British stormed inside and bayoneted 67 Americans dead before they accepted a surrender.

Then the Indians were turned loose. By New Year's Day of 1814 Buffalo was a cinder smoking in the snow and Black Rock, Lewiston, Youngstown, Manchester, Schlosser and Tuscarora village were black heaps of rubbish. An area 12 miles wide and 36 miles long had been devastated, and as the cold and hungry survivors mourned their slain, the country was treated to the spectacle of Wilkinson and Armstrong engaged in public acrimony which ended with Wilkinson making his customary demand for a court-martial that would fix the blame elsewhere.

It would have been hard for Wilkinson to find a clean scapegoat. At the time, a New York newspaper printed the names of 13 discredited generals, headed by Granny Dearborn, along with a refrain which became popular during the court-martial of General Hull:

> Pray, General Dearborn, be impartial,
> When President of a Court-Martial;
> Since Canada has not been taken,
> Say General Hull was much mistaken.
> Dearborn himself, as records say,
> Mistaken was the self-same way.

And Wilkinson, and Hampton, too.
And Harrison, and all the crew.
Strange to relate, the self-same way
Have all mist-taken Canaday.[41]

Only one general of reputation remained. He was in the South, and
his name was Andrew Jackson.

7

☆

Andrew Jackson had already run afoul of Wilkinson and
Armstrong. During Burr's trial he had denounced Wilkinson to his
face as a "double traitor," and sneered: "Pity the sword that dangles
from his felon's belt, for it is doubtless of honest steel!"[42] Even so, at
the end of 1812 Jackson, a major general of militia, had not hesitated
to lead 2,000 Tennessee volunteers south to support Brigadier
General Wilkinson in New Orleans.

But Wilkinson had no intention of allowing a detested militia
officer of superior rank to enter New Orleans. He directed Jackson
to halt near Natchez in present-day Mississippi. Throughout January
of 1813 the highhearted Tennessee troops cooled their heels, and then
were coldly dismissed from service by John Armstrong two days after
he took office as Secretary of War.

Jackson, never a man to hold his temper long, flew into a fury.
He refused to disband his men 1,000 miles from home and personally
led them back to Tennessee, gaining, en route, his famous nickname
of "Old Hickory." Even so, the patriotic Jackson still offered to take
these self-same repudiated troops up north. "I have a few standards
wearing the American eagle," he wrote to Armstrong, "that I should
be happy to place upon the ramparts of Malden."[43] The offer was
ignored, and Jackson dismissed his men in Nashville in May of 1813.

That same month Jackson acted as second for his friend William
Carroll in a duel with Jesse Benton, younger brother of Thomas
Hart Benton, later a Senator from Missouri. Young Benton fired

first, missed and panicked. Turning, he doubled up and offered Carroll the seat of his pants. Taking deliberate aim, Carroll fired a ball into Benton's behind. The injury done to Jesse Benton's body was superficial, but the wound in his pride was deep. He became the butt of Tennessee's broad humor, and eventually, with his brother, he magnified Jackson's part in the affair and blamed him for the indignity.

On September 4, 1813, the Bentons came into Nashville wearing two pistols each. They went to the City Hotel. Jackson and his close friend, the gigantic John Coffee, went there also. Both were armed, and Jackson carried a whip. Seeing Thomas Benton in a doorway, Jackson brandished the whip and roared: "Now, defend yourself, you damned rascal."[44] Benton reached for his pistol, but before he could draw, Jackson's gun was at his breast. Step by step, Jackson backed Benton through a corridor. Suddenly, Jesse Benton came up behind him, drew and fired. Jackson pitched forward, firing as he fell. His powder merely burned Thomas Benton's sleeve, but blood was streaming from Jackson's left side. More shots were fired, blades were drawn, and the huge John Coffee entered the fight—but out of the smoke and shouting emerged one clear fact: General Jackson was badly wounded.

Jackson barely understood the doctors asking permission to amputate his arm, but when he did, he muttered, "I'll keep my arm."[45] He lay in great pain in his bed in the Hermitage, and he was still there when news of the Creek rising reached Tennessee.

It was the dream of Tecumseh that sent the peaceful Creeks on their nightmare war against the United States. Tecumseh hoped to bring the Southern Indians into his confederacy, and in 1811 he visited the Creek country in present-day Alabama. He taught the young and more warlike braves the dance of the Indians of the lakes, which became their symbol, and the sorcerers he brought with him infected the Creeks with a religious fanaticism which compensated for Creek deficiencies in firearms and fighting confidence. Tecumseh made a deep impression upon the half-breed Billy Weatherford, a bold and intelligent leader who boasted of French, Scottish, Spanish and Creek ancestors but "not one drop of Yankee blood." Weatherford became Tecumseh's lieutenant in the South.

Not all the Creek chiefs were persuaded by Tecumseh. Big Warrior did not hesitate to denounce him. Tecumseh told Big Warrior that he would feel the stamp of his foot as he entered Detroit. After his departure and the elapse of about the time required for his homeward journey, an earthquake shook Alabama. Tecumseh won many converts.

Returning in 1812, he won many more, for he brought the exhilarating news of the British-Indian victory at Detroit. He promised the Southern Indians aid from both the British in the North and the Spanish in the South. His influence spread, and then, late in 1812, Chief Little Warrior led a band of warlike Creeks all the way to Canada. They participated in the River Raisin massacre, and on the way home they slaughtered two white families living at the mouth of the Ohio.

The American government demanded that the Creeks hand over Little Warrior and his companions. In council, the elders under Big Warrior's lead decided to execute the murderers themselves. Little Warrior and his followers were hunted down and killed, and this act precipitated nothing less than a civil war among the Creeks.

The Upper Creeks, living in the higher valleys of the Gulf Coast streams, wanted Little Warrior avenged. The Lower Creeks, living along the lower Chattahoochee and Apalachicola rivers, feared war with the whites and tried to stay aloof. When Big Warrior sent a message calling for an end to "fooleries" among the Upper Creeks, the messenger was killed and a general uprising began. All Little Warrior's executioners were either driven into the forests or killed, and 29 of 34 Upper Creek towns declared for war. The warriors seized the crimson war clubs from which they took their name of Red Clubs or Red Sticks, and they swung them in wrath against every vestige of the white man's civilization as well as those kinsmen who refused to do the same.

In July of 1813 the half-breed chief Peter McQueen led a party of warlike Creeks into Pensacola. They brought war booty to exchange for provisions as well as a letter to the Spanish governor from the British authorities at Malden. The governor gave the Indians powder and bullets, merely for "hunting purposes," he said. American settlers already under attack could guess who the hunted might be, and they intercepted McQueen's party at a place called Burnt Corn, capturing some of the pack mules carrying the ammunition.

Two half-breeds, Major Daniel Beasley and Captain Dixon Bailey, had been among the Americans who ambushed the ammunition train, and now the Creek civil war became also a half-breed war. Hatred fed upon hatred as Billy Weatherford and Peter McQueen rallied 800 braves to avenge themselves upon the lovers of white men. They marched for Fort Mims, a stockade about 40 miles north of Mobile held by the detestable Beasley and Bailey and crowded with 550 refugees from the Red Stick uprising. Beasley commanded this motley of whites, half-breeds, Indians and Negroes, old and young, women and men, of whom perhaps 175 were armed militia. On August 30, 1813, Beasley wrote that he could "maintain the post against any number of Indians," but on noon of that day when the drum beat for dinner there were no patrols out, the gates were open, and the eastern gate, blocked by a mound of drifted sand, could not be quickly closed.

Suddenly there were whooping Indians swarming toward the fort. Beasley rushed for the gates, reached them, was tomahawked on the spot, and the yelling Indians rushed through to begin the butchery. Fifteen persons escaped, and most of the Negroes were spared for slaves, but everyone else in Fort Mims was cut down.

It was of this massacre that Andrew Jackson was informed by a committee of public safety hastening to the sick room in the Hermitage. Some 250 white scalps—a grisly harvest rare in the annals of Indians north or south—had excited the ferocity of the Creeks. And here lay Old Hickory, conscious "that he had squandered in a paltry, puerile, private contest, the strength he needed for the defense of his country."[46] Yet, without hesitation, he immediately ordered volunteers to rendezvous at Fayetteville on October 4. Propped against a pillow, he wrote:

"The health of your general is restored. He will command in person."[47]

The Creeks were not a formidable military force. At most there were about 4,000 Red Stick warriors, of whom never more than 1,000 could be assembled for a single battle. They had no artillery, and the men who did have muskets fired them only at the outset of combat, after which they relied upon bows and arrows, tomahawks and clubs. Yet they defied the United States for a year, and that was because the difficulty was not in fighting them but in reaching them. They dwelt within inaccessible strongholds. The heart of the Creek country, the sacred Hickory Ground at the forks of the Coosa and Tallapoosa, was 150 miles away from the nearest American base.

Major General Thomas Pinckney, commanding the Southern Department, discovered these problems in wilderness logistics after two columns—one moving from Georgia, the other from Mobile—failed to accomplish much. Yet these two forces passed over easier routes than the 2,500 men whom Tennessee sent south under Andrew Jackson.

The difference was Jackson. Haggard, his arm in a sling, Benton's bullet still lodged in his shoulder to make him wary of those sudden movements which sent a thrill of agony twanging through his body, Old Hickory took command of his infantrymen on October 7. Many of them were the volunteers who had marched to Natchez and back. Among them were Ensign Sam Houston and that legendary frontiersman Davy Crockett, "the merriest of the merry, keeping the camp alive with his quaint conceits and marvelous narratives."[48] John Coffee, Jackson's closest friend and ablest lieutenant, had already advanced with the cavalry.

Coffee may have been a better general than Jackson; he was at least an instinctively superior tactician. He gave Jackson his first victory at Tallushatchee on November 3, 1813. Like Daniel Morgan before him, Coffee executed a Cannae in miniature. He placed his men in a semicircle and sent forward a small body to lure the Indians into it. As the Red Sticks attacked, the advance force retreated, the end of the semicircle swung shut—and over 180 Creeks were killed. Coffee lost 5 dead and 14 wounded. Six days later Jackson tried the same tactic, but his lines failed to hold and 400 of 700 Creeks escaped. Jackson's losses were 15 killed and 85 wounded.

Had Old Hickory been able to follow up these strokes, he might have ended the Creek War there and then. But he, too, was having his supply problems. As the year came to an end, the old American difficulty of short-term enlistments arose to plague him.

The men who had been to Natchez believed that their time expired December 10, 1813. They counted the months they had spent at home between Natchez and the Creek War as served time. Jackson disagreed. One stubborn company began marching home. Jackson, still unable to lift a musket because of the bullet in his back, rested his gun across the neck of his horse and threatened to shoot the first man who moved. The militiamen stood sullenly, glaring at him, but no man moved.

To everyone but Jackson the Creek War appeared hopeless. Governor Willie Blount wrote to him recommending a retreat. Jackson, who had dined on acorns at least once, flew into his customary passion at the perfidy of politicans. He composed a long letter to Blount, reminding him that he had "bawled aloud for permission to exterminate the Creeks," and asking: "And are you my Dear friend sitting with yr. arms folded . . . recommending me to retrograde to please the whims of the populace? . . . Let me tell you it imperiously lies upon both you and me to do our duty regardless of consequences or the opinion [of] these fireside patriots."[49] Angrily sketching the consequences of a retreat that would send thousands of hitherto friendly but wavering Creeks, Choctaws and Cherokees flocking to the Red Stick cause, he concluded:

Arouse from yr. lethargy—despite fawning smiles or snarling frowns— with energy exercise yr. functions—the campaign must rapidly progress or . . . yr. country ruined. Call out the full quota—execute the orders of the Secy of War, arrest the officer who omits his duty . . . and let popularity perish for the present. . . . What, retrograde under these circumstances? I will perish first.[50]

The letter together with a supporting thrust from the War Department stiffened Blount's spine. More troops came south. Although they were only 60-day men, Jackson made good use of them in a pair of sharp but indecisive engagements at Emuckfaw and Enotachopco creeks. In February of 1812 Jackson's army rose to 5,000 men, and the arrival of the 39th U.S. Infantry and the execution of a rebellious militiaman put steel into hitherto slouching ranks. Then Jackson learned that some 800 Red Sticks had fortified a position at Horseshoe Bend on the Tallapoosa River. They awaited all-or-nothing battle, and Old Hickory marched at the head of 2,000 men to give it to them.

The Horseshoe was a peninsula of about 100 acres of brush and small timber furrowed by gullies. Across its neck the Indians had built a zigzag row of logs pierced with double gun ports. At its rear they had drawn up hundreds of canoes in the event they were forced to flee. Jackson arrayed his main body and artillery opposite the log breastwork, and sent Coffee's cavalry across the river to cut off retreat.

Coffee's Cherokee scouts swam the river and stole the Creek canoes. Then the impetuous Coffee used them to cross and attack the Indian rear. To the front, Jackson's artillery plunged harmlessly into the breastwork's soft pine logs. Old Hickory called for a frontal assault.

Major Lemuel Montgomery, a relative of General Montgomery who was killed with Arnold at Quebec in 1775, was the first on the works. The Red Sticks shot him dead. Next came tall Sam Houston, leaping onto the breastwork, waving his sword and jumping down. A fierce fight at the rampart followed. Gradually, the Red Sticks were pressed back. They fought on bravely. Their prophets had told them that the Great Spirit promised victory. The sign would be a cloud in the heavens, said the priests, moving among them, chanting their incantations, falling as the warriors fell.

In the middle of the afternoon the cloud appeared—just as Jackson's messenger arrived offering pardon to all who surrendered. The aroused Creeks nearly killed the messenger, and the battle was renewed with redoubled ferocity. At dusk one band held out in a fortress at the bottom of the ravine. Jackson called for volunteers to take it. Sam Houston stepped forward, and was hit by two musket balls before he was carried from the field. After Jackson set the fort afire with flaming arrows the battle came to an end. More than 550 Indians had fallen on the field, and perhaps 200 more had perished in the river. Jackson's losses were 49 killed and 157 wounded.

With the Battle of Horseshoe Bend the Creek War came to an end. Led by Billy Weatherford the Red Sticks made their peace. Jackson summoned all the chiefs to the fort he had built at the confluence of the Coosa and Tallapoosa. They came, the friendly Creeks expecting rewards, the hostiles anticipating harsh punishment from "Sharp Knife," but none dreaming of such brutal terms as Jackson offered. Half of the Creek country, 23 million acres comprising three-fifths of Alabama and one-fifth of Georgia, were to be ceded to the United States. The Creeks protested, and Jackson replied that through this territory led "the path that Tecumseh trod. That path must be stopped. Until this is done your nation cannot expect happiness, mine security."[51]

On August 9, 1814, the sorrowing Creeks signed the Treaty of

Fort Jackson. Andrew Jackson wrote to his wife Rachel back in the Hermitage that the "disagreeable business" was done and "I know you humanity would feel for" a fallen nation robbed of half its patrimony.[52]

8

☆

It is to John Armstrong's credit that in 1814 the graybeard generals at last gave way to young and vigorous men. Whereas in 1812 there had been eight top generals averaging 60 years of age, in 1814 the ranking nine averaged only 36.

Among these was Major General Jacob Brown, the commander who had repulsed Prevost at Sackets Harbor the year before. Brown was ordered to make a new invasion of Upper Canada, aiming at Burlington Heights on Lake Ontario.

Speed was to be the essence of this campaign, for Britain had brought the Napoleonic Wars to a triumphant conclusion. In April of 1814 Napoleon abdicated as emperor, and at least 14 of Wellington's veteran regiments were free for service in America. By June Brown was ready with about 3,500 men.

Opposing them was the energetic Lieutenant General Sir Gordon Drummond with about an equal number. But Drummond's force was spread thin over a vast frontier. About 1,000 men were kept in York to be rushed to any threatened point, while another 2,600 were strung out along the Niagara under Major General Phineas Riall. Obviously, to respond quickly to American movements would require hard marching from the British. However, the British had little fear of the Americans.

But this was a different Yankee army. Its soldiers saluted smartly and took pride in their uniforms, and its brigade commanders were Winfield Scott; Peter B. Porter, the aggressive war hawk Congressman; and Eleazer Wheelock Ripley, one of many New Englanders whose loyalty during the war preserved their region's honor. Scott the scientific had been particularly active drilling his troops. He put them in neat uniforms, albeit of militia gray, for Scott could not obtain cloth for regulars' blue.

On July 3, 1814, General Brown threw this force across the river and invested Fort Erie. It was surrendered in the afternoon, and Brown spent the Fourth of July moving north along the Niagara.

Riall, however, had moved swiftly. Gathering his garrisons, he came south with about 2,000 men, halting at Chippewa 18 miles above Fort Erie. Here, the next day, he attacked the American camp.

Porter's militia-Indian brigade drove off a Canadian force, but the British regulars routed Porter in turn. General Brown ordered Scott's brigade, fortunately already drawn up for evening parade, to give battle. With American and British guns already dueling counterbattery, Scott led his men over a creek and deployed. Marching steadily, tall in their trim gray uniforms and high hats, Scott's soldiers spread out in a concave line to put a converging fire into the redcoated British drawn up in column, two regiments abreast. The British opened fire. Americans toppled. But the gaps were quickly closed and the long gray line came on. Seventy yards apart the two forces halted and fired. Now there were gaps in the British line, and the Americans charged with the bayonet to break and rout Riall's redcoats.

British losses in the Battle of Chippewa were 500 men, while the Americans lost 300. It was not an important victory, but its psychological effects were stunning and enduring. For the first and only time in the war regulars of both sides had met and maneuvered on an open plain, and the Americans had won. At Chippewa the *esprit* of the United States Army was born, and the battle is commemorated in the gray uniforms worn by cadets at the U. S. Military Academy.

Brown followed up Scott's victory by pressing the British back to Fort George and Burlington Heights. Encamping at Queenston, he awaited the heavy guns needed to reduce the enemy forts. They were slow in coming from Chauncey at Sackets Harbor, and Brown was forced to return to Chippewa on July 24.

In the interval, General Drummond had hurried to the Niagara from Kingston. He now ordered his 3,000-man force out in pursuit of the Americans. While Riall followed Brown, another force crossed the river to menace Brown's supplies. Brown became worried. He sent Winfield Scott down the Canadian side of the river in hopes of forcing the enemy to recall his troops from the American side. Scott came upon Riall at Lundy's Lane, a point a mile below the falls, and immediately attacked.

Such was Scott's audacity that Riall was forced to retire. But just then Drummond came up with the rest of his army, ordering the cross-river detachment to rejoin him. Drummond put his artillery on a hill, with his infantry in line slightly to the rear.

Scott attacked again, directing his brigade against the British center and left. On the left, the Americans temporarily turned the British flank, capturing the wounded Riall while doing so. But the British eventually recovered there, while in the center they hurled back charge after charge. Still Scott hung on, until, at about five o'clock, Brown arrived with the rest of his army.

Brown ordered another attack. The lines swept forward in a darkness shimmering with the flashes of the British guns, but they could not seize the hill and the British battery blazed on. Brown ordered Colonel James Miller of the 21st Infantry to take the British works. While the enemy guns thundered at an American column moving along the river, Miller's regulars slipped forward through the darkened scrub. Coming to within a dozen yards of the enemy, they crashed out a close volley, charged with the bayonet and seized both hill and battery. Now Brown brought his entire army up to the hill, and the astonished Drummond counterattacked.

Three times the dark silhouettes of the British regulars swept upward, and three times the muzzles of American muskets and the captured guns flickered and flamed to drive them back again. Brown and Scott were both hit and evacuated. Around midnight, Brown ordered Ripley, now commanding on the hill, to withdraw for water and ammunition. He did, but he also left some of the enemy guns behind. With daylight Drummond quickly reoccupied the height and turned the guns around—restoring the situation of the preceding day except that both sides were battered and bleeding and each minus about 900 men.

In the Battle of Lundy's Lane the Americans might just possibly have won a tactical victory, but they suffered strategic defeat. Lundy's Lane put out the ardent flame enkindled by Chippewa and forced Brown to abandon all hope of conquering Upper Canada. He withdrew into Fort Erie. The energetic Drummond assaulted him there on August 15, but the Americans repulsed him. On September 17 Brown led a sally out of the fort to seize and spike the British guns. No less than 500 men fell on both sides during this bitter flare-up, and now both Brown's and Drummond's armies were exhausted remnants. Drummond issued orders proclaiming a victory, and then fell back to Chippewa. Less than two months later the Americans acknowledged the futility of fighting on the Niagara frontier by blowing up Fort Erie and recrossing the river to American soil.

All had not been in vain, however, if only for the gleam which Chippewa, Lundy's Lane and Fort Erie gave to a young but thus far lusterless military tradition. The cost had been high. James Miller, the hero of Lundy's Lane, wrote a friend: "Since I came into Canada this time every major save one, every lieutenant-colonel, every colonel that was here when I came and has remained here has been killed or wounded, and I am now the only general officer out of seven that has escaped."[53]

But now the guns fell forever silent along the 40-mile strait separating New York and Ontario. For the focus of the war had long ago shifted east, where the weight of British arms flowing to the United States from victorious European battlefields was bearing the fledgling American eagle to the earth.

9

☆

By the summer of 1814 military defeat, blockade, internal dissension, a near-empty treasury and the prospect of British invasion coupled with no real confidence in Brown's expedition into Canada had brought the United States to the point where peace talk would have been sweet indeed. But by then it was too late.

America's first chance had come in 1812 when the British suspended the Orders in Council and ordered Admiral Warren to attempt to negotiate a cease-fire. At that time Secretary of State

Monroe bluntly informed Warren that the outrageous practice of impressment must be dropped first, and that, of course, was not possible.

Another opportunity appeared in March of 1813 when John Quincy Adams, U.S. Minister to Russia, transmitted Czar Alexander's offer to mediate the Anglo-American dispute. By then, Canadian defeats had chastened the Americans, and Madison, without waiting for British reaction to the Czar's offer, appointed Albert Gallatin, his capable Secretary of the Treasury, and James Bayard, a Federalist, as peace commissioners. Journeying to St. Petersburg, Gallatin and Bayard, together with Adams, were to conclude a peace which would still insist upon the end of impressment. Then, as American arms won victories at York and on the Niagara frontier, Monroe wrote to Gallatin: "These successes ought to have a salutary influence on your negotiations, [and] it might be worthwhile to bring to view the advantage to both countries which is to be promised by a transfer of the upper parts and even the whole of Canada to the U.S."[54]

Bumptiously confident as Mr. Monroe might have been, the commissioners soon found the realities to be that the Czar was out of town fighting Napoleon and the British were not interested in mediation of what, so far as impressment was concerned, was to them a domestic question. Yet Britain held the door open for direct negotiation, and Madison added Jonathan Russell and Henry Clay to the delegation. Gallatin and Bayard, meanwhile, left St. Petersburg, bumped around Europe for a bit, and entered England in April—just as Napoleon fell from his imperial throne. Bayard wrote home: "The whole nation is delirious with joy, which was not indulged without bitter invectives against their remaining enemies: the Americans. They consider [the war] as an aid given to their great enemy at a moment when his power was most gigantic. . . . They thirst for a great revenge and the nation will not be satisfied without it."[55] Gallatin wrote: "To use their own language, they mean to inflict on America a chastisement which will teach her that war is not to be declared against Great Britain with impunity."[56] Gallatin urgently advised Madison to drop the impressment issue.

Madison did. While war hawks still muttered darkly about maritime grievances and banners proclaiming "FREE TRADE AND SAILORS' RIGHTS" still fluttered from the masts of American ships, the issue which had called forth all the blood and bullets was quietly dropped in a Cabinet meeting of June 27. Instructions to that effect were sent to the peace commissioners gathered in the (now Belgian) city of Ghent to await the pleasure of their British counterparts. And while the Americans cooled their heels, Mother England raised the rod which was to despoil, as well as discipline, her runaway, impudent daughter.

If carried out, Britain's strategy probably would have left her in possession of New England, part of New York, the Great Lakes and the Louisiana Territory. Then she would have been able to bargain at Ghent on the basis of "the state of possession" at the close of hostilities.

Three expeditions were to achieve this position. The first and major force would invade New York at Lake Champlain. In support, to divert the Americans from Champlain, an army-navy team would attack American coastal cities. Finally, a third force would seize New Orleans.

In none of these plans was there a word about revenge or reprisals, and yet the first force to move, the army-navy team under Vice Admiral Sir Alexander Cochrane, went into action with retaliation as an objective.

In July of 1814 Cochrane in Bermuda received a letter from Sir George Prevost reporting that American troops had pillaged Canadian communities on Lake Erie. The raid was unauthorized, but Prevost, without waiting for the explanations and reparations which actually did follow, asked Cochrane to "assist in inflicting that measure of retaliation which shall deter the enemy from a repetition of similar outrages."[57] On July 18 Cochrane informed his squadrons: "You are hereby required and directed to destroy and lay waste such towns and districts upon the coasts as you may find assailable."[58]

A few weeks later Cochrane sailed for Chesapeake Bay at the head of 4 ships of the line, 20 frigates and sloops and more than 20 transports carrying 4,000 regulars. Major General Robert Ross commanded the troops. He was one of Wellington's finest professionals and a gentlman renowned for his "easy and beautiful manners." Reaching the bay, Cochrane and Ross conferred with a less cultivated commander, the irascible despoiler of the Chesapeake, Rear Admiral Sir George Cockburn.

Cockburn's temper had not been softened by the invective poured upon his name in the American press, and he had a particularly active hatred for the Washington newspaper, the *National Intelligencer*. It was not surprising, then, that Cockburn should propose the American capital as the first object of retaliation. Cochrane, however, wished to move first against an American gunboat flotilla commanded by the aggressive Commodore Joshua Barney. After that, a choice would be made between Washington and Baltimore.

On August 18 the British fleet began sailing up the Patuxent River with Barney's gunboats fleeing before it. Next day General Ross's soldiers and marines began going ashore. A column was formed to march parallel with the ships in pursuit of the gunboats. On August 22, finding himself trapped, Barney blew up his boats. The British were now free to punish either Washington or Baltimore, and on the night of the 23rd Ross chose the American capital.

For five days an enemy army had marched and countermarched around the capital without a finger raised against it. Few nations have submitted to insult so spinelessly, and yet few nations have been served in their peril by leaders such as John Armstrong and James Madison.

Armstrong, with his eyes fixed on Canada, had done next to nothing about Washington's defenses. He had no plan, very few regulars, and depended upon militia requisitioned from the neighboring states. Moreover, Armstrong was certain that Washington would not be attacked. "Baltimore is the place, sir," he told a militia general. "That is of so much more consequence."[59] He was right, but just because he had left America's front door open, he had invited Ross to swerve toward Washington.

At last Madison, who lacked the courage to dismiss Armstrong, placed defense of the capital in the hands of Brigadier General William Winder. A lawyer whose chief military distinction was his disgraceful capture at Stony Point the year before, Winder was chosen because he was the cousin of Levin Winder, the Federalist Governor of Maryland upon whom most of the requisitions for militia would fall. At the outset, however, General Winder found that the states were willing to defend themselves but not the capital. He called for 3,000 men and got not 300. He asked for more, but Armstrong refused to approve his call. Winder, it appeared, commanded only himself and his horse—and he nearly killed that poor beast when, starting on July 5, he rode for nearly a month over the terrain he was to defend, returning to Washington on August 1 to proclaim the obvious: Washington was poorly defended.

Its only regular force was a half-trained District Brigade. At Bladensburg on the Washington road, the obvious point to stop Ross and his 4,000, there were only 450 troops holding entrenchments voluntarily dug by the exasperated citizens of the capital. Alarmed at last, President Madison issued a call for more militia, and Brigadier General Tobias Stansbury began marching down from Baltimore to Bladensburg with about 2,000 militia. As they did, Washington flew into a first-class flap.

Citizens and clerks fought each other for wagons to carry off private or governmental valuables. Families boarded up their homes and buried the silver under the shrubs. Dolley Madison, the President's charming and saucy wife, left off scolding her neighbors for foolish talk about evacuation and busied herself moving things from the residence of her friends, the Gallatins. And as General Winder rode everywhere at breakneck speed, Secretary of War Monroe, the only official who had constantly feared an attack on Washington, mounted his horse to ride to Benedict, where he spent two days personally scouting the enemy's movements.

On August 21 both Winder and Monroe joined the District Brigade camped at the Woodyard roughly midway between Bladensburg in the north and Benedict in the south. On August 22, the day Barney blew up his boats, Winder and his cavalry rode south toward the British at Nottingham. They came upon the enemy moving north to Upper Marlboro. For perhaps an hour the Americans sat their horses watching the perspiring redcoats marching through the fields. Then they galloped back to the Woodyard and the entire force retreated out of Ross's way to Oldfields (now Forestville, Maryland). They were now about ten miles below Bladensburg. About half that distance east lay the British at Upper Marlboro. At Oldfields, meanwhile, Winder was joined by Barney with about 500 sailors and 150 marines under Captain Samuel Miller. That evening President Madison and his Cabinet rode out from Washington.

In the morning of August 23 the President reviewed Winder's troops, and rode back to Washington. After he left, Winder rode north to Bladensburg. He had not gone far before a messenger overtook

him to inform him that the British were marching on the army he
had left. Wheeling, Winder galloped back to Oldfields in time to see
Ross's columns approaching and to give the order for retreat.

It was not an orderly withdrawal. Winder's army simply turned
tail and ran west to the capital. Ross, perhaps startled by his enemy's
sudden disappearance, did not pursue. Instead, he marched south
to the Woodyard, and it was there that he decided to attack Washington on the following day.

Winder's retreat to Washington had brought him to the Navy
Yard on the east branch of the Potomac. He came there, he said,
because he believed the enemy might move on the city by the river.
Winder had no thought of Bladensburg, the true avenue of approach.
Neither, apparently, did Bladensburg's defender: General Tobias
Stansbury. As the hot sun of August 24, 1814, rose in the Maryland
sky, Stansbury pulled his troops out of that vital little village and
began marching to join Winder at the Navy Yard.

President Madison and his Cabinet had already reached Winder's
camp. They spoke for fruitless hours with the distracted general,
until, at ten o'clock, a scout came clattering over the bridge with news
that the British had been marching for Bladensburg since dawn and
were nearly halfway there.

Secretary of State James Monroe immediately mounted his horse
and rode hard for Bladensburg, seven miles away. After him streamed
President Madison and the rest of the Cabinet, then Winder and his
army, and then, after blowing the Navy Yard Bridge, came the
resolute Barney with his sailors and big naval cannon.

Fortunately, the retiring General Stansbury was also alerted to
the British approach. He turned and hastened back to block the
Washington road west of Bladensburg. That road ran out from the
town, crossed a bridge over the eastern branch, ran level through a
marsh and gradually ascended rolling hills. Stansbury certainly had
time to destroy the bridge, but he did not. Instead, he placed artillery
and about 500 men in a position overlooking it. His main body was
placed west of the marsh.

At about eleven o'clock Monroe came galloping down the hill.
Without consulting Stansbury, he altered the general's dispositions—
to their ultimate disadvantage. Some Maryland militia arrived at about
the same time. Next came Madison and his Cabinet, Secretary Arm-

strong repeatedly asking for command and being just as frequently refused. The President jogged through Stansbury's lines toward the bridge and inevitable capture, until a scout headed him off. Then Winder came puffing up, placing his men on a ridge too far behind Stansbury to assist him. Thus there were three lines consisting of perhaps 6,000 men to oppose Ross's 4,000. But there was no real organization. The units had no understanding of their relations to each other, some were in excellent position to fire on their comrades, and everyone was exhausted and confused by the marching of the past few days.

At one o'clock British scarlet streamed into Bladensburg and Stansbury's artillery opened fire. Then the British light brigade rushed the bridge. Immediately, Stansbury's sharpshooters opened up. Redcoats fell, but most of them got across. Tearing off their knapsacks and tossing them into squad piles, the British formed files of skirmishers ten paces apart. They came on at the trot, and it was then that there was a gurgle, a screech and a whoosh overhead.

Ross had fired his Congreve rockets at Stansbury's second line. The first few sputtered harmlessly overhead. Then their trajectories were flattened out and the American men and mules were seized with a mad, superstitious fright. There was little to be feared from the Congreves, a weapon so innocuous that it soon ceased to frighten even savage tribes. They were all bark and no bite, yet, without a single one falling among the Americans, they put Stansbury's left and center to rout. Soldiers threw away their guns and fled, and the only casualty was a captain who ran himself to death.

Not all the Americans fled so quickly. At one point, some of them even forced the redcoats back to the cover of the river bank. But then Ross fed another regiment into the battle, and after this unit forded the stream and threatened to turn the American left, the rout became complete. The battle had not lasted a quarter-hour. President Madison, watching the stampede from a hill, suggested to Secretary Armstrong that it would be wise "to take a position less exposed." Whereupon the American Cabinet joined the American Army in a flight that did not stop until it was at least 16 miles beyond Washington.

Startled once again by his enemy's trick of vanishing, Ross regrouped and began marching west to Washington—and ran into Commodore Barney's sailors and marines.

Barney had arrived on the field as Winder was being swept away. He set up his cannon and put his men into line about a mile west of Bladensburg. By his own account:

At length the enemy made his appearance on the main road in force and in front of my battery, and on seeing us made a halt. I reserved our fire. In a few minutes the enemy again advanced, when I ordered an 18-pounder to be fired, which completely cleared the road. Shortly after, a second and a third attempt was made by the enemy to come forward, but all were destroyed. They then crossed over into an open field, and attempted to flank our right. He was met there by three 12-pounders, and marines under Captain Miller, and my men acting as infantry, and again was totally cut up. By this time not a vestige of the American army remained, except a body of five or six hundred posted on a height on my right, from which I expected much support from their fine situation.[60]

But Barney got no such support. Even though his men actually counterattacked, crying "Board 'em! Board 'em!" to drive the world's finest troops before them, the militia on the height to his right broke and quit the field. Now the British got into Barney's rear. Barney was himself wounded. Even so, his men fought on. Some of them were bayoneted at their guns with fuses still in their hands. They would have stayed until the end had not Barney, lying in a pool of his own blood, ordered them to retreat.

It was a magnificent stand, and it cost Ross about 250 casualties against Barney's 26 killed and 51 wounded. The slightest follow-up of Barney's counterattack might have produced an American victory. As it was, the road to Washington now lay open, and Ross, accompanied by Admiral Cockburn, led two tired regiments down it into the heart of the American capital.

It was dark as Ross and Cockburn and their troops entered the deserted city. Yet bullets flew at them from the house once occupied by Gallatin, and Ross's horse fell dead beneath him. Angered, the perfect gentleman had the house burned. Under the urging of Cockburn, he next sent troops to the Capitol. Using gunpowder and rockets, the British set the symbol of American sovereignty blazing in the blackness. Now Ross and Cockburn and 200 men marched through the eerily silent darkness to the White House. No one was inside. Dolley Madison had long since fled with most of the plate and valuables, although the table was set for dinner for forty. Decanters of wine stood on the sideboards, and in the kitchen, spits loaded with joints were turning before the fire, and the pots were filled with sauces and vegetables. Subaltern George Glieg, who was present, has written: "You will readily imagine that these preparations were beheld by a party of hungry soldiers with no indifferent eye. An elegant dinner . . . was a luxury to which few of them . . . had been accustomed."[61] So they ate it, after which they disposed of the immemorial problem of cleaning up by setting fire to the White House. Meanwhile, the Navy Yard and all the vessels in the eastern branch were put to the torch, along with the War and Treasury buildings. Before midnight the blazing city cast flickering red light over those Virginia and Maryland hills into which the American government and its army had crept. Then a violent thunderstorm sprang up to quench the flames and all fell dark again.

In the morning Dolley Madison hurried to meet her husband 16 miles up the Potomac. En route she stopped off at what appeared to be a friendly farmhouse. She went upstairs while her attendants announced her presence to the housewife. Enraged, the woman ran to the stairs and shouted up them: "Mrs. Madison, if that is you, come down and get out. Your husband has got mine out fighting, and damn you, you shan't stay in my house! So get out!"[62] Dolley went, her humiliation symbolizing the low estate into which the American presidency had fallen.

In Washington, meanwhile, the firebrands were up early to rekindle the dampened ruins, making certain this time that the Library of Congress inside the Capitol was also destroyed. Admiral Cockburn was delighted. Riding an uncurried white brood mare with a black foal trotting by her side, he made for the office of the *National Intelligencer*. He ordered the newspaper's library heaped in the street and lent his own hands to the burning of the books. Then he ordered his men to scatter the type, shouting gleefully, "Be sure that all the C's are destroyed so that the rascals cannot any longer abuse my name!"[63]

At noon the sky darkened and a rare tornado struck the city with a dreadful howl. It increased the havoc, but it also put out the fires. Shortly afterward an explosion at the Navy Yard injured many of Ross's redcoats and placed a final check on "retaliation." At about nine o'clock that night, leaving their campfires burning and marching in extreme silence, the British departed the dishonored capital.

10

☆

      In its psychological consequences the burning of Washington first appalled and then angered and briefly united the American nation, but diplomatically it was of no consequence whatever.

News of the event simply came too late to influence the peace commissioners of either side then meeting in Ghent. If the Americans had known that their capital had been contemptuously burnt like any stinking pirate's lair, they might not have been so firm in rejecting Britain's demand; but as it was, on August 24, the very date of the "Bladensburg Races," they flatly rejected them.

Britain had asked for an Indian buffer state to include one-third of Ohio, two-thirds of Indiana, and nearly the entire area from which Illinois, Wisconsin and Michigan were formed. They also demanded parts of Maine, control of the Great Lakes, forfeiture of American fishing rights in the North and other exactions equally humiliating. Asked what would be done with about 100,000 Americans then living within the area of the buffer state, the British shrugged and said that they would have to shift for themselves. So the Americans bluntly stated that the demands were inadmissible, and declared: "A treaty concluded on such terms would be but an armistice."[64]

The American reply jolted the British. Lord Liverpool, the Prime Minister, was afraid that if negotiations were broken off the British would be blamed and the war would become popular in America and unpopular in Britain. He wrote to the Duke of Wellington: "It is very material to throw the rupture of the negotiation, if it is to take place, upon the Americans."[65] So the British, who had also not yet heard of Washington, retreated from their dictatorial stand. They did not change their demands, but neither did they reiterate them as *sine qua nons*. They also sought to adjourn rather than break off the negotiations. In the meantime, British arms would bring the "impudent" Yankees to heel. "If our commander does his duty," Liverpool wrote, "I am persuaded we shall have acquired by our arms every point on the Canadian frontier which we ought to insist on keeping."[66]

Liverpool's policy of writing the peace with the point of a sword got off to an excellent start on September 1, when a British fleet entered Penobscot Bay and took Castine. At the cost of one man killed and eight wounded all of Maine east of the Penobscot River gradually fell into British hands. One hundred miles of seacoast was restored to the dominion of the King of England, while all its male inhabitants meekly, often eagerly, took an oath of allegiance to him. To nail down these acquisitions and to tidy up the Canadian frontier in a southern direction, Sir George Prevost began moving down Lake Champlain.

Sir George's army was the most splendid ever sent by Britain to America. In all of Canada he commanded some 29,000 regulars, and for the Lake Champlain expedition alone he had about 18,000 redcoats, not counting Canadian militia. The problem of feeding this host might have been insuperable but for some of Prevost's friendly enemies to the south. "Two thirds of the army are supplied with beef by American contractors, principally of Vermont and New York,"[67] Prevost reported. One commissary official noted on June 19, 1814: "I have contracted with a Yankee magistrate to furnish this post with fresh beef. A major came with him to make the agreement; but, as he was foreman of the grand jury of the court in which the Government prosecutes the magistrates for high treason and smuggling, he turned his back and would not see the paper signed."[68] Major General George Izard, commanding at Plattsburg, reported: "On the eastern side of Lake Champlain the high roads are insufficient for the cattle pouring into Canada. Like herds of buffaloes they press through the forests, making paths for themselves. . . . Were it not for these supplies, the British forces in Canada would soon be suffering from famine."[69]

Such complicity made it difficult for Prevost to decide whether to attack down the New York or Vermont side of Champlain. But then Vermont's ardor in its enemy's cause won him over, and he wrote: "Vermont has shown a disinclination to the war, and as it is sending in specie and provisions, I will confine offensive operations to the west side of Lake Champlain."[70]

On August 31, leaving behind a rear guard of about 5,000 men, Prevost led 11,000 across the border into New York. On his eastern or left flank sailed a fleet which, headed by the 36-gun *Confiance,* was nearly as formidable as his army. And in Washington far below him he possessed in the person of John Armstrong an unwitting ally perhaps the equal of either.

Although the Washington fiasco had forced Armstrong to resign (Madison still had not the courage to dismiss him), before he did so he stripped the land defenses of Lake Champlain nearly naked by ordering General Izard to take 4,000 men from Plattsburg to the Niagara frontier. Izard obeyed, while protesting that Plattsburg on Champlain was the enemy's objective. So Brigadier General Alexander Macomb was left to man Plattsburg's forts with about 1,500 effectives. Fortunately for America, Prevost was as dilatory as Armstrong was devious, and even more happily there had come to Lake Champlain a sailor in the mold of Lawrence and Oliver Hazard Perry.

Lieutenant Thomas Macdonough had been born in Delaware, the son of a physician in the Revolutionary Army. He had helped Decatur burn the *Philadelphia* at Tripoli. Before the outbreak of war he had been one of those commanders who refused to allow British captains to impress their seamen. He was handsome, devout, self-disciplined— and very thorough.

As Prevost and his veterans moved south on Plattsburg, Macdonough brought his squadron into tiny Plattsburg Bay. He realized that he could not hope to meet Captain George Downie's British fleet in long-range battle out in the open water. He hoped, rather, to lure Downie into a close-up fight fought at anchor. So he anchored his biggest ships—flagship *Saratoga, Eagle, Ticonderoga* and *Preble* —across Plattsburg Bay and put his gunboats behind him to fill the gaps. Next he carefully rigged his ships for battle at anchor, using kedges and hawsers so that he might at any time "wind" them around to bring unused broadsides to bear. This, in effect, gave him double the firepower of his 86 guns against the British 90. For Downie to enter Plattsburg Bay against such precautions was for a bowman to enter an alley full of knives with one arm in a sling. Yet he did enter— because Sir George Prevost insisted upon it.

Prevost did not understand the niceties of naval warfare, and therefore he insisted that Downie put to sea even though his flagship, 36-gun *Confiance,* was not ready to sail. So *Confiance* came down the lake with riggers and carpenters still at work on her decks, in the company of the big *Linnet*, two sloops *Chub* and *Finch*, and a dozen gunboats and row galleys. As they did, the Americans harassed Prevost's advance.

Having gathered his detachments, and been reinforced by about 800 New York militia, Macomb had about 4,000 men holding Plattsburg. They dismantled both bridges over the Saranac River and fell back south of the stream into three well-built forts. On September 6 the British probed briefly at these defenses, after which Prevost decided to sit back and await the arrival of Captain Downie.

He marked time for five days, and then he ordered a land-sea assault! America had already given pathetic demonstration of what happens to armies when civilians play soldier, and Prevost was about to show that there is something even worse: the civilian-soldier playing sailor. Prevost possessed the strength to storm the American positions, after which he could turn the captured guns on Macdonough's ships and drive them out into the unequal combat of the open lake. Macdonough had prepared well, but he had also offered Prevost the opportunity of defeating himself and Macomb in detail. But Prevost did not see it. He only saw that as he crossed the Saranac his left flank would be exposed to the fire of the American gunboats, and so he ordered Downie to sail into Macdonough's ambush.

At eight o'clock in the morning of September 11, 1814, the British fleet rounded Cumberland Head. The wind turned foul, as Macdonough had hoped, and *Confiance, Linnet, Chub* and *Finch* crept toward their anchorages with limp and flapping sails. The Americans opened fire.

Downie, disregarding his long-range superiority, had intended to lay *Confiance* alongside *Saratoga*. But now the raking fire of Macdonough's carronades forced him to anchor 300 yards away, or about 50 yards beyond the point-blank range of a carronade. Then *Confiance*'s gun ports blazed and half of Macdonough's crew was felled on *Saratoga*'s decks. Soon the battle became general and scattered. *Linnet* battled *Eagle, Chub* was sent drifting out of control among the American gunboats where she struck, and *Ticonderoga* and *Preble* fought what appeared to be a losing battle with *Finch* and the British gunboats. All depended now on the dreadful duel between *Confiance* and *Saratoga*. At first it went poorly for the British. Captain Downie was killed when an American gun sent a shot plunging into his groin. Then the British long-range superiority began to tell. The American left was turned when *Linnet* drove *Eagle* to refuge between *Saratoga* and *Ticonderoga,* and joined *Confiance* in battering *Saratoga.* By then *Saratoga* could not work a gun on her starboard side.

Now Macdonough's forethought came into the scales. Ignoring the battle, he directed the winding of his ship. Slowly, one by one, *Saratoga*'s port guns were unmasked and Macdonough fired on *Confiance* with one gun after another as *Saratoga* bore around. *Confiance* tried desperately to wind ship herself. Failing, she struck her colors— and her three smaller sisters were forced to surrender, although the gunboats escaped.

In the meantime, Prevost's redcoats had gotten over the Saranac at an upper ford. They were coming down on the forts when American shouts running upriver like a jubilant powder train proclaimed Downie's defeat. Prevost all but panicked. He could have, in the words of a subordinate, gone on to take Plattsburg in 20 minutes. But the news of the lake reverse so distressed him, as he explained later, that he decided to retire to the border to see what use the Americans would make of their naval superiority. Once launched on the retrograde, however, he did not stop until the last of his splendid troops crossed into Canada. Meanwhile, Thomas Macdonough reported to the Secretary of the Navy:

"Sir: The Almighty has been pleased to grant us a signal victory on Lake Champlain. . . ."[71]

It was indeed more significant than Macdonough might imagine, and two days later an event more memorable though less momentous in American history was to be written in the red glare of rockets bursting over Fort McHenry.

11

☆

In that September of 1814 mannerly Robert Ross and George Cockburn with 4,000 redcoats sailed up the Chesapeake toward Baltimore, intending to launch a demonstration which, if successful, could be converted into all-out assault upon that wealthy "nest of pirates."

At the same time General William Winder rode north from Washington expecting to take command of Baltimore's defenses. He was rebuffed, however, by Senator Samuel Smith, a militia major general who had no intention of placing the city's fate in the hands of the starter of the Bladensburg Races. Smith was a rarity: he was 61 and a Revolutionary War veteran, but he had not forgotten his military lessons and he still wanted to fight.

Because the vengeful Cockburn had diverted Ross to Washington, Baltimore, the true object of the expedition, had been granted time to prepare its fortifications. They were built by the citizens themselves, and held by as many as 16,000 men under General Smith. Baltimore's harbor, a busy privateering base, was protected by Fort McHenry.

The British plan was to bombard McHenry into submission while Ross advanced overland against the city. On September 12 the fleet anchored off North Point at the tip of the peninsula between the Back and Patapsco rivers and Ross's impatient redcoats went ashore.

Ross was confident and in high spirits. Breakfasting with Cockburn at a Maryland farmhouse, he toyed with the idea of making Baltimore his winter quarters. As he departed, the farmer asked him if he would be back for supper.

"No," Ross said, "I'll have supper tonight in Baltimore," and then, in afterthought, "or in Hell."[72]

The first conjecture seemed more likely as Ross's eager redcoats swept briskly up the peninsula. But then his scouts ran into a force of riflemen sent forward by Brigadier General John Stricker, who had marched out from Baltimore with about 3,200 raw militia. Shots were fired, the British spread out, flanked the Americans and drove them off.

General Ross hurried up with his advance guard. Two American marksmen who had not fled—Daniel Wells and Harry McComas—fired their last shots. One bullet hit Ross. He lurched back into the arms of his aide, calling his wife's name, and then he spoke no more. His body was laid under an oak tree, and the troops moving up to the attack saw it as they passed. "A groan came from the column," according to Subaltern Glieg, and it was obvious after Colonel Arthur Brooke took command that "the army had lost its mainspring."[73]

The Americans under Stricker made an unusually firm stand at

Godly Wood. Musket fire blazed out from both lines in a battle which brought death to Wells and McComas, the men who shot at Ross, and which eventually ended in a British victory. But British casualties were 300 against 200 for the Americans, and on the next day, after Brooke saw the formidable entrenchments in front of Baltimore, he stopped short to await support from the fleet.

By then, midday of September 13, 1814, Admiral Cochrane's bombardment ships were at work battering Fort McHenry. For 25 hours the British ships rained shells and Congreve rockets upon the sturdy little bastion. The Americans fired back briefly, but could not make the range. Luckily, neither could the bigger British vessels because of a barrier of sunken ships. Some 1,800 projectiles fell upon the Americans, but they could not bring about the fort's submission.

Ashore Brooke feinted twice to no avail and a British landing party was driven away from Fort Covington. McHenry had held, along with the Baltimore defenses, and the British fleet eventually sailed back to Halifax and the troops returned to Jamaica.

Such was the British failure at Baltimore, and it might not have merited more than a passing notice in the annals of American arms had not a Washington lawyer named Francis Scott Key watched the bombardment of Fort McHenry from a British cartel boat.

At one time a pacifist so fierce that he would write in 1812 of his willingness to accept "any disgrace or defeat," Key had changed his attitude and was now on a patriotic mission to obtain the release of Dr. William Beanes, a Maryland physician whom the British had caught in the act of imprisoning redcoats straggling out of Washington. Even the just General Ross had been intent upon seeing the elderly Dr. Beanes hanged in Halifax, but Key's diplomacy, together with reports that Beanes had been kind to British wounded, changed his mind. He granted the old man's release.

Throughout the night of September 13-14 Beanes and Key stood on the deck of the enemy ship watching British rockets and shells bursting over and upon the ramparts of Fort McHenry. Even at that distance Key could see the fort's huge flag illuminated again and again by the explosion flashes, and he began to jot down his impressions on the back of a letter. But old Dr. Beanes could not see so well. As dawn began to break, and the British bombardment subsided, he kept asking anxiously: "Is the flag still there?"[74]

The question triggered in Key's mind the theme of a poem, and he began to expand his jotting into verses. After he and Dr. Beanes were allowed to go ashore, he revised and expanded them and then took the completed poem to his brother-in-law, Judge J. H. Nicholson. The judge had been in Fort McHenry during those dreadful 25 hours. He had seen "the rockets' red glare" and had had his stomach squeezed by the shock of "bombs bursting in air." He had lived Key's poem, and he saw at once that it could be sung to the melody of a popular drinking song called "Anacreon in Heaven." Nicholson suggested immediate publication, and a young printer's devil named Samuel Sands set it in type and it came forth anonymously in a handbill entitled "Defence of Fort M'Henry." It was published on September 20 in the Baltimore *Patriot;* soon soldiers began singing it, and it spread gradually—though not suddenly—across the country. But not until March 3, 1931, did the United States Congress adopt "The Star-Spangled Banner" as the American national anthem.

If the War of 1812 had not given Americans much to brag about, it had at least given them a song to sing.

12

☆

Toward the end of October, 1814, news of the repulse at Baltimore and the Battle of Plattsburg reached London. The British were badly shaken, although they did not abandon their demand that negotiations at Ghent be conducted on the basis of "the state of possession" at the end of hostilities.

The Americans, who had already firmly rejected that demand, felt their own insistence on the *status quo ante bellum* fortified by news so stimulating that John Adams at first refused to believe it. Only a few months before, the London *Times,* reminding Lord Liverpool of his sacred duty to punish the Americans, had solemnly adjured him: ". . . oh may no false liberality, no mistaken lenity, no weak and cowardly policy, interpose to save them from the blow! Strike! Chastise the savages, for such they are!"[75] On October 19, printing the news of

Plattsburg, the *Times* observed gloomily: "This is a lamentable event to the civilized world."[76] Lord Liverpool could not agree more, for that "civilized world" was in distress both at home and abroad.

At home the loss of the American market caused by the blockade was already being severely felt, and the success of American privateers in the Irish Sea had made shipping insurance rates three times higher than they were during the war with Napoleon. Prevost's defeat meant that the war would have to be continued another year, at an estimated cost of £10 million. To raise such a sum meant extension of the detested property tax, then due to expire in a few months. Liverpool knew that his ministry could not survive, much less obtain, continuation of a tax "for the purpose of securing a better frontier for Canada."

Abroad the coalition which had conquered Napoleon was coming apart at the seams. Western Europe not only was troubled by the perils of reconstruction, but was also menaced by the new power of Russia. Diplomats at the Congress of Vienna, no longer impressed by British talk of the "contemptible Americans," would not fail to take note of the fact that some of Britain's finest regiments were beyond reach in far-off America. Czar Alexander's battalions were very close indeed.

Still, Liverpool faced up to the fact that the unpopular and unpleasant American war could yet be settled by a military decision. He asked the Duke of Wellington to assume command. Napoleon's nemesis replied: "That which appears to me to be wanting in America is not a general, or a general officer and troops, but a naval superiority on the Lakes."[77] On the diplomatic side, Wellington said: "In regard to your negotiation, I confess that I think you have no right, from the state of the war, to demand any concession of territory. . . . Why stipulate for the *uti possidetis?* You can get no territory; indeed the state of your military operations, however creditable, does not entitle you to any."[78]

The first soldier of Britain was not alone in his pessimism: all around Liverpool the country was giving way to a war weariness which quickly changed to outright opposition after the Americans cleverly made public Britain's outrageous territorial demands. Even the London *Times* was displeased, and liberals in Parliament bitterly castigated the Tory government for making demands it had no power to enforce. Recognizing reality, Liverpool moved to bring the distasteful war to a close, almost at the very moment when the dearest objects of British policy—American economic collapse and rupture of the American union—seemed to be taking place.

By the fall of 1814 it appeared that the federal government had run out of both men and money.

All attempts to establish a dependable regular army seemed to have failed. Although the paper strength of the U.S. Army was raised to 62,000 men, by the end of September the actual strength was only 34,000 men.

Secretary of State Monroe, who had taken over the War Department, boldly recommended conscription; but Congress had not the courage to give the nation its first draft. Instead, it raised the land bounty for enlistments, thereby encouraging desertion for the purpose of re-enlisting under another name to claim the bounty. At the end of 1814 the country staggered along with 34,000 regulars and the six-month militia of the various states.

By then, however, even the despised militia could not be counted upon to take the field, let alone remain there in the face of an enemy. Led by Massachusetts—possessor of the finest militia, which she would use only for her own defense—Connecticut, Pennsylvania, Maryland, Virginia, South Carolina and Kentucky began to form or to plan the formation of state armies.

Even more deplorable was the federal government's financial position, which was, in that fall of 1814, probably at its lowest point in the history of the nation. Although Congress had doubled imports at the outset of the war, while reviving some excise taxes and imposing direct taxes on dwellings and slaves, it proposed to finance the war by borrowing money. After the first year of defeat and retreat the only way the Treasury could borrow money was by selling its stock at greater and greater discounts. It has been estimated that of $80 million borrowed between 1812 and 1816, the government actually received only $34 million in specie value.

While the national debt rose, a Congress afraid to draft soldiers was also too timid to levy the taxes that would cover expenditures. Moreover, the Treasury had no national administrative system. It was not even able to transfer its deposits from one section of the country to another. Millions of banknotes collected in Middle and Southern banks had to be left on deposit there while debts in Boston and New York remained unpaid.

Finally, the section of the country which had the most cash was the center of opposition to the war. A variety of factors—not all of them so obvious or so culpable as the practice of playing quartermaster to the enemy—had enriched New England. Specie holdings in Massachusetts alone jumped from $1,709,000 in June of 1811 to $7,326,000 in June of 1814. Massachusetts, unalterably opposed to the war from the beginning, hoped to end it by withholding financial support.

When her war profits were shut off and British fleets menaced her shores, she called that quasi-secessionist assembly known as the Hartford Convention.

It is not fair to blame New England alone for the national government's shortages in men and money. Except New York, Kentucky, Tennessee, and perhaps Ohio, no state gave the war its full and earnest cooperation. Moreover, many patriots from New England volunteered for the regular Army and some of its finest regiments were recruited there. Nevertheless, the conduct of the Federalists who controlled New England is not to be admired. They gave the war the least support and took the largest profits. Shippers took advantage of Britain's licensing system to supply Britain and her allies in the Peninsular War against Napoleon, who, if he was not an American ally, was at least fighting the American enemy. Although these same ships later turned privateer to attack British shipping, their purpose was prizes not patriotism. Because of New England's antiwar spirit Britain had at first excluded her coasts from the blockade, enabling her to gain a monopoly of the import trade. Finally, New England so openly and effectively supplied the enemy in Canada that Congress had to pass a law forbidding the coastal trade.

Outraged, New England came to a boil of town meetings, just as in the days of King George, only now it was the Republican "Jacobins" and "that little man in the Palace" who were denounced. Profiteering and smuggling were cloaked in the righteous mantle of assistance to the Lord's anointed—Britain—standing at Armageddon against the Napoleonic antichrist. However, after the devil incarnate had been defeated and exiled to Elba, there was still no lessening of opposition to the war. Even after Britain extended the blockade to New England—thereby cutting war profits—the Federalists could describe the British peace terms as "moderate" and recommend relying upon British magnanimity. But then, in September of 1814, those merciful cousins from across the sea seized 100 miles of Maine seacoast and a British fleet prepared to descend upon Boston.

Massachusetts was not only dumbfounded but left to her own resources. Two years before, Governor Caleb Strong had refused to put the state militia under the War Department. Now, as the national government offered to maintain the militia so long as it was commanded by regular Army officers, Strong replied that he would call out the militia only *to defend Boston,* providing the state retained control and the United States paid the bills. The answer, of course, was no. And so Massachusetts sent out an invitation to other New England states to confer at Hartford upon "their public grievances and concerns" and to concert plans for interstate defense.

The Hartford Convention met in secret session from December 15, 1814, to January 5, 1815. Delegates from Massachusetts, Connecticut and Rhode Island attended, with only a scattering from Vermont and New Hampshire. At the outset the moderates gained control, and the issues of secession or a separate peace were almost at once ruled out. Nevertheless, the Hartford Convention pointed a pistol at the heart of the Union. In simplest terms, New England proposed to defend herself with her own forces financed by federal tax monies collected within her borders. As the Federalists well knew, what New England could do the other sections might also do, and that would be the end of *"e pluribus unum."* If Congress did not accept this and other proposals, New England would then hold another convention at which, it was safe to infer, the final step of secession would be taken.

In the minds of many Federalists there was no doubt that secession was the ultimate solution, and there were many Republicans who despaired of any means of preserving the Union. The news of the gradual softening of the British position at Ghent had not yet been received in America. What was known, as the Hartford Convention's three "ambassadors" rode off to Washington to inform Congress of New England's pleasure, was that a large British force had invested New Orleans. Even Thomas Jefferson expected that city to fall and to be held indefinitely by the British. And if New Orleans fell, then a federal government unable to pay its army or its navy or even the interest on its national debt could certainly be expected to topple too.

Britain sought New Orleans first to command the mouth of the Mississippi and to deprive the American West of its outlet to the sea, and second as a prize either valuable in itself or as a counterweight at the peace table. Some 10,000 soldiers eventually were gathered for an army to be commanded by Robert Ross, but after his death command passed to Sir Edward Pakenham, the brother-in-law of the Duke of Wellington.

To defend against this most formidable British armada to sail against a New World city, the United States had a few regiments of regulars, the Western and Southern militia and Major General Andrew Jackson. Jackson took command at his headquarters in Mobile on August 15, 1814, and promptly looked eastward away from New Orleans toward Pensacola in Spanish East Florida. Here a small British force had seized the fortifications, and Jackson, immediately calling for 2,500 Tennessee militia, proposed to expel them. Before he could, the British forces there moved against Mobile—only to be repulsed by the gallant stand of Fort Bowyer. Incensed, still looking away from New Orleans, ignoring a petition from its citizens imploring him to come there, and without authority to invade Spanish possessions, Old Hickory attacked and seized Pensacola. That was on November 7, 1814, after which he returned to Mobile.

Jackson simply could not believe that anyone would be foolish enough to mount an amphibious assault directly against New Orleans. He set this conviction down on paper, writing: "A real military man, with full knowledge of the geography of this country, would first possess himself of [Mobile], draw to his standard the Indians, and march direct to the Walnut Hills [present-day Vicksburg] . . . and being able to forage on the country, support himself, cut off all supplies from above and make this country an easy conquest."[79] Old Hickory was right. New Orleans could be defended easily against amphibious invasion, but it could not survive if its communications with the back country were cut off by a strong army above the city. However, Old Hickory probably was not aware of how powerfully the lust for prize money could influence the counsels of British admirals. It was Cochrane who decided to attack New Orleans directly, and inasmuch as he knew that the city was crammed with the produce of the American West valued at £4 million, and because he did include barges in his fleet, it is not too much to suggest that considerations of private gain as well as of public glory helped to make up the admiral's mind. On November 26, without waiting for Pakenham and with Major General John Keane commanding the troops, Cochrane sailed from Jamaica for New Orleans.

Four days before that Andrew Jackson had at last begun moving west. Big John Coffee went riding on ahead to Baton Rouge with 2,000 mounted riflemen; another 1,000 troops were left in Mobile; and with 2,000 under his own command, Old Hickory marched for New Orleans 130 miles away. On December 1 he was received outside the city by a New Orleans merchant who, together with the cultivated Creole lady who prepared his house for the reception, seems to have been surprised to observe: "A tall, gaunt man, very erect . . . with a countenance furrowed by care and anxiety. A small leather cap protected his head, and a short blue Spanish cloak his body, whilst his . . . high boots [were] long innocent of polish or blacking. . . . His complexion was sallow, and unhealthy; his hair iron grey, and his body thin and emaciated like that of one who had just recovered from a lingering sickness. . . . But a fierce glare [lighted] his bright and hawk-like eye."[80] The Creole lady complained: "Ah! Mr. Smith . . . you asked me to . . . receive a great General. I make your house *comme il faut,* and prepare a splendid *déjeuner* . . . all for . . . an ugly old Kaintuck flat-boatman."[81]

It was Jackson's energy and determination, not his unkempt appearance, which impressed the mostly French population of New Orleans after he entered the city next day to throw himself headlong into organizing its defenses. Forts protecting the city were strengthened, bayous leading into it were blocked by felled trees or filled with mud, and troops were placed in positions so that they might be concentrated at the first alarm. On December 18 Jackson put on a new uniform, mounted a splendid horse and rode out to review his colorful army of regulars, militia, free Negroes, gaudy Creoles, painted Choctaws and fierce Baratarian pirates. The last, headed by the audacious and charming Jean Laffite, had been among the most enthusiastic volunteers to Jackson's standards, but they had not been readily accepted. Jackson bluntly rejected these "hellish banditti" until Laffite personally confronted him and offered his services. Fiction has made much of this meeting, but all that is known is that Jackson, unable to resist a man who had his own habit of looking another squarely in the eye, found that Laffite's trained gunners "could not fail of being very useful." On December 20 John Coffee's dragoons clattered in from Baton Rouge, and a few hours later 3,000 Tennessee volunteers under William Carroll came floating down the yellowish broad river on flatboats. By December 23 Jackson could write home: "All well." He did not seem to be upset by the British capture of five gunboats on Lake Borgne, the watery link between the Gulf and the left bank of the Mississippi just below New Orleans. Jackson was confident that every bayou from Borgne to the river bank was blocked and guarded.

Shortly after noon a young Creole named Augustin Rousseau flung himself from his lathered horse outside Jackson's headquarters and burst upon the general with the report that the British were inside his defenses. It was incredible. As Jackson retired to his sofa to ponder such astounding news, a sentry rapped at his door to announce three gentlemen having "important intelligence." They rushed in, breathless and mud-stained. From the lips of Major Gabriel Villere fell a torrent of French. From the lips of an interpreter, Jackson heard: "The British have arrived at Villere's plantation! Major Villere was captured by them and has escaped!"[82]

Jackson listened in astonishment. Unseen, the British had landed on the western shore of Lake Borgne. They had found the thing Jackson believed to be nonexistent—an unblocked and unguarded bayou—and had passed through five miles of swamp to appear in force only seven miles below the city. Eyes flashing, Jackson sprang from his sofa, struck the table with his fist and cried: "By the Eternal, they shall not sleep on our soil!"[83]

Suddenly calm again, he gave his visitors wine to sip, called his aides and announced: "Gentlemen, the British are below. We must fight them tonight."[84]

If it is difficult to forgive Jackson for having allowed himself to be so completely surprised, as it certainly is, then it is also just to praise his quick and decisive reaction. To surprise he was offering counter surprise. He could not know that General Keane had rejected advice to push on immediately to New Orleans with his vanguard of 2,400 men. But he did accurately surmise that the British would pause, and he decided to strike them suddenly and at night when British discipline operated at least advantage.

Jackson had about 4,000 men available, as well as the schooner

Carolina. He had helped himself plentifully to Jean Laffite's guns and gunners, and the weight of *Carolina*'s broadsides forced her low in the water. In the gathering dusk, *Carolina*'s shadowy bulk began sliding gently downstream toward Villere plantation on her left. Captain Daniel Patterson would not need to search for targets. The British, drenched for days like swamp rats, had been busily gathering wood and lighting fires which blazed cheerfully in the darkness fallen on the Villere flats. Patterson was to open fire at 7:30; a half-hour later, giving the enemy enough time to conclude that the main assault would come from the river, Jackson would attack.

A cold fog rising from the river closed in on *Carolina* as she floated away on the current. Mist dimmed the moon and enshrouded the enemy campfires. Suddenly, a great glob of red glowed through the fog, followed by the muted roar of *Carolina*'s guns. For a moment, Britain's veterans came close to panic as the earth bucked and roared and men screamed. Some of them tried to douse their fires, but most ran for the cover of the Mississippi levee. *Carolina* roared on, and then, at eight o'clock exactly, the Americans attacked.

The higher voice of American 6-pounders joined the deeper-throated chorus of *Carolina*'s guns downstream. Then *Carolina* fell silent, not wishing to catch friend and foe alike in her raking fire. The Americans stumbled on against an enemy who had turned to fight, and the battle became a lieutenant's melee: squad by squad, platoon by platoon, men seeking each other in the darkness with clutching fingers or drawn knife, rifles twinkling and cannon muzzles gushing flame, and the cries of men mingling with the neighing of Coffee's horses. At one point the British threatened to capture the American 6-pounders. Jackson rushed into the fight, shouting, "Save the guns!"[85]

Marines and a company of the 7th Infantry rallied around Jackson and saved the cannon.

"Charge! Charge!" yelled the Americans, and the Creoles cried, *"A la baïonnette!"*[86]

At midnight the black battlefield became suddenly silent. Jackson, correctly suspecting that the enemy was being reinforced, decided to withdraw. Unknown to himself, he had dealt the British a blow from which they never completely recovered. British casualties of 46 killed, 167 wounded and 64 captured did not seem very heavy, even though they exceeded American losses of 24 killed, 115 wounded and 74 captured, but the very audacity of the American assault had shaken the redcoats' conviction that "the Dirty Shirts" at New Orleans would run just as fast as their Bladensburg brothers. And so, as the dawn of December 24, 1814, disclosed his assault force safely drawn up behind the dry Rodriguez Canal, Old Hickory sent into the city for those lowly shovels which, more than rifles, bayonet or cannon, are the soul of every defensive stand.

In Ghent that night the British and American negotiators signed the Peace of Christmas Eve. On November 18 Liverpool had dropped his policy of continuing the war to gain territory. Opposition in Parliament, financial strain, the difficulty of extending the property tax, unrest in the interior of France, the lack of progress at the Congress of Vienna, and, perhaps most important of all, the attitude of the Duke of Wellington had all conspired to make him change his mind. In the following month, America's astute diplomats led by Gallatin slowly forced the British away from their position of "the state of possession," until both sides finally agreed to the *status quo ante bellum*.

The Treaty of Ghent was a simple cessation of hostilities. Every principle or issue for which the War of 1812 was fought was ignored. The rights of neutrals and impressments, American fishery or British navigation rights, questions of boundaries or armaments on the lakes, all were referred to commissions for future settlements. All, in effect, was left to the healing power of time; and that was a wise decision. Henry Clay may have called the agreement "a damned bad treaty," but it has been one of the most enduring in history. Unfortunately for the men still confronting one another in this wretched, futile war, it was weeks before news of the Peace of Christmas Eve reached American shores.

Christmas Day in New Orleans began with a salvo of artillery from the British camp. Americans building their mud rampart behind the canal dropped their spades, seized their rifles and jumped to the firing platforms. Then they relaxed. The salvo was only a salute to Sir Edward Pakenham, who had arrived to·take command from Keane.

Pakenham's presence gave a lift to his bedraggled redcoats. The boyish, brilliant hero of Salamanca was popular with the army. Moreover, he was confident and eager for a victory that would make him the royal governor of Louisiana with an earldom to match. His wife waited at sea, as did many other ladies accompanying a force "prepared to take over the civil administration of New Orleans, with appointments from tide-waiter to collector of customs already designated."[87] Sir Edward apparently wanted to withdraw from the present poor position and land elsewhere. But he was overwhelmed by the scorn of Admiral Cochrane, who vowed that his sailors alone could defeat the Dirty Shirts and "The soldiers could then bring up the baggage."[88] So Pakenham agreed to attack Jackson's fortifications.

On December 27 the British batteries opened on the American ships *Louisiana* and *Carolina. Louisiana* narrowly escaped but *Carolina* blew up with a roar that rattled windows in New Orleans. On the same day the Americans dragged their own artillery into position while Jackson began construction of a second line of defense two miles behind the first. Next day the British showered the American lines with rockets and sent two columns forward in assault.

On the American left, the redcoats came very close to turning the sector held by Coffee's and Carroll's men standing almost waist-deep in the swamp. On the right, the enemy column moving along the river bank was raked dreadfully by the guns of *Louisiana*. Rampart guns, manned chiefly by Laffite's red-shirted pirates, thickened the fire from *Louisiana* and the assault on the American right was dealt a bloody repulse. As it halted, so too did the threat to the left flank— and Pakenham's first attempt failed. Although he tried to excuse it as a "reconnaissance in force," one of his aides wrote later: "In spite of our sanguine expectations of sleeping that night in New Orleans, evening found us occupying our negro huts at Villere's, nor was I sorry that the shades of night concealed our mortification from the prisoners and slaves."[89]

The last three days of 1814 were ones of back-breaking toil on both sides. The Americans fortified the other side of the river with three batteries of naval guns and the mud line's cannon rose from five to twelve. Cotton bales were sunk into the mud flats and wooden platforms placed over them. The faces of the gun embrasures were protected by cotton bales stiffened with dried mud. As Jackson's defenses grew, he continued to send "hunting parties" into the British lines every night. His men lay still in the cane stubble between the lines, rising suddenly to shoot or tomahawk a careless sentry.

On the British side Cochrane's sailors had brought off an incredible feat of labor, bringing forward naval guns from the fleet 70 miles away. On New Year's Eve, a black and foggy night, these big pieces of ordnance were put into position 700 yards away from the Americans. Protected by mounds of earth and hogsheads of sugar, the British guns were to silence the American artillery and blast a breach in the rampart through which the redcoats, their bellies now pinched by hunger, might stream to victory.

New Year's Day, 1815, was still foggy. Nevertheless, General Andrew Jackson persisted in his intention to review his troops. Visitors from the city, among them ladies, streamed into the camp. A band played. Troops assigned to parade had cleaned up their uniforms. Suddenly the fog became suffused with scarlet, there came a thunder that was not the roll of drums, and as the mist became slashed with showers of rockets and civilians went scurrying frantically cityward while soldiers sprinted for the ramparts, the British bombardment began to work over the American camp.

One hundred balls struck and shattered Jackson's headquarters, a supply boat was crippled, cotton bales on the ramparts were set ablaze, a gun carriage was shattered, a 32- and a 12-pounder were knocked out, and a caisson loaded with ammunition was blown up. With that, the British infantry waiting to attack sent up a cheer and their gunners, satisfied that they had silenced the enemy, suspended fire. To their astonishment, through clouds of billowing, pungent smoke that blotted out everything, came the American answering fire.

It began faintly at first and then rose with a gradually ascending roar. Converging from Jackson's line and the batteries across the river, 15 guns in all answered Britain's 24, and Subaltern Glieg has described their effect:

> The enemy's shot penetrated these sugar-hogsheads as if they had been so many empty casks, dismounting our guns and killing our artillery-men in the very centre of their works. There could be small doubt, as soon as these facts were established, how the cannonading would end. Our fire slackened every moment; that of the Americans became every moment more terrible, till at length, after not more than two hours and a half of firing, our batteries were all silenced. The American works, on the other hand, remained as little injured as ever, and we were completely foiled.[90]

The Dirty Shirts had slugged toe to toe with the pride of the fleet and driven them to cover, and Andrew Jackson jubilantly wished his troops a Happy New Year with the message: "Watch Word: Fight On—The Contractor will issue half a gill of whiskey around."[91]

A week passed during which both sides were reinforced: a brigade for the British, 2,400 Kentuckians for the Americans. Pakenham now had about 8,000 men and Jackson 5,700, although Old Hickory was startled to hear that most of his Kentuckians were unarmed.

"I don't believe it," he exclaimed. "I have never seen a Kentuckian without a gun and a pack of cards and a bottle of whiskey in my life."[92]

Nevertheless, only one man in three had a firearm, so Jackson sent about 500 of them across the river to act as reserve for the 550 Louisiana militia who defended Patterson's batteries there under Brigadier General David Morgan. For a while Jackson was undecided about where to expect the enemy's next attack. News that the British were dragging boats from Lake Borgne to the Mississippi suggested that they might cross the river to strike Morgan. But then the sight of redcoats bundling cane stalks into fascines and making ladders made it clear that the enemy might try to cross the canal and scale the rampart of Jackson's main position.

In truth, Pakenham meant to do both. The boats were for Colonel William Thornton, the officer who led the charge at Bladensburg, to take 1,400 men across the river to overwhelm Morgan, seize the guns and turn them on Jackson's rear. Meanwhile, three columns would hit the canal and rampart: General Keane on the British left by the river, Major General Sir Samuel Gibbs on the right by the swamp, and Major General John Lambert in the center to be rushed wherever needed. It was a good plan, especially the cross-river thrust for the American guns. Artillery playing on Jackson's rear could be decisive. However, British fear of Dirty Shirt marksmanship had dictated that the assault take place in the confusion of darkness.

At the outset Thornton got only half of his men into boats on time and was quickly swept downriver below his landing place. Then Gibbs on the right discovered that his men had forgotten their fascines and ladders. Before dawn broke, only Keane on the left was ready. Nevertheless, Pakenham fired a rocket, that *"fatal ever fatal rocket"* signaling the attack of January 8.

Andrew Jackson and his aides had been up since one o'clock in the morning inspecting the lines. They came to the battery commanded by the fierce and dandified little pirate captain, Dominique You. Dominique's red-shirts were cooking coffee and Jackson said, "That smells like better coffee than we can get." He turned to Dominique. "Smuggle it?"

"Mebbe so, General," the little captain grunted, filling a cup for his commander.

"I wish I had five hundred such devils in the butts,"[93] Jackson muttered, passing on until he came to his Tennesseans under Coffee and Carroll on the left. He was there, standing on the parapet, when Pakenham's rocket burst in a bluish-silver shower overhead. Another from Keane answered from the river bank, and Jackson peered intently into the opaque wall of mist before him. Then a providential breeze sprang up, opening patches in the fog through which Jackson could now see the British advancing.

They were coming through a cane stubble silvery with frost. They came on bravely, cross-belts forming a white X on scarlet tunics, and Jackson issued the order: ". . . . aim above the cross plates."[94]

American cannon spoke first, then the British answered, and the fog again glowed red. Soon smoke spoiled the aim of the American riflemen, and Jackson ordered two leftward batteries to cease firing. The air cleared and the British could be seen coming at a run 300 yards away. American cannon to Jackson's right angled a scything fire into the British ranks. The red ranks shuddered, closed up and came on. Now the gleaming cross plates were just a hair above the sights of American rifles.

"Fire!"

Flame and flash and single crack, and the first rank of riflemen stepped down to reload while the second took its place.

"Fire!"

The second rank gave way to the third.

"Fire!"[95]

Scarlet coats lay crumpled among the stubble. Gibbs's oncoming column had been splayed out into skirmish line as though a giant hand had slapped it. Again and again the American fire ripped into them, until the foreranks turned to the rear. "Never before had British veterans quailed," an English officer wrote later. "The leaden torrent no man on earth could face."[96]

Sir Edward Pakenham came galloping up to his shattered right flank, had his horse shot dead beneath him and flung himself upon his aide's black pony. A second assault was formed, led by a "praying regiment" of Highlanders, every man six feet tall—coming on with swinging kilts, and going down among the silver stubble. Perhaps 70 of these brave men gained the bank of the canal, perhaps 30 got across it and clambered up the parapet. But none of them survived.

That was the end of Gibbs's attack. Gibbs himself was dying, Keane had been shot through the neck, and Pakenham had received his third and mortal wound. On the British left a splendid charge had carried through an American bastion, but penetrated no farther. In the center, General Lambert ignored Pakenham's dying orders to throw in the reserve and began withdrawing the stricken British Army from the field.

In all, the British had suffered more than 2,000 casualties against only eight Americans killed and 13 wounded. At half-past eight it was all over at the Rodriguez Canal. "I never had so grand and awful an idea of the resurrection," said General Jackson, "as . . . [when] I saw . . . more than five hundred Britons emerging from the heaps of their dead comrades, all over the plain rising up, and . . . coming forward . . . as prisoners."[97]

The battle was not entirely over. Across the river, Colonel Thornton drove steadily through Morgan's militia. Jackson's elation over the British failure at his main position changed to alarm as he saw the Americans across the river give way completely. Cross-river cannon fire still raking the British in front of Jackson suddenly ceased. Captain Patterson was spiking his guns. Night came and Jackson still held his breath. He had moved too late to counter Thornton, and now the British held an advantage which might easily be exploited. But in the morning Lambert recalled Thornton to the east bank. On the night of January 18, leaving their campfires burning, the British returned the way they had come. Ahead of them went the body of General Pakenham "in a casket of rum to be taken to London. What a sight for his wife who is aboard and who had hoped to be Governess of Louisiana."[98]

Three days later the majestic notes of the *Te Deum* reverberated around the stone walls of the cathedral in New Orleans.

News of the deliverance of New Orleans traveled even slower than news of the Treaty of Ghent. Up North, the "ambassadors" of the Hartford Convention were still supremely confident of American defeat as they rode toward Washington. They still intended to speak plainly to Mr. Madison. Three black crows preceded their coach into Washington, but the ambassadors remained unshaken, for Puritans took no stock in the "auguries" of a superstitious past. At Baltimore, however, they heard of the victory at New Orleans. Though shaken, they rode on to Washington. On February 13, 1815, news of the Treaty of Ghent was received in the capital. Stunned, the Hartford emissaries hung around Washington for about a week, after which, no longer able to sit still as the butt of war hawk barb and caricature, they rode back to New England.

On February 17, 1815, President Madison declared the War of 1812 at an end.

PART IV

The War with Mexico

1

☆

In February of 1815, a week after the War of 1812 came to an end, Napoleon Bonaparte escaped from Elba. Four months later he met the Duke of Wellington at Waterloo and went down to his last defeat.

Thus ended the Anglo-French duel which had extended over nearly two centuries. Six times—four times with the British, twice against them—the Americans had been drawn into that world-wide conflict; but now this new nation, hating war yet born and bred to battle, was at last free of "the broils of Europe."

America was free because Waterloo had conferred upon Britain an immense, world-wide prestige and had ushered in the *Pax Britannica,* that relatively peaceful century during which Britain "controlled extra-European events and localized European wars."[1] It is one of the great paradoxes of American history that the British Navy which had so insulted America by its insistence on the right to impress her seamen would now by its mastery of the seas enable the United States to embark unmolested upon an era of territorial expansion and internal development.

The year 1815, then, was a great turning point. Relations with Great Britain became friendly, and the so-called Era of Good Feeling commenced with the election of James Monroe as President in 1816. So also began a spirit of nationalism, which seems to have sprung from the common experience through which Americans had just passed as well as from a reaction against the selfish sectional strife which had characterized the war. Albert Gallatin, returning from Ghent, said this of his countrymen: "They are more American; they feel and act more like a nation; and I hope that the permanency of the Union is thereby better secured."[2]

Nationalism buried the states' rights Federalists in the grave dug by the Hartford Convention. Once nationalism had been the very soul of Federalism, as it was the *bête noire* of Republicanism, but the Federalists had since shifted to states' rights, and the Republicans, observing to what depth their rivals had been interred, quickly switched to nationalism. The movement's leaders, John C. Calhoun and Henry Clay, had a formula called "the American system," which included a protective tariff for the manufacturing industry developed during the war, a home market for national products and improved transportation.

Good transportation was vital to the new westward surge begun when American settlers flowed into the lands taken from Tecumseh and the Creeks. Four new states—Indiana (1816), Mississippi (1817), Illinois (1818) and Alabama (1819)—were admitted to the union. Unfortunately, territorial expansion raised the ghost of slavery extension. An even balance between slave and free states had been maintained by alternately admitting slave-soil and free-soil territories. After Alabama's entry there were 11 each. But then, in 1819, Missouri sought admission as a slave state, and this most divisive of sectional issues came alive with an acrimonious vigor which threatened to shatter the nationalist honeymoon.

Outraged Northerners insisted that the entry of Missouri, which lay north of the line then dividing slavery and freedom, was a Southern attempt to increase its voting power. Southerners, who had not yet come to defending slavery on moral grounds, claimed that they had the right to take their property, i.e., slaves, into Missouri. Both sides talked secession. Eventually the Missouri Compromise was agreed upon. Under its terms, Missouri was admitted as a slave-holding state, while Maine, which had detached itself from Massachusetts, was admitted as a free state. More important, slavery was prohibited in unorganized territory north of Missouri's southern boundary of 36°36′. Thus the South provided for the eventual admission of Florida and Arkansas as slave states, while the North guaranteed freedom in the huge unsettled stretches of U.S. territory.

Whatever the Missouri Compromise may have done in restoring a fatally deceptive tranquillity to the Era of Good Feeling, it had also driven home for the first time the fact that the question of slavery was not a political or economic problem but a moral one. Thomas Jefferson saw this, and wrote: "This momentous question, like a fire bell in the night, awakened and filled me with terror. I considered it at once as the knell of the Union."[3] John Quincy Adams, now Secretary of State, informed his diary: "I take it for granted that the present question is a mere preamble—a title page to a great, tragic volume."[4] Much of the dreadfully involved wrangle over Missouri was actually a struggle to control the trans-Mississippi West, an area finally delineated by Adams after Jackson tore Florida out of the hands of Spain.

In the fall of 1817 the first of the wars with the Seminole Indians broke out, and Andrew Jackson marched to battle again at the head of about 2,500 Tennessee militia. Breaking the power of the Seminoles, he kept marching south until he had taken Pensacola and ejected its Spanish governor, after which he went back to Tennessee a hero. In Washington, however, there were powerful men who remembered Julius Caesar and wished to have Jackson disgraced or at least reprimanded.

Adams was not one of them. He stood behind Old Hickory, insisting that Spain had long ago shown her inability to govern Florida. Spain seemed to agree, for negotiations to sell the troublesome province were begun. They concluded in the Transcontinental Treaty of February, 1819, under which, in return for $5 million, Spain ceded all her lands east of the Mississippi together with her claims to the Oregon territory. The treaty also traced the boundary between the United States and Mexico, and because it recognized an American line to the Pacific running west from the Rockies along the 42nd parallel, it made the United States of America a continental power. Mexico, however, the last Spanish province in North America, remained enormous. It included not only its present-day lands but the modern American states of California, Nevada, Utah, Arizona, New Mexico, Texas and parts of Wyoming and Colorado. Mexico was roughly equal in size to the United States itself—bigger if the Oregon territory which America jointly claimed with Britain was excluded —and Mexico a few years later was herself a free republic.

Mexican independence climaxed a seven-year eruption of revolutions which convulsed Latin America after the fall of Napoleon. One by one, under the leadership of José de San Martín, Simon Bolívar and Bernardo O'Higgins, Spain's colonies in the New World renounced allegiance to the mother country and set themselves up as free republics. Unfortunately, they did not unite as the North Amer-

ican colonies had. Such a multipilicity of young and unsteady republics, all open to the intrigues as well as the commerce of the
older powers, created a dangerously unstable situation. Britain took
the lead in attempting to stabilize it by asking the United States to
join her in a declaration barring France from South America. But
the Americans went Mother England one better. They decided to
bar *everyone* from South America, and on December 2, 1823, in his
annual message to Congress, President Monroe laid down the Monroe
Doctrine warning all European powers against attempting to interfere with nations in the "Western Hemisphere." The United States,
of course, had no power to enforce such a declaration. Only British
sea power was capable of patrolling the shores of both continents.
Yet Britain was at that moment deeply interested in preserving the
peace in South America, just as she was not interested in expanding
at the expense of the new Latin republics. So the Monroe Doctrine
stood up—propped up, as it were, by the British Navy—gradually
solidifying into one of the pillars of American foreign policy as the
nation itself grew in power and prestige.

On this note, the Era of Good Feeling came to an end.

2

☆

Mexico and the United States were sister republics in name
only. A better term is neighboring republics: they bordered each
other from the Pacific to the Gulf, that was all.

One spoke English, the other Spanish; one was Protestant, the other
Catholic; one, colonized on British lines, was organized by a strong
federal government, was energetic, proliferating and expanding; and
the other, colonized in the Roman way, had little unity, was torpid,
thinly populated, and already weakened by an oppressive clergy and
upper class and by the immemorial Latin custom of celebrating today's
revolution by toasting tomorrow's. Such differences were not disputes,
and none was a valid reason for going to war. But the two republics
were neighbors—one strong, the other weak—and it is only in recent

times, under the Sign of the Mushroom Cloud, that strong neighbors have acted as though they thought they should feed rather than eat the weak. In a sense, Mexico was to America what Ireland was to England. Again, it was a geographical fact, sheer proximity; Americans had yearned for Canada, and now, in the two decades (1825-45) following Monroe's administration, they turned their eyes from their northeastern border to the southwestern one.

This desire was never so conscious or deliberate as that illustrated by the war hawk raid on Upper Canada. Nor was the American government—at least not before President Polk—its instrument. Its agents—it might almost be said its advance guard or fifth column— were the pioneers and the backwoodsmen who crossed the Mississippi and came upon the northern outposts of Mexico.

The provinces of Upper California (the modern state of California), New Mexico and Texas were sparsely populated and bound to the parent government in the city of Mexico by the weakest of ties. Neither California nor New Mexico welcomed Americans, but in Texas they were not only welcomed but actually imported. Why, is difficult to answer. Even if it was imperative that Mexico should encourage migration to people her huge unsettled lands, it is inexplicable why she chose Americans. Europeans, especially from countries more nearly Mexican in customs, race and religion, would have been far safer. But only a few Germans were so encouraged; in the main it was *los Yanquis* who poured into Texas.

Their leaders were the *empresarios* to whom Mexico granted great tracts of land for settlement. By 1834 one such colony organized by Stephen Austin numbered 20,000 whites and 2,000 slaves and outnumbered the native Mexicans four to one. Few of these pioneers became Catholics as they had promised to do, and none heeded Mexican laws abolishing slavery; and as much as they might try to adhere to the laws of their adopted land, they found them forever changing in the wake of the latest revolution. As much as they might admire, say, the horsemanship of their adopted countrymen, they had the Anglo-Saxon's deep-seated faith in the superiority of the fair-skinned and soon came to despise the "greasers" as a lazy, superstitious lot. In turn, the Mexicans came to resent *los gringos* with their cold, condescending, acquisitive ways. They were *los hereticos,* and thus it might have been New France and New England colliding again beneath a sunnier sky.

Within the United States, especially in the Mississippi Valley, there were many Americans who believed their nation had a claim to Texas. After John Quincy Adams was elected President in 1824 he offered to buy the province. So did Andrew Jackson following his election in 1828. Both times the Mexicans angrily refused. But then the peaceful pioneers were joined by their less savory migratory twins, the hard-fighting, hard-drinking, straight-shooting frontiersmen, those "ring-tailed roarers, half-horse and half-alligator" who lived on "whiskey and bear's meat salted in a hailstorm, peppered with buckshot, and broiled in a flash of forked lightning."[5] Davy Crockett was one of them and so were the Bowie brothers of Louisiana, famous for slave-smuggling and the long knife—or short sword—that they had designed. Such men could not fail to fan the flames of hatred between Mexicans and Texans.

By 1836 there were 30,000 Americans in Texas, and Mexico, at last awake to the danger, sought to stem the onrushing tide of frontiersmen. By then the fiery and energetic revolutionary, General Antonio López de Santa Anna, had become virtual dictator of Mexico. He proclaimed a constitution which swept away states' rights and imposed an iron control on the Yankees north of the Rio Grande. The Texans replied by declaring their independence on March 2, 1836. They set up a provisional government under the Lone Star flag and expelled the Mexican garrison from San Antonio de Bexar.

Santa Anna promptly collected an army of 3,000 men and marched on San Antonio. There, less than 200 Texans took refuge in an abandoned adobe mission called the Alamo. Among them were Crockett and Jim Bowie. Their leader was Colonel William Travis. In his last message addressed "To the People of Texas and all Americans in the world," Travis declared: "I shall never surrender or retreat. . . . I am determined to sustain myself as long as possible and die like a soldier who never forgets what is due to his own honor and that of his country —VICTORY OR DEATH."[6]

For ten days the heroic men of the Alamo held off the Mexicans. Santa Anna's losses were frightful, but he pressed the assault. In the gray dawn of March 6, 1836, his entire remaining force swept forward with wild yells. Twice more they were beaten back. But on the third charge they swarmed over the Alamo's walls and fell upon its handful of survivors. Step by step, with knife and clubbed rifles, the Texans fought them off. In the end, not one of the Alamo's defenders was left alive. Colonel Travis had chosen victory or death, but he had been given both: less than 200 Texans had killed 1,544 Mexicans to turn Santa Anna's laurels into thorns, and the rallying cry of "Remember the Alamo!" that thrilled all Texas was at the least a moral victory. Three weeks later, after the Mexicans cold-bloodedly shot down 350 Texan prisoners at Goliad, all Texas burned with a thirst for revenge.

That desire was to be slaked by Sam Houston, the valiant giant who had led Andrew Jackson's charge at Horseshoe Bend. Putting himself at the head of the tiny Texas army, Houston awaited Santa Anna in a grove of live oak near the San Jacinto River. Here, on April 21, 1836, shouting "Remember the Alamo!" the Texas cavalry charged and broke Santa Anna's line and the Texas infantry put the Mexicans to rout. Santa Anna was captured and forced to sign treaties (which he did not intend to honor) by which he agreed to evacuate Texas and use his influence to obtain Mexican recognition of an independent Texas with a southern boundary at the Rio Grande. Mexico, of course, refused to recognize these claims.

In the meanwhile, the new republic elected Sam Houston as its first president, legalized slavery and sent an emissary to Washington to ask for recognition or annexation to the United States. It was a delicate question, and Old Hickory in the White House moved cautiously.

First, John Quincy Adams with the help of Henry Clay and Daniel Webster had formed the Whig Party now supplanting the old Republicans. The Whigs opposed recognition of Texas, and Northern abolitionists were crying that the Texas revolt was a plot to extend the area of slavery. By then Arkansas and Michigan had been admitted to the union, making 13 slave and 13 free states. But Florida was the last slave state remaining to the South, and there were three free territories —Wisconsin, Iowa and Minnesota—awaiting their turn. Obviously, the South would soon be outnumbered, and so Southern leaders such as Calhoun began thundering for outright annexation of Texas.

In such a situation Old Hickory was careful not to do anything to harm the chances of Vice President Martin Van Buren, his hand-picked presidental candidate. So Jackson waited until after "Little Van" was elected in 1836, and then, on March 3, 1837, his last day in office, he recognized the Lone Star Republic.

Van Buren did little about Texas, and his successor, William Henry Harrison, had no time to do much about anything. With John Tyler of Virginia as his running mate ("Tippecanoe and Tyler, too!"), the old Whig general had defeated Van Buren in 1840, but one month after

"Tip and Ty" took office, Tip was dead of a cold caught at his inauguration and Ty, a slave-holding man who was no friend of the Whigs, was the President. Tyler wanted Texas, but, like Jackson, he had to wait until his last day in office before he could inform San Houston that Texas had been admitted to the Union by a joint resolution of Congress.

Next day, March 4, 1845, James K. Polk came into the White House. And Polk not only wanted Texas; he wanted California, too.

James Polk was the first "dark horse" presidential candidate in American history. He was a protégé of Andrew Jackson's, he had been in Congress and been Governor of Tennessee—but he was still, in 1844, a colorless gray squirrel of a man alongside the sleek, beaverish Van Buren or the leonine Henry Clay. Yet the dispute over Texas killed off both Van Buren and Clay.

Van Buren, confident of the Democratic nomination, had proposed to Clay, who was certain of the Whig choice, that they should make public their opposition to the annexation of Texas on the ground that it would mean war with Mexico. There was no doubt that Mexico would so react to annexation; to keep the peace, Clay agreed. But neither man had accurately gauged the extent of expansionist sentiment in the country. Van Buren felt its strength first at the Democratic Convention when Polk the unknown was given the nomination chiefly because he was an annexationist. Clay was bowled over next when Polk won the election by a close vote aided by antislavery Whigs voting for an abolitionist candidate.

The White House has had few occupants as cheerless and friendless as James K. Polk. Yet, for whatever he may have lacked in charm, wit, good health or brilliance, he was nonetheless courageous, tenacious and purposeful. He knew what he wanted and he knew how to get it. Chief among his desires was California, and he yearned to acquire it before France or Britain obtained it from Mexico. Above all he hoped to obtain it by peaceful purchase; but this, for the simple reason that Mexico had no wish to sell, was not to be.

Mexico was so offended by the American offer to annex Texas that she broke off diplomatic relations with the United States shortly after Polk took office. After Texas did join the Union, Mexico resounded to cries for war with the United States. Polk replied by ordering General Zachary Taylor to a position "on or near" the Rio Grande to repel invasion. Taylor took station at Corpus Christi, on the south side of the Nueces River. Thus he highlighted the continuing Texas-Mexico border controversy.

Texas claimed the Rio Grande as her southern boundary. But Mexico, still claiming Texas, insisted that the southeastern limit of Texas had always been the Nueces River farther to the north. As a Mexican department, Texas had never extended beyond the Nueces. Land south and west of that river had belonged to the department of Tamaulipas. At the very best Texas had a highly doubtful claim to territory below the Nueces, yet here was an American army encamped there—much as if a Canadian army had crossed the Niagara River into New York to "defend" Ontario.

It was against this background, and even using the border dispute as a lever, that President Polk made his second, most persistent effort to buy off Mexico's northern outposts.

Recent civil wars in Mexico had, among other things, resulted in the ouster of Santa Anna as well as property damage to American nationals estimated at about $4.5 million. In 1845 Polk offered to assume that debt if Mexico would be willing to recognize the Rio Grande as the southern boundary of Texas. Another $5 million would be offered for New Mexico, and for California "money would be no object." Polk's minister to Mexico, John Slidell, was instructed to be tactful with Mexico's feeble and distracted government. So Slidell left for Mexico City in November of 1845, and when he arrived he found the nation so aroused by the Texas affair that posters were appearing charging that he had come to buy Texas and California and that any negotiation with him would be treason.

In the meantime, expansionist fever over what was known as "Manifest Destiny" had seized and inflamed the American imagination. In December of 1845 the editor of the New York *Morning News,* John O'Sullivan, wrote of "our manifest destiny to overspread and to possess the whole of the continent which Providence has given us for the development of the great experiment of liberty and federated self-government."[7]

Manifest destiny! It had a Godly as well as a golden ring to it. Not only was wealth to be had in California but the will of God was to be executed there by His newly Chosen. Here once again was the crusading spirit which had energized the colonials against their French and Indian foes. Here was "the right of our manifest destiny,"[8] as one Congressman put it, and even abolitionists, regarding expansion as a Southern plot to erect a new "slavocracy" in the Southwest, could not resist the lure of that magical, mystical phrase. By the end of 1845 the *American Whig Review* could ask: "Why not extend the 'area of freedom' by the annexation of California? Why not plant the banner of liberty there?"⁹

The answer to that question was that in Mexico City the latest government was fruitlessly appealing to France and Britain for assistance, for it did not dare receive Minister Slidell. To do so would have meant its downfall. Even so, it did topple—on the ground that it was treating treasonably with the United States! Into the office strode General Mariano Paredes. He promised no concessions to America and he proceeded to whip Mexico into a hate-America frenzy.

In Washington, hearing of Slidell's rebuff, President Polk ordered General Taylor to move his little army down to the left bank of the Rio Grande. Taylor, mistakenly believing that torrential rains barred his path, did not move south until two months later. On March 24, 1846, he reached a point on the Rio Grande opposite Matamoros and 33 miles inland from Port Isabel. Taylor assured the Mexicans that he had come only to protect American property. They replied that he was on Mexican soil, a fact which automatically created a state of war. General Pedro de Ampudia demanded that Taylor withdraw to the Nueces. Taylor refused, building a fort, training his guns on Matamoros and blockading the mouth of the Rio Grande to cut off Mexican supplies.

Thus was the powder keg built and stuffed. Texas had seceded from Mexico, making very doubtful claim to a southern boundary at the Rio Grande. Mexico recognized neither secession nor claim, and was enraged by American annexation of Texas and infuriated by attempts to buy New Mexico and California. Yet American troops now stood on soil which Mexico believed belonged to her. Opposing those Americans were Mexican soldiers. All that was needed now to explode the powder keg was the spark of war: blood.

No one appreciated this better than James K. Polk. On May 8 he had been informed by Slidell that force was now the only expedient left to the United States. Next day Polk met with his Cabinet. He found all but one in favor of his proposal to ask Congress for a declaration of war. Some, Polk included, would have liked it better if Mexico had committed some act of aggression. That very night the President learned that the Mexicans had, if one can be an "aggressor" on soil considered to be one's own.

On April 24 General Mariano Arista took command in Matamoros and promptly sent a force across the Rio Grande above Taylor's camp. Next day the Mexicans ambushed 63 American dragoons under Captain Seth Thornton, killing 11, wounding others and capturing most of the rest. On April 26, 1846, General Taylor informed Washington that "hostilities may now be considered as commenced," and called upon Texas and Louisiana for volunteers.

Taylor's 11th-hour message was a *casus belli* far superior to Mexico's failure to pay American claims or to receive Slidell, and on May 10, a Sunday, Polk worked on his war message before and after church, regretting "the necessity . . . for me to spend the Sabbath in the manner I have."[10] The following day he told Congress: "The cup of forbearance has been exhausted. After reiterated menaces, Mexico has passed the boundary of the United States, has invaded our territory and shed American blood upon the American soil."[11] Congress then declared that "by the act of the Republic of Mexico, a state of war exists between that government and the United States," authorized Polk to accept 50,000 volunteers and appropriated $10 million for war purposes. The vote was 174 to 14 in the House, 40 to 2 in the Senate. On May 13, 1846, Polk signed the war bill into law.

Five days earlier, however, Mexican and American soldiers north of the Rio Grande had made the war a flaming fact.

3

☆

Outnumbered by the United States—20 million to 7 million—Mexico nonetheless was supremely confident of victory.

Her generals, chief among them Dictator Paredes, shared the general European contempt for American military prowess. That was why Paredes, who had come to power promising to chastise the gringos, had ordered Arista to gain the victory over Taylor that would strengthen his hold on the nation.

Paredes was not being vainglorious; he merely mistook size for strength. In 1845 the Mexican Army included about 30,000 men against less than 5,500 effectives in the American establishment. However, much of Mexico's artillery was outmoded, command of her rank-heavy units* was held by officers exalted by their dexterity in changing sides rather than diligence in matters military, and the men themselves, though brave and very hardy, were poorly trained. Mexican soldiers usually shot from the hip to avoid the recoil of muskets so overcharged with powder that they generally fired high. These defects, of course, were of the hidden kind that only become apparent during the stress of battle. Thus, having heard that Taylor's troops were a rabble of undisciplined foreigners, it was no wonder that one of Arista's generals could say, "Those adventurers cannot withstand the bayonet charge of our foot, nor a cavalry charge with the lance."[12]

In truth, 47 percent of the regulars in Taylor's army of 4,000 men were foreigners. Irish alone made up 24 percent of his force, 10 percent were Germans, 6 percent English, 3 percent Scots and a scattered 4 percent were from Canada and Western Europe. But they were far from being without discipline. While at Corpus Christi, Taylor had hammered them into an efficient fighting force. A young lieutenant named Ulysses S. Grant could write home that "a better army, man for man, probably never faced an enemy."[13] Taylor's flying artillery composed of 12 horse-drawn 6-pounders under the innovating Major Samuel Ringgold was a daringly modern weapon. Moreover, the entire U.S. Army—now commanded by tall Winfield Scott, the hero of Lundy's Lane—was fortunate in possessing what was and still is the finest group of young officers in the nation's history. Most of them had been trained at West Point, and to read their names is to call the roll of generals in the Civil War. Grant is one of them, and Robert E. Lee, Thomas, Beauregard, Hooker, J. E. Johnston and Albert Sidney Johnston, Burnside and Bragg, Kearny, Pope, Meade, McClellan, McDowell, Stonewall Jackson and Jefferson Davis, Longstreet, Pickett, Armistead, Hebert, Pemberton, Simon Bolivar Buckner,

---

* At one time in her history, Mexico had 24,000 officers commanding 20,000 men.

Sherman and Halleck, both Hills, Reynolds, Hancock, Buell and Ewell and Jubal Early—and among the admirals Du Pont, Buchanan and David Glasgow Farragut. Not all of these men were still in service or with Taylor, but many of them were—and some of them were troubled by what Sam Grant called the "unholy" character of their mission. One considered the march to Matamoros to be "of itself an act of hostility." He saw no Texans or Americans south of the Nueces. "All were Mexicans, acknowledging none but Mexican laws. Yet we . . . drove those poor people away from their farms, and seized their custom-house at Point Isabel."[14]

The march itself was a grueling ordeal of 150 miles beneath a blazing sun which "streamed upon us like a living fire."[15] The light blue jackets and trousers of the infantrymen became caked with soft white powdery dust, and soon those stiff-necked cavalrymen who rode above the choking clouds were calling the foot-sloggers "adobies" after the white Mexican huts along the river. It was a short step to "dobies" and after this to "doughboys," and thus the immortal nickname was born. And the floury dust that had christened the doughboys also coated their tongues and clogged their nostrils to aggravate a thirst that was terrible for both men and animals. A whole day's march often lay between ponds of potable water, and yet even the agony of thirst and sunburn might be forgotten in the universal delight to behold the wide blue sky filled with "mirages": ships and islands reflected from the Gulf 60 or more miles away.

It was on this march that Zachary Taylor endeared himself to his troops. "Old Rough and Ready" made no attempt to avoid the hardships suffered by his men. His hawkish nose was also white and peeling beneath his old straw hat, and he rode along on Old Whitey, often with one leg nonchalantly slung over the pommel, looking as military as a mounted sack of flour. One day his slouching body was clothed in a blue-checked gingham coat, another in a dusty green coat, then an old brown coat or a linen waistcoat or yet again a soldier's light blue overalls.

At last, on March 23, Taylor's suffering doughboys formed into columns four abreast and went marching through a prairie now thick with grass and red and gold with blossoming cactus. On March 28 they saw the blue mists of the Rio Grande ahead of them. At ten-thirty that morning they came to the river bank and stared across the water at Matamoros.

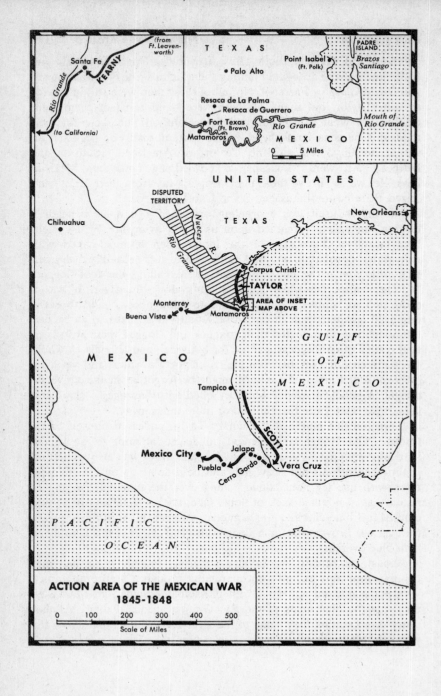

TEXAS

Palo Alto

Point Isabel
(Ft. Polk)

PADRE
ISLAND

Brazos
Santiago

(from
Ft. Leaven-
worth)

Santa Fe

KEARNY

Rio Grande

Resaca de La Palma
Resaca de Guerrero

Fort Texas
(Ft. Brown)

Matamoros

Rio Grande

MEXICO

(to California)

Mouth of
Rio Grande

0   5 Miles

UNITED   STATES

Chihuahua

DISPUTED
TERRITORY

Nueces R.

TEXAS

New Orleans

Rio Grande

Corpus Christi

TAYLOR

AREA OF INSET
MAP ABOVE

Monterrey

Buena Vista

Matamoros

MEXICO

GULF

OF

MEXICO

Tampico

SCOTT

Mexico City

Jalapa

Puebla   Cerro Gordo

Vera Cruz

PACIFIC

OCEAN

ACTION AREA OF THE MEXICAN WAR
1845-1848

0   100   200   300   400   500

Scale of Miles

They saw Mexicans standing in curious throngs atop the town's tiled rooftops. They saw red roses climbing snow-white walls. They heard bands blaring, bugles pealing, dogs barking and church bells ringing in a medley counterpointed by the liquid Spanish of excited civilians and drilling soldiers—but most of all they saw the cool blue waters of the Rio Grande and many of them stripped and went bathing in it.

That was when they saw the Mexican girls come laughing down to the opposite bank to step out of their skirts and chemises and go naked in the water, and with that a difficulty unforeseen by Zachary Taylor had begun.

"Efforts are continually [being made] to entice our men to desert," Taylor reported on April 6, "and, I regret to say, [they] have met with considerable success."[16]

By then, 30 of Taylor's soldiers had crossed to Matamoros. Naked Mexican lasses splashing in the water had not been the only attraction, nor had the girls been official sirens but only local maidens following a Matamoros custom which happened to coincide with Mexican policy. The Mexicans had guessed that many of the foreigners in Taylor's army were Roman Catholics, and they made a powerful appeal to their religious loyalties. Nearly every day Matamoros celebrated a saint's day with masses, music and processions. Taylor's troops were encouraged to desert to claim bounties starting at 320 acres. Old World allure was also complemented by the contempt and cruelty which too many American officers visited upon their foreign soldiers. And so, as sex, saints and sadism began to whittle the army he had worked so hard to build, Old Rough and Ready acted. He got tough and began shooting soldiers trying to desert, starting with a Frenchman and a Swiss. Such draconic measures—taken, incidentally, before the state of war which justifies such executions had begun—plugged the leak at last. But desertions among regulars was a continuing problem for Taylor, and those who turned their coats at Matamoros were to form the nucleus of that San Patricio or Saint Patrick's Battalion which turned out to be Mexico's finest fighting unit.

In the meantime, both sides crowned the Rio Grande with fortifications, General Arista arrived to take command, to order the ambush which provided President Polk with his *casus belli,* and to cross the river downstream to cut Taylor's communications with Port Isabel.

On May 1 Taylor received word that Arista was beginning to cross the river downstream. Alarmed for the safety of his supply line, Taylor immediately struck camp and began marching for Port Isabel. Left behind in Fort Texas were about 500 men under Major Jacob Brown.

Fortunately for Taylor, Arista did not have enough boats to get his force quickly across the river. Before he could intercept Taylor the American led his exhausted command into Port Isabel. There he began filling 250 empty wagons with supplies needed to maintain his position at Matamoros, and there on the morning of May 3 he heard the dull booming of cannon from the direction of Fort Texas. The Mexicans were bombarding Major Brown's little garrison. Down at Port Isabel, some of Taylor's young officers swallowed nervously to hear their first hostile cannon. Sam Grant later admitted: "I felt sorry that I had enlisted."[17]

General Taylor was not concerned. Scouts had returned with assurances from Major Brown that the fort could hold out. So Taylor ignored the pleas of commanders wild to march to the fort's relief and continued to load his wagons while strengthening the defenses of Port Isabel. On May 6 the first recruits from New Orleans arrived, together with 500 sailors and marines from Commodore David Conner's blockading squadron. That morning Brown received his mortal wound at the position which was henceforth to bear his name and become the city of Brownsville, Texas. Defense of Fort Brown continued under Captain Edgar Hawkins, who rejected a Mexican surrender demand by explaining that he could not speak Spanish, "But if I have understood you correctly, my reply is that I must respectfully decline to surrender."[18]

At three o'clock that afternoon Taylor was ready to march. There was a moment of comedy when old Colonel William Whistler wrathfully rounded upon "a young officer of literary tastes" who had dared to put a case of books into a wagon.

"That will never do, Mr. Graham," he snapped. "We can't encumber our train with such rubbish as books."

At this point Lieutenant Charles Hoskins nervously admitted that, not being well, he had taken the liberty of inserting a keg of whiskey in the wagon, and the old colonel murmured: "Oh, that's all right, Mr. Hoskins. Anything in reason. But Graham wanted to carry a case of *books!*"[19]

With the recruits and the seamen left behind to guard the base, whips snapped, pennants fluttered, wheels turned, feet fell—and wagons and men went swishing through waist-high grass. Throughout that day and the next the Americans saw no Mexicans. Then, through the shimmering heat of noon of May 8, 1846, they saw the enemy. At first they were only a line of gleaming metal drawn up on the plain of Palo Alto, the "Tall Timbers" which rose dramatically behind them. Then they were distinguishable: the sun danced on the needle points of lances in the grasp of mounted men, it burnished the brass of cannon drawn up between masses of tall-hatted infantrymen. They seemed an enormous host, but actually, having raised the siege of Fort Brown, General Arista had little more than 4,000 men on the field.

Old Rough and Ready commanded less than 3,000. But these men had an unshakable faith in their indomitable old general, sitting there on Old Whitey with his leg hooked around the pommel while he waited for his wagon train to close up. Then he advanced to within half a mile of the Mexicans, where he halted and ordered a platoon from each company to stack arms and collect their comrades' canteens and fill them from a nearby pond. The men relaxed and forgot their tension.

Opposite them, General Arista rode across his lines waving his sword. The men shouted *"Viva!"* and lifted their banners. At three o'clock in the afternoon, the Mexican cannon began firing. At first the round brass balls came bounding through the tall grass so slowly that they could be easily sidestepped. As the Americans continued to advance, however, the missiles came faster and thicker. Lieutenant Grant gasped to see a ball knock off the under jaw of a captain standing next to him. Then General Taylor halted his advance and sent his own artillery into action.

Major Ringgold's battery went flying to the right, Captain James Duncan took his galloping to the left, and into the center went two bulky 18-pounders, each towed into place by ten yoke of oxen. Now the Americans had the range and their fire was devastating. Again and again American shot cut a swath through the massed Mexican infantrymen, and each time the enemy ranks closed up bravely. But the field artillery, which the Americans were using with a precision unrivaled since the time of Napoleon, prevented almost every Mexican effort to advance. The only attempt was a cavalry charge at the American right.

A thousand lancers with two guns came sweeping through the grass, but Taylor's flank regiments rapidly formed a square and cut the Mexican riders down with musket fire while Lieutenant Randolph Ridgeley led a section of Ringgold's battery to the rescue on the run, unlimbering and blasting the Mexican guns before they could fire a shot.

Palo Alto had become strictly an artillery duel, with the Americans holding the upper hand. American doughboys who had expected to charge with the bayonet merely stood at order arms, cheering as their artillery tore gaps in the enemy lines, or carefully watching for the Mexican solid shot so as to step out of its way. Then smoke obscured the battle. A flaming wad from one of Duncan's guns had set the grass on fire, and the breeze from the Gulf swept the choking smoke toward the Mexican line. Under cover of the prairie fire, Taylor advanced his right. But Arista threw his own right forward, so that the relative position of the lines was little changed. However, Duncan's battery had also moved under cover of the smoke, swinging out to the left to take the enemy right under an enfilading fire.

It was the moment for the American foot soldiers to press forward with the bayonet, but the opportunity had come too late. Darkness veiled the field of Palo Alto, and both sides withdrew. Nine Americans had been killed—among them the invaluable Major Ringgold—and 44 had been wounded. But Mexican losses had totaled 250, and in the early morning darkness of May 9 Taylor gathered his leaders in a council of war and asked them if he should press the attack.

It is in councils of war that the cautious are most aggressive, and this one was no exception: seven of ten officers wanted to wait for reinforcements. But then Captain Duncan rode past, and Taylor called to him to ask his opinion.

"We whipped 'em today and we can whip 'em tomorrow!" Duncan snapped, and Taylor said, "That is my opinion, Captain Duncan. Gentlemen, you will prepare your commands to move forward. The council is dissolved."[20]

The Mexican withdrawal from the field of Palo Alto began at sunup. Taylor did not pursue until he had arranged for the protection of his precious—and distracting—wagon train. At noon his men plunged into the gloomy chaparral which had masked Arista's retreat.

Here the terrain differed sharply from the level plain of Palo Alto. Here were dense thickets broken by resacas, or remnants of river beds. Some were sunken lagoons and others were dry trenches, and as such they were excellent for defense. Two of them, the Resaca de la Palma across which the American attack was launched, and the Resaca de Guerrero inside which the Mexicans made their defense, have given their names to the same battle of May 9, 1846.

The Resaca de Guerrero which Arista occupied extended east and west across the road to Matamoros. It was about 200 feet wide and of a depth of three to four feet at the banks. Within it were a few narrow ponds surrounded with bushes and small trees. To either flank and to its rear it was protected by thick chaparral. Arista put his infantry on each side of the road behind the resaca. To his right or east of the road he stationed three or four guns. Then the Mexican general went back to his headquarters tent to attend to paper work. He did not believe the Americans would attack.

They did, however, coming chiefly against the Mexican artillery. Here Taylor, slouching on his horse, was delighted by the spectacle of Lieutenant Ridgeley, now commanding Ringgold's battery, charging down the road with horse-drawn guns unprotected by infantry. Ridgeley deliberately drew the fire of Mexican infantry and artillery, blasting back at their smoke. Meanwhile, the battle had become a sergeant's war. Small parties of men stumbled through the chaparral and tore at each other shot for shot and blade for blade. The Americans went forward yelling like fiends, and the Mexicans—who had not eaten for 24 hours—fought them off bravely.

In all, however, possession of Arista's guns was to mean victory or defeat. Sensing this, Taylor called upon Charles May, a dashing captain of dragoons, to lead his squadron down the road. May went trotting off to form his troopers, but he soon found that the enemy artillery was better emplaced than he had thought. He rode back to General Taylor and asked for new orders.

"Charge, Captain!" Taylor roared. "Charge, *nolens volens!*"[21]

May dashed off, his long black beard streaming in the wind. Ridgeley called to him: "Hold on a minute, Charley, till I draw their fire!"[22] Again Ridgeley lured the Mexicans into giveaway fire, and May's dragoons, observing their position, went sweeping forward in four columns.

Down the road they clattered, down into the resaca, up its opposite bank, over the guns and beyond them—too far beyond them. Before they could stop their hard-bitted horses, the Mexican gunners came swarming out of the chaparral to reclaim their pieces and to cut up May's squadron as it returned to the American lines.

Taylor was furious. He called his infantry forward and roared: "Take those guns, and by God keep them!"[23] Bayonets leveled, the infantry obeyed orders. Ridgeley's gunners followed in behind them to turn the captured cannon on the Mexicans—and it was then, with its flanks slowly giving way to stubborn Americans clawing through the chaparral and its center cracking, that the Mexican line broke. It snapped and flew backward like a broken bow. Even General Arista's tent and possessions were abandoned in the mad rush to the rear. En route to the Rio Grande and Matamoros, the fleeing Mexicans were taken under a bloody enfilade by the guns of Fort Brown. Within the river itself many of them drowned. A priest named Father Leary tried to calm a crowd of crazed fugitives aboard a big flatboat, but then a party of fleeing lancers spurred their horses aboard the boat and swamped it. The last sight the pursuing Americans saw was the priest's upheld crucifix slowly sinking beneath the water.

Now was the time for Taylor to cross the river and to crush the enemy army. He might have ended the war then and there. But Old Rough and Ready was old in his ways. He told his younger officers that the enemy had taken all the boats to the other side, and because he was an "old 'un" he had little time for engineers clamoring for permission to build new ones. No, Zachary Taylor had won two fine fights. His casualties for both totaled 48 dead and 128 wounded, perhaps not one-sixth of Arista's losses. And so, on the evening of May 9, he retired to his tent to write his report.

Even as President Polk far to the northeast was working on his war message, Taylor set down the concluding words: "The enemy has recrossed the river, and I am sure will not again molest us on this bank."[24] Arista not only failed to molest Taylor again; he eventually gave up Matamoros without a fight.

4

☆

The long-range effect of Zachary Taylor's victories at Palo Alto and Resaca de la Palma was to give to American arms a tradition of offensive success which has lasted to this day. Up until May of 1846, American troops had seldom sought and defeated an organized foe. Excepting Trenton, which was hardly more than a raid, and Yorktown, which could not have been won without the French, American victories had been gained in defensive stands or in retreats which averted disaster. But now Americans were attacking and winning, and the American nation, no less than the French placing the laurels on Napoleon's brow, was quick to idolize Old Rough and Ready.

Cities and towns across the nation passed resolutions nominating Zachary Taylor for President. Toasts were raised everywhere to "Old Zack," and the fact that he had no known political preferences meant nothing to those delirious Whigs who at once embraced him as their own. No result could have been more abhorrent to James K. Polk. He realized immediately that he, a Democrat, might be waging war to make a Whig President. But there was nothing Polk could do. Even if he had wanted to recall Taylor, he could not have dared it, for it would have made Old Zack a martyr. And with whom would he replace Taylor? Certainly not Winfield Scott, with whom Polk had already quarreled and whom he had removed from field command, for Scott was an active Whig who had once tried to obtain his party's nomination. And so, in this era of extreme partisanship when a political general was a commonplace, Polk turned to making Democratic generals in the faint hope that one of them might outshine Old Rough and Ready.

Meanwhile, a tidal wave of enthusiasm rolled across the country. Everywhere except in New England, where the annexation of Texas was still resented, volunteers rushed to the colors in the tens of thousands. In New York City walls were plastered with placards proclaiming "Mexico or Death" or "Ho, for the Halls of the Monte-zumas!" America's streets reverberated to the roll of drums and squeal of fife and the tramp of marching men roaring out such songs as:

> Come all ye gallant volunteers
> Who fear not life to lose,
> The martial drum invites ye come
> And join the Hickory Blues.[25]

In Indianapolis Lew Wallace raised a company in three days by parading the street with a four-sided sign inscribed: "For Mexico: Fall In!" Ohio, unhappy with both annexation and the war itself, nonetheless sent 3,000 of her sons to war in less than two weeks. Illinois volunteered 14 regiments instead of four, North Carolina tripled her quota and Tennessee gained her nickname of "Volunteer State" after 30,000 men responded to a call for 2,800 and the rejects angrily tried to buy their way in.

It was not only patriotism or a sense of Manifest Destiny that solved the manpower problem. Privately recruiters excited almost every passion with promises of "roast beef, two dollars a day, plenty of whiskey, golden Jesuses, and pretty Mexican girls."[26] The charming customs of the maids of Matamoros were presumably not excluded from such recitals. And so the highways were black with thousands hurrying off to the Halls of the Montezumas where life was lazy, lush and golden, and dark-eyed señoritas were obliging.

This time, however, the men were not diverted into those state militias which had been Washington's bane and Madison's mortifica-tion. This time the federal government avoided collisions with state authority by enlisting men in volunteer units separate from the regular Army but still liable to foreign service. They were as yet untrained and still given to the pernicious practice of electing their own officers. A soldier in the Alton (Illinois) Guards has described how one such candidate for command recommended himself to the men:

Fellow Citizens! I am Peter Goff, the Butcher of Middletown! I am! I am the man that shot that sneaking, white-livered Yankee abolitionist son of a bitch, Lovejoy! I did! I want to be your Captain, I do; and I will serve the yellow-bellied Mexicans the same, I will! I have treated you to fifty dollars worth of whiskey, I have, and when elected Captain I will spend fifty more, I will![27]

He was elected, he was—even as President Polk made another attempt to satisfy his territorial desires by peaceful means.

Polk planned to smuggle the exiled General Santa Anna into Mexico on his promise to deal with the United States. On August 4, 1846—the day on which General Paredes fell from power, and while Santa Anna was still in Havana—Polk asked Congress for a secret appropriation of $2 million to be used as an advance payment in bribing Santa Anna to cede California. In the House an obscure representative from Pennsylvania named David Wilmot attached to the measure a prohibition against slavery in any lands acquired from Mexico. This was the famous Wilmot Proviso, another "fire bell in the night" such as the Missouri Compromise had been, and though it would clang wildly during the clamorous debate which, a decade later, nearly rang out the Union, its net effect in August of 1846 was to torpedo Polk's plan. Although the House eventually approved the Wilmot Proviso, the whole appropriation measure was filibustered to death after it went to the Senate.

Polk was furious. He had no doubt that he might have stopped the war and gained California with the money, which would have gone toward supporting Santa Anna's army against a public uproar likely to follow such a deal with Uncle Sam. So ended whatever chance there might have been to end the war by peaceful means. In the meantime, the Stars and Stripes were already waving over California—and over the Oregon Territory as well.

One reason Mexico went to war with the United States was because the Mexicans hoped to have British support, if not directly, at least in an Anglo-American war which would draw off Yankee power to the Oregon Territory.

Since 1818 both Britain and the United States had jointly occupied this vast area. But then the British made the same mistake as the Mexicans: they encouraged settlements in the area of their trading posts, and the emigrants, of course, were hardy Yankees, traveling northwestward this time over the rugged Oregon Trail. In the 1840s the Manifest Destiny fever also inflamed these people, and a clamor arose for the assertion of American claims as far north as Russia's southern limit at the Alaskan Panhandle. This was the line 54°40′ which gave rise to the slogan: "Fifty-four forty or fight!"

James Polk did not want to fight, but he still believed that "the only way to treat John Bull is to look him straight in the eye."[28] Thus, after Britain rejected his offer to accept the 49th parallel as a compromise line, Polk returned to the 54-40 claim and served notice of his intention to terminate joint occupation. John Bull, however, stared straight back. Aware that war between Mexico and the United States was imminent, conscious that Polk's extreme position might split his party, the British rattled the saber. Polk naturally did not want war on two fronts, and so he renewed his 49th parallel offer and a conciliatory British government decided that this was an honorable compromise after all. On June 15, 1846, the Senate ratified the Oregon Treaty whereby the future states of Washington, Oregon and Idaho, as well as part of Montana and Wyoming, became American territory. Except for minor revisions made later on, the 49th parallel became the permanent dividing line between the United States and Canada west of the Lake of the Woods.

A few months later both California and New Mexico were in American hands. The first fell on August 7 when Commodore John Sloat merely raised Old Glory over the customhouse at the capital of Monterey. However, the Californians later rose in revolt, only to be put down by the timely appearance of Colonel Stephen Kearny and 150 dragoons.

Kearny had earlier invaded New Mexico by marching with a much larger force from Fort Leavenworth over the Santa Fe Trail. Having annexed the lonely province by proclamation of August 15, he sent out expeditions against the Navajos and into Chihuahua while setting out for San Diego himself. He arrived there after an epic and grueling trek, was worsted by the Californians in a skirmish at San Pasqual, but nevertheless managed to join forces with Commodore Robert Stockton, the new Pacific naval commander. Between them Kearny and Stockton ended the revolt by defeating the Californians at the Battle of the San Gabriel River on January 8, 1847.

Before that date, however, the province was all but subdued. And Mexico, shaken by the march of American victories, was by then in the hands of the returned Santa Anna.

Between his defeat at San Jacinto in 1836 and his return to power, Antonio López de Santa Anna had lost a leg. He lost it in 1839 to French gunners when France, angered by Mexico's failure to pay claims similar to those American ones which had helped provoke the present war, sent a squadron to bombard the fort at Vera Cruz. The event made a national hero of Santa Anna, although it could not prevent his eviction from his country in December of 1845.

During his exile in Havana he was able to convince President Polk that if he were allowed to steal back into Mexico he would seize power and sign the sort of treaty Polk wanted. And so, still vigorous at 52, limping on his peg leg, accompanied by his 17-year-old second wife, General Santa Anna went aboard the British steamer *Arab* in Havana Harbor on the night of August 8, 1846.

As instructed, the American blockading squadron allowed *Arab* to slip through its line into Vera Cruz Harbor. Santa Anna went ashore to be greeted by a carefully staged military celebration in which "not one *viva* was heard."[29] Next he issued a proclamation which made it clear that for once the calculating James Polk had miscalculated:

"Mexicans! There was once a day, and my heart dilates with the remembrance, when . . . you saluted me with the enviable title of Soldier of the People. Allow me again to take it, never more to be given up, and to devote myself, until death, to the defense of the liberty and independence of the republic."[30]

Then Santa Anna retired with his young wife to his enormous estates, while in Mexico City the way was cleared for his return to power and along the Rio Grande Old Rough and Ready Taylor made ready to strike still deeper into Mexico.

Zachary Taylor had been swamped by volunteers. They came in a steamboat flood down the Mississippi, out onto the Gulf and across to Port Isabel and thence up the Rio Grande to Matamoros or Taylor's advanced base at Camargo about 70 air miles farther west. The first arrivals were useless. They had been enlisted for six- or three-month terms, and by the time most of them arrived it was time for them to go home. Then, in July and August, 1846, the 12-monthers came whooping into camp.

They murdered; they raped, robbed and rioted. A Texas colonel thought the Tennessee men were worse than Russian Cossacks; Taylor himself thought the Texans "were too licentious to do much good"; testy little Lieutenant George Meade considered all volunteers to be "full of mutiny"; and the Mexican priests called them "Vandals vomited from Hell."[31] When they did not attack Mexican civilians or fight each other, they fought the regulars. They defied their officers and helped their comrades to escape from the guardhouse. They dressed as they pleased. The "Volunteers of Kentucky" wore full beards, three-cornered hats and hip boots faced with red morocco. Elsewhere the various "Guards," "Rifles," "Killers," "Gunmen," "Blues" and "Grays" who came crowding in on the long-suffering Taylor appeared in colors ranging through gray, green, blue and white with trimmings of red, yellow and pink. When their gorgeous going-away raiment wore out, they objected to putting on regulation blue. "Let 'em go to hell with their sky blue," swore an Indiana soldier. "I'll be blowed if they make a regular out of me."[32] Volunteers who were slaveholders expected the despised "foreigners" among the regulars to wait on them, and many of them, bitter because they did not get more than regular pay of seven dollars a month, cursed themselves as "seven-dollar targets." Gradually, in the immemorial way of indisciplined troops, they fell sick.

Camargo, at which some 15,000 American troops were assembled by August, came to be known as a "Yawning Grave Yard." It was too far from the Gulf to be cooled by sea breezes, and the rocks rimming the encampment round made it a caldron in which men were baked and boiled to death. All day long the troops heard the crashing of three volleys over the grave of some soldier, and as one officer said: "The Dead March was played so often on the Rio Grande that the very birds knew it."[33]

With the volunteers there arrived those "Democratic generals" appointed by Polk in his peeve against Winfield Scott and his fellow Whigs. One of them arrived in a fancy buggy which he expected to use in the campaign, and Polk's former law partner, Brigadier General Gideon Pillow—"Polk's spy," as he was sometimes called—provoked a howl of derision among the regulars when he built an entrenchment with the parapet on the wrong side of the ditch.

Such trials were suffered by Taylor with the outward calm which was his chief characteristic. Inwardly, he was a disturbed man: he had orders to move deeper into Mexico, and he not only had military misgivings about such a move; he also believed that his sudden popularity had given rise to an "intention to break me down." Nevertheless by mid-August he was ready to attack Monterrey, the capital of Nuevo León. His army numbered 6,000 men, half of them regulars commanded by bull-necked, big-voiced Brigadier General David Twiggs and the valorous though erratic Brigadier General William Worth; the other half volunteer horse and foot under Major General Pinckney Henderson and William Butler, a pair of part-time soldiers who out-ranked the professional Twiggs and Worth on the strength of their party loyalty. On August 18 the move to Monterrey began, and on September 19 the little army was in camp at Walnut Springs three miles outside the city.

Monterrey was as near a fortress city as might be found in Mexico. Its stone-walled houses stood on high ground forward of the little Santa Catarina River, which effectively guarded its rear. Most of the houses were loopholed and the streets were barricaded. Forts and redoubts covered the city's northern front and eastern flank, while to the west were two fortified heights between which ran the road from Saltillo. General Pedro de Ampudia, who had replaced the disgraced Arista, commanded at Monterrey; and he had 7,000 men and 40 guns to defend his fortifications. Thus the city was a very tough nut to be cracked by only 6,000 Americans without any proper siege train.

Zachary Taylor, however, now that he had reached his objective, was as confident as though he were still fighting Seminoles. In Win-field Scott's belief "few men ever had a more comfortable, labor-saving contempt for learning of every kind"[34] than Old Rough and Ready. But if his igorance was invincible, his courage was indom-itable, and thus, relying on the bayonet, as always, and dividing his command, as always, he prepared simultaneous assaults on the city's eastern and western flanks.

On September 20 Worth took 2,000 regulars and Texas cavalry on a long swing north to come in on the two fortified hills to the west. Running into difficult going, the column could make only five miles in the first four hours, and at nightfall the men encamped in the hills northwest of the city. Taylor's force was now split and separated, vul-nerable to defeat in detail; but Ampudia, who had seen his precious opportunity, made no move to sally from the city.

Next morning, September 21, 1846, the Battle of Monterrey began in earnest. Worth in the west repulsed a determined charge of Mexican lancers and began attacking Federation Hill on the southern side of the Saltillo road. By nightfall the position was taken with a loss of less than 20 men, and the Mexican guns were turned against Independence Hill across the road. In the east, however, the Americans were not so fortunate.

Here the city was guarded by the bastioned Black Fort 1,000 yards to its northern front and on the fort's east by a series of redoubts chief of which was Fort Tenería, or the Tannery. Here red-necked Dave Twiggs's regulars were to charge almost without artillery preparation. But Twiggs was not with them. He was sick, and command passed to Lieutenant Colonel John Garland.

Garland was to create a diversion for Worth engaged to the west. Whatever the purpose, the regulars pressed forward bravely—bayonets against bastions—and they were scourged from the Black Fort on the right, the Tannery on their left and loopholes and housetops in front of them. Americans flew into the air or stumbled and fell to pour out their blood on the hot earth. Scurrying low, the broken Americans sought shelter where they could find it, until, unit by unit, they could withdraw. One small unit which had gotten into a building behind the Tannery remained to pour musketry into that redoubt.

A second charge surged forward and was also broken in blood. Mexican marksmen picked off the Yankee officers with dreadful accuracy. Lieutenant Hoskins, he whose keg of whiskey had once won transportation priority over a case of books, came gasping up to Lieutenant Grant to borrow his horse. Minutes later he was shot dead from the back of the beast. Now, as the second line withdrew, General Twiggs came onto the field in "very unmilitary garb" to explain why he arrived late.

"I expected a battle today," he said, "but didn't think it would come off so soon, and took a dose of medicine last night as I always do before a battle so as to loosen my bowels. A bullet striking the belly when the bowels are loose might pass through the intestines without cutting them."[35]

No one then appreciated the humor of the situation, for a third attempt, at a fortified bridge farther to the right, had also been hurled back. Now Taylor turned to his volunteers. Brigadier General John Quitman sent the Tennessee and Mississippi regiments through a canefield which shielded them from enemy fire until the final dash at the Tannery. The moment they became visible, the Mexican guns roared. One solid shot killed seven volunteers and wounded others. One of the wounded clutched his rent abdomen while he crawled onto a rock, crouching there to sing a death psalm as he held in his intestines. But now the regulars behind the Tannery were picking off the Mexican gunners while the volunteers charged.

"Now is the time!" Jefferson Davis roared at his men. "Great God! If I had 30 men with knives I could take the fort!"[36]

It was taken with a final rush, Tennesseans and Mississippians tumbling in together. They would quarrel for a decade over who had been the first inside. Now the field artillery came flying into the suburban streets, one battery becoming caught and rendered useless, another driving off Mexican lancers who rode over the field spearing American wounded and killing medical attendants. And then it was night, and Taylor, who had won a little fort at the cost of nearly 400 casualties, ordered everyone back to camp except the troops holding the Tannery.

Before daylight, the attack was resumed. Worth's men, who had gone for two days without food and who had crouched all the rainy night at the base of Independence Hill, began crawling softly up its slopes. With dawn they charged and drove the Mexicans off its summit.

To the east there was no action, except that General Ampudia, having lost his western outposts, decided to abandon all his fortifications except the Black Fort and to concentrate his defense in the blocks of stone houses surrounding the Plaza. On September 23 the Americans renewed the assault on the east.

They did not move through shot-swept streets, but instead had their artillery shoot down them while doughboys armed with picks and crowbars burrowed through the walls of the houses. Worth, meanwhile, hearing the firing and having no orders, pressed in from the west and began shelling the Plaza. Caught between two fires, General Ampudia next day offered to surrender.

After a day of haggling over terms, Taylor accepted. His conditions —allowing the Mexican Army to withdraw intact with its arms, even agreeing to an armistice of eight weeks—were more than generous, and the armistice itself was angrily rejected by President Polk. But as much as Taylor was criticized, he could hardly have done better. His little army was down to 5,000 effectives, he was running short of supplies and ammunition, he was deep in enemy country, and if renewed assaults against a still superior enemy should fail, he would run the dreadful risk of retreating through a jubilant and vengeful countryside. If anyone was to be censured, it was Ampudia for giving up so readily.

And so, on September 25 the Mexican flag over Monterrey came down and Old Glory went up. The Mexican soldiers, neat in trim uniforms and freshly pipe-clayed belts, came marching out; and the Americans, "as dirty as they could be without becoming real estate,"[37] went marching in to the tune of "Yankee Doodle."

5

☆

Although Taylor's victory at Monterrey exalted him politically, it did not set the nation exulting as had his earlier triumphs.

Monterrey made it plain that Mexico was not going to be defeated easily. Bereft of Texas, shorn of New Mexico and California, and now menaced by American arms south of the Rio Grande, Mexico took courage from the wrathful oratory of General Santa Anna, spurning all offers to negotiate and swearing to fight on.

Thus the United States gradually became disenchanted with the war. Even Taylor privately proposed a defensive stance, holding just enough Mexican territory to force payment of claims. The idea was popular enough to attract Polk, who feared what an extended war might cost in men and money; if, indeed, he could persuade the nation to support it. But then it also became clear that to surrender the initiative to Mexico would incur a great loss in trade, prestige and national honor. Seizing a neighbor's provinces and holding them for ransom might strike the world as piracy. And so Polk and his advisers—who had begun the war with no real plan—at last decided on the obvious step of striking at the enemy's heart in Mexico City.

From the outset it was obvious that the route from the Rio Grande, an advance across 800 rugged miles, was out of the question. The best approach was from Vera Cruz on the Gulf. Cortez himself had followed this route in his campaign against the Aztecs. It had been recommended to Polk by no less a person than General Santa Anna in the days when the new Mexican commander in chief was talking treason. Taylor was for it, and so were Winfield Scott and the powerful Senator Thomas Hart Benton. But it took a Whig victory in the Congressional elections of 1846 to make Polk realize, at the repeated urgings of Senator Benton, that "a rapid crushing movement" was necessary to win the war and retrieve Democratic political fortunes.

Next came the question of a commander. Again in the partisan spirit of his times, Polk looked around for a trustworthy Democrat. But there was no such general acceptable to the Army. There were only Taylor and Scott, and because Taylor was in the habit of criticizing Polk's administration, and because Scott, clearly Taylor's superior in generalship, was also now considered politically harmless, it was Scott who received the command.

Certainly there were considerations of a nobler cast motivating Polk's decision, chief among them the fact that Scott still outranked Taylor, together with Taylor's belief that the season of the yellow fever—*el vómito*—was too near to make an attempt on Vera Cruz. Nevertheless, Scott had inadvertently qualified by committing political suicide during his dispute with Polk the preceding spring.

Polk had then ordered Scott to take command on the Rio Grande. Scott intended to obey, but about that time the alarmed Polk was also preparing to name a half-dozen Democratic generals. Scott thought he "smelt the rat" and bluntly told Secretary of War Marcy that he saw "the double trick, to supersede me, and, at the end of the war . . . disband every general who would not place Democracy above God's country."[38] Next Scott explained his failure to move quickly to the Rio Grande by informing the Secretary: "I do not desire to place myself in the most perilous of all positions:—*a fire upon my rear, from Washington, and the fire, in front, from the Mexicans.*"[39] That ended Scott's brief career as field commander, for the infuriated Polk directed him to remain in Washington. Scott's political career was concluded by his next epistolary indiscretion. He explained to Marcy that he had not been in his office to receive him one day because he had stepped outside "to take a hasty plate of soup."[40] The remark tickled the country and Scott, in a pun upon the name of the great French soldier, Marshall Turenne, became known as "Marshal Tureen." As the Boston *Courier* announced, Scott had "committed suicide with a goose-quill."[41] Still, Scott endured these professional and political setbacks with an admirable dignity. He remained devoted to his task of organizing and directing the expanding army. He might have been too fond of plans and calculations, as his nickname "Old Fuss 'n' Feathers" suggests; he may actually have been so prim and prissy that, as one general's wife disdainfully observed, you could cover his mouth with a button; but he was nevertheless the most professional and scientific soldier the United States had yet produced—and without him there might not have been much of an army.

So Scott hurled himself into the Vera Cruz expedition. On November 14 the Navy presented him a splendid gift: the port of Tampico, which would make an excellent staging area for America's first joint amphibious operation. On November 24 Scott departed for the Rio Grande and a hoped-for conference with Taylor at Camargo.

He had not been long gone before President Polk had reservations about appointing him. He still did not like him, and he liked less the prospect of seeing a second Whig trailing clouds of martial glory. Polk was not himself seeking re-election, yet he naturally wanted a Democrat to succeed him. And so it occurred to him to ask Congress to create the post of lieutenant general for Senator Benton, who would then supersede Scott. Congress, however, refused. The harsh, domineering Benton had made too many enemies among his own party, and no Whig would desert Scott.

This "vile intrigue," as Scott called it, so infuriated Old Fuss 'n' Feathers that he was later to write: "A grosser abuse of human confidence is nowhere recorded."[42] So the Polk-Scott rift widened, even as a Scott-Taylor quarrel began developing.

Scott had written to Taylor of his intention to come to Camargo. But his letters either went astray—one was intercepted by Santa Anna—or arrived after Scott did. In the meanwhile, General Taylor had slanted off on a southwestern excursion against Victoria, the capital of Tamaulipas. Why, is not clear. Inland Victoria was of no use to Taylor. To march on it was only to weaken his position on the Monterrey-Saltillo-Parras line. Yet the march did have the effect of taking him away from Camargo, and Scott on his arrival there was unable to inform Taylor personally of the disagreeable truth that he needed his troops. Instead, he had to tell him by letter that he was taking most of Taylor's regulars and half his volunteers for the Vera Cruz–Mexico City operation, and that Taylor would have to act "for a time" on the "strict defensive."

Taylor blew up. He was not only a general being stripped of his troops and stopped in his tracks; he was also a candidate halted in mid-career. Full of wrath, he accused Scott of "worming himself" into the chief command by promising to kill him off as a presidential candidate. He said he was being sacrificed to the ambition of others, meaning the partisan Polk and the sly Scott, and although Taylor was himself on record as believing that Vera Cruz required 25,000 men, 10,000 of them regulars, this was but a puny piece of logic which would not even scratch the gorgeous campaign theme of "The Martyrdom of Old Zack." So if Taylor did lose half an army, he did advance another giant step toward the White House—even as Santa Anna began advancing north against him with a brand-new army.

Antonio López de Santa Anna had been elected President of Mexico. Technically, however, he was not free to exercise both political and military command, and so executive power had passed to Vice President Gómez Farías while Santa Anna, the self-styled Liberator of Mexico, took the field with a brand-new army.

Santa Anna had no fears about the side door at Vera Cruz, for he seems to have believed that the season of the yellow fever would arrive there before the Americans could. Rather, he fixed his eyes on the front door in the north. Here he hoped to gain a single, smashing victory, after which he would bar the road while worrying the "war-weary" Americans to such an extent that they would be crying for peace before the winter of 1846-47 was over. For Santa Anna, like many other Mexicans, had listened at long distance to the rising clamor of antiwar sentiment in America and concluded that his enemy was faltering.

Opposition to the war in America, forced underground by Taylor's victories, had erupted after the Whig Congressional triumph, and its leaders included Northern Democrats as well. As in 1812, New England was the center of the movement, where it had powerful support from influential religious sects such as the Quakers, Congregationalists and Unitarians. Unitarian William Henry Channing went so far as to say that if he served in this "damnable war" he would be on the side of Mexico.[43] Once again the cry of a "slavocracy plot" was raised, and the poet James Russell Lowell warned his Yankee neighbors:

> They jest want this Californy
>   So's to lug new slave-states in
> To abuse ye, an' to scorn ye,
>   An' to plunder ye like sin.[44]

Less restrained were the remarks of Senator Tom Corwin of Ohio, who declared: "If I were a Mexican, I would tell you, 'Have you not room in your own country to bury your dead men? If you come into mine, we will meet you with bloody hands, and welcome you to hospitable graves.' "[45]

Outraged American soldiers might hang "Black Tom" Corwin in effigy, but the net effect of his speeches—and those of Daniel Webster—was to create in Mexico the expectation of a joint pronunciamento from Whigs and Northern Democrats forcing the American government to withdraw its troops. Meanwhile, Santa Anna was busily trying to raise his army, and in this he was again aided by the activity of his enemy.

This time it was the volunteers, more ferocious at Monterrey than they had been at Matomoros. Their severest critic, Lieutenant Meade, wrote home of them:

They are sufficiently well-drilled for practical purposes, and are, I believe, brave, and will fight as gallantly as any men. But they are a set of Goths and Vandals, without discipline, laying waste the country wherever we go, making us a terror to innocent people. . . . They cannot take care of themselves; the hospitals are crowded with them, they die like sheep; they waste their provisions, requiring twice as much to supply them as regulars do. They plunder the poor inhabitants of everything they can lay their hands on, and shoot them when they remonstrate, and if one of their number happens to get into a drunken brawl and is killed, they run over the country, killing all the poor innocent people they find in their way, to avenge, as they say, the murder of their brother.[46]

The cause, Meade said, "was the utter incapacity of their officers to control them or command respect."[47] and the cause of this was the old evil root of elected officers: men simply will not curb men who were once their civilian equals, their clients and their customers, and who will soon be so again. So the volunteers remained rapacious, making it easier for Santa Anna to recruit troops among the northern Mexicans they had ravaged.

Even so, the Liberator had to struggle against the hatred of those northern states which remembered him as their old oppressor. They refused him men and money, and even tried to combine against him. In San Luis Potosí members of a secret society called the Red Comet swore: "Nobody is bound to obey one who has no right to command."[48] For a time even the federal government seemed powerless to help him. The treasury was empty, and the Liberator was forced to the final expedient: seizure of Church property. As might be expected, such a measure raised little funds while alienating the Church and setting the old anticlerical fires blazing. And yet, by forced loans, seizures, remittances from state and federal governments and his personal credit, Santa Anna raised enough money to support an army of 20,000 men. Few generals in history have possessed the Liberator's capacity for making an army stand where none had stood before, even if, like the soldiers of Ivan the Fool, many of its men were made of straw. On January 27, 1847, then, Santa Anna's army started marching north from San Luis Potosí.

"Let them come," General Taylor said of the Mexicans. "Damned if they don't go back a good deal faster than they came."[49] But it was Taylor who went back, once his scouts reported Santa Anna to his front. Fearing that the Liberator might outflank him and strike Saltillo in his rear, Taylor withdrew ten miles to an excellent defensive position at the Buena Vista ranch about eight miles south of Saltillo. Actually he was a mile and a half below Buena Vista, at a place called La Angostura or "The Narrows." Here the Saltillo road became a narrow defile passing through a ravine-slashed plateau on the east, or Taylor's left, and a maze of gullies fronting a mountain on the west, or right. Because the right was considered impassable, it was the left that was fortified.

The road itself was barred at the Narrows, after which infantry and artillery stretched away east on the plateau in a rough arrowhead pointing south. The left or eastern side of this arrowhead was more vulnerable because there were not enough units to form a continuous line there. Still, it was a strong position; the ravines would nearly paralyze the Mexican cavalry and artillery and hamper their infantry. Thus, thought Taylor, Santa Anna's numerical superiority of about 15,000 to 5,000 would be largely discounted. Santa Anna, however, did not agree. He warned Taylor that he was surrounded by 20,000 men and would meet catastrophe unless he surrendered. His letter was carried under a flag of truce by a German surgeon, and after it was interpreted, Old Zack snorted, "Tell Santa Anna to go to hell!"[50] Turning to his chief of staff, he said, "Major Bliss, put that in Spanish and send it back by this damned Dutchman."[51] It was done, with considerably more courtesy, and in late afternoon of Washington's Birthday, 1847, Santa Anna attacked.

His artillery began roving over the American lines while his right, under General Ampudia, tried to gain the slopes of a mountain above the lightly held American left. Both sides skirmished until after dark, when the Americans withdrew to the valley.

That night Taylor returned to Saltillo with an infantry regiment and a squadron of dragoons. He feared that the Mexicans might have flanked him and be moving on the city. Finding himself in error, he started back toward Buena Vista next day—February 23—just as the Mexicans gained the summit of the mountain and opened on the American left with long-range artillery. Brigadier General John Wool at once began shifting his troops to the threatened left. Volunteer riflemen and a battery of artillery under Lieutenant John Paul Jones O'Brien rushed toward the left-center where two Mexican divisions were coming up a slope. O'Brien's trio of guns dashed forward to within musket range of the Mexicans, unlimbered and began battering the enemy. In turn, a Mexican battery on his flank struck at O'Brien. To his rear, the American riflemen had quit the field— most of them retreating all the way back to Buena Vista ranch. O'Brien and his gunners stayed on, stemming the Mexican tide until he had no more cannoneers. Then, leaving one gun behind among its dead gunners and horses, he pulled the other two out.

But now there was a break in the American left-center, and the Mexicans quickly began driving in the entire Yankee left. Only the right continued to face south, both center and left being bent back to face east. Masses of Mexican cavalry and infantry were moving along the base of the mountain to strike at Buena Vista in the American rear. At this moment, Taylor trotted up on Old Whitey. He went directly to the center of the line to direct the battle, and also, by his calm presence, to steady his men. Meanwhile, the riflemen he brought back with him checked the Mexicans in the center, while a composite command of horse, foot and guns was rushed to the rear to block the Mexican cavalry moving on Buena Vista.

With a gathering gallop, the Mexican lancers came charging forward. The Americans countercharged and split the enemy column in two. From American sharpshooters on Buena Vista's rooftops and behind her walls came a withering small-arms fire that emptied Mexican saddles and sent one wing of the broken column flying back the way it came, and the other fleeing west to make a complete circuit around the American position.

Now a second, more serious threat developed. A column of lancers prepared to charge the American infantry forward of Buena Vista. For a time Captain Braxton Bragg's guns broke up the enemy formation, but eventually it came on. At once two regiments of volunteers formed a V with the open end to the enemy. Into those yawning jaws came the lancers, at first at a trot, and then slowing to a walk, and the storm of fire that came from each side of the V of Buena Vista annihilated the head of the enemy column and broke the tail in a dozen pieces.

With its cavalry repulsed, the Mexican infantry withdrew. The tide of battle had flowed to the Americans, but then, for reasons never made known, a flag of truce passed between both armies and firing ceased. In that interval, Santa Anna prepared his last stroke. It came against what had been the American center and was now the left, and it fell just as three volunteer regiments were deploying. Once again, it was the guns of Lieutenant O'Brien, together with one gun under Lieutenant George Thomas (not yet "The Rock of Chickamauga"), which flew into the breach. With blown horses and weary men, the American artillerists drove forward to a position from which they could rake the enemy rear. After volunteer units came running forward to plug the gap, the Mexican tide halted and flowed back again.

The Battle of Buena Vista was over. A handful of artillerists backed up by volunteers fighting bravely when bravely led had repulsed a superior force executing a well-conceived and well-nigh successful turning movement. Taylor's losses were high—746 killed, wounded and missing—but Santa Anna's were five times higher. And on the morning of February 24 he turned his troops and began his horrible retreat to San Luis, arriving there with half of the force he had led north and with the next best thing to victory: the announcement of one.

As might have been expected, those materialist critics who always overlook the moral factor of war thought Taylor never should have fought Santa Anna. But Buena Vista denied the Liberator that single smashing victory which he desired so desperately, while reviving the drooping spirits of the American nation. That new determination to go on with the war and win it was solemnized by the poet Theodore O'Hara, celebrating Buena Vista in the lines:

> On Fame's eternal camping-ground
> Their silent tents are spread,
> And Glory guards, with solemn round,
> The bivouac of the dead.

After Buena Vista the Mexican War shifted to the side door at Vera Cruz, and Zachary Taylor, who had fought his last battle, raised his sights still higher on the presidency. To the newspapers who rebuked his partisans for their unseemly haste in discussing Old Zack's candidacy before the Whig National Convention, one Kentucky volunteer replied: "National convention be damned! I tell ye, General Taylor is going to be elected by spontaneous combustion!"

6

☆

On February 21, 1847—the day on which Taylor's scouts sighted Santa Anna's banners below Buena Vista—General Scott reached his staging area at Lobos Island about 50 miles south of Tampico.

Here Scott found nothing like the 20,000 troops he had been promised, but only a few thin formations of volunteers already ravaged by smallpox. Although he had organized his campaign against Vera Cruz and Mexico City down to such thoughtful details as special landing boats built to fit inside one another in "nests" of three, the inevitable delays attendant upon this first amphibious operation in American history were unraveling all his finely spun plans. Meanwhile, Scott was frantic to be off to Vera Cruz before the season of *el vómito* should arrive to turn the city into a pesthouse.

Gradually his troops arrived. Worth and Twiggs came to Lobos in transports loaded with their regulars. There was another volunteer division under Major General Robert Patterson, a wealthy Democrat to whom Polk at one time wanted to give the chief command. There were also the volunteer brigades of Quitman, Pillow and Shields.

Scott had culled the cream of the West Point corps for his command. His most valued officers were the engineers, men such as the stocky, aristocratic Lieutenant P. G. T. Beauregard or testy George Meade, but most of all the splendid Captains Joe Johnston and Robert E. Lee, two old friends who were both 40 and who bunked together aboard Scott's flagship, the steamer *Massachusetts*. Crusty Jubal Early was at Lobos, too, along with Sam Grant and the tall young artillerist, Lieutenant Tom Jackson. The future would bestow the nickname of "Stonewall" on Jackson; now he was known for a painful reserve broken only by such terse remarks as: "I should like to be in one battle."[52] Tom Ewell was Jackson's exact opposite. He liked to laugh, and he was convulsed at a camp along the Rio Grande one day when Old Fuss 'n' Feathers rode up to praise the "scouts" he had seen "peering at him from behind every bush." Ewell knew that the men were not on duty but rather doing their duty, for, as he wrote home: "The water here . . . opens the bowels like a melting tar."[53]

At last some 10,000 men and about 80 ships were assembled, and on March 2 the fleet of paddle-wheelers and sailing ships—plus one queer steamer driven silently through the sea by an underwater propeller—upped anchors and made away for Vera Cruz about 200 miles south. On March 5 the vanguard ships began arriving at Antón Lizardo, 12 miles below the target city. Two days later Commodore Conner took Scott and his general and engineers aboard the little steamer *Secretary* to reconnoiter Vera Cruz and its huge stone fortress of San Juan de Ulúa on a reef across the bay. This was the 128-gun fort which British naval officers swore could "sink all the ships in the world," yet little *Secretary* slipped in close until Ulúa began to puff and roar and raise splashes all around her, whereupon she turned and sped for safety. Back on his flagship, Scott announced that he would land his army on beaches a few miles southeast of Vera Cruz and out of Ulúa's range.

March 9, 1847, was a glittering blue day. Far away west the snowy peak of Mount Orizaba glistened like a noble beacon for the soldiers and sailors of the American fleet moving north for the landing beach. Off Vera Cruz men with glasses swarmed through the rigging of the foreign war vessels while ladies twirling parasols crowded the rails. At one o'clock in the afternoon Conner's bombardment ships with double-shotted cannon were in place offshore. In closer were seven gunboats armed with grape. Now 4,500 regulars led by Worth began clambering over the sides of their steamboats into 65 of Scott's surfboats. Ashore, a few hundred Mexican lancers cantered nervously along the beach. In Vera Cruz, housetops and walls were black with humanity. All American eyes turned toward Orizaba. The moment the setting sun touched the mountain's peak the assault would commence. It happened: red ball met white mountain, from *Massachusetts* came the flash of a signal gun, from Vera Cruz and Ulúa came the roar of cannon making futile dimples on the silken sheen of the Gulf, from the American ships came the thunder of guns driving off the Mexican cavalry, and as cheer after cheer and the crashing of bands bursting into "The Star-Spangled Banner" chased the sound of the cannon across the water, the American soldiers ducked their heads beneath their gleaming bayonets while the sailors bent to their oars.

Men and officers still aboard ship watched anxiously as oars bit and flashed and the line of boats caught the swell of the Gulf. "Why don't they hit us?" a salty old sailor muttered. "If we don't have a big butcher's bill, there's no use in coming here."[54]

But the enemy beach was silent. Suddenly, the boat carrying Worth shot out in the lead. It grounded with a lurch and the impetuous general leaped out, followed by his officers. Now the Americans were jumping into the surf, holding muskets and cartridge boxes high overhead. They waded in, sprinted up the sand to the crest of the first dune, raised their standards and burst into cheers. From the fleet offshore came answering huzzas, and as the bay reverberated to the triumphant cries and music of the Americans, Conner's blue-jackets rapidly brought another 5,500 troops ashore.

By midnight Vera Cruz was invested without the loss of a single man and 10,000 Americans were eating pork and biscuit in the sand. It was a splendid feat, so dazzling that General Scott could scarcely believe that he had been able to bring it off unopposed.

The first American D-Day had been a stupendous success simply because Santa Anna had chosen to fight Taylor elsewhere and because

Mexico had been shaken by the *"Polko* Rebellion."

This complicated conflict was in essence a struggle between the *"Puros,"* those doctrinaire democrats who, coming to power under Acting President Farias, "passed sentence of death" on Mexican society, and the equally fanatic *"Polkos,"* conservative merchants, professional men, craftsmen, clerks and, chief of all, the clergy. The *Polkos* got their names from the polka music played by the bands of the four independent battalions they had formed, as they said, to defend private property against the designs of the *Puros*. Actually, the *Polkos* were clericals and the *Puros* anticlericals, and the *Puros-Polkos* duel was in many ways an adumbration of the bloody factional strife of the Spanish Civil War as well as the dualism which still divides Latin America.

The apple of discord was Church property. The Mexican government, inept as well as corrupt, and so eaten by loan sharks that in 1845 it was entitled to only 13 percent of the money entering its treasury, was at last bankrupt. But the Church was still wealthy, and even other parties such as the *Moderados* regarded her property as the solution to the problem. The thinking of many Mexican leaders, not only the ferociously anticlerical Farias, who would just as soon cripple the Church as defeat the invaders, was best expressed by the Congressman who said: "If the Yankee triumphs, what ecclesiastical property or what religion will be left us?"[55]

But the Church could not agree, and so, after Congress passed laws levying on her estates, she secured the allegiance of the *Polko* battalions. This was in February of 1847, by which time all of Mexico was aware of the impending American invasion of Vera Cruz. Farias, not daring to disarm the *Polkos,* decided to get rid of them by ordering them to march to the defense of the imperiled city. The *Polkos* refused. When Farias and the *Puros* attempted to disarm them, the *Polkos* took to the barricades. Bloodcurdling cries arose from either side, there was much firing back and forth, but, as had happened so often in Mexican uprisings, most of the casualties were among innocent civilians.

President Santa Anna, meanwhile, refrained from taking sides openly. Secretly, however, he worked for the downfall of Farias and toward a *rapprochement* with the Church. Although the hierarchy distrusted him, he was obviously a lesser evil than Farias; and the *Moderados,* believing in his "victory" at Buena Vista, also rallied to his support. And so President Santa Anna came to Mexico City, a *Te Deum* was sung to celebrate his defeat of the Americans, and on March 23, 1847, he formally superseded Farias in office.

Thus the penultimate result of the tragicomic *Polko* Rebellion. The last step completed the farce: to get rid of Farias the office of Vice President was abolished, and a *Moderado* "substitute president" was appointed while Santa Anna again put aside the politician's coat-and-collar to vest himself in "glory and the robes of war." But before he could march to the rescue of Vera Cruz, American cannon were already smashing at the city's walls.

Winfield Scott had all but placed the siege of Vera Cruz in the hands of his engineers. Day after day they went out—Lee, Johnston, Beauregard, George McClellan and the others—to study the city's defenses and terrain and to site gun emplacements. Sometimes Sam Grant of the infantry went along to watch them work. Once Grant and Beauregard were inside an adobe hut when a Mexican shell slammed into it and exploded. They were only stunned, for Mexican shells were notoriously weak.

Gradually, American soldiers, toiling in sweat and ankle-deep sand, built an investing line in the sand hills behind Vera Cruz, while others cut the city's water supply or dragged artillery into position. Many of Scott's officers fretted at the delay. The idea of a siege bored them and they were impetuous for a charge.

"Ugh," General Twiggs snorted, "my boys'll have to take it yet with their bayonets."[56]

But Scott still wanted to take Vera Cruz "by headwork, the slow, scientific process."[57] He did not want to lose more than 100 men, and said: "For every one over that number I shall regard myself as his murderer."[58]

On March 22, with his cannon emplaced, Scott summoned Vera Cruz to surrender. The Mexicans refused and the American siege artillery opened with a rising roar. Yankee gunboats began bombarding the city from the water, running in so close that Ulúa began growling again. Commodore Matthew Perry—the younger brother of Perry of Lake Erie—had relieved Conner the day before, and he at once recalled his overbold gamecocks. Soon heavier naval cannon were brought ashore, and Perry's sailors, trained in the naval way not to flinch at the flash of cannon, eventually learned that on land it was no disgrace to take cover: one day four sailors standing erect in the open had the tops of their heads blown off.

Night and day the guns roared until the artillery load rose to 180 shells an hour and there were fires burning throughout the city. On March 26 a white flag fluttered at Vera Cruz. Scott sent Generals Worth and Pillow to meet the Mexican commissioners. Worth came back grumbling: "General, they're only trying to gain time—they don't mean to surrender. They evidently expect forces from the interior to come to their aid and compel us to raise the siege, or else to keep up dilly-dallying until the yellow fever does it for them. You'll have to assault the town, and I'm ready to do it with my division."[59]

Scott thanked Worth, took from him the Mexican note and called for interpreters with the remark: "Now, let's hear the English of what these Mexican generals have to say."[60] To his annoyance, but not entirely his surprise, Scott heard language indicating that the Mexicans merely wanted to save face. He at once dictated acceptable terms, and on March 29, 1847, both the city of Vera Cruz and the fort at San Juan de Ulúa surrendered.

Scott the scientific had been better than his word. He had lost only 67 killed and wounded against what were at first reported as enemy losses of 400 soldiers and 500 to 600 civilians. He was criticized, of course, particularly in the foreign press, for his "inhumanity" in bombarding the city into submission. His traducers, ignoring the plain fact that Vera Cruz was a fortified city which had refused to surrender, presumably wanted Scott to take it by syllogism. They certainly could not have wanted him to storm it, for to have done so would have been to guarantee a frightful slaughter. Actually, the British naval commander on the scene estimated that the Mexican Army lost 80 men killed and that civilian deaths numbered about 100.

Few shooting sieges have been less bloody, and yet Scott was soon to learn that the America of his day really loved a big butcher's bill. Upon the announcement of the capture of Vera Cruz in New Orleans, a man in the crowd called out: "How many men has Scott lost?" The reply was: "Less than a hundred," and the man cried: "That won't do. Taylor always loses thousands. He is the man for my money."[61]

7

☆

While Winfield Scott exercised his formidable organizing skills to turn Vera Cruz into a base of operations against Mexico City, President Polk in Washington decided that there should be a peace commissioner attached to Scott's army.

The man chosen was Nicholas Trist, whose title of chief clerk made him the second in rank in the State Department. Trist departed for Vera Cruz on April 16, convinced, apparently, that although he had never met General Scott he disliked him most heartily.

Scott, meanwhile, was in a rage to get his army out of the coastal flats and into the highlands before the dread *vómito* arrived in mid-April. His immediate objective was Jalapa, 75 miles away and 4,000 feet above sea level, but his immediate difficulty was in obtaining animal transport. Washington had failed to forward 500 draft horses needed to pull the siege guns, and so, as a poor substitute, Mexican mustangs were rounded up. On April 8 Twigg's division stepped out on the march to Mexico City, 260 miles west.

"Old Davy" Twiggs, a man with an oxen back and matching brain, "led" his foot soldiers on horseback. Paced by a horse, floundering in sand, broiling in a brazen sun and ravaged by diarrhea, the men simply melted away. By the end of the first day's march a third of the division was missing, and the route was strewn with abandoned equipment. On the second day the Americans came to the national highway, the way of Cortez, which the Spaniards had graded, paved and guttered and used for three centuries. Now, however, it was in disrepair; but it was nevertheless a better road than most of the Yankee soldiers had seen. To either side of it, all the way from Vera Cruz to Jalapa, were the estates of Santa Anna. Here the going was not only easier but also gorgeous, and the step of the soldiers quickened and their eyes brightened to behold the birds and flowers and

trees of the exotic paradise through which they tramped. On April
11 they crossed a stone bridge into the village of Plan del Río,
where the road winds and begins to climb the highlands. Here the
Americans sighted Mexican lancers. Next day, Captain Joe Johnston
and his engineers went scouting. Johnston came back with bullet
holes in his right thigh and arm and the report that Santa Anna
was at the pass of Cerro Gordo.

Limping on his wooden leg, the Liberator had left the capital
on April 2, and by April 5 had reached Jalapa. Here he took command of about 6,000 men, most of them the veterans of his northern
campaign, and led them about 20 miles east to the point where
Cerro Gordo—the "Big Hill"—guards the brow of the cordillera.
Here he expected to bar the American advance and keep the invaders so far down the slopes that they would be within reach of
the *vómito*.

Santa Anna's position was a good one. To the right or south of
the road was a heavily fortified ridge. To the left or north was Cerro
Gordo itself, also fortified, and a half-mile to the northeast was
another fortified hill, Atalaya. Thus the Americans trying to climb
the road would be caught between two plunging fires. They could
not get behind the fortified ridge on the south for its rear was guarded
by a canyon and the Plan del Río. And Santa Anna thought the
north flank was protected by terrain so impenetrable that a rabbit
could not get through it.

Although the Americans were much bigger than cottontails, they
were also a bit more rational. Since General Scott had arrived at
Cerro Gordo his engineers—Lieutenants Beauregard and Zebulon
Tower the first among them—had been probing the Mexican front
in the region Santa Anna thought impassable for rabbits. On April
15 Captain Robert E. Lee continued the reconnoiter.

Lee probed far to his right, slowly working his way up the ravines.
He came to a spring and a well-trampled path leading from the south.
He heard voices speaking Spanish and saw a party of Mexican
soldiers approaching the spring. Silently, he dropped to the ground
behind a log. The voices grew louder. There were more of them.
Lee lay still in the moist heat while insects whirred in his ears and
stung his flesh. Suddenly a Mexican sat on the log. Then another.

Their backs were not three feet from the American. Then they arose and walked away. But more soldiers came and went and Captain Lee lay still until dark. Then he lifted his stiffened limbs and crept away. Down the treacherous ravine he went, moving stealthily with that intuitive feel for ground which is among the greatest of soldierly qualities. At last he reached headquarters and reported: it seemed possible that the Mexican left could be turned.

Encouraged, Scott ordered Lee to reconnoiter the area again on the 16th. He did, using a party of pioneers to cut a path still farther to the right. Next day he began to guide Twigg's division around the enemy left.

Sweating soldiers in light blue toiled up and down chasms so steep that animals could not climb them. Artillery was let down the steeps by rope and hauled up the same way. Suddenly, at noon, the Americans were discovered by Mexicans on Atalaya. A sharp fight for the hilltop began. Both sides fed in forces, until Colonel William Harney, a man as fiery in color as a red fox, led a charge over and around Atalaya. In fact, the charge was too impetuous. It carried forward to the slopes of Cerro Gordo, where the Americans were pinned down and picked off until light artillery from Atalaya enabled them to break off and withdraw.

Now Scott reinforced Twiggs with Shields's volunteer brigade. Under Lee's direction, they dragged three 24-pounders onto Atalaya's crest. That night Scott issued his battle orders: Twiggs was "to move forward before daylight, and take up position across the national road in the enemy's rear, so as to cut off a retreat towards Jalapa."[62] Pillow's brigade was to attack the Mexican right on the fortified ridge. Worth's division was to follow Twiggs and Shields.

On April 18 the attack began. Twiggs sent the brigades of Shields and Colonel Bennett Riley on a swing right to get at the Mexican camp in the rear of Cerro Gordo and Atalaya. Shields moved directly on target, but Riley veered to his left and struck the western flank of Cerro Gordo. As both brigades moved, Colonel Harney's regulars went yelling down Atalaya, swept across the intervening hollow, and charged up Cerro Gordo's slopes. Within 100 yards of the crest, they threw themselves down to catch their breath, jumped erect and followed the shouting Harney over the enemy's breastworks.

As the Mexicans fled, Captain John Magruder turned their abandoned guns on them. At this moment, Shields's troops burst upon the Mexican camp. A blast of grapeshot carried clear through Shields's body to deal him a wound that was miraculously not mortal; but his men rallied and routed the startled enemy. At the same time, Pillow's brigade, delayed in its advance to a jumping-off point, fell upon the Mexican right. Here the Americans suffered their severest losses, and Pillow was himself wounded in the arm. But once the Mexicans here realized that they were cut off to the rear, they surrendered.

By noon the Battle of Cerro Gordo was all over. Scott lost 63 killed and 337 wounded, but half of Santa Anna's army was captured and many others must have fallen. The Liberator did not wait to tally his losses. He fled toward Jalapa leaving his baggage wagon behind. Inside it the Americans found his military chest containing coin to pay his soldiers, cooked chicken and—most precious prize of all—Santa Anna's spare wooden leg. Soon, in the tradition of the more grisly "Tecumseh razor strops," "Santa Anna legs" became fashionable in the States.

And within a few days Winfield Scott's triumphant little army was safely inside Jalapa. Behind the Americans lay the *vómito* and before them the exposed capital of a stunned nation.

8

☆

Scott was eager to pursue the retreating Santa Anna, but before he could leave Jalapa he had to reorganize and eliminate shortages which had begun to afflict his army.

The first was in troops. On April 27 he was informed that the "new" regulars recruited under the Ten-Regiment Bill were being diverted to Taylor on the Rio Grande. Next his 12-month volunteers began clamoring to go home. Most of them had only a month or six weeks left to serve, and they objected that if they waited until their discharge date they would have to leave the country through Vera Cruz just when the yellow fever was raging strongest. General

Scott accepted the force of this argument, and on May 4 about 3,000 men, the remnant of seven volunteer regiments, left Jalapa for the Gulf.

Scott's next shortage was in ready money with which to pay his troops and to purchase supplies. He also lacked cavalry and did not have enough teamsters and wagon masters, specialists who in those days were hired civilians rather than soldiers trained for the task. But even such serious problems as these were as nothing to the one raised with the arrival in Jalapa of a communication from Polk's peace commissioner, Nicholas Trist.

The Honorable Mr. Trist seems—with ample cause—to have become convinced of the magnitude of his mission and the importance of his person. He had been given the grandiloquent title of "Commissioner Plenipotentiary," he had been taken into the confidence of President Polk—where he was informed that General Pillow, not Scott, was the man to trust—and it had been intimated to him by Secretary Buchanan that if he was successful in concluding a peace with Mexico he might become the next Democratic candidate for President. Upon his arrival in Vera Cruz, therefore, Trist did not go forward to Scott's headquarters as instructed. Instead, he wrote him a letter which may stand as a model of how a civilian may harry an already harassed soldier into apoplexy.

Trist told Scott that he, Trist, "was clothed with such diplomatic powers as will authorize him to enter into arrangements with the government of Mexico *for the suspension of hostilities.*"[63] With this he sent a *sealed* letter for Scott to forward to the Mexican minister.

Scott flew into a rage. A rash letter-writer himself, he dashed off a reply stating that the "Secretary of War proposes to degrade me, by requiring that I, the commander of this army, shall defer to you, the chief clerk of the Department of State, the question of continuing or discontinuing hostilities."[64] The sealed letter, which was nothing more than a refusal of earlier Mexican demands, together with a notice that a peace commissioner was now with the American Army, was disdainfully returned.

It was all a dreadful misunderstanding, chiefly due to Trist's preconceived notion that he disliked Scott and his inflated sense of his own importance. If he had met the general personally and shown him the confidential papers in his care, as he was instructed to do, he would not have provoked a rancorous quarrel which bid fair to have most destructive consequences for the government they both sincerely served. But after Trist's first letter, all was cross-purposes. Scott, already aggrieved by the diversion of the "new" regulars to Taylor, became, like Taylor, convinced that all Whig generals were to be crucified. He wrote to Secretary Marcy and asked to be recalled, and at one point he wrote to Trist: "The Jacobin convention of France never sent to one of its armies in the field a more amiable and accomplished instrument. If you were armed with an ambulatory guillotine you would be the personification of Danton, Marat, and St. Just, all in one."[65]

Fortunately, the good offices of the British minister in Mexico helped to heal the rift. Scott and Trist met, found that they liked each other, and then, after Trist fell ill and Scott sent him a peace offering in the form of guava marmalade, they became close friends.

By then, mid-June, Scott had lost the friendship of his old comrade-in-arms, William Worth. After the army had advanced to Puebla, about 150 miles west of Vera Cruz, Worth issued an ill-founded warning to his men that the Mexicans were mixing poison with the food they sold them. Scott ordered Worth to recall his circular, and Worth demanded a court of inquiry to judge his action. The court found him in error and subject to reprimand, and although Scott sought to soften the censure, Worth could not forgive him. Nor could he abide the fact that John Quitman and Gideon Pillow had been breveted to major generals senior to him.

Such difficulties made it ever more plain to Scott that he dared not tarry much longer at Puebla. He had already written to Secretary Marcy: "Like Cortez, finding myself isolated and abandoned, and again like him, always afraid that the next ship or messenger might recall or further cripple me, I resolved no longer to depend on Vera Cruz, or home, but to render my little army a self-sustaining machine."[66] Like Cortez, he was burning his boats. He had received enough volunteer reinforcements, among them a brigade under Brigadier General Franklin Pierce, one of the few Easterners to lead combat troops in "Mr. Polk's War." He had now about 10,500 effectives to march against an enemy city of 200,000 persons defended by a force he believed to be three times his own.

On August 7, 1847, the drums beat, bugles blew and the long lines of men in faded blue went swinging away to the Halls of Montezuma. In Europe the Duke of Wellington said: "Scott is lost. He cannot capture the city, and he cannot fall back upon his base."[67]

The Mexican government had passed through another convulsion, only to lay quiescent once more beneath Santa Anna. The Liberator had outmaneuvered his numerous enemies by offering his resignation as a "sacrifice," after which, gratified by the public protest, he made the second sacrifice of withdrawing it. "What a life of sacrifice is the General's," a Mexican newspaper sneered. " A sacrifice to take the power, to resign, to resume; ultimate sacrifice; ultimate final; ultimate more final; ultimate most final; ultimate the very finalest."[68]

Amid such dissension, Santa Anna prepared his defense of the capital. He did not have 30,000 men, as Scott thought, but rather about 25,000. Nevertheless, he disposed them artfully in a system of defenses—both natural and artificial—which made the hearts of the Americans sink as they marched down the road into the magnificent Valley of Mexico in which lay the capital city of their desires.

Scott's engineers could give him nothing but discouraging reports on the screen of lakes and marshes guarding Mexico City. Passage between the lakes was possible only on causeways raised above the marshes, and most of these were heavily guarded. Santa Anna had been careful to fortify the area around Lake Texcoco and the hill El Peñon in the north, for he expected Scott to come in here from the east. But Scott saw clearly that such an attempt would mean frightful losses. He ordered reconnaissances south of Lakes Chalco and Xochimilco. Here a rough but passable road was discovered, and on August 15 the army began movement to the village of San Agustín, modern Tlalpan, nine miles south of the city.

Here also the Americans seemed stymied. A few miles ahead of them was the well-fortified hacienda of San Antonio, and two miles farther north a fortified bridge over the canalized Río Churubusco. Supporting the bridge was the thick-walled convent of San Mateo, inside which were the deserters of the San Patricio Battalion—excellent gunners who would lovingly blast away at their former tormentors of the parade ground. The route north, then, seemed barred. Could it be turned? Not on the right or east where Xochimilco lay, nor, it seemed, on the left through the Pedregal, a great gray field of lava looking like a storm-tossed sea of stone. What about the other side of the Pedregal? There was a road there—the San Angel road —but there also seemed no way across the Pedregal.

Scott kept probing, however. On August 18 a party of engineers under Captain Lee entered the Pedregal, while others pushed north toward San Antonio escorted by dragoons under Captain Seth Thornton, the man whose ambush on the Rio Grande a year ago had touched off the war. From the hacienda came cannon fire, and the first shot cut Thornton in two. As the Mexican cannonade continued, the Americans withdrew.

Captain Lee, meanwhile, had found a tiny track in the Pedregal. Following it, he came to a piled-up mass of volcanic rock called Zacatepec. He climbed it and saw the San Angel road to the west. There were enemy troops on the slope of the hill at the village of Padierna to his left. Suddenly Lee heard firing. His escort had met a Mexican picket and exchanged shots. Realizing that these men had come from the San Angel road, Lee concluded that he could get there too, and that was the gist of his report to General Scott.

That night Scott decided to try to improve the Pedregal track so that guns and wagons might move over it. Early in the morning of August 19 working parties were sent out, and by one o'clock in the afternoon a road had been brought to within range of Padierna. But then enemy soldiers were met once more and cannon shot fell among the Americans. Padierna, it was seen, was now held in force by the Mexicans.

They were there because of the insubordination of General Gabriel Valencia, commander of the army of the north. After Santa Anna had seen that Scott was not going to attack in the north, he had sent Valencia south to block the western road at San Angel. Valencia, however, had his own ideas and his own pretensions to glory. On August 18 he moved south from San Angel to the slope at Padierna, refusing, that night, to obey Santa Anna's orders to return to San Angel. By the afternoon of August 19 he was emplaced on the hill in full view of American officers standing atop Zacatepec.

To these officers it seemed that Valencia's left could be turned. General Pillow gave the word to Riley to take his brigade to the right, cross the San Angel road and cut off Valencia's retreat to Mexico City. Then he ordered Brigadier General George Cadwalader to follow Riley, after which Brigadier General Persifor Smith, moving on his own initiative, took his brigade along the same route. By late afternoon all three units—about 3,500 men in all—were safely across the San Angel road. By then General Scott had come out to Zacatepec to approve what had been done, and also to see about 3,000 Mexican reinforcements start coming south from Coyoacán to take up station at San Angel.

The Americans west of the San Angel road were now caught between Valencia to their left or south and the reinforcements on the north. But neither Scott nor Persifor Smith, who had taken command west of the road, appeared to be concerned. Scott merely sent Captain Lee to Smith and calmly awaited developments.

They began after dark when Smith told Lee that he was going to move around Padierna during the night and attack it from the rear before daybreak. He told Lee that he would like a diversionary attack to be launched in front of Padierna, and Lee volunteered to carry that request to Scott. In rain and lightning, Lee crossed the road and began working east across the Pedregal. As he did, Santa Anna sent orders to Valencia to spike his guns and return to San Angel in darkness before an American attack in the morning should cut him off. Valencia, certain that he won a "victory" that afternoon, scornfully disobeyed the order.

On the rain-swept Pedregal, meanwhile, Captain Lee and a few men picked their way among lava rocks and chasms, leaping across fissures when they saw them outlined in fitful flashes of lightning, guiding on the gloomy bulk of Zacatepec when it, too, was thrown into relief. Lee's greatest fear was of blundering into a trigger-happy American sentry. Once, hearing the tramp of feet ahead of him, he paused, and saw in a glare of lightning that they were the men of General Shields moving to reinforce Smith. Detailing a man to guide them, Lee plunged on. At last he came to Zacatepec. But Scott was not there. Weary and bruised, soaked to the skin, Lee pressed on to San Agustín, where he found his general.

Scott approved Smith's plan and ordered Franklin Pierce's troops to make diversion in front of Padierna. Pierce himself was injured, and command passed to Colonel Trueman Ransom. Lee found Ransom's men bivouacked on the Padierna and guided them into position.

West of the road, the arrival of Shields raised the American strength to 4,000 men. At three o'clock in the morning, of August 20, 1847, the rain-plastered Yankee soldiers began moving out. Once again those invaluable engineers showed them the way. Slipping and stumbling on the slippery track, they stole into Valencia's rear.

In front of Valencia, Ransom's men opened up. Valencia's soldiers returned the fire. Suddenly, they heard wild yelling to their rear. A tide of blue was flowing down the hill toward them, led by the huge Riley. Firing as they came, the Americans rushed headlong into the Mexican position. For a while the Mexican gunners worked wildly to reverse their guns. But then they broke and ran, joining the infantry already being trampled by fleeing Mexican horse. In 17 minutes the battle was over. Day had hardly dawned before the San Angel road was black with Mexican soldiers streaming north. Among them somewhere was General Valencia, who had disappeared at the commencement of the battle. Left behind were 700 dead, more than 800 prisoners and a great store of military supplies.

The Americans had lost less than 60 killed and wounded, and now General Scott was free to push up the San Angel road to come down upon San Antonio in the rear.

General Santa Anna did not sit still for his envelopment at San Antonio. Instead, learning of Valencia's defeat, he abandoned the position and ordered its troops to withdraw to inner defenses behind the Churubusco River. Other soldiers moved into those *garita,* or gates, which guarded the heads of the causeways and which were actually fortified stone buildings used as police and customs stations. It was at the Churubusco bridgehead-and-convent complex, however, that the main defense was concentrated, and here the pursuing Americans smacked "butt-end first" into the stubborn enemy.

Worth's division took the San Antonio road: Garland's brigade moving through a cornfield to the right of the road, Colonel Newman Clarke's men advancing up the road itself. On the left of the road was Cadwalader's brigade, trying to punch between bridgehead and convent. Cadwalader could not, and his men finally crossed the road into the cornfield. Farther left, Smith's brigade struck at San Mateo, while still farther left Riley hit the convent in flank.

Across the Churubusco Franklin Pierce, barely able to keep to his saddle, faced his brigade east and tried to cut the Mexican line of retreat. Pierce was eventually reinforced by Shields, and by riflemen and dragoons guided into battle by Captain Lee.

Santa Anna was now engaged across his entire front, and he fought back skillfully, rapidly countering Scott's cross-river attempts to turn him. For three hours the battle raged. From San Mateo, where the deserters were "fighting with a halter around their necks,"[69] came a dreadful drumfire. The hoarse cries of stricken men were counterpointed by the mad screaming of horses and mules. Smoke drifted everywhere, and in the cornfield the sound of bullets popping stalks was counterpointed by the uglier one of lead smacking flesh. Across the river Franklin Pierce was down again with a twisted knee, but he urged his men on until consciousness left him.

By three o'clock in the afternoon Scott had shot his bolt. All his available men were engaged—6,000 against 18,000—they were falling by the hundreds, and they seemed stopped. One officer near Scott said to himself, "We must succeed or the army is lost."[70]

But the Mexicans were low on ammunition, and the Americans had worked their way into position for the final heave. Almost at once, they arose on three fronts and charged—and they were irresistible. Only at San Mateo did the fight continue, and here the deserters fought with clubbed muskets until at last there were only 80 of them alive to be taken prisoner. With his bridgehead gone, the convent fallen and his line of retreat threatened, Santa Anna ordered another withdrawal.

Mexican soldiers went streaming north for the safety of the San Antonio Gate, and the American infantry let them go. Suddenly bugles blew a charge and a squadron of American dragoons under hawk-nosed Captain Philip Kearny, nephew of the conqueror of New Mexico, went clattering up the road in full pursuit. They were a stirring sight, matched iron-grays moving nose to tail with their riders ramrod-straight and grasping gleaming sabers that rested, blade up, against their right shoulders. On toward the gate they charged, into a storm of enemy fire, with Kearny unaware that behind him Colonel Harney had blown recall and his rear horsemen were dropping off by fours.

Kearny had only Richard Ewell and a handful of troopers with him when he reached the gate, dismounted and tried to force it on foot. But the Americans were fighting at the cannon's mouth. Blast after blast cut them to the ground. They withdrew, with Kearny clinging to his mount with the one arm that was to remain to him and Ewell escaping on his third horse.

Perhaps the chance to enter the San Antonio Gate and drive straight into the city of Mexico had been missed. At any rate, the Battle of Churubusco was over. Chiefly because of the dreadful fire of the San

Patricios, it had been far more costly than Padierna: about 1,000 casualties in all. Santa Anna's losses for the day were about 3,200 soldiers captured, among them eight generals, and 4,000 killed and wounded, plus a paralyzing loss of arms and ammunition.

Winfield Scott, convinced that he had "overwhelmed the enemy," did not occupy the capital, as he might easily have done. Instead, he agreed to a cessation of hostilities during which Nicholas Trist and his Mexican counterparts might negotiate a peace. But the armistice lasted only two weeks. Trist's territorial demands provoked the Mexicans into advancing unacceptable terms of their own, and on September 7, learning that Santa Anna had used the truce as a breather in which to refresh his forces, Scott brought the armistice to an end.

The Molino del Rey, or "King's Mill," was part of the bastion of Chapultepec which guarded the western approaches to Mexico City. Chapultepec Castle itself stood on the brow of a hill about 200 feet high. To its west was a park and then the massive Molino del Rey built in a north-south line. About 500 yards west of the Molino lay another strong building, the Casa Mata. Between the two was an artillery battery supported by infantry. Perhaps 8,000 Mexicans held the entire position.

Scott decided that he must have this most formidable strong point after observing Mexican troop movements in that direction and hearing that Santa Anna was using the Molino as a foundry in which to cast cannon out of church bells. So he ordered General Worth to take it and destroy its contents.

Worth had a force of about 3,250 men, nearly half the 7,000 soldiers to which Scott's army had been reduced. He also had nine guns, but Worth, perhaps even more than Twiggs, scorned artillery when bayonets could be used. Cold steel, not exploding shells, was Worth's solution to stone walls. Thus the Americans jumped off in the morning of September 8, 1847, with the barest bombardment. As Molino's walls glowed white in the dawning day, two 24-pounders barked ten times apiece—and then the blue lines swept forward.

The entire Mexican front blazed with musketry and cannon. The blue lines were riddled and ripped apart. In the center, 11 of 14 officers were struck down and the ranks suffered in proportion. On the left at the Casa Mata two commanding officers fell, followed by a third. Broken, the left rallied—just as swarms of Mexican cavalry appeared across a ravine on the left. If the Mexican horse could get across the ravine under cover of Casa Mata's guns, they could charge the American left and perhaps roll up the entire line.

American bugles blew and 250 dragoons swept toward the enemy lancers. Galling fire from Casa Mata and a battery to their right emptied 40 American saddles, but still the dragoons rode on, bluffing and outmaneuvering the more numerous Mexicans.

On the right, at the southern end of the Molino, battle was confused, with units advancing independently and fighting other units in the swirl of smoke. Finally a gate was battered in and shouting Americans went pouring into the murk of the Molino. They chased the enemy up on the roofs of the buildings.

Up on the left, even as the reinforced center was returning to the attack, the enemy was also cracking. Mexican guns unwisely left outside the Casa Mata were captured and turned against the enemy. Still fighting stubbornly, the Mexicans twice mounted counterattacks. Beaten back, they began retreating east from the Casa Mata to Chapultepec.

The position was now completely in American hands, and Worth, scenting total victory and glory, asked permission to press on to Chapultepec itself. Scott refused, repeating his order to destroy the enemy "cannon" and withdraw. But there were no newly cast cannon, not even any old church bells. And the Mexican church bells which caroled away joyously in the mistaken belief that an all-out assault on Chapultepec had been repulsed seemed to mock Scott's decision to launch the attack at all.

Even though the enemy lost 680 prisoners and between 1,000 and 2,000 casualties, Worth's losses were close to 800 men, or a quarter of his attacking force and nearly an eighth of Scott's army. As one of Scott's officers wrote in his diary: "We were like Pyrrhus after the fight with Fabricius—and a few more such victories and this army would be destroyed."[71]

One result of the "victory" at Molino del Rey was that some of the men who had fought most gallantly decided to desert. They thought the American position was desperate, they had no wish to scratch stone walls with bayonets again, and they stole away even in the face of the example made of the San Patricio deserters.

A general court-martial on September 8 found 80 Patricios guilty of desertion and sentenced 54 to death by hanging, while the rest, men who had deserted before war was declared, were ordered to be flogged, branded on the cheek with the letter D and imprisoned at hard labor until the end of the war.

The first 18 to be hanged were brought by wagon to scaffolds erected outside the beautiful church of San Angel. Their necks were noosed, a drum was tapped, and the wagons rolled away. The fall, however, was not great enough to break their necks, and the condemned men choked and squirmed to death. Next came the lighter punishment. Captain Thomas Riley, chief of the deserters, was given 50 lashes, the others 25. Hot irons were pressed into their cheeks. Because Riley's D was burned in upside down, he was given a second.

Thus the examples set at San Angel, and they outraged the enemy's sensitivities and stiffened his spine. However just the sentences, however normal the punishments for the armies of that day, to have carried them out so ineptly in front of a church and in the eyes of a people who regarded hanging as a profanation of the crucified Christ was a vengeful and thoughtless variation from the considerate and humane face which Scott had tried to show the Mexicans since he landed at Vera Cruz.

The executions continued, however, while the American command considered where to deliver the next blow.

Winfield Scott had to attack. His position, if not desperate, was at least sobering. Here were the Americans, down to 7,000 men and at the end of a 250-mile supply line whose base at Vera Cruz was useless until the *vómito* vanished in November. Before Santa Anna became alive to the possibilities of this vulnerable line, Scott had to seize the enemy capital. The question at the conference of September 9, then, was not when to attack but where.

The volunteer generals and Captain Lee favored the southern approaches, but the regular generals and Lieutenant Beauregard preferred Chapultepec in the west. Beauregard argued forcefully that the fall of Chapultepec would unmask two easily traversed causeways into the city. Hearing him, Franklin Pierce changed his vote to Chapultepec and Scott declared: "Gentlemen, we shall attack by the western gates."[72]

On the morning of September 12 American soldiers seized the vacant Molino del Rey and Casa Mata on the western end of the

Chapultepec complex. With daylight, American artillery roared, battering Chapultepec's buildings and walls in the fiercest bombardment of the war. Inside, General Nicolas Bravo called for reinforcements. But Santa Anna had no wish to feed more troops into what might become a slaughter pen. He kept some 4,000 troops available on the western causeways, but they did not enter Chapultepec. Santa Anna's eyes were fixed south, where a convincing diversion by Twiggs had deceived him as to the American intent. So Bravo had to hold with less than 1,000 men, of whom 100 were cadets quartered at the Military College in Chapultepec.

Against them came Pillow's division issuing out of the Molino and Quitman's division moving north from Tacubaya against Chapultepec's eastern end. On the west the Americans met a withering fire as they dashed whooping through a grove of giant cypresses. Here Pillow was wounded, and his men were brought to a cowering halt in a ditch beneath the castle, and here it was found that the storming party had forgotten to bring scaling ladders. In desperation Pillow called for Worth to bring up his division before all was lost. But then the scaling ladders arrived, and the Americans leaped into the ditch, swung the ladders against the stone wall and went swarming up them.

Lieutenant James Longstreet, rushing up with a flag in his hand, fell to the ground wounded, and the colors were caught up and carried forward by Lieutenant George Pickett.

On the left of Pillow's advance, Mexican musketry had cut down the men following Lieutenant Tom Jackson as he tried to manhandle a single gun forward. Alone among dead gunners and kicking horses, the tall young officer called to his vanished troops: "There's no danger! See, I'm not hit!"[73] But his gunners heard the peening of the enemy bullets and they returned only after more guns and a column of regulars appeared.

On the east, Quitman was attacking and taking heavy casualties. Colonel Ransom died, so did Major Levi Twiggs of the Marines. The fight was hand to hand, with crossed swords and clubbed muskets, and the Mexicans stood firm for a time. But then all gave way.

All but the cadets of the Mexican Military College, many of whom fought on to the death and entered Mexican history as *"Los Niños."* Six of them, aged 13 to 19, gave up their lives rather than surrender. One of these, 18-year-old Agustín Melgar, battled the Americans step by step, dueling with them up the stairways until he reached the roof of the college where American bayonets ended his gallant young life. Over his prostrate form stepped Lieutenant Pickett to haul down the green-red-and-white Mexican tricolor and run up the Red, White and Blue.

The men on the rooftop cheered. Below them other Americans already advancing along the causeways toward Mexico City also burst into huzzas. And from the plain of Mixcoac, some two miles to the south, came other cheers—but for the Mexicans.

At Mixcoac the last 30 of the Patricios condemned to death were waiting to be hanged. They sat hand-and-foot bound in wagons with ropes around their necks. They were to die the moment the American flag should fly above Chapultepec. Colonel Harney, who had learned the executioner's skill in Florida, where he ravished Indian girls by night, stringing them up to the limbs of oaks by day, had saved them for that moment. He was furious because, so far from showing contrition, they taunted and jeered him. When one of them sarcastically asked for a last pull on his pipe, Harney struck him in the mouth with his saber hilt. Spitting blood and teeth, the man mock-moaned: "Bad luck to yez! I shan't be able to hold a pipe in me mouth as long as I live!" About then the flag was seen, and as the Patricios roared with laughter, Colonel Harney, snarling curses, sent them to their death.

The battle was now a race for Mexico City, Quitman versus Worth. Quitman had the closer route, for he moved along the causeway running directly east to the Belén Gate. Worth had to follow one causeway north before turning hard east to drive on the San Cosmé Gate. General Scott had sent both generals reinforcements, personally joining Worth, accompanied by Captain Lee. But Captain Lee, on his feet or in the saddle for nearly three days without respite, suddenly fell from his horse exhausted and unconscious.

Both of the causeways the Americans followed carried an arched aqueduct down their middles while roadways ran to either side. Both were barricaded and covered with troops and artillery. Nevertheless, the Americans slugged ahead. At 1:20 P.M. Quitman's troops crashed through the Belén Gate into the city's outskirts. The Mexicans fought back from the massive Citadel and Belén Prison. They were led by Santa Anna, who had hurried north from his fruitless vigil in front of Twiggs. At Belén the Americans hung on desperately against mounting casualties.

Worth also took losses as he slugged north and then swung east. Once again the Americans began burrowing through houses with picks and crowbars. They drove up to the San Cosmé Gate. Alarmed, Santa Anna rushed to San Cosmé, but his presence made no difference. The Americans burst the barrier and kept on fighting after nightfall.

Aware, now, that Mexico City's defenses had been breached, Santa Anna returned to the Citadel at Belén. Here, in a council of war, he decided to evacuate the city. He still had 5,000 infantry and 400 cavalry, but he chose to move north to Guadalupe Hidalgo. Before he did, some 2,000 convicts were "liberated" to prey upon the invading gringos.

In the morning of September 14, 1847, General John Quitman prepared for a stiff fight at the Citadel. His left foot bare from the stress of the previous day's fighting, he was sending his units forward when a flag of truce appeared with notice of Santa Anna's flight. Quitman quickly took possession of the Citadel, and then, hearing that the freed prisoners were plundering the city, the half-shod Quitman put himself at the head of his men and marched into the Grand Plaza. He formed them on the great square in the shadow of the Cathedral and gave to the Marines the mission of cleaning the National Palace of thieves and vagabonds.

Atop the Palace itself, the legendary "Halls of Montezuma," Marine Lieutenant A. S. Nicholson cut down the Mexican flag and ran up the Stars and Stripes, unwittingly giving to his famous Corps the first line of its hymn. And then at eight o'clock in the morning there came the sound of bugles, the rising clatter of horses' hooves. General Winfield Scott, superbly mounted and splendidly uniformed, swept into the Plaza escorted by dragoons with bared sabers. His officers followed, his bands played, his soldiers presented arms and whooped, and even his Mexican audience waved handkerchiefs.

It was the high point of a great career, and Scott had earned it. He had led one of the most momentous fighting marches in all history. Cortez may have conquered Mexico City for Spain, but the Mexican nation is no longer Spanish; whereas Winfield Scott in conquering the same capital was the chief instrument in adding 1,193,061 square miles of territory—an area more than five times the size of France—to the national domain of the United States.

That area was ceded after Nicholas Trist negotiated the Treaty of Guadalupe Hidalgo, signed on February 2, 1848. Trist had been recalled by Polk, but after Santa Anna abdicated, Trist saw his opportunity and deliberately disobeyed orders. In return for the ceded land, the United States agreed to assume the unpaid claims and pay Mexico $15 million.

All this was achieved by a repudiated diplomat and a discredited general, for Polk the superb expansionist soon became "Little Jimmy Polk" the petty politician: he relieved Scott with a Democratic general and dismissed Trist from the State Department.

Nevertheless, except for Alaska the area of the continental United States was now rounded out. Now the "firebell in the night" could clang anew over whether the new lands should be slave or free. Almost all of the great protagonists in the dreadful debate lying ahead—especially the generals trained in the Mexican War—were on the scene. They were already taking sides and even changing tunes. One young Whig Congressman, in criticizing "Mr. Polk's War" as unconstitutional, discussed the right to revolt in terms that could never have fallen from his lips a decade later.

"Any people anywhere," he said, "being inclined and having the power have the right to rise up and shake off the existing government, and form a new one that suits them better. . . . Any portion of such people that can may revolutionize and make their own of so much of the territory as they inhabit."[74]

The name of the speaker was Abraham Lincoln.

PART ☆ V

The Civil War

1

☆

True to his word, President Polk did not seek re-election in 1848. In his place the Democrats nominated Lewis Cass of Michigan, an old soldier who had been with Hull at Detroit in 1812 and was then a veteran politician enrolled in that numerous company of Northerners with Southern sympathies. The Whigs, remembering their success with Tippecanoe, passed over Henry Clay once again and named Zachary Taylor.

Old Rough and Ready swept to victory assisted by a third party of Free-Soilers. Led by Martin van Buren, this coalition of antislavery Whigs and Democrats took enough New York votes away from Cass to give that vital state to Taylor. Thus, for the fourth time in its 60-year history, the antimilitarist American nation had bestowed its highest office on a military hero.

Taylor's inauguration in 1849 seemed to open what was literally an American Golden Age, for gold had already been discovered in California and hordes of fortune-hunting "forty-niners" were converging on the Sacramento Valley. It was glamorous with the gleaming white sails of the Yankee clipper ships, then the admiration of every sea, and it was bright with the hope rising in the breasts of thousands of Old World immigrants following new roads and railways west to fill up the vast and empty empire taken from Mexico and the Indians. The nation was prospering, too: in the North the Industrial Revolution gave manufactures a golden shove, while Europe's insatiable hunger for cotton crowned that staple king of the South. Eli Whitney's invention of the cotton gin seemed to have guaranteed that the South should have economic as well as political dominance over the North, and none but a few thoughtful Southerners noticed that it had also rescued the institution of slavery from the slow death they had desired for it. Nor had Manifest Destiny perished. It had yet another decade of bumptious life, calling itself Young America while its prophets cast covetous eyes on Cuba or lectured kings and emperors on their duty to abdicate in favor of the common man.

In truth, the common man in America seemed then to be the envy of the world. He was in fact what he has since become in legend: an independent small farmer dwelling in rural order and blissful plenty. He lived better than his father had and he confidently expected his son to live even better. In the old way, of course, because most Americans then expected the old ways to continue. They did not know—few Americans did—that new winds were blowing over the world and breaking up the old ways; nor could they have suspected that the fruits of the Mexican victory were already sour with sectional discord.

To organize the new territory was to reopen the old question of slavery expansion. The South, led by Calhoun, had long ago declared that the Missouri Compromise of 1820 prohibiting slavery in territories north of 36°30′ was unconstitutional. Congress, said Calhoun, not only had not the right to restrict slavery, it had the positive duty to protect it. Slaves were property, just like cattle, and a slaveowner had the right to take this property into any corner of the Union and to expect it to be protected there. Slavery, then, followed the flag.

Such was the Southern position, and although it begged the question of the morality of slavery, it was allowed to do so simply because both sides were engaged in a political-economic power struggle. First, the South feared to lose control of the government. There had been a time when the South hoped to continue in the ascendancy by gaining the allegiance of the new states now known as the Midwest through trade up and down the Mississippi River. But then the new railroads began tying the Midwest to Eastern ports. Calhoun saw clearly that the North, that is to say the Midwestern and Eastern states, was becoming stronger. Its population was skyrocketing: immigrants did not go south to compete with slave labor but stayed east or went west. If slavery were to be prohibited in the new territory north of the Missouri Compromise line, the ranks of the free-soil states would be swelled and the North would become invincibly powerful.

Thus the virus of sectionalism, which had weakened the United

States since colonial times. North and South were as different as people sharing the same language and generally the same religion and ancestry can be. The South was agricultural, the North industrial. The North wanted high import tariffs to protect its products against cheap European imports, while the South sought low tariffs or none at all so that it might import European goods in exchange for its cotton. Moreover, the South also planted crops with money borrowed in the North. Finally and most important, the agrarian debtor of the South employed slave labor while the capitalist creditor of the North hired free men. It may be, as the South came to maintain, that the wage-earner of the North often was little better than an industrial serf. He certainly had little bargaining power. But what he did have dignified him, it gave him political power at the ballot box, and the last thing he desired was to have this smallest corner of economic freedom threatened by the introduction of slave labor into the North.

Such differences were extreme enough, but they were eventually to be made even sharper and irreconcilable by the gradual shift of argument from an economic to a moral plane. Down deep the problem was moral. If slaves *were* property, then a slaveholder did have the right to take his slaves into any corner of the Union and expect the government to protect him in his possession of them there. But if it was wrong to make chattels of human beings, then at the very least the nation could not permit this evil to spread. Outright abolition, of course, was hardly even discussed by those Northern leaders who wished to preserve the Union. The South had some $2 billion invested in slaves and followed a way of life which despised labor as fit only for bondmen. Southerners considered their society superior to the North's, and it is highly doubtful that they would have accepted even compensatory emancipation—that is, to have the government repay them at the "market value" of their freed Negroes. To remove the "peculiar institution" from the fabric of Southern society was just not possible, because that fabric was woven with the thread of slavery. Northern leaders, then, recognized this seemingly ineluctable fact, just as they preferred to ignore or remain indifferent to the question of the morality of slavery.

The abolitionists of the North were not indifferent. At first they were temperate in their criticism of slavery. They considered it an incongruity in a free society and resented the fact that much of the South's political power sprang from the fact that three-fifths of the slave population was counted in apportioning slave-state representation. Gradually, however, the moderates gave way to extremists such as William Lloyd Garrison, who founded his antislave newspaper in 1831 with the declaration: "On this subject I do not wish to think, or speak, or write, with moderation. . . . I will be harsh as truth and as uncompromising as justice. . . . I am in earnest—I will not equivocate—I will not excuse—I will not retreat a single inch. AND I WILL BE HEARD."[1]

He was heard, and eventually the South began censoring abolitionist literature pouring through the mails and proposed a gag on antislavery petitions in Congress. But the abolitionist movement grew, and as it did it grew less temperate. In ever more strident tones its disciples denounced slavery as a crime and a curse and quoted the Bible as well as the Declaration of Independence to prove that all men were created equal. They harried the slave-catchers who were sent north by the masters of escaped slaves (and who sometimes also kidnaped free Negroes under the pretext that they were fugitives), and they organized the famous Underground Railroad by which escaped Negroes were passed from house to house at night until they reached some far Northern sanctuary or even crossed into Canada. They were not always popular in the North, these crusaders burning with a thirst for justice, and Ralph Waldo Emerson once advised them to love their neighbors a little more and their Negro brethren less. But they would not leave their more apathetic neighbors alone so long as slavery flourished in the United States. Hating bondage with such a fierce, deep hatred that they sometimes seemed just a little hateful themselves, disdaining compromise and ready to accept even disunion as a consequence of their goal of abolition, these fanatics nevertheless made more and more Americans realize that slavery was both a social injustice and a dreadful moral evil; and if they rubbed some delicate natures the wrong way, they also kept the public conscience awake.

They also drove the South to the position of defending slavery as a moral right and a social good. The glories of those ancient civilizations which had rested on slavery were extolled, while the Bible was quoted not only to sanction bondage but to demonstrate that God had deliberately created inferior races such as the Negroes to be the servants of superior people such as the white "cavaliers" of the South. In the South the wants of the Negroes were more than cared for, it was argued, while in the hypocritic North a wage-earner was rarely paid enough to purchase the necessities of life.

So the gap widened. More and more Southerners became willing to pick up the gauntlet of disunion thrown down by the abolitionists, and the South began to dream of a great slaveholding republic stretching from sea to sea. Then, in 1849, California decided to skip the territorial phase of organization and requested admission to the Union as a free-soil state with a constitution prohibiting slavery—and with that the South talked openly of secession.

Henry Clay, the "Great Pacificator" who had brought off the Missouri Compromise, came forward once again to preserve the Union. Clay realized that the Union was not yet ready to deal with secession. In January of 1850 he proposed a set of this-for-that compromises which touched off one of those great debates which have been characteristic of American history from the time of the Federalists to the Truman-MacArthur controversy during the Korean War.

It took place in the Senate, among the old lions—Clay, Calhoun, Webster—and such rising young leaders as Jefferson Davis of Mississippi, Stephen Douglas of Illinois, William Seward of New York and Salmon P. Chase of Ohio.

With all his conciliatory skill, Clay pleaded with the North not to insist on the Wilmot Proviso prohibiting slavery in the new territories, and to return fugitive slaves. He told the South that secession was not constitutional and would not be tolerated.

After Clay spoke, Calhoun's ultimatum was issued. "T have, Senators, believed from the first that the agitation of the subject of slavery would, if not prevented by some timely and effective measure, end in disunion."[2] The words were spoken by Calhoun's friend, Senator Mason of Virginia. Calhoun himself sat silent, wrapped in his cloak like a ghostly hawk, dying of catarrh. But his words were a clarion to the South: the North must "cease the agitation of the slave question."

Now it was the turn of Daniel Webster. It was his last great appearance. He spoke once again with that marathon grandiloquence which was typical of his time, with all his old oratorical skill: the thunderous voice and the imposing figure and massive head, the pointing finger and the questioning eye. "I wish to speak today," he began, "not as a Massachusetts man, not as a Northern man, but as an American. . . . I speak today for the preservation of the Union. 'Hear me for my cause.' "³ Webster supported Clay's compromise proposals, even a more stringent Fugitive Slave Law, repugnant as it was to him. And he warned the South that it could not expect secession without strife. "Sir, your eyes and mine are never destined to see that miracle! . . . There can be no such thing as a peaceable secession."⁴

Senator Seward, a spokesman for the antislavery faction, and a leader-to-be of the yet unborn Republican Party, opposed the compromise and appealed to "a higher law than the Constitution." Seward's appeal to the Almighty—which disgusted Webster—had little effect on the debate. Webster's masterly speech and the powerful support of Douglas of Illinois carried the day for what has been called the Compromise of 1850.

Resolutions was adopted providing (1) admission of California as a free-soil state; (2) organization of the territories of New Mexico (including Arizona) and Utah without reference to slavery; (3) a new and stringent fugitive slave law; (4) abolition of the slave trade in the District of Columbia.

President Taylor did not like the Compromise, and might have vetoed it—except that as the debate raged he fell victim to a combination of Fourth of July oratory and medical exuberance. After listening to a two-hour speech in the boiling sun, Old Zack tried to cool off with large helpings of cucumbers washed down with cold milk. He became ill with acute gastroenteritis, from which he might have recovered had not his doctors sprung to his side to stuff him full of calomel, opium, ipecac and quinine, after which they bled and blistered him until, on July 9, 1850, the Angel of Death came to his rescue.

His successor, Vice President Millard Fillmore of Buffalo, was a man more friendly to compromise. He was also the perfection of mediocrity. The measure of his outlook and insight was his expressed hope that the slavery question had reached its "final settlement."

Although the new Fugitive Slave Law all but silenced secessionist talk in the South, it stuck in Northern throats. "This filthy enactment," Emerson called it, and declared: "I will not obey it, by God."⁵ Actually the law defeated the purpose of the Compromise. In placating the South it infuriated the North, and thus guaranteed that "agitation of the slave question" would not cease—as the South demanded as the price of Union—but would increase. And then, in 1852, Harriet Beecher Stowe published *Uncle Tom's Cabin.*

No book written in America has even approached *Uncle Tom's Cabin* in its influence on American history.* Serialized in a magazine at first, each installment was eagerly awaited by millions of readers. In book form it sold 300,000 copies in less than a year, and eight presses were kept busy day and night catching up with the demand. *Uncle Tom* was also translated across the world, and plays based upon it gave additional millions the opportunity to hear Mrs. Stowe's message. Slavery, she said, debases all: master as well as slave and the society that permits it. She said this in a style that was ordinary, and through characters who were crude caricatures of the good and gentle Negro or the cruel, crass master, yet her theme erupted in the American conscience with titanic force; and after it was published it was no longer possible for Northerners to remain indifferent to slavery or for Southerners to pretend that the problem had been settled.

Alarmed and angered as the South was, it still kept its political head. In 1852, the year of *Uncle Tom's* publication, the all-powerful Democratic Party bowed to Southern wishes and nominated Franklin Pierce for President. Although Pierce was from New Hampshire, he was regarded as a "doughface," a Northern man with Southern principles. His opponent was his old military chief from Mexico City days, General Winfield Scott. The Whigs, torn by factions, had decided to go with the old war-hero formula again. But Franklin Pierce won by a margin wide enough to contain the corpse of the expiring Whig Party, and Scott's defeat—his second—seems to have demonstrated that except for the unique George Washington generals seeking to be President had better be rough-and-ready rather than full of fuss-and-feathers.

Pierce was the third mediocre President in a row. Without real convictions of his own and always persuaded by the last man to talk to him, especially if it was Secretary of War Jefferson Davis, he was the butt of friend and foe alike. Yet his was one of the stormiest of administrations, chiefly because Stephen Douglas, the Senator from Illinois who had once hailed the Missouri Compromise as a "sacred

---

* When Mrs. Stowe visited the White House during the Civil War, Lincoln greeted her with the remark: "So this is the little lady who made this big war."[6]

thing, which no ruthless hand would ever be reckless enough to disturb,"[7] lifted his own to kill it.

Stephen Arnold Douglas, the "Little Giant" from Illinois, five feet of plump bounce and brilliance, was a heavy speculator in Western lands and a presidential aspirant. On the first count he wanted the transcontinental railway to follow the central route from Chicago, and on the second he sought an explosive political issue for 1856.

To gain approval of the central railway route he needed the support of Southern Senators. So in a bill to divide the territory through which the railroad would pass into the future states of Kansas and Nebraska, he introduced the idea of "popular sovereignty." This meant that local residents could decide whether or not their regions would be free- or slave-soil. However, Nebraska and Kansas lay north of that Missouri Compromise line and were thus "forever" closed to slavery. In order to open them to that possibility, the "sacred" Missouri Compromise would have to be repealed. Douglas wanted this done by implication, but the Southern Senators whose support he needed for the central railway route insisted that it be repealed outright. Douglas consented, and when he did he got a political issue explosive enough to blast the Union in two.

Pride and passion, the twin terrors of human nature, were newly roused by the proposal to repeal the Missouri Compromise. This was the one agreement which had kept the peace between the sections for a generation. To attempt to overturn it, even to touch it, as Douglas seems to have known before he became blinded by ambition, was to break that peace. And it was broken: Southern pride now demanding that slavery follow the flag further inflamed Northern passion already aroused by the Fugitive Slave Act.

Yet Democratic party discipline pushed the Kansas-Nebraska Act through Congress, and the Compromise was repealed.

Next day in Boston an angry mob tried to prevent the return of a fugitive slave. A battalion of artillery, four platoons of marines and 22 companies of militia were required to get the runaway down to the ship. Thousands of civilians lined the streets, hissing and groaning and crying, "Kidnapers! Kidnapers!" Buildings were hung with crepe and church bells tolled—tolled the death of the Fugitive Slave Act, for henceforth in the hardening antislavery North a man felt it was his duty not to obey that law but to violate it.

Douglas's moral obtuseness had another result. On February 28, 1854, antislavery forces had met in a schoolhouse at Ripon, Wisconsin, to recommend formation of a "Republican party." On July 6, 1854, that party was formally organized at Jackson, Michigan. Beneath its standard were gathered Whigs, Free-Soilers and anti-Nebraska Democrats. That very fall these new Republicans gained a majority in the House, an astonishingly rapid victory that was in great part due to the scandal of "bleeding Kansas."

Even before the Kansas-Nebraska bill became law, proslavery groups had moved into Kansas from Missouri and antislavery colonists began preparing to enter the territory. Both sides sent representatives to Congress, both sides drew up constitutions and awaited admission to the Union—and both sides were armed. Civil war was the result: a small-scale dress rehearsal for the titanic conflict that was to convulse the nation. On balance, the proslavery "border ruffians," as the Free-Soilers called them, seemed to have been guilty of more violence; although the antislavery settlers from the Ohio Valley were far from adverse to squeezing the triggers of the new and accurate breech-loading Sharpe's rifles they carried. "Popular sovereignty" had become not a matter of voting slavery in or out by ballot but of shooting it either way by bullet. In Washington a Northern Senator placed the blame for this tragedy squarely on the shoulders of the South.

Senator Charles Sumner of Massachusetts made the accusation on May 19, 1856, in his sensational speech, "The Crime Against Kansas." Sumner sought to prevent the admission of Kansas as a slave state. As insensitive and insulting as he was eloquent and erudite, Sumner excoriated the "Slave Power" and directly impugned Douglas and Senator Butler of South Carolina. A few days later Butler's nephew, Representative Preston Brooks, walked up to Sumner in the Senate Chamber and caned him into bloody insensibility.

Now the North erupted in wrathful indignation again. Its passion had already been inflamed by the news that on May 21 a proslavery mob had sacked the antislavery settlement of Lawrence, Kansas, and on May 24 its own answer of violence was given by a lantern-jawed egomaniac named John Brown. His was an Old Testament creed of an eye-for-an-eye, a tooth-for-a-tooth, and after the Lawrence bloodletting he told his four sons and three other followers that "something must be done to show these barbarians that we too have rights."[8]

Then, presumably in the name of the civilized and righteous, these eight men lifted old artillery broadswords and stole off to a proslavery settlement at Pottawatomie Creek where they hacked to death five innocent men who had actually come to Kansas to get away from slavery.

Now it was the South that seethed with rage. The name John Brown was uttered like an epithet, just as "damn-Yankee" became a single word and a curse. The gulf between the sections widened: Southerners traveling in the North felt uneasy, Northerners visiting the South sensed hostility. In the South especially there developed a rising current of nationalism. Students enrolled in Northern schools came home to study, the myth of the "Cavalier" South and the peasant or plebeian North was extended and exaggerated, and Southerners were exhorted to eschew all that was not of Southern origin. In effect, two distinct nations were beginning to emerge within the boundaries of the United States. The North would not—could not—cease agitating the slavery question; and the South, driven back on herself, grew ever more rigid and inflexible in slavery's defense. The cleavage even cut the Baptist and Methodist churches into Northern and Southern branches. Even had a conciliator such as Henry Clay been alive, a reconciliation would have been impossible.

Yet the sectional showdown was avoided for another four years because the Democrats gave the South another "doughface" for President. This time it was James Buchanan of Pennsylvania, for neither Franklin Pierce nor his party desired his renomination. The "black Republicans" named John Charles Frémont, a national idol whose sobriquet of "Pathfinder" has been modified by modern historians to "Pathmarker." Frémont's campaign slogan was: "Free speech, free soil and Frémont." If he had won, the South probably would have seceded then and there. But victory went to the ponderously vacillating Buchanan, the fourth successive mediocrity to occupy the White House and the one who, having done most to get there, did least after his arrival. Nevertheless, the sectional storms were also to howl around his ears—and this was because even before his inauguration he connived at the Dred Scott decision.

Dred Scott was a Negro slave whose master took him from Missouri to Illinois and Minnesota Territory for two years. Upon his return, Scott sued for liberty in the Missouri courts on the ground that residence in a free state and a territory north of the Missouri

Compromise line automatically conferred freedom on him. The case reached the U.S. Supreme Court, and Buchanan and Chief Justice Taney with four Southern justices saw in it the opportunity to extend slavery throughout the nation. In a decision announced March 6, 1857, only a few days after Buchanan took office, the Court denied Dred Scott's claim on three grounds: (1) Negroes could not be United States citizens, therefore they could not sue in federal courts; (2) the laws of Illinois could not affect him in Missouri, where he now lived; (3) his residence in Minnesota Territory north of the Missouri Compromise line could not confer freedom because the Compromise was unconstitutional.

The Dred Scott decision shook the North like a thunderclap, and the area simply refused to be guided by it. Legislatures repudiated it and New York proclaimed the freedom of any slave who reached its precincts and promised up to ten years in prison to anyone who even passed through the state attended by a slave. To the young Republican Party the decision brought another increase of power, while to the South it brought determination to ram Kansas into the Union as a slave state.

In that year of 1857 the free-soil residents of Kansas outnumbered the proslavery settlers by nearly ten to one. Yet the Senate had rejected an antislavery constitution for the state-to-be and accepted one permitting bondage. Here Stephen Douglas, who had done so much to unsettle the Union, rose to the heights to preserve it. He led the fight to allow the people of Kansas the right to vote on the proslavery constitution, and when they rejected it by a margin of six to one they fulfilled the Little Giant's prediction: "Kansas is to be a free State."[9] For his stand on principle, Douglas became known as "a traitor to the South." In the following year, 1858, Douglas ran for re-election to the Senate against the surprisingly strong opposition of a rising Republican lawyer named Abraham Lincoln.

But for his gangly tall frame and his uncommonly homely face, Abraham Lincoln might have been just another prairie lawyer-politician. He was a Whig who had been to the Illinois legislature and been to Congress, where his opposition to the Mexican War cost him his seat in the House. He looked upon slavery as an evil, but he also regarded abolitionist agitation as harmful to the Union. The South could have its institution, Lincoln thought, but it should not be allowed to extend it. Holding this conviction, common enough among Whig Free-Soilers, Lincoln retired from politics in 1849.

In 1854 the Kansas-Nebraska Act brought him back, and he was a different man. Now he was attacking the morality of slavery itself: "Slavery is founded on the selfishness of man's nature—opposition to it in his love of justice. These principles are in eternal antagonism, and when brought into collision so fiercely as slavery extension brings them, shocks and throes and convulsions must ceaselessly follow."[10] Three years later, as a Republican, Lincoln attacked the Dred Scott decision as a reversal of the principles of the Declaration of Independence, and then, on June 16, 1858, he said:

" 'A house divided against itself cannot stand.'

"I believe this government cannot endure permanently half slave and half free.

"I do not expect the Union to be dissolved—I do not expect the house to fall—but I do expect it will cease to be divided.

"It will become all one thing or all the other.

"Either the opponents of slavery will arrest the further spread of it and place it where the public mind shall rest in the belief that it is in the course of ultimate extinction; or its advocates will push it forward until it shall become alike lawful in all the States, old as well as new, North as well as South."[11]

With this speech Lincoln became the Republican candidate challenging the Democrat, Douglas. Eventually the two agreed to discuss the issues in a series of debates across the state. Famous for their cogency, the Lincoln-Douglas Debates might be equally celebrated for the contrasts in the debaters. Here was Douglas, a bristling bulldog dressed in fine clothes, the man of power and position riding into town on a special train and very likely firing off signal cannon to herald his arrival. There was Lincoln, six feet four inches tall, his big bony hands and feet sticking out from his ill-fitting trousers as he awkwardly rides a horse toward the platform. If anyone impresses, it is Douglas, with his powerful bark and sure movements of the hands; but then, as one observer reported, Lincoln speaks and "his eye glows and sparkles, every lineament, now so ill-formed, grows brilliant and expressive, and you have before you a man of rare power and of strong magnetic influence."[12] His rough good humor softens the bite but not the point of his logic and he "*takes* the people every time."[13]

The outstanding meeting was at Freeport, where 15,000 people heard Lincoln ask Douglas how he could square his doctrine of popular sovereignty with the Dred Scott decision that slavery follows the flag. Douglas replied that residents of a Territory had it in their power to prevent or protect slavery by local police regulations. This was the "Freeport Doctrine" by means of which Douglas sidestepped the moral issue of the right or wrong of slavery. It guaranteed his reelection, but also so mortally offended the South that he lost all chance of gaining the Democratic presidential nomination in 1860.

In the intervening period, the North continued to agitate and the South to protest until fanatical old John Brown ended all hope of moderation.

"Caution, sir!" John Brown had growled before his Pottawatomie Massacre. "I am eternally tired of hearing that word caution. It is nothing but the word of cowardice."[14]

Coward he was not, maniac he was—and on the night of October 16, 1859, he and his followers again lifted their avenging swords and attacked and seized the federal arsenal at Harpers Ferry, Virginia. Their hope was to take the captured arms southward to stir up a revolt of Negro slaves, but the reality was that Colonel Robert E. Lee and a company of marines rushed to Harpers Ferry to overwhelm Brown and take him prisoner.

Within two weeks John Brown was brought to trial and convicted of insurrection, murder and treason. On December 2, 1859, content "to die for God's eternal truth," he was hanged.

In John Brown the Northern extremists saw a noble martyr while their Southern counterparts saw the embodiment of all their fears. "He wanted to arm the slaves!" secessionists said, in effect, to moderates and Unionists. "That's what the North *really* wants." It made no difference that most Northern newspapers and leaders from Douglas to Lincoln denounced Brown's acts as lawless; the voices that the South heard were those of the firebrands shouting that John Brown had been sacrificed on the altar of slavery. Not many Northerners seem to have understood the full extent of Brown's plans to raise the slaves. His earlier murders at Pottawatomie were either forgotten or ignored. Even so serene a sage as Emerson lost his customary balance long enough to hail "that new saint . . . [who] will make the gallows glorious like the cross."[15]

But John Brown left no legacy of love; rather he put hatred in the saddle and sent it galloping wildly across the land. In the South the radicals had complete control when the Democratic Party held its convention in April, 1860. They tried to "stop" Douglas, and failed; tried to get a proslavery platform adopted, and failed—and then, as had been concerted beforehand, eight Southern delegations walked out. Douglas was easily nominated, but the renegade Southerners countered by nominating their own candidate, John C. Breckenridge of Kentucky. A more moderate group named John Bell of Tennessee.

Ironically, the Southern radicals, dreading the triumph of the antislavery Republicans, had guaranteed their victory. They knew as well as Douglas that a divided Democratic Party had no chance. Yet they split it. Why? Probably because the Southerners believed that their backs were to the wall and that now it was a case of rule or ruin. It has been said that the South hoped that a "deadlock" in the Electoral College might throw the decision into Congress where Southern parliamentary skill would produce a proslavery President. But this was truly a hopeless hope. More likely the South believed that the gauntlet had to be thrown down and for the last time.

In May of 1860 the Republican Party named Abraham Lincoln of Illinois as its candidate. Seward of New York had come to the convention confident of victory, but Lincoln and his managers cleverly trotted out "Honest Abe" in the homey garb of "the rail-splitter" while making the customary behind-the-scenes political deals to gain real support. Lincoln won on the third ballot, and some Southern states announced that his election would be tantamount to secession.

Lincoln was elected. On December 20, 1860, South Carolina seceded from the Union. A few weeks later she was followed out by Mississippi, Alabama, Georgia, Florida, Louisiana and Texas. On February 8, 1861, delegates from the seven seceded states met in Montgomery, Alabama, to form the Confederate States of America and to name Jefferson Davis as its first President.

It had come. Innate differences dividing Northern and Southern societies from their very beginnings had pushed the two sections farther and farther apart until at last Southern pride and Northern passion had cut the last remaining bonds. As Mrs. Mary Chesnut of South Carolina was to say: ". . . we are divorced, North from South, because we have hated each other so."[16]

2

☆

Secession was a fact; the question now was: Would there be war?

In the new Confederacy war was not desired. The South wished to be free to consolidate and to gain recognition and allies among those European nations who were both dependent on her cotton and eager to see the American experiment in self-rule come to a ruinous end.

In the North the Federal government floundered because of the deficiencies of President Buchanan and a system which placed four long months between a President's election and his inauguration.* Lincoln could do nothing until March 4, 1861, and Buchanan—beguiled by the Southerners in his Cabinet—did next to nothing until then because he also feared to provoke powerful Virginia into joining the Confederacy.

There were, of course, movements toward reconciliation, but these were torpedoed by hotheads and even the famous Crittenden Proposals were unacceptable to Lincoln because they included the extension of slavery to the Pacific. In the meantime, the governors of seceded states seized Federal mints, forts, shipyards, customhouses and other installations. In Texas, "Old Davey" Twiggs ignominiously handed over all his posts with their men and equipment without firing a shot and while still wearing the sash of a United States general. Eventually the South held all but three of the Federal forts in the Confederacy—and one of these three was Sumter off the Charleston coast.

Fort Sumter was still in Union hands while Abraham Lincoln traveled slowly from Illinois to Washington to take possession of his House Divided. He had been advised to crush the Confederacy or to let "our erring sisters depart in peace," and the New York *Herald*

---

* March 4 remained the inauguration date until Franklin Roosevelt began his second term on January 20, 1936.

had also advised him to resign in favor of a more "acceptable" man
or else "totter into a dishonored grave . . . leaving behind him a memory more execrable than that of [Benedict] Arnold."[17] In the South
similar voices of sweet reason were shouting: "Resistance to Abraham
Lincoln is obedience to God."[18] So the cleft nation, its eyes on Sumter,
awaited Lincoln's speech for omens of war or peace. Lincoln clearly
stated that he intended to preserve the Union, but he also told the
South:

> In your hands, my dissatisfied fellow-countrymen, and not in mine, is
> the momentous issue of civil war. The government will not assail you.
> You can have no conflict without yourself being the aggressors. You
> have no oath registered in heaven to destroy the government, while I
> shall have the most solemn one to "preserve, protect, and defend" it.[19]

Having uttered these magnificent words, Lincoln did little to back
them up. For weeks he vacillated nearly as badly as Buchanan. But
then he made up his mind to hold the Federal forts and especially
Sumter. Troops and provisions were collected for Sumter's relief.
Yet Lincoln was careful to inform the South that no troops would
land unless provisioning was resisted or the fort was fired upon.
Clearly, the new President was adhering to the American principle
of allowing the other side to strike the first blow.

The South, also loath to be the aggressor, hesitated. But the South
had Virginia and other wavering slave states to be considered. Strike
a blow, some men urged, fire a shot—and Virginia and the rest will
be inside the Confederacy within an hour. On April 10, Jefferson
Davis ordered General P. G. T. Beauregard*—the old campaigner
from Mexico City—to demand Sumter's surrender and to seize it
should he be refused. He was refused, by Major Robert Anderson of
Kentucky, who loved both North and South and had no heart to see
them fight. However, Anderson also admitted that his lack of supplies would soon force him to capitulate, and Beauregard telegraphed
this information to the Confederate government. Still reluctant to
start a civil war, the South now instructed Beauregard to hold off
the bombardment if Anderson would specify at what date he would
evacuate the fort.

Anderson replied to this by saying that he could not hold out past

---

* For clarity, the names of Confederate leaders henceforth will be printed
in capitals and small capitals.

April 15 unless he received prior instructions from his government or additional supplies. The men who heard this answer were young firebrands, empowered to determine whether or not it was satisfactory. They decided that it was not and so informed Anderson. He told them courteously that if he did not see them again in this world he hoped to meet them in Heaven, and they returned to Charleston.

At 4:30 A.M. in the morning of April 12, 1861, a red speck rose from a mortar on the Charleston shore. It could be clearly seen describing its fiery loop, going up and over, coming down with a whoosh and exploding over Fort Sumter.

The Civil War had begun.

The shots fired at Sumter—and the fort's fall the following day—-outraged and unified the North. The flag had been fired upon, that was treason, and now the cry arose: "The Union forever!" The issue of slavery was all but forgotten as the drums beat the patriotic pulse higher and young men rushed to answer Lincoln's call for 75,000 90-day volunteers.

Sumter also electrified the South, and there was a surge of Southern youth to fulfill President DAVIS's earlier call for 100,000 men. As expected, Sumter brought Virginia into the Confederacy, followed by Arkansas, North Carolina and Tennessee. But then there was a secession in reverse: the non-slaveholders of Virginia's western mountains, long resentful of slaveholder domination, organized their territory into a loyal section that was admitted to the Union in 1863 as the state of West Virginia.

Like the North, the South ignored the slavery issue. "States' rights!" was her rallying cry. The Union was merely a loose compact of states with nothing sacred about it, any member of which had the right to secede. To prevent secession was unjust, it was an invasion of the South. Thus both sides unconsciously sidestepped the very issue which had divided them. In the South it was probably easier to get men to fight for "our rights" rather than for the institution many of them instinctively despised, and in the North most of the abolitionists were cheerleaders at heart and the true fighting men would rather risk their flesh for the sacred Union than for distant Negroes whom they loved as little as their Southern opponents. This is not to mock the motives of the men of the Civil War armies. No soldiers were ever more noble or idealistic; but Johnny Reb did not put on Confederate gray or butternut to fight for Southern chivalry any more than Billy Yank vested himself in Union blue to stamp out slavery.

But with what a mixture of highhearted gaiety and religious fervor did they go to war! Farmer's sons, most of them, with a generous leaven of Germans and Irish—especially in the North—they cheered and sang and swore such mild oaths as "dang" and "durn," carrying their Bibles in breast pockets to ward off enemy bullets and attending daily services where they prayed—especially in the South—with a fervor unequaled since the Puritans of Oliver Cromwell.

In them aristocratic paternalism was meeting democratic nationalism, and if most of them found this conflict difficult to grasp, all of them regarded their own cause as sacred. In the North fathers presented swords to their sons with the command to bring them back stained to the hilt, while kneeling officers wept to receive regimental colors from the hands of little girls garlanded with flowers. In the South "gentlemen privates" enrolled themselves and their horses beneath the new nation's bold red banner—the colorful Stars and Bars, as pretty a flag as ever caught the wind—and a man's capacity to command was measured by the number of bales of cotton stacked on his wharf. Dixie, it would seem, had little need for the first conscription law in American history: the Southern woman was the Confederacy's recruiting sergeant. Mother, wife, sister, sweetheart, "she was the South's incarnate pride,"[20] and it was her smile the soldier sought, her stony contempt the slacker feared.

Once again regiments of "Guards" and "Zouaves" and "Tigers" and "Invincibles" in colorful uniforms followed the tap of the drum and the squeal of the fife into camp, but now they were peeling off into rival armies, flocking to state capitals above and below the Mason-Dixie Line, surrounding Washington and the new Confederate capital of Richmond 100 miles south with serried rows of tents. On both sides the armies were raised by calling upon the states to furnish militia to be enrolled in Federal or Confederate service. As is customary in American military history, both sides envisioned a short spectacular land war (although the Union Navy did possess 40 seagoing ships, on the strength of which President Lincoln proclaimed a blockade), and both sides thought themselves prepared.

They were not, of course. Until March, 1861, the South had no army; and the Federal Army was a splendid 16,000 strong, barely enough to police the frontier and man the coastal guns. Each side also thought itself superior, blinding itself to the other's advantages.

In fairness, it is hard to blame the North for her confidence. After all, in 19 Northern states lived nearly 19 million people, compared to 9 million in 11 Confederate states. In the North were nine-tenths of the nation's industrial power, two-thirds of its rails with most of its rail manufacturing capacity, most of its mineral resources, and a growing surplus of foodstuffs which, through Northern sea power, could be exported to Europe just as surely as the Southern exportation of cotton could be cut off. In the end, finding the right combination of political and military genius, such advantages had to be overwhelming. But in the beginning they blunted political and military judgment and were also offset by certain Southern superiorities either unseen or unsuspected.

Foremost were Southern courage and zeal. Next came its feudal society, which by its very structure, like the French Canada of Frontenac and Montcalm, lent itself to the martial spirit and rapid mobilization. Then, much as the proportion of slave population might seem to reduce the South's actual strength in fighting men, it also produced a stable labor force while freeing almost every white male between 16 and 60 for duty in the field. Another hidden advantage was that the South would be fighting a defensive war, thus requiring the North to mass a larger army and risk the higher casualties which usually befall the invader. The North, of course, *had* to attack. Lincoln desired to preserve the Union and to do this he had to crush the Confederacy. The South was fighting to defend herself until that magic moment in history when King Cotton—as JEFFERSON DAVIS so fondly and foolishly kept on hoping—would force the nations of Europe to intervene on her side. In this defensive war, then, the South possessed the advantage of interior lines and terrain which the god of war had made for defensive fighting. It was in this very crosshatch of hills and gullies, of swamps and forests and mountains laced with curling, racing rivers, that Nathanael Greene had taught Lord Cornwallis the lesson of his military life. To defend such eminently defensible terrain the South possessed commanders of a quality equal to Greene. Chief among them was ROBERT E. LEE. One of the heroes of the Mexican War, LEE had refused command of the Northern armies proffered him by his old chief, General Winfield Scott, with the remark that he would only draw his sword in defense of his native Virginia. After that state seceded, LEE became a Confederate general, joining the distinguished company of BEAUREGARD, the two JOHNSTONS, both HILLS, LONGSTREET, STONEWALL JACKSON and many others. Never, before or since, has a nascent nation possessed such swords with which to cut its course in history; and yet they had once been Federal officers!

The U.S. Army, while compelling its enlisted men to remain loyal, had permitted its officers to resign, and about 270 of 900 followed their conscience South. Moderns might well gasp at such a mad and noble gesture, for no modern government would do less than imprison commanders of such proven worth and plain disloyalty. But this was the last of the gentlemanly wars, and the Union, recognizing that a man's first loyalty was to his conscience and his God, not yet committed to the brutal logic of total war, permitted them to go. Thus, at garrisons across the nation, men in the same uniform exchanged toasts of farewell and wrung each other's hands while their wives exchanged misty-eyed kisses, all knowing that the next meeting would be on the battlefield with unsheathed swords. Thus the South gained one of its greatest assets, and the Civil War one of its chief characteristics: the commanders frequently knew each other and made moves based on that knowledge.

Another Confederate asset seemed to be its President, JEFFERSON DAVIS. He, too, was a military man, a West Pointer, veteran of Mexico, and Secretary of War under Franklin Pierce. Tall, thin, handsome in an ascetic way, he was a man carved of stone, a creature who might be broken but never bent, and he was the apotheosis of mansion and magnolia just as Abraham Lincoln was the embodiment of prairie and melting pot. Like Lincoln he had been born in Kentucky, and at about the same time that the child Abraham was being taken North to become the leader of the new nationalism, the child JEFFERSON was being taken South to become the spokesman of embattled aristocracy. But DAVIS was not the military asset he was thought to be: he treated his Secretary of War as a clerk, quarreled with such capable officers as JOE JOHNSTON and BEAUREGARD, and kept the military reins so tightly in his own hands that it was not until the war's end that LEE received the powers of general in chief. DAVIS's grand strategy was also errant in imposing an embargo on cotton exports in the belief that this would create such a demand that England, at least, would go to war on the Confederate side just to get cotton. But the fact was that Europe had built up a backlog of cotton supplies and later found new sources in India and Egypt. If the Confederacy had rushed her bumper crops to Europe in 1861, she might have obtained the money to buy badly needed munitions. But she did not, nor did the timid Confederate Congress levy any taxes that year; and here was another unseen Southern weakness.

States' rights, the very cause, would help to kill the Confederacy. By what right, stormed a Governor BROWN of Georgia or a Governor VANCE of North Carolina, did the central government presume to seize state supplies or enforce taxes? DAVIS, agreeing with them in principle, could only answer: none. He was so much the man of abstract conviction, of high unbending principle, that he could not see that the revolution he was leading required revolutionary tactics. States' rights could only be protected by insisting on a temporary cession of them. This, however, DAVIS refused to accept; and as the South's chief executive remained forbearing, its Congress stayed timid.

Thus, as Southern terrain, tacticians and society offset Northern industrialism, population and resources, so the lack of cohesion in the Confederacy was the equal of Lincoln's own struggles with Peace Democrats and radical, antislavery Republicans. But there was one other Southern disadvantage, and that was the South's complete contempt for the North's fighting prowess. To too many Southern commanders the "damn-Yankees" were a crowd of cunning rabbits who could not and would not fight. Probably the most perfect expression of this foaming contempt was the "Southern Series" of mathematical problems worked out by the educator-general, D. H. HILL. For example: "A Yankee mixes a certain quantity of wooden nutmegs, which cost him one-fourth cent apiece, with a quantity of real nutmegs, worth four cents apiece . . ."; or "Buena Vista is six and a half miles from Saltillo. Two Indiana volunteers ran away from the field of battle at the same time. . . ."[21] Such a habit of mind—the eternal autocrat despising the "frivolity" of free men—is bound to cripple judgment, and it did.

Fervor, hatred and overconfidence, then, were the hallmarks of the Civil War then beginning in April of 1861. Because of these it became the most ferocious and bloody war in American history: 540,000 deaths out of a total white population of 25 million. Yet it might have been worse had it been a true civil war in which the entire population, civil as well as military, rends itself. In most civil wars the strife is internal as the factions seize or hold regions from which they seek to extend their influence. It is not only brother against brother but neighbor against neighbor. The American Civil War, however, was unique in that not only two different forms of society but two separate nations fought each other. Each was a geographical entity and each had sufficient resources to make war. True enough, in this war fathers fought sons and brothers split off into rival camps, but not to any degree comparable to, say, the Spanish Civil War. In America no city or region divided into factions, each bathing the other in blood. South and North were both solid, with every state, city and town remaining loyal; and although spies proliferated on both sides, there were no governors or generals standing ready to betray.

Only in the border states was there the possibility of internal strife.

No single factor in the Civil War was more determining than possession of the slaveholding border states of Maryland, Kentucky and Missouri. When war broke out, their allegiance was divided: some people were strong for secession, others for Union. How they swung was vital. If it was South, then the Confederacy's frontiers would be advanced to the Ohio River, the Northwest would be menaced and the Federal capital at Washington would become a Northern island in a Southern sea. If they went North, then they aimed a Union dagger at the heart of the Confederacy.

Maryland forced the issue when, on April 19, a mob of Southern sympathizers collided with a Massachusetts militia regiment marching crosstown through Baltimore to change trains for Washington. Bricks and paving stones were hurled at the startled soldiers. Pistols were fired at them. They answered with muskets. Four soldiers and 12 civilians were killed. On to Washington moved the Northern troops, the bodies of their fallen packed in ice for martyrs' burial at home; and after they departed, pro-South mobs blew the railroad bridges linking Washington and the North and cut the telegraph. Washington was isolated. There were rumors that BEAUREGARD was marching on the capital at the head of 100,000 men. There was even talk among the fainthearted of replacing the "feeble" Lincoln with a dictator. Lincoln, however, could play that hard-handed role himself.

He sent troops under Major General Benjamin Butler, a devious, cross-eyed Bay State politician-turned-soldier, into Baltimore. Butler restored the bridges and arrested the mayor, 19 state legislators and numerous other secession-minded Marylanders and threw them into jail. When Chief Justice Taney issued a writ of habeas corpus for one of these improperly imprisoned men, Lincoln merely ignored it. Bullets, not legal briefs, were now defending the Constitution; and by this and other dictatorial moves Lincoln kept Maryland firmly in the Federal camp.

West Virginia was kept there, too, after the young and brilliant Major General George McClellan defeated a Confederate force which had come there to reclaim it for the South. Though minor, this action was decisive—and in McClellan's Napoleonic prose it became a major victory.

Farther west, the Union moved softly. Kentucky was Unionist both in its people and its legislature, but secessionist Governor MAGOFFIN tried to hold off the North by issuing a proclamation of neutrality. Lincoln did move against MAGOFFIN because Kentucky would probably go as Missouri went, and there the Union cause was progressing.

Secessionist Governor CLAIBORNE JACKSON and Captain Nathaniel Lyon were the antagonists in Missouri. Lyon, a pugnacious little redhead and a born revolutionary, had not the rank to match JACKSON. That belonged to General William Harney, the bluff, red-necked old cavalryman who had hung the Patricios at Mexico City. But Harney could not believe that Governor JACKSON coveted the Federal arsenal as a means of controlling the state. Captain Lyon did, and so did his associate, Frank Blair, whose brother sat in Lincoln's Cabinet. Through Blair's influence, General Harney was called out of St. Louis so that Captain Lyon might confront Governor JACKSON.

JACKSON began the struggle by calling out about 700 Missouri militia and putting them into camp near St. Louis on the pretext of drilling them. Captain Lyon concluded otherwise. He disguised himself as a woman and clattered into camp in a carriage, a basket of eggs on his lap and beneath the eggs a half-dozen loaded revolvers. Lyon saw enough to convince him that JACKSON was preparing to seize the arsenal and take Missouri out of the Union. Returning to St. Louis, he began swearing the city's numerous Germans into the Federal service. With them, and with a few companies of regulars, he surrounded the militia and forced them to surrender.

All went peacefully enough, until Lyon attempted to march his prisoners into town through gathering crowds of angry secessionists. As in Baltimore, civilian pistols were fired, then military muskets—

and before nightfall the cobblestones of St. Louis were stained with the lifeblood of 28 Americans. Still, Lyon had kept the Federal arsenal in Federal hands, and by the middle of June he had driven Governor JACKSON out of the state capital and placed Missouri temporarily, if not firmly, in the Federal camp.

The struggle for the border states was not fully appreciated by either side. In the South sectional pride exaggerated the importance of the Confederate victory at Big Bethel, Virginia, in the first skirmish of the war, and the North did the same with McClellan's triumph in West Virginia. Both sides were also mesmerized by the cries of "On to Richmond!" or "Forward to Washington!" They believed that capture of the enemy's capital, not destruction of his army or his will to fight, would end the war.

Winfield Scott was not so misled. Still general in chief at a dropsical 75, Scott advised Lincoln that "300,000 men under an able general might carry the business through in two or three years."[22] Scott's plan was to seize New Orleans while sealing up the Southern ports, after which one large army would move down the Mississippi and cut the Confederacy in two while another menaced Richmond and so contained the Southern forces in Virginia. This, in effect, is the plan that was eventually adopted. It provided for nothing less than strangulation of the enemy economy, but because this took time, men and money, Lincoln would have none of it. After it was made public, the same press that had howled at Winfield Scott as "Marshal Tureen" derided his "Anaconda Plan." For some reason—perhaps because he sat too tall in the saddle—Winfied Scott's countrymen found him uproariously funny. So the nation clamored for immediate action, and on July 4 the New York *Tribune* thundered: "Forward to Richmond! Forward to Richmond! The Rebel Congress must not be allowed to meet there on the 20th of July! By that date the place must be held by the National Army!"[23]

Lincoln the politician had to heed such voices. Moreover, his own capital seemed to be threatened by the force gathering in Virginia under BEAUREGARD. So he directed Brigadier General Irvin McDowell to move quickly against the Confederates.

Irvin McDowell was no better and no worse than the run of generals available to the Union cause that summer of 1861. Tall and

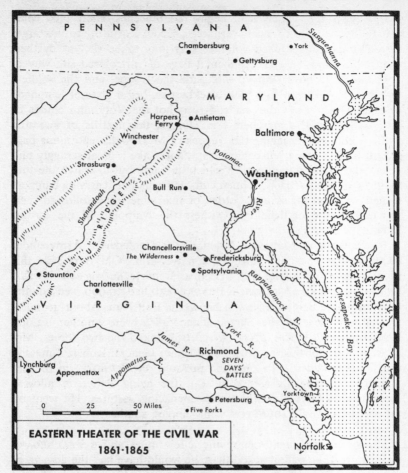

EASTERN THEATER OF THE CIVIL WAR
1861-1865

handsome, tailor-made for statues, he was a bluff, hearty man famed for his gargantuan appetite. (He once polished off a huge meal by consuming an entire watermelon that he found "Monstrous fine!") Like every Civil War leader save Winfield Scott, he had never commanded large bodies of troops. Still, he was a fighter, and he ordered his 35,000-man army to move south on July 16.

It was a parade of amateurs, this gaudy, straggling procession of half-trained 90-day men. It was American innocence marching to its grave. Here were Zouaves in baggy red breeches, short blue coats and yellow or scarlet sashes, veritable peacocks strutting to the target area. With them marched volunteers in gray to be shot at by their own men. Bands played, regimental flags of varicolored silk waved, dogs and little boys skipped alongside the troops, and the soldiers themselves broke ranks to pick blackberries, beg a glass of lemonade or take a breather in the shade. It was hot that July, and clouds of dust settled on the marchers and clogged the nostrils of sweating mules and horses dragging the wagons of McDowell's enormous baggage train stretching out behind his infantry like a great scraggly tail. A few days later the elite of Washington came out to watch the fun. By gig and on horseback, in linen cuffs and crinoline, carrying hampers stuffed with delicacies and bottles of fine wine, they followed their warriors to the battlefield to witness the whipping of the upstart Rebels.

Below them at Manassas Junction, the Confederate Army under BEAUREGARD was only hardly less naïve. But "Old Bory," as this broad-shouldered soldier with the imperial mustache was called, was a little less green than McDowell. BEAUREGARD had 20,000 men holding a ten-mile line behind a stream known as Bull Run. About 40 miles to the northwest in the Shenandoah Valley were another 12,000 Rebels under JOE JOHNSTON. A railroad linked the two forces. McDowell, aware of this, had instructed Major General Robert Patterson with 18,000 Federals to keep the pressure on JOHNSTON to prevent him from joining BEAUREGARD. But the aging Patterson allowed JOHNSTON to bluff him with a few menacing gestures. He went on the defensive, while JOHNSTON went slipping southeast.

McDowell arrived at Centreville a few miles above BEAUREGARD on July 18. If he had attacked then, he would have had the advantage of numbers. But he frittered away two days while JOHNSTON reinforced BEAUREGARD. When he did attack, on July 21, 1861, the two forces were nearly even.

Both commanders planned to strike each other's left, and it was the Federals who got there first. Hours late, two Union infantry divisions with artillery and a handful of cavalry crossed Bull Run above BEAUREGARD's lightly held left and began to roll it back.

They came out of the trees, the Federals, advancing bravely for raw troops who had been blundering through the woods for five hours on a hot day. For such an army, not too many men hid in the woods, but neither did too many keep order. It was difficult for the officers to maintain discipline with the complicated maneuvers of those days. Opposing them was a fragmented Rebel brigade under Colonel NATHAN EVANS, who had observed the Union turning movement, wheeled left and gone rushing into the breech.

Far to the right, BEAUREGARD heard the rising clamor of battle to his left and saw clouds of gunsmoke drifting skyward. Alongside him was JOHNSTON, who urged him to forget about his own turning movement and to reinforce his left. "The battle is there," JOHNSTON said. "I am going!"[24] BEAUREGARD hurriedly checked movements which had been going forward with even less precision than McDowell's. Columns of men in gray wheeled about and began marching toward the sound of battle. Among them was THOMAS JACKSON's brigade.

Fortunately for the Rebel commander, his subordinates had acted with rare initiative. Brigadier General BARNARD BEE and Colonel FRANCIS BARTOW went hurrying to the assistance of EVANS, whom the hurrahing Federals had been pressing steadily back. They formed in line on his right, but they too were driven backward. Then a Union brigade under Colonel William Tecumseh Sherman crossed Bull Run on their right and struck them hard. They were in danger of being routed. The Union cause appeared triumphant, and the Rebels began falling back on Henry House Hill where JACKSON had taken position with his infantry and a battery of artillery.

Resolute, not at all the "panic-stricken Unionists" of the school history books, the Federals pursued through the smoke and keening bullets. The Rebel lines were being whittled. BEE rode up to JACKSON, who was struck twice that day, and cried, "General, they are beating us back!" JACKSON replied, "Sir, we'll give them the bayonet," and BEE tried to rally his remnant with the shout: "There is JACKSON standing like a stone wall. Let us determine to die here, and we will conquer."[25] BEE did die that day, after conferring the undying nickname of "Stonewall" on THOMAS JACKSON.* Many more Confederates fell as the Rebel forces drew still farther back, and then two Union batteries—11 guns—came out of the smoke at a splendid gallop,

---

* D. H. HILL, JACKSON's brother-in-law, called this account, printed in the Charleston *Mercury,* "sheer fabrication." But it has been generally accepted in history, and HILL may have resented a nickname which he considered least suitable to the swift, tigerish JACKSON.

rolled up the Henry House slope, unlimbered and began battering the Rebel artillery.

Union infantry support was slow in forming to the right of its guns and was driven off by cavalry led by Colonel J. E. B. STUART. Still, the Union guns roared—apparently swinging the tide of battle. It was then that a line of blue came out of the smoke toward them. But these men were Rebels, still dressed in blue uniforms, and the Union officers allowed them to get close enough to shoot down every gunner and drive off supporting marines and Zouaves. Still, the Federals rallied and retook the lost position, and the critical moment of the battle approached.

BEAUREGARD had received more reinforcements in Brigadier General KIRBY SMITH's brigade, which had arrived at Manassas by train from Winchester and had immediately marched to the battlefield. Even so, at four o'clock in the afternoon the Confederate left still seemed in danger of giving way. BEAUREGARD looked anxiously to his left. Through his glass he could see a column of marching men. But whose? A courier rode up with a report that it was Patterson's Federals believed to have followed JOHNSTON from Winchester. BEAURE-GARD's heart sank. He started to give the orders to break off the action and await nightfall when he might reorganize his lines. Still, he kept his eyes on that column to his left. Suddenly he called to his messenger: "Let us wait a few minutes to confirm our suspicions before resolving to yield the field."[26] It was then that the wind caught and spread the red Confederate banner below him, and BEAUREGARD realized that Colonel JUBAL EARLY had arrived with the reserve.

All along that line rose the high shrill call of the fox hunter— the famous Rebel yell—and as these fresh troops and a battery of guns rolled around the Union right, BEAUREGARD pressed the Union front. The Federals broke. Again, they did not panic. They had merely fought themselves into exhaustion and were not in the mood for further battle. They just quit the field and recrossed Bull Run and were going down the Warrenton Turnpike toward Centreville when a Confederate battery ranged in on a bridge between them and their base. Then a wagon was upset on the bridge, blocking it—and panic did begin.

Congressmen and gentlemen and ladies who had flocked gaily to the "fun" were caught and entangled in that milling mass of fleeing soldiers. Knapsacks, guns and canteens fell among hampers and cushions abandoned along the roadway. Foot soldiers cut mules and draft horses out of their traces and rode away with the harness clinging to the heels of their mounts. Negro servants fled on their masters' chargers. Unwounded soldiers crowded into ambulances or swarmed aboard wagons which they had emptied of their contents. Animals and vehicles, all went churning and rolling through a shouting, cursing stream of frightened human beings on foot; and every time it appeared that a quiet had come upon this flood of frightened humanity, the cry arose, "The cavalry! The cavalry are coming!" and it was convulsed by a fresh tremor of terror.

McDowell's broken army did not stop until it straggled into Washington the next day under a drenching rain. And Washington itself might have fallen, if STONEWALL JACKSON had had his way. "Give me 5,000 fresh men, and I will be in Washington City tomorrow morning,"[27] he cried to President DAVIS, who had arrived on the battlefield. But DAVIS demurred, and BEAUREGARD, his own army disorganized and his judgment unsettled by false alarms, decided not to pursue.

Thus, with 2,900 Union casualties against 2,000 for the Confederates, ended the first real battle of the Civil War: the one the North mourned as Bull Run and the South celebrated as Manassas.

3

☆

The effects of Bull Run were immediate and enormous. The South's triumph impressed Europe and confirmed the Confederacy not only in its confidence but in its contempt for Northern arms. It thus tended to give the South a sense of false security.

Not so in the North, where national pride had been scorched by the humiliating retreat to Washington. Bull Run awakened the Union to the reality of a long and dreadful war, and the day after it was fought Lincoln called upon George McClellan—the hero of West Virginia—to take command of an enlarging army of long-term volunteers and regulars. Reliance on short-term militia and carefree soldiers in baggy red pants had been buried deep in the grave of American innocence.

That was the deeper significance of Bull Run: it ended the era of romantic war, or at least a romantic attitude toward war, and introduced modern warfare. War had already been democratized by the American and French revolutions. France's famous *levée en masse* commanding the hands, hearts and heads of every French man, woman and child had regimented liberty in a soldier's suit, and the huge armies of Napoleon were a result of this. But the Napoleonic Wars were fought before the Industrial Revolution made it possible for large armies to devour each other with the swift and horrible efficiency now open to both North and South. Steel and steam were to make monster killing machines of massive national armies, and the telegraph, the steamboat and the railroad were to mobilize them and get them at each other's throats more rapidly.

So now, as Northern industry cranked up and the South began its herculean struggle to build a war plant while making war, both sides drew deeper on their manpower reserves. The North voted an army of 500,000 men and the South one of 400,000. At one time or another some 900,000 men would wear Confederate gray, while 1,500,000 put on Union blue. In the South there was as yet no single general in chief to direct this growing host. PIERRE BEAUREGARD, by his impolitic propensity for bombarding his War Department with strategic proposals, which, though sound, were also infuriating to the despotic DAVIS, gradually fell from favor.

In time, he went west to assist ALBERT SIDNEY JOHNSTON, and to be replaced in Virginia by JOE JOHNSTON.

In the North there was a new and dashing young general in chief, after the aging Winfield Scott resigned to make room for George McClellan.

George Brinton McClellan—"Little Mac" to his adoring Army of the Potomac—probably wrote the epitaph of his own military career when he said: "It probably would have been better for me personally had my promotion been delayed a year or more."[28] Perhaps it was a case of too much too soon, obtained at too little cost.

A veteran of Mexico, an American observer of the Crimean War and a successful railroad president, McClellan at 35 had brought off those West Virginia successes which catapulted him into national prominence. He had arrived in Washington hailed as the savior who would redeem all, and he wrote to his wife: "I find myself in a new and strange position here: President, cabinet, Gen. Scott and all deferring to me. By some strange operation of magic I seem to have become the power of the land."[29] There was so little humility in McClellan that he was not above snubbing Lincoln, and yet he did have organizing ability.

Camps were organized around Washington, the service of supply was made efficient, and the men were drilled daily. At intervals McClellan held huge reviews, with the newly formed brigades and divisions all drawn up with glittering bayonets and gleaming brass and waving flags—all breathlessly awaiting the arrival of "Little Mac." Suddenly he would appear, and they would cheer, as they had been trained to do; and he would ride down the line, this dapper little general on the big black horse, gazing fiercely at them as though looking each and every man straight in the eye—and they cheered and hurrahed themselves hoarse. They loved Little Mac. He had made soldiers of them and given them back their self-respect. He was the very soul and spirit of that Army of the Potomac that he was creating.

But the soul had hidden self-doubts and the spirit was one of caution. Loath to recognize this, Lincoln was at first patient. "Never mind," he told aides angered by Little Mac's hauteur, "I will hold General McClellan's horse if he will only bring us success."[30] But then December came, and McClellan was still "getting ready," and because of a minor Union debacle at Ball's Bluff the hair shirt of the radical and inquisitorial Committee on the Conduct of the War was hung around Lincoln's neck. Exasperated at last, Lincoln said, "If General McClellan does not want to use the army, I would like to borrow it."[31]

When 1862 arrived, McClellan was still marking time, and it was in the West that battle was resumed.

Command of Union forces in the West was held by Major General John Charles Frémont, the glamorous pathfinder who had been the Republican Party's first presidential candidate. Frémont took charge on the day of Bull Run, just before the South opened its western offensive.

On August 10, 1861, resurgent Confederates in Missouri met a

Union army under Nathaniel Lyon at Wilson's Creek, defeating the army and killing Lyon. The following month the Rebels seized Columbus, Kentucky, and ended that state's neutrality. Frémont's task, then, was to seize the Mississippi, stabilize Missouri and wrest Kentucky and Tennessee from the Confederate grasp. And he was not up to it.

Frémont was not a trained military commander like his capable opponent, ALBERT SIDNEY JOHNSTON. He was not adept at handling large bodies of troops and he was one of those men who dream of great, bloodless victories gained by outmaneuvering some pliant enemy who does just what the plans call for. Frémont's down-to-earth Midwesterners did not like the gold-braided European revolutionaries who crowded around the general in a babble of broken English. The Southerners considered Frémont's incompetence "a guarantee against immediate peril," but, fortunately for the North, his fondness for sending bold words ringing down the wind removed him from command.

On August 30, 1861, General Frémont proclaimed martial law in Missouri and ordered confiscation of the slaves and property of all Confederates. This was too much for Lincoln, who realized that shooting civilians would only bring Southern reprisals and that to free the slaves would erase all Union sentiment along the border. Slavery was still a very delicate issue. As Lincoln was to write to Horace Greeley a year later: "My paramount object in this struggle is to save the Union, and is not either to save or destroy slavery."[32] So Frémont was asked to modify his proclamations, and when he refused, a coldly furious Lincoln replaced him with Major General Henry Halleck.

At about the same time the Department of Ohio was created and given to Don Carlos Buell. So two Union forces now menaced General JOHNSTON in the west. One under Halleck at St. Louis was poised opposite JOHNSTON's left flank along the Mississippi, and the other under Buell headquartered at Louisville menaced JOHNSTON's right anchored far away in the Cumberlands. The right cracked first, after George Thomas, acting on Buell's orders, defeated the Confederates at Mill Springs, Kentucky, on January 19, 1862. And then in February an unknown Union general named Ulysses S. Grant began moving against the Rebel left.

When the Civil War began, General RICHARD EWELL of the Confederacy said to a friend: "There is one West Pointer, I think in Missouri, little known, and whom I hope the Northern people will not find out. I mean Sam Grant. I knew him well at the Academy and in Mexico. I should fear him more than any of their officers I have yet heard of. He is not a man of genius, but he is clear-headed, quick and daring."[33]

The Union very nearly did not "find out" about Sam Grant. Bored by the peacetime garrison life that followed the glory of Mexico City, Grant had begun to drink and had been forced out of the Army rather than face a court-martial for drunkenness. Next he failed as a farmer on "Hardscrabble Farm" in Missouri, failed at selling real estate, was a down-and-outer selling firewood in St. Louis, and drifted toward the brink of despair as a despised clerk in the family harness shop in Galena, Illinois. No one thought much of Grant except when horses were to be gentled or an armed customer to be subdued, for his was one of those natures that fade like a dying ember in periods of calm only to be blown glowing and ablaze by the winds of adversity. Grant was also the very opposite of the self-confident McClellan. After Sumter, he told a friend: "To tell you the truth, I would rather like a regiment, yet there are few men really competent to command a thousand men, and I doubt whether I am one of them."[34] Such doubts were not shared by Governor Yates of Illinois, who made Grant a colonel of volunteers at 39.

But Colonel Grant's men had their doubts when their commander arrived in camp dressed in an old civilian coat worn out at the elbows and wearing a ragged hat. "What a colonel!" they howled, but they, too, were brought to observe Grant's straight hard line of mouth, his calm glance and the amazing clarity of both his voice and his orders.

Yet Grant still had doubts as he led his regiment against a Rebel force in Missouri under a Colonel HARRIS. As he neared HARRIS's camp, he became afraid. But he kept on, and then, to his surprise, found that his enemy had fled his approach. "It occurred to me at once," Grant wrote later, "that Harris had been as much afraid of me as I had been of him. This was a view of the question I had never taken before; but it was one I never forgot afterwards."[35]

This bloodless victory earned Grant a brigadier's commission, and in the fall of 1861 he was assigned to Cairo, Illinois, at the vital junction of the Mississippi and Ohio rivers. From Cairo, Grant saw the importance of Paducah, Kentucky, which lay 25 miles eastward up the Ohio and controlled the exits of the Tennessee and Cumberland as they flowed into that river. On his own initiative, Grant seized Paducah. Now he was in position to pierce the heart of the Confederacy, for the Tennessee was navigable as far south as Alabama and the Cumberland could be ascended into east Tennessee.

The Rebels, aware of this, had built forts to guard these rivers: Fort Henry on the Tennessee and Fort Donelson on the Cumberland, about ten miles distant from each other. Grant asked General Halleck for permission to attack these forts, and it was granted.

The Army-Navy teamwork which had already distinguished Union arms during the attack upon Hatteras Inlet in North Carolina the previous summer was continued in the west under Grant and Commodore Andrew Foote. The general and the commodore liked and respected each other, and were in complete harmony when, on February 2, 1862, the Union fleet of gunboats and transports shuttling 15,000 men moved up the Tennessee. On February 5 they were in position to attack Fort Henry, and Foote invited Grant and his generals aboard his flagship *Cincinnati* to inspect the fort's defenses.

The river was full of floating mines—torpedoes, as they were called then—and Foote's sailors had brought one aboard. An armorer began disassembling it, and it suddenly began to hiss ominously. In an instant the deck was cleared, Grant and Foote racing each other for the ladder topside. Reaching the upper deck and realizing that the mine was not going to explode, the general and the commodore exchanged sheepish glances while Foote said, "General, why this haste?"

"That the Navy may not get ahead of us,"[36] Grant replied.

Next day the assault began, with Grant moving his troops ashore while Foote's armored gunboats laid down a preliminary bombardment. Fort Henry boomed back in defiance, and a ship-to-shore gun duel began. But the Rebel commander, wisely judging Fort Henry indefensible, had already sent most of his men back to Fort Donelson ten miles east, and he surrendered Henry to Foote after a token defense.

Elated, Grant notified Halleck of his victory and began moving his men overland to take Fort Donelson. Here, as he knew, he had a far harder nut than Henry to crack. ALBERT SIDNEY JOHNSTON, aware of the danger to his left flank, had sent 12,000 reinforcements to Donelson so that the fort was defended by about 15,000 men against Grant's 15,000.

Commodore Foote had gone back to Cairo. Then he took his

ironclads up the Ohio to the Cumberland, swung right and ascended
that river to bombard Donelson. But Donelson was on high ground
with well-mounted and well-manned guns, and Foote bored in too
close. If he had kept off and slugged it out at long range, he might
have battered the fort's flag down. But, like commanders everywhere,
he fought this new battle with the successful tactics of the last one,
and he closed to point-blank range as at Henry.

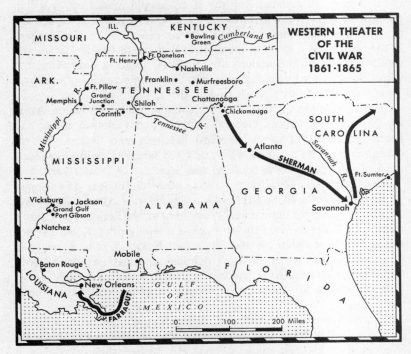

As a result, his gunners overshot, sending their shells howling harmlessly over the fort while the Confederates took deadly aim and sent
theirs plunging into the ironclads. Two of Foote's six gunboats were
forced out of action, the others were damaged. Foote himself was
badly wounded, and as the gunboats withdrew, Grant settled down to
a siege.

Though disappointed, he was not disheartened. He knew his
opponents. JOHN FLOYD, the commander, had been Secretary of War
under Buchanan, and gray-whiskered GIDEON PILLOW, of course, had

been "Polk's spy" in Mexico. "I had known General PILLOW in Mexico," Grant said, "and judged that with any force, no matter how small, I could march up to within gunshot of any entrenchments he was given to hold. . . . I knew that FLOYD was in command, but he was no soldier, and I judged that he would yield to PILLOW's pretensions."[37]

Grant was right. With the fort pinned down in front by Union naval forces still commanding the river, he did march up to within gunshot of Donelson and surround its landward rear and flanks. On the right was a division under the politician-general John McClernand, in the center was a division under Lew Wallace of Mexico fame, and on the left was a third under salty old C. F. Smith, a ramrod regular with flowing white mustaches who had been commandant of cadets at West Point when Grant was a student there.

Inside Donelson on that bitter cold night, while the Union Army lay shivering on its arms, General FLOYD called a counsel of war and heard General PILLOW recommend breakout and escape. FLOYD, fearing capture by a Union which detested him for having weakened the Federal striking force while he was Secretary of War, agreed.

Next morning, February 15, 1862, while Grant was downstream conferring with the wounded Foote, a Confederate column sallied out of Donelson's entrenchment and struck hard at McClernand on Grant's right. The Federals were driven back, especially after Rebel cavalry under the redoubtable NATHAN BEDFORD FORREST rode down their flank. After two hours of hard fighting an escape route between McClernand and the river had been opened. A Rebel brigade under SIMON BOLIVAR BUCKNER swept into a rear-guard position to protect the getaway.

Hurrying upriver to Donelson, Grant was met by a staff officer "white with fear." He saw at once the disaster threatening his right wing in this, his first major action. He flushed slightly. Suddenly crushing the papers he held in his hand, his face cleared and he spoke quietly to McClernand and Wallace. "Gentlemen, the position on the right must be retaken."[38] Then he rode to his left toward Smith, shouting to his bewildered soldiers: "Fill your cartridge-boxes, quick, and get into line! The enemy is trying to escape; he must not be permitted to do so."[39]

While Wallace's men rushed to help McClernand's division swing the escape door shut, Grant ordered Smith to attack. Smith put his regiments in line and rode ahead of them, crying, "Damn you,

gentlemen, I see skulkers! I'll have none here. Come on, you volunteers, come on! This is your chance. You volunteered to be killed for
love of country, and now you can be. You damned volunteers—I'm
only a soldier and I don't want to be killed, but you came to be
killed and now you can be!"[40]

Taunting them, shaming them into battle, riding forward with his
hat on his sword point, Smith led his men into the tangle of trees
felled by the Confederates—and at this point General FLOYD faltered.
Seeing the Union troops shutting his escape route, unsettled by Smith's
attack, and aware that Grant had been reinforced to the strength of
25,000 men, he ordered his men back into the Donelson position. That
night, another ordeal of cold for the Union soldiers, FLOYD and
PILLOW made their own escape. So did NATHAN BEDFORD FORREST,
but this hard and hardy guerrilla genius took his troopers with him,
leading them to safety through an icy, waist-deep backwater. Thereafter FORREST and his cavalry raiders taught Grant many a lesson in
the perils of an exposed line of communications.

A little past midnight, Grant, in a small cabin he shared with
General Smith, received a note from General BUCKNER asking surrender terms. "What answer shall I send to this, General Smith?" he
asked his old instructor, and Smith barked, "No terms to the damned
Rebels!"[41] Grant chuckled and sat down to write: "No terms except
an unconditional and immediate surrender can be accepted. I propose
to move immediately upon your works."[42]

Protesting against Grant's "ungenerous and unchivalrous terms,"
BUCKNER next morning surrendered the fort and 11,500 men with all
their equipment.

One of the most damaging blows of the war had been struck against
the Confederacy. The Rebel front in the West had been burst asunder,
the road to Vicksburg and control of the Mississippi opened, and the
defense of New Orleans weakened by drawing Confederate forces
north.

A thrill of hope ran through a Union accustomed to defeat and
retreat. U. S. Grant became a national hero, and because "unconditional surrender" fitted his initials, he received that nickname. The
phrase had a hard edge to it, and it cut deep into the mind of
Abraham Lincoln.

Grant's fame was wormwood to Henry Halleck. An ambitious,
bookish soldier known irreverently as "Old Brains," and also well

described as "a large emptiness surrounded by an education,"[43] Halleck seems not to have trusted Grant from the start; and because he, Halleck, had already failed to wangle over-all command in the West, he was now at pains to remove a rival for that honor from the field. St. Louis was rife with rumors that Grant was drinking heavily. Halleck himself told McClellan that "General Grant had resumed his former bad habits,"[44] and was disobeying orders. After Halleck removed Grant from his command, however, President Lincoln entered the controversy by ordering Halleck to make specific charges. Unable to do so, Halleck quickly smoothed the matter over and returned Grant's army to him with the exhortation to "lead it on to new victories."[45]

Grant's next move was against JOHNSTON's army in Corinth, Mississippi. Sending his advance guard to Pittsburg Landing on the Tennessee 20 miles north of Corinth, Grant set up his own headquarters in Savannah about ten miles farther north. He was waiting for Buell to join him, after which they would move down to Corinth to crush JOHNSTON.

The Confederate commander, however, was not sitting still for his destruction. BEAUREGARD had convinced him that Rebel fortunes might be retrieved by a signal victory. Grant was the target because he was well forward of his base, was unsupported and had divided his forces. On April 3 JOHNSTON put his 40,000-man army on the road for Pittsburg Landing.

It was a disorganized movement, made with the carefree, whooping, straggling indiscipline typical of a Rebel army on the march. It took so long that the day of battle had to be postponed from April 4 to the 5th and then the 6th—and BEAUREGARD, who had proposed the attack, now wanted to call it off on the ground that the enemy could not help but be forewarned. JOHNSTON disagreed, and said: "I would fight them if they were a million."[46]

They were actually about 33,000, and their defenses were even sloppier than the Confederate approach had been. Between Shiloh Church and Pittsburg Landing two miles to the northeast Grant had stationed five divisions. A sixth under Lew Wallace was at Crump's Landing five miles north.

Most of the regiments in the Shiloh-Pittsburg force were green and knew little about scouting and outpost duty. As a result, JOHNSTON's noisy army was able to bivouac two miles to their front without being detected. Worse, neither William Tecumseh Sherman at Shiloh nor Grant himself back at Savannah anticipated a Rebel attack. Both were overconfident, and Grant wrote to Halleck on the night of April 5: "I have scarcely the faintest idea of an attack (general one) being made upon us, but will be prepared should such a thing take place."[47]

April 6, 1862, was a Sunday, but there were no services in Shiloh Church, standing empty and silent on a hillside near the banks of the Tennessee. Around its bleak log walls were serried the white tents of the Union Army, neat, in a dreadfully prophetic way, as gravestones in a cemetery. Similar encampments lay to the rear of Shiloh or stretched eastward to the river. In all of them men in blue were cooking breakfast or cleaning equipment for Sunday morning inspection. Birds sang, for it was a bright clear day with the sun glistening on grass wet with the previous night's rain.

Near Shiloh, a suddenly anxious Sherman had sent patrols probing to his front. They blundered into Confederate pickets, exchanged shots, and came running back to announce an enemy attack. At once, Sherman formed his regiments in front of the tents, with his guns on higher ground. Far to his left, however, the Union men thought the gunfire was from green troops shooting at shadows or firing off muskets to see if the rain had dampened their powder. But then came the hollow baying of artillery, and on the hillsides at Shiloh the men in blue felt the enemy's shells crash among them and saw the Confederates approaching in two long lines of butternut.

JOHNSTON had not achieved complete surprise, as he had hoped, but the momentum was his. His troops smashed into Sherman's left-flank units around Shiloh Church and broke them. Whole regiments fled the field. One colonel called, "Fall back and save yourselves,"[48] before dashing to the rear. Many of these men came back to fight, as their cowardly officers did not, but at the first impact they gave way so completely that Sherman was forced to call upon McClernand to plug his collapsing left.

Ten miles downstream, Grant at breakfast heard the gunfire. Getting painfully to his feet (his horse had fallen on him two days ago), he hobbled down to the river and boarded a steamboat. Before leaving Savannah, he had directed one of Buell's divisions to move to a point opposite Pittsburg Landing, and now, reaching Crump's

Landing, he paused to notify Lew Wallace to stand by for battle. Then he hastened upriver, reaching the battlefield at 8:30 A.M., two hours after the fighting began.

By then the fury of the Confederate assault had driven the Union soldiers back from their camps. Jubilant Rebels pursued them, running into the tent streets and stopping there to loot and eat. In that interval, the Union divisions reorganized. In the center of the line a division under Benjamin Prentiss fell back through a peach orchard to a sunken road about two feet deep, taking position in this ready-made trench.

In the Union rear, however, all was chaos. The roads running back to the river landing were a tangle of terrified soldiers and wagons, guns, horses and ambulances. Into this backwash of near-disaster rode U. S. Grant moments after he reached the landing, and he set out at once to form a straggler line and return his demoralized remnants to battle, organizing a line of guns on high ground to protect the landing—where he expected to receive reinforcements—and sending orders to Lew Wallace and Buell's troops to hurry to the rescue.

Meanwhile the lines of gray and butternut flowed into those of blue again. Cannon boomed, canister spewed their shrieking shot, bullets whizzed or made that ugly smacking sound of lead striking flesh, while the screams of stricken horses and men mingled with the high fierce cry of the Rebel yell or the hurrahing of the Northerners. Shiloh was one of the fiercest battles in the war, and it was also battle at its most uncontrolled. Both sides green as well as gallant, the two armies struggled back and forth like two great "fighting swarms." Control was all but lost at the regimental level. Colonels fought on foot like privates and privates led companies. Units were cut off and captured only to be freed after their captors blundered into captivity. Only the battle flags fluttering in and out of drifting clouds of dirty white smoke gave the commanders any sense of unity.

Gradually, however, the Confederates drove the Federals back again—except for Prentiss at the sunken road. Here the Union troops held an excellent position and had been ordered to hold at all costs. Grant needed time to straighten out his battle line, to receive reinforcements, and Prentiss and his men gave it to him. The Rebels, instead of pinning down and by-passing the sunken road—or "Hornet's Nest," as they called it—were diverted by it. Some 60 guns collected in the peach orchard thundered at the Hornet's Nest, and 12 separate attacks—one led by JOHNSTON himself—were hurled against it. But

Prentiss fought on, "as cool as if expecting victory,"[49] and it was not until 5:30 P.M. that he surrendered.

By then JOHNSTON had died of wounds, to be replaced by BEAUREGARD, and the Rebels had missed the opportunity for victory. At one point they had turned Grant's left and had Pittsburg Landing within their grasp. Seizing this, they could have prevented reinforcements from reaching Grant and might have pressed the Union Army back against two creeks. But BEAUREGARD had no reserve available and some of his units were out of ammunition. Before nightfall, a gallant Rebel bayonet charge against the landing was repulsed, and that was the end of battle.

As night closed in, Lew Wallace finally arrived (he had taken the wrong road), and Buell's advance guard reached the landing. Niether force was in time to change the course of battle, but they would be of use when it was resumed in the morning.

That night the rain fell in torrents, aggravating the agony of the wounded and magnifying the ordeal of stretcher bearers and surgeons. General Grant made his headquarters under a tree a few hundred yards from the river. But the rain, the throbbing of his swollen ankle and the booming of the gunboats *Tyler* and *Lexington* firing down the length of the Confederate line made it impossible to sleep. So the general moved back to the shelter of a log house which had been taken as a hospital. Here, the cries of the wounded and of men undergoing amputation seemed to Grant "more unendurable than encountering the enemy's fire,"[50] and he returned to his tree in the rain.

In the morning, with General Buell and two more divisions arrived on the field, the Union Army attacked. BEAUREGARD was surprised. He had already informed Richmond of a great victory and had passed the night in Sherman's captured tent. But here were the Federals rolling toward Shiloh, and the second day of battle around that historic little meetinghouse was nearly as bloody as the first.

By midafternoon the tide turned against the Confederates. BEAUREGARD's army was exhausted and outnumbered. "General," an aide asked BEAUREGARD, "do you not think our troops are very much in the condition of a lump of sugar thoroughly soaked with water, but yet preserving its original shape, though ready to dissolve?"[51] BEAUREGARD agreed, and began his retreat to Corinth.

Grant let him go. His own army was fought out, and as Sherman later said: ". . . we had quite enough of their society for two whole days, and were only too glad to be rid of them on any terms."[52]

At Shiloh were fought two of the bloodiest days in Civil War history. Union losses were 13,700, Confederate 10,700. Tactically, Shiloh was a standoff; strategically it was a Union victory: the Rebels had been forced to withdraw with a shattered army and the way was clear for a larger Union army to pursue.

Henry Halleck led that "pursuit." Having treated Grant shabbily after Donelson, he did the same after Shiloh, taking personal command at Pittsburg Landing and advancing on Corinth with such pick-and-shovel caution that his troops swore he was trying to get there by burrowing. On May 30 Halleck arrived in Corinth to find the town evacuated. He had taken 31 days to march 20 miles!

Grant, meanwhile, found himself once more under fire. It was said that he had been drunk at Shiloh and he was described as a heartless butcher who sacrificed men to redeem his own errors. One high-placed Republican came to Lincoln to obtain Grant's dismissal. He spoke at length on the general's faults. After he had finished, Lincoln sank into prolonged silence. Suddenly he looked up, and cried: "I can't spare this man—he fights!"[53]

4

☆

In the summer of August, 1861, a Swedish inventor named John Ericsson wrote to President Lincoln offering to design and build an ironclad warship capable of wrecking the Rebel fleet in Norfolk.

In time, Ericsson's offer was accepted, although some naval officers scoffed at his plan for a ship with but two guns mounted in a revolving turret and a water line so low that it seemed any passing wave might sink her. One officer said that to worship Ericsson's model of his *Monitor* could not possibly be idolatry "because it was in the image of nothing in the heaven above or in the earth beneath or in the waters under the earth."[54] Lincoln himself held the model in his hand and said: "All I have to say is what the girl said when she put her foot into the stocking. It strikes me there's something in it."[55]

Before Ericsson went to work on the *Monitor,* however, the Confederate Navy had raised the sunken 40-gun U.S. frigate *Merrimac,* covered her with 4-inch iron plates and fitted her prow with a formidable cast-iron ram. It did not seem that Ericsson's bizarre little toy could possibly oppose this big ironclad, and even as a tugboat began towing *Monitor* south from New York in March of 1862, *Merrimac* moved out of Norfolk against the wooden Union warships *Congress* and *Cumberland,* blasting and battering them into floating wrecks. *Minnesota,* also wooden, was forced aground. Next day she too would be smashed and the Rebel ironclad would be free to move on Washington.

Terrified Federal authorities nearly panicked, and no one was more frightened than Secretary of War Edward Stanton. Now everyone in authority lamented the time and money wasted in the crack-brained *Monitor* experiment. Moreover, they asked, where *is* the *Monitor?*

She was limping south, storm-tossed. One fierce blow had sent black waves breaking over her low decks. Water tumbled down her blowers to swamp the engines, and Lieutenant John Worden and his crew hurriedly rigged hand pumps. Then a second storm threatened to part her towline. But at last *Monitor* made Hampton Roads and came to the side of stranded *Minnesota.* At dawn of March 9, 1862, *Merrimac* came out to finish *Minnesota,* and tiny *Monitor* sailed straight toward her.

Federal troops at Newport News cheered when the little raftlike Union vessel came at the big roof-shaped Confederate. Rebel sailors in the harbor laughed in astonishment at this upstart "cheesebox on a raft" this "tin can on a shingle," this David challenging Goliath two guns to ten. Lieutenant CATESBY JONES, acting captain of *Merrimac,* ordered broadside after broadside hurled at the little Yankee —but most of the Rebel shot screamed harmlessly over her low silhouette, or rattled off her turret like pebbles.

Inside that turret the Union sailors heard a monster metallic clanging, and some were stunned by the impact of the enemy shells. But they kept on firing their brace of 11-inchers. Each time the guns were withdrawn into the turret for recharging, metal stoppers were swung into place to seal the gun ports. Each time the turret began to revolve, the guns were fired "on the fly" for it was not possible to stop or reverse the turret once started.

Although the battle began at a mile range, the two ironclads gradually closed the distance until they were 100 yards apart, sometimes scraping up against each other. Once the *Merrimac* tried to ram. But her iron beak had been twisted off the day before, and she struck only a glancing blow which started a leak in her own armor. Next the audacious little *Monitor* tried to ram *Merrimac!* But she missed.

After four hours of inconclusive thundering, the two ships drew away. History's first contest between ironclad battleships had ended in a draw, although both sides claimed a victory. In a sense, the Union cause had been better served, for the menace of the *Merrimac* had been ended for good and the Federal Navy now had the time in which to build a fleet of ironclads.

Eventually the Confederacy was forced to blow up *Merrimac,* and with her passing the South's chief threat to Union naval supremacy came to an end. One day after Shiloh, Island Number 10 in the Mississippi River was surrendered to Union gunboats and General John Pope, and the Rebels' river defense was forced back on Memphis. After Union gunboats and rams wrecked a makeshift Confederate fleet off Memphis, the defense fell back farther to Vicksburg.

And then the very mouth of the Mississippi fell into Union hands when Admiral Farragut made a nighttime assault on the forts guarding New Orleans and compelled the city to surrender. New Orleans, the great port that was to send out cotton and take in guns, was in Federal hands by the end of April.

Throughout that black-bordered spring of 1862, the South felt the North's amphibious whip strip her of positions on the Atlantic coast. For a time, much was hoped from the Confederate raider *Alabama* which put to sea from Liverpool, England, on July 29, 1862. *Alabama* was a veritable sea scourge, but one ship could not win a war, and even this gallant vessel went to her doom under the guns of the *Kearsage* two years later. And when the Confederates attempted to have other ships built in France and huge rams constructed in Scotland, Yankee diplomacy ruined both ventures.

By the summer of 1862, then, it was plain that the Union held a clear-cut naval superiority. Even with her enormous coastline, the South had never had the sense of sail possessed by the Middle and New England states. She had always let the British or the Yankees carry her cotton over the seas. She had never understood sea power, and now, with the Union blockade drawing the economic noose ever tighter around her throat, with her very life depending upon control of the Mississippi, she was beginning to pay a fearful price for that mistake.

5

☆

It had not been a pleasant winter for George McClellan. True, there had been the pleasure of seeing the entire Union Army expand and improve under his own hand. But he had also been harried by a revival of the cry, "On to Richmond!" as well as by Radical Republicans who did not scruple to suggest that Little Mac deliberately dragged his feet to serve the South.

More by accident than design (at least at this time), McClellan had become identified with those Northern Democrats who wanted the war won only to restore the Union. But among Republicans there was a growing conviction that the secession could only be crushed by stamping out slavery. To the Democrats, this was a harsh position; to the Republicans anything less than this was soft. Thus the Republicans distrusted the Democrats, if not as outright traitors at least as fainthearted patriots or Southern sympathizers, and each new delay on the part of McClellan was looked upon as another proof of doubtful loyalty. Thus, also, the Republican government was not in harmony with its Democratic general in chief.

On March 11, in fact, McClellan was relieved of over-all command, ostensibly so that he would have more freedom for action in the field. The real reason was McClellan's refusal to move until he was ready, capped by his failure to move against JOE JOHNSTON's army while it was concentrated around the old Bull Run battlefield. On March 9 the wily JOHNSTON pulled his 40,000-man force back behind the Rappahannock River. Union soldiers entering his abandoned trenches and log-hut encampments found evidence that McClellan's army had been more than twice as big as JOHNSTON's, and that cautious Little

Mac had been bluffed by dozens of dummy wooden cannon—"Quaker guns," as they were called. Lincoln, who had taken to complaining, "He has got the slows,"[56] was now exasperated. Unfortunately, no new general in chief was appointed for four months, and the military reins remained firmly in the hands of the President.

One result of this was a clumsy command setup. Between them two political generals, Nathaniel Banks and John Charles Frémont, had about 28,000 troops in the Shenandoah Valley and West Virginia. Both men were coequal to McClellan and any coordination of their movements had to come from Washington. This was to work to McClellan's disadvantage, as was the fact that Lincoln and Secretary of War Stanton, being politicians first and military men second, were both unduly concerned with the defense of Washington. Stanton, a fierce man outwardly who was constantly threatening generals with dismissal, was inwardly timid. The slightest Confederate gesture toward Washington brought him close to panic.

Thus STONEWALL JACKSON was able to do McClellan a great disservice when he tangled with a Union force under James Shields at Kernstown in the Shenandoah Valley. JACKSON was defeated, but his presence in the valley so upset Lincoln and Stanton that when McClellan finally did begin moving south, they withheld 35,000 troops under Irwin McDowell to stand guard in upper Virginia.

McClellan, disappointed in his hopes to drive overland against the Confederate capital, had decided to steam down to Fortress Monroe on the tip of the York Peninsula. Landing not far from the site of Washington's victory at Yorktown, he would march quickly up the peninsula between the York and the James rivers and so take Richmond from the side door. The Union Navy, meanwhile, would guard his flanks.

It was a pretty plan, except that the *Merrimac* still barred the James, and Rebel batteries inside the York were too strong to pass. The Navy could offer McClellan only token support, and it could not get around Yorktown, the anchor for a line of fortifications stretching across the peninsula to the James. McClellan would have to breach this line, and on April 4, 1862, he ordered an advance. Next day, he changed his mind.

There were only 15,000 men in the Rebel line, opposing 53,000 under McClellan, but they were commanded by that consummate actor, JOHN BANKHEAD MAGRUDER. McClellan might well have remembered "PRINCE JOHN's" penchant for theatricals, and might have regarded the constant marching and countermarching of the Rebel Army as a stage production. Instead, he was deceived into thinking MAGRUDER led a large force, and he at once settled down to siege warfare. No less than 150 huge mortars, among other big guns, were mounted in the Union lines opposite MAGRUDER; and no less than a solid month was lost, during which JOHNSTON gathered his forces and placed them between Richmond and the Army of the Potomac. In joyous amazement, JOHNSTON told LEE, "No one but McClellan could have hesitated to attack."[57] On May 4, when Little Mac finally did give the order to bombard the line he considered "one of the most extensive known to modern times,"[58] his shells fell into empty trenches. JOHNSTON had waited until the last moment, and then, on the preceding night, had quietly fallen back on Richmond.

McClellan now ordered a pursuit, while preparing an amphibious force to sail up the York and cut off JOHNSTON's retreat. But he was too slow in getting his enveloping movement water-borne, and JOHNSTON, anticipating him, defeated his forces when they attempted to land at West Point. On land, the pursuing Federals ran into a Rebel rear guard under JAMES LONGSTREET near Williamsburg. LONGSTREET, wounded 15 years before while carrying the colors at the Molino del Rey, was at once attacked by a division led by Joseph Hooker, who had earned his "Fighting Joe" nickname in Mexico. LONGSTREET hurled Hooker back, and then, counterpuncher that he was, attacked himself—and that was when a third hero of the Mexican War came galloping up the muddy road.

Fiery Phil Kearny had fought for the French in Africa and Italy since he lost his left arm at the San Antonio Gate. Fierce as ever, sword in hand and reins in his teeth, he led his division to Hooker's rescue—and found the road blocked by wagons mired in the mud. "Tip those wagons out of my way!"[59] he roared, and when an officer tried to explain that the wagons were stuck, he bellowed: "Move them, I say—or I'll put the torch to them!"[60] The wagons were dragged aside, and Kearny's men sloshed forward to see their general go dashing across the Confederate line like a flame in the saddle and deliberately draw the fire that gave away the enemy positions. At that juncture, the Yankee-hating D. H. HILL—who had helped storm the heights of Chapultepec—brought his division to LONGSTREET's side. The battle raged on inconclusively, until Winfield Scott Hancock

—who had been with HILL at Chapultepec—took his Union division wide to the right and found an opening on LONGSTREET's flank and rear. Under cover of darkness, the Confederates withdrew.

Tactically, the battle had been a Confederate victory, for LONGSTREET had held off the Federals long enough to cover the withdrawal of JOHNSTON's precious supply trains. Measured by Civil War standards, however, Williamsburg had not been a major battle. Yet in miniature it possessed all those elements which were to be characteristic of the dreadful, three-year struggle between the Army of the Potomac and the force that LEE named the Army of Northern Virginia. Bull Run had shown what the war was not to be like, Williamsburg showed what it would be. At Williamsburg men who had fought together in Mexico as lieutenants and captains now fought each other as generals, and they commanded troops whose fighting qualities probably have never been surpassed. Because both sides now realized that the enemy was in earnest, because both had a supply of trained commanders who wanted passionately to win and a reservoir of men who wanted fiercely to kill, the battles in the East —like those already fought in the West—were to be to the finish. Very few commanders were going to be bluffed or maneuvered off the field. Most of them were going to stay until beaten. And that, of course, meant a blood bath of three years' duration.

Williamsburg, a delaying action, was therefore only a smaller blood bath. But the Federals occupying the field that night were nevertheless horrified by the black and bloated dead, as well as by the cries of the wounded and the sound of surgeons sawing off limbs whose bones had been shattered beyond repair by the huge bullets of .58 caliber and more fired by both sides. There was also the customary horror of battlefield theft. In the morning the pockets of friend and foe alike had been turned inside out, and even the buttons cut from their uniforms. Such ghouls and scavengers have marched with every army since Agamemnon's, and the men of the Army of the Potomac were only being introduced to another of the ancient horrors of war when they heard a swag-stuffed Union soldier simper: "I wish there was a battle every week."[61]

McClellan now had another chance. He had broken through the defenses of Yorktown and forced the evacuation of Norfolk, which opened the James River to him. With Norfolk gone, *Merrimac* had no home. The big ironclad's draught was too deep for her to flee up the James, and so, at the end of an eventful two-month career, she had to be blown up. But then the Union Navy was dealt one of its rare reverses. Attempting to reduce the Rebel forts at Drewry's Bluff seven miles out of Richmond, its ships were driven off. For nearly three years the river approach to Richmond was to remain in Rebel hands, and McClellan was thus denied that convenient avenue to the capital.

Yet McClellan had 105,000 men against JOHNSTON's 60,000, and he still did not move until another month elapsed. Depending on intelligence reports supplied by the woefully inept private detective, Allan Pinkerton, he believed that JOHNSTON's strength was double his own. Perhaps he unconsciously wanted to believe Pinkerton. He certainly accepted the detective's incredible calculations without a murmur of surprise, and he failed to question methods that may have been fine for catching bank robbers but which were dreadful for counting enemy heads. Throughout the Civil War there was never a time when any single army in the field numbered as many as 150,000 men; in fact, the peak strength of the entire Confederate Army, reached in June, 1863, was only 261,000 men. Yet in May of 1862 McClellan believed or preferred to believe that JOHNSTON alone commanded from 250,000 to 300,000 soldiers.

That was the tragedy of McClellan. Personally, of course, he was brave. But if he could organize and train a great army, even get it to the battlefield, he would not risk it. Defeat was worse than death to him. Vain rather than proud, with his Napoleonic prose and imperial mustache, he resembled the great Corsican in mere physical size only. He was truly a little man on a big horse. Night after night in letters dramatically dated "Midnight" or "1 A.M.," he writes to tell his young wife how firm he is, how resolved, how inexorable—and then some self-pitying bleat escapes him: ". . . the necessity for delay has not been my fault. I have a set of men to deal with unscrupulous and false."[62] He is like a man who lifts one hand to strike and with the other points out the reasons why he cannot.

Yet McClellan did have some excuses. First, the weather was wretched, making movement difficult and his men miserable. Second, he was thwarted in his desire to have McDowell's force of 40,000 sent south to join him in front of Richmond. In this the villain was again General STONEWALL JACKSON.

TOM JACKSON had thought of living in Mexico for a while, but then, deciding that "Spanish was meant for lovers,"[63] he came home, resigned from the army, and began teaching at Virginia Military Institute. His students thought him a dullard who taught from the book and they called him "Tom Fool." But JACKSON was strange rather than foolish, a silent awkward figure forever sucking a lemon, riding his shambling sorrel horse with his big clumsy feet turned out in the stirrups, only the lemon and his brown beard visible beneath a mangy forage cap pulled down so that the broken visor concealed the cold blue eyes of the killer.

During battle, those icy eyes gleamed with an intense light, the fire of the burning bush, for STONEWALL JACKSON was a warrior out of the Old Testament. He was a pious soldier who could spend hours on his knees praying to the God of Battles, or write a clergyman in lengthy explanation of why he fought on the Sabbath. He was also brutal, as successful soldiers must be, and when an officer protested that his men would be annihilated if they obeyed an order of JACKSON's, STONEWALL replied: "General, I always endeavour to take care of my wounded and to bury my dead. You have heard my order—obey it!"[64] In his soft, gentle voice, Jackson could call a colonel a "wicked fellow" for swearing at his men, or murmur to an officer who regretted having to kill brave Federals: "No, shoot them all, I do not wish them to be brave."[65] Such a man, fierce, swift and relentless, was just the commander to carry out ROBERT E. LEE's plan to prevent McDowell from joining McClellan.

LEE, now a full general, was military adviser to President DAVIS. LEE knew that a juncture of the Union armies in front of Richmond could prove fatal to the Confederacy. So he decided to play on Northern fears for the safety of Washington by sending STONEWALL JACKSON into the Shenandoah Valley to make a bloody diversion.

Moving with a celerity which was to make his troops famous as "JACKSON's foot cavalry," STONEWALL led a small force west to the Alleghenies, where he jumped the unsuspecting Frémont. Then, turning his back, reinforced to a total of 15,000 men, he swept toward the lower valley and practically annihilated Banks's flank guard at Front Royal, ripped up his rear guard at Winchester, and drove the Union general clear back to the northern side of the Potomac.

Once again, Washington was in a state of near-panic. It was rumored that JACKSON was going to invade the North. Frantic telegrams went out alerting Northern governors to the danger, and McDowell, Frémont and Banks were ordered to converge on JACKSON.

By then STONEWALL was heading home, his mission accomplished.

He had lowered Northern morale and had moved Lincoln to cancel McDowell's orders to join McClellan. Instead, that vital reinforcement went into the valley.

As a second result of JACKSON's famous Valley Campaign, McClellan was caught astride the flooding Chickahominy River.

Little Mac had sent one part of his army south of the Chickahominy to hold a bridgehead, while keeping the larger part on the north bank to protect his base. After McDowell arrived, he would move the entire army across the river. That was all right. But then McDowell was diverted to the valley, and McClellan still clung to this vulnerable position. So General JOHNSTON decided to try to wipe out the small Union force south of the river before the larger force north of it could come to the rescue.

Heavy spring rains worked to JOHNSTON's advantage. They turned the Chickahominy into a raging torrent that threatened to sweep away the bridges built by McClellan's engineers. Confederate staff work, however, redounded to JOHNSTON's disadvantage. LONGSTREET, in charge of the main attack, took the wrong road and fed in his units piecemeal.

The battle began on May 31, 1862, and ended the next day. It was fought over and around a railroad station known as Fair Oaks and a farm called Seven Pines, and bears both those names. In the end, the Rebels got so thoroughly in each other's way that they were too late to stop Union reinforcements from rushing over bridges which did hold, despite the flood. Fair Oaks–Seven Pines was as bloody as it was confused and inconclusive: some 5,700 Rebels dead or wounded, some 4,400 Union casualties. One of these Confederate casualties was the oft-wounded JOE JOHNSTON himself. And that was a great calamity for the North, because command of the Army of Northern Virginia then passed to ROBERT E. LEE.

"Army of Northern Virginia, fabulous army," sang Stephen Vincent Benét, and now it was LEE who led these gaunt and dauntless Rebels, this "army of planters' sons and rusty poor-whites";[66] it was ROBERT EDWARD LEE, the flower of Southern chivalry and the last White Knight of the battlefield. In the words of Winfield Scott he was the hero of the Mexican War and "the greatest military genius in America";[67] in the eyes of his brother officers he had been "the handsomest man in the Army";[68] in the affections of his men he was

"Marse Robert"—but when he rode among them on his great gray stallion Traveler, they did not whoop and cheer but rather stood in awe or removed their slouch hats while gazing reverently at this tall, white-bearded patriarch of a soldier. "I've heard of God," one Confederate lady said, "but I've *seen* General LEE." In LEE's own eyes he was perhaps the earthly representative of George Washington: LEE's father, Light-Horse Harry Lee, had been one of Washington's intimates, and LEE's wife, Mary Randolph Custis, was the great-granddaughter of Washington's wife. Washington had been a Virginian, and LEE was first and foremost a Virginian. Hating slavery, he had drawn his sword not to defend that detestable institution but in the service of the beloved soil that made him.

LEE had seen his duty, and to LEE duty was paramount—above all duty to the will of God. Not since the Middle Ages, when reference to God was often as perfunctory as a genuflection, have the orders of a chief been so full of supplication to the will of God. They are like a litany: God gives victory or defeat, and if it is success He is to be praised, and if failure the Army of Northern Virginia is exhorted to search its soul to see where it has sinned. In this, there are a fatalism and submission that are perhaps not good for a commander of armies.

There were also in LEE a strange gentleness and a compassion alien to the field of combat. He was more at ease in the company of women, delighting especially in the gentleness of young girls, and those women whom he scrupulously honored felt toward him a reticence as cool and proper as an outstretched hand. "LEE was a great soldier and a good man," Mary Chesnut wrote, "but I never wanted to put my arms around his neck, as I used to want to do to JOE JOHNSTON."[69] If STONEWALL JACKSON was the avenging sword of the Old Testament, then ROBERT E. LEE was the warrior of the New.

JACKSON might mutter, "No quarter!"—as he did—but LEE could take the hand of a wounded but defiant Union soldier, look lovingly into his eyes and say, "My son, I hope you will soon be well."[70] Some of JACKSON's hardness, however, might have made LEE an even greater commander. In his very real humility, he deferred almost without deviation to JEFFERSON DAVIS. In his gentleness, he could not be severe, and therefore found it difficult to dismiss incompetent officers or to settle disputes over authority or to discipline those magnificent scarecrows whom he loved to the depths of his being. And in his simplicity, in his very desire to live no better than any private soldier, he was sometimes unapproachable. Too many Confederates thought of ROBERT E. LEE as a saint, and because human beings, prone to mistake goodness for saintliness, are also afraid of sanctity, they kept away from him.

Such were the virtues that sometimes tended to become defects when mounted in the saddle of the commander in chief, and they are detailed here only because the personality of ROBERT E. LEE seems to be buried beneath an avalanche of bronze statues, LEE memorial days and the uncritical adulation of worshipful biographers. LEE the man is frozen inside a marble myth. Great soldier that he was, he was not matchless; and he might have been even greater had his idealism been tempered with an understanding of the holes in human nature. Nevertheless, his nobility of character made him the soul of his army. No commander ever possessed a greater capacity for inspiring troops, for electrifying them by his very presence on the field of battle. Nor was any commander more masterful in defense, in devising fortification—or more audacious in attack.

McClellan, still convinced that he was outnumbered, made no offensive moves after Fair Oaks. He seems to have been preparing to take Richmond by siege operations. But LEE was busy, building fortifications with that energy and skill that caused his men to call him the "King of Spades," and drawing up a plan to strike McClellan.

First he needed to know McClellan's exact position, and for this information he called upon JEB STUART. A man of great physical strength and presence whose West Point nickname of "Beauty" was in joking reference to his homely face and big bold nose, JEB STUART was the Southern cavalier par excellence. For all his homeliness and huge brown beard curling down below his breastbone he was the darling of the Southern ladies, whose delight it was to garland his bridle with roses or to make some contribution to a costume that made the hussar getup of the flamboyant Federal cavalryman, George Custer, seem funereal garb indeed. Beneath a broad gray hat looped with a gold star and adorned with a plume, STUART wore a short gray jacket bright with buttons and braid. A gray cavalry cape trailed from his shoulder, around his waist was an ornate and tasseled yellow sash from which a light French saber hung, great leather gauntlets reached almost to his elbows, on his legs were enormous jack boots with gold spurs, while his saddle held a pistol and a bright red blanket. When

STUART gave commands, it was in a voice that carried like a bugle call, and he was in good voice, singing "Kathleen Mavourneen," as he led some 1,200 horsemen in a spectacular ride around McClellan's entire army. Upon his return from this 150-mile circuit he brought the information LEE required, although he also developed a taste for the sensational which was to prove harmful in the future.

Nevertheless, LEE now knew that McClellan had moved most of his army south of the Chickahominy but had left one corps under Fitz-John Porter on the north bank at Mechanicsville. LEE decided to have 25,000 men under the actor JOHN MAGRUDER hold down McClellan's main body of 60,000, while hurling 65,000 men against Porter's 30,000. To do this he ordered JACKSON to march down from the valley and hit Porter's right flank. As he did, A. P. HILL would cross the river at Mechanicsville to clear the town. After this, LONGSTREET and D. H. HILL, across the river above the town, were to come in behind JACKSON and A. P. HILL in support. Together, the four commanders would roll Porter down the river bank before McClellan could come to his rescue.

It was a fine plan, but as had happened to JOHNSTON, it went awry. JACKSON was slow in arriving and did not get his men into action. A. P. HILL, despairing of JACKSON's arrival, went rushing across the river without orders and charged smack into the formidable Union line. The result was miniature disaster. The Battle of Mechanicsville ended in 1,500 Confederate casualties against 250 for the Union.

LEE was annoyed but not dismayed. MAGRUDER had succeeded in deceiving McClellan again, and the bulk of the Rebel Army was north of the river in position to crush Porter. Next day, June 27, 1862, at Gaines's Mill, the attack was renewed. Again and again the Confederates charged the Union line, only to be repulsed each time. Artillery thundered throughout the day, and Union guns south of the Chickahominy reversed aim to hurl shells into the onrushing Rebels. Rifle fire was so thick that the brush and saplings were cut down as though scythed.

Just before sunset there was a lull. Weary Union soldiers thought the battle had ended in a Rebel defeat. But LEE, across the river, had assembled every available man for a general assault. Behind a sudden crash of artillery, screeching the Rebel yell, they came running forward—and this time the Federals broke and ran.

Gaines's Mill was a victory for LEE, but it had cost another 8,750 casualties against 4,000 for the Union. Yet, if Porter had not been crushed, as expected, then McClellan had been cowed. South of the river that night, where he had held his main body inactive all day, McClellan ordered a retreat to the James River.

Once again MAGRUDER had fooled him with one of his typical productions—marching men in full view, sending out patrols and skirmishers, firing off cannon—but he had not beguiled Hooker or Kearny, who knew PRINCE JOHN too well. These two division commanders had the audacity to burst into McClellan's headquarters, and when Little Mac curtly demanded the reason for such behavior, Kearny burst out: "The enemy lines around Richmond are thin. They can and must be broken. An order to retreat is wrong! Wrong, sir! I ask permission to attack MAGRUDER at once."

"Denied," McClellan snapped, and after Kearny renewed his arguments, he said: "Nothing has changed, General. The retreat will be made on schedule." With that, according to General Hiram Berry, who was present: "Phil unloosed a broadside. He pitched into McClelland with language so strong that all who heard it expected he would be placed under arrest until a general court-martial could be held."[71]

McClellan, however, merely allowed Kearny to calm down, and let him go without a word. That night, the supply trains of the Army of the Potomac began the retreat.

One of ROBERT E. LEE's favorite maneuvers was to strike the flanks of a moving enemy, and he tried it repeatedly against the retiring Federals. Once, at Frayser's Farm, there was an opportunity to gain a splendid victory. But for the fourth time since LEE began his campaign STONEWALL JACKSON was slow in moving. Throughout June 29, he stayed in his camp and wrote a letter to his wife telling her how much to contribute to their church. That night he fell asleep while eating, and when he did move out the following day the opportunity was lost. Either because he thought the enemy's position too strong, or because he had lost too much of the sleep his frail physique required, STONEWALL had failed the leader whom he idolized as "the only man whom I would follow blindfold."[72]

LEE never got over the missed opportunity at Frayser's Farm, and when JUBAL EARLY expressed concern that McClellan was escaping, he lost his habitual self-control and snapped: "Yes, he will get away because I cannot have my orders carried out."[73]

McClellan did make it safely to Harrison's Landing on the James.

Here his supply line was safely in the hands of the Union navy, and his front was guarded by Malvern Hill, blocking the road to the James.

Malvern Hill was a natural fortress. With his fine engineer's eye, LEE saw this at once as he rode forward to sweep the position with his glasses. Still, he thought so little of McClellan that he believed one more blow might crumple the enemy. He became more confident after LONGSTREET reported that a Confederate crossfire could silence the Union artillery so that the butternuts could charge the Federals off their 150-foot hilltop. D. H. HILL disagreed, saying, "If General McClellan is there in strength, we had better let him alone."[74]

He was there in strength. Massed infantry held every strongpoint, and there were divisions in reserve. Artillery was abundant, with some 100 fieldpieces parked hub to hub to blast any Confederate assault. Still, on July 1, 1862, LEE attacked—and it was the Confederate artillery, not the Union, that was knocked out. Throughout the war, Union artillery was to dominate the Confederate, and Malvern Hill was probably its finest hour. One by one, the Southern fieldpieces were silenced. And when the gallant gray lines surged forward, the Union guns shredded them, maimed them, pulped them—and then a storm of rifle fire broke them in blood. Some 5,500 Rebels fell in those dreadful wasting attacks, and next day a horrified Federal officer looked down the slopes and saw: "A third of them were dead or dying, but enough of them were alive and moving to give the field a singular crawling effect."[75] Long afterward, D. H. HILL wrote of Malvern Hill: "It was not war, it was murder."[76]

6

☆

General HILL was right, but the great tragedy of the Civil War was that neither he nor General LEE nor U. S. Grant nor any other high commander ever came to realize why it was that war had become "murder," or, in the phrase of William Tecumseh Sherman, "all hell."

The rifle bullet was the reason. The bullet had given the advantage to the defense. It had dethroned the bayonet, the shock weapon of the assault, and together with its handmaidens, the ax and the spade, had made the defense just about invincible.

The point that had been missed was that the bullet ended the era of headlong assault. In the days of edged or pointed weapons—the sword, the battleax and the lance—the assault was the ultimate tactic because all fighting was hand to hand. An attacker had little difficulty in approaching his enemy. This situation might have been ended by the bow and arrow, except that the invention of gunpowder came so close upon perfection of the English longbow that the possibilities of this silent missile were not fully realized.* But after muskets appeared the bullet was subordinated to the bayonet.

This was because the effective range of the smooth-bore flintlock was only from 30 to 100 yards. It was not accurate, and it took so long to load and fire that most commanders regarded it as a noise-and-smoke-making machine. The first volley would both frighten the enemy and produce a smoke screen under cover of which the assaulters could charge, risking at most a single volley from the defense before achieving "the bayonet clinch, the flash of steel, the stab and the yell of victory."[77]

Shock tactics made rapid decisions possible. The bayonet did not so much kill men as make men run. But the slaughter of Wellington's finest, the red-coated conquerors of Napoleon, at the Battle of New Orleans was a dreadful adumbration of the inevitable outcome when bayonets charge entrenched rifles. The lesson was ignored, however, and even the battles of the Mexican War were fought with the shock tactics of the past. One reason for this was the difficulty of making a satisfactory bullet for long-range muzzle-loading rifles.

A muzzle-loader bullet had to be small enough to permit it to be dropped down the bore and rammed home. The problem, then, was to design a bullet which would expand into the bore's grooves and utilize the power of the powder gases forming behind it. This was solved by the Minié ball named for the Frenchman who designed it, and when it was, the bullet's effective range rose from 100 to 500 yards. With the killing zone extended five times, the defense was five times more effective and the assault five times more dangerous. When to this were added trenches and rifle pits and all the other

---

* Kit Carson once said that he never fully realized what a weapon the bow was until he had arrows fired at him in the dark.

products of ax and spade, the assault was penalized further. All of the attacker's body was exposed as compared to about a fifth of the defender's. More, improved rifles could fire at a rate of three times a minute, and toward the end of the war, breechloaders even faster. This also favored the defense; *any* increase in range or firepower *had* to favor the defense simply because the defender was underground and the attacker aboveground. Obviously, then, the bayonet charge was a bloody anachronism. Civil War soldiers sensed this, derisively describing their blades as "candlesticks" (when thrust into the ground the bayonet's upturned socket was just the right size to hold a candle). Civil War generals, however, did not realize that the bullet had ushered in the horrible era of trench warfare, that all shock tactics, including cavalry charges, were actually a thing of the past. Even artillery was being chased off to a respectful distance by the bullet's increasing range, while its effect was being reduced by the spade's increasing protection.

What was needed were new weapons and tactics whereby the defense could be pinned down in its entrenchments while its flanks were turned, or the attack might advance to within assault range at a minimum risk. These were not developed, and it would be far from fair to fault either LEE or Grant for failing to understand the revolution worked by the bullet. It was not understood in the West as late as World War I and beyond, when automatic weapons and barbed wire made the power of defense even greater, and the famous "*banzai* charges" of the Japanese during World War II were even bloodier repetitions of the shock tactics which reddened the slopes of Malvern Hill.

LEE's explanation for these assaults was that he believed the enemy to be demoralized. Granting him the universal failure to grasp the limitations now imposed upon the attack, his judgment must be upheld. During the Seven Days' Battles begun at Mechanicsville and ended at Malvern, LEE had suffered 20,000 casualties against 16,000 Union losses, and yet it was McClellan, not LEE, who was backing off.

He ordered a general retreat to Harrison's Landing on the James. His decision enraged many of his officers, none more than Phil Kearny, who slammed his famous kepi into the mud, and roared: "I, Philip Kearny, an old soldier, protest this order for retreat. We ought, instead of retreating, to follow up the enemy and take Richmond. And in full view of all the responsibility of such a declaration, I say to you all, such an order can only be prompted by cowardice or treason."[78]

Neither accusation, of course, was true. Phil Kearny was one of those fighting generals who walk in a two-tone world and whose contempt for politics often conceals an inability or reluctance to swim in those conflicting currents. McClellan missed his great chance because he was still adding up the disadvantages and therefore submitting to the moral mastery of ROBERT E. LEE. Besides, he was playing politics.

Not long after the withdrawal, President Lincoln came down to Harrison's Landing and McClellan gave him a letter which was nothing less than a blueprint for running the war. In effect, he advocated those very policies which Republicans detested as "soft" and intimated that his army, McClellan's army, the fighting force molded by McClellan in McClellan's image, would not fight to destroy slavery. Lincoln, who was already coming to the conclusion that some form of emancipation was necessary, read the letter in McClellan's presence and put it in his pocket without a word. He never replied to it, masterpiece of self-important insolence that it was, and a few days later he lifted Henry Halleck out of the West and brought him to Washington as general in chief. Halleck assumed command of all the armies on July 11, 1862. In Virginia he confronted this situation.

On June 26, because of failures in the valley and command complications there, Lincoln had created the Army of Virginia under General John Pope. Pope had a threefold mission: to protect Washington, to guarantee the safety of the valley, and, by threatening LEE's rail communications, to draw troops off from Richmond and thus make McClellan's task easier. McClellan, however, continued to mark time at Harrison's Landing, and so Halleck went down to see him.

Once again, Little Mac wildly overestimated his enemy's strength, claiming that LEE had 200,000 men when he actually had fewer than McClellan's own 90,000. He asked for 30,000 more men, but Halleck told him he could have only 20,000 and would that be enough to take Richmond. McClellan answered modestly that there was a "chance." Halleck at once concluded that if LEE's army was so big it would be madness to allow him to sit between McClellan's and Pope's divided forces. So he ordered McClellan to return to his Washington base and then unite with Pope.

That, of course, meant an ignominious end to George McClellan's Peninsular Campaign, and a victory for ROBERT E. LEE. And as the Army of the Potomac began its ponderous slow movement north, the audacious LEE moved at once to strike at Pope.

John Pope had become famous for his victory at Island Number 10 on the Mississippi. He was a dashing figure, especially on horseback. He was also given to bluster, and he did not make the men of the Army of Virginia love him when he issued the order: "I have come to you from the West, where we have always seen the back of our enemies. . . ."[79] His reported remark, that his headquarters would be "in the saddle," left the salty Confederate soldiers, even, it is said, ROBERT E. LEE, shaking with laughter at the general who had his headquarters where his hindquarters ought to be.

Otherwise, General LEE did not find General Pope comic. Pope's harsh orders regulating Confederate civilians within the Union lines angered LEE, and he observed that Pope would have to be "suppressed." To do this, even before McClellan began retiring from the James, LEE sent STONEWALL JACKSON north.

JACKSON began the business on August 9, 1862, at Cedar Mountain. Here he met Pope's advance guard under Nathaniel Banks and was rocked back on his heels by a fierce Federal rush against his left flank. The Confederates were on the verge of being routed when A. P. HILL's division arrived, after which JACKSON mounted a counterattack to drive off the outnumbered Banks. Next day Pope's main body came up and JACKSON drew off to await the arrival of LEE.

LEE was quick in coming. As soon as McClellan's withdrawal from Harrison's Landing began, leaving only two brigades behind, he hurried to join STONEWALL with the rest of his army in hopes of carrying out the "suppression" before Pope could be joined by McClellan.

LEE, however, was surprised to find Pope countering all his own maneuvering skill with an equal mastery. Marching and countermarching was wearying LEE's troops and would soon wear down their fighting edge. Something had to be done, and that something was triggered in LEE's mind by one of JEB STUART's typical exploits.

LEE's cavalry leader had been piqued at the loss of his famous red-lined cape and plumed hat to the Federals. In retaliation, he raided Pope's headquarters and there found not only the Union general's dress coat but also many of his papers and a dispatch book. From these LEE learned that overpowering reinforcements were en route to Pope, who even then outnumbered LEE 75,000 to 55,000. If LEE was to move, it must be quickly. So he called STONEWALL JACKSON to his headquarters and ordered him to take 25,000 men on a wide sweep around Pope's right flank to get in his rear, and to cut his communications to Washington.

No more daring move could have been devised. Even today there are critics who say it was foolhardy to violate the sacred canon of concentration of forces by committing the cardinal sin of dividing them in the face of a superior foe. But the audacious LEE was a gambler. Throughout his leadership of the Army of Northern Virginia he was guided by the principle that he must take long chances to offset an enemy superior in men and munitions. He was not, however, contemptuous of Pope, as has also been said. He was merely trying to make him retreat by getting on his line of communications in his rear. He did not then intend to give battle. Only after the grasp of the situation slipped suddenly from Pope's fingers did he move to strike.

JACKSON worked that change. After a two-day march his "foot cavalry" came out of the Bull Run mountains to fall upon Pope's supply base at Manassas Junction. With glad yells and shouts of famished glee, they gorged and looted, and then they filled their wagon trains with ammunition and rations, put the torch to the rest, cut the railroad—and vanished. Pope sought them frantically. In the interval JACKSON took a strong position on Stony Ridge overlooking the old Bull Run battleground while LEE hurried to his side with LONGSTREET and 30,000 veterans.

On August 29 Pope found JACKSON and began battering him with steady, heavy attacks. He also finally began to think about the rest of LEE's army and sent a force to hold them off while he disposed of JACKSON. But he had not sent enough, and before the first day of battle had ended, LONGSTREET was in position on JACKSON's right. That was the moment for LEE to swing hard at Pope's unsuspecting left. Three times LEE declared to LONGSTREET that the magic moment had come, and three times the solid but slow "Old Pete" declared against it. Because the gentle LEE could not bring himself to order

Longstreet forward, the moment passed—and Jackson spent the day fighting for his life against determined Federal attacks.

That night Pope became convinced that the Confederates were withdrawing. He jubilantly telegraphed Washington that the Rebels were in retreat, and next day he ordered a pursuit. But when the "pursuing" Federals came up against Jackson's right wing, Longstreet's artillery came plunging among them and broke them. Lee, seeing his opportunity reappear, did not delay this time. He at once ordered Longstreet forward, and the gray lines smashed Pope's left flank so thoroughly that his entire army was broken and sent reeling back on Henry House Hill, the place where Stonewall Jackson had won his nickname the previous year.

This time there was no Federal panic, and next day Pope began an orderly withdrawal. Hoping to strike at his rear again, Lee sent Jackson on another sweep. But the Federals were prepared, and on September 1, 1862, a savage battle was fought at Chantilly mansion. As a storm-tossed night closed in, Confederate riflemen under A. P. Hill heard a horse galloping toward them. A flash of lightning illuminated a Federal officer. The Rebels opened fire, the horseman turned—and then fell with a bullet in his spine. Hill ran to the fallen man and peered at him by the light of a lantern.

"You've killed Phil Kearny," he gasped. "He deserved a better fate than to die in the mud."[80]

7

☆

Lee had won a fine victory. If Second Bull Run (Manassas) had not been decisive, it had at least cleared most of Virginia of the locust-like Federals and had again demoralized Union forces in the East. The question was: What now?

Lee did not think he could wait and thus surrender initiative to the enemy. If he did, a larger Army of the Potomac might move south again. No, Lee decided, the thing to do is to invade the North.

His reasons seemed cogent. First, by entering Maryland and Pennsylvania the enemy could be drawn away from his Washington defenses. With Maryland held by the South, no Federal army based on Washington would would dare move against Richmond again and Virginia would be free.

Lee also believed that most Marylanders were sympathetic to the Southern cause and would flock to his standards. He was convinced that an invasion of the North would widen the gulf between the Peace Democrats and Republicans, and, most of all, bring to fulfillment that fondest dream of Confederate diplomacy: friendly intervention by France and England.

So far, the two chief powers of Europe had sat on the fence. Neither King Cotton nor Southern diplomacy had budged them. The nearest thing to a break had occurred in the fall of 1861 during the celebrated Mason-Slidell affair.

JOHN SLIDELL, who had been President Polk's emissary to Mexico, and JAMES MASON had been appointed to represent the Confederacy abroad. Slipping out of Charleston on a blockade-runner, they reached Havana, where they took passage on the British mail steamer *Trent*. On November 8, 1861, the U.S. frigate *San Jacinto,* Captain Charles Wilkes, fired a pair of shots across *Trent*'s bow, sent a crew aboard, and bore off Messrs. MASON and SLIDELL to the United States.

Britain became enraged. The fleet was put on a war footing and 11,000 troops were rushed to Canada. In the North there was many a firebrand who was willing to take on the British, but Abraham Lincoln had a cooler mind, and he apologized to the British and released MASON and SLIDELL. It was a wise move, for neither MASON in Britain nor SLIDELL in France was able to gain recognition for their country.

Except for Queen Victoria, who favored the North, the effective rulers of both nations were sympathetic to the South, if only to see America permanently divided. While detesting slavery, the aristocracies of both nations felt a kinship for the genteel South, especially the English, who scorned the Yankee North as a rude polyglot and looked upon the Confederate cavaliers as true-blooded English. But the middle and lower classes, again especially the English, were solidly for the North.

However, not many Englishmen believed that the North could subdue the South. In August of 1862, during and after Second Bull

Run, England and France were considering a proposal to effect a peace based on the independence of the Confederacy. A successful invasion of the North, then, could not fail to give impetus to such a movement, and that is why President DAVIS gave tacit approval to LEE's plan.

LEE knew that there were risks involved. For one thing, if he had just inflicted 14,500 casualties on the Federals, he had lost 9,500 himself. He was short on rations, thousands of his men were shoeless and many of his horses were worn out. Nevertheless, on September 5, only three days after Chantilly, LEE's sunburned, tobacco-chewing scarecrows went splashing across the Potomac singing, "Maryland, My Maryland."

They received a frosty reception. Secessionist sentiment had had 17 months to cool in Maryland, and even those who still sympathized with the South were repelled by the sight of these ragged and ravenous "liberators." In Frederick City, Dame Barbara Fritchie, nearly 100 years old, remembering the Revolution, is supposed to have leaned from her window to shake the Stars and Stripes at STONEWALL JACKSON's troops. Whittier immortalized her with the lines: " 'Shoot if you must this old gray head, but spare your country's flag,' she said." As Carl Sandburg has observed, no Confederate poet has done the same for the woman who stood on her doorstep with tears in her eyes, crying, "The Lord bless your dirty ragged souls!"[81]

But there were not many like her, and ROBERT E. LEE was dismayed. He pressed on, however, full of confidence in himself and contempt for George McClellan.

Little Mac was back. He had never really been removed from command, although his command had been taken from him bit by bit and fed to John Pope. After Pope was discredited, however, McClellan was reinstated, and the beaten men of the Army of the Potomac shuffling north from Chantilly shouted and cheered and threw their hats and their knapsacks into the air when they heard a general call out, "Boys, McClellan is in command of the army again! Three cheers!"[82] Throughout that night of defeat and retreat they straightened their backs and cheered themselves hoarse as the magical little man on the big black horse rode among them. Incredible as it may seem, these men actually did love this simulacrum of a general, this splendid hesitator. They knew nothing of his failings;

they knew only that he had once made soldiers of them when they were men of straw, and here he was to do it again when they were straws of shame. McClellan understood this and he returned their affection, saying, "We are wedded and should not be separated."[83] Thus, for all of his shortcomings in the field, McClellan had twice saved the Union Army from despair. Soon he had again effected its rejuvenation, and then, with 95,000 men, he marched northwest from Washington in search of General LEE.

They did not find him, at first, but two of McClellan's soldiers— Corporal Barton Mitchell and First Sergeant John Bloss—made a find of their own in the sleepy town of Frederick. It was a prize, three cigars wrapped in a paper, and that meant a smoke apiece with perhaps a flip for the odd one. Then Corporal Mitchell noticed the paper, smoothed it out and began to read:

SPECIAL ORDERS NO. 191

Headquarters, Army of Northern Virginia,

September 9, 1862

The army will resume its march tomorrow, taking the Hagerstown road. General Jackson's command will . . .

There were other generals mentioned—LONGSTREET, STUART, D. H. HILL—and the two soldiers jumped to their feet in excitement and ran for the captain. The captain dashed for the colonel, the colonel jumped on his horse and clattered away for the general, and thus, with a speed not always characteristic of the Army of the Potomac, the deployment ordered by ROBERT E. LEE was very shortly known to George Brinton McClellan.

LEE had again divided his forces. Confident that McClellan was still marking time around Washington, and anxious to protect his line of communications to Virginia, LEE had ordered STONEWALL JACKSON to capture Harpers Ferry and then rejoin him at Hagerstown before McClellan could move. McClellan, at Frederick, read of this deployment with rising jubilation. Here was a heaven-sent opportunity to destroy LEE's army in detail. LEE was not only fragmented, but the fragments were closer to McClellan than they were to each other! Waving the captured order, McClellan cried: "Here is a paper with which, if I cannot whip Bobbie Lee, I will be willing to go home."[84]

Resolving to strike at the Hagerstown fragment, McClellan began to move with what he probably considered to be speed. But it was not quick enough. Although he did break through South Mountain in a savage fight, he could not prevent LEE from withdrawing to Sharpsburg on the Potomac. Nor could he stop JACKSON from taking Harpers Ferry and rejoining LEE at Sharpsburg. Thus the great opportunity was lost. Knowledge of LEE's deployment had enabled McClellan to wreck LEE's invasion, but a 16-hour delay in attacking had ruined his own chance to destroy Marse Robert.

Nevertheless, McClellan with some 70,000 troops followed LEE to Sharpsburg. There he found him with 39,000 men, the Potomac to his back and across his front a sluggish creek called the Antietam.

As at Shiloh, there was a little church at Antietam. It was a Dunker church, standing white and peaceful along a road with a wood to its rear and across the road a cornfield and another wood. Here, on the morning of September 17, 1862, McClellan attempted to break LEE's left wing under STONEWALL JACKSON.

Fighting Joe Hooker led off for the Federals. Three dozen guns cleared the cornfield and cut it to the ground, after which a full corps swept furiously up to the little church. But then JACKSON fed in reinforcements and the Union troops were driven back to their starting point. Now another corps, under red-faced, white-haired Joseph Mansfield, came swinging into the battle—and after Mansfield was killed and Hooker wounded, these men also failed. Still neglecting to concentrate, still feeding in his units piecemeal, McClellan ordered in Edwin Sumner's corps. For a time, old Bull Sumner seemed to have gained possession of the church, but once again JACKSON hurled in fresh troops. They struck Sumner's flank and rear and rolled him back. Now, with the cornfield cut down, the wood lots riddled, the rail fence along the road draped with corpses, Sumner shifted his attack farther left toward a sunken lane held by the Confederates. And so another sunken lane entered Civil War history, this one to be known as Bloody Lane, for after it was taken by Sumner's men it was found to be stuffed with bodies.

Everywhere, now, the cooling autumn earth was warmed and soaked with blood and the air was vile with the reek of death. In the cornfield were so many dead that one soldier said it was possible to walk from one end to the other without touching the ground. Wounded men who had crawled from the battle to take refuge under haystacks were burned alive when the hay caught fire. The body of one Confederate soldier hanging over a fence in Bloody Lane contained no less than 57 bullets, and the Hagerstown road in front of the church was so horribly cluttered with carcasses and corpses that a colonel riding through it next day observed how his horse "trembled in every limb with fright and was wet with perspiration."[85]

Yet the battle raged on, and LEE's center grew weaker and weaker. The lines there were so thin that LONGSTREET and his staff were firing guns and D. H. HILL seized a musket to lead a counterattack. If McClellan hurled in fresh troops, he might burst through. But he hesitated, and the roar of battle began to shift gradually from the center of LEE's line to his right, where Ambrose Burnside with four divisions was trying to force the Antietam crossings.

Burnside also committed his divisions one at a time, and they met four bloody repulses. Still, Burnside pressed the attack, crossed the river and by two o'clock in the afternoon ROBERT E. LEE faced disaster. JACKSON on the left could do nothing against the Federals, his center was nailed down and his right was crumbling under steadily rising Union blows. He had no reserves. He had only the hope that A. P. HILL might arrive in time from Harpers Ferry, 17 miles away. Then, at 2:30, a courier galloped up breathless with the news that HILL's men were only an hour off. Could the butternuts hold?

It did not seem so. At three o'clock a fresh Federal assault broke with a roar against LEE's right. Standing in the high echoing streets of Sharpsburg, LEE could see the Federal columns plunging forward under a pall of smoke. He pointed to a distant column and asked a lieutenant named JOHN RAMSAY, "What troops are those?" RAMSAY focused his telescope and replied: "They are flying the United States flag." LEE pointed to another column on his right and repeated the question. RAMSAY answered: "They are flying the Virginia and Confederate flags." LEE, his breast swelling with a vast thanksgiving, said quietly: "It is A. P. HILL from Harpers Ferry."[86]

It was only half of HILL's division, for the other half was strewn along the roadside half-dead from the man-killing pace of the march. But there were enough men to turn the tide, to flow straight into battle and to strike Burnside in the flank, forcing him to halt, to withdraw and call for reinforcements that never came. Thus in the high drama of a roaring and critical twilight, the Battle of Antietam, the bloodiest single day in the Civil War, came to its close.

LEE had suffered 13,700 casualties against 12,350 Union losses, and that night LONGSTREET and other generals came to LEE and urged him to withdraw. "Gentlemen," he said calmly, "we will not cross the Potomac tonight. . . . If McClellan wants to fight in the morning, I will give him battle again. Go!"[87] It was the White Knight of the Confederacy who spoke; it might have been another Roland preparing another Roncesvalles, except that ROBERT E. LEE knew his man. McClellan did not give battle again. Next day he had it within his power to overwhelm LEE's exhausted and riddled Army of Northern Virginia, but something in those calm and reorganized lines awaiting him across the debris and stench of no-man's land unsettled his nerves. He did not see LEE with his back to a river but only LEE with his face to the front, and that night the Confederate Army slipped across the Potomac and returned to Virginia.

Antietam (Sharpsburg) was not so much a Union victory as a Confederate defeat, but however it may be described its effects were more far-reaching than those of any other battle in the war. First, by forcing LEE to withdraw from Maryland, it caused Britain and France to postpone a decision on intervention. Second, it called forth the Emancipation Proclamation.

Since the war began Abraham Lincoln had moved cautiously on the slavery issue. The loyal slave states of Maryland, Delaware, Kentucky, Missouri and West Virginia were highly sensitive on the question, and they had blocked Lincoln's cherished proposal for compensated emancipation. In some ways, the Negroes themselves were forcing Lincoln closer and closer to a major decision. Whenever Union arms entered Confederate territory, the Negroes flocked to the Stars and Stripes, thus enraging their masters and embarrassing Federal commanders. For a time this problem seemed solved when Ben Butler used his lawyer's mind to classify the slaves as "contraband of war," and the "contrabands" were organized into labor battalions.

Such a legalism might have been a good joke on the South, but it resembled a solution to the slavery problem about as much as a cough resembles an earthquake. And Abraham Lincoln had come to realize that only the cataclysm would do. He had asked himself: Of what avail to restore the Union without destroying the slavery that divided the House? His answer was: "The moment came when I felt that slavery must die that the nation might live."[88]

On July 22, 1862, Lincoln informed his Cabinet that he intended to free the slaves effective next New Year's Day. After Secretary of State Seward pointed out that to make such a declaration on the heels of defeat would sound like the "last shriek of the retreat"[89] from Richmond. Lincoln then decided to wait until the Union had won a victory. Antietam was that victory, and on September 22, 1862, President Lincoln issued the Emancipation Proclamation proclaiming that as of January 1, 1863, all slaves held in any state then in rebellion would be "then, thenceforward and forever free."

The proclamation did not free a single slave, simply because they were all in Rebel hands; it was of doubtful legality under the President's vague "war powers"; and if abolitionists thought it was not strong enough, the loyal slave states and the Northern Democrats thought it went too far. Yet the Emancipation Proclamation is among the most profound and revolutionary events in history. It opened the world-wide struggle for racial equality, and it opened it within the one country which, possessing in miniature all those colors and creeds, prejudices and fears which divide humanity, had it therefore in its power to produce the model solution.

In its immediate effects, the proclamation isolated the Confederacy. No foreign power responsible to public opinion dared enter the war against a nation now dedicated to the destruction of slavery, and henceforth all the South received from abroad was sympathy. Henceforth, also, the Civil War was a war to the death.

In the South, Emancipation Proclamation was spelled *Unconditional Surrender*. A wave of fury swept the Confederacy. Lincoln was accused of violating the sacred rights of property, of encouraging Negroes to rise in murder and rapine. Members of the Confederate Congress talked wildly of running up the black flag and killing all enemy wounded and prisoners. In effect, the Southern spine was stiffened to fight to the end.

So was the North's. Abraham Lincoln had lifted the North's purpose from the cause of Union to the high call of the crusade to crush slavery. Soldiers in blue now marched to a nobler end than the cry of "Home and Rights" which drew the butternuts into the field. And they also sang a nobler marching song. It had been "John Brown's Body" until Julia Ward Howe replaced that monotonous litany to a murderer with her magnificent "Battle Hymn of the Republic."

> Mine eyes have seen the glory of the coming of the Lord:
> He is trampling out the vintage where the grapes of wrath
>   are stored;
> He hath loosed the fateful lightning of his terrible
>   swift sword:
>   His truth is marching on.

Only the men of the Civil War could have sung such a song. Only the sons of a nation just shedding its innocence could have been exalted, rather than embarrassed, to cry aloud: "Oh! be swift, my soul, to answer Him! be jubilant, my feet!" or to attest in song that they were where Abraham Lincoln always said he wanted to be: on the side of the Lord. So they went down the lanes on that crusade and singing that song; and if ROBERT E. LEE was the last of the generals to enter battle submissive to the will of God, then the Union soldiers were the last to march to it with His name on their lips.

Abraham Lincoln had strummed a mystic chord within the nation's soul. He had truly "sounded forth the trumpet that shall never call retreat."

Unfortunately for Lincoln, he possessed no trumpet which could call George McClellan into battle again. Having permitted LEE to depart Antietam unmolested, McClellan allowed six weeks of splendid autumn marching weather to slip by before crossing the Potomac in pursuit. Even then, he was annoyed by Lincoln's importunate messages to get going. "I feel that I have done all that can be asked in twice saving the country,"[90] he wrote to his wife after Antietam.

Abraham Lincoln could not agree, and in his mind he prepared a test for McClellan. If Little Mac should permit LEE to cross the Blue Ridge and interpose his army between Richmond and the Army of the Potomac, George Brinton McClellan would be through. That happened, and on the night of November 7, 1862, two men stumbled through a driving snowstorm to reach General McClellan's tent near Rectortown.

One of the men was General Burnside and the other was Adjutant General C. P. Buckingham. Burnside seemed nervous and embarrassed. McClellan understood why after Buckingham handed him a message relieving him of command and ordering him to turn his army over to Burnside.

8

☆

Where, it has often been asked, did Abraham Lincoln find Ambrose Everett Burnside? The answer is that he had been around all the time. All the other generals of reputation—McDowell, McClelland and Pope—had failed, Grant seems to have been still beneath the cloud of Shiloh and Henry Halleck had no intention of crossing swords in the field with ROBERT EDWARD LEE.

Lincoln may have been impressed with Burnside's record as an independent commander of a successful amphibious operation along the North Carolina coast, and at Antietam he had done at least as well as any other corps commander. Yet Burnside had never shown any capacity for high command, and he knew very well himself that a good corps commander does not always make a good leader of armies.

Twice Burnside told Lincoln that he was "not competent to command so large an army,"[91] and he was so shocked by the President's final order that he had to be talked into obeying it by George McClellan himself.

Perhaps it was Burnside's very candor and modesty that impressed Lincoln. Certainly Burnside had much to be modest about. As a young officer in Mexico and against the Indians he was renowned for his poor skill at cards; he had had the unique experience of leading a young lady to the altar only to have her decline at the last moment with a loud and ringing "No!"; and as a civilian he went broke trying to manufacture a breech-loading rifle he had invented. George McClellan, then a railroad president, rescued him from the last misfortune, and Burnside was treasurer of McClellan's road when war broke out.

Burnside was a strong, handsome man, although completely bald at 39. His face, however, was not hairless, and even in this most mustachioed and bearded of wars he possessed facial foliage and was also unique. It was neither beard nor mustache but a growth that began beneath his nose and spread back to either ear in two great bushy loops. The style was named "the burnsides" in his honor, and has since flip-flopped into the dictionary as "sideburns." In dress, Burnside wore a high, well-crowned hat and a musty frock coat that made him appear, in modern eyes, the prototype of the Keystone Cop. Even in those days there must have been something faintly ridiculous about Ambrose Burnside, something that might have been slapstick, had not the lives of 113,000 men been in his keeping.

Burnside's plan was to threaten Richmond directly by crossing the Rappahannock River at Fredericksburg. After Halleck sidestepped the responsibility of deciding on this proposal, Lincoln gave it his reluctant approval with the words, "It will succeed if you move very rapidly, otherwise not."[92] Burnside did move fast, at first. By November 17 his advance guard under Sumner was on the Rappahannock opposite Fredericksburg. Old Bull Sumner wanted to ford the river at once, brush aside the handful of Rebels in the town and seize the high ground to its rear. Burnside hesitated. Heavy rains were falling and the pontoon train he needed to bridge the stream had gone astray. He decided to wait for the pontoons, and thus became the fourth Federal commander to sit unwisely still in front of LEE.

LEE quickly gathered his forces in Fredericksburg. He probably would have preferred to oppose Burnside farther back, where there was room for maneuver, but JEFFERSON DAVIS was as insistent upon the distant defense of Richmond as Abraham Lincoln was eager for its quick capture. So LEE mustered 75,000 veterans, the peak strength of the Army of Northern Virginia, under JACKSON and LONGSTREET. He watched the Federals build their bridges over the Rappahannock and allowed them to cross into the little city without much more than token opposition from sharpshooters and a few cannon. LEE knew his position was secure, and he could hardly believe that Burnside would actually attack the heights which he held behind the town.

On his right flank was JACKSON with A. P. HILL's massed artillery, and it was here that LEE expected the brunt of the Federal attack. He could not conceive that anyone would dare LONGSTREET on the left. Here was a death trap, here was another sunken road, even deeper than those at Shiloh or Antietam. The side facing the Federals

was lined with a stone wall four feet high forming a perfect parapet
for the Rebel riflemen. Behind the road rose Marye's Heights,
crowned by LONGSTREET's artillery. To approach this position the
Federals had to cross open, uphill country. It was no wonder one
of LONGSTREET's artillerists said to him: "General, we cover that
ground now so well that we comb it as with a fine-tooth comb. A
chicken could not live in that field when we open on it!"[93]

LONGSTREET laughed, just as he had chuckled when STONEWALL
JACKSON appeared that day wearing a handsome new gold-braided
dress coat. "Old Jack's" men whooped and hollered at the sight:
"Come here, boys! STONEWALL has drawed his bounty and has
bought himself some new clothes."[94] Watching the midmorning sun
burn off the mists above Fredericksburg, seeing the steeples appear
and the streets filled with marching Federals, LONGSTREET jokingly
asked JACKSON if he was not afraid of all those Yankees. No man
for a joke, JACKSON growled: "Wait till they come a little nearer, and
they shall either scare me or I'll scare them."[95] One of STONEWALL's
aides thought the general was allowing the enemy to get too close,
but JACKSON said: "Major, my men have sometimes failed to *take*
a position, but to *defend* one—never!"[96]

Burnside had two grand divisions, one under Hooker which was
to attack LONGSTREET, and the other under William Franklin, which
was to strike JACKSON. Franklin moved first, plastering JACKSON
with artillery before his blue files began skirmishing. But JACKSON's
answering artillery broke up the Federals.

It was then that Hooker's divisions swept toward LONGSTREET
holding the sunken road and Marye's Heights. From the stone parapet
came a crash and a flash of flame, from the hill behind it a roar
of artillery—and the carnage was begun. Again and again these
gallant Union soldiers obeyed those remorseless, heartless, mindless
orders to conquer a very hell of flame and steel. They were like lead
soldiers storming a stove. They had only their blouses between their
hearts and the bullets of the entrenched Rebels, yet onward they
came, flesh flowing against lead, brigade after blue brigade, and the
Rebels standing four deep behind the stone wall loaded and fired,
loaded and fired, shattering the blue lines into fragments, scattering
them across the frozen mud.

Such was the charge at Marye's Heights, a tragedy of high courage at the abuse of high incapacity. Even the Rebels were thrilled by the bravery of their enemy, and GEORGE PICKETT later wrote his wife: "The brilliant assault . . . of their Irish brigade was beyond description. Why, my darling, we forgot they were fighting us, and cheer after cheer at their fearlessness went up all along the line."[97] Fearlessness, however, cannot conquer entrenched rifles, and some 7,000 Federals fell before Marye's Heights.

On LEE's right, more Yankees were falling as Franklin renewed his assault on JACKSON. Here a Confederate counterattack was launched, and LEE, standing on a hill, heard the weird high cry of the Rebel yell and saw a line of ragged butternuts come running out of a wood in pursuit of a body of fleeing Federals. LEE's eyes flashed, but then the gentler, truer side of his nature came uppermost and he murmured: "It is well that war is so terrible—we should grow too fond of it!"[98]

On that cold, clear night the aurora borealis blazed in white splendor upon horrors which a Confederate soldier on burial detail described two days later as:

Eleven hundred dead bodies—perfectly naked—swollen to twice the natural size—black as Negroes in most cases—lying in every conceivable posture—some on their backs with gaping jaws—some with eyes large as walnuts, protruding with glassy stare—some doubled up like a contortionist—here one without a head—there one without legs—yonder a head and legs, without a trunk—everywhere horrible expressions—fear, rage, agony, madness, torture—lying in pools of blood—lying with heads half buried in mud—with fragments of shell sticking in the oozing brain —with bullet holes all over the puffed limbs.[99]

Many more than 1,100 were buried during the truce LEE granted for such purposes. In all, Union casualties were 12,600 against Rebel losses of 5,300. The Army of the Potomac was so stunned that LEE might have counterattacked and broken it that very night, or at least the next morning. JACKSON is said to have counseled a night attack, with the Rebels stripping naked so as to avoid confusion in the dark. LEE, however, perhaps overwary of the Union artillery across the river, did not move—thus missing the same opportunity that McClellan failed to grasp after Antietam.

Burnside, who had shed real tears of grief at the slaughter of his soldiers, wanted to lead a fresh attack personally the next day, but his generals dissuaded him from this possibly expiatory course. Suddenly turning tenacious, he decided to move farther up the Rappahannock and get around LEE's left. On January 20, 1863, his army started to march, just as three days of icy, pouring rain began. Wagons, horses and soldiers sank into the bottomless mud of the Virginia roads. The impossibility of movement was described by the officer who requested "50 men, 25 feet high to work in mud 18 feet deep."[100]

Drenched and dispirited, the Army of the Potomac slogged back into camp, and with the ludicruous "Mud March" to cap the holocaust of Fredericksburg, Ambrose Burnside was relieved of his command.

9

☆

The Union defeat at Fredericksburg brought the Lincoln administration close to disaster. The fall elections had already gone against the Republicans, the Peace Democrats were gaining strength, and in the Northwest war weariness was so great that Lincoln was told he must open the Mississippi or face a demand for a negotiated peace.

It was to the West, then, that the eyes of the Union turned. Here, Grant with his Army of the Tennessee was poised to move against Vicksburg on the Mississippi in the campaign that would open the great river to New Orleans and cut the Confederacy in two. Just below Nashville, Tennessee, was the Army of the Cumberland, now commanded by William Rosecrans.

Rosecrans had replaced Buell after that general had failed to pursue BRAGG on his retreat from Kentucky. Red-faced, heavy, excitable and devout, "Old Rosy" was a favorite with the men. He liked to drill them personally and to offer such gems of battlefield advice as: "Never turn your backs to the foe; cowards are sure to get shot." "When you meet the enemy, fire low."[101] Rosecrans was also a fighter, and in December he began moving down into central Tennessee to get at BRAXTON BRAGG's army based at Murfreesboro.

JEFFERSON DAVIS was in Murfreesboro at the time, savoring the good news from Fredericksburg as a vindication of his defensive strategy. The Confederate President was also enjoying a gay Christmas season in Murfreesboro, a red-hot Rebel town where gallant soldiers and charming girls sang songs such as "The Bonny Blue Flag" or danced to the sentimental strains of "Lorena." The highlight of the season was the wedding of 37-year-old JOHN MORGAN, the fabled leader of Rebel cavalry, to young Martha Ready, daughter of a Tennessee member of the Confederate Congress and also a determined young lady who had resolved to marry MORGAN before setting eyes on him. The marriage was sanctified by portly General LEONIDAS POLK, who was also an Episcopal bishop. After the wedding, in that cavalier abuse of cavalry characteristic of both sides, MORGAN was allowed to gallop off on another flamboyantly useless raid and leave BRAGG without scouts or the services of 4,000 proven fighters. In all, BRAGG had about 38,000 men and Rosecrans 45,000, when, on December 31, 1862, the two armies collided at Stones River a few miles west of the town.

Both generals planned to swing their left flank, a situation which would give the advantage to the first to strike. In this case, it was BRAGG. His butternuts drove into Rosecrans's right wing and might have crushed it but for the battle put up by a division under a cocky young general named Philip Sheridan. One by one, Sheridan's brigade commanders were killed, and yet his division responded to his orders "as if on parade."[102] Still, Rosecrans was forced to retire his right to re-form it and he was able to do so while George Thomas, the stolid general from Virginia, held steady in the center.

It was a bloody day, this final 24 hours of 1862, and at one point the thunder of guns and muskets was so great that Rebels charging through a cotton field stopped to pick the raw cotton and stuff it in their ears. Night fell with the Union Army badly bent and seemingly beaten. BRAGG did proclaim a great victory, but found the stubborn Rosecrans still on the field on New Year's Day. BRAGG neglected to strike until January 2, 1863, after which, having been repulsed, he abandoned both the field and Murfreesboro to the enemy.

It is difficult to say what was achieved by the slaughter at Murfreesboro (Stones River). Losses were equal, both armies suffering about 12,000 casualties, yet Rosecrans might have been the technical victor because he occupied the field. Otherwise nothing substantial was gained. Both armies went into winter quarters and BRAGG's army still blocked Rosecrans's objective at Chattanooga. Meanwhile, the war shifted farther west to Vicksburg.

Vicksburg was the key to the Mississippi, if not to the entire war. If it fell, the great waterway would be in Union hands, but if it held out, as Abraham Lincoln said: "We may take all the northern ports of the Confederacy and they can still defy us from Vicksburg. It means hog and hominy without limit, fresh troops from all the States of the far South, and a cotton country where they can raise the staple without interference."[103] Vicksburg, however, was a very tough nut, especially from the water. It stood on high bluffs on the eastern bank commanding a great bend in the river, while on its eastern or landward side it was protected by the valley of the Yazoo, a watery labyrinth of swamps and bayous.

Eager to get at Vicksburg, U. S. Grant finally received word from Halleck: "Fight the enemy when you please."[104] However, as he made ready to move his Army of the Tennessee into an overland assault, his problem was complicated by an intrigue behind his back.

The political general John McClernand, a faithful War Democrat high in Lincoln's favor, had gone to Washington to ask the President to place him in command of a force to sail straight down the Mississippi and capture Vicksburg. McClernand told Lincoln that unless the great river was opened soon, the Northwest would drop out of the war. Eager for a victory, Lincoln consented—although he did not give McClernand exactly the carte blanche command he desired.

Grant learned of this design through newspaper rumors, and found himself forced to put his Vicksburg plans into premature operation. First, he ordered Sherman to sail downriver from Memphis before McClernand could arrive to supersede him. Then he began advancing into Mississippi with the intention of drawing JOHN PEMBERTON, the Confederate commander, away from Vicksburg and thus weaken the city for Sherman's assault. However, by then an alarmed JEFFERSON DAVIS had appointed JOE JOHNSTON to over-all command in the West. JOHNSTON wisely ordered his cavalry into action against Grant's rear, capturing both his supply base and wrecking his communications. Out of touch with Sherman, Grant was unable to inform him of what had happened, and on December 29 the far-from-weakened Confederates dealt Sherman a bloody repulse at the Battle of Chickasaw Bluffs.

Grant's plans were now completely upset. Moreover, he could see that political considerations had ruled out the easier overland approach in favor of the more difficult river route. Thus, doubting McClernand's competence to command, he requested and received permission to take charge on the Mississippi himself. On January 30, 1863, he arrived at Young's Point, about 20 miles above Vicksburg on the western bank.

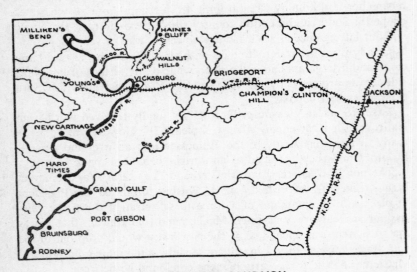

THE VICKSBURG CAMPAIGN

Few generals have faced a more bleak outlook than Grant at that moment. JEFFERSON DAVIS had already hailed the defeat at Chickasaw Bluffs as proof that Grant would slink back to Memphis. Grant was himself still under the stigma of Shiloh, still rumored to be a drunkard, and still the object of infamous attack in the Eastern press. Moreover, unable to turn back from the river approach, he could neither storm Vicksburg frontally nor establish a base below the city until the spring rains ceased. Least of all, he could not sit still for four or five months to give his enemies proof of his "timidity" or to allow his army of 45,000 men to fall apart. Thus, to keep his men occupied, to perplex PEMBERTON in Vicksburg, and also just on the chance of finding a chink in the city's armor, he made four flanking attempts.

Opposite Vicksburg was a peninsula formed by the river's great hairpin bend. It seemed that if a canal were cut across its base the river might flow into it and thus by-pass the city. However, after the channel was dug, the Father of Waters refused to enter it. Next, Grant tried to deepen and connect a chain of lakes and streams which wound west from Lake Providence above the city to a re-entry point in the river 150 miles below it. Here, two months of hard work ended in failure. So did two similar attempts undertaken in the labyrinthine Yazoo above the city to the east. So the outcry against Grant continued. He was "pronounced utterly destitute of genius or energy; his repeatedly baffled schemes [were] declared to emanate from a brain utterly unfitted for such trials; his persistency was dogged obstinacy, his patience was sluggish dullness."[105]

During this ordeal of frustration, however, Grant had come to suspect that the country might be prosperous enough to support his army on the march, and this fact was at the back of his mind when he proposed to march his troops down the river's western bank to a point below Vicksburg where a crossing to the eastern bank might be made. Grant's top generals, especially William Tecumseh Sherman, objected to such an advance. Sherman insisted that the only way to take Vicksburg was to return to Memphis and follow the line of the Mississippi Central Railroad. But Grant was not to be dissuaded, and so, to confuse PEMBERTON, he ordered Sherman to make a diversion north of Vicksburg, while 1,700 cavalry under Colonel Benjamin Grierson went on a raid through central Mississippi, tearing up railroads and upsetting PEMBERTON's troop deployments. In the meantime, the bulk of the army slipped down the western river bank to Bruinsburg. Here Grant awaited the arrival of the Union fleet which was to run the gantlet of Vicksburg's guns so that it might carry his army to the eastern bank. On the night of April 16-17, 1863, the fleet under Admiral David Dixon Porter made its move.

With lights dowsed and engines silent, the ships began floating downstream. The dark, wooded shores of the peninsula were on their right as they headed for the end of the hairpin turn. Reaching it, the Union fleet suddenly found itself illuminated by the flickering light of a house set ablaze on the peninsula and a calcium fire lighted on a Vicksburg hill. Stealth was not possible now, and Vicksburg's batteries were already booming. Thundering back with their own guns, the Yankees cracked on steam. One by one—armored gunboats, turtle-backed rams and steamboats belching fire and smoke from their tall funnels—the Union ships swept through the Rebel shot and shell. Soon the cotton bales which served as "armor" for some of the transports caught fire, and as the stricken *Henry Clay* staggered downstream she trailed a wake of fiery bunches of cotton that made Admiral Porter think "a thousand steamers were coming down."[106] But all the other ships had come safely through, and on April 30 the crossing of the Mississippi was begun. "When this was effected," Grant wrote, "I felt a degree of relief scarcely ever equalled since. . . . I was on dry ground on the same side of the river with the enemy. All that campaigns, labors, hardships and exposures from the month of December previous to this time that had been made and endured, were for the accomplishment of this purpose."[107]

Now Grant's clear-sightedness and daring came into play. Although he had about 33,000 men against PEMBERTON'S 23,000, the enemy army in Vicksburg was linked to the interior by rail and could be easily reinforced or supplied. Grant decided to attack the city's rear, its supply base to the east in Jackson, then held by JOE JOHNSTON with about 6,000 men. The Union chief proposed one of the most audacious moves in history: to cut loose from his base, seize Jackson, and then, still living off the land, turn west to invest Vicksburg. Thus, as Grant moved east toward Jackson, the bewildered PEMBERTON sallied from Vicksburg to "cut" the nonexistent Yankee supply line. In the meantime, Sherman's corps went crashing into Jackson, JOE JOHNSTON went dashing out, and on the night of May 14 Grant slept in the room which JOHNSTON had occupied the night before.

About-facing, posting a sizable force in his own rear to block JOHNSTON should he attempt to return, Grant moved on Vicksburg. On May 16 PEMBERTON tried to halt him at a place called Champion's Hill, but the Confederate commander was hurled back and finally driven inside his defenses at Vicksburg. On May 18 Grant stood on the Walnut Hills overlooking Vicksburg. Beside him an admiring Sherman cried: "Until this moment I never thought your expedition a success. I never could see the end clearly, until now. But this is a campaign; this is a success, if we never take the town."[108]

Next day Grant ordered a full-scale assault, which failed completely. Unfortunately, Grant also failed to learn the lesson of the new invincibility of the entrenched defense, and he ordered a second, bloodier assault on the 22nd. This also failed, after which the Union commander settled down to siege warfare.

Vicksburg was caught in a noose. On the river, gunboats kept up a steady slow shelling of the city; on land, the Union trenches spread their strangling arms wider, and gun batteries wormed their way ever closer. Within the city, the garrison and the people lived like cave-dwellers. Cave-digging became a regular business, and a woman wrote: "The hills are so honey-combed with caves that the streets look like the avenues in a cemetery."[109] Clothes and shoes wore out, and were replaced with homemade ones of rags. There was little to eat but corn bread and mule meat. Soldiers lived on spoiled bacon and bread made of pea flour. Those with hardy stomachs trapped and ate rats, comparing their flesh to spring chicken. When the tobacco gave out, they smoked sumac leaves. Throughout it all, there was hardly a glimmer of hope: the Union fleet held the river and Grant held the land. No reinforcements or supplies could possibly get through, and on July 4, 1863, PEMBERTON finally surrendered.

Not many campaigns in history can compare to Grant's capture of Vicksburg. His losses were 9,400 compared to Rebel losses of 10,000 dead and wounded and 31,000 prisoners, including 15 generals. Within 18 days of his Mississippi crossing he had fought and won five battles and marched 200 miles with but five days' rations. He had cared promptly for the wounded on both sides, and treated Confederate prisoners with a compassionate understanding which gives the lie to that still-undying legend of Grant "the brutal butcher."

But most of all, he had cut the Confederacy cleanly in two. Not long after Vicksburg fell, the fortress of Port Hudson to the south also surrendered, and Abraham Lincoln could say with deep satisfaction: "The Father of Waters again goes unvexed to the sea."[110]

10

☆

On January 26, 1863, the Army of the Potomac came under the command of Fighting Joe Hooker. A hard-drinking, profane driver, Hooker was also easily the most handsome general in the Union Army, a square-shouldered Adonis with his curling blond hair and clean-shaven face of a complexion "as delicate and silken as a woman's."[111]

Abraham Lincoln had his good reasons for making Hooker his fifth choice in his search for the soldier who would lay the prize of Richmond at the Union's feet, but Lincoln was also aware of some of Hooker's defects, and he did not hesitate to detail them in writing what must certainly be among the most extraordinary letters of promotion ever composed by a commander in chief:

I have placed you at the head of the Army of the Potomac. Of course I have done this upon what appears to me to be sufficient reasons, and yet I think it best for you to know that there are some things in regard to which I am not quite satisfied with you. I believe you to be a brave and skillful soldier, which, of course, I like. I also believe you do not mix politics with your profession, in which you are right. You have confidence in yourself, which is a valuable, if not an indispensable, quality. You are ambitious, which, within reasonable bounds, does good rather than harm; but I think that during General Burnside's command of the army you have taken counsel of your ambition, and thwarted him as much as you could, in which you did a great wrong to the country and to a most meritorious and honorable brother officer. I have heard, in such a way as to believe it, of your recently saying that both the Army and the Government needed a dictator. Of course, it was not for this, but in spite of it, that I have given you the command. Only those generals who gain successes can set up dictators. What I now ask of you is military success, and I will risk the dictatorship. The Government will support you to the utmost of its ability, which is neither more nor less than it has done or will do for all commanders. I much fear that the spirit which you have aided to infuse into the army, of criticizing their commander and withholding confidence from him, will now turn upon you. I shall assist you as far as I can to put it down. Neither you nor Napoleon, if he were alive again, could get any good out of an army while such a spirit prevails in it. And now beware of rashness. Beware of rashness, but with energy and sleepless vigilance go forward and give us victories.[112]

To Lincoln's gratified surprise, Hooker proved himself an unusually able organizer. He raised his army's drooping spirits and halted a disastrous flow of desertions by introducing a system of furloughs and improving the food, living conditions and hospitals. Scrapping Burnside's unwieldy "grand divisions," he reorganized the army into seven infantry and one cavalry corps, and by thus concentrating his mounted strength he made better use of it than those predecessors who had dissipated it by attaching it to the infantry. However, Hooker did decentralize his artillery to his later disadvantage.

All in all, the Army of the Potomac was a fine striking force of 94,000 effectives when, in April of 1863, it moved against Richmond again. In the Army of Northern Virginia, still concentrated along the Rappahannock near Fredericksburg, there were only 53,000 effectives, for LEE had found it necessary to send LONGSTREET south to guard the Virginia-Carolina coast.

Hooker's basic plan was to draw LEE out of his fortified defenses. John Sedgwick with 40,000 men was to demonstrate in front of Fredericksburg and hold LEE there while Hooker took the remaining 54,000 men up the Rappahannock to cross and come down on LEE's left. If LEE retreated, he would make, in effect, a flank march across Hooker's front and could be struck and annihilated. Joe Hooker had already announced that it was up to God to have mercy on the Confederates, because he would have none, and now he prepared his own superior brand of fire and brimstone.

At first, Hooker's maneuver was carried out with such skill and speed that he had three full corps over the river and advancing on LEE's left rear before the Southern chief realized what had happened. On April 29 Hooker was in Chancellorsville, a place which was hardly more than a long name for a little lone brick house at a tiny crossroads within a murky tangle of forest called "the Wilderness." Here, stands of second-growth oak and pine were choked with underbrush and laced with narrow, swampy streams, and here visibility was very poor and movement most difficult for large bodies of troops. Here, also, Hooker made the mistake of pausing, while the restless LEE gradually saw through Sedgwick's sound and fury at Fredericksburg. Realizing that his left rear was imperiled, LEE left 10,000 men under JUBAL EARLY to contain Sedgwick and hurried to halt Hooker with the rest of his army.

LEE did not, however, move fast enough. His advance units were pushed back by the Federals, and his right flank was gravely menaced by an entire corps under George Gordon Meade. The usually irascible Meade was so overjoyed that he cried: "Hurrah for old Joe! We're on LEE's flank, and he doesn't know it!"[113] Even better, Hooker's observation balloons had detected how weakly JUBAL EARLY was holding Fredericksburg. Here was the golden moment of Joseph Hooker's career. On his own front he had LEE outflanked and outnumbered, at Fredericksburg he had 40,000 men who could easily brush EARLY aside and crash into LEE's rear. What did he do? He let Sedgwick sit still and he ordered his own troops back to Chancellorsville.

Long ago in California an officer had noticed how "Hooker could play the best game of poker I ever saw until it came to the point where he should go a thousand better, and then he would flunk."[114] Hooker had flunked at Chancellorsville. He might say, with an outward assurance, "The enemy is in my power, and God Almighty cannot deprive me of them,"[115] but some of his indignant generals were already convinced that this was the bluster of the beaten man.

LEE was not yet convinced, although STONEWALL JACKSON was. Slowly, gradually, suspecting such an easy victory, LEE followed Hooker to Chancellorsville. By sunset of May 1, however, he had changed his mind.

No mere card-player who risks only money on the turn of a pasteboard, but a gambler willing to hazard armies and his own life and reputation on the bold move that can change the destiny of nations, LEE was again dividing his forces! JUBAL EARLY had 10,000 at Fredericksburg, LEE would keep another 14,000 at Chancellorsville in front of Hooker, while STONEWALL JACKSON took 28,000 on a sweep around the Union right flank to strike Hooker in the rear. To separate his force into three parts, none of which was superior in numbers to any enemy force, was audacious even for ROBERT E. LEE; yet LEE had inexhaustible faith in JACKSON, as JACKSON had in LEE, and between the one to conceive and the other to execute there has never existed a more perfect command collaboration in history.

On the morning of May 2, 1863, as JACKSON's corps began the long turning movement, the two men met briefly at a crossroads. JACKSON's Sorrel shambled forward toward LEE mounted on Traveler. JACKSON pointed ahead. LEE nodded, and JACKSON rode off. Throughout the day, JACKSON's butternuts marched across the Union front. They were detected by both scouts and observation balloons, yet Hooker did little to strengthen his right flank held by the one-armed Oliver Howard. It seemed that the very terrain there was too difficult for an enemy to penetrate. Hooker himself was extremely confident, touring his lines and repeatedly murmuring, "How strong! How strong!"[116] It was his expressed hope that the Confederates would attack him; and yet, as dusk began to gather, there had appeared no move.

The sun was low on the Union right. Soldiers who had stacked arms to eat dinner might have noticed, as they squatted on their knapsacks, how the blue of their uniforms grew less vivid. Suddenly groups of deer came running out of the woods to their right. The soldiers whooped and cheered, never bothering to wonder what had frightened the deer. Then came a riffle of rifle shots, the spine-chilling keen of the Rebel yell, thick rolling volleys of musketry, the boom of cannon —and into their midst came the first waves of a butternut flood.

With one great smashing blow, JACKSON shattered the Union right. An entire Federal corps was sent reeling back, and as it did, LEE, far to the east, pressed forward to hold Hooker's left. It might have been complete disaster for Hooker, except that night soon fell, the Confederates became disorganized, STONEWALL JACKSON was wounded by the fire of his own men, A. P. HILL was also wounded, and Federal artillery massed in the Union center struck viciously at the Confederates throughout the night.

In the morning JACKSON's attack was resumed under JEB STUART. Hooker, stunned by a falling pillar in the Chancellorsville mansion, failed to grasp the fact that his bigger army lay between LEE's fragments and that he could turn defeat into victory. Instead, his lines were bent back into a horseshoe holding his bridgeheads over the Rappahannock. He was so obviously eager to escape that when Sedgwick burst through EARLY at Fredericksburg on May 3, LEE calmly turned his back on him and went east to hurl Sedgwick back over the river. Turning again, he marched up to Hooker's horseshoe to complete the rout of the Army of the Potomac. But Fighting Joe Hooker had had enough of Marse Robert. He got his divisions safely across the Rappahannock, returning to the roost opposite Fredericksburg and there allowing the campaign which was to make the Lord blush for his mercy dwindle away to ignominious failure.

Federal losses at Chancellorsville were 17,000, compared to 13,000 for the Confederates. Yet LEE was soon to suffer an irreparable loss. At first it had seemed that the wounded JACKSON would quickly recover from his wounds. However, word soon came to LEE that JACKSON's left arm had been amputated and that he had displayed signs of pneumonia. Grieving, LEE told JACKSON's chaplain: "Give my affectionate regards, and tell him to make haste and get well, and come back to me as soon as he can. He has lost his left arm, but I have lost my right."[117] Inside the little cottage where he lay, STONEWALL JACKSON worsened, drifting in and out of delirium. May 10,

1863, arrived and JACKSON whispered: "It is the Lord's day. . . . My wish is fulfilled. I have always desired to die on Sunday."[118] He sank back into unconsciousness. Suddenly, clearly, softly, his voice rose from the bed: "Let us cross over the river, and rest under the shade of the trees."[119]

He did cross, and LEE the Jove of war had lost his thunderbolt.

Chancellorsville has been called the high noon of the Confederacy. Actually, in retrospect it may be seen that there never was a Confederate high noon. Southern victory had followed Southern victory, but none had been decisive, each had merely postponed the inevitable and thus prolonged the war. ROBERT E. LEE, splendid commander that he was, had not struck that shattering blow that annihilates armies and which can be marked by the wholesale surrender or desertion of enemy soldiers. ROBERT E. LEE has been compared to Hannibal, to whom a Carthaginian general said on the morrow of Cannae: "You know how to gain victory, but not how to use it."[120]

It may be that LEE, having drawn his sword for Virginia, could not see that the Confederacy was then, in that May of 1863, in serious trouble. The noose of the Federal blockade was slowly strangling the Southern economy and seaport after seaport was falling to the Union. In the central theater, Rosecrans and BRAGG neutralized each other, but along the Mississippi Grant had driven PEMBERTON into his corner at Vicksburg and slammed the door. LEE, of course, was not responsible for all this, because he was not the general in chief. Yet LONGSTREET did not hesitate to advise the Confederacy to rescue the Mississippi by taking advantage of its interior lines. Troops could be shifted from place to place by rail faster than the Federals could counter, he said. LEE should use two corps in Virginia to contain Hooker, and send all other troops west to help crush Rosecrans. Such a victory would stun the North and force the withdrawal of Grant from Vicksburg, argued LONGSTREET. The proposal was reasonable, although it overrated the capacity of the Confederacy's "worn-out" railroads.

LEE, however, preferred to defend the Confederacy in Virginia rather than on the Mississippi. To do this, he proposed to invade Pennsylvania, believing, as he had in 1862 when he invaded Maryland, that his movement north would draw the Federals away from Richmond. LEE was also convinced that the growing peace movement in the North would be strengthened, perhaps decisively, by a successful invasion. Moreover, he simply could not feed his army on the Rappahannock. He had to enter the North for provisions, if nothing else; and there, beyond doubt, is the proof that the "high noon" is a midday mirage. An army which invades to ease its hunger does not march under the banner of a prospering cause. Yet JEFFERSON DAVIS, troubled at the time by calls for troops at Vicksburg, also favored another invasion. The only officer of rank who opposed it was, again, JAMES LONGSTREET.

It is possible that LONGSTREET had grasped the enormous advantage which the bullet and the spade had conferred on the defense. When he rejoined LEE after Chancellorsville, he argued that the invasion of the North should be offensive in strategy and defensive in tactics. As he wrote later:

I suggested that, after piercing Pennsylvania and menacing Washington, we should choose a strong position, and force the Federals to attack us, observing that the popular clamor throughout the North 'would speedily force the Federal general to attempt to drive us out. I recalled to [LEE] the battle of Fredericksburg as an instance of a defensive battle; when, with a few thousand men, we hurled the whole Federal army back, crippling and demoralizing it, with trifling loss to our own troops.[121]

LEE listened, but was not persuaded. Unfortunately, for both men and the cause they served, LEE did not directly refuse the advice. LONGSTREET, in his vanity, mistook courtesy for consent—and left the interview convinced that the invasion would be conducted along the lines he had recommended.

Meanwhile, LEE reorganized his army into three infantry corps under LONGSTREET and A. P. HILL and one of JACKSON's old division commanders: RICHARD STODDART EWELL.

Bald-headed, long-nosed, pop-eyed and shrill-voiced, DICK EWELL had lost a leg at Second Manassas to complete his appearance as one of nature's jokes. Yet he was a fighting soldier whose perverse humor and sulphurous tongue made him a favorite with the men. "Old Baldhead," they called him, laughing at the thought that if he had lost a leg he had, in the period of his convalescence, gained a wife. However, EWELL, like A. P. HILL, was better with a division than a corps, although he led LEE's invasion off well enough by defeating the Federals at Winchester and clearing the way for an advance to the Potomac.

To the rear at Brandy Station, JEB STUART was to have screened LEE's right flank with his cavalry. But on June 9 STUART was surprised by a strong Union force of cavalry under Alfred Pleasonton. The biggest cavalry battle ever fought on the American continent began, 10,000 sabers to a side hacking at one another and firing pistols point-blank from heaving saddles. Gradually, STUART gained the upper hand; but he did not pursue Pleasonton, and the result was that Brandy Station burnished the tarnished pride of the Union horsemen and so stung STUART's vanity that he eventually took off on one of those sweeping "ride-arounds" he enjoyed so much. He did not screen LEE's flank; in fact, he allowed the Union Army to get *between him and Lee.*

Deprived of the eyes of his army, LEE entered Pennsylvania as though blindfolded and under the optimistic assumption that the Army of the Potomac was still sitting still on the south side of the Potomac.

On the night of June 28, however, a spy reached him with the news that the enemy army was across the Potomac around Frederick, squarely on LEE's flank, and that it had a new commander.

Like McClellan, Fighting Joe Hooker had been a casualty of Henry Halleck's fixation on Harpers Ferry. Halleck wanted to hold it, Hooker wanted to abandon it as indefensible and use the troops elsewhere. Actually, Hooker had been getting a little frantic about troops, complaining that LEE's army of 76,000 men outnumbered his own force of 115,000 men. Thus, when Hooker hotly sent off a telegram of resignation, it was quickly accepted. In the black early morning of June 28, 1863, an official from the War Department went to George Meade's tent and awakened that sleeping soldier. Meade thought he was being placed under arrest and tried to think of what he could have done wrong. It was only after a while that he realized he had been placed in command of the Army of the Potomac.

Like Burnside, he tried to decline, only to be informed that he could not disobey orders. So it was that this tall, hawk-nosed, hot-tempered, modest and competent general became the sixth man to command in the East. He was taking charge at a difficult time, on the eve of impending battle and with his army loosely scattered. Such difficulties were well appreciated by ROBERT E. LEE when he heard that night of his old comrade's promotion. Yet he could say: "General

Meade will commit no blunder in my front, and if I make one he will make haste to take advantage of it."[122]

Thus, on the following day, LEE hastened to concentrate his own forces. In the afternoon he spoke quietly to his officers: "Tomorrow, gentlemen, we will not move to Harrisburg, as we expected, but will go over to Gettysburg and see what General Meade is after."

General Meade was after General LEE. He was cautiously poking north from Maryland into Pennsylvania, with two corps moving toward Gettysburg. On June 30 two blue brigades of cavalry under John Buford rode into the town. A few leading riders clattered west of it on the Chambersburg Pike.

East along the dusty pike came the butternuts of A. P. HILL's corps, lean, bearded, sunburned men in mismatching shirts and pants, some without hats, others without shoes. They were after shoes, these men of JAMES PETTIGREW's brigade in HARRY HETH's division. They had heard that there was a big store of shoes in Gettysburg. Outside the town, however, they ran into Buford's outriders and were driven back. PETTIGREW reported the skirmish to HETH, and HETH received HILL's permission to take his entire division to Gettysburg the following day to "get those shoes."

Meanwhile, dismounted Union cavalrymen carrying breech-loading carbines were fanning out in a heavy picket holding the Chambersburg Pike. From his headquarters in a theological seminary, John Buford messaged General Meade that he had found enemy infantry and that he thought there might be trouble at Gettysburg the next day.

Buford's troopers were up early on July 1. Part of them patrolled roads north of Gettysburg, but most of them held the ridges west of town. Here one man in four stood 50 yards to the rear holding the horses, while the others took cover. There were not many of them, but their stubby new breechloaders would enable them to fire faster than the enemy, and because they need not make telltale motions of the arm ramming bullets home as was necessary with muzzle-loaders, they could remain concealed. They also had artillery, six guns in the center of their line.

It grew light and breezy, and the Federals saw the enemy column approaching. Ahead of it were skirmishers fanned out to both sides of the road and coming three deep through the fields. One of the Union guns was aimed at a group of mounted officers three-quarters of a mile off. The gunner pulled his lanyard, there was a flash and a bucking roar—and the Battle of Gettysburg was joined.

Soon Confederate guns began baying. ROBERT E. LEE, riding into Cashtown about six miles west, heard that distant grumble. Artillery! Leaving LONGSTREET behind, he urged Traveler forward into Cashtown. There he found A. P. HILL, pale and sick that day, who told him only that HETH had gone ahead under instructions not to bring on battle until the rest of the army came up. LEE's forces were scattered: LONGSTREET to the rear, HILL at Cashtown, and EWELL north of Gettysburg. Fearing an escalating fight, a "meeting engagement" for which he was not prepared, LEE galloped toward the sound of the guns.

On and on he rode, "like a blinded giant,"[123] absolutely in the dark about where the Federals were or what his own forces were doing. Louder rose the sound of the guns, counterpointed now by the roll of musketry and the sharp spatting of the Yankee carbines.

South of Gettysburg, couriers from Buford brought the news of battle to John Reynolds. He, too, galloped toward the sound of guns, ordering his corps to follow. He rode toward the seminary. Buford saw him from the belfry. "There's the devil to pay!"[124] he yelled, and clattered down the stairs. Reynolds took charge. His soldiers went into line with Buford's troopers on Seminary Ridge west of the town. He called for help from General Howard and his corps, and messaged Meade that the enemy was attacking Gettysburg but "I will fight him inch by inch. . . ."[125]

Reynolds's units arrived just in time, just as the butternuts drove back Buford's exhausted troopers. Counterattacking savagely, the blue-clad infantrymen wrecked two Confederate brigades. Then a Rebel sharpshooter killed the gallant Reynolds, but then also, at noon, Howard arrived with his corps to block the northern road down which EWELL had begun to advance.

Below Seminary Ridge, ROBERT E. LEE had reached the battlefield. He could learn nothing except that two of HETH's brigades had been shattered. Then, to the left of HETH's lines, LEE saw a long gray column emerge from a wood. It was one of EWELL's divisions, forming on HETH's left. It could not have happened better if LEE had planned it. Still, he hesitated.

"No," he told an eager general, "I am not prepared to bring on a general engagement today—LONGSTREET is not up."[126]

It was then that LEE saw, still farther left, another of EWELL's divisions form up, and he hesitated no longer. With a yell and a roll of musketry, the gray lines swept forward, and the blue ranks were broken and forced into a stubborn retreat through Gettysburg to Cemetery Hill south of town.

LEE saw that if he could take Cemetery Hill he would control the entire position. A. P. HILL, however, said that his men were too exhausted to fight. LEE asked EWELL to make the attack, and then LONGSTREET rode up and LEE showed him Cemetery Hill where blue columns were massing. Studying the height through glasses, LONGSTREET said: "All we have to do is to throw our army around by their left, and we shall interpose between the Federal army and Washington."[127] Obviously, LONGSTREET still clung to his theory of offensive strategy and defensive tactics, but LEE answered him at once: "If the enemy is there, we must attack him."[128]

There was no further action that day, however, because EWELL had delayed and LONGSTREET's corps was still marching toward the battlefield. Meanwhile, two more Federal corps had arrived, together with Winfield Scott Hancock whom Meade had sent forward to take command. Howard objected. He had been distinguished that day, riding over the field with a battle flag stuck under his stump of right arm, and he was senior to Hancock. At length, the two generals agreed to cooperate in organizing the position. Culp's Hill to the right of Cemetery Hill was fortified, and so was Cemetery Ridge to the left.

At midnight George Meade arrived. Somewhat regretfully, he decided to accept the fight forced upon him. The successful holding action begun by Buford and continued by Reynolds and Howard had given him time to bring more of his forces forward. LEE's numerical superiority had been whittled and Meade now held a slight edge. LEE realized this. He, too, had accepted battle reluctantly, if he was not actually forced into it by eager subordinates.

Neither EWELL nor HILL had served LEE particularly well that day, and he was beginning to doubt LONGSTREET to the extent that for once a cry of complaint escaped him: "LONGSTREET is a very good fighter when he gets in position, but he is so slow!"[129] Even if LONGSTREET had been right about getting around the Federal left and standing on the defensive there, LEE, with only a few thousand cavalry, knew so little about Meade that he could not be sure that such a maneuver might not end in disaster. No, there was nothing for LEE to do next day but strike with all his strength before the entire Federal Army arrived on his front.

That night a full moon shone upon the armies massed opposite each other. It illuminated the dreadful debris of battle and shone palely on the sign at the graveyard gate warning that a five-dollar fine would be imposed on anyone caught discharging a firearm in the cemetery.

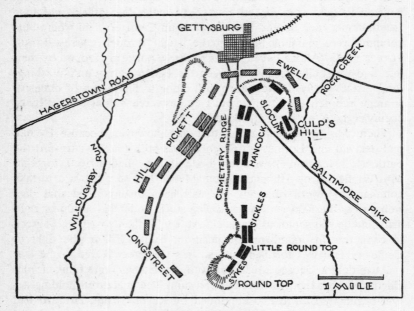

BATTLE OF GETTYSBURG

July 2 came in hot. Sweat stained the armpits of Federals putting the finishing touches on their log breastworks, and darkened the homespun shirts of Confederate soldiers marching over dusty roads or into sultry fields where the sunlight hung heavy in suffocating folds. Any way the Rebels looked at it, either from their left where EWELL's men were going at Culp's Hill and Cemetery Hill, or from their right where LONGSTREET was to storm Cemetery Ridge, the advance was going to be uphill over rocky slopes and into massed guns.

It did not, however, begin on time. Longstreet was again late. When he did arrive, he renewed his argument for the turning movement around the Yankee left. Lee, who wanted to attack first thing in the morning, was still for immediate battle. After Lee left him, Longstreet said to General John Hood: "The General is a little nervous this morning. He wishes me to attack. I do not wish to do so without Pickett. I never go into battle with one boot off."[130]

Longstreet's other boot was not on until three o'clock in the afternoon, when his artillery began firing. An hour later his men swept forward, coming against a peach orchard and high ground which extended the Yankee flank farther left.

Here was a corps under the legendary Dan Sickles, a duelist and political general who also had his own ideas of how a battle should be fought. On his own initiative Sickles had occupied this new ground with its apex in a peach orchard. The position was too extensive to be defended by a single corps, and because of its wedge shape it could be struck on either side by Rebel artillery. An infuriated George Meade snapped all these defects into Sickles's teeth after the rumble of Longstreet's guns brought the Union commander galloping to his embattled left. By then it was too late to withdraw. The Confederate bombardment was rising in fury, taking off one of Sickles's legs and beheading the little peach trees. Federal guns bellowed back, and then the Confederates charged.

Back and forth swayed the battle, through the splintered peach orchard, into a wheat field, around a jumble of boulders to be known as the Devil's Den. Men and horses dashed in and out of choking blue clouds of powder smoke. Confederate and Federal knelt to blast away at each other at point-blank range. Officers peered anxiously into the smoke, trying to follow the course of the battle by a glimpse of battle flags. Everywhere was the deafening and dreadful clamor of combat, the crash of gun and shell, the hoarse high cries of men or the terrible screaming of stricken horses; and everywhere also the varied voices of invisible death: the keen of the bullet, the wail of the shell and the shrieking of shards of stone. At first the Federals were forced back. Reinforced, the blue lines regained the lost ground, only to be thrown back again by a furious Confederate counterattack. Now a great hole gaped in Meade's left, until another Federal corps rushed forward to plug the gap.

On Meade's right, EWELL's attack did not spring forward until shortly before dark. The Rebels came struggling up smoke-drifted hills, and were spun and scythed to the earth or toppled and sent rolling down the slopes. At one point, the Confederates seized a foot-hold; but they could not hold it, and when night fell only their fallen remained on Cemetery Hill.

That night JEB STUART's weary horsemen at last rode into the Con-federate camp, and the fresh troops of GEORGE PICKETT's division also arrived. With these reinforcements, LEE resolved on a supreme effort to crush the Army of the Potomac. STUART was to take all the cavalry and strike the Union rear while LONGSTREET hurled himself once more upon the Federal left. Again, on that fateful morning of July 3, 1863, JAMES LONGSTREET protested—and for the same reasons. LEE, how-ever, was determined; but because of LONGSTREET's reluctance he shifted that general's attack to the Federal center. And so, as JEB STUART and his veteran troops rode off to an inconclusive saddle-to-saddle joust with Federal cavalry in Meade's rear, LONGSTREET began massing 160 guns and 15,000 infantry opposite the Yankee center on Cemetery Ridge. Objective for both men and guns was a grove of umbrella-shaped chestnuts: the center of the center which, if it gave, would break Meade's army in half.

Noon came, and all was in readiness on Seminary Ridge where the Confederates had massed. A mile away, across a little valley, the Federals waited, sweating under the same sun, their own cannon massed, their eyes fixed on the ranked red battle flags. The moment had arrived for the boom of artillery and the long quavering yell, but it was slow in coming because JAMES LONGSTREET could not bring himself to give the final order for the charge. To his artillery chief, EDWARD ALEXANDER, he wrote: "If the artillery does not have the effect to drive off the enemy or greatly demoralize him, so as to make our effort pretty certain, I would prefer that you should not advise PICKETT to make the charge."[131] ALEXANDER, loath to accept his gen-eral's responsibility, demurred. There was an exchange of notes, until ALEXANDER finally wrote: "General: when our fire is at its best, I will advise General PICKETT to advance."[132]

At 1 P.M. the Rebel guns began bellowing. A mile away, Union cannoneers ran to their pieces. The mightiest bombardment of the war was under way, a monstrous metallic clanging that filled the little valley with the fog of war and spread death and destruction on both ridges. Twenty minutes after it began, ALEXANDER notified PICKETT: "If you are to advance at all, you must come at once or we will not be able to support you as we ought. But the enemy's fire has not slackened materially and there are still 18 guns firing from the cemetery."[133] A few minutes later, through a rent in the smoke, ALEXANDER saw the Federal batteries withdrawing from the chestnut grove, and he wrote to PICKETT: "For God's sake come quick. The 18 guns have gone. Come quick or my ammunition will not let me support you properly."[134]

PICKETT was standing beside LONGSTREET when he received ALEXANDER's first note. He handed it to the general. LONGSTREET read it without a word, and PICKETT asked: "General, shall I advance?"[135] LONGSTREET glanced away, turned back and slowly nodded his head. PICKETT saluted. "I am going to lead my division forward, sir,"[136] he said, and galloped away. LONGSTREET walked back to a fence and sat on it to watch the battle which had commenced against his wishes and without his having spoken a single word of command. At one point, learning that ALEXANDER was low on ammunition, he thought of halting PICKETT. "I don't want to make this charge," LONGSTREET said. "I don't see how it can succeed. I would stop PICKETT now but General LEE has ordered it and is expecting it."[137]

So PICKETT was not detained, and he rode among his butternuts shaking his long hair and crying, "Up men, and to your posts!"[138] Seizing their muskets, the Confederates walked through their now silent gun batteries and began dressing ranks. The time had come.

Across the valley, the Federals sensed it. Their guns, too, had fallen still; not because they had been silenced or withdrawn, as ALEXANDER thought, but because the Union gunners wanted to conserve ammunition until the moment when the Confederate lines were caught helplessly out in the valley. Now the Rebel skirmishers could be seen emerging from the woods of Seminary Ridge. Now the whole line was visible, dressing almost perfectly . . . coming on, a moving forest of steel, bayonets glittering in the sunlight. Now there was a gap between right-flank units, but still they came on . . . 100 yards they came . . . 200 yards . . . not quite 300—

With a dreadful roar the full fury of massed Union guns struck that gallant host. Flags went down, men sank to the ground, horses fell or galloped riderless over the field, but PICKETT's charge pressed forward. Because they were coming at the Union center, the Rebels could be enfiladed from both sides, and the Union guns savaged them mercilessly. Their lines broken and ragged, with units forward and back, they stopped to redress once again, and kept on. Then they were at the hill beneath a stone fence and charging up it. There was a twinkling of flame from the wall and the men in butternut were toppled and spun. From the remnant came a ragged Rebel yell, and LEWIS ARMISTEAD put his hat on his sword, cried, "Follow me!" and leaped the stone wall to die with his hand on a Union cannon. But few followed him.

PICKETT'S charge had been broken by Union artillery and long-range musketry before it could even gain momentum. Only the great bravery of such soldiers and the gallantry of such officers could have brought it so far as the stone wall on Cemetery Ridge. Now, however, the broken bits of regiments and brigades were washing back down the valley. Now there was the opportunity for a Federal counterattack. LEE, sensing this, rushed to meet PICKETT to tell him to put his division behind a hill and prepare for a Federal sally. "General LEE, I have no division now," PICKETT said sadly, "ARMISTEAD is down, GARNETT is down, and KEMPER is mortally wounded."[139]

"Come, General PICKETT," said LEE, "this has been my fight and upon my shoulders rests the blame."[140] Still preparing for the Federal thrust, LEE rode among the returning butternuts, crying to them, rallying them, and whenever he met a man only lightly wounded, calling to him, "Bind up your hurts and take a musket."[141]

General Meade, however, was content with his defensive victory, and he remained in position. That night LEE prepared to retreat to Virginia. His second attempt at invasion had ended more disastrously than the first. As a rainy night fell upon the bloodiest battlefield in American history, the exhausted LEE walked Traveler through the silent tents of his sleeping army. Reaching his headquarters, he suddenly burst into a cry of admiration: "I never saw troops behave more magnificently than PICKETT'S division of Virginians did today in that grand charge upon the enemy! And if they had been supported as they were to have been—but for some reason not yet fully explained to me, were not—we would have held the position and the day would have been ours." LEE paused, and then, in a loud and agonized voice, he cried: "Too bad! *Too bad!* OH, TOO BAD!"[142]

11

☆

Gettysburg remains the most famous battle in the Civil War, chiefly because of the immortal Gettysburg Address delivered there by Abraham Lincoln on November 19, 1863, and because it was such a dreadful blood bath. Union losses totaled 23,000, while the Confederates, reporting 20,400, probably suffered closer to 28,-000. That was no less than one-third of LEE's force, and if Meade had pursued vigorously he might have made Gettysburg a truly decisive victory.

Meade, however, followed so cautiously that LEE got safely back to Virginia. "We had them within our grasp," Lincoln lamented. "We had only to stretch forth our hands and they were ours. And nothing I could say or do could make the Army move."[143] Gettysburg, then, merely ended for all time Southern hopes for that victory on Northern soil which would bring help from abroad. It was Vicksburg, which fell the day after PICKETT's charge, that gave the Confederacy its mortal wound. Lincoln was aware of this when, on August 26, he wrote of the great event with such sprightly jubilation:

Thanks to the great Northwest for [Vicksburg]. Nor yet wholly to them. Three hundred miles up they met New England, Empire, Keystone, and Jersey, hewing their way right and left. The sunny South, too, in more colors than one, also lent a hand. On the spot, their part of the history was jotted down in black and white. The job was a great national one; and let none be banned who bore an honorable part in it. And while those who have cleared the great river may well be proud, even that is not all. It is hard to say that anything has been more bravely and well done than at Antietam, Murfreesboro, Gettysburg, and on many fields of lesser note. Nor must Uncle Sam's web-feet be forgotten. At all the watery margins they have been present. Not only on the deep sea, the broad bay and the rapid river, but also up the narrow muddy bayou, and wherever the ground was a little damp, they have been, and made their tracks. Thanks to all. For the great republic—for the principle it lives by, and keeps alive—for man's vast future—thanks to all.[144]

Lincoln's elation over Vicksburg, however, was tempered considerably by the realization that Meade's failure to destroy LEE's army had prolonged a war growing ever more unpopular in the North. Only the previous July a mob howling "To hell with the draft and the war!"[145] had terrorized New York City for three wild and bloody days. Burning homes, public buildings, churches, police stations, stores, factories, saloons, even an orphanage, murdering Negroes and battling police and soldiers hand to hand in the streets or from behind barricades, driving draft officials from their offices and wrecking draft apparatus, the rioters exploded in a fury of resentment against "a rich man's war and a poor man's fight." In the end, the draft was suspended in New York and regiments from the Army of the Potomac marched into the city to quell the mob. But not before 400 persons had been killed or wounded and $5 million lost in property damage.

In truth the rioters, incited by antiadministration newspapers as well as by such personages as Franklin Pierce and Governor Horatio Seymour, had much to resent in a draft law that permitted anyone to buy an exemption for $300 or to hire a substitute to go in his place. Obviously the law was designed for well-heeled lip-servers of the Union cause, most notable among them being Grover Cleveland, who hired a substitute to fight his fight for the nation which he was twice to lead as President. In New York City some $5 million was siphoned from the city treasury for draft-evasion purposes, the money going to politicians, lawyers, examining physicians, fixers and other patriotic types who would thus see to it that the "right people" would be deferred. Thus, of 292,441 men called in New York, 39,877 failed to report, 164,394 were exempted, 52,288 bought exemption for $300 apiece and 26,002 hired substitutes. Only 9,880 men—about one out of 30—who either lacked political pull or possessed true patriotism went off to fight. No wonder the mob rose in fury! No wonder there were similar though not nearly so violent protests throughout the North, especially in New England where sanctimonious "blue noses" often bought exemption and then, once the war was over, piously prevailed upon local legislatures to repay them for this patriotic outlay. The humorist Artemus Ward ridiculed such coat-holders with the remark: "I have already given two cousins to the war, & I stand reddy

to sacrifiss my wife's brother, ruthurn'n not see the rebellion krusht.
And if wuss comes to wuss, I'll shed every drop of blood my able-
bodied relations has got to prosekoot the war."[146] So it was the farmers, the wage hands, and especially the immigrants, who arrived in
the North to the number of 800,000 during the war years, who
shouldered the Union muskets.

Meanwhile, enormous profits were being made by war contractors.
Among those famous fortunes founded during the Civil War were
Armour in meat-packing, Borden in dairy products, Carnegie in iron
and steel, Marshall Field in merchandise, Huntington in merchandise
and railroads, Remington in guns, Rockefeller in oil and Weyer-
haeuser in lumber. Profiteering naturally contributed to inflation, and
wages, without benefit of organized unions, trailed far behind skyrocketing prices. In purse as well as in person, then, it was "a rich
man's war and a poor man's fight."

Among Lincoln's other difficulties in that summer of 1863 was the
intrusion of France into Mexico, where Napoleon III hoped to set up
a puppet government with the young Austrian Archduke Maximilian
as his emperor. Little Napoleon had flagrantly violated the Monroe
Doctrine, but there was not very much that Lincoln could do about it
until after the war. Nor was there much that either Lincoln or JEF-
FERSON DAVIS could do about the defeatism and disloyalty which grew
stronger in each camp with every passing month.

Some of the opposition to both Presidents was provoked by the
ruthlessness with which they enforced conscription. Some of it came
from persons honestly convinced that peace could be achieved by
negotiation, and some from those fainthearted or selfish persons for
whom plotting or treason always has seemed the way of safety or
profit. Thus both sides organized secret societies. In the Northwest
the "Knights of the Golden Circle" terrorized loyalists with midnight
raids or met with Southern spies to plot fifth-column uprisings for
which they really had no stomach, and in the South the "Heroes of
America" gave more surreptitious aid and comfort to the North. On
both sides, opposition was too formidable for either President to move
against it.

DAVIS's chief difficulties came from states' rights governors such
as JOSEPH BROWN of Georgia, who suspended the draft and raised a
militia of 10,000 men to defend his state alone. Governor VANCE of
North Carolina was only less obstructionist, and he acted in that

fashion because his state was so full of antiwar sentiment that at one point there was open talk of seceding from the Confederacy. Much as the gentlewoman had been the South's chief recruiter, too many beloveds had been coming home in coffins. Mrs. Chesnut wrote: "Is anything worth it—this fearful sacrifice; this awful penalty we pay for war?"[147] Another wife of a Confederate officer wrote: "I am for a tidal wave of peace—and I am not alone."[148]

The North's peace movement was more open and better organized. In the Northwest, where intense patriotism and open treason flourished side by side, it was led by those antiwar Democrats called Copperheads from their lapel insignia of an Indian head carved from a copper penny. A former Ohio Congressman named Clement Vallandigham was the Copperhead leader. While in Congress the proslavery Vallandigham had taunted Republicans with the remark: "War for the Union was abandoned; war for the Negro openly begun, and with stronger battalions than before."[149] While campaigning for governor of Ohio in 1863 he had characterized the war as being fought "for the purpose of crushing out liberty and erecting a despotism."[150] Lincoln would have been content to let Vallandigham talk himself out, rather than make a martyr of him; however, the blunt General Burnside was now in command in Ohio and he had Vallandigham arrested, tried by a military court and sentenced to jail for the rest of the war. With keen good humor, Lincoln changed the sentence to banishment within the Confederacy. The Copperheads replied with a 40,000-member mass meeting in Lincoln's home town where they resolved "that a further offensive prosecution of this war tends to subvert the Constitution and the Government."[151] They also assailed Lincoln's treatment of Vallandigham, to which he gave the grim answer: "Must I shoot a simple-minded soldier boy who deserts and not touch a hair of the wily agitator who induces him to desert?"[152]

By then the North was shooting deserters a half-dozen at a time, and with such solemnity and deliberation as would strike fear into the hearts of soldiers massed to witness the executions. Desertion was a problem for both sides—one out of nine enlistments in the South deserted, one out of seven in the North—but the Union Army had to deal with defeatists who systematically encouraged soldiers to desert and mailed them packages containing the civilian clothes and railroad tickets which would facilitate their disappearance. Most despised deserters of all were the bounty jumpers, men who enlisted in one state or locality to claim a bounty, and then deserted to claim another one in a different place.

The bounty system was another Union headache. To reduce the number of men needed to be drafted from any state or city, bounties were paid to men who would volunteer. However, the bounties rose to as high as $1,000 per man after reluctant draftees began to bid against states and cities for the services of a substitute. Next there entered the inevitable middleman, the sly, grasping bounty broker who for a fee would find a man willing to enlist. Too often the broker operated like a waterfront crimp, getting his man drunk and inducing him to sign away his bounty rights for a pittance and then rushing him through the enlistment process. Some did not scruple to scour the slums of Europe for recruits. As a result, the dregs of society were often draped in Federal blue, to the indignation of one recruiting officer who protested against putting the uniform "upon branded felons; upon blotched and bloated libertines and pimps; upon thieves, burglars and vagabonds; upon the riff-raff of corruption and scoundrelism of every shade and degree of infamy which can be swept into the insatiable clutches of the vampires who fatten upon the profits of the execrable business."[153] Naturally, the chief concern of such "soldiers" was how best to avoid fighting and how quickly to get out of uniform; and so, as the war grew older, they were treated with increasing harshness by a government which still had not the moral courage to draft outright all those shrinking, perfumed patriots who had purchased their own safety with these decrepit or debased human beings.

Although the South was not so hypocritical in waging "a rich man's war and a poor man's fight," it nevertheless did discriminate to a lesser degree. Substitute-buying, though not as widespread, was permitted; and to the numerous exempt classes was added that of the plantation overseer at the rate of one to every 20 Negro slaves. This was the infamous "20-nigger law" which enraged the poorer whites, and helped to raise the rate of deserters and men absent without leave. In June of 1863 the proportion of absentees from the Confederate Army was nearing one-third, and President DAVIS proclaimed an amnesty for all who would return to their units. Few, however, came back; nor did many respond after Gettysburg evoked a repetition of the offer. Confederate arms, then, appeared to be in desperate straits when Union forces in the West began driving for Chattanooga.

Chattanooga was one of the South's vital east-west railroad junctions, it was the gateway to Georgia, and possession of it by the North would liberate pro-Union populations in east Tennessee and northern Georgia. Chattanooga was the objective of William Rosecrans, as its defense was the mission of BRAXTON BRAGG. Since the Battle of Murfreesboro, however, Old Rosy and his Federals had built what appeared to be a permanent camp around the town while BRAGG and his Rebels had gone into similiar hibernation at Tullahoma 20 miles to the south.

On June 23, 1863, after months of inaction, Rosecrans and his Army of the Cumberland began moving toward BRAGG and Chattanooga. As they did, they were swamped by torrential rains. "No Presbyterian rain, either," a soldier said, "but a genuine Baptist downpour."[154] Yet the army stumbled on, and Rosecrans, maneuvering with rare skill, was able to threaten BRAGG's rear and force him to retreat all the way to Chattanooga.

Old Rosy, however, wasted the next two weeks at Tullahoma, bickering by long-distance telegraph with General Halleck over reinforcements. Curtly ordered to resume his advance, he moved out on August 16. Again he maneuvered deftly, getting his army across the Tennessee by demonstrating above Chattanooga while his main body crossed the river below the town. BRAGG, again fearing for his rear, evacuated Chattanooga and fell back into Georgia.

To Rosecrans, this withdrawal looked like a retreat. He resolved on headlong pursuit to catch and crush BRAGG, and because the terrain below Chattanooga was a most difficult land of huge ridges offering few passes, he divided his forces to facilitate their movement. But BRAGG was not retreating. He was actually concentrating his army for battle, receiving reinforcements being rushed to him from Kentucky and Mississippi. Far away in Virginia, President DAVIS, at last conceding the importance of the West, had put JAMES LONGSTREET and most of his corps aboard rickety trains and sent them by a roundabout route to BRAGG's side. When they arrived in September, BRAGG outnumbered Rosecrans by 70,000 to 60,000; and he saw that the Federal commander's rash dispersion was his own opportunity.

The battleground was to be in the valley of Chickamauga Creek. Here, BRAGG first struck at the separated Union right under George Thomas and Alexander McCook. But the Confederate commanders, unaccustomed to any celerity from BRAGG, moved with the usual deliberation and failed. Their failure alerted Rosecrans, who began frantically pulling his forces together on his left a few miles south of Chattanooga. BRAGG evolved another plan: swing hard against the Union left before it could concentrate, driving it away from Chattanooga into a jumbled wilderness where it could be fragmented and beaten to death by bits.

BRAGG as usual delayed, and Rosecrans rapidly moved Thomas's corps into position on the left of Thomas Crittenden's. So the Army of the Cumberland seemed prepared when BRAGG began attacking on September 19, and the opening Confederate blows were blunted. Next morning the Rebels struck again, the right under the battling bishop LEONIDAS POLK coming against Thomas with crushing fury. Fighting desperately, the Federals held. But Thomas was hurt and he kept calling for reinforcements. Rosecrans tried to feed him a division from his quiet right flank, but the unit went astray and never reached Thomas. Thomas, however, renewed his pleas for help, giving Rosecrans the impression that a Confederate tidal wave was rolling against his left. In fact, POLK had been beaten back, and it was Rosecrans's *right* that was endangered.

Here JAMES LONGSTREET had prepared his customary set-piece haymaker. Under cover of woods, he had formed his troops in a column of brigades. When they hit, they would hit in a series of hammer blows. And now, opposite LONGSTREET, chance was entering the battle.

Rosecrans had received an erroneous report that there was a gap to the right of his center. He ordered one division to "close up" on another to plug the gap, but the division commander, knowing that there was no gap, construed the "close-up" order to mean he should get *behind* the other division. So he pulled out of the line, leaving a gaping void, and as he did LONGSTREET's brigades came rolling into the hole.

They struck Union brigades as they were leaving the line, Union brigades as they were entering, and they came yelling against them on their flanks. The result was sheer catastrophe. The Union right was swept away. Rosecrans, his staff, even Assistant Secretary of War Charles Dana were jostled off toward Chattanooga on a struggling flood of soldiers, ambulances, baggage wagons and artillery. When Dana saw the devout Rosecrans crossing himself in supplication, he concluded that all was lost.

But all was not lost. George Thomas, the solid general from Virginia, was hanging on. While LONGSTREET and POLK eagerly closed around him, he reorganized around Horseshoe Ridge. LONGSTREET might cry jubilantly, "They have fought their last man and *he* is running,"[155] but the fact was that the Federals were rallying, tightening their lines beneath the smoke, waving their flags defiantly at the oncoming Rebels. In the hollow of a hill, Thomas stood feeding his horse corn, impassively following the battle. At one point Thomas told a colonel that his hill must be held at all costs, and the colonel replied: "We'll hold it, General, or we'll go to heaven from it."[156]

The hill held, Thomas held—like a rock, to receive the immortal nickname of "the Rock of Chickamauga"—and the Army of the Cumberland was saved from destruction. That night Thomas retired, and the Confederates failed to pursue. Nevertheless, the South was thrilled to hear of BRAGG's great victory at the Battle of Chickamauga. It seemed that he had turned the tide in the West, and even the price of 18,450 Confederate casualties as against 16,170 Union losses seemed not too high to pay for such a great reversal of fortunes. Moreover, BRAGG had Rosecrans's army penned up in Chattanooga, and it seemed only a matter of time before the Federals capitulated.

Unfortunately for the South, BRAGG had also succeeded in bringing U. S. Grant into the field against him.

News of the defeat at Chickamauga and fears for the safety of the Army of the Cumberland all but panicked the Washington government. Two full army corps were immediately detached from Meade and sent west under Joe Hooker, while Sherman was ordered east from Memphis with part of the Army of the Tennessee. Finally, Lincoln named Grant chief of all Union forces between the Allegheny Mountains and the Mississippi,* with the option of choosing Rosecrans or Thomas to command at Chattanooga. Grant chose Thomas, until, on October 23, he arrived there himself.

Grant found the Union forces caught in a trap and in danger of being starved into surrender. A vast Confederate semicircle enclosed the Federals. It ran around Chattanooga from the Tennessee upstream, following the heights of Missionary Ridge south and then swinging west again to Lookout Mountain and a bit beyond to the Tennessee. To the north of the Union rear ran wild, mountainous country

* Except for the force in New Orleans under Banks.

penetrated only by a single cart track. Thus there was no way out if a retreat were contemplated, and no way in for supplies.

The situation could hardly have been worse, and for Grant, whose spirit thrived on adversity, that was tantamount to never being better. Almost at once he determined to open a supply line. On the night of October 26 about 1,500 Federals surprised a Rebel force at Brown's Ferry to the west, seized a beachhead and threw a pontoon bridge over the river. From here, Joe Hooker led a march overland to Bridgeport, the Union supply depot on the Tennessee. Thus was opened the famous "cracker line" over which troops and supplies came into Chattanooga. BRAGG, failing to grasp the importance of this breach in his investing line, did little to retake Brown's Ferry. Instead, he detached LONGSTREET and 15,000 badly needed veterans, sending them 150 miles east to attack General Burnside in Knoxville, Kentucky.

Now Washington actually did panic, bombarding Grant with shrill requests to do something to relieve Burnside. On November 7 Grant asked Thomas to attack BRAGG's right flank so as to compel him to recall LONGSTREET. Thomas, however, grimly alluded to the fact that he had not enough mules or horses (10,000 of them had died during the siege) to draw a single piece of artillery. Grant agreed to wait until Sherman arrived. Once Sherman was on the scene, Grant began attacking.

His plan, which evolved as the situation changed, was to bring off a double envelopment. Hooker was to strike the Confederate left at Lookout Mountain while Sherman hurled himself at the Rebel right on the upper end of Missionary Ridge. In the meantime, Thomas's men were to put the pressure on the center at Missionary Ridge to prevent BRAGG from reinforcing his flanks.

The battle began November 24, 1863, with Hooker meeting immediate and spectacular success. His men outnumbered the Rebels by five or six to one, and they swarmed up Lookout Mountain's rocky slopes and meadows to drive the defenders off the summit. Below them, war correspondents gazed in enchantment at the mountaintop alive with the winking of thousands of deadly fireflies, and then after a fog drifted in between valley and crest, giving Lookout a circlet of smoke infused with flame, the phrase "battle fought above the clouds" was born.[157] Actually, Hooker had not done much more than knock BRAGG's left anchor loose.

Meanwhile on the right, BRAGG's men were breaking Sherman's attack into fragments. Here, there was not one continuous ridge as Grant and Sherman believed, but a jumble of separated small hills. The Rebels fought from behind excellent fortifications, sometimes rolling big boulders down upon their luckless attackers. With nightfall, Sherman had not made much of a dent in BRAGG's right.

Next day, November 25, the double assault was renewed. This time Hooker's men descended the other side of Lookout Mountain and blundered into futility on a wooded plain, while Sherman once again could get nowhere on the right. In fact, Sherman was so convinced that BRAGG was reinforcing from his center that he asked Grant for help. Grant's reply was to order Thomas to press forward against the Rebel center on Missionary Ridge.

Here were bristling lines at the foot of the 500-foot hill and on its crest. Thomas had some doubts about taking even the rifle pits at the bottom, but Grant prodded him forward. Standing on a hill smoking a cigar, Grant watched Thomas's men start for the blazing pits. Into a tangle of felled trees they poured, 20,000 strong, breaking through in several places to strike the dismayed Rebels on opened flanks and exposed rear. In an instant, the Confederates broke and fled up the ridge. Into the abandoned pits jumped the aroused Federals, men of the Army of the Cumberland who had fought hard at Chickamauga only to find themselves the butt of endless needling by the unbeaten dandies of Sherman's and Hooker's units. Now they looked eagerly up the ridge to the Confederate guns.

Cocky little Phil Sheridan, resplendent in dress uniform, sat his horse and looked at the guns. He drew a flask from his pocket and toasted a group of Confederate officers above him, crying, "Here's at you!"[158] At once, the Rebel guns roared at Sheridan, striking close enough to shower him and his officers with dirt. Sheridan's face darkened. "I'll take those guns for that!"[159]

And then, suddenly and in a rush, the Federals went charging up the ridge, straight into a storm of enemy fire, and right before the incredulous eyes of U. S. Grant on his hilltop. Wheeling in anger, Grant snapped: "Thomas, who ordered those men up the ridge?"

"I don't know," Thomas replied slowly, and then, addressing one of his corps commanders, Gordon Granger: "Did you order them up, Granger?"[160] Slowly at first came the answer, "No, they started up without orders," and then, with a flash of pride: "When those fellows get started all hell can't stop them!"[161]

Growling something to the effect that someone would suffer if the attack failed, Grant turned to watch the charging Cumberlands, and saw to his delight that all hell indeed could not stop them. The great battle line was now a series of V's struggling upward behind fluttering battle flags, for the regiments were racing each other for the crest. On through the Rebel fire and smoke they came, sometimes pausing for breath, but sweeping inexorably closer until Confederate astonishment turned to alarm, then to fear—and they broke and ran. Jubilant Federals chased them, beckoning their comrades forward and calling, "My God! Come and see them run!"[162]

Butternuts had never before been routed like this, but they had been through much, these weary fighters of BRAGG's army. So they gave completely away, a two-mile hole was punched in BRAGG's center, and the Battle of Chattanooga ended with BRAGG retreating into Georgia and the Union forces in full possession of the West.

Chattanooga, with 5,820 Union casualties and 6,600 Confederate, also placed the reputation of U. S. Grant beyond reach of his numerous traducers. Abraham Lincoln had already suggested that perhaps those timid generals who deplored "Grant's drinking" might do well to try Grant's brand of whiskey. After the winter of 1863-64 passed without another Union success, the President called Grant to Washington and placed him in command of all the armies.

12

☆

On March 9, 1864, Ulysses S. Grant received the revived rank of lieutenant general and took command of all the Union armies. After four years of fruitless searching, Abraham Lincoln had at last found *his* general: a man of single purpose and ruthless driving energy who would ignore politics and concentrate upon destroying the Confederate Army.

Under Grant there was to be a common plan, with all forces acting in concert, and armies, not cities, were to be the objective. These targets were the Army of Northern Virginia with 60,000 men under

LEE and the Army of Tennessee with about the same number now under JOE JOHNSTON, who had replaced the feckless BRAXTON BRAGG. William Tecumseh Sherman with 100,000 men in Chattanooga was to go for JOHNSTON while Grant with 120,000 in Virginia went for LEE. In effect, Grant would hold LEE by constant attack while Sherman maneuvered against his rear by pushing JOHNSTON back toward Atlanta. Thus neither Confederate force could help the other; each would be worn down until one or the other was crushed, and then both Union forces would unite to destroy the survivor. Thus, also, the Confederacy would be forced to contend with those high casualties which were its daily dread.

Actually, George Meade still led the Army of the Potomac; however, inasmuch as Grant had decided to accompany this force in the field, it came to be known as Grant's army and by his continued presence often did come under his direct control. Grant was always the general in chief. The plan was his; the war, in effect, was his; and to make it total he ordered Ben Butler to take the Army of the James against Richmond and a Shenandoah army under Franz Sigel to move on Staunton and threaten LEE's railroads. Phil Sheridan was also brought east to command Grant's cavalry. In the simplest terms, the pressure was to be applied everywhere and made unbearable. LEE would not be permitted to maneuver, and he would be thrown on the defensive with the inevitable results.

In eight weeks, then, U. S. Grant put together his war machine, oiled and geared it, and on May 4, 1864, he sent it clanking toward the foe.

LEE's army had passed a frightful winter. The men were in rags, half-starved and freezing in their miserable huts along the Rapidan. Food was so scarce that when LEE had guests one day he could serve nothing but stringy bacon and cabbage. Because there was obviously not enough bacon to go around, the diners politely declined it. Next day there was even less to eat. Lee, remembering the untouched bacon, asked his steward about it and was told that it had been borrowed in the first place and had already been returned to its hungry owner.

Shortages in hay and fodder also caused the death of thousands of horses. When LONGSTREET left for Georgia, he was not able to take his guns, and half the animals in JEB STUART's horse artillery were dead.

Unbelievable as it may seem, this incredible army had not yet lost its fighting spirit. Nor had its commander, when, on April 6, he successfully divined Grant's plans. Immediately, LEE ordered BEAUREGARD to defend Richmond against Butler and scraped together a scratch force to hold off Sigel in the valley. He would attend to Grant himself, letting him cross the Rapidan and then hitting him in the flanks as his ponderous slow army struggled through the steaming tangle of the Wilderness.

As Grant moved, LEE moved, and on May 5 they collided.

Only a year ago the armies of LEE and Hooker had swirled through this maze of swamp and swale, leaving it a monster burial ground. Here eyeless sockets stared from the bleached skulls of men and horses, there a skeletal hand or leg rose from a half-finished grave; every thicket was strewn with rusty guns and canteens and every bush seemed to blossom with rotten bits of bloodstained clothing. Even the bullet-nicked trees bore mute testimony to the savagery of Chancellorsville, and the entire scene startled the Federals of Gouverneur Kemble Warren's corps as that unit came poking south from the Rapidan. They quickly recovered from their horror, however, when they blundered into the butternuts of DICK EWELL's corps who had come marching east along a turnpike. Gradually this chance encounter built up into full-scale conflict, the opening notes of the Battle of the Wilderness, and within a few hours it had become a blind, black struggle over which neither commander exercised much control.

In a field near Wilderness Tavern, U. S. Grant sat on a stump, smoking a cigar and whittling on a stick, issuing the orders that fed more and more soldiers into the fight. In the Confederate rear, ROBERT E. LEE calmly rode with A. P. HILL as that general's corps came rushing up on EWELL's right. LEE also sent orders for LONGSTREET to hurry up from Gordonsville, 42 miles away. So the battle grew and grew, the Rebels trying to get around the Union Army, the Federals building up their left flank to contain them. Soon rolling clouds of smoke intensified the forest gloom. Now soldiers merely fired blindly into the smoke and murk, others groped their way forward or crawled on their bellies. A horizontal rain of bullets three feet high swept the battlefield. Then the woods took fire, and the crackle of flames mingled with the wild screams of men and animals being burned alive.

By midafternoon Grant had the corps of Sedgwick, Warren and Hancock, right to left, opposed to EWELL and HILL. He resolved to crush the Confederate right under HILL and sent Hancock crashing forward. Once again, the Wilderness was the Rebel ally. It quickly fragmented solid formations into bits, while the outnumbered Confederates, better woodsmen who knew every path and fastness by heart, riddled the Union attack. By nightfall, however, two of HILL's divisions were badly battered.

That night LEE realized that he had met his most aggressive adversary. All day long the Federals had attacked, attacked, attacked; never surrendering the initiative and never once giving LEE the opportunity to maneuver. He had been held in place as never before, and now his right flank was badly damaged. Still, he hoped that LONGSTREET would arrive next day in time to turn the tide. Early on May 7, however, the roar of enemy guns told LEE that HILL's weakened divisions were once again being assaulted.

LEE mounted Traveler and rode toward the guns. He rode through stragglers, and then, to his mounting alarm, through a butternut flood pouring away westward. LEE's right was shattered. Not since Antietam had he faced such a crisis. LEE rode back to consult A. P. HILL and to look anxiously for LONGSTREET. HILL shouted at his artillery to fire off 12 loaded guns before withdrawing the pieces from danger. The guns bucked and roared and hurled shells into the woods and the approaching Federals only 200 yards away. Smoke swirled around LEE. The Federals came on, and then, through the smoke behind him, LEE saw a score of ragged soldiers dash forward with muskets in their hands.

They were Texans. Texans! That meant they were from JOHN B. HOOD's famous brigade in LONGSTREET's corps. LONGSTREET had arrived! In rare excitement ROBERT E. LEE spurred Traveler forward through the gun pits. He came up with his advancing reinforcements as though to lead them forward. "Go back, General LEE, go back!" they cried. He ignored them, and they shouted: "We won't go on unless you go back!"[163]

Persuaded at last, LEE reined in Traveler, waved his hat at the onrushing Texans, and rode back to see LONGSTREET. That stolid general bluntly told LEE to go farther behind the lines, and then came forward himself to stop the Yankee attack—and to be wounded badly by the fire of his own men.

So the Battle of the Wilderness ended as Antietam had ended, with the eleventh-hour arrival of reinforcements to save LEE's crumbling right. Would it also end as had all other drives on Richmond? Would the Army of the Potomac turn north, recross the river and regain Washington to refit and regroup before shuffling south again? It seemed so to many of the Union soldiers lying weary and heart-broken in the darkness. When they were ordered to take the road, it seemed only that the command to retire had come sooner than usual. It was another Chancellorsville, they told each other. Then they came to a crossroads. If they turned left, they would be retreating again. They turned right, and suddenly those tired men lifted their heads and a great cheer rose in the night. They capered in the dust and tossed their caps in the dark and shouted with a wild fierce joy until U. S. Grant reined in his great war horse Cincinnati and told his staff to tell the men to stop cheering or else the enemy would realize that the Army of the Potomac was slipping away south.

Neither LEE nor Grant had fought with distinction, only with determination; and if casualties measure victories, then LEE had won: Union losses were between 15,000 and 18,000, Confederate estimated at between 7,750 and 11,400. Casualties, however, measure only the costs of battle. It was Grant who was the victor. He had achieved his objective: he had held LEE, had fixed him, had thrown him on the defensive. All LEE's moves hereafter were to be in response to Grant's. Yet Grant the slugger was stalking LEE the boxer and must inevitably become bruised and lacerated, while the very success of Grant's policy was to call forth from LEE all that mastery of defensive warfare which was uniquely his. A field engineer by education, LEE had spent decades building forts and dredging rivers. He had a marvelous feel for terrain and here, in the Wilderness, he was fortifying his own back yard. "When our line advances," an aide of Grant's wrote, "there is the line of the enemy, nothing showing but the bayonets, and the battle-flags stuck on top of the works. It is a rule that when the Rebels halt, the first day gives them a good rifle pit; the second a regular infantry parapet with artillery in position; and the third a parapet with an abattis in front and entrenched batteries behind. Sometimes they put this three days' work into the first twenty-four hours."[164] Thus did the "King of Spades" make bloody woe of Grant's progress south, and on that very night that the Union chief sideslipped left to come up under LEE's right at Spotsylvania Court House, LEE shifted right to race him for that position. The Confederate commander won, and on May 8 Grant found his path once again blocked.

It was blocked because the Confederate advance guard had marched with lightning speed and because the Union cavalry had dawdled clearing the road through Spotsylvania. Meade blamed this failure on Sheridan, and when the little cavalry chief appeared at his headquarters the towering commander of the Army of the Potomac lost his temper with a roar that could be heard by every orderly with a pretext for being within hearing distance. Black-eyed Phil Sheridan, five foot three inches of pure pugnacity, yelled back with an insubordinate vigor that rattled the chain of command and warmed the orderlies' hearts. It was Meade's fault, Sheridan shouted, because Meade countermanded his orders and used his cavalry as scouts and errand boys rather than as a fighting corps. What Sheridan wanted, Sheridan shouted, was to go and whip JEB STUART clear out of his saddle. Somewhat startled, Meade took the dispute to Grant and Grant said: "Did Sheridan say that? Well, he generally knows what he is talking about. Let him start right out and do it."[165] So Grant ordered Sheridan to "cut loose from the Army of the Potomac, pass around the left of LEE's army and attack his cavalry."[166] He was also to cut LEE's communications. Thus, shortly after noon of May 8, Sheridan led more than 10,000 troopers on a jingling swing around the Union right and then made due south as though bound for Richmond.

In the meantime, the Battle of Spotsylvania was swelling from an advance-guard encounter into a rolling, roaring eight-day battle which eventually embroiled both armies. While the conflict developed, LEE skillfully entrenched himself between the Po and Ny rivers in a line roughly resembling an inverted V. This enabled him to put most of his troops on the line and to move them to and from either face of the upside-down V as the situation required. Trees and underbrush concealed most of his works, and his skirmish line was pushed far enough forward to prevent Union scouts and officers from reconnoitering it. This made it difficult for Grant to gauge the extent of the opposition, and with Sheridan's cavalry gone he was, like LEE at Gettysburg, fighting nearly blindfolded.

Confederate sharpshooters also kept Federal artillery at a respectful distance, or pinned down those gunners rash enough to drag their pieces within sniping range. On May 9 John Sedgwick tried to rally his nervous artillerists by standing erect among the pinging bullets and crying, "Don't duck, they couldn't hit an elephant at this distance!"[167] A minute later Sedgwick was down and dying with a sniper's bullet under his left eye. Command of his corps passed to Horatio Wright, and it was Wright who seems to have decided that the weakest point of LEE's heretofore impregnable line was the west face of the V, or "the Mule Shoe," as the Rebels called it. Although the works there were strong, they could be enfiladed by Union artillery, and there was a stand of trees that would enable a Federal force to come within 200 yards of the works undetected. It seemed to Wright that the Mule Shoe could be taken by a sudden, silent rush, and he organized a special force of 12 regiments under an intense young colonel named Emory Upton.

Upton was among the most professional commanders in the Union Army. Free to criticize, he was himself very hard to fault because of his capacity for taking pains. He planned his assault carefully, taking his commanders forward to study the ground, organizing four lines of three regiments each. The first line was to pierce the outermost Confederate line and widen the gap so that a second line could rush through to assault the second Rebel position. The last two lines were to form a reserve, lying down beneath the Confederate breastworks until called for.

Late in the afternoon of May 10, 1864, Union artillery began pounding the Rebel positions. At 6:15 P.M., Upton's blue lines charged and drove straight through as planned. But then the Rebel guns scattered the Union reserve, which had formed in the open contrary to orders, and Upton was left isolated inside the Confederate position. He hung on until nightfall, assisted by another attack on the Federal right, and then withdrew. Yet he had proved that the salient at the Mule Shoe could be penetrated. Obviously, a larger force might break it and split LEE's army in two. That was what U. S. Grant meant when he said to Meade: "A brigade today—we'll try a corps tomorrow."[168]

It was two days later and with two full corps that Grant attacked the Mule Shoe. Hancock's corps came straight down against the tip of the V while Wright's hammered away at the western face, and throughout that day and night of May 12,1864, there raged probably the most vicious battle ever fought on American soil, and possibly one of the most ferocious fought anywhere. It was worst on Wright's front, "the Bloody Angle," as it was called. It was hand to hand. Men fired muskets muzzle to muzzle, and struck at each other with battle flags. The Rebels ran their guns right up to the parapets and sprayed double canister shot into rank after falling rank of Yankees. Fence rails and logs in the breastworks were actually splintered by the hail of Minié balls, and trees over a foot and a half in diameter were cut in two by them. Skulls were smashed with clubbed muskets, men were stabbed to death by swords and bayonets thrust between the logs of the parapets separating the forces, and the wounded were entombed alive by the crush of dead bodies toppling upon their wriggling, helpless forms. Night fell and a fierce rainstorm broke, and still the struggle convulsed the Bloody Angle until at last, at midnight, both sides sank on their arms in exhaustion.

At the point of the V, meanwhile, it appeared that Hancock's massed Federals had won the day. They bore straight down on the Mule Shoe, broke it, captured artillery pieces and took prisoners and swept on until momentarily checked by an incomplete line of breastworks. Here ROBERT E. LEE came riding on Traveler, faced once again with disaster. He rode straight to the center of the division commanded by JOHN GORDON, and GORDON thought that "LEE looked a very god of war."[169] Then LEE turned his horse's head as though to lead the desperation charge needed to shatter Hancock's advancing front.

At once GORDON spurred his horse across Traveler's front and grasped LEE's bridle. Lifting his voice deliberately so that his men might hear, GORDON said: "General LEE, you shall not lead my men in a charge. No man can do that, sir." Turning to his men, GORDON asked if they would fail LEE. "No, no, no!" they roared back, "We'll not fail him!" Turning back to LEE, GORDON shouted: "You must go to the rear," and his men echoed him with a thundering shout: "General LEE to the rear, General LEE to the rear!"[170] Crowding around the beloved Marse Robert, some clutching his bridle, others holding his stirrups, they forced Traveler around with such vehemence that GORDON believed that if LEE had resisted they would have carried both horse and rider to the rear. But LEE submitted to their pressure, and GORDON's division rolled forward with cyclonic force to shiver Hancock's lines and eventually force the Federals out of most of the Mule Shoe.

In the meantime, while attacks by Warren on the Federal right and Burnside on the left were also repulsed, LEE hurried construction of a new line at the base of the Mule Shoe. By nightfall the Confederate position was out of danger.

By then also JEB STUART had overtaken Sheridan's cavalry at Yellow Tavern about ten miles above Richmond. Outnumbered two to one, STUART tried to hold off the Union horse until infantry reinforcements could arrive from Richmond. But the Federals were too strong, they were scattering the Rebels aside, and STUART personally led a mounted countercharge. As he did, a dismounted Yankee trooper ran past him, fired his pistol at him and vanished. STUART slumped in the saddle, gravely wounded.

That had been on May 11, and Sheridan's cavalry had broken through, riding through Richmond's outer defenses and eventually making a complete circuit of LEE's army. On the night of the 12th while the Mule Shoe battle still raged, LEE learned that STUART was dying. LEE's voice was trembling when he told his staff: "He never brought me a piece of false information."[171] Later, he was told that STUART had died. Grief-stricken, LEE retired to his tent with the remark: "I can scarcely think of him without weeping."[172] It was a black night for ROBERT E. LEE, who had lost his right arm, JACKSON, a year ago and tonight "the eyes of the army." JACKSON dead, STUART dead, LONGSTREET wounded, A. P. HILL sick and EWELL weakening. All the old faces were vanishing. Two of his corps were in the hands of men as yet untried to high command: RICHARD ANDERSON and JUBAL EARLY. Yet LEE must hang on—and he did, assisted by four days of rain that enmired Grant's subsequent attempts to burst the Rebel line.

Nevertheless, Ulysses S. Grant had not given up. His casualties at Spotsylvania totaled between 17,000 and 18,000, against between 9,000 and 10,000 for LEE. Yet on May 19 he sat down to write his famous report: "I purpose to fight it out on this line if it takes all summer."[173]

On the following night he sideslipped left again in another attempt to draw the King of Spades outside his invincible earthworks.

Although Grant was successfully holding LEE while Sherman in Georgia had begun to drive JOHNSTON before him, Union movements elsewhere were being decisively defeated. Ben Butler's advance on Richmond was blocked by BEAUREGARD at Bermuda Hundred, after which Butler allowed himself to be trapped on the Bermuda Hundred peninsula, corked up neatly in a bottle, as Grant phrased it, thus releasing troops to LEE. In the Shenandoah Valley, Franz Sigel, a Union general by virtue of his abhorrence of slavery, had met JOHN BRECKINRIDGE at Newmarket and been defeated in a battle distinguished by the fighting of a corps of cadets from Virginia Military Institute. It was now up to Grant alone to keep the pressure on his opponent. He did, compelling LEE, in fact, to follow him; yet never succeeding in drawing Marse Robert out into the open.

LEE's counter to Grant's second sideslip was to move into another V-shaped position prepared the previous winter inside the steep-banked North Anna River. Again LEE was able to move troops from face to face of the V, making such clever use of the terrain that if Grant tried to move from flank to flank he would have to cross the river twice. Grant had no desire to be so discomfited, and after a few days of light skirmishing he sideslipped left again. Skirmishing once more to Totopotomoy Creek, he stepped left a fourth time and finally came up against LEE at a place called Cold Harbor.

Here Grant came to the conclusion that because LEE had not attempted an offensive he was beaten. The time had come for the crusher, Grant thought, and he ordered an all-out frontal assault. However, he had failed to reconnoiter LEE's lines, and had given LEE an extra day in which to fortify. Now he attacked *all along the line* rather than massing at a single point. No less than LEE at Gettysburg or Burnside at Fredericksburg, Grant had failed to grasp the new and awesome power of the defense. As a result, the Battle of Cold Harbor fought on June 3, 1864, was a Federal butchery.

Charge after charge was broken up, some in less than a quarter-hour. In one sector an outraged company commander, believing that his men had basely taken cover, ran over the field indignantly prodding them with his sword only to discover that they were all dead. Taken in their flank by enemy fire, some Union lines collapsed one upon the other like toppling dominoes. Across their entire front all the Federals could see were the black slouch hats of the Rebels and the flash of their muzzles. In less than an hour Grant lost 7,000 men against 1,500 for the Confederates, and he finally called off the assault.

It was an incredible defeat, made more doleful next day by the cries of "Water, water, for God's sake, water!"[174] breaking from the agonized lips of Grant's wounded outside the Confederate lines. LEE did not attack over this ground, but neither did Grant ask for a truce until June 6, and it was not until the night of June 7 that one was agreed upon. By then those wounded who had not been rescued by their comrades were all dead.

Cold Harbor closed a month of battle such as neither the Army of Northern Virginia nor the Army of the Potomac had ever before experienced. Many Union soldiers and some officers saw nothing but senseless slaughter. "For thirty days it has been one funeral procession past me," cried the sensitive General Warren, "and it is too much!"[175] It was not too much for U. S. Grant. True enough, he would one day write: "I have always regretted that the last assault at Cold Harbor was ever made."[176] Though shaken, he was not dismayed, and he saw in his defeat proof that frontal assault against LEE would never succeed. Instead, he decided to attack LEE's rear, to move all the way down to the south bank of the James River and cut off LEE's source of supply.

Here was an audacity worthy of ROBERT E. LEE. Grant was going to break contact with the watchful LEE and march undetected into LEE's rear, moving through LEE's own country swarming with LEE's own spies. To do this he must march 50 miles through swamps and across two rivers—including the half-mile-wide tidal James—always risking attack from that masterly commander whose favorite tactic was to strike an army on the move. Yet Grant had confidence in himself and his men, and he believed that the Rebel Army was no longer capable of those lightning adjustments which once had been its specialty. Whittling his sticks, gazing throughtfully through clouds of cigar smoke, Grant formulated his plans.

First, a force under Sheridan went into the Shenandoah Valley to disrupt LEE's supply lines there. Next, Meade prepared a second line of entrenchments to the rear of Cold Harbor under cover of which the army might slip away. Then William ("Baldy") Smith was ordered to take his corps by water up the James to seize Petersburg, holding it until Grant arrived with his main body.

Petersburg was the key to Grant's scheme. It was a vital rail junction lying 20-odd miles south of Richmond. If it fell and the Shenandoah line was blocked, Richmond could not be held and the specter of starvation would drive LEE's army into the open for a finish fight.

On the night of June 12 the Army of the Potomac began slipping away, moving as much like clockwork as is possible for 100,000 human beings. Every crossroad was strongly held to screen the army's movements. The James was spanned by one of the greatest military bridges in history, a pontoon crossing 2,100 feet long built to resist a strong tidal current and to adjust to a four-foot tidal rise and fall. Even Confederate gunboats on the upper James were contained. It was truly a magnificent maneuver, and LEE was left in the dark.

On the morning of June 13 his scouts reported the enemy trenches at Cold Harbor were empty. LEE did not know exactly where to look for Grant's vanished army. He had already moved to check the Union build-up in the Shenandoah, and he had also sent JUBAL EARLY there to threaten Washington and play the old game of panicking the North. Thus LEE was looking north while Grant was moving south, and he had weakened himself at a time when he needed to be strongest.

BEAUREGARD, holding the Petersburg defenses, had divined Grant's intentions and had pointed out that Petersburg was in great danger. Eventually LEE came to realize this, and when he did he began rushing reinforcements south in a race against time.

From the Union viewpoint, all depended now on Baldy Smith. He arrived with his corps by water at Bermuda Hundred on July 14 and was reinforced by a division of Negro troops and one of cavalry. He had about 10,000 men, but BEAUREGARD had only about 2,200 holding Petersburg. If Smith moved swiftly, he could crack BEAUREGARD's thinly held defenses and walk into the city. But it was not until 4 P.M. of July 15 that he ordered his attack. Then it was discovered that the artillery horses had been sent to water, and another two hours passed before the supporting guns could be hauled into position. Finally, with a division of Rebels marching madly to BEAUREGARD's rescue, with Hancock's corps coming toward Smith, the Federal assault began.

The Rebels were overrun, and the Negro troops were so jubilant that they danced in triumph around their captured cannon. Petersburg was Smith's for the taking, but he decided to hold what he had and wait for Hancock. When Hancock did arrive, Smith advised him not to attack, and so these fresh, eager soldiers merely relieved

Smith's weary men. They had marched toward Petersburg crying, "We'll end this damned rebellion tonight!"[177] but after they realized that the golden chance had gone glimmering and that tonight's weak enemy would be tomorrow's strong foe, they cursed and ground their teeth in anguish. "The rage of the enlisted men was devilish," a soldier wrote. "The most bloodcurdling blasphemy I ever listened to I heard that night, uttered by men who knew they were to be sacrificed on the morrow."[178]

With the eternally true instincts of cannon fodder, the men were right. During the night BEAUREGARD moved all his troops from Bermuda Hundred across the Appomattox River to reinforce Petersburg. This unbottled Butler, who could have placed himself between Richmond and Petersburg and perhaps, like Baldy Smith, won the war. But Butler only justified BEAUREGARD's contempt for him, making a few token moves before retiring in the face of reinforcements from LEE. In the meantime, BEAUREGARD's butternuts held off three entire Federal corps the next day, the 16th. They did the same on the 17th. On the 18th BEAUREGARD pulled back and the Union assault struck thin air. By the time the Federals regrouped, LEE had arrived with more reinforcements and Petersburg was too tough to storm.

Thwarted by his subordinates, baffled by BEAUREGARD, Grant settled down to a siege.

13

☆

A siege, ROBERT E. LEE had said, would make it "a mere question of time"[179] for the Army of Northern Virginia. Yet time was exactly what the Army of the Potomac was not supposed to grant the enemy.

Abraham Lincoln needed a quick victory, one that would come soon enough to influence the presidential election. Not only Lincoln's office was at stake on November 8 but the very fate of the nation as well: the election would also be a vote for or against continuing the war, and if the North said no to the war, that meant that the Union stood dissolved, perhaps permanently.

Discontent and disenchantment were spreading, and for different reasons. On the one hand were those radical Republicans who thought the war was not being fought hard enough, and they had already nominated John Charles Frémont as their own candidate for President. Such a splinter party could not fail to hurt Lincoln, who had been nominated by the so-called Union Party and had chosen a War Democrat, Andrew Johnson of Tennessee, as his running mate. On the other hand were those Peace Democrats, Copperheads, strict Constitutionalists and others who thought the war ought to be waged less harshly or else abandoned outright. Then there was the great bulk of the people who favored prosecution of the war but were dismayed by the sight of so many limbless veterans and the sound of so many funeral bells, and were wondering if the South was not actually unconquerable.

The Confederacy did seem unshaken in the summer of 1864. It was in truth a hollow shell, its insides eaten away by economic ills, but most people only saw that hard outer rind. Grant may have done exactly what he had proposed to do in fixing LEE on the defensive, but to many Northerners it appeared that he had only advanced to the James at the cost of a stunning butcher's bill of 60,000 men. Nor did Sherman seem to have done much better against JOHNSTON.

True, Sherman did not suffer so many losses and he had driven JOHNSTON deeper and deeper into Georgia. Yet JOHNSTON's army, his true objective, remained undefeated; and because the Rebels gathered in reinforcements as they retreated, it had grown even stronger. By the middle of July, 1864, Sherman had reached the outskirts of Atlanta, but he seemed to be stalled there.

At the same time, JUBAL EARLY came bursting out of the Shenandoah to menace Washington. This, of course, turned out to be only a passing scare. "Old Jube" knew very well that if he took his men into Washington he probably would never come out again, and after Grant calmly sent a corps north by water to attack him, EARLY quickly turned about and headed for home. Still, this last play of ROBERT E. LEE's capital card had not helped Northern war nerves. Nor were they eased when Grant made his last attempt to take Petersburg by literally blasting his way in.

A regiment of miners had dug a 500-foot tunnel under the Confederate lines and had planted four tons of gunpowder beneath the enemy's works. At dawn of July 30 the mine went up with a dreadful roar. Bodies, dirt and guns flew into the air. A huge crater was opened in the Confederate lines and defenders to either side of it fled in terror. Once again, the North had a chance to walk into Petersburg. However, instead of going around the crater, the troops went into it and found a 30-foot bank at the end. They could not climb it, they had no ladders, and as they milled around in confusion more and more troops were jammed into the pit, two of the Federal commanders took drunken refuge in a bombproof to the rear—and the Confederates rallied to counterattack. Before the Battle of the Crater was over the Federals had lost another 4,400 men, and Northern resolve to continue the war received another blow.

Such defeats nourished defeatism to the extent that the Radical Republican editor Horace Greeley could announce flatly: "Mr. Lincoln is already beaten. He cannot be re-elected."[180] Lincoln himself was deeply pessimistic. On August 23 he mystified his Cabinet by asking its members to sign a folded paper which would probably have flabbergasted them had they read it. It said:

This morning, as for some days past, it seems exceedingly probable that this administration will not be re-elected. Then it will be my duty to so co-operate with the President-elect as to save the Union between the election and the inauguration; as he will have secured his election on such ground that he cannot possibly save it afterward.[181]

In effect, "such ground" was virtual Copperhead control of the Democratic Convention gathered at Chicago that month. Led by Clement Vallandigham, who had slipped back into the North, the Peace Democrats denounced the war in the most violent terms and poured personal vituperation on the head of Lincoln. In the immemorial American way delegates took the convention floor to shout that free speech had been suppressed, and one of them avowed that his right to speak his mind openly had been denied on "the infamous orders of the gorilla tyrant that usurped the Presidential chair."[182] In the end George Brinton McClellan was nominated on a peace platform. McClellan did not actually accept that platform, however, only the support of those who formulated it. And as August ended it appeared that universal war weariness would put Little Mac in the White House.

With hindsight it can be seen that the flood of Federal misfortune —rather of apparent misfortune—had turned to the ebb long before Vallandigham and his bellicose pacifists made common cause with the pacific warrior McClellan. As the month of August began, the Southern façade began to crack and bulge under the strain of inexorable Federal pressure, and the first fissure appeared at Mobile.

Mobile had always seemed to Ulysses S. Grant one of the cornerstones of Confederate power. In 1863 he had told Halleck that an expedition from Mobile could detach Mississippi, Alabama and most of Georgia from the Confederacy. After he took command on March 9, 1864, Grant had wanted to seize Mobile so as to threaten JOHNSTON in his rear while Sherman pressed him on the front. The troops for such an expedition were then on the Red River Campaign under Nathaniel Banks. Their mission was to invade Texas for the sake of cotton and of frightening Napoleon III out of Mexico. However, they were defeated by the Rebels at Sabine Crossroads, Louisiana, on April 8, 1864, and Grant thereafter changed his plan.

Mobile, meanwhile, became an objective of the Union Navy. It was the Confederacy's last port on the Gulf of Mexico and it sheltered a Rebel gunboat flotilla and the big ironclad ram *Tennessee*. On August 5 a Federal fleet of wooden sloops, monitors and gunboats under Admiral Farragut entered Mobile Bay.

Farragut had climbed into the rigging of his flagship *Hartford* for a better view, and the ship's skipper, remembering the admiral's attacks of dizziness, had had him lashed there as a precaution. From the leading ship, *Brooklyn,* came a warning that the bay was filled with mines (torpedoes they were called then), and from Farragut came the famous reply: "Damn the torpedoes! Four bells! Captain Drayton, go ahead! Jouett, full speed!"[183] One by one the Rebel gunboats were sunk, the ram *Tennessee* was crippled and captured, and on August 23, the day of Lincoln's deepest pessimism, Fort Morgan was taken by assault.

The Confederacy, severed east from west by Union possession of the Mississippi, was now nearly shut off from the sea. As the month ended, William Tecumseh Sherman tried to cut it again, north from south.

". . . Mr. DAVIS had an exalted opinion of his own military genius," U. S. Grant was to write. "On several occasions during the war he came to the relief of the Union army by means of his *superior military genius.*"[184]

One of these occasions came that July, when DAVIS angrily relieved JOE JOHNSTON of command of the Army of Tennessee and replaced him with JOHN B. HOOD. The Confederate President could not see that JOHNSTON had been skillfully fighting the only kind of campaign possible, which was to refuse to attack Sherman until he had him at a disadvantage. DAVIS wanted action, for he, too, was in political trouble, and HOOD was the kind of man who would give it to him.

Sherman was delighted. HOOD was a valiant fighter who had lost a leg and had an arm crippled in the forefront of battle, but he was also reputed to be rash and reckless. Sherman hoped that he would attack him as JOHNSTON had not, and HOOD did.

Three times within a week—July 20 to July 28, 1864—the Confederates struck at the Federals, hitting them hard north, east and west of Atlanta. Each time they were repulsed, and HOOD was forced to fall back on Atlanta. Sherman followed him and opened a siege, subjecting the city to heavy bombardment. Refusing to assault the Rebel works, Sherman drew his noose tighter and tighter. At the end of August he moved south and southwest to sever HOOD's communications, and with that the Confederate commander evacuated the city. On September 2 jubilant Federals marched into a city half-wrecked by Union guns and retiring Rebel dynamiters, and a few days later Sherman made his report beginning: "So Atlanta is ours, and fairly won."[185]

News of the capture of Atlanta electrified the North. It stunned the soft-war forces which had rallied around McClellan and silenced the plotters in Lincoln's own party who had been secretly preparing to repudiate the President in favor of "some candidate who commands the confidence of the country."[186] Down at Petersburg, an overjoyed U. S. Grant ordered a loaded 100-gun salute fired at the Rebel batteries.

Obviously, the Union's pressure on the Confederacy was becoming unbearable, and before the month was over it had opened another seam in the beautiful and prosperous Shenandoah Valley.

Here was one of the South's great assets. It not only provided food and forage for LEE's army but aimed a dagger at the Federal heart in Washington. Because the valley ran southwest to northeast, a

Confederate army marching down it would be moving directly toward the Union capital; but a Union army ascending the Shenandoah would only be going farther away from Richmond. Again and again LEE had taken advantage of this geographical accident. STONEWALL JACKSON and others had gone repeatedly into the valley to frighten Washington and draw Union troops away from Richmond for the Northern capital's defense. It might almost be said that LEE defended Richmond in the valley, just as he also supplied his army from there.

Of these facts U. S. Grant was well aware. He wanted the valley cleared of Rebels and an army of hungry Federals to "eat out Virginia clear and clean as far as they go, so that crows flying over it for the balance of the season will have to carry their provender with them."[187] The man eventually selected to carry out this mission was Philip Sheridan.

At first Grant had ordered that no houses were to be burned and that the valley's inhabitants—many of them pacifists with a religious horror of war—though notified to move, were to be treated justly. Sheridan echoed these instructions. However, such compassionate reservations are not possible to an army ordered to make "a desert" of a lush and smiling garden, and it is difficult not to suspect that they were advance disclaimers for the excesses that both Grant and Sheridan must have known were inevitable.

One reason that excesses were inevitable was that by the summer of 1864 the American Civil War had followed the logic of warfare, which argues that when the enemy does not quickly submit, then more and more brutal means must be brought to bear to compel his submission. A thickening fog of hatred had also descended upon both camps, especially after both sides learned of the horrible treatment of their captured soldiers. The South's infamous camp at Andersonville, where 10,000 Yankee prisoners died in seven months, was probably the most notorious of these dreadful pestholes; yet there were places in the North such as the camp at Elmira which were only a bit less miserable. There were also atrocities committed by both sides, and again the South led the way with the burning of Lawrence, Kansas, by Colonel WILLIAM QUANTRILL's raiders and the massacre of the Union garrison at Fort Pillow carried out by NATHAN BEDFORD FORREST. Many of these soldiers were Negroes, and FORREST reported: "The river was dyed with the blood of the slaughtered for two hundred yards. . . . It is hoped that these facts will demonstrate to the Northern people that negro soldiers cannot cope with Southerners."[188] Irregular bands such as QUANTRILL'S were another reason that the soldiers of Sheridan's Army of the Shenandoah were not going to fill the hypocritical bill of a gentle desolation. Many of these guerrillas operating in the Shenandoah were little better than outlaws. Deserters and desperadoes, they had no stomach for the battle line but preferred the sudden midnight swoop and the quick getaway; and they were detested as much by Confederate commanders as they were dreaded by Federal soldiers. The fires of hatred, then, had crept into that last calm crevice of war: the breast of the common soldier. Johnny Reb and Billy Yank had openly fraternized from Vicksburg to Petersburg, swapping jokes and comic taunts and trading Confederate tobacco for Yankee newspapers and coffee. But now they hated, if not each other, at least the other side; and in this growing mood of savagery the Union picked up the red-hot iron of total war and pressed it down hard on the Shenandoah.

The results were red and smoking scars. From mountain to mountain billowing clouds of smoke shut out the sun by day, and by night the shadows danced and flickered in the light of glowing bonfires. Stacks of hay and straw were burned, barns filled with harvested crops were set blazing, all supplies of use to man or beast were set afire and all cattle were driven off. Everywhere that Sheridan's troops lifted the torch they were met by throngs of weeping old men, women and children, but the work of scorching the enemy's earth went on inexorably. As a Union chaplain wrote: "The time had fully come to peel this land and put an end to the long strife for its possession."[189]

The strife, however, was not yet over. Alarmed, LEE sent JUBAL EARLY to drive Sheridan out of the valley. Tall, thin, twisted, with a rasping wit to give bite to his misanthropic jibes, "Old Jube" had begun to distinguish himself as one of the ablest of that able company of lieutenants who served ROBERT E. LEE. Above all, EARLY was impetuous, and he did not hesitate to hurl his 15,000 lean veterans against Sheridan's 45,000.

The two forces met at Winchester, where EARLY caught Sheridan's advance guard and drove it back. Riding forward on his great black horse Rienzi, Sheridan built up his battle line and pressed the Rebels back. Not since the days of Fighting Phil Kearny had Federal soldiers seen a Union general so far forward. Waving his little flat hat, crying out, "Come on, boys, come on," disdaining enemy fire, laughing when a shell burst directly overhead, the fiery little general on the big horse infused his army with a dash and daring hitherto unknown among the Federals of the Shenandoah. Just before dusk, a splendid Union cavalry charge struck the Confederates in their left flank and rear to roll them back—and Winchester was another Union victory to lift Lincoln's reviving political stock still higher. Three days later, on September 22, Frémont withdrew from the presidential race.

Sheridan pursued EARLY up the valley, still spreading devastation as he moved, and still harassed by the attacks on his supply line made by the masterful Confederate partisan chieftain JOHN MOSBY.

MOSBY played on Sheridan's line like a virtuoso, forcing the Union general to detach large bodies of troops to protect his rear.

By mid-October Sheridan's army was encamped at Cedar Creek 20 miles south of Winchester. Sheridan had gone to Washington for a brief visit. He did not think that the twice-beaten EARLY would dare attack his powerful army. On the night of October 18, Sheridan was back in Winchester—and the daring EARLY had already made up his mind to strike the Union left at Cedar Creek the next morning. Out of the misty dawn the Confederates poured on that memorable October 19, 1864, rolling back the surprised Federals and threatening to rout Sheridan's entire army. Up in Winchester, an officer awakened Sheridan and told him he had heard artillery. "It's all right," Sheridan said, explaining that a scouting force was "merely feeling the enemy."[190] Two and a half hours passed before Sheridan was mounted on Rienzi, and it was then that he heard the roar of artillery to the south. Leaning forward in his saddle, he heard it grow at a rate indicating that his own army must be falling back. He had heard:

> The terrible rumble, grumble and roar
> Telling the battle was on once more—
> And Sheridan twenty miles away![191]

Sheridan did not go galloping wildly all the way down that road, as Read's poem says, but he did urge his horse forward into the frantic backwash of a beaten army. Wagon trains, sutlers and camp followers, walking wounded and artillery wagons, stragglers and skulkers, all

flowed back toward Winchester, their hurry and their fright eloquent
of a disaster at the front. Sheridan rode faster, now, coming at a
gallop in front of some 50 mounted men. Now he saw real soldiers
retreating, and he drew rein to shout at them: "Turn back! Face the
other way! If I had been here with you this morning this wouldn't
have happened."[192] On he rode, crying, "Turn back! Turn Back!"
swinging his little cap and calling for more and more speed from the
tireless Rienzi. Then he fell silent, his face setting into stone while
his piercing black eyes took on the dull red stubborn glint of a spirit
defiant in defeat.

Suddenly, Sheridan had reached the battlefield. Across the battle
line he galloped while a thunderous great cheer broke from the
throats of his army. "Sheridan! Sheridan!" his soldiers shouted, as
though the mere repetition of his name would avert disaster. Such
emotional outbursts rarely occur on modern battlefields, but there
were men there who swore that Sheridan's presence meant: "No more
doubt or chance for doubt existed; we were safe, perfectly and un-
conditionally safe, and every man knew it."[193]

Regrouped, revitalized, the Union Army swept forward; and it
was irresistible. The redoubtable JUBAL EARLY and his veterans
could not contain such furious waves of blue, and the fact of Sheridan's
ride was thus equal to the legend: by his sudden appearance the Union
general turned defeat into victory and closed the Shenandoah to the
South forever.

Mobile, Atlanta, the Shenandoah, they were names that stuck in
the minds of Northern voters going to the polls on that fateful
November 8, 1864. There, with ballots not bullets, the real battle
was being fought. There, in an event unique in history, a democracy
engaged in a dreadful civil war was electing a President. At Washington on that rain-swept night Abraham Lincoln awaited the result
in the war telegraph office. He was confident. He told of another rainy
election night, when he had lost to Stephen Douglas. Walking home
on a slippery hogback, "my foot slipped from under me, knocking
the other one out of the way, but I recovered myself and lit square,
and I said to myself: 'It's a slip and not a fall.' "[194] Toward midnight
Abraham Lincoln knew that he had been re-elected. Well-wishers
besieged the telegraph office with a brass band and demands for a
speech.

"It is no pleasure to me to triumph over any one," Abraham Lincoln said, "but I give thanks to the Almighty for this evidence of the people's resolution to stand by free government and the rights of humanity."[195]

14

☆

As the year 1864 came to a close the Civil War possessed all those hideous features that make the Medusa of modern war. It had begun with gay flags and blaring bands and pink-cheeked farm boys in baggy red pants, and it was ending with sabered pigs and burnt barns and weeping women shoved rudely aside by gaunt men with hollows in the cheeks where innocence had bloomed.

Along the way the Civil War had introduced the breech-loading rifle, barbed wire, hand grenades, winged grenades, wooden wire-bound mortars, rockets and even booby traps. Magazine rifles were invented and also the Requa machine gun. At Mobile the Confederacy had built a submarine, the 35-foot *R. L. Hunley* which was propelled by a screw worked from the inside by eight men, and on February 17, 1864, the *Hunley* torpedoed and sank the U.S.S. *Housatonic* and went down with her. The first battle of ironclads had been fought between *Monitor* and *Merrimac*, while on land there were armored trains as well as land mines. Trench warfare as grim and dirty as any in World War I had already started outside Petersburg, and poison gas was foreshadowed by the Confederate officer who toyed with the notion of a stink-shell to give off "offensive gases" and cause "suffocating effect." Flag and lamp signaling also was used, as well as field telegraph, while both sides maintained observation balloons. In fact, "the meanest trick of the war" occurred when the North captured a Rebel balloon made of silk dresses donated by patriotic ladies. Finally, the restless mind of Ben Butler had come up with the forerunner of the flame-thrower, a "small garden engine" squirting Greek fire. "Also he is going to get a gun that shoots seven miles and, taking direction by compass, burn the city of Richmond with shells of Greek fire."[196] In this, the concepts of Big Bertha and of fire-bombing are rolled into one, and Butler may have been unique in thinking of constructing an auger to bore a tunnel five feet in diameter and thus dig his way into Richmond. Except for tanks, airplanes and atomic bombs, then, the foundations for the arsenal of modern warfare had been laid; and a week after Lincoln was re-elected the very tactics of frightfulness which moderns condemned as evil incarnate when they were used in the service of Nazi Germany were being put into effect by Sherman in the state of Georgia.

Of all the remarkable leaders of the Civil War the most original was William Tecumseh Sherman. Many military historians acclaim him as the first of the modern strategists. Certainly he was the first to see that industrialized war shifted the target from the military to the economic and moral. A nation must be struck in its capacity to fight and its will to fight, Sherman reasoned. This meant by-passing its armies and attacking its industrial potential and its population; this meant nothing less than deliberate desolation and demoralization: this was blitzkrieg.

The man who conceived this strategy was not, as the descendants of his Southern victims maintain, the reincarnation of Attila the Hun. He was rather an unusually perceptive, gifted and complicated human being, in whose character and career can be found perhaps more marks of genius than in those of any other American commander before or since. Chief of all, he cared nothing for human respect. He wore rumpled, muddy, mismatching uniforms; he conceded a russet beard to the chin fashions of the day but kept it close-cut; he was tall, lanky, awkward, given to shoving his hands into his pockets or rubbing up his thatch of coarse red hair; his face was wrinkled, his nose pointed and red, and his little eyes black and sharp. "Uncle Billy," as the soldiers called Sherman, talked rapidly in a high voice about a host of subjects, his features often all but obscured by clouds of "segar" smoke and his clothing covered by a fine film of cigar ash. One young lieutenant who met him thought him the "ideal Yankee," while admitting that he had "experienced almost an exhaustion from the excitement of his vigorous presence."[197]

In Sherman were combined so many seemingly conflicting qualities that he would seem to have been crippled by that inconsistency which is "the hobgoblin of little minds." Actually he was balanced: quick in thought and careful in detail, visionary in planning and practical in execution, dynamic yet reflective, warmhearted but coolheaded, Sherman was one of those unique double personalities who are at once the man who thinks and the man who feels. Neither gained the ascendancy, but such a struggle between head and heart must necessarily carry a man very close to insanity, and so it was no wonder that he was often thought "crazy" or that he, too, was touched with that divine discontent which sank him deep in despondency or sent him soaring to the heights of inspiration. "A dead cock in a pit," he called himself before the war, although he had already been reared in the household of the famous Senator Ewing of Ohio, educated at West Point, trained in the law, soldier in Mexico, voyager around the Horn, Indian fighter, banker, battler for law and order in lawless San Francisco, and, finally, president of a military academy in Louisiana. After Louisiana seceded, Sherman remained loyal; and Lincoln liked him because he said he did not want appointment to high rank, preferring instead to work his way up while he learned the art of war.

By the fall of 1864 he knew it well enough to make one of the boldest gambles in military history. By then, Hood had shown that he could prevent Sherman from destroying his army. By then also, Sherman had learned that his long supply line back to Louisville was becoming a costly nuisance. First NATHAN BEDFORD FORREST had gone into Tennessee to tear up railroads and cause enough trouble to compel Sherman to send Thomas and 30,000 men back to Nashville to contain him. Then Hood himself had begun to maneuver against the Union supply line north of Atlanta, hoping to draw Sherman north. Hood did not hurt the supply line much, but neither did Sherman ever catch Hood in a finish fight. Finally, with the boldness born of desperation, Hood began marching his entire army toward Tennessee in the belief that Sherman would now have to abandon Atlanta and come after him.

Sherman's response to Hood's gamble was an even bolder decision. He proposed to ignore the enemy army and attack instead the spirit of the South. He decided to abandon his supply line and lead some 60,000 men from Atlanta to Savannah and the sea. An army of human locusts would devour the food so badly needed by LEE's hungry soldiers in Petersburg and then destroy what they could not eat or carry off. They would make the people of Georgia feel the harsh hand of war in their very homes, and they would make the entire South feel helpless at the sight of a Union army moving unchecked through its heartland. "I can make the march, and make Georgia howl!"[198] Sherman told Grant, and eventually both Grant and Lincoln agreed.

On November 15, then, as HOOD marched north toward Tennessee, Sherman set his face in the opposite direction: the seacoast. First, however, he burned Atlanta. It is said that Sherman only intended to wreck and burn railroad installations and factories, that he wanted to spare shops and stores and private homes. Nevertheless, as the South still maintains with much justice, Sherman's soldiers were "a mite careless with powder and fire," and most of Atlanta went up in flames.

Nor were Sherman's soldiers very careful about property rights as they moved on a 60-mile front through a rich land where the harvest was in, the barns were stuffed with corn and forage, smokehouses bulged with hams and bacon, and the fields were full of cattle. Each morning each brigade detached a forage company of about 50 men to comb the countryside a few miles to either side of the brigade's line of march. Seizing farm wagons and carriages, they loaded them with bacon, eggs, cornmeal, chickens, turkeys and ducks, sweet potatoes—whatever could be carried off—and delivered their loads to the brigade commissaries at the end of each day. Meanwhile, other units drove off livestock. What they could not take, they killed. To save ammunition, they sabered pigs and poleaxed horses and mules between the ears. From sunup to sundown lean veterans accustomed to hardtack and salt pork gorged themselves on ham and yams and fresh beef, and as they advanced across the state they grew fat and sleek. So did the Negroes to whom they gave the plantation masters' food, and who frolicked on the heels of the advancing host in the living embodiment of the famous ditty:

> Say Darkies has you seen old Massa
> Wid de muffstache on his face
> Go long de road sometime dis mornin'
> Like he gwine to leave de place?
>
> De massa run, ha-ha!
> De darkey stay, ho-ho!
> I tink it must be Kingdom Coming
> And de year ob Jubilo.

It was indeed the Year of Jubilo for the Negroes, just as for Sherman's laughing veterans the march had become a picnic promenade, but to the South it seemed a wanton and barbaric ruin that cried out to heaven for vengeance. From wing to wing 60 miles apart there rose columns of smoke as the advancing army trailed its own somber clouds of destruction. Warehouses, bridges, barns, machine shops, depots and factories were burned. Not even houses were spared, especially not by the "bummers," those deserters, desperadoes and looters, North and South, who were drawn to the march for the sake of loot. These were the men who forced old men and helpless women to divulge the secret places where silver, jewelry and money were hidden. They danced with muddy, hobnailed boots on snow-white linen or gleaming table tops, smashing furniture with gun butts, slashing feather beds with sabers and shattering windows and mirrors with empty bottles. Sherman, who might have restrained them, did little to stop them. "War is cruelty, and you cannot refine it,"[199] he had told the people of Atlanta, and it was his intention to demonstrate that the Confederacy was powerless to protect its people against it.

Railroad-wrecking was another object of the march, and to this, Sherman wrote, "I gave my personal attention."[200] After the rails had been pried up they were heated over bonfires of crossties and then twisted around trees to be left useless, and the countryside was festooned with "Sherman hairpins" or "JEFF DAVIS neckties." Thus like a flow of molten lava 60 miles wide and 300 miles long, the Union Army marched to the sea.

Meanwhile, General HOOD had begun a successful drive into Tennessee. On November 29-30 near Franklin he nearly trapped a Federal army under John Schofield, but the Federals eventually escaped after savage fighting which caused the death of five Confederate generals. HOOD pursued toward Nashville, where Thomas blocked his path. Thomas, in fact, was in position to destroy HOOD; and a jittery U. S. Grant ordered him to do so before the Rebel Army could by-pass Nashville and invade the North. Such a maneuver might upset all Grant's plans and thus prolong a war which seemed on the verge of being won. But the stolid Thomas moved in his own good time, so slowly, in fact, that Grant resolved to relieve him. On December 15, however, Thomas struck HOOD with such fury that the Confederate Army was sent south in headlong retreat. That was the South's last gasp in the West, and six days later, when Sherman's sleek tatterdemalions poured jubilantly into Savannah, the death rattle of the Confederacy was clearly audible on both sides of the Mason-Dixon Line.

JEFFERSON DAVIS was not the man to listen to his own death rattle. Unbending die-hard or eleventh-hour savior, he would not in either case be conscious of impending defeat. As the year 1864 came to a close the Confederacy had shrunk to the Carolinas and Virginia, HOOD's army was a wreck, Sherman was poised to march north to join Grant's swelling Army of the Potomac, and Sheridan was ready to ride down to Petersburg with all his immense and veteran horsemen. Surely the South, for all its splendid fighting spirit, should fight no longer. Its economy was crippled, and its government so powerless to wage war that even the gentle ROBERT E. LEE raged against Congressmen who "do not seem to be able to do anything except to eat peanuts and chew tobacco, while my army is starving."[201] LEE's army was also cold and poorly clothed, and its ranks were dwindling. Desertions were now at their height, because when Sherman menaced a hearth in Georgia or the Carolinas he twisted a heart at Petersburg. Moreover, as Grant inexorably extended his lines to his left, the outnumbered LEE had to move right to contain him, and this thinned his lines. Yet JEFFERSON DAVIS had no thought of capitulation, not even after the Union seized Fort Fisher on January 15, 1865, and thus sealed off Wilmington, North Carolina, the Confederacy's last major port.

The Confederate President, a son of the eighteenth century, if not an earlier age, still saw the war as a contest between armies, soldier to soldier, not as a conflict between nations in which capacity to fight is paramount, or a war between democracies in which the will to fight is major. Attrition and blockade had scuttled the Confederate capacity, while hunger, defeat and calculated frightfulness had worn down the will. Southern morale had also been weakened by disputes over DAVIS's frequent suspensions of the writ of habeas corpus, and many a brave butternut left the trenches and headed home after being informed that the Confederate commissary was stripping his farm of food and animals. Under these conditions a peace movement was begun under the leadership of DAVIS's archfoe and obstructionist, Vice President ALEXANDER STEPHENS. DAVIS agreed to ask for a peace conference, but actually only in the hope of provoking a harsh statement of Union war aims that would stiffen the Southern spine.

On February 3, 1865, STEPHENS and two others met Lincoln and Seward on the *River Queen* in Hampton Roads. STEPHENS proposed that the two camps make peace to join in evicting the French from Mexico in defense of the Monroe Doctrine. Lincoln replied that he could not enter negotiations unless the Confederacy agreed to return to the Union and abolish slavery. Such proposals, of course, could not even be considered by the Confederates—and the war went on.

It continued with JOHNSTON recalled to block Sherman's northward march through the Carolinas, and with ROBERT E. LEE at last the Confederate commander in chief. Popular resentment against DAVIS's conduct of the war had led to creation of this position, but the gesture came as the hands of the clock neared midnight. LEE knew that the Confederacy was teetering on the edge of disaster. Desertions had so drained his armies that the Confederacy passed a law conscripting slaves. With splendid irony the South offered Negroes the equal opportunity of fighting shoulder to shoulder with whites in a war begun to preserve their own enslavement.

Nevertheless, JEFFERSON DAVIS was determined to go down to utter defeat rather than accept any terms that did not recognize Southern independence, and because it was not LEE's habit to challenge the President on matters of policy, LEE also decided to fight on. Ever the gambler, he resolved on a last, desperate chance: a breakout from Petersburg followed by a lightning march south to join JOHNSTON and overwhelm Sherman, after which both armies would return north to defeat Grant. General JOHN GORDON, the hero of Spotsylvania, was ordered to lead the assault on Union-held Fort Stedman directly east of Petersburg. An hour before daylight on March 25, 1865, the Rebels attacked.

They went in with a silent rush, surprising and seizing Stedman and sending a spearhead ahead to pierce the Federal secondary line. If they could widen their breakthrough and hold it, LEE's army could pour through the breach and get clean away to North Carolina. But the Federals rallied. Forts to either side of Stedman refused to fall, a counterattack was launched on Stedman, and Union artillery shattered the Rebel front. By midmorning LEE's last sally had been broken and hurled back with losses of 5,000 men. Now it was the turn of U. S. Grant.

Before GORDON's attack Grant had seen that he must crush LEE's right flank, seizing the roads and railways by which the Confederates might escape south. Heavy rains had delayed putting his plan into operation, but after Philip Sheridan arrived at Petersburg with all his cavalry Grant began to move swiftly.

On March 29 a full corps began striking LEE's right, while Sheridan led a corps of cavalry and one of infantry in a wide sweep toward Five Forks still farther to the Rebel right. If he could get in behind LEE, he would cut off the Confederate escape and practically guarantee LEE's defeat. LEE reacted swiftly, sending PICKETT to oppose him. On March 31 the Confederates halted Sheridan's forces short of Five Forks at a place called Dinwiddie Court House. But the little Union general was not defeated. He had wisely retired to await reinforcements, and Grant sent him Warren's corps.

Next day Sheridan chafed at Warren's delay. Sheridan smelled victory, he could win the war that day, and he cried aloud: "This battle must be fought and won before the sun goes down!"[202] In simple terms, Sheridan wanted to crush and scatter PICKETT's force and seize the Southside Railway to his rear. If this was done, it was all over with LEE and probably for the Confederacy.

At last Warren's veterans began moving into line. Sheridan was everywhere among them. When one of his skirmish lines was staggered and seemed ready to fall back, he galloped toward his faltering soldiers, shouting, "Come on—go at 'em—move on with a clean jump or you'll not catch one of them!"[203] A soldier beside him was hit in the throat. "I'm killed!" he cried, blood spurting thickly from his jugular vein. "You're not hurt a bit!" Sheridan roared. "Pick up your gun, man, and move right on!"[204] Obediently, the soldier trotted forward—and fell dead. Now the battle line was formed, and Sheridan shouted: "Where's my battle flag?"[205] It was brought forward, and the general raised his little swallow-tailed red-and-white banner high over his head and rode black Rienzi up and down the line.

A bullet pierced the flag, and the sergeant who had brought it fell. Sheridan rode forward, spurring his horse toward the Rebel earthworks. After him came the yelling Federal infantry. Sheridan put Rienzi over the works in a splendid leap, and his infantry swarmed in after him. Now a perfect rage of battle had come over Sheridan, in the midst of which he relieved the unfortunate Warren of his command. It was brutal, it was probably not just, but Sheridan realized with Grant that the end of the war was within the Union grasp, and a general should be ready to press forward as obediently as the private whose lifeblood poured from his throat.

"What I want is that Southern Railway," Sheridan roared repeatedly. "I want you men to understand we have a record to make before the sun goes down that will make Hell tremble!"[206]

Capture of the vital railway that day was not to be. Yet PICKETT's force had been completely shattered and Five Forks fell to Sheridan. A jubilant Grant cabled the information to Lincoln, who relayed the information to the press. For the next few days an eager North read with drawn breath of the progress of that single win-the-war battle that had eluded the nation for four years.

Next day, April 2, Grant attacked all along the line. Row upon row of Federal gun batteries began baying in a voice of rolling thunder, hurling a dreadful weight of death and destruction upon the Rebel positions. Then came silence. Thousands upon thousands of Federal soldiers moved forward. Slowly, with a gathering rush, they struck the Confederate lines, and in the weakened center they tore them apart. One by one clusters of Rebel muskets winked out in that predawn darkness, and black gaps opened in the Southern line. Into the open spaces rushed the Federals, widening them, and a quarter-hour after Wright's corps attacked in the center a decisive breakthrough was achieved.

To the rear A. P. HILL heard of the penetration while discussing the battle with LEE. He rode forward, to receive a bullet in the heart and strip from LEE yet another of his great lieutenants. Tears in his eyes, LEE called upon LONGSTREET. But "Old Pete" and his valiant men could not stem the rising Federal tide.

As the Sunday of April 2, 1865, grew lighter, LEE prepared to abandon Petersburg. He still hoped to join JOHNSTON. It was a forlorn hope, and LEE doubtless knew it, yet his sense of duty kept him loyal to President DAVIS's designs. As 30,000 red-eyed and starving survivors of the Army of Northern Virginia began streaming west, LEE dictated the long-dreaded telegram to the War Department.

Meticulously dressed in gray, cold as a marble statue, JEFFERSON DAVIS sat in the family pew at St. Paul's Episcopal Church. Surrounded mostly by women, many dressed in black, DAVIS heard the preacher say: "The Lord is in His holy temple; let all the earth keep silence before Him."[207] Into that churchly silence there crept the tinkle of spurs. An officer holding his saber came striding down the aisle. He handed DAVIS a paper. The President unfolded it and read: "I advise that all preparation be made for leaving Richmond tonight. I will advise you later, according to circumstances."[208]

With tight-lipped calm, DAVIS pocketed LEE's message of doom and walked majestically from the church. Going to the War Department, he telegraphed LEE that to move the Confederate government that night would "involve the loss of many valuables." LEE received the protest in the field, and angrily tore it to bits with the remark: "I am sure I gave him sufficient notice."[209] Regaining his composure, he notified DAVIS that it was "absolutely necessary" to move that night.

Richmond learned swiftly that the government was fleeing. Throughout that Passion Sunday civilians fought government clerks for possession of carts and wagons, carriages and gigs, while crowded streets echoed to rolling wheels or the rumbling of departing trains. The Confederate treasury—less than a half-million dollars in bullion—was placed in charge of a battalion of naval cadets. Civilians able to flee joined the government exodus. Those who could not, locked their doors and closed their shutters and sat down in despair to await the Yankee invasion. Night fell and the city began to tremble to the detonation of bridges and arsenals.

Soon the city was afire. So was neighboring Manchester. They blazed like beacons in the dark while the James lay glittering between them. Inevitably, those people of Richmond whom inflation and food shortages had transformed into wild, half-starved creatures turned to looting. Commissary depots were full of supplies never delivered to LEE's hungry army, and now that they were left unguarded they were broken into and plundered. Barrels of whiskey were also found, and soon there were drunks capering in the reflected flames of burning cotton or tobacco warehouses. Then the mob began breaking into shops and storehouses, sotted women fought each other for ostrich plumes, drunken men shot each other over boots and sashes. So the flames and the frenzy spread, and soon the only safe place in Richmond was in the green hills of Capitol Square. Here women in shawls clasped frightened children to their bosoms, and here, while the night winds whipped the fires, as tall flames roared and drunken revelers shrieked, like a shower of sparks from a falling building, the capital of the Confederacy collapsed.

ROBERT E. LEE had a headstart of one day in his race against the tenacious Grant. With this advantage, LEE believed he could get his army to Danville, the pleasant little city on the Dan River to which JEFFERSON DAVIS had already moved the government. Here he could be joined by JOHNSTON.

On April 3 it did not seem to LEE that Grant was pursuing too rapidly. That night his ragged veterans staggered into Amelia Court House, 21 miles west of Petersburg. There, to his dismay, LEE found not a single ration to feed 30,000 agonizingly hungry men. He had no recourse but to halt next day while forage wagons searched the countryside for food. In the meantime, the day's headstart was lost. Federal cavalry were everywhere. Close behind them hurried three eager corps of Union infantry, marching a few miles south of LEE on a straighter, parallel route. That night of April 4 some of Sheridan's riders menaced Amelia.

On the morning of April 5 the forage wagons came in, and LEE saw with concealed despair that they were nearly empty. His men must march now on their nerves alone, their hearts nourished by LEE's spirit but their bellies empty and growling with hunger. Another delay ensued: EWELL and ANDERSON were slow in closing up. Finally, the army moved south from Amelia Court House—and found Federal infantry and cavalry barring the way.

There was nothing left to do but to shift west toward Farmville, where there was hope of receiving rations from Lynchburg. This meant a night march that killed a good part of LEE's army. It was a slow stumble over crowded roads made by men with leaden limbs, men who moved like sleepwalkers. Many fell out never to return. Many were captured by Federal cavalry, which never left off nipping at LEE's heels. Grant was clinging to LEE's army, and he would not let go.

Still, LEE pressed on. On April 6 the Federals caught up at a place called Sailor's Creek. Here they overwhelmed GORDON, who was covering the Confederate trains, capturing the greater part of LEE's wagons, and here, as LEE watched in agony, they broke EWELL's and ANDERSON's corps. Sitting on Traveler and holding a red battle flag, LEE saw the wreck of shattered regiments come backwashing toward him, and he cried aloud: "My God, has the Army been dissolved?"[210] That day LEE lost between 7,000 and 8,000 men. That night LEE's army was down to 15,000 muskets and sabers to oppose 80,000 Federal infantry and cavalry. On April 7, however, his pale and pinched veterans struggled into Farmville, where they received their first rations since the retreat began. From Farmville, LEE continued his withdrawal. He got safely across the Appomattox River and burned the bridges behind him. Some of them were saved by the Federals, however, and once more Union cavalry began to bite on LEE's rear. That night LEE received Grant's invitation to surrender. He handed it to LONGSTREET, who replied: "Not yet."[211]

There was still hope. If LEE could get to a place called Appomattox Station, he could feed his men from four trains of food from Lynchburg, and then swing south to safety at Danville.

On April 8 LEE was forced to fight another rear-guard action to save his remaining wagons. As he did, Sheridan's cavalry and infantry under E. O. C. Ord swept past his southern flank and drove into Appomattox Station. They captured LEE's ration trains and put themselves across his line of march. That night LEE's army reached Appomattox Court House. Below them, across their path, lay Sheridan's force. If it was only cavalry, it might be brushed aside and the army yet saved. But if infantry was there in force, the Army of Northern Virginia was doomed.

April 9, 1865, was a Palm Sunday. Very early that morning ROBERT EDWARD LEE put on a new gray uniform, a sash of deep red silk, the jeweled sword given him by ladies in England, beautiful red-stitched spurred boots and long gray gauntlets. An officer expressed surprise, and Lee said: "I have probably to be General Grant's prisoner and thought I must make my best appearance."[212]

To the east, riding anxiously toward Appomattox over sloppy roads came a slender brown-bearded man wearing a mud-spattered private's blouse. His face was strained, for he had a bad headache and had been up all night bathing his feet in hot water and applying mustard plasters to his neck and wrists. Still, Ulysses S. Grant was hopeful that today would see an end to four years of blood and agony.

Yet Palm Sunday was beginning with the roar of guns. Down from Appomattox Court House charged the butternuts under General GORDON. They brushed aside the Federal outriders, and saw a solid blue phalanx of glittering bayonets to the rear. The Army of Northern Virginia had come to the end of the road. Back to LEE went GORDON's message that he could do nothing without reinforcements. "Then," said ROBERT E. LEE calmly, "there is nothing left for me to do but to go and see General Grant, and I would rather die a thousand deaths!"[213]

It was the end. With cries of anguish, protesting men and officers clustered around LEE. One general proposed that the army disperse and turn to guerrilla warfare. LEE replied that to do so would make mere marauders of his soldiers and inflict anarchy upon the South. He was prepared to sacrifice his own invincible pride for the safety of his country, and as the messages went out to Grant, Phil Sheridan opposite LEE grew impatient. He had massed both his men and horse with the passionate cry: "Now smash 'em, I tell you, smash 'em!"[214] Now his bugles blew and his blue lines leaned forward, and out from those pitiful gray ranks huddled beneath a host of battle flags a lone rider galloped. He carried a flag of truce and he told Sheridan that LEE was waiting to see Grant in the McLean House.

Skeptical at first, Sheridan finally ordered a cease-fire. Dazed, the two armies sat down and contemplated each other. In the spring stillness they suddenly heard bird song rather than bullets. Then General Grant rode up to Sheridan. He inclined his head toward the village and asked, "Is General LEE up there?" Sheridan said, "Yes," and Grant said, "Well, then, let's go up."[215]

They "went up" to that McLean House which, ironically, had brought the war full circle. It was at the home of Wilmer McLean that BEAUREGARD made his headquarters during the First Battle of Bull Run. To get away from the war, McLean sold out and moved to Appomattox. Now it was in McLean's front parlor that Grant met LEE.

Grant came in alone and saw LEE with two aides. Taking off his yellow thread gloves, Grant stepped forward to shake LEE's hand. He was aware of his own mud-stained appearance and LEE's splendor, but he gave no sign of it. Both men sat at tables while a half-dozen of Grant's generals entered with tinkling spurs and clanking sabers to stand behind their chief. LEE gave no sign of disapproval of their presence.

Grant spoke: "I met you once before, General LEE, while we were serving in Mexico, when you came over from General Scott's headquarters to visit Garland's brigade, to which I then belonged. I have always remembered your appearance, and I think I should have recognized you anywhere."

"Yes," Lee said, "I know I met you on that occasion, and I have often thought of it and tried to recollect how you looked, but I have never been able to recall a single feature."[216]

Grant talked eagerly of Mexico, perhaps to soften the impact of the request that he must make, and LEE, probably anxious to be done with the ordeal of surrender, brought him back gently with the words: "I suppose, General Grant, that the object of our present meeting is fully understood. I asked to see you to ascertain upon what terms you would receive the surrender of my army."[217]

Without changing countenance, with not a hint of exultation or gloating in his voice, Grant quickly outlined his terms: ". . . the officers and men surrendered to be paroled and disqualified from taking up arms again until properly exchanged, and all arms, ammunition and supplies to be delivered up as captured property."[218]

Next Grant set down his terms in writing. LEE read them, courteously corrected an unintentional oversight, and agreed. There was, however, the matter of the horses, which were the private property of his cavalrymen and artillerists. Would the men be permitted to retain them? At first Grant said that the terms allowed only officers to keep private property, but then, seeing how much this request meant to LEE, he promised "to let all the men who claim to own a horse or mule take the animals home with them to work their little farms."[219]

LEE was relieved and grateful. "This will have the best possible effect on the men," he said. "It will be very gratifying and will do much toward conciliating our people."[220] In Grant's generosity LEE saw not a vindictive but a compassionate conquerer.

ROBERT E. LEE knew then that the South had fallen. Even though the army which he formally surrendered a few minutes later was only his own, even though combat might sputter on until May 26, the fighting soul of the South died with LEE's signature on that Palm Sunday of 1865.

After he signed, LEE arose and shook hands with Grant. He bowed to the others in the room and strode silently out the door. On the porch of the McLean House he paused to draw on his gauntlets. He gazed sadly toward the hillside where his little army lay, faithful and fearless to the last. Twice, with slow and savage ruefulness, LEE drove his fist into his palm. Then, crying for Traveler in a hoarse and choking voice, he mounted and rode out of sight.

PART ☆ VI

Indian Wars,
the Spanish-American War
and the Philippine Insurrection

1

☆

What was to be done with the fallen South?

She had been crushed. She had gone down before the North's superior firepower, manpower and industrial power, and now she lay prostrate. In those areas where the armies of both sides had fought and marched, her railroads were demolished, her cities devastated and her countryside ravaged. Her warrior pride had been humbled and her manhood mutilated. Her economy was wrecked: land values had collapsed, the currency was worthless and some 3.5 million slaves "valued" at $2 billion had been freed without compensation for their "owners."

Empty warehouses and rusting river boats, rotten wharves and deserted plantations, these were what remained to the land of cotton; and while former Confederate generals plowed their own fields or hawked homemade pies along grass-grown streets, many of the emancipated Negroes loafed in their cabins or roamed the roads in enjoyment of their new-found freedom. Who could blame them? The defeat of the Confederacy had struck away their chains, and to them this meant only that they would no longer have to work. An idle labor force, however, meant that the land lay barren, and soon hunger followed poverty in the wake of ruin.

Politically, what was to be done with the South? Military victory had in no way solved the problem of states' rights. It had only quelled rebellion. But were the Rebels to be punished? Had the Confederate states actually left the Union and thus forfeited statehood? Were they to be treated as conquered territories or as errant equals? Above all, what of the Negroes: they were free, but were they to be the white man's social and political peers?

To all these questions Abraham Lincoln hoped to give a compassionate answer. There had been enough bloodshed: at least 540,000 dead in battle, in prisons and in hospitals. The legacy of hate —useless, festering hate—was large enough, and Lincoln would not add to it. Again and again he had advised his generals, "Let 'em up easy," and in his second inaugural address he had said: "With malice toward none; with charity for all; with firmness in the right, as God gives us to see the right, let us drive on to finish the work we are in; to bind up the nation's wounds; to care for him who shall have borne the battle; and for his widow, and his orphan—to do all which may achieve and cherish a just and lasting peace among ourselves, and with all nations."[1] On the night of April 11 Lincoln stood on the White House balcony to announce the most merciful terms granted by any victor. The rebellion was to be forgotten and every Southern state was to be readmitted to full privileges in the Union after 10 percent of its electorate took an oath of allegiance and organized a state government. Of Negro suffrage Lincoln said that he preferred to confer the vote at that time only on the "very intelligent" and those who had served as Union soldiers.

On the 14th, Good Friday of 1865, Lincoln told his friends of having had the same dream which had preceded some of the great battles of the war. An unfamiliar ship seemed to be carrying him toward an unknown shore. That night, with his wife and two friends, the President went to Ford's Theater to see the play *Our American Cousin.* He entered the presidential box and sank into an upholstered rocking chair. Although the door to the box was closed, the President's guard left his post there to watch the play.

At half-past nine the actor John Wilkes Booth entered Ford's Theater. He slipped along a back corridor to the presidential box. Stooping, he peered through a tiny hole he had previously drilled in the door and saw the President in his chair. Entering silently he aimed his six-inch brass derringer at the back of Lincoln's head and fired.

Lincoln slumped forward. Booth leaped to the stage below, breaking his leg. In an instant he was up, brandishing his pistol and shouting, "*Sic semper tyrannis!*" and before the stunned audience could move he had rushed through a rear exit and made his escape by horseback.

Unconscious, Lincoln was carried across the street to a lodging house. He lay diagonally across a bed that was too short for him, breathing with slow full breaths, his pale gaunt features calm and striking. At 7:22 A.M. April 15 he breathed his last. "Now he belongs to the ages,"[2] said Secretary Stanton, while in the South a

Confederate leader heard the news and cried aloud: "God help us if that is true."[3]

No event could have been more inimical to Southern recovery or national harmony than the assassination of Abraham Lincoln. His murder not only deprived the Union of the one man whose rare combination of vision, common sense and compassion might have led the nation through the difficult period of Reconstruction, but also unleashed those very forces of hatred and vengeance which he alone might have restrained.

For three weeks following his death Secretary Stanton conducted a spiteful little reign of terror. The North was provoked into crying for the blood of the captured Jefferson Davis and other "conspirators" such as Robert E. Lee. Not until John Wilkes Booth was killed resisting capture and three of his accomplices were executed, along with the unfortunate woman who harbored them, did the hysteria subside. Davis, meanwhile, was imprisoned in Fortress Monroe, where he spent two unrepentant years before his release. The only Southern war criminal executed was Captain Henry Wirz for his cruelties at Andersonville.

Nevertheless, hatred for the South still lingered, and nowhere did it rankle more than in the breasts of the Radical Republicans. These were the men who were determined upon a harsh peace. They sought equal rights for Negroes as well as almost unlimited power for themselves. Even today historians have difficulty separating their sincere aspirations from their selfish ambition, and this is probably because the one served the other. Negro suffrage meant that the Negroes would certainly vote for the Republicans who had enfranchised them, and never again would the Democrats of the South join their Northern colleagues to control Congress.

Such, simplified, was their policy; and just because these political split personalities pursued it so often in the language of hatred, the face that has come down to posterity is that of a hideous political Mr. Hyde, who wanted to crucify the South, rather than that of a humanitarian Dr. Jekyll, who wanted to give the Negroes free schools, free homesteads and the vote. In their defense, it should be remembered that the times were full of hate. The war had ended with a shriek of hatred—though not among the generals—for Lincoln had been felled by a mad dog, and the North was now engulfed by a flood of loathsome literature full of false tales of Southern atrocities.

Emerson thought that "General Grant's terms look a little too easy,"[4] while the House heard George Washington Julian of Indiana declare: "As for Jeff Davis, I would indict him, I would convict him and hang him in the name of God; as for Robert E. Lee, unmolested in Virginia, hang him too. And stop there? Not at all. I would hang liberally while I had my hand in."[5] True, noncombatant politicians are often quick to call upon God to help tie the hangman's knot, yet the sober *New York Times* did not hesitate to say of the starving South: ". . . if we should feed them, we would make them insolent and they might think it unreasonable in us to stick bayonets in them afterwards in order to make them sincerely sorry for their rebellion."[6] Eventually, it did come to bayonets, but not until after President Andrew Johnson clashed with the Radical leaders, Sumner of Massachusetts and Stevens of Pennsylvania.

It was Charles Sumner whose vituperative speech, "The Crime Against Kansas," had fanned the flames of sectional hatred in 1856 and led to his being caned into insensibility by a Southerner on the Senate floor. It was more than three years before Sumner recovered from that attack, and now, the most powerful man in the Senate, he was his old moralistic and dogmatic self, pursuing his humanitarian ideals under the impression that debate means monologue and that "There is no other side."[7] Even more powerful, even more vitriolic, was Representative Thaddeus Stevens. Tall and bent by his 74 years, his white face a death mask beneath his dark brown wig, trailing the club foot that seems to have envenomed him since birth, Thad Stevens had none of Sumner's idealism. Although his concern for the Negro was genuine, it could also be traced to the fact that his closest companion for most of his bachelor life was a handsome Negro woman, while his hatred for the South might have sprung from the destruction of his Chambersburg property by Lee's soldiers in 1863. When Thad Stevens fought for Negro rights, then, it was not only to secure justice for a downtrodden people whom he actually did love, but also to avenge himself upon a section that had injured him; and the certainty that both of these objectives converged in guaranteeing "perpetual ascendancy to the party of the Union,"[8] i.e., the Republicans, only made their attainment that much more desirable. So the scornful Sumner and the harsh Stevens prepared their prescription for Southern political impotence, and at first it seemed that they had the President's approval of it.

Andrew Johnson, the self-taught tailor from Tennessee, had succeeded to the presidency because Lincoln had wanted a loyal Democrat as his running mate. Johnson's reputation as Vice President
had been that of an honest, forthright and courageous public servant.
He was an ardent Unionist whose constantly repeated remark, "Treason is a crime and must be made odious,"[9] had an ominous ring for
the South. In fact, when the Radicals first conferred with Johnson,
Senator Ben Wade exclaimed: "Johnson, we have faith in you. By
the gods, there will be no trouble running the government."[10] But there
was trouble. The Radicals were mistaken in their conviction that
Johnson's hatred for the Southern aristocracy would lead him to support their program of Negro suffrage. As a Southerner, Johnson had
no desire to destroy white man's rule and he favored only a limited
suffrage for Negroes. Moreover, he was convinced that the Radicals
meant to hobble the white South to protect Northern industrialists,
and he had no more love for tycoons than for planters. Finally, Johnson sincerely believed that the Radicals' civil rights program was
unconstitutional. He felt that such matters were the concern of the
state governments. Thus Andrew Johnson gradually came to embrace
the lenient policy laid down by Abraham Lincoln, and after he did
there was joined a political battle unrivaled in American history.

The conflict began when the Radical-dominated Congress refused
to seat members from Southern states recognized by Johnson. In
essence, Congress specified that no Southern state would be readmitted until it had guaranteed civil rights and the vote for Negroes, while
disqualifying many ex-Confederates and repudiating the Confederate
war debt. In the fall of 1866 the battle between the presidential
veto and Congressional majorities shifted to the ballot box, and it
was here that the Radicals were aided by the ineffable stupidity of the
"Bourbon South."

Moderates such as Wade Hampton of South Carolina and General
Beauregard of Louisiana had counseled the South to confer the vote
upon its educated freedmen, of whom there were about a half-million
employed as farmers, barbers, mechanics or small business men. This
cadre could then be used to educate the great mass of newly freed
but illiterate slaves. Such a gesture might also go a long way toward
placating the North. But, no, the Bourbon reply was the infamous
Ku Klux Klan by which the Negro was frightened away from the
polls, and the Black Codes by which the Negro, valuable for his

labor, was permitted to stay in the South—if he was not actually compelled to—but prevented from becoming "uppity," that is, attempting to better himself.

Black Codes were most severe in states such as Mississippi, South Carolina and Louisiana, where Negroes outnumbered whites. In Mississippi, Negroes were required to sign contracts binding them to service with their employer for a full year, and the law stated: "Every civil officer shall, and every person may, arrest and carry back to his or her legal employer any freedman, free Negro or mulatto who shall have quit the service of his or her employer before the expiration of his or her term of service without good cause. . . ."[11] This was not slavery, merely involuntary servitude, and to the Radicals it was proof positive of the South's intentions to replace bondage with legal serfdom. "We tell the white men of Mississippi," the Chicago *Tribune* trumpeted, "that the men of the North will convert the State of Mississippi into a frog pond before they will allow such laws to disgrace one foot of soil in which the bones of our soldiers sleep and over which the flag of freedom waves."[12]

The Black Codes, as well as Southern race riots in which hundreds of Negroes were murdered, swung Northern sentiment solidly toward the Radical Republicans. Johnson supported the Democrats, many of whom had been Copperheads, and the astute Radicals, temporarily soft-pedaling the issue of Negro suffrage, made the issue one of "patriotism" versus "rebellion." They attacked Johnson with a vigor which exhausted the art of invective. He was a drunkard and a traitor, they cried, and Charles Sumner declared: "Jefferson Davis is in the casement at Fortress Monroe, but Andrew Johnson is doing his work."[13] Enraged, the President struck back. "If I have played the Judas," he cried, "who has been my Christ that I have played the Judas with? Was it Thad Stevens? Was it Charles Sumner?"[14] Such unbridled language did not fall gracefully from the lips of an American President, and bluff, tactless Andrew Johnson, never a man to charm an electorate, was roundly repudiated. The election gave the Radicals enough votes to override the President on any issue, and the new Congress had not been long in session before they had need of all of them.

In March of 1867 Congress passed the first Reconstruction Act carving the South into five military districts commanded by Federal generals. Johnson at once took up the challenge. Four times he vetoed Reconstruction Acts, and four times the defiant Radicals overrode him. They also began a campaign to strip the presidency of much of its power, even reaching out to control his own Cabinet by a Tenure of Office Act making dismissal of Cabinet officers subject to approval of the Senate. Stubborn bulldog that he was, Johnson fought back—and in 1868 the Radicals picked up the ultimate weapon: impeachment.

The pretext for impeaching Johnson was his dismissal of Secretary of War Stanton, who had constantly betrayed Cabinet secrets to the Radicals. Before the bar of the Senate it was charged that Johnson had broken the new Tenure of Office Act. There were other trumped-up charges, but this was the main accusation. Johnson's reply was that the act was unconstitutional, a position later upheld by the Supreme Court. The Radicals, however, were not interested in legality, only in bringing down the presidency and making it subservient to Congress. Once again, they covered Johnson with shameless and lying invective. Their position was best expressed by the credo of Thad Stevens: "Throw conscience to the Devil and stand by your party."[15] In the end, that was what it came down to: party loyalty versus conscience. In the end, seven courageous Republican Senators sacrificed their political careers on the altar of truth and voted for acquittal. One more vote for conviction, and Johnson would have been removed from office. A precedent would have been set by which any future Congress differing from the President might move to impeach and silence him.

Unfortunately for President Johnson's own peace of mind, it was many years before he was vindicated by some of the very men who had impeached him; and by then Radical Reconstruction had been fixed upon the South at the point of the bayonet.

Each of the South's five military districts was held by an army of occupation and commanded by a general with full responsibility for law and order. Moving swiftly, the generals removed six of the state governors, dismissed thousands of local officials and purged legislatures of those conservative members who might block the policies of the Radicals. New state governments were elected with the Negroes voting, and by 1870 all 11 states of the old Confederacy were regulated by such governments.

With these developments, and the disfranchising of many ex-Confederates, power was transferred from the old aristocracy to the new triumvirate of Negro, "carpetbagger" and "scalawag." A carpetbagger was one of those Northern opportunists who had come swarming South with their possessions supposedly crammed inside a single carpetbag, and a scalawag was a white Southerner who made common cause with the Radicals. Between them they often controlled the more numerous, but politically inexperienced Negroes, and the results were frequently scandalous. Spoilsmen and profiteers were allowed to debauch the state treasuries. They played upon the Negro legislators' very human desire to make the most of their new-found prestige. A Negro majority in the South Carolina legislature kept a fancy restaurant and bar open from 8 A.M. to 2 A.M. at a cost of $125,000 for a single session. They voted themselves free wine, whiskey and food, fine furniture, gold watches and perfume. They refurbished the state capital at a cost of $200,000, but after they were replaced by a conservative legislature the state's property was valued at a total of $17,000.

Such were the extravagances and corruptions that have made Reconstruction a nightmare memory in the mind of the white South; and yet much good was accomplished by Reconstruction governments. The new state constitutions abolished property qualifications for holding office, reapportioned legislatures on more equitable lines and established free public education for all children. The new governments also repaired war damage, built railroads—a chief source of graft—constructed roads, softened harsh penal codes and undertook public works. If the carpetbaggers and the scalawags stole, such was the public morality of the times, and they could not equal Boss Tweed of Tammany Hall who stole more than $100 million from New York City alone.

Nevertheless, the Reconstruction governments were anathema to most of the white South. Inevitably, a counterattack was launched. The objective was the voting Negro who gave the carpetbag governments their power, the tactics were pure terror, and the troops were the white-sheeted night riders of the Ku Klux Klan. They kidnapped, horse-whipped or hanged Negroes who clung to their rights. Eventually, the Klan's "lynch law" became so widespread that the South recoiled and the Klan was officially disbanded in 1869. But it continued unofficially on its career of terror, doing as much if not more to restore white supremacy than the devices of poll taxes and literacy tests which also kept the Negroes away from the voting booths. As Negro suffrage became a mockery, factional fights among the Radicals further weakened their hold upon the legislatures.

By 1872 the North had wearied of its attempt to impose its will on the South. By then also Ulysses S. Grant was in the White House. In 1868, backed by his "Boys in Blue" and the Negro vote, Grant had defeated his Democratic opponent, Horace Greeley, to become the fifth war hero in 80 years to receive the "peace-loving" American nation's highest office. Grant was to prove himself among the weakest of Presidents, yet he understood that the public was tired of Reconstruction. In 1872 he ordered the occupation troops not to interfere in Southern politics. Without Northern support, the Radicals were swept away by the resurgent Democrats of the South. By 1876 only three states remained under Radical control.

These also went Democratic after the disgraceful—or at least dubious—election of 1876. In this, the Democratic candidate Samuel J. Tilden of New York appeared to have defeated the Republican, Rutherford B. Hayes of Ohio. Prematurely, the Democrats rejoiced. But then the votes of the three remaining carpetbag states, South Carolina, Florida and Louisiana (together with Oregon), were called into question because of returns from rival election boards. Without these disputed states, Tilden had only 184 votes in the Electoral College. With them, Hayes had 185. The Republicans immediately declared that they had won and telegraphed their election boards to hold the line.

Now the election was thrown into Congress, where a special electoral commission made up of five Senators, five Representatives and five justices of the Supreme Court was appointed to study the disputed votes. Dividing on exact party lines, the commission voted 8 to 7 in favor of Hayes. For a time the Democrats refused to accept the verdict. There was talk of insurrection, and it was then that the Southern Democrats parted company with their Northern colleagues. They agreed to support Hayes at the price of a more generous policy toward the South. This ultimately resulted in the expulsion of the Radicals from the last three carpetbag states and creation of the so-called "Solid South" with all its political implications for the Negro and the nation. It was not until 1890, and after, that "Jim Crow" made the social suppression of the Negro complete. Long before then, in 1877, President Hayes kept his word by recalling the last of the Federal troops from the South.

They were needed to help suppress the Indians.

2

☆

Two and a half centuries had passed since Samuel Champlain fired those fatal shots on the shore of the lake that bears his name. It was in the flash of his firelocks and the fall of the painted Iroquois that the wars of America had begun, and now, eight wars later,* the clash of two incompatible civilizations was at last coming to its conclusion.

It had been an unequal struggle. From the outset the white man had been better organized and better equipped, possessing all the advantages of a superior civilization. In the days when he had been outnumbered, his discipline had enabled him to cling to his toeholds, his "beachheads," in effect, on the red man's continent. Thereafter, Indian indiscipline had led to the red man's defeat in detail. Tribe by tribe, outpost by outpost, the dispersed Indians went down before the concentrated white men. It never occurred to Indians of the interior that the tribes of the East Coast were fighting their battle, that they were resisting the white invasion "at the water's edge." No, they went their own way until the white tide flowed over the mountain barriers and engulfed them, too. So each tribe or confederation fought the white man alone, and each time they were conquered the white man expanded his beachhead, that is, he advanced his frontier farther westward and received more "reinforcements," i.e., immigrants from the Old World and his own progeny.

Such reinforcements swelled the white man's forces while the treaties of peace were in effect, and in retrospect it can be seen that the In-

* King William's, Queen Anne's, King George's, French-and-Indian, Revolutionary, 1812, Mexican and Civil.

dians never should have granted a single treaty. It was not so much that they would be dishonored—that was inevitable, granting the white man's purpose of conquest—it was that they gave the white man time to dig deeper, to consolidate and expand, until at last he had transformed his tenuous beachhead into a secure base.

After that happened, the outcome was foreordained. French in the North, English in the center, Spaniards in the South, the white men began the inexorable process of eviction and extermination. Of the three, the English and their American descendants were the most savage and successful. Seeking the land for itself, rather than for its gold or furs, they were more prone to evict than to exploit. And when the evicted resisted and struck back, extermination followed. The Iroquois and King Philip, Pontiac and Tecumseh, Creek and Seminole, all these and more had fallen victim to this insatiable lust for land, and as the Civil War was succeeded by the last and largest westward movement, this hunger began to feed on the tribes of the Great Plains.

There were some 200,000 of these Indians, the Sioux, Northern Cheyenne and Arapaho in the North, the Comanche, Southern Cheyenne, Kiowa and Apache in the South. Peerless horsemen, excellent shots, hardy and brave, they may have been the finest light cavalry in history. Mounted on fast ponies, they swept down upon settlements or mining camps, loosed their flights of arrows and then were gone before the whites could strike back. If they had had a Genghis Khan to organize them, they might have blocked or at least long delayed the American westward expansion. But at the time of their wars with the United States, they had only good tactical captains to follow, no unifying, visionary chief such as Tecumseh.

Up until 1861 the Plains tribes had been relatively peaceful, but in that year the appearance of settlers on the upper Mississippi and Missouri and the entry of miners into Colorado resulted in open warfare. In 1862 the Sioux of the Dakotas took to the warpath, ravaged the Minnesota frontier and had to be put down by a Union army under John Pope. For the next quarter-century Indian warfare raged practically unabated. Both sides fought ferociously, and both sides committed atrocities. In 1866 a force of 80 soldiers was massacred at Fort Phil Kearny, Wyoming, by Indians under Red Cloud, and even veteran Indian fighters found that the mutilations inflicted on the fallen were indescribable. So too did a force of Colorado militia treacherously destroy a band of Indians while peace negotiations were under way. A white man who witnessed the carnage reported: "They [the Indians] were scalped, their brains were knocked out; the men used their knives, ripped open women, clubbed little children, knocked them in the head with their guns, beat their brains out, mutilated their bodies in every sense of the word."[16]

Such reports enraged the American public, particularly in the distant East. Reformers and churchmen demanded a more humane policy toward the Indians, and in the midst of the uproar the mistake of rapid demobilization went unnoticed. An army of 25,000 men was hardly able to occupy the South and cope with the intrepid Plains Indians, who were made even more formidable by the modern breech-loading, magazine rifles sold to them by Western carpetbaggers and even Indian agents themselves. All the sympathy, however, was for the red men; and the ill-paid, sometimes unpaid American regular with his converted muzzle-loader struggled through what has been called "the dark ages" of the U.S. Army.

In the meantime, attempts were made to clear the main line of Western advance by taking the Plains Indians away from the roads and settling them on reserved lands in the Black Hills of Dakota and in Oklahoma. The Indians, however, refused to step aside. They preferred roaming the prairie to settling down on a reservation. On the open plains they could hunt the buffalo which provided them with food, clothing, weapons and even fuel. Unfortunately, the buffalo was vanishing at a rate accelerated by the appearance of railroad interests in the Plains. Railroad gangs joined hunters and miners in the slaughter of the herds, all but depriving the red men of their means of subsistence.

In 1875 prospectors discovered gold in the Black Hills. Here was the holy ground of the Sioux which the U.S. government had promised to hold inviolate. But no government in Washington, no puny, scattered army could restrain the rush of greedy miners into the Indian lands. With this, the Sioux lifted the hatchet again and went on the warpath under Crazy Horse and Sitting Bull. General Phil Sheridan, then commanding the army, organized a force to destroy them.

On June 17, 1876, 1,000 regulars and 250 friendly Indians under George Crook, probably the greatest of all Indian fighters, caught up with Crazy Horse and 6,000 Sioux and Cheyenne at the Rosebud River in Montana. The Indians were driven off, and their retreat took them across the path of other American columns. One of these was commanded by the young and vainglorious Colonel George Custer. Custer's orders were to get behind Crazy Horse and await the arrival of the main body. However, on June 25, 1876, having found the enemy, with a force of only 212 men at his own disposal, Custer rashly attacked Crazy Horse at the Little Big Horn. The result was the annihilation known as "Custer's Last Stand."

Not an American survived, but neither did Crazy Horse's army long survive this famous victory. In January of 1877 the regulars defeated him and his war came to an end. That same year discovery of gold on the Salmon River brought a characteristic rush of miners into the western Idaho lands held by the peaceful Nez Percé.

Led by the noble and eloquent Chief Joseph, the Nez Percé struck back. But they were defeated, after which Chief Joseph led his people on a masterful fighting retreat over 1,500 miles of mountain, plain and river. Just short of sanctuary in Canada, he was overtaken and compelled to surrender on October 5, 1877. His farewell was memorable: "Hear me, my chiefs, I am tired; my heart is sick and sad. From where the sun now stands, I will fight no more forever."[17]

In the meantime, the Southwest had become inflamed by the Apache uprising under the legendary Geronimo. Once again it was the redoubtable Crook, together with the capable Nelson Miles, who brought the Apache to submission. In 1886 Geronimo surrendered, but border warfare blazed fitfully until 1890. In that year, Sioux under Sitting Bull danced "the ghost dance" and put on the "ghost shirts" which they believed would protect them against white men's bullets. Orders went out to arrest Sitting Bull, but the old medicine man resisted and was killed. With that, his Sioux broke out of their Dakota reservation, only to be brought to bay at a place called Wounded Knee. There, in December of 1890, 300 Indian men, women and children were slaughtered by machine guns in the hands of the regulars.

As it had begun nearly three centuries before, so had it ended: from firelock to machine gun, the Indian fought a hopeless fight. He had been brave, but courage cannot master technocracy. He went down—he had to go down—because his indolent civilization could not possibly coexist beside the most dynamic in history. He had been too content, too conservative, satisfied for centuries with his continental Eden. It may be that the white man played the very devil in driving the Indians from their virgin paradise—certainly the ruthlessness of the Indian conquest remains the blackest page in American annals—yet only a sentimental romantic could maintain that the passing of this primitive society was not inevitable.

So the long, long battle between the hunter and the settler, between communal land and private property, had ended in the utter defeat of the hunter. When it did, so also ended the period in which American wars were fought on American soil.

3

☆

With the end of the Civil War on May 26, 1865—the date of the Confederate surrender west of the Mississippi—the nations of Europe expected the United States to turn upon France or Britain.

The triumphant Union had scores of able generals, millions of trained soldiers, almost unlimited reserves of the most modern weapons and a gigantic new munitions industry. With such a war machine, Europe reasoned, President Johnson would certainly seize Canada in retaliation for official British sympathy for the Confederacy and in compensation for shipping losses inflicted by Confederate raiders built in Britain. But Johnson did not move against Canada, and the shipping claims were amicably settled with an award of $15.5 million.

Neither did Johnson order an invasion of Mexico to evict the French and their puppet emperor, Maximilian. Instead, Phil Sheridan and 50,000 men marched to the Rio Grande as a reminder that the Monroe Doctrine was still in force. France took the hint, withdrawing her troops and abandoning Maximilian to the Mexican republicans, who had him shot to death.

Instead of foreign adventure, then, the triumphant Union quickly disarmed. There were a million men under arms at the Appomattox surrender, but there were only 183,000 seven months later—and by the end of 1866 the United States Army was down to 25,000 men, and the Navy was reduced to a few wooden sloops of war and ironclad monitors. Europe was astonished. Her own nations embarked upon a great imperialist scramble for colonies in Asia and Africa, she could not understand why the United States did not make similar acquisitions. Nor could she understand—as modern despotisms still do not understand—that a nation may be martial without being militarist. The fact was that the United States was sick of war and was looking inward. Manifest Destiny, although not dead, was at least asleep. Secretary of State Seward discovered this after he made his singlehanded deal to purchase Alaska from Russia for what would today be considered a paltry $7.2 million. The howl of derision at "Seward's Folly" forced the imperialistic Secretary to abandon schemes to annex Hawaii, the Danish West Indies and even Santo Domingo. Foreign adventures, then, were anathema in America. Foreign policy was so little respected that the New York *Sun* advocated abolition of the diplomatic service. "It is a costly humbug and sham," the paper said. "It is a nurse of snobs. It spoils a few Americans every year, and does no good to anybody."[18]

Isolation, George Washington's injunction to beware of the broils of Europe, was still the American watchword. Isolation had enabled the American nation to throw down political roots, to expand at the expense of Mexico and the Indians and to pass through a terrible Civil War without outside interference. Now isolation would continue so that the Midwest could become a global breadbasket, the two oceans might be linked by transcontinental railroads and a new-born industrial giant could be nursed to mammoth manhood.

There was, unfortunately, very little to admire morally about the new colossus. Where railroad magnates openly bought legislatures like penny candy, industrialists herded millions of migrants to the Land of Opportunity into dreadful mines and mills and there sweated their labor out of them for a dollar a 14-hour day. These were the days of the gilded tycoon and bloated robber baron. Because the notions of Darwin expressed by the phrase "survival of the fittest" had been applied to the world of business and there given free rein, it was thought proper that the men who built the railroads and created the nation's industrial plant should do so by ruthless suppression of competition and methods of corruption that would shame a pirate. "Nothing is lost save honor!"[19] cried big Jim Fisk at the conclusion of one particularly shameful railroad deal. Yet the nation did grow mighty under the guidance of such men, and historians are still divided over whether it could have done so in any other way, whether the bitter dregs of wholesale corruption and widespread waste and extravagance had not to be taken with the sweet tonic of a powerful industrial system.

Closer scrutiny from the White House and more responsibility in the Congress probably would have made the history of postwar internal development less of a stench in the nostrils of posterity, but, as Henry Adams observed: "No period so thoroughly ordinary had been known in American politics since Christopher Columbus first disturbed the balance of American society."[20] With the possible exception of Grover Cleveland, the Presidents from Grant through McKinley passed over the sands of American political history like men without feet. All Republicans, they allowed the Republican Party of such noble origin to become the complete captive of big business.

Grant was so indifferent toward the scandals that shook his two terms in office that the word "Grantism" has gone into the political lexicon as the ultimate in permissiveness. Hayes also cultivated the hands-off attitude, as did his successor, James A. Garfield, and Chester A. Arthur, who stepped up to the presidency after Garfield was assassinated by a disgruntled office-seeker. Cleveland's opposition to the tariff alienated big business and brought about his defeat by Benjamin Harrison, the grandson of old Tippecanoe; although Cleveland did manage to "make a comeback" and defeat Harrison next time to become the only President to succeed his successor. Laissez-faire in their domestic policy, then, all these men were naturally isolationist in foreign policy. Cleveland also avoided foreign commitments, and in his first inaugural he declared for "the policy of neutrality, rejecting any share in foreign broils and ambitions upon other continents and repelling their intrusion here. It is the policy of Monroe and of Washington and Jefferson—'Peace, commerce and honest friendship with all nations; entangling alliances with none.' "[21]

Yet, even as Cleveland charted this uncompromising isolationist course, a nascent imperialism was gaining converts in America, and five years later the disappearance of the frontier produced a profound change in the nation's attitude.

In 1890, just as the Indian war whoop and the peal of cavalry bugles subsided into history, the director of the census announced that the frontier had ceased to exist. Probably the Indian conquest and the closing of the frontier were associated, for each new westward thrust had had to contend with hostile Indians. Now, with the Indians gone, settlement had reached clear to the Western ocean and the land frontier had vanished. But the expansionist spirit did not disappear. The itch to move on, to grow, to settle new lands was far too deeply ingrained in the American character to perish merely upon the exhaustion of the supply of free land. Instead, expansionism changed its name to imperialism and began to wonder if new lands might not be found beyond the ocean barriers. Captain Alfred Thayer Mahan, the naval strategist and exponent of sea power, declared openly: "Whether they will or no, Americans must now begin to look outward."[22] Gradually, business leaders began to accept Mahan's doctrines. The enormous growth of American industry suggested the need for foreign markets to absorb the surplus from the nations' farms, mines and factories. Naturally this did not mean that foreign markets could not be acquired through normal economic or diplomatic processes rather than through conquest or seizure, but the fact was that the imperialists of Europe were already using the force of arms to exploit Asia and Africa, and it was argued that if the United States did not join the ranks of the aggressors she would be left far behind. Eventually, and inevitably, a divine mandate was invoked for imperialism. The American sense of crusade which had carried the colonists of Boston to the cliffs of Quebec two centuries before was revived, together with the jingoist cant of Anglo-Saxon supremacy. The Congregationalist minister Josiah Strong wrote: "This race of unequalled energy, with all the majesty of wealth and numbers behind it—the representative, let us hope, of the largest liberty, the purest Christianity, the highest civilization—having developed peculiarly aggressive traits calculated to impress its institutions upon mankind, will spread itself over the earth."[23] Specifically, Strong charted a course to "move down upon Mexico, down upon Central and South America, out upon the islands of the seas, over upon Africa and beyond."[24] Finally, the internal discontent of the 1890s was another powerful force making for imperialism. Ill-paid industrial workers and farmers scourged by dust storms, insect plagues and falling grain prices found that looking outward could be a form of escapism, just as the leaders who were unable to satisfy demands for reform found the golden dream of imperialism a convenient diversion.

In 1893, with Benjamin Harrison in the White House, imperialism reached out toward Hawaii. There a group of powerful Americans revolted against Queen Liliuokalani and seized power. Their chief motive was annexation to the United States in order to escape the import duties on sugar. President Harrison appeared to favor annexation, but he was a lame duck defeated the previous year by Grover Cleveland. The new President was still a moderate in foreign policy, and he believed that the dispatch of American Marines to Hawaii during the revolt had been a wrongful intervention in the affairs of a foreign state. So he withdrew the treaty of annexation, merely recognizing the new Republic of Hawaii organized by the revolutionaries.

Mild and restrained in 1893, Cleveland was a fire-breathing jingoist two years later after Great Britain rejected his attempt to mediate her dispute with Venezuela over the boundaries between that nation and British Guiana. American "mediation" consisted of a reminder that the Monroe Doctrine was still in force and that Britain actually had no right to colonies in Latin America. "Today the United States is practically sovereign on this continent," the British Foreign Office was bluntly informed, "and its fiat is law upon the subjects to which it confines its interposition. . . . Its infinite resources combined with its isolated position render it master of the situation and practically invulnerable as against any or all other powers."[25]

Britain, however, replied that the Monroe Doctrine had nothing to do with the border dispute, and an angry Cleveland called upon Congress to vote funds for a commission to determine the boundary line of British Guiana. The President declared that the nation must be ready to prevent Britain from ruling any territory that "we have determined of right belongs to Venezuela."[26] Cleveland's challenge, for such it was, was ignored by a Britain too deeply involved elsewhere in the world, and perhaps also too deeply aware of the new and powerful navy at Cleveland's back, and as the clamor for war in America gradually subsided, the dispute was submitted to arbitration. Nevertheless, the crisis had been significant and prophetic. Captain Mahan said: "It indicates as I believe and hope, the awakening of our countrymen to the fact that we must come out of our isolation, which a hundred years ago was wise and imperative, and take our share in the turmoil of the world."[27]

To enter that turmoil the United States need look no farther than Cuba, where a revolt against Spanish rule had begun.

Cuba had been among the first of the Spanish colonies in the New World. She had been discovered by Columbus in 1492, and Spain had been in "the pearl of the Antilles" since 1511. But the once proud Spanish empire deteriorated; Spain's South American colonies dropped away from her one by one. Cuba, taking note, wished to do the same. Her people arose in 1868, only to be put down in a bloody ten years' war. Thereafter Spanish rule grew more oppressive. Taxation maintained a corrupt bureaucracy and an occupying army, while a blind colonial policy imposed strangling commercial regulations. From America came relief in the form of a tariff admitting raw sugar duty-free. Then a tariff in 1894 imposed a heavy duty on sugar. Since four-fifths of the wealth of Cuba was invested in sugar production, this action by her chief customer provoked a severe depression. This, together with Spanish misrule, brought on the revolution of 1895.

Americans at once sympathized with the revolutionaries. Cuban patriots centered in New York played skillfully upon this sympathy. They spread stories of Spanish atrocities and successfully appealed for funds. They also threatened to destroy American property in Cuba unless its owners contributed to the rebel cause, and they launched filibustering expeditions from American shores. Thus they early involved the American people, if not their government, in the Cuban Revolution.

In Cuba itself, a cruel war was being fought. The policy of the rebels was to wreck the economy to cripple Spanish resources, force the unemployed into the ranks of the revolution and starve the Spanish garrison. In reply, General Valeriano Weyler, the Spanish Governor General, adopted a policy of "reconcentration." The Cuban people were ordered to come to the towns occupied by the Spanish troops or else face trial as rebels. When the poor uprooted peasantry obeyed, it was found that the Spanish could not feed them. There was much suffering, and yet the policy of reconcentration was hardly crueler than the rebels' program of merciless ruin. However, the Cuban patriots in the States were careful to see that only the stories of Spanish barbarity were circulated.

Pro-Cuban sentiment grew strong enough to demand direct intervention, but Grover Cleveland had by then recovered his balance and he ignored the jingos. Interest in the Cuban Revolution also waned during the famous election of 1896 in which the silver-tongued William Jennings Bryan, the Democrat, stumped the country crying that mankind would not be crucified "upon a cross of gold," while the Republican, William McKinley, sat on his front porch in Ohio to chat with carefully screened delegations from across the nation. McKinley won, and promptly declared that there would be "no jingo nonsense" in his administration. However, McKinley did not reckon upon the influence of such stout expansionists as the powerful Senator Henry Cabot Lodge or the bellicose Theodore Roosevelt, and especially not upon America's "yellow press."

Though a new factor in world affairs, the popular press had already shown its power to detonate a political powder keg by its part in triggering the Franco-Prussian War of 1870. By the end of the nineteenth century its standards of accuracy and decency were decidedly lower than those of today, and in America no newspaper was more shamelessly sensational than Joseph Pulitzer's New York *World* or the New York *Journal* of William Randolph Hearst. Both Pulitzer and Hearst were locked in a bitter circulation battle, and they found the Cuban Revolution a source of the sensational kind of news that would sell newspapers. They seized upon "every incident calculated to shock, horrify, titillate, or disgust their readers and blew it up to fantastic proportions."[28] Out of history's dust bin came the Anglo-Saxon caricature of the Spaniard—swarthy, leering, cruel and cowardly— and his atrocities were detailed with a lip-smacking sense of outrage that was not deterred by the realization that many of them had been fabricated by the Cuban revolutionaries. Pulitzer and Hearst were absolutely without conscience. To an artist who cabled from Cuba, "There is no trouble here. There will be no war. I wish to return," Hearst issued his famous reply: "Please remain. You furnish the pictures and I'll furnish the war."[29]

Thus, while Hearst's *Journal* described the Spanish commander as "Butcher" Weyler, "the devastator of Haciendas, the destroyer of families and the outrager of women," Pulitzer's *World* printed such "reports" as this:

The horrors of a barbarous struggle for the extermination of the native population are witnessed in all parts of the country. Blood on the roadsides, blood on the fields, blood on the doorsteps, blood, blood, blood! The old, the young, the weak, the crippled—all are butchered without mercy. There is scarcely a hamlet that has not witnessed the dreadful work. Is there no nation wise enough, brave enough to aid this blood-smitten land?[30]

Certainly not all of the American press was so irresponsible, yet the fact remained that the warmongering *World* and *Journal* had a combined circulation of 1,560,000 against 225,000 for the total anti-war press based in New York, and because most of the nation's news-papers took their editorial leads from New York, the result was that the screams of the war hawks drowned out the cooing of the doves. In such an atmosphere it was impossible for the American people to maintain a calm, detached judgment, nor was the situation improved after Hearst triumphantly printed a letter of the Spanish Ambassador's which criticized President McKinley as "weak and a bidder for the admiration of the crowd."[31]

By then, February of 1898, the American nation was on the brink of war, brought there by the jingo press, the evangelical zeal of Josiah Strong, Captain Mahan's dreams of world power, Senator Lodge's political aspirations and Theodore Roosevelt's love of adventure. Moreover, the American people were eager for a diversion which might efface the memory of a recent depression and the ugly class conflict which arose during the election of 1896. Agrarian reformers who had followed Bryan to defeat at the hands of Eastern capital welcomed the prospect of a fresh crusade against a foreign foe. Nevertheless, not one or all of these reasons combined was enough to push America into another war. Neither Hearst nor Pulitzer had been able to demon-strate that the United States was in any way endangered by the Cuban Revolution, and sympathy for the Cuban people was just not enough to detonate a war. What was needed was that extraneous spark that comes flashing out of nowhere.

Spain did not seem likely to provide it. She had hardly protested after McKinley sent the battleship *Maine* into Havana Harbor during a riot there. The Spanish authorities thought that the *Maine*'s presence in Cuban waters might result in an incident that could cause war. "We are trying to avoid it at any cost,"[32] they told McKinley. Then, on the night of February 15, 1898, a terrific explosion shook the *Maine* and sent her to the bottom with 250 men. Back in New York William Randolph Hearst heard the news, and told his editor: "This means war."[33]

It did indeed, even though it is still not known who sank the *Maine*. Theodore Roosevelt said, "The *Maine* was sunk by an act of dirty treachery on the part of the Spaniards,"[34] a charge which, without a shred of evidence, was echoed and embellished upon by the press. But the fact is that the *Maine* could have been sunk by an internal accident, by Cubans eager to draw America into their failing fight, by some misguided, bumbling Spanish "sympathizer," or—least of all, probably not at all—by Spain herself. The last thing that decrepit old Spain wanted was war with powerful young America, yet this was the first thing guaranteed by the sinking of the *Maine*. Spain might immediately express regrets and condolences, even allow the American dead to be buried in Cuban soil, but nothing would now placate those Americans who, motivated either by ulterior purpose or a belief in comic-strip causality, were bellowing that the national honor must be avenged.

Diplomacy was useless. By April 9 Spain had acceded to every American request except Cuban independence: she had released every American prisoner, recalled General Weyler, recalled her offending ambassador, revoked the reconcentration order, agreed to furnish food for Cuba and finally granted an armistice. Still the press and the imperialists thundered on, and the Congressional mail reeked of sulphur. McKinley had not the strength to resist the tide making for war. On April 11 he asked Congress for authority to use force to intervene in Cuba. On April 19, 1898, Congress jointly declared Cuba free and independent, demanded Spanish withdrawal from the island, and granted McKinley the power to secure both objectives. On April 21 Spain broke off diplomatic relations with the United States, and on April 25 Congress declared that a state of war had existed since that day.

4

☆

A war for an island by contending offshore powers has to become a naval war, or at least be decided by sea power. Because part of the Spanish fleet was halfway around the world in the Philippines—where a native insurrection was also in progress—the Spanish-American War became a two-ocean naval war.

For once America was prepared. Her Navy was three times as large as Spain's and was far more efficient. The American Navy had four first-class battleships and one second-class one, against a single

Spanish first-class battleship, which, laid up for repairs, never saw service. American cruisers and other warships were vastly better equipped and served than those of the Spanish Navy. Never before or since has the American Navy sailed to battle with such superiority, and much of this was due to the theories of Captain Mahan and the driving energy of Theodore Roosevelt.

Mahan, of course, persuaded many influential Americans to adopt his theories of imperialism backed up by a powerful navy. Roosevelt, whom McKinley made Assistant Secretary of the Navy in 1897, was his chief convert. Proud, energetic and brilliant, warm and outgoing by nature, "Teddy" Roosevelt had struggled for years to overcome the handicap of a frail body and a weak constitution. By the strength of his will and his devotion to the "strenuous life" he had so changed his physical appearance that many of his contemporaries regarded him as the epitome of the clean-living American. Others saw in Teddy's buck-toothed grin, walrus mustache and bright eyes twinkling behind little glasses the features of "perpetual adolescence." Yet even his detractors would grant Roosevelt's driving energy and his leading role in preparing the American Navy for war.

Actually, it was Roosevelt who put part of it on a war footing two months before hostilities commenced. On February 25, 1898, shortly after the *Maine* was sunk, while Secretary John Long was away, Roosevelt ordered Commodore George Dewey to take the Asiatic Squadron to Hong Kong and there stand by to attack the Spanish squadron in the Philippines. It has been charged that Roosevelt's unauthorized action is proof of an imperialist clique's plot to annex the Philippines. In fact, Secretary Long, though infuriated to discover Roosevelt's cable, did not rescind it. By then the entire American government was resigned to war—and Commodore Dewey quickly cleared his decks for battle.

His white ships—cruisers *Olympia, Boston, Raleigh* and *Concord,* gunboat *Petrel*—were painted battle gray. Coal colliers were purchased from Britain and arrangements were made for an emergency base off the south China coast. The cutter *McCulloch* arrived April 17 and was also painted. Meanwhile, Dewey waited impatiently for the arrival of cruiser *Baltimore* with a load of ammunition. If she did not appear before war was declared, the neutral British authorities in Hong Kong would order him to sea without her. On April 22 *Baltimore* arrived from Yokohama, and in 48 hours she was docked, scraped, repaired, painted, coaled and provisioned—to the astonishment of the British.

Even so, the British did not believe that Yankee energy was enough to humble Spain. It was hard for Europe to forget the noble naval history of the voyaging Iberians, and Dewey himself wrote: "In the Hong Kong Club it was not possible to get bets, even at heavy odds, that our expedition would be a success, and this in spite of a friendly predilection among the British in our favor."[35] On April 24 Dewey cleared Hong Kong. A few more days were spent off the Chinese coast. Ammunition was distributed. Spars, chests, hatch covers and other flammables of wood were sent to the colliers. On April 27 the U.S. Asiatic Squadron sailed for the Philippines.

Rear Admiral Patricio Montojo y Pasaron, commander of the Spanish squadron in Manila Bay, was like most Spanish naval officers: utterly brave and utterly defeatist. He knew that he served but the shell of an empire, and that his seven ships—flagship *Reina Cristina*, *Castilla*, *Don Juan de Austria*, *Don Antonio de Ulloa*, *Luzon*, *Cuba* and *Duero*—were no match for Dewey's six. Yet he was prepared to go down fighting. To prevent the bombardment of Manila, he stationed his ships in the shallow but unprotected waters off Cavite, a few miles away. There, in gloomy resolution, he awaited the Americans.

Commodore Dewey had looked into Subic Bay. Finding it empty, he made for Manila—arriving off the city on the last night of April. The moon was up, drifting through light clouds; nevertheless Dewey decided to run the channel. Just before midnight the mouth of the bay was sighted. It yawned darkly between two dark headlands. Corregidor Island's grim bulk loomed farther back in the space between. Flagship *Olympia* leading, the American ships steered straight in. Sailors who had been called stealthily to their stations by word of mouth rather than blaring bugles steeled themselves for the sound of gunfire. Suddenly, the soot in *McCulloch*'s funnel caught fire. Flames shot up, died down, shot up again. . . . Still, no enemy gun spoke until well after midnight. The shells did no damage, the Spaniards stopped firing, and by daybreak the American squadron had safely sailed the 23 miles to Manila.

The seven Spanish ships were in line. American sailors heard cheers rising from the enemy decks and saw Spain's historic red-and-orange battle flags catch the wind. The Spanish fired first: wild and high. A shell burst above *Olympia,* and the ship's crew cried: "Remember the *Maine!*" Commodore Dewey spoke to *Olympia*'s captain: "You may fire when ready, Gridley."[36] At a distance of 5,500 yards *Olympia*'s starboard 8-incher belched smoke and flame. Soon all the American ships were firing. Deliberately and with slow majesty, Dewey paraded his bellowing ships before the Spanish ships. Five times they promenaded, three times west and twice east, until the smoke of battle obscured the stricken enemy. As Dewey broke off the action for breakfast, an excited *Olympia* gun captain cried: "For God's sake, captain, don't let us stop now! To hell with breakfast!"[37]

Nevertheless, the respite was taken, and at 11:16 A.M. Dewey stood in to renew battle. By then the Spanish fleet was dying. *Cristina* was a blazing shambles, *Castilla* had to be abandoned and *Ulloa* soon went down with colors flying. After the Sangley Point batteries above Cavite were knocked out, light-draft *Petrel* ran boldly into the inner harbor to complete the enemy's destruction.

Petrel found most of the Spanish ships abandoned or sunk. Her crew set fire to those ships beyond hope of salvage, and her 6-inch guns quickly brought the Spanish flag fluttering down the pole at Cavite Navy Yard. Upon threat of bombardment of the city, the Spaniards agreed to silence their shore batteries.

It was all over. Dewey's squadron took up unchallenged command of the bay, masters of Manila and of the entire Philippine archipelago as well. In seven hours, with not a man killed and only eight lightly wounded, the United States had become a world power and had embarked on her Asiatic career.

5

☆

America went wild over Dewey's victory at Manila Bay. North and South, coast to coast, there was a rush to join the colors. Old soldiers who had fought each other in the Civil War were reunited in regulation blue. Once again there were tootling bands and emotional farewells. Women adorned departing troop trains with sheaves of lilies and bouquets of daffodils, while perspiring young men in hot woolen uniforms bought kisses with brass buttons cut from their tunics.

Camping grounds blossomed at state capitals across the nation. Such was the invincible innocence of this post-Civil War generation that one governor opposed letting his militia camp in the field with the question: "But what if it rains?"[38] Inclement weather could not dampen the ardor of William Jennings Bryan, who took well-publicized command of a Nebraska "silver" regiment which the government discreetly kept far away from any headline-harvesting field of battle. Theodore Roosevelt quickly resigned from the Navy Department and telegraphed Brooks Brothers in New York for a "blue cravenette regular Lieutenant-Colonel's uniform without yellow on the collar and with leggings."[39] Then Teddy joined a regiment of volunteer cavalry which was commanded by the competent Colonel Leonard Wood but which was forever known as Roosevelt's Rough Riders. After drilling one of the squadrons on a hot afternoon at San Antonio, Teddy, who liked his wars jolly or "bully," bought beer for the men—and that night the irate and professional Colonel Wood made Roosevelt's conduct the subject of a lecture on discipline. If the abashed Roosevelt could apologize, however, there was very little the Army as a whole could do to escape the coils of confusion wound around it by such enthusiastic amateurism.

Unlike the Navy, the Army was unprepared. Kept to 25,000 men throughout the Indian Wars, after the *Maine* was sunk it had been raised to a paper strength of 28,000, not a formidable force to oppose 155,000 better-trained and better-equipped Spanish troops in Cuba. After war broke out, the regular Army was expanded to 61,000 men, and President McKinley called for 125,000 volunteers and again for 75,000. Before the end of November, 1898, more than 223,000 men had enlisted. Once again the volunteer system with all the mistakes of the Mexican and Civil Wars was put into service. Instead of using the regulars as cadres around whom the volunteers could be formed into new units, the regular formations were left intact and the volunteers were assembled in huge camps of instruction. Without the regulars to temper them, to impart to them something of their own toughness and respect for the soldier's hard calling, the volunteers counted themselves veterans the moment they put on those romantic broad-brimmed campaign hats or those prosaic suspenders and leggings.

Confused as such a call-up would have been under any circumstances, it became chaotic under the genial misrule of the politician who ran the War Department. Russell Alger seems to have been the sort of man who meets a problem in logistics with a cheerful smile. Under him an Army shrunken by neglect was racked by growing pains. There was not enough of anything, especially of the new Krag-Jorgensen magazine rifles which fired a .308 caliber bullet using smokeless powder. The food was so bad that the soldiers swore they were fed "embalmed beef," and because of inadequate sanitary and medical facilities disease carried off 2,565 men, more than seven times the 345 men who died in battle. Volunteers arrived at the camps without arms, blankets or tents, while heavy equipment disassembled and packed in unmarked boxes was scattered in hundreds of railroad cars parked on quiet spurs and side tracks.

Still, the Army had a plan. Havana, the seat of Spanish authority, was to be the objective. The regulars were to be assembled at New Orleans, Mobile and Tampa while the volunteers were being trained. A detachment of about 5,000 regulars under Major General William Shafter was to sail from Tampa for Cuba to make a reconnaissance in force and bring supplies to the Cuban rebels. In the meantime, the powerful Atlantic fleet at Key West was to blockade Cuba and seize control of the sea. After this happened, a huge expeditionary force would embark for Cuba.

That was the original plan, changed, of course, by events on the sea.

Spain had two fleets in the Atlantic, the smaller one in home waters, and the larger one in the Cape Verde Islands under Admiral Pascual Cervera. On May 29 Admiral Cervera sailed from St. Vincent with four cruisers and three torpedo boats. His mission was to break the American blockade of Cuba. Opposing him was Rear Admiral William Sampson at Key West with a powerful fleet of three battleships, two cruisers and numerous smaller vessels. Eventually, Sampson's strength would be augmented by the mighty new battleship *Oregon*, just launched at Bremerton, Washington, and then steaming around the Horn at flank speed.

Unfortunately for Sampson, the public and the jingo press became so jittery over rumors that the Spaniards were sailing to attack the East Coast that he was forced to detach a powerful "Flying Squadron" from his fleet and send it north on patrol duty off Hampton Roads, Virginia. Still, he searched the Caribbean for Cervera. The Spaniard hoped to refuel at San Juan, Puerto Rico, but after he arrived at Martinique he learned that there was no coal there. Cervera decided to make for Curaçao, where he expected to find coal colliers, but when he arrived the colliers were not there. In despair, in great need of fuel, he sailed for Santiago de Cuba, the only open port in which he might obtain coal, and after he entered the harbor on May 19 the American fleet under Sampson found him there and bottled him up.

Now the American plan of campaign was changed. Sampson dared not risk forcing the harbor to get at Cervera's squadron. Even though many of Santiago's land batteries were obsolete, the Spaniards still possessed a few modern guns, the narrow channel was sown with mines and Cervera's ships might be able to "cross the T," that is, put themselves broadside to the Americans advancing in column and concentrate all their firepower upon them. Finally, American relations with foreign powers were so strained at that time that the United States could not afford to lose a single ship. Sampson had special instructions not to risk the fire of land batteries.

At first, he tried long-range bombardment of the shore positions, but without success. Next, facing a prolonged blockade, he moved to establish a coaling base on Cuban soil. Marines were sent to seize Guantánamo Bay, about 40 miles east of Santiago. They succeeded, and drove off a Spanish counterattack in the first land battle between the two nations. Yet, even before this happened, it had become clear to U.S. authorities that a continued blockade would not solve the problem. Inside the harbor at Santiago, Cervera was being supplied from the interior. He could hold out indefinitely, immobilizing Sampson and thus blocking the entire American expedition to Cuba.

What was needed now was an attack on Santiago from the landward side. On May 30, 1898, instructions went south from Washington to General Shafter at Tampa: "You are directed to take your command on transports . . . to the vicinity of Santiago de Cuba . . . to capture or destroy the garrison there; and . . . with the aid of the navy capture or destroy the Spanish fleet. When will you sail?"[40]

General Shafter blithely informed Secretary Alger that he could sail in three days, after which he took personal charge of efforts to unravel the logistics tangle at Tampa. He moved his headquarters to the pier at Port Tampa, where a packing case served him as a desk and two boxes supported his 300-pound bulk. There he sat, his huge stomach hanging between his legs, gasping like a beached whale in the hot Florida sun, while the process of "mounting out" America's greatest military expedition went forward with a chaos born of Shafter's confidence that his colonels could each get his own men and animals, guns and supplies, aboard his own ship in his own way.

Here was the antithesis of Winfield Scott with his minute preparations for Vera Cruz. Though a brave and determined officer, Shafter was an old frontier fighter whose experience with small units and local actions had ill prepared him for the complexities of a large amphibious operation. Shafter left the embarkation up to the colonels, and they, discovering that the ships would carry only 18,000 out of Tampa's 20,000 men, immediately raced each other for the transports. Tents were struck, camps were policed, and tired, hungry men with bedding rolls slung over their shoulders were marched off to the railroad stations. Only a few regiments found trains waiting for them; one marched to an appointed track, found no train, marched to another track, again found nothing and finally commandeered a coal train; another seized a cattle train and sent its soldiers rolling to the docks ankle deep in soft stinking filth. At the water's edge the rush to commandeer ships began. There were no assigned transports, merely a process of first-come-first-served, and Theodore Roosevelt took a squad of Rough Riders to hold the gangplank of the *Yucatan* against another regiment. So it took eight days, not three, to sail; but on June 8 with all his ships loaded and moving down the bay, Shafter was notified by Alger to wait for further orders.

The ships were recalled, while the Navy searched for two Spanish ships reported in waters between Florida and Cuba. They were not there, in fact they did not exist, and while the "Phantom Fleet" was thus pursued, Shafter's soldiers sweltered and sickened in their hot, airless holds. On June 14, with the false alarm over, General Shafter and a force of 17,000 men in 32 transports steamed south.

The vessels formed in three long lines, escorted by battleship *Indiana* and other warships, but they soon were spread out over 30 or 40 miles. After five and a half days of uneventful sailing beneath

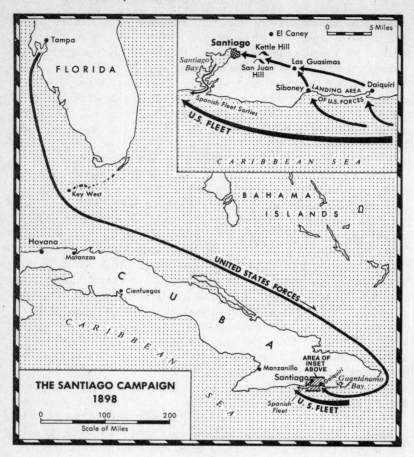

THE SANTIAGO CAMPAIGN
1898

0   100   200
Scale of Miles

bright suns and starry skies and over a glassy sea, they joined Admiral Sampson's fleet off Santiago. Here Sampson came aboard Shafter's ship and sailed with him 18 miles west to a rendezvous with General Calixto García, the Cuban rebel leader. At a council of war held in a palm-frond hut, Sampson suggested that Shafter land his men on both sides of the entrance to Santiago Harbor. The doughboys would then charge up steep slopes to capture Morro Castle and the sister forts at Socapa.

General Shafter demurred. En route to Cuba he had read an account of a disastrous British expedition to Santiago in the eighteenth century. He had no wish to repeat the bloody mistake of charging a stone fort perched atop a 230-foot cliff. Instead, he would land 15 miles east of the city at Daiquirí, and advance overland on Santiago. He would have to strike quickly, before the yellow fever arrived, and he would have to land over open beaches beneath high, fortified bluffs. Still, General García had informed Shafter that there were only 300 men at Daiquirí and that his own rebels could drive them off. It was agreed then to land at Daiquirí, while the Navy distracted the Spanish by bombarding other points along the coast and one of Shafter's two divisions feinted a landing west of Santiago.

On June 22, 1898, the landings began.

Lieutenant General Arsenio Linares, commanding in Santiago Province, had 36,500 troops distributed throughout the area. Of these, 12,000 were in the city of Santiago itself, with some 5,000 stationed between the town and Daiquirí. If General Linares had ordered this latter force to oppose the American landing, he might have dealt the *Yanquis* one of the bloodiest defeats in their history. Even 300 men fighting from the fortified stone bluffs above the Daiquirí beaches could have raked and ripped the go-as-you-please amphibious assault launched on that sparkling, sunlit morning. Yet Linares had chosen to withdraw even that bare garrison, to fight only delaying actions while he concentrated most of his forces around the city for a major defense closer in.

So the American naval guns belched smoke and gouts of orange flame and sent huge red blobs screaming into the Cuban hillside, uprooting trees and smashing cliffs—but hitting no military objectives —while boatloads of men in blue raced through the swells without one Spanish bullet to dig up a spurt in the sea.

The sprint for shore became anticlimactic after a Cuban ran out on the iron pier at Daiquirí to wave a white flag in signal that the Spanish had fled. The swarm of correspondents present, who would eventually write more words on the campaign that was then beginning than there were bullets fired in it, were disappointed. Not so the soldiers who jumped safely onto the iron pier or leaped into the surf of the Daiquirí beaches, setting up a wild cheer that was picked up by every ship in the fleet and carried for miles out on the ocean. Meanwhile, the horses were "unloaded" by throwing them into the water, where boatmen seized their halters to lead them ashore. When a group of cavalry horses began swimming out to sea, buglers on the beach blew the calls that turned them in the right direction. Before nightfall, the Navy had put 6,000 troops ashore with most of their equipment at a loss of only five horses drowned.

On the two days following the landing, the Spaniards continued to fall back on Santiago, while the Americans pushed forward to Siboney to set up their base. The road they followed was a rut in the jungle, passable only two abreast and so densely overgrown to either side that it was not possible to put out scout flankers. Two weeks of shipboard life had already weakened the Americans, and as the moist, oozing tropic heat drenched them in their own sweat and drew upon them the stinging torments of clouds of mosquitoes, their pace slowed perceptibly so that the long blue line snaking back through the brush became an easy target for Spanish ambuscade. The Spanish, however, were interested only in a delaying action while the entrenchments around Santiago were strengthened.

To delay the invaders, a force of about 2,000 men held the height of Las Guasimas about five miles inland from Siboney and astride the road to Santiago. General Shafter had no desire to attack Las Guasimas. He wanted his advance division to halt at Siboney and hold it until enough supplies were built up for the push to Santiago. However, Brigadier General Joseph Wheeler thought otherwise. Wheeler was a veteran Confederate commander of cavalry who had shared prison life with Jefferson Davis, and he gloried in the nickname of "Fighting Joe." Thus, early in the morning of June 24, 1898, the old Rebel led a division of dismounted cavalry northwestward from Siboney and ran into the Spanish at Las Guasimas.

Wheeler sent one column up against the Spanish front while another tried to get around the enemy's right flank. The Spaniards fought back grimly. A blind, hot, wearisome fight ensued. American soldiers and artillery mules thrashed through tangles of creeper, fern and vine while Spanish bullets clipped the branches overhead. Before it was over, Wheeler called for reinforcements, but by then the Spaniards were retreating.

"We've got the damned Yankees on the run!"[41] Wheeler yelled, momentarily forgetting his new allegiance, while mistaking the Spaniards' motive. They were only carrying out an orderly fallback to prepared positions.

Nevertheless, a wild outburst of overheated press copy celebrated

Las Guasimas as a splendid American victory, although American casualties of 16 killed and 52 wounded, against Spanish losses of 10 dead and 18 wounded, certainly do not suggest anything but a skirmish. Yet the fighting did teach the Yankee invaders that "the Dons" were willing fighters indeed, while restraining the impetuous Wheeler long enough for Shafter to come ashore and take command. So Las Guasimas, probably the most formidable of all the excellent positions which General Linares was so easily relinquishing, was occupied by the Americans while Siboney grew as a base.

As it did, the Americans began to lose some of their enthusiasm for their Cuban companions in arms. At the Daiquirí landing, the two races had exchanged glad cries of *"Viva Cuba libre"* and *"Viva los Americanos."* The Yankee deliverers did all they could to help ease the misery of these ragged, barefoot, hungry *amigos.* But at Siboney they began to resent them, because, as a British correspondent wrote: ". . . the Cuban insurgent regarded every American as a kind of charitable institution, and expected him to disgorge on every occasion. The Cuban was continually pointing to the American's shirt, coat, or trousers, and then pointing to himself, meaning that he desired a transfer of property."[42]

Meanwhile, there was a halt at Siboney. It was probably due to Shafter's illness. He was not only prostrated by the heat, but suffered so from the gout that he moved about with his foot in a gunny sack and was unable to get his great bulk aboard a horse. In the interval, General Linares opened a series of rifle pits on San Juan Heights about a half-dozen miles from Shafter's advanced base at Sevilla, and also fortified the little village of El Caney to the left or north of San Juan. A few miles behind these positions lay Santiago.

Shafter's plan was to take El Caney with Henry Lawton's division, and then, two hours later, to move against San Juan Heights with the rest of the command. In the meantime, General García and his Cubans would block the road west from Santiago to prevent the arrival of Spanish reinforcements. By these movements, Shafter hoped to penetrate Santiago's outer defenses and the city would be cut off from its water supply.

Shafter's plan was limited in seeking only the enemy's outer works, and unwise in assigning nearly half of his force to securing his right flank at El Caney. As Shafter knew, the village was held by fewer than 600 men. Instead of sending Lawton's entire division to storm it, he could have contained it while using most of Lawton's men as a reserve to crash straight into Santiago once San Juan was reduced. As it turned out, the men at El Caney under the gallant Joaquín del Rey held off Lawton's division for most of the day. The slender little Spaniards in straw sombreros and blue coats fought with stubborn bravery, especially at a small stone fort south of the town. An American artillery battery of four 3.2-inch guns tried to batter the fort down, but without success. Marking the smoke rising from some Americans firing old-fashioned black-powder cartridges, the Spaniards opened up with their smokeless Mausers and drove a regiment back. At ten o'clock General Lawton gave his exhausted doughboys a rest. Three hours later he renewed the assault, and once again the Spaniards repulsed them.

To the south, meanwhile, the assault on San Juan was stalled awaiting news that El Caney had fallen and that the American right flank was secure. Alarmed, Shafter notified Lawton to leave El Caney and join the main attack. By then, however, Lawton's force was too deeply engaged to withdraw.

Still, the Americans closed in on the El Caney blockhouse. About 150 yards from the fort orders were issued for only marksmen and sharp-shooters to fire. Thirty or 40 of them crept forward to fire at every rifle pit, window, door and gun port in sight. Some Spaniards threw down their rifles and ran. An American sergeant bellowed, "Remember the *Maine!*" Four Spaniards were shot down at the door of the fort. Another waving a white flag ran out and was felled. A second seized the flag and was also shot. Then, suddenly, there was a silence.

The fort had fallen. A half-hour later El Caney surrendered. Only a little thatched-roof fort west of the town held out under General del Rey. Here the Spaniards fought heroically, until del Rey was killed, after which all resistance at El Caney came to an end.

To the south, a division of American infantry under Jacob Kent moved against San Juan Hill on the left while a division of dismounted cavalry under Samuel Sumner went up against Kettle Hill on the right. This was the San Juan Heights complex, and the Americans approached it in a slow and confused advance. First, an observation balloon towed along the ground made an excellent aiming point for Spanish artillery, which had already registered on the existing roads. Next, American artillery firing in support sent up clouds of giveaway smoke from black-powder ammunition and was quickly silenced by the Spanish. Finally, the entire assault was delayed by difficult terrain and the unexpected stubbornness of the Spaniards at El Caney. It did not actually begin until ten o'clock in the morning, when the Spaniards shot down the observation balloon.

It sank into the treetops on the left near the ford of the San Juan River. The Spaniards, aware that American troops must be near it, aimed a converging fire at it and panicked an entire volunteer regiment. Regulars were sent to push through the demoralized volunteers. The point of a regiment of dismounted Negro cavalrymen came up, led by a hard-bitten lieutenant named John J. Pershing. Then came the Rough Riders. The panicked volunteers cheered at the sight of Theodore Roosevelt, now in command, but Teddy replied tartly: "Don't cheer, but fight. Now's the time to fight."[43]

Once across the river, the units of troopers were shifted to the right until they were directly in front of Kettle Hill. At about one o'clock, Sumner ordered them up.

Roosevelt, splendidly mounted on his horse Little Texas, paraded in front of his dismounted troopers. Joined by other regiments of cavalry, Negro as well as white, the Rough Riders went up Kettle Hill with a rising cheer. They quickly drove the Spaniards from the ranch buildings at the summit, and seized the heights of San Juan beyond. But on their left, at San Juan Hill, the Americans were in trouble.

Here an open plain led up to San Juan's steep slopes, and three batteries of American artillery had failed to silence the Spanish riflemen and gunners who made it a no-man's land of shot and shell. A blockhouse crowning the hill also survived the bombardment. To cross the plain and charge the hill appeared to be a suicidal assignment, until a battery of three Gatling machine guns under Lieutenant John Parker swept daringly forward. Firing at ranges of from 600 to 800 yards the famous "coffee grinders" began to drive the Spaniards out of their trenches. With that, the American infantry broke from cover and began the ascent famous in history as "The Charge at San Juan Hill."

It was not, however, a charge—rather a creeping ascent in the face of steady enemy fire, and therefore even more dangerous. Foreign military attachés present were astonished. "It is very gallant, but very foolish,"[44] one of them cried. But the blue lines went forward, the soldiers holding their rifles across their chests and climbing heavily. In the forefront were just a few, spread out like a fan, then came the more regular lines. Slipping and stumbling in the smooth high grass, while the hillside and hilltop flashed with flame, they crept upward. Some fell, sinking suddenly from sight or rolling downhill, but not as many as might have been expected, for the Spaniards, rattled by the Gatlings and shaken by the Americans' silent, inexorable ascent, were firing high. Suddenly, nearing the summit, the blue fragments joined and gained momentum, and the Spaniards fired a final volley and fled.

At nightfall, with Lawton moving down from El Caney to hold the American right, all of San Juan Heights was in American hands and the road to Santiago appeared open. In the morning, however, General Shafter discovered that the inner defenses prepared by General Linares appeared to be very strong. On June 2, while Shafter extended his lines almost to Santiago Bay and thus surrounded the city on its landward side, there was more fighting. Casualties rose to 143 killed and 1,010 wounded. By July 3, still sick himself, fearing the advent of the yellow-fever season, Shafter was so dispirited that he considered withdrawing for five miles. Yet on that same day he called upon the Spanish to surrender, just as Admiral Cervera's squadron sortied from the harbor in a desperate dash for freedom.

Admiral Cervera had hoped to escape from Santiago by night, until Admiral Sampson began to illuminate the harbor mouth with floodlights. Upon the arrival of the American Army, however, Governor General Blanco in Havana urged Cervera to leave lest Santiago fall and the squadron be included in the surrender. On July 2, alarmed by the American victory at San Juan, Blanco bluntly ordered Cervera to depart—and the admiral sailed the following morning.

No one in the American blockading fleet expected Cervera to come out. Sampson certainly did not. He had sent battleship *Massachusetts* and smaller *Suwanee* to Guantánamo for fueling, and on July 3 he sailed east with flagship *New York* and two smaller ships to confer with Shafter. Nevertheless, Commodore Winfield Scott Schley still commanded a formidable force: battleships *Iowa, Indiana, Oregon* and *Texas,* his own flag cruiser *Brooklyn* and the armed yachts *Vixen* and *Gloucester.* At 9:35 in the morning, the Spanish ships began coming out. Flagship *Maria Teresa* led, followed by the cruisers *Vizcaya, Cristóbal Colón* and *Oquendo,* and destroyers *Pluton* and *Furor.* Because of the shallow, narrow channel, partially blocked by the sunken American collier *Merrimac,* the Spaniards came out slowly, one at a time, at intervals of about ten minutes. *Iowa* was the first to sight *Maria Teresa* rounding Smith Cay, her magnificent battle flag flying in the wind. *Iowa* closed and began firing while the other startled American ships got their engines turning and sounded general quarters.

Aboard *Teresa,* Captain Victor Concas ordered the bugles blown for battle. "Poor Spain!" he murmured to Admiral Cervera beside him, and the admiral looked away in agony, aware, as Concas said later, that he was hearing the last echo of the bugles sounded at the fall of Granada four centuries ago, and that Spain "was becoming a nation of the fourth class."[45]

Almost immediately, Americans shells began to rack *Teresa.* Cervera's flag cruiser shuddered, and there were dead on her decks as she swung to her right or westward. She made directly for *Brooklyn,* the westernmost American. Cervera hoped to knock out *Brooklyn* and open a gap through which his squadron might escape to Cienfuegos halfway down the island or perhaps even around to Havana on the opposite coast.

For ten minutes gallant *Teresa* was alone beneath the concentrated fire of the American fleet, able to fight back with only two of her guns. Five miles to the east, Admiral Sampson heard the thunder and turned *New York* around. Before he could come up, *Teresa* had been knocked out of action, deliberately beached on Cervera's orders. Meantime, *Vizcaya* and *Colón* had come out and had taken advantage of the attention paid to *Teresa,* gaining a good lead under cover of the gun smoke. Not so the unfortunate *Oquendo,* sortying just as the Americans finished *Teresa* and looked for new targets. Battered and smashed like the flagship, *Oquendo* was forced to run ashore only a half-mile beyond *Teresa.*

By then mighty *Oregon* had shown surprising speed, forging well ahead of *Texas* and keeping pace with the swift *Brooklyn.* These three Americans pursued escaping *Vizcaya* and *Colón.* At the harbor mouth now, little destroyers *Pluton* and *Furor* poked out, and fell victim to a dreadful converging fire. Salvo after salvo from *Texas, Iowa* and *Indiana,* even from distant *Oregon* and the fast-arriving *New York,* fell upon them, while *Gloucester* came boldly close to finish them off.

Within a few minutes *Pluton* was forced onto the rocks, where she blew up, and the riddled *Furor,* almost cut in two by a shell from *Iowa,* sank beneath the surface.

To the west, the running fight continued, the Americans gaining and scoring hits, the Spaniards firing high. Smoke was everywhere across the American path, smoke from funnels, from guns' muzzles, from explosions. It got into the sailors' ears and noses, choked them, blinded them, but the pursuit was pressed. *Vizcaya* was dropping behind. Soon she was crippled, and at eleven o'clock she staggered inshore and was grounded.

Iowa went in to watch her, *Indiana* sailed back to guard the harbor mouth, and *Oregon, Brooklyn* and *Texas* with *New York* coming hard concentrated on the fleeing *Colón.* Soon *Colón* was out of range of *Brooklyn*'s 8-inchers. But mighty *Oregon* was armed with huge 13-inchers firing an 1,100-pound shell. Just before one o'clock *Oregon*'s forward turrets bellowed. On her sixth shot, at a range of five miles, a huge geyser of water rose just ahead of *Colón,* and with that near-miss as a hint of more accurate fire to come, *Colón* turned and headed for shore. A few minutes later another 13-incher struck under *Colón*'s stern, and her colors dropped in a heap.

Cheer after cheer rose from the American ships and the bands began playing the "Star-Spangled Banner"; but aboard *Texas* a compassionate Captain John Philip cried: "Don't cheer, men—the poor fellows are dying."[46] Soon the Americans who had just been killing Spaniards were rushing to their rescue, taking them off their stricken ships. Of 2,200 Spanish seamen, 323 Spaniards died, 151 were wounded, and most of the rest were taken prisoner. American losses were one killed and one wounded. Jubilant, ignoring Schley's role in the battle, Sampson telegraphed Washington: "The fleet under my command offers the nation, as a Fourth of July present, the whole of Cervera's fleet."[47] And while America rejoiced at the death of the Spanish Navy, the dubious General Shafter took heart and messaged Secretary Alger: "I shall hold my present position."[48]

Day by day, Shafter extended his lines around Santiago. More and more guns pointed at the city, more and more troops filled the American rifle pits, while Santiago's supplies and strength sank lower and lower. From this position, Shafter began to negotiate for Santiago's surrender, dealing with General José Toral, who had replaced the wounded Linares.

At first, a truce was arranged for the exchange of prisoners and it appeared that the Spanish were willing to surrender. However, Spanish law did not permit a commander to capitulate as long as he had ammunition and food, both of which Toral possessed. Moreover, he was to uphold the honor of Spanish arms. Gradually, however, the hopelessness of the situation was borne in upon the Spanish, especially after American field and naval artillery bombarded the city on July 10-11. From his sickbed General Linares appealed to Madrid for permission to surrender. The arrival of Major General Nelson Miles, the Army's commanding general, with a brigade of reinforcements also helped make up the Spanish mind. At last, after more delays and misunderstandings, General Toral agreed to lay down his arms.

On July 17, 1898, Shafter, now able to mount a horse, rode with a troop of cavalry to a field outside Santiago. He met Toral with a company of 100 men. The Spaniards presented arms, and the Spanish flag which had floated over the ancient New World city for 382 years was hauled down and furled.

6

☆

There was no more fighting in Cuba. Yellow fever was the new enemy, and as the Americans sickened and died in their camps, fear of a yellow-fever epidemic forced the withdrawal of Shafter's men. They were replaced by the "Immune Regiments," so called because they were composed of Southerners believed to be immune to the disease.

Meantime, General Miles had taken his command to Puerto Rico, which he occupied in an almost bloodless operation, and on July 26, 1898, Spain made overtures for peace through the French Ambassador. On August 12 preliminary arrangements were completed, and on the same day—August 13 on the other side of the International Date Line—Manila fell to the Americans.

Here there had been difficulties of a different nature. Ships of all nations had scrupulously observed Dewey's blockade, except for a German squadron of five ships under Vice Admiral Otto von Diederichs. The German commander openly communicated with the Spanish and Filipinos ashore without consulting Dewey. Annoyed, Dewey told a German officer: "Does Admiral von Diederichs think he commands here, or do I? Tell your Admiral if he wants war I am ready."[49]

Although the Germans were as powerful as Dewey, they did not want war—only a few choice scraps from Spain's crumbling Pacific empire. But the presence of a British squadron prevented this, and Dewey was left to deal with the other problem of the Filipino *insurrectos.*

The American admiral had already brought Emilio Aguinaldo, the insurgent leader, to Manila from Hong Kong. Once ashore, Aguinaldo gathered his Filipino forces, capturing towns and proclaiming a republic with himself as president. Aguinaldo was anxious for Dewey to make an alliance or an agreement which would recognize Filipino freedom. This Dewey carefully avoided, until American ground troops at a strength of 8,500 arrived under Major General Wesley Merritt. The fact was that if the United States was planning to make Cuba *libre,* she was also preparing to keep the Philippines for herself. Hawaii had already been annexed in July of that year, Guam had fallen without a fight, and America was fairly embarked on a career of imperialism.

Yet, if Aguinaldo and his 10,000 insurgents were a hindrance to Dewey and Merritt, they also turned out to be a help in bringing about Manila's fall. The Spaniards knew that the oppressed Filipinos were eager to sack the city. Therefore, they preferred to surrender to the Americans, saving, of course, their military honor.

This was spared by the shots fired at Fort San Antonio Abad by Dewey's ships, operating on the left or water flank of Merritt's columns as they drove northward into Manila. The Americans met only token opposition, quickly capturing the city and successfully preventing Aguinaldo's men from entering it on its eastern side.

Gradually, however, the Filipinos pressed in upon the Americans. They demanded joint occupation of the city. They began to rob, beat and burn. The American Army of 8,500 men found itself in the position of having to guard 13,000 Spanish prisoners while 10,-

ooo infuriated Filipinos gradually penetrated their lines and clamored for Spanish spoils. At last, General Merritt ordered Aguinaldo to withdraw his army. Angered, but helpless against the guns of Dewey's squadron, the Filipino President moved his government to Malolos. He was not cowed, however, but merely making a prudent retirement while awaiting the outcome of the peace talks between America and Spain. Neither Aguinaldo nor his countrymen had any intention of exchanging the despotism of the Spanish oppressor for the paternalism of the American liberator. Even silken chains form a yoke, and they wanted a freedom as complete as Cuba's. Unfortunately for them, the new American imperialist party had grown too powerful.

American isolation died with the annexation of Hawaii. It did not perish, however, without a fight from the anti-imperialists who pleaded with McKinley and Congress to heed the advice of Washington and Jefferson and remain within the ocean barriers. McKinley's reply was: "We need Hawaii just as much and a good deal more than we did California. It is Manifest Destiny."[50] It was argued that acquisition of the islands would not only advance Mahan's program for American control of the Pacific but also promote trade and commerce. In reply, the opposition charged that the true motive was the old "unconquerable Anglo-Saxon lust for land," and Manifest Destiny was described as "the specious plea for every robber and freebooter since the world began."[51] Nevertheless, on July 7, 1898, Hawaii was annexed.

Armed with this precedent, the imperialists opened the struggle for the annexation of the Philippines. Gradually, they won over business interests heretofore reluctant, convincing them that the European powers were trying to close the door to American trade in China, and that possession of the Philippines would give America a base in eastern Asia.

Another new ally was Albert Beveridge, soon to be elected Senator from Indiana, who declared: "It is God's great purpose made manifest in the instincts of our race, whose present phase is our personal profit, but whose far-off end is the redemption of the world and the Christianization of mankind."[52] Religious leaders echoed the cry of Christianizing the Filipino, ignoring the fact that the Roman Catholicism professed by almost all of them was a fairly well-known form of that faith. McKinley was also persuaded. The man who had once wanted "no jingo nonsense" could not resist the imperialist tide, the public clamor to obey Rudyard Kipling's injunction to "take up the white man's burden."

McKinley's own description of his conversion to imperialism was given a few years later to a group of visiting clergymen:

> I thought first we would take only Manila; then Luzon; then other islands, perhaps, also. I walked the floor of the White House night after night until midnight; and I am not ashamed to tell you, gentlemen, that I went down on my knees and prayed Almighty God for light and guidance more than one night. And one night it came to me this way—I don't know how it was, but it came: (1) That we could not give them back to Spain—that would be cowardly and dishonorable; (2) that we could not turn them over to France or Germany—our commercial rivals in the Orient—that would be bad business and discreditable; (3) that we could not leave them to themselves—they were unfit for self-government —and they would soon have anarchy and misrule over there worse than Spain's was; and (4) that there was nothing left for us to do but to take them all, and to educate the Filipinos, and uplift and civilize and Christianize them, and by God's grace to do the best we could by them. . . . And then I went to bed, and went to sleep, and slept soundly.[53]

After this memorable night of illumination, McKinley did indeed "take them all," and Spain reluctantly agreed to terms by which Cuba became free, and Guam, Puerto Rico and the Philippines were ceded to the United States for $20 million. In signing, Spain observed sorrowfully, "This demand strips us of the very last memory of a glorious past and expels us . . . from the Western Hemisphere, which became peopled and civilized through the proud deeds of our ancestors."[54]

The treaty was not ratified without a bitter battle, however. An Anti-Imperialist League was organized by Americans such as Grover Cleveland and William Jennings Bryan, steel tycoon Andrew Carnegie, labor leader Samuel Gompers, and many leading educators and writers such as Mark Twain and William James. Like Rome before her, these men argued, America was embarking on the road to ruin. Imperialism was not only unconstitutional; it was certain to require an expensive army and navy to maintain it. From William Vaughn Moody came the haunting lines:

Tempt not our weakness, our cupidity!
For save we let the island men go free
Those baffled and dislaureled ghosts
Will curse us from the lamentable coasts
Where walk the frustrate dead. . . .
O ye who lead,
Take heed!
Blindness we may forgive, but baseness we will smite.

The imperialist reply was made by Senator Beveridge in his maiden Senate speech. Maintaining that the Pacific would be paramount in the twentieth century, he said: "The power that rules the Pacific, therefore, is the Power that rules the world. And, with the Philippines, that Power is and will forever be the American Republic."[55] But it was politics, not oratory, that decided the issue: the defection of the Democrat, Bryan, to the ranks of the imperialists. Bryan urged Democratic Congressmen not to oppose annexation, and on February 6, 1899, the Treaty of Paris was ratified and the Spanish-American War formally came to an end.

"It has been a splendid little war,"[56] John Hay wrote, but most of the world seemed to prefer the observation of Bismarck: that there was a special Providence for drunkards, fools and the United States of America. Yet both Hay and Bismarck were wrong. The splendid little war just ended was among the most expensive in American history, for hundreds of thousands of veterans needlessly mobilized and never sent into action have drawn pensions valued at close to $5 billion, and 60 years later there were still 10,000 of them receiving a total of $150 million annually. Nor was Bismarck's special Providence at work then; on the very eve of the war's end, the longer and bloodier Philippine Insurrection began.

Major General Ewell Otis commanded in Manila. Tall, bulky, wearing sideburns, the tedious Otis knew less about the Philippines than he did about controlling them. He had the faculty of alienating people, including the homeward-bound Admiral Dewey who called him a pincushion of an old woman; and his brilliant but arrogant division commander, Arthur MacArthur, who said that Otis resembled an upside-down locomotive. Still, Otis was determined to keep the peace in the islands, and he had the Navy and 21,000 troops to back him up. About 14,000 of these soldiers formed two divisions under MacArthur and Thomas Anderson. Armed with artillery and those detested .45 caliber Springfields that kicked like a mule, as well as with modern Gatling and Hotchkiss machine guns, these two formations held Manila.

Opposed to them was Aguinaldo's army of 80,000 Filipinos, of whom 30,000 surrounded Manila in a four-mile arc that had its north and south terminals on the bay. This force possessed a few Krupp guns, but a third of the men were without rifles. They carried machetes or bolo knives and wooden spears. Of the riflemen not many knew how to shoot. Some of them threw away their rear sights as a nuisance. Thus they would inevitably fire high. Yet they were confident. They assured themselves that they had defeated the Spaniards and that they would have no difficulty with the Americans. On the night of February 4 they attacked.

There was very little method in the assault. The insurgents merely sallied from their trenches and blockhouses to make random thrusts at the Americans, while the Sandatahan or fifth column created panic inside the capital. Only two concerted rushes were made, and they were shattered as the hard-kicking Springfields spewed bullets of such dreadful shocking power that they tore huge holes in the Filipinos' bodies and nearly tore off their heads. Meanwhile, the Sandatahan uprising also failed, and in the morning the Americans counterattacked.

The *insurrectos* were astonished. During the centuries that they had fought the Spaniards, all combat had taken place in the cool of the night, with both sides retiring at daybreak to avoid the heat of the day. Yet the *Americanos* were advancing by daylight behind an artillery barrage. Shattered as well as startled, the Filipinos on the northern half of the line fled. MacArthur's division pursued them into the hills and captured the reservoir. On the northern sector, General Anderson's division was even more successful, and the Filipinos learned the dreadful folly of anchoring a flank on water patrolled by a hostile navy. The ironclad *Monadnock* and smaller ships shelled positions ahead of the American line, which was marked by a red flag. Aiming through new telescopic sights, *Monadnock*'s gunners sent 500-pound shells screeching in upon the *insurrectos,* driving them out of their trenches and barricades so that the pursuing Americans could pour rifle fire into their backs.

The Filipinos were utterly crushed. Their casualties were probably five times higher than American losses of 59 killed and 278 wounded.

In this second battle of Manila it was clear that the insurgent army could never fight the Americans in orthodox wars of maneuver and massed assault, a fact which became plainer on February 10 after MacArthur took the rail center of Caloocan several miles north of the city. South and east there were also easy victories. It seemed certain that the insurrection was on the verge of collapse.

Actually, as the Spaniards might have told the Americans, it had only begun. Since 1551 Spaniards had been beating the Filipinos in open battle, but had never crushed them. To the elusive and hardy *insurrectos* formal defeat was merely the signal to begin guerrilla warfare, to fragment their forces, vanish into the wild interior, and conduct a hide-and-seek, hit-and-run harassment designed to exhaust American patience. Such warfare naturally depended upon a loyal populace, and the Filipinos were loyal to the insurrection; almost fanatically faithful to the revered Emilio Aguinaldo, who was himself an adept in the art of irregular war. No, the Spaniards might have said, "You will not stamp out the insurrection so soon; you will have no great and decisive blaze of battle but hundreds of small brush fires flaming up all over the islands."

General Otis, however, did not ask for Spanish advice but pursued the Filipinos with confidence in orthodox warfare. On Luzon, the rebel capital at Malolos was seized and burnt, but the government escaped to San Isidro. On the other islands capitals were also occupied, but the insurgents faded into the mountains. Sometimes the Filipinos turned and gave battle, and then there were American casualties. By June 10, 1899, losses were nearly 2,000. Not counting the sick and the dead of disease, this was more than the entire Cuban campaign.

American sick lists were appalling. After the doughboys entered San Fernando in May it was found that of 4,800 combat troops in the area 2,160 were on sick report. One regiment had 70 percent of its men in the hospital. The heat, the bad food, the endless exertion of chasing a tireless, indomitable enemy, all wore upon the will of the Americans. Then, in June, the rains came. From May to October no less than 70 inches fell. Roads were washed out, bridges collapsed, low-lying lands and rice paddies became temporary lakes and where the ground was not under water, it was often an impassable paste of mud. In such weather operations broke down, men sickened and soldiers who were well turned sullen. Now the Americans hated the Filipinos with a fierce black hatred. They killed all they found, frequently failing to distinguish between soldier and civilian. In truth, it was hard to do so. The *insurrectos* no longer wore their gingham uniforms. At one moment a Filipino might be an enemy insurgent aiming his Mauser out of the bush; at the next, hiding his rifle, he might be a friendly civilian with a smile on his face, welcoming the Americans with cries of, *"Amigo! Amigo!"* So the Americans decided: "There are no more *amigos.*"[57]

Sometimes the doughboys entered villages where their comrades had been held captive, only to find tortured bodies boloed to pieces. Their reply was to burn the village and slaughter its men, women and children.

They became what they fought. The Filipinos were fighting the kind of war that is based on terror; the Americans fought back just as cruelly. They developed a "water torture" that made even the Spanish cringe. If a captured Filipino refused to divulge military information, four or five gallons of water were forced down his throat until his body became "an object frightful to contemplate."[58] Then the water was forced out by kneeling on his stomach. The treatment was repeated until the prisoner talked or died. Almost all of them talked. Thus did the Americans civilize their "little brown brothers," and as one historian of the insurrection has observed: "What Otis was now doing to the Filipinos was almost what 'Butcher' Weyler had done to the Cubans; and the paradox was all the greater since we had gone to war with Spain to put an end to such abominations."[59]

Yet the Filipinos still resisted, and as the dry season set in General MacArthur went smashing through the central Luzon plain in an attempt to crush them. In November of 1899 the latest insurgent capital at Tarlac fell and MacArthur wired Otis: "The so-called Filipino Republic is destroyed."[60] But it was not, and the vanished Aguinaldo's army continued to raid American camps, tear up railroads, steal supplies and slaughter surprised American garrisons in the little outpost towns. By the spring of 1900, Filipino casualties were up around 17,000, but American losses were at least one-fifth of that, and as the war that was "won" continued without respite, reports of American suffering and of American brutality began to slip through the strict censorship imposed by General Otis.

A good part of the country was dismayed. Even the jingo *World* turned anti-imperialist and parodied Kipling's injunction with the lines:

We've taken up the white man's burden
Of ebony and brown;
Now will you tell us, Rudyard,
How we may put it down?[61]

Tales of torture, looting, wanton destruction of property and the summary execution of Filipinos by drumhead courts shocked the national pride and so disturbed President McKinley that he looked around for a civil governor to take control of the islands out of the hard hands of the generals. His choice fell upon Judge William Howard Taft, an elephantine man of more than 300 pounds and a reputation for largeness of mind and heart as well. Like Otis and the others, Taft knew nothing of the Philippines. Nor did he want the job. But McKinley prevailed upon him to accept. In April, 1900, at the head of a five-man commission, Taft sailed for Manila. In May the mortified Otis offered a resignation which was speedily accepted.

MacArthur succeeded Otis in his military duties, and was very much annoyed when Taft arrived armed with not only civil power but the right of financial control over the military. Although the two men never did get along, Taft was able to organize a model administration. Schools were constructed, public works begun, graft was abolished, and Filipinos who took the oath of allegiance began to participate in the government. Such benign tactics, it would seem, were bound to disarm the insurrection.

Yet this could not be, not for as long as the vanished Aguinaldo remained free. In his breast the fires of freedom burned strongest, and in his brain was the capacity to organize and direct the fight for it. So the guerrilla war continued without letup, while Aguinaldo based his hopes on a Democratic victory in the American presidential election of 1900.

Opposition to the war in the Philippines was carried on chiefly by the Democrats, who again nominated Bryan for the presidency, joined by the Anti-Imperialist League. Bryan, who had again changed his mind, went so far as to demand the military defeat of his own country, while the Anti-Imperialists stated flatly: "We demand the immediate cessation of the war against liberty, begun by Spain and continued by us. . . . We propose to contribute to the defeat of any person or party that stands for the forcible subjugation of any people."[62] They bombarded soldiers in the Philippines with leaflets, advising them: "Boys, don't re-enlist. Insist [upon] immediate discharge."[63]

The flaming Anti-Imperialist Edward Atkinson published a series of pamphlets describing the war as criminal, quoting American soldiers as saying that the Spaniards were appalled by Yankee cruelty, predicting that 8,000 American soldiers would die in the first year and that in two years the country would be bankrupt, and quoting a mother's description of McKinley as an unadulterated murderer. Atkinson tried to ship his pamphlets to the troops in the Philippines, but the War Department intercepted them. Indignant, Atkinson cried that free speech was being suppressed, and once again an American nation at war was faced with the problem of discovering at what point criticism ceases to be such and becomes treason.

Bryan and Atkinson and the other Anti-Imperialists were aware that the insurgents constantly quoted their remarks to encourage the Filipinos to fight on. In effect, they gave aid and comfort to the enemy Even if they were sincerely convinced that the war was wicked, to continue to say so cost more American lives. Thus the problem of conscience versus country, one which always haunts a divided democracy at war. Insoluble in 1812, 1847 and during the Civil War, the dilemma remained unsolved in 1900.

McKinley's reply in the fall campaign was to stress America's new prestige, the victory over Spain, prosperity and the pretext that the Philippine situation was well in hand. With some very handsome assistance from his highly popular running mate, the ebullient Teddy Roosevelt, who stumped the country in his Rough Rider hat, McKinley was easily re-elected, and with the defeat of Bryan the insurrection began to lose heart.

Although the insurrection had begun to falter, Aguinaldo was still at large. Unless he were captured or killed, the guerrilla war, though dwindling, might drag on for years and some new spark might set all the old fires blazing again. Yet no one knew of Aguinaldo's whereabouts. By February of 1901, after two years of insurrection, the Americans had not been able to find a single traitor among eight million Filipinos. But then one of Aguinaldo's couriers was captured. His name was Cecilio Segismundo, and it was he who revealed the hideout of his chief.

Aguinaldo later charged that Segismundo did not talk until after he had been given the water cure twice, but American officers insisted that he gave his cooperation voluntarily. However that may be, a daring scheme began to evolve in the romantic mind of Frederick Funston, a short, red-haired and muscular brigadier general of volunteers. From the dispatches taken from Segismundo, Funston learned that Aguinaldo was expecting guerrilla reinforcement at his headquarters at Palinan in northeastern Luzon. Funston would provide them.

His Maccabebe Scouts, a tribe of bloodthirsty mercenaries who had fought their brother Filipinos for Spain and now served America, were dressed as *insurrectos.* Their leaders were Segismundo, Hilario Tal Placido, a renegade insurgent, and a disguised Spanish secret service officer named Lazaro Segovia. Into their custody went Funston and four other American officers playing the part of "prisoners." With MacArthur's approval, on February 6, 1901, this bogus band set sail for lonely Casiguran Bay. Just after midnight of February 14, they were set ashore, to begin a 100-mile, five-week trek through the unknown wilds of Aguinaldo's own country.

Passing from village to village, often hailed as heroes, sometimes received with brass bands and full municipal honors, but never suspected, the guerrillas moved on Palinan. Word was sent ahead to Aguinaldo that his reinforcements were arriving with American prisoners. At once the wily Aguinaldo, fearing that the Americans might learn of his whereabouts, dispatched a force of his followers to take charge of them. With this, the Maccabebes hid Funston and his friends in the bush and told the loyalists that the Americans were back in Casiguran. The loyalists pressed on to Casiguran, while Funston's pretenders pushed on to Palinan.

Here Aguinaldo sat in a room on the second floor of a little house overlooking the village square. Two bodyguards were with him. Below, in the square, was a group of armed loyalists. As the Maccabebes came up they faced the loyalists with lowered rifles while Segismundo, Placido and Segovia walked boldly into the house. In a moment, Segismundo came out and departed. On the second floor, Placido told stories and cracked jokes while Segovia stood at the window watching the Maccabebes maneuver into position around the loyalists. Segovia nodded, and the Maccabebes opened fire. Annoyed, thinking his men were firing their weapons to welcome the reinforcements,

Aguinaldo walked to the window and shouted: "Stop that foolishness. Don't waste your ammunition."[64] With that, the burly Placido hurled himself on the slender Aguinaldo, while Segovia began shooting at the bodyguards. One fell wounded and the other fled. Aguinaldo was thrown to the floor. Placido sat on him until Funston came running upstairs to inform him that he was a captive.

Almost with relief, Aguinaldo gave himself up. On March 28 he was brought to Manila in triumph, and on April 19, 1901, finally coming to see the futility of fighting on, he took the oath of allegiance to the American government and called upon his followers to lay down their arms.

Still, the fires of insurrection once lighted are not quenched with a word. Although Luzon became quiet, resistance moved to the southern islands, especially among the fierce Mohammedan Moros. Inevitably, Moro massacres were succeeded by American reprisals every bit as ferocious. "Kill and burn" were the orders for Samar, and the ordeal of battle there was so intense that for years veterans of it were introduced at officers' mess with the salute: "Stand, gentlemen, he served on Samar."

At length, after 4,230 Americans had died, with hundreds more later dying of disease, and more than 20,000 Filipinos had perished, the Philippine Insurrection was ended by presidential proclamation on July 4, 1902. The proclamation did not instantly end the shooting, nor had it the power to prevent an *insurrecto* from shooting a campaign hat off the head of General MacArthur's dashing young son, Lieutenant Douglas MacArthur. Yet it remains the official date of the end of the Philippine Insurrection.

The President who issued it was named Theodore Roosevelt. On September 6, 1901, William McKinley was assassinated in Buffalo by an anarchist fanatic, and Roosevelt became the fourth Vice President and the sixth war hero to move into the White House. With his assumption of the presidency the new imperialism was confirmed with all of 43-year-old TR's free-swinging vigor. Some Republicans were appalled. They had believed that when troublesome Teddy accepted the empty office of Vice President he had taken the political veil.

"Now look!" one of them cried. "That damned cowboy is President of the United States!"[65]

Notes

☆

PART I: THE COLONIAL WARS

1. Francis Parkman, *The Pioneers of France in the New World* (Boston: Little, Brown, 1888), p. 350.
2. Francis Parkman, *The Jesuits in North America* (Boston: Little, Brown, 1888), p. 247.
3. *Ibid.,* p. 248.
4. Michael Kraus, *The United States to 1865,* "The University of Michigan History of the Modern World" (Ann Arbor: University of Michigan Press, 1959), p. 91.
5. Alvin M. Josephy, *The Patriot Chiefs: A Chronicle of American Indian Leadership* (New York: Viking, 1961), p. 58.
6. *Ibid.,* p. 59.
7. Francis Parkman, *Count Frontenac and New France under Louis XIV* (Boston: Little, Brown, 1888), p. 15.
8. *Ibid.,* p. 214.
9. *Ibid.,* p. 233.
10. *Ibid.,* p. 268.
11. *Ibid.,* p. 270.
12. Francis Parkman, *A Half-Century of Conflict* (Boston: Little, Brown, 1892), Vol. I, p. 135.
13. *Ibid.,* p. 171.
14. *Ibid.,* p. 174.
15. *Ibid.,* p. 177.
16. Alfred Thayer Mahan, *The Influence of Sea Power upon History 1660–1783* (New York: Hill & Wang, 1957), p. 200.
17. *A Half-Century of Conflict,* Vol. II, p. 70.
18. *Ibid.,* p. 102.
19. *Ibid.,* p. 124.
20. *Ibid.,* p. 132.
21. *Ibid.,* p. 133.

22. Douglas Southall Freeman, *George Washington* (New York: Scribner, 1948), Vol. I, p. 310.
23. *Ibid.*, p. 318.
24. *Ibid.*
25. Francis Parkman, *Montcalm and Wolfe* (Boston: Little, Brown, 1888), Vol. I, p. 218.
26. *Ibid.*, p. 225.
27. *Ibid.*
28. *Ibid.*, p. 308.
29. *Ibid.*, p. 309.
30. *Ibid.*, p. 506.
31. *Ibid.*, p. 510.
32. *Montcalm and Wolfe*, Vol. II, p. 46.
33. *Ibid.*, p. 97.
34. Christopher Hibbert, *Wolfe at Quebec* (New York: World, 1959), p. 1.
35. *Ibid.*, p. 34.
36. *Ibid.*, p. 37.
37. *Ibid.*, p. 25.
38. *Montcalm and Wolfe*, Vol. II, p. 205.
39. *Ibid.*
40. *Ibid.*, p. 206.
41. Hibbert, p. 76.
42. *Ibid.*, p. 100.
43. *Ibid.*, p. 113.
44. C. P. Stacey, *Quebec, 1759* (Toronto: Macmillan, 1959), p. 179.
45. *Ibid.*, p. 35.
46. *Ibid.*, p. 276.
47. *Ibid.*, pp. 285–86. Some historians have challenged this incident, but none with proof that it did not occur. It does not seem likely that the scrupulous Parkman would have been taken in by a fable.
48. Hibbert, p. 135.
49. *Ibid.*
50. *Ibid.*, p. 136.
51. *Montcalm and Wolfe*, Vol. II, p. 291.
52. *Hibbert*, p. 149.
53. *Montcalm and Wolfe*, pp. 296–97.
54. *Ibid.*, p. 297.
55. *Ibid.*, p. 308.
56. Major General J. F. C. Fuller, *A Military History of the Western World* (New York: Funk & Wagnalls, 1955), Vol. II, p. 270n. (Hereinafter referred to as Fuller, MH.)

PART II: THE WAR OF THE REVOLUTION

1. Christopher Ward, *The War of the Revolution* (New York: Macmillan, 1953), Vol. I, p. 7.
2. Bruce Lancaster, *From Lexington to Liberty*, "Mainstream of America Series" (New York: Doubleday, 1955), p. 17.
3. Lawrence Henry Gipson, *The Coming of the Revolution*, "New American Nation Series" (New York: Harper & Row, 1954), p. 67.
4. *Ibid.*, p. 68.
5. *Ibid.*, p. 219.
6. Ward., Vol. I, p. 13.
7. *Ibid.*, p. 16.
8. Lancaster, p. 67.
9. *Ibid.*, p. 68.
10. Gipson, p. 227.
11. Henry Steele Commager and Richard B. Morris, eds., *The Spirit of 'Seventy-Six: The Story of the American Revolution as Told by Participants* (Indianapolis, New York: Bobbs-Merrill, 1958; new edition, Harper & Row, 1967), Vol. I, p. 65. (Hereinafter referred to as Commager.)
12. *Ibid.*, pp. 108–09.
13. Ward, Vol. I, p. 22.
14. Commager, Vol. I, p. 67.
15. Ward, Vol. I, p. 35.
16. Commager, Vol. I, p. 69.
17. Ward, Vol. I, p. 37.
18. *Ibid.*
19. *Ibid.*
20. Lancaster, p. 99.
21. Ward, Vol. I, p. 43.
22. *Ibid.*
23. *Ibid.*
24. *Ibid.*
25. Lancaster, p. 110.
26. John C. Miller, *Triumph of Freedom: 1775–1783* (Boston: Little, Brown, 1948), p. 42.
27. Commager, Vol. I, p. 103.
28. Ward, Vol. I, p. 68.
29. *Ibid.*
30. Freeman, Vol. III, p. 427.
31. Willard M. Wallace, *Appeal to Arms: A Military History of the Revolution* (Chicago: Quadrangle Books, 1964), p. 32.

32. Miller, p. 8.
33. Ward, Vol. I, p. 56.
34. Lancaster, p. 129.
35. *Ibid.*
36. *Ibid.*, p. 130.
37. Ward, Vol. I, p. 74.
38. *Ibid.*, p. 86.
39. Thomas J. Fleming, "Battle at Bunker Hill," *Reader's Digest,* July, 1960, p. 259.
40. Ward, Vol. I, p. 88.
41. Fleming, p. 263.
42. *Ibid.*
43. Commager, Vol. I, p. 133.
44. *Ibid.*, p. 137.
45. *Ibid.*, p. 130.
46. Fleming, p. 271.
47. *Ibid.*
48. Ward, Vol. I, p. 103.
49. Freeman, Vol. III, p. 520.
50. Ward, Vol. I, p. 195.
51. *Ibid.*, p. 194.
52. Miller, p. 82.
53. *Ibid.*, p. 58.
54. *Ibid.*
55. Commager, Vol. II, p. 1071.
56. Commager, Vol. I, pp. 313–14.
57. Burton Stevenson, *Home Book of Quotations* (New York: Dodd, Mead, 1958), p. 62.
58. Russel Blaine Nye, *The Cultural Life of the New Nation,* "New American Nation Series" (New York: Harper & Row, 1960), p. 198.
59. Ward, Vol. I, p. 205.
60. Wallace, p. 113.
61. Lancaster, p. 215.
62. Miller, p. 132.
63. Ward, Vol. I, p. 232.
64. Wallace, p. 122.
65. *Ibid.*, p. 123.
66. Commager, Vol. I, p. 500.
67. *Ibid.*, p. 503.
68. *Ibid.*, p. 504.
69. Freeman, Vol. IV, p. 309.
70. Ward, Vol. I, p. 298.

71. Lancaster, p. 245.
72. Freeman, Vol. IV, p. 321.
73. Ward, Vol. I, p. 305.
74. Lancaster, p. 249.
75. Commager, Vol. I, p. 520.
76. Wallace, p. 133.
77. Ward, Vol. I, p. 317.
78. Commager, Vol. I, p. 517.
79. Miller, p. 166.
80. *Ibid.*
81. *Ibid.*, pp. 165–66.
82. Ward, Vol. I, p. 347.
83. *Ibid.*
84. *Ibid.*, p. 351.
85. *Ibid.*, p. 354.
86. Commager, Vol. I, pp. 625–26.
87. *Ibid.*
88. *Ibid.*
89. Miller, p. 206.
90. Lancaster, p. 238.
91. Ward, Vol. I, p. 351.
92. *Ibid.*, p. 423.
93. Stevenson, p. 66.
94. Lancaster, p. 279.
95. Wallace, p. 164.
96. Lancaster, p. 238.
97. Wallace, p. 170.
98. Lancaster, p. 335.
99. Wallace, p. 140.
100. *Ibid.*, p. 181.
101. Lancaster, p. 354.
102. Ward, Vol. II, p. 584.
103. Freeman, Vol. V, p. 59.
104. Ward, Vol. II, p. 681.
105. Miller, p. 405.
106. Dudley Knox, *A History of the United States Navy* (New York: Putnam, 1948), p. 35.
107. Miller, p. 481; Lancaster, pp. 380–81.
108. Miller, p. 483.
109. Commager, Vol. II, p. 804.
110. John Richard Alden, *The American Revolution*, "New American Nation Series" (New York: Harper & Row, 1954), p. 220.
111. *Ibid.*, p. 221.

112. Miller, p. 518.
113. Ward, Vol. II, p. 724.
114. Miller, p. 524–25.
115. Lancaster, p. 369.
116. Miller, p. 527.
117. *Ibid.*, p. 528.
118. Ward, Vol. II, p. 741.
119. *Ibid.*, p. 742.
120. *Ibid.*
121. *Ibid.*
122. *Ibid.*, p. 760.
123. *Ibid.*, p. 761.
124. *Ibid.*
125. Bruce Lancaster, *The American Heritage Book of the Revolution* (New York: Simon & Schuster, 1958), p. 321.
126. Commager, Vol. II, p. 1217.
127. *Ibid.*, p. 1218.
128. Ward, Vol. II, p. 890.
129. Commager, Vol. II, p. 1233.

PART III: THE WAR OF 1812

1. Commager, Vol. II, pp. 1243–44.
2. Wallace, p. 266.
3. *Ibid.*
4. Samuel Eliot Morison, *The Oxford History of the American People* (New York: Oxford, 1965), p. 270. (Hereinafter referred to as Morison, O.)
5. William Addleman Ganoe, *The History of the United States Army* (New York: Appleton, 1928), p. 101.
6. Glenn Tucker, *Dawn Like Thunder: The Barbary Wars and the Birth of the U.S. Navy* (Indianapolis, New York: Bobbs-Merrill, 1963), p. 26.
7. *Ibid.*, p. 115.
8. Glenn Tucker, *Poltroons and Patriots: A Popular Account of the War of 1812* (Indianapolis, New York: Bobbs-Merrill, 1954), Vol. I, p. 224. (Hereinafter referred to as Tucker, PP.)
9. Henry Adams, *The War of 1812*, ed. by Major H. A. De Weerd (Washington: Infantry Journal Press, 1944), p. 1.
10. Harry L. Coles, *The War of 1812*, "The Chicago History of American Civilization" (Chicago: University of Chicago Press, 1965), p. 45.

11. Adams, p. 24.
12. *Ibid.*, p. 34.
13. Coles, p. 80.
14. Tucker, PP, Vol. I, pp. 174–75.
15. *Ibid.*
16. Adams, p. 43.
17. Tucker, PP, Vol. I, pp. 174–75.
18. Coles, p. 84.
19. Tucker, PP, Vol. I, p. 230.
20. *Ibid.*, p. 231.
21. Adams, p. 57.
22. Tucker, PP, Vol. I, p. 299.
23. *Ibid.*, p. 267.
24. Coles, p. 121.
25. Tucker, PP, Vol. I, p. 315.
26. Josephy, p. 168.
27. Coles, p. 120.
28. Tucker, PP, Vol. I, p. 327.
29. *Ibid.*, p. 331.
30. *Ibid.*, p. 337.
31. Josephy, pp. 169–70.
32. Tucker, PP, Vol. I, pp. 338–39.
33. Josephy, p. 170.
34. *Ibid.*, p. 171.
35. Ganoe, p. 132.
36. Adams, p. 91.
37. *Ibid.*
38. *Ibid.*, p. 92.
39. *Ibid.*, p. 93.
40. *Ibid.*, p. 102.
41. Tucker, PP, Vol. II, p. 427.
42. Marquis James, *The Life of Andrew Jackson* (Indianapolis, New York: Bobbs-Merrill, 1938), p. 130.
43. Tucker, PP, Vol. II, p. 439.
44. James, p. 153.
45. *Ibid.*, p. 154.
46. Tucker, PP, Vol. II, p. 442.
47. James, p. 154.
48. Coles, p. 197.
49. James, p. 165.
50. *Ibid.*, p. 166.
51. *Ibid.*, p. 178.

52. *Ibid.*
53. Coles, p. 163.
54. *Ibid.,* p. 248.
55. *Ibid.,* p. 249.
56. Alfred Thayer Mahan, *Sea Power in Its Relation to the War of 1812* (Boston: Little, Brown), p. 332. (Hereinafter referred to as Mahan, 1812.)
57. Adams, p. 218.
58. *Ibid.*
59. *Ibid.,* p. 215.
60. *Ibid.,* p. 225.
61. George Robert Glieg, *The Campaigns of the British Army at Washington and New Orleans* (London: 1821), p. 132.
62. Tucker, PP, Vol. II, p. 483.
63. Adams, p. 227.
64. *Ibid.,* p. 332.
65. *Ibid.,* p. 334.
66. *Ibid.,* p. 335.
67. Mahan, 1812, p. 364.
68. *Ibid.*
69. Adams, pp. 201–02.
70. Mahan, 1812, p. 364.
71. Tucker, Vol. II, p. 635.
72. *Ibid.,* p. 590.
73. *Ibid.,* p. 591.
74. *Ibid.,* p. 589.
75. Neil H. Swanson, *The Perilous Fight* (Toronto, New York: Farrar & Rinehart, 1945), p. 504.
76. Adams, p. 338.
77. *Ibid.,* p. 340.
78. *Ibid.,* p. 341.
79. Coles, pp. 206–07.
80. James, p. 201.
81. *Ibid.*
82. *Ibid.,* p. 217.
83. *Ibid.*
84. *Ibid.*
85. *Ibid.,* p. 225.
86. *Ibid.*
87. *Ibid.,* p. 228.
88. *Ibid.*
89. *Ibid.,* p. 236.

90. Adams, p. 313.
91. James, p. 239.
92. *Ibid.*, p. 240.
93. *Ibid.*, pp. 241–42.
94. *Ibid.*, p. 244.
95. *Ibid.*
96. *Ibid.*, p. 245.
97. *Ibid.*, p. 247.
98. *Ibid.*, p. 249.

PART IV: THE WAR WITH MEXICO

1. Fuller, M. H., Vol. II, p. 541.
2. George Dangerfield, *The Awakening of American Nationalism, 1815–1828*, "New American Nation Series" (New York: Harper & Row, 1964), p. 4.
3. Morison, O, p. 405.
4. *Ibid.*
5. Kraus, p. 424.
6. *Ibid.*, p. 421.
7. Ray Allen Billington, *The Far Western Frontier: 1830–1860*, "New American Nation Series" (New York: Harper & Row, 1956), p. 149.
8. *Ibid.*
9. *Ibid.*, p. 148.
10. Morison, O, p. 561.
11. *Ibid.*
12. Justin H. Smith, *The War with Mexico* (Gloucester: Peter Smith, 1963), Vol. I, p. 159.
13. Edward J. Nichols, *Zach Taylor's Little Army* (New York: Doubleday, 1963), p. 35.
14. Lloyd Lewis, *Captain Sam Grant* (Boston: Little, Brown, 1950), p. 137.
15. Robert Selph Henry, *The Story of the Mexican War* (New York: Ungar, 1961), p. 41.
16. *Ibid.*, p. 45.
17. Lewis, p. 142.
18. Henry, p. 47.
19. Lewis, p. 143.
20. *Ibid.*, p. 147.
21. Henry, p. 62.
22. *Ibid.*

23. *Ibid.*
24. *Ibid.*, p. 63.
25. Smith, Vol. I, p. 194.
26. Lewis, p. 160.
27. Samuel E. Chamberlain, *My Confession* (New York: Harper & Row, 1956), p. 31.
28. Glyndon G. Van Deusen, *The Jacksonian Era: 1828–1848*, "New American Nation Series" (New York: Harper & Row, 1959), p. 210.
29. Henry, p. 103.
30. *Ibid.*
31. Lewis, pp. 161, 168.
32. *Ibid.*, p. 161.
33. *Ibid.*, p. 162.
34. Lt. Gen. Winfield Scott, *Memoirs* (New York: 1864), Vol. II, p. 383.
35. Lewis, p. 175.
36. *Ibid.*, p. 176.
37. Smith, Vol. I, p. 260.
38. Henry, pp. 68–9.
39. *Ibid.*, p. 69.
40. *Ibid.*, p. 70.
41. Scott, Vol. II, p. 401.
42. *Ibid.*
43. Van Deusen, p. 240.
44. Morison, O, p. 562.
45. Lewis, p. 200.
46. Henry, p. 174–75.
47. *Ibid.*, p. 175.
48. Smith, Vol. I, p. 376.
49. *Ibid.*, p. 374.
50. Chamberlain, p. 116.
51. *Ibid.*
52. Lewis, p. 193.
53. *Ibid.*
54. *Ibid.*, p. 196.
55. Smith, Vol. II, p. 10.
56. Lewis, p. 199.
57. Scott, p. 423.
58. Lewis, p. 199.
59. Lewis, p. 201.

60. *Ibid.*
61. Scott, p. 425.
62. Henry, p. 287.
63. *Ibid.*, p. 296.
64. *Ibid.*
65. *Ibid.*, p. 305.
66. Scott, p. 460.
67. *Ibid.*, p. 466.
68. Smith, Vol. II, pp. 84–5.
69. Lewis, p. 234.
70. *Ibid.*
71. *Ibid.*, pp. 241–42.
72. *Ibid.*, p. 244.
73. *Ibid.*, p. 245.
74. Henry, p. 381.

PART V: THE CIVIL WAR

1. Kraus, pp. 445–46.
2. Morison, O, p. 571.
3. Kraus, p. 438.
4. *Ibid.*
5. Morison, O, p. 573.
6. Edmund Wilson, *Patriotic Gore: Studies in the Literature of the American Civil War* (New York: Oxford, 1962), p. 3.
7. Kraus, p. 451.
8. Bruce Catton, *This Hallowed Ground: The Story of the Union Side of the Civil War,* "Mainstream of America Series" (New York: Doubleday, 1956), p. 8. (Hereinafter referred to as Catton, HG.)
9. Kraus, p. 469.
10. *Ibid.*, p. 472.
11. *Ibid.*, p. 473.
12. *Ibid.*
13. *Ibid.*
14. Catton, HG, p. 8.
15. Morison, O, p. 602.
16. Clement Eaton, *A History of the Southern Confederacy* (New York: Macmillan, 1962), p. 17.
17. Carl Sandburg, *Storm Over the Land: A Profile of the Civil War* (New York: Harcourt, Brace & World, 1942), pp. 5–6.
18. *Ibid.*, p. 8.

19. Morison, O, p. 610.
20. Stephen Vincent Benét, *John Brown's Body* (New York: Holt, Rinehart & Winston, 1962), p. 141.
21. Douglas Southall Freeman, *Lee's Lieutenants* (New York: Scribner, 1942), Vol. I, p. 20. (Hereinafter referred to as Freeman, LL.)
22. Fuller, MH, Vol. III, p. 12.
23. Sandburg, p. 54.
24. Freeman, LL, Vol. I, p. 61.
25. Clifford Dowdey, *The Land They Fought For: The Story of the South As the Confederacy, 1832–1865*, "Mainstream of America Series" (New York: Doubleday, 1955), p. 121.
26. Freeman, LL, Vol. I, p. 72.
27. Lt. Col. Matthew Forney Steele, *Campaigns of America* (Washington: Combat Forces Press, 1951), Vol. I, p. 72.
28. Bruce Catton, *Mr. Lincoln's Army* (New York: Doubleday, 1962), p. 53. (Hereinafter referred to as Catton, MLA.)
29. Bruce Catton, *The American Heritage Picture History of the Civil War* (New York: American Heritage, 1960), Vol. I, p. 111. (Hereinafter referred to as Catton, AH.)
30. Morison, O, p. 636.
31. *Ibid.*
32. *Ibid.*, p. 616.
33. Maj. Gen. J. F. C. Fuller, *Grant and Lee* (Bloomington: Indiana University Press, 1957), p. 59. (Hereinafter referred to as Fuller, G–L.)
34. *Ibid.*
35. Ulysses S. Grant, *Memoirs of U. S. Grant* (New York: Webster, 1894), p. 149.
36. Catton, HG, p. 94.
37. Grant, p. 173.
38. Fuller, G–L, p. 72.
39. Grant, p. 181.
40. Catton, HG, p. 97.
41. *Ibid.*, p. 98.
42. Grant, pp. 183–84.
43. Fuller, G–L, p. 140.
44. Catton, HG, p. 103.
45. *Ibid.*, p. 104.
46. *Ibid.*, p. 111.
47. Col. Vincent J. Esposito, ed., *The West Point Atlas of American Wars* (New York: Praeger, 1959), Vol. I, 1689–1900, Map 33.
48. Catton, HG, p. 114.

49. Grant, p. 201.
50. *Ibid.*, p. 206.
51. Fuller, G–L, p. 75.
52. *Ibid.*, p. 148–49.
53. Sandburg, p. 112.
54. *Ibid.*, p. 119.
55. *Ibid.*
56. *Ibid.*, p. 149.
57. Catton, AH, Vol. I, p. 142.
58. *Ibid.*
59. Irving Werstein, *Kearny the Magnificent* (New York: John Day, 1962), p. 202.
60. *Ibid.*
61. Henry Steele Commager, ed., *The Blue and the Gray* (Indianapolis: Bobbs-Merrill, 1950), p. 337. (Hereinafter referred to as Commager, B–G.)
62. Catton, AH, Vol. I, p. 141.
63. Lewis, p. 266.
64. Fuller, G–L, p. 129.
65. *Ibid.*
66. Benét, p. 165.
67. Fuller, G–L, p. 107.
68. *Ibid.*, p. 102.
69. *Ibid.*, p. 101.
70. *Ibid.*, p. 100.
71. Werstein, pp. 224–25.
72. Fuller, G–L, p. 129.
73. Richard Harwell, *Lee: An Abridgment of the Four-Volume R. E. Lee by Douglas Southall Freeman* (New York: Scribner, 1961), p. 215. (Hereinafter referred to as Harwell-Freeman.)
74. Catton, AH, Vol. I, p. 165.
75. *Ibid.*
76. *Ibid.*
77. Fuller, G–L, p. 250.
78. Werstein, p. 231.
79. Kenneth P. Williams, *Lincoln Finds a General* (New York: Macmillan, 1964), Vol. I, p. 252.
80. Werstein, 235–36.
81. Sandburg, p. 144.
82. Catton, MLA, p. 50.
83. Catton, HG, p. 161.
84. Catton, MLA, p. 217.

85. *Ibid.*, p. 318.
86. Harwell-Freeman, p. 261.
87. Fuller, G–L, p. 169.
88. Morison, O, p. 653.
89. *Ibid.*
90. Commager, B–G, p. 200.
91. Sandburg, p. 158.
92. Esposito, Vol. I, Map 71.
93. Freeman, LL, Vol. II, p. 346.
94. Dowdey, p. 234.
95. *Ibid.*
96. *Ibid.*
97. Kraus, p. 500.
98. Harwell-Freeman, p. 278.
99. Morison, O, p. 656.
100. Catton, AH, Vol. I, p. 281.
101. Catton, HG, p. 191.
102. Williams, Vol. II, p. 555.
103. Sandburg, p. 181.
104. Esposito, Vol. I, Map 102.
105. Fuller, G–L, p. 180.
106. Richard S. West, Jr., *Mr. Lincoln's Navy* (New York: Longmans, 1957), p. 221.
107. Grant, p. 284.
108. Fuller, G–L, p. 183.
109. Commager, B–G, p. 663.
110. *Ibid.*, p. 677.
111. Bruce Catton, *Glory Road* (New York: Doubleday, 1952), p. 140. (Hereinafter referred to as Catton, GR.)
112. Commager, B–G, pp. 250–51.
113. Catton, GR, p. 165.
114. *Ibid.*, p. 141.
115. *Ibid.*, p. 169.
116. *Ibid.*, p. 177.
117. Harwell-Freeman, pp. 301–02.
118. Freeman, LL, Vol. II, p. 681.
119. *Ibid.*, p. 682.
120. Fuller, G–L, p. 128.
121. Freeman, LL, Vol. III, p. 46.
122. Harwell-Freeman, p. 321.
123. *Ibid.*, p. 322.
124. Catton, GR, p. 270.

125. *Ibid.*
126. Harwell-Freeman, p. 323.
127. *Ibid.*, p. 325.
128. *Ibid.*
129. *Ibid.*, p. 326.
130. *Ibid.*, p. 329.
131. *Ibid.*, p. 336.
132. *Ibid.*
133. *Ibid.*, p. 337.
134. *Ibid.*
135. Commager, B–G, p. 627.
136. *Ibid.*
137. *Ibid.*, pp. 627–28.
138. Harwell-Freeman, p. 338.
139. *Ibid.*, p. 340.
140. *Ibid.*
141. *Ibid.*
142. Commager, B–G, p. 1074.
143. Williams, Vol. II, p. 730.
144. Commager, B–G, p. 677.
145. Sandburg, p. 206.
146. *Ibid.*, p. 207.
147. Eaton, p. 271.
148. *Ibid.*
149. Catton, GR, p. 228.
150. *Ibid.*, p. 231.
151. Morison, O, p. 659.
152. Catton, GR, p. 233.
153. Bruce Catton, *A Stillness at Appomattox* (New York: Doubleday, 1953), p. 24. (Hereinafter referred to as Catton, S.)
154. Catton, HG, p. 273.
155. Commager, B–G, p. 887.
156. Catton, HG, p. 285.
157. *Ibid.*
158. Commager, B–G, p. 907.
159. *Ibid.*
160. *Ibid.*
161. *Ibid.*
162. Catton, HG, p. 300.
163. Harwell-Freeman, p. 376.
164. Fuller, G–L, p. 216.
165. Catton, S, p. 100.

166. Esposito, Vol. I, Map 126.
167. Sandburg, p. 252.
168. Catton, S, p. 116.
169. Commager, B–G, p. 998.
170. *Ibid.*, pp. 998–99.
171. Harwell-Freeman, p. 388.
172. *Ibid.*
173. Sandburg, p. 252.
174. Harwell-Freeman, p. 408.
175. Catton, S, p. 169.
176. Grant, p. 503.
177. Catton, S, p. 191.
178. *Ibid.*
179. Harwell-Freeman, p. 411.
180. Catton, S, p. 289.
181. *Ibid.*
182. Sandburg, p. 306.
183. West, p. 267.
184. Grant, p. 388.
185. Catton, HG, p. 352.
186. *Ibid.*, p. 348.
187. Catton, S, p. 275.
188. Grant, p. 417.
189. Catton, S, p. 285.
190. Commager, B–G, p. 1055.
191. Thomas Buchanan Read, "Sheridan's Ride," quoted in Stevenson, p. 2118.
192. Catton, S, p. 312.
193. *Ibid.*, p. 315.
194. Sandburg, p. 315.
195. *Ibid.*, p. 316.
196. Fuller, G–L, p. 50.
197. Commager, B–G, p. 925.
198. William Tecumseh Sherman, *Memoirs* (Bloomington: Indiana University Press, 1957), Vol. II, p. 152.
199. *Ibid.*, p. 126.
200. Sandburg, p. 331.
201. Harwell-Freeman, p. 447.
202. Sandburg, p. 384.
203. Catton, S, p. 355.
204. *Ibid.*
205. *Ibid.*
206. *Ibid.*, p. 357.

207. Sandburg, p. 390.
208. *Ibid.*
209. Harwell-Freeman, p. 466.
210. *Ibid.*, p. 475.
211. *Ibid.*, p. 479.
212. *Ibid.*, p. 483.
213. *Ibid.*
214. Catton, S, p. 378.
215. Fuller, G–L, p. 61.
216. Harwell-Freeman, p. 489.
217. *Ibid.*
218. *Ibid.*, p. 490.
219. *Ibid.*, p. 492.
220. *Ibid.*

PART VI: INDIAN WARS, THE SPANISH-AMERICAN WAR
AND THE PHILIPPINE INSURRECTION

1. Morison, O, p. 702.
2. *Ibid.*, p. 704.
3. Hodding Carter, *The Angry Scar*, "Mainstream of America Series" (New York: Doubleday, 1959), p. 31.
4. *Ibid.*, p. 25.
5. *Ibid.*
6. *Ibid.*
7. Foster Rhea Dulles, *The United States Since 1865*, "The University of Michigan History of the Modern World" (Ann Arbor: University of Michigan Press, 1959), p. 13. (Hereinafter referred to as Dulles, US.)
8. *Ibid.*, p. 14.
9. Grant, p. 641.
10. Carter, p. 94.
11. Dulles, US, p. 15.
12. *Ibid.*
13. *Ibid.*, p. 14.
14. *Ibid.*, p. 18.
15. *Ibid.*, p. 14.
16. *Ibid.*, p. 41.
17. Josephy, p. 340.
18. Foster Rhea Dulles, *America's Rise to World Power*, "New American Nation Series" (New York: Harper & Row, 1955), p. 19. (Hereinafter referred to as Dulles, WP.)
19. Dulles, US, p. 55.

20. *Ibid.,* p. 126.
21. Dulles, WP, p. 20.
22. Dulles, US, p. 159.
23. Harold U. Faulkner, *Politics, Reform and Expansion,* "New American Nation Series" (New York: Harper & Row, 1959), p. 217.
24. *Ibid.*
25. Dulles, WP, p. 27.
26. *Ibid.*
27. *Ibid.*
28. Faulkner, p. 225.
29. W. A. Swanberg, *Citizen Hearst* (New York: Bantam Books, 1963), p. 127.
30. Dulles, US, p. 165.
31. Faulkner, p. 227.
32. *Ibid.,* p. 229.
33. Swanberg, p. 162.
34. Faulkner, p. 230.
35. Frank Freidel, *The Splendid Little War* (New York: Bramhall House, 1959), p. 14.
36. Freidel, p. 22.
37. Knox, p. 338.
38. Freidel, p. 33.
39. Faulkner, p. 235.
40. Freidel, p. 59.
41. Wolff, Leon, *Little Brown Brother* (London: Longmans, 1961), p. 277.
42. Freidel, pp. 94–95.
43. *Ibid.,* p. 153.
44. *Ibid.,* p. 163.
45. *Ibid.,* p. 194.
46. *Ibid.,* p. 224.
47. *Ibid.,* p. 231.
48. *Ibid.*
49. Knox, p. 361.
50. Dulles, WP, p. 43.
51. *Ibid.,* p. 44.
52. *Ibid.,* p. 46.
53. *Ibid.,* p. 51.
54. Faulkner, p. 248.
55. Dulles, WP, p. 55.
56. Faulkner, p. 248.
57. Wolff, p. 252.
58. *Ibid.,* p. 253.

59. *Ibid.*
60. *Ibid.*, p. 279.
61. *Ibid.*, p. 271.
62. *Ibid.*, p. 276.
63. *Ibid.*, p. 274.
64. *Ibid.*, p. 344.
65. Morison, O, p. 810.

Recommended Reading

THE COLONIAL WARS

Freeman, Douglas S., *George Washington*, New York: Scribner, 1948. Although inflated, Freeman's seven-volume biography remains the definitive work on Washington. Vols. I and II relate to the Colonial Wars.

Josephy, Alvin M., Jr., *The Patriotic Chiefs*, New York: Viking, 1961. A colorful chronicle of American Indian leadership beginning with King Philip in the Colonial Wars and ending with Chief Joseph in 1877.

Mahan, Alfred Thayer, *The Influence of Seapower upon History, 1660–1783*, New York: Hill and Wang, 1957. The chief book of the "bible" of seapower also gives a demonstration of its decisive role in the Colonial and Revolutionary Wars.

Morison, Samuel Eliot, ed., *The Parkman Reader*, Boston: Little, Brown, 1955. An excellent short trot with Parkman for those without the time to take the entire trip.

Parkman, Francis, *France and England in North America*, Boston: Little, Brown, 10 vols. 1887–88, 2 vols. 1892.* Parkman's work remains the classic on the Colonial period. Of the 12 volumes cited here, those dealing directly with the Colonial Wars are:

The Pioneers of France in the New World.
Count Frontenac and New France under Louis XIV.
A Half-Century of Conflict, 2 vols.
Montcalm and Wolfe, 2 vols.
The Conspiracy of Pontiac, 2 vols.

Stacey, C. P., *Quebec, 1759,* Toronto: Macmillan, 1959. A clear style and the most up-to-date research combine to present the best single account of the climactic battle of the Colonial Wars.

* All the editions cited here are those used by the author.

THE WAR OF THE REVOLUTION

Commager, Henry Steele, and Richard B. Morris, eds., *The Spirit of 'Seventy-Six*, 2 vols., Indianapolis: Bobbs-Merrill, 1958. A mine of documents, diaries, letters and eyewitness accounts of events of the Revolution.

Freeman, *op. cit.*, Vols. III, IV and V.

Lancaster, Bruce, *The American Heritage Book of the Revolution*, New York: Simon & Schuster, 1958. Text and lavish illustrations join to make an absorbing popular account of the Revolution.*

———, *From Lexington to Liberty*, New York: Doubleday, 1955. Although Lancaster's narrative here is neither so disciplined nor so lucid, the book is still crammed with entertaining incident and anecdote.

Miller, John C., *Triumph of Freedom, 1775–1783*, Boston: Little, Brown, 1948. The most complete single-volume work on the Revolution, and especially recommended for the balance struck between battle front and home front.

Wallace, Willard M., *Appeal to Arms*, New York: Harper, 1951. The finest short history of the Revolution, a brilliant small gem of military writing.

Ward, Christopher, *The War of the Revolution*, 2 vols., New York: Macmillan, 1953. This is a complete and masterful narrative, perhaps the best on the subject.

THE WAR OF 1812

Adams, Henry, *The War of 1812*, Washington: Infantry Journal Press, 1944. This excerpt from Adams's nine-volume history of the United States remains the most complete account of 1812.

Coles, Harry L., *The War of 1812*, Chicago: University of Chicago Press, 1965. A clear and concise narrative which should be attractive to modern readers.

James, Marquis, *The Life of Andrew Jackson*, Indianapolis: Bobbs-Merrill, 1938. One of the best biographies in American letters, and invaluable for its portraits of Jackson in the Creek Wars and at New Orleans.

Tucker, Glenn, *Dawn Like Thunder*, Indianapolis: Bobbs-Merrill, 1963. A stirring account of the Barbary Wars and the birth of the U.S. Navy.

———, *Poltroons and Patriots*, 2 vols., Indianapolis: Bobbs-Merrill, 1954. A highly readable popular history of the war.

* Again because of space limitations, the author is compelled to cite only American authors.

THE WAR WITH MEXICO

Henry, Robert Selph, *The Story of the Mexican War*, New York: Ungar, 1961. An affectionate and accurate narrative, with much emphasis on the character of the individual American soldiers.

Lewis, Lloyd, *Captain Sam Grant*, Boston: Little, Brown, 1950. A fascinating study not only of the young U. S. Grant but also of his comrades-in-arms who were to be the generals of the Civil War.

Nichols, Edward J., *Zach Taylor's Little Army*, New York: Doubleday, 1963. A short colorful account of the fighting in northern Mexico.

Smith, Justin H., *The War with Mexico*, 2 vols., Gloucester, Mass.: Peter Smith, 1963. Although flawed by a prejudice against things Latin, this remains the most complete work on the subject.

THE CIVIL WAR

Catton, Bruce, *The American Heritage Picture History of the Civil War*, 2 vols., New York: American Heritage, 1960. This is Catton's finest work, a lucid narrative that covers all the ground and is superbly served by marvelous maps and photographs.

Eaton, Clement, *A History of the Southern Confederacy*, New York: Macmillan, 1962. A short history notable for its accuracy and impartiality.

Foote, Shelby, *The Civil War*, 3 vols, New York: Random House, 1958, 1963. An exhaustive study of the war from a Southern viewpoint. The third volume has not yet been published.

Freeman, Douglas S., *Lee's Lieutenants*, New York: Scribner, 1942–43–44. A detailed account of the war waged in the East by the Confederate Army.

Fuller, Major General J. F. C., *Grant and Lee*, Bloomington: Indiana University Press, 1957. One of the most perceptive military writers of the century makes a fascinating study of generalship which challenges many of the conventional judgments on the war's two great protagonists.

Harwell, Richard, *Lee*, New York: Scribner, 1961. This is an excellent and readable abridgment of Freeman's four-volume study of the great Virginian.

Sandburg, Carl, *Storm Over the Land*, New York: Harcourt, Brace, 1942. Taken from Sandburg's four-volume *Abraham Lincoln: The War Years*, this profile of the Civil War is a colorful account of Lincoln's conduct of the war.

Williams, Kenneth P., *Lincoln Finds a General*, 5 vols., New York: Macmillan, 1956–64. A factual and sometimes controversial work, which, when read in conjunction with Freeman's volumes, presents a detailed and balanced account.

INDIAN WARS, THE SPANISH-AMERICAN WAR AND
THE PHILIPPINE INSURRECTION

Crook, General George, *His Autobiography,* edited by Martin F. Schmitt, Norman: University of Oklahoma Press, 1960. All the flavor of the frontier is present in this remarkable personal narrative by "the greatest Indian fighter of them all."

Downey, Fairfax, *Indian Wars of the U.S. Army, 1776–1865,* New York: Doubleday, 1963. A stirring account of the Indian Wars of the "middle period."

————, *Indian-Fighting Army,* New York: Scribner, 1941. The same author carries the narrative to the end of the nineteenth century and also presents a picture of the regular army which later fought the Spanish-American War. Read with Parkman and Josephy, these two books complete the story of Indian warfare.

Freidel, Frank, *The Splendid Little War,* Boston: Little, Brown, 1958. This popular account of the Spanish-American War is also available with pictures in a book of the same title published by Bramhall House, New York, 1958.

Schott, Joseph L., *The Ordeal of Samar,* Indianapolis: Bobbs-Merrill, 1964. A chilling story of the vicious guerrilla fighting characteristic of the Philippine Insurrection.

Wolff, Leon, *Little Brown Brother,* London: Longmans, 1961. A skillful presentation of both sides of the unpleasant coin of American imperialism.

Index

☆